COLONIAL
POLICY AND PRACTICE

COLONIAL
POLICY AND PRACTICE

A Comparative Study of
Burma and Netherlands India

by

J. S. FURNIVALL

NEW YORK UNIVERSITY PRESS

First published in Great Britain by Cambridge University Press 1948
in cooperation with
The International Secretariat, Institute of Pacific Relations
First United States edition 1956

Library of Congress catalogue card number: 56-10677

Manufactured in the United States of America

CONTENTS

PREFACE

THIS book originated in a request from the Government of Burma at the end of 1942 for my views on reconstruction, with particular reference to features of colonial rule in Netherlands India that might suitably be adopted in Burma. One cannot transplant administrative machinery without reference to the environment; in a new environment it may work better or worse, but it certainly will not work in the same way. It was necessary therefore to emphasize the fact that British and Dutch colonial policy are founded on different traditions. Two basic principles of British colonial policy are the rule of law and economic freedom, whereas Dutch colonial policy has aimed at imposing restraints on economic forces by strengthening personal authority and by conserving the influence of custom.

In modern Burma under British rule there were five notorious evils: the failure of western self-governing institutions; the growth of debt and agrarian distress; the multiplication of litigation and crime; the rise of disaffection and unrest among the Buddhist clergy; and widespread corruption in the judicial and administrative services. I suggested that these can all be traced to a common cause: the disintegration of social life through the inadequacy of law to control the working of anti-social economic forces. Although in other respects Dutch rule is open to criticism which does not apply to Burma, yet in all these matters Netherlands India presents a notable contrast. We would not, even if we could, abandon what is valuable in the traditions of British rule, and in any case we cannot break suddenly with old traditions, or escape the consequences of the past. But the contrast indicates that we ought to incorporate in our policy the principle of controlling economic forces in the interest of social welfare. I tried accordingly to show how, by adapting certain devices of Dutch administrative machinery, this principle might be applied to cure the ills of modern Burma, and to lay the basis of a new and constructive policy.

While formulating these proposals it occurred to me that the comparison between Burma and Netherlands India might be of somewhat more general interest. In presenting it to a wider public there was, however, one obvious difficulty. The officials for whom the original note was written shared with the writer a common knowledge of Burma and its administration. For readers without such special knowledge it was necessary to trace the course of development more closely and to illustrate the results more clearly, even at the risk of multiplying tedious detail. Another difficulty, still more formidable, may be less obvious. For undesirable features of British rule in Burma, British officials, conscious of their good intentions, naturally tend to blame the Burman; Burmans, no less naturally, blame the British. Similarly in Netherlands India we find mutual recriminations between Dutch and Indonesians. Only by eliminating so far as possible all personal and local factors can one arrive at a just estimate of any particular experiment in colonial rule. It seemed necessary therefore to frame the comparison between Burma and Netherlands India in a general survey of colonial policy and practice. For such a survey, however, they provide a convenient introduction by presenting respectively extreme types of the alternative systems of direct and indirect rule.

In venturing further afield one was inevitably treading on uncertain ground. I was at home in Burma. After more than twenty years in the Civil Service, I was occupied for some time in business and in the direction of an agricultural bank, and also had the privilege of being associated with the University of Rangoon and the Education Department in various educational experiments. With the ready assistance of Dutch and Indonesian authorities I have made some study of Netherlands India, and I have visited Malaya, Siam and Cochin China. I also have some personal acquaintance with administration in British India. But of Africa, the other great field of colonial rule, I knew nothing at first hand. Fortunately it was possible to turn for information to Lord Hailey's great *African Survey*, and the extent of my debt to it will be readily apparent. It would be hard to say how much I owe to the voluminous writings of Dutch colonial experts, but among them I must mention in particular Dr J. H. Boeke, Professor of Tropical Economy in Leiden University, and Mr Meijer Ranneft, formerly Vice-President of the Raad van Indië. It is impossible for me to express adequately my gratitude to my friend Mr G. E. Harvey, for the care with which he read the first proofs of this book and for his generous comments and criticisms, and also for allowing me to use his unpublished extracts from the records of early British rule in Arakan.

The book was written during the late war, and completed early in 1945. The delay in publication has been due partly to the difficulties of the present time, partly to imperfections in the original script; and in this connection I must gratefully acknowledge the help and patience of the University Press. During the interval there have been great changes but, as the Japanese invasion of the Tropical Far East must certainly mark a turning-point in colonial rule, and subsequent events are still too close to be reviewed in due perspective, it seemed expedient merely to revise the tense in references to the war.

One change however calls for comment. Britain has granted Burma independence. On both parts this may seem bold even to the point of rashness. Some contend that we have been too ready to throw off the responsibilities of Government and Burmans over-ready to assume them. It is a tumbled house that they inherit, and there is urgent need to repair the damage, moral and material, inflicted on Burma in a war during which it was twice invaded. Exports have fallen by two-thirds of the pre-war figure of £37 million. The annual revenue covers only one-third of the current expenditure, and the national debt of over £110 million, about seven times the revenue, is rapidly increasing. Despite the general inexperience of Burmans in modern industry and commerce, their new leaders must enable Burma, so far as national interest allows, to make a due contribution to world welfare by the development of its resources. Moreover, in a country where the tradition of military service has long been suffered to decay, they must train the people to defend their freedom. Now also it will fall on them to deal with problems long-standing and hitherto insoluble: to adapt western institutions to an eastern people, provide remedies for agricultural debt and land alienation, reduce litigation and crime to healthy proportions, restore order among the Buddhist clergy, and purify the administration of corruption. In a troubled world, though less acquainted with affairs than their old rulers, they face a situation far more difficult. In these circumstances it is impossible to contemplate the future without misgivings, and we may well regret that in the past more was not done to equip the people and their leaders for the responsibilities of independence.

Some advocate Dominion status as an alternative. But, for countries such as Burma, Dominion status is an unmeaning formula. The British Dominions are countries potentially able to stand alone but preferring to be associated on equal terms with the other major partners in the Commonwealth. Burma is not in that position. The racial divisions and sharp conflict of interest and sentiment, which weakened the former Government, would still continue and are incompatible with Dominion status. On the other hand, if the Burman leaders had accepted it, they would have split their party, strengthened their rivals, especially the so-called Communists, and conferred on the prevalent dacoity the halo of patriotism and the semblance of civil war. It is lamentable that we failed to capture the imagination of the people so as to inspire an instinctive loyalty to the British connection, but we cannot escape the consequences of the past. In purporting to grant Dominion status, we would have been promising something that we could not give in return for support that the leaders of the people were unable to command. Once again we would have been committed to the ungrateful task of pacification; more difficult now, and far more costly, than after the wars of 1852 and 1885 when we could employ Indian troops.

I hold then that on both parts the decision in favour of independence was as wise as it was bold, not only in their interest but in ours. Nothing less than independence could transform nationalism from a destructive fever into a creative force. Yet national independence is not a cause or guarantee of welfare. Burmans still need help, and by our long connection we can do most to give the help they need. But we can help them only on terms acceptable to both parties. If we can help Burmans to stand alone securely, we may perhaps look forward to a time when they will welcome a more intimate association. However that may be, we can at least feel that we have done our best to meet whatever difficulties lie ahead by responding boldly to the challenge of a new age.

J. S. FURNIVALL

24 *October* 1947

LIST OF ARTICLES CITED

BROEK, JAN O. M. Indonesia and the Netherlands (*Pacific Affairs*, 1943, pp. 329–38).

CREUTZBERG, K. F. Education in the Netherlands East Indies (*Asiatic Review*, 1934, pp. 118–26).

FIELD, Dr M. J. Some Difficulties of Indirect Rule (*Man*, 1943, p. 90).

FISCHER, I. A. Hospital Accommodation in the Netherlands Indies (*Bulletin of the Colonial Institute of Amsterdam*, 1939, pp. 24–36).

FURNIVALL, J. S. Land as a Free Gift of Nature (*Economic Journal*, 1909, pp. 554–62).

The Organisation of Consumption (*Economic Journal*, 1910, pp. 23–30).

Education and Economics (*Economic Review*, 1912, pp. 380–92).

Economic Surveys in Netherlands India (*Economic Journal of India*, 1934, pp. 295–312).

Administration in Burma and Java (*Asiatic Review*, 1935, pp. 625–33).

The I.C.S. (*Koloniaal Tijdschrift*, 1938, pp. 273–81).

The Political Economy of the Tropical Far East (*Royal Central Asian Journal*, 1942, pp. 195–210).

Manu in Burma (*Journal of the Burma Research Society*, 1940, pp. 351–70).

India and a Regional Council for the Tropical Far East (*Asiatic Review*, 1944, pp. 265–75).

Mass Education in Netherlands India (*Proceedings of the Anglo-Netherlands Society*, 1944–45, pp. 7–15).

HART, G. D. H. International Co-operation in the Colonial Sphere (*Asiatic Review*, 1941, pp. 625–33).

HINDEN, Dr RITA. Imperialism To-day (*Fabian Quarterly*, 1945, pp. 5–12).

HUGHES, T. L. The Campaign in and Evacuation of Burma (*Royal Central Asian Journal*, 1944, pp. 80–92).

INNES, Sir CHARLES. The Separation of Burma (*Asiatic Review*, 1934, pp. 193–215).

The Future of Burma (*Asiatic Review*, 1937, pp. 177–90).

LEACH, F. BURTON. Autonomy on Trial in Burma (*Asiatic Review*, 1939, pp. 631–43).

Burma's War Effort (*Asiatic Review*, 1940, pp. 745–50).

Burma (*Quarterly Review*, 1944, pp. 83–96).

MEIJER RANNEFT, J. W. Indische Economie (*Koloniale Studiën*, 1928, pp. 151–61).

MOOK, H. J. VAN. International Aspects of the Future of Africa (*Journal of the Royal African Society*, 1943, pp. 177–81).

PORTER, CATHERINE. The Future of Philippine-American Relations (*Pacific Affairs*, 1943, pp. 261–76).

WILDE, A. N. DE. Dutch Policy in the East Indies (*Asiatic Review*, 1934, pp. 216–33).

CHAPTER I

THE BACKGROUND OF COLONIAL POLICY AND PRACTICE

1. COLONIES AND DOMINIONS

ONE outstanding feature of world history during the last few centuries is the expansion of Europe. In some regions, chiefly in North and South America, settlements of European origin have become independent powers. Other settlements, in what are now the British dominions, are independent in all but name and sentiment, though owing a voluntary allegiance to the Crown. But wide areas, mostly in the tropics, still remain under the rule of a few western powers, reckoning as western powers the countries and dominions of western origin. Some, at the outset of the late war, were ruled by Japan, which had recently established itself in the position of a western power. In law these subordinate regions exhibit a wide variety of status, but they may all conveniently be termed colonies, and the powers that have assumed responsibility for their welfare may be termed colonial powers. Colonization originally implied settlement, but the tropics have been colonized with capital rather than with men, and most tropical countries under foreign rule are dependencies rather than colonies, though in practice both terms are used indifferently. Some tropical countries, such as Siam, though in law politically independent, resemble colonies because, in their economic relations, they are largely dependent on the West.

Up to the end of the last century, or even later, tropical peoples seemed, after the initial troubles of pacification, to accept, and even to welcome, foreign rule. Of British dependencies it has been said that 'a sentiment of alienation or estrangement has seldom shown itself in the earlier days of British administration.... Where the sentiment occurs, it has tended to manifest itself most clearly as the people of the dependencies advance in education and standards of living.'[1] That is generally true of tropical dependencies in their relations with colonial powers. Towards the end of the nineteenth century impatience of foreign control appeared both in India and the

---

[1] Hailey, Lord, *Britain and Her Dependencies* (1943), p. 36.

Philippines, and during the present century a reaction against western rule, and even against western civilization, has spread rapidly and widely. This raised new problems for those concerned directly in the administration or development of tropical countries, but it hardly touched the ordinary man except to suggest that his investments might be safer elsewhere. Recent events, however, and especially the rapid collapse of western rule throughout the Tropical Far East, have thrown down a rude challenge to western dominion in the tropics, and even those who know little of the outer world, beyond what they gather from the newspaper, have come to feel that colonial policy and practice need reconsideration.

The general growth of discontent and unrest, and the general sudden collapse in the Pacific, suggest a common cause in some defect inherent in colonial relations. The situation is all the more remarkable by the striking contrast between the dependencies and the dominions. Formerly it was held that colonies resembled fruit which falls from the parent tree when it is ripe. Yet the links of interest and affection between Britain and the dominions seem to grow stronger, while dependencies clamour for independence even when to outside view they seem unripe for it, and we have come to regard it as natural and right that they should claim independence. It would seem possible for Burma to gain much more than Canada from an association with Britain. But, as a former Chief Secretary to the Government of Burma said recently, 'it may be candidly admitted that our rule was not beloved by the Burmans'.[1] Why should the ties with Canada grow closer while Burma finds them irksome? What common factor is there making for estrangement with the dependencies? All human relations have a particular character arising out of the personality of those concerned, and this is no less true of colonial relations. The relations between Englishmen and Hindus cannot be identical with the relations between French and Annamese, or between Dutch and Javanese. Yet Europeans have much in common that contrasts with features common to tropical peoples in general, and colonial relations in themselves present many common problems that are little if at all affected by the particular nationality or race of those concerned. Let us then glance briefly at some of the common factors in colonial policy and practice.

<hr>

[1] Leach, *Quarterly Review*, Jan. 1944, p. 50.

2. The Background of Colonial Policy

It would appear superfluous to argue that the western powers which have come to exercise dominion in the tropics have a fundamental unity. No one would suggest that Portuguese and Spaniard, Dutch, English, French and American are all alike; all have their distinctive national character which is an invisible export on every ship from Europe. The towns which they have built in the tropics are as different as those who built them. Similarly, each colonial power has stamped its own imprint on its system of administration. But the West has a common civilization derived from Greece and Rome under the vitalizing impulse of Christianity. When this civilization first made contact with the tropics the rebirth of reason had already begun to liberate fresh sources of material power by the rationalization of economic life; from that time onwards there has been a growing tendency in the West to base economic and social relations on reason, impersonal law and individual rights.

Similarly, throughout the tropics one finds everywhere a basic resemblance in the social structure. There is a wide range of variation, from primitive tribal communities to settled agricultural societies with a complex social and political organization, yet in all the variations, from the most primitive to the most advanced, one can trace a common pattern. Under native rule everywhere, even in settled agricultural communities, social and political relations were customary, not legal; authority was personal, based on Will and not on Law; and both custom and authority were closely bound up with religion. The social order rested not on impersonal law and individual rights, but on personal authority and customary obligations, and authority and custom derived their sanction not from reason but from religion.

Wherever a western power has gained dominion in the tropics, or even, as in Siam, a large measure of economic control without actual political sovereignty, an intimate contact has been established between these two contrary principles of social life: between the eastern system, resting on religion, personal authority and customary obligations, and the western system, resting on reason, impersonal law and individual rights. That is a common feature of all colonial relations. And it is common to them also that the contact has been established for the advantage of the colonial power, and that the first condition of establishing dominion is the maintenance of order.

Ordinarily, the motive of colonial expansion has been economic advantage. Considerations of prestige and military strategy have played their part, but in the main economic considerations have prevailed. It is, indeed, generally true that colonization has arisen out of commerce, and not commerce out of colonization: the doctrine that trade follows the flag is quite modern, and in history the flag has followed trade. During the earlier stages of its expansion Europe produced little that tropical peoples required, and the main object of colonial policy was to get tropical produce at the lowest cost. That was the economic end of empire in the days of Portugal and Spain. The same end was attained more effectively by the great chartered companies, concentrating on economic activities, enjoying, as regards their nationals, a monopoly over eastern produce, and exercising sovereign powers which enabled them to obtain part of their supplies free of cost as tribute. But, with the growing rationalization of life in the western world, man has achieved a greater mastery over material resources, and there has been a continual readjustment of colonial policy to meet new conditions arising through economic progress. The first great change was the Industrial Revolution, which enabled Europe to sell its products in the tropics. This required a new colonial policy, no longer directed towards obtaining tropical produce cheaply through chartered companies, but towards opening up markets for the sale of European manufactures by the encouragement of native enterprise. Further economic development in Europe built up large-scale enterprise, needing a secure command over vast quantities of raw materials which natives working by their own methods were unable to supply; at the same time it created a surplus of capital available for overseas investment. Thus, from about 1870, with the opening of the Suez Canal, the tropical market ceased to be the main object of colonial policy, which now aimed at obtaining the necessary raw materials of industry by the rapid development of the tropics through western enterprise. Meanwhile, in some of the more closely populated regions, the abundant supply of cheap unorganized labour was attracting capital to oriental industry and manufacture, with the result that during recent years imports from India and Japan have reduced the value of the tropics as a market for cheap European manufactures, though increasing rather than diminishing their demand for capital goods. This has encouraged in the colonial powers a more sympathetic attitude towards local manufactures in their dependencies, and towards economic nationalism; but the full effect on colonial policy of this new trend, which was interrupted by the recent war, is not yet clearly visible. In this gradual transformation of world economy during the building of the modern world, all colonial powers and all dependencies have been involved, and it has been necessary, as a condition of survival, that colonial powers should revise their policy to meet the challenge of new circumstances.

The course of economic progress has had a further reaction on colonial policy by its effect on domestic politics within the colonial powers. In Britain the transition from a policy of endowing a chartered company with a monopoly over tropical products to a policy of opening a free market for British goods signalized, and was partly the result of, the transfer of power from the aristocracy and London merchants to the manufacturers of Manchester. When, in due course, policy turned in the direction of developing the natural resources of the tropics by western enterprise, Manchester had to meet the growing rivalry of heavy industry in Birmingham, and of financial interests in the City. But at this stage a new factor intervened. In order to secure its interests against the increasing power of capital, labour entered politics. For some time this had no obvious reaction on colonial policy. Manchester and Birmingham alike furnished employment, and imports of tropical produce encouraged production and reduced prices; colonial rule was profitable, more or less, to all classes. But the clash between labour and capital in Parliament encouraged a tendency towards colonial autonomy under capitalist control, answered by labour with demands for colonial autonomy on a democratic basis. Then, with the growth of tropical industry and manufacture, the conditions of labour in the tropics became a matter of economic interest to various classes in Britain, and welfare measures began to assume a new importance in colonial policy. In other lands, also, colonial policy has been moulded by the interplay of conflicting domestic interests, and in general on much the same pattern, though in some countries the rivalry of industry and agriculture has had a greater influence on colonial policy than in Britain.

Naturally, colonial policy is framed with reference to the interests, real or imagined, of the colonial power. But modern colonization is an affair of capital and not of men, and capital knows no country. The capitalist, the owner of capital, may be swayed by national or ethical considerations, but reason impels him to disregard them and lay out his capital where, on a long view, it will obtain the best return, and within recent times capitalist activities, reaching out rapidly beyond national boundaries, have acquired an extra-national character. Labour interests have had to counter this by uniting in an international association with a common policy. Out of the adjustment of the relations between capital and labour on an international plane has arisen a common recognition that the economic development of the tropics is a matter of world welfare.

Not infrequently, however, there is a conflict between world welfare and particular national interests, and colonial powers, pursuing their own interests, tend to disregard world welfare and the interests of other powers. The danger of rivalry in the colonial sphere first found public recognition in the Berlin Conference of 1884–5, which marked a new stage in the evolution of a common colonial policy. Before that one can trace a common resemblance in the colonial policy of different powers because they all had *similar* interests; from the closing years of the nineteenth century the common features of colonial policy are accentuated because colonial powers recognize, at least in name, a *common* interest in the development of backward areas. Colonial policy, though still directed with primary reference to the interests, real or imagined, of the colonial power, must now be justified to world opinion with reference to world welfare.

But colonial policy is only one aspect of national policy; each generation evolves its own social philosophy with no direct reference to colonial affairs, and inevitably colonial policy is framed in terms of the broad general conceptions which dominate the national outlook, and reflects the emergence of new general ideas. Moreover, although colonial relations arise out of the search for material advantage, men like to justify their activities on moral grounds and colour them with the warm glow of humanitarianism. 'I do not pretend', says the historian of the Portuguese Empire, 'that our sole aim was to preach, if others will allow that it was not only to trade.' When men came to accept the principle of freedom of person, property and trade, consistency required that it should be extended to colonial relations. Similarly, the idea of social justice that took shape in Europe during the nineteenth century permeated colonial policy, and so likewise did the ideas of democracy and self-determination or nationalism. It was self-determination in Europe for which Asquith drew the sword in 1914, but before the war was ended the right of colonies to self-determination had been recognized in principle. Again, popular Darwinism of the last century held that progress was achieved through the survival of the fittest, of the more efficient; accordingly, in the name of progress and efficiency, men set themselves to run the colonies on more business-like, efficient, lines. Thus colonial policy tends to follow, even if at a distance, domestic policy. Liberty, Social Justice, Democracy, if approved as sauce for the domestic goose, are served up a little later with the colonial gander; Free Trade is good for Britain, and good, therefore, for India; social legislation protects British labour and should, therefore, promote welfare in the tropics; democracy strengthens the political fibre of Europe and should, therefore, help dependencies towards autonomy. As one aspect of national policy, colonial policy reflects ideas transcending economic aims. It is true that, in retrospect, ideals claiming a moral basis have often worked in practice to the advantage of the colonial power rather than of the dependency, and men are apt to dismiss the humanitarianism of a former age as humbug and its zealous advocates as hypocrites. That is partly because on the whole morality is a paying proposition; yet, though it pays to be honest, men are not honest merely because it pays. For ideas have an independent vitality; men accept them even to their apparent prejudice. And the ideas may outlast the empire which they help to build, just as Roman law survived the fall of Rome and provides a steel framework to the fabric of the modern world, and as in the Spanish colonies the Faith survived the fall of Spain. So in Asia and Africa the ideas of Law and Liberty and Social Justice may have a longer life than western rule. But the point immediately relevant is that the succession of these general ideas is common to western civilization and therefore to all western colonial powers, and forms a common feature in the evolution of colonial policy.

If, then, colonial relations have so much in common, and colonial policy reflects the application to colonial relations of ideas which are common to all colonial powers, it might seem that a comparative survey of pronouncements on colonial policy should lead to the enunciation of certain principles of colonial rule. But the matter is not so simple. One obstacle to the progress of the social sciences is the difficulty that students find in maintaining an objective attitude. The rules for statesmen which the economist prescribes in his academic cloister reflect his political opinions; educationists vehemently debate what education should and might be, and what it could or must do with little heed to what education actually is and does; 'political philosophy has chiefly concerned itself with how men *ought* to live, and what form of government they *ought* to

have, rather than with what *are* their political habits and institutions '.[1]
Similarly, projects of colonial policy lay down the goal at which it
ought to aim, but the measures advocated to attain the goal, even if
free from unconscious bias and likely to succeed in Europe, often
lead in tropical dependencies in a different or even a contrary direction. In policy, as in law, men must be held to intend the natural
consequences of their acts, and it is from the results of colonial
policy rather than from statements of its objects that its true character
may be ascertained. In the study of colonial affairs statements of
policy need scrutiny in the light of practice. That is far more
difficult. For if a survey of colonial policy reveals a fundamental
identity in colonial relations, the study of colonial practice gives a
first impression of diversity.

3. THE BACKGROUND OF COLONIAL PRACTICE

In respect of colonial practice, however, one can distinguish two
factors characteristic of colonial relations in general. Since colonial
relations are predominantly economic, colonial practice is conditioned
by economic laws, and we shall see that in the tropics the working
of these laws has certain features common to all dependencies.
The second factor common to all colonial practice is that the
responsibility for maintaining order is assumed by the colonial
power; an organic autonomous society maintains order with more
or less success in virtue of its inherent vitality, but a dependency
is kept alive, as it were, by artificial respiration, by pressure exercised
mechanically from outside and above. These two factors are common
to all colonial relations, though it is in connection with them that
divergences in colonial practice first arise.

The prime care of any colonial power must be to maintain order,
for order is essential to such advantages as it anticipates from imposing its rule on the dependency. In maintaining order the colonial
power must choose between the western principle of law and the
tropical system of relying on personal authority, between direct and
indirect rule. Secondly, to attain the prospective advantages the
colonial power must choose between the western principle of freedom
and the tropical system of compulsion. These are the two main lines
along which colonial practice divides, and the line actually followed
is a resultant of complex factors. General ideas carry some weight:

[1] Fortes, M. and Evans-Pritchard, E. E., *African Political Systems* (1940), p. 4.

compulsion will be less uncongenial in an age which values welfare more than freedom. So also do national traditions: reliance on authority will be less uncongenial to a western power with a strongly centralized administration. Of greater importance is the relative strength of the ruler and the ruled: a chartered company reinforced once a year by a small fleet of sailing vessels must show more regard to native sentiment than a Governor who at need can summon by radio the assistance of modern naval and military forces. These things affect colonial practice, but the dominating factor is the nature of the advantage envisaged by the colonial power from its relations with the dependency; whether it is chiefly concerned to sell its own goods or to obtain tropical produce. All these conditions vary from one colonial power to another, from one dependency to another, in different dependencies of the same colonial power, and in the same dependency at different times; and colonial practice varies accordingly. Naturally then in any comparison of colonial relations it is the diversity of practice which first impresses the observer, and only by tracing their evolution can the first impression be corrected.

Yet even a historical study may be misleading. For colonial relations arise out of the impact of western civilization on the tropics, and the violence of this impact varies with the width of the gap between the particular western and tropical cultures, and the rate at which the process of bringing them together is effected. In their mastery over the material world, India and Europe in the sixteenth century were far closer together than modern Europe and the modern tropics; the connection dates from before the Industrial Revolution, and both have grown up in the modern world together. Again, Indian society stands alone in resting on the institution of caste, which has fortified it to some extent against the impact of the West. For both these reasons care is needed in drawing parallels between conditions in India and in the tropics generally. Where tropical conditions elsewhere resemble those of India, one may presume that they are inherent in colonial relations. For example, one feature of the modern tropics that is not confined to India is the growth of agricultural indebtedness; another feature is the increasing impatience of foreign rule. On the other hand, if India is in some measure exempt from the 'atomization' of society that is found elsewhere in the tropics, the explanation may lie in the fact that the impact of the West has been less violent, and that caste has afforded a considerable measure of protection.

Still it remains true that, if one would understand colonial practice, one must study it both comparatively and historically. Such a survey could hardly be compressed within the limits of a single volume, even of the dimensions of Lord Hailey's *African Survey*, and would need abilities to which the present writer can make no pretence. It is, however, as a contribution to such a study that the following comparison of British rule in Burma with Dutch rule in Netherlands India is intended. It is a comparison with many points of interest. Both countries came under the effective rule of the home Government shortly after the Industrial Revolution had transformed the economic, and therefore the social and political, relations between Europe and the tropics, and when the social philosophy of Europe was dominated by liberal ideas; in both, therefore, it is possible to trace the reaction on colonial practice of subsequent economic progress and of the procession of general ideas. Both countries, like the tropics in general, lacked the consolidating bond of caste to protect them against the solvent influence of western thought and economic forces. In these things both countries are alike. But in respect of colonial practice they show a striking contrast. In Burma the British have from the first relied on western principles of rule, on the principles of law and economic freedom; in Netherlands India the Dutch have tried to conserve and adapt to modern use the tropical principles of custom and authority. In each case the choice was dictated in the first instance by the interests of the colonial power. When Britain first established contact with Burma it could already sell its produce in the East and looked to Burma as a market. The Dutch at that time had neither manufactures nor capital; they wanted tropical produce at the lowest cost and could best obtain it through the native chieftains. For an understanding of subsequent developments it is necessary to have some knowledge of physical conditions and past history in the two regions.

4. BURMA

The dominant factor in the social life of Burma is immediately apparent on a first glance at the map. It is cut off from the world by mountains and the sea. Though marching with India, China and Siam, land traffic with these countries on any considerable scale is almost impossible. From the mountains on the north two rivers run throughout the length of Burma, the Irrawaddy and the Salween, and between them is a third river, the Sittang, rising in the middle of Burma and also running south. The mountains and hills, separating these rivers and on either side of them, are covered with forest, and are sparsely inhabited by backward hill tribes. Apart from the hill country there are five natural divisions: Burma Proper, the central tract of rolling uplands; the Shan Tableland, open country in the eastern hills; Pegu, comprising the deltaic plains; Arakan, a broken strip of land along the Bay of Bengal, cut off from Burma by the Arakan Hills; and Tenasserim, the southern projection towards the Malay Peninsula. Burma Proper, the Shan Tableland and the surrounding hills are known as Upper Burma; the rest of the country, comprising Pegu, Arakan and Tenasserim, is known as Lower Burma. The Salween, forcing its way through narrow mountain gorges, is of little use to commerce, but the Irrawaddy is navigable by steamboats for nearly a thousand miles, and its main tributary, the Chindwin, is also open to steam navigation. The Sittang, owing to a bore, is difficult of navigation, but is open to large country boats for some two hundred miles. Thus within Burma, even under primitive conditions, it has always been easy to travel north and south, and the facility of communications has favoured the growth of a common social life, while at the same time the difficulty of communications between one valley and the next has been an obstacle to the permanent establishment of a common political authority. The only part of Burma where a man may pass easily in all directions is the centre, commanding the valleys of the Chindwin, the Irrawaddy and the Sittang. Farther south the level plains formed in the deltas of the rivers are cut up by innumerable creeks, and the heavy rainfall promotes dense forest growth, but in the centre of the country there are few streams, and the arid climate allows only of scrub jungle that forms no barrier to traffic. Natural conditions, therefore, mark out Central Burma as the seat of political authority. This has had an unfortunate reaction on the course of social evolution, for, in a country naturally isolated, social life has centred in the region most remote from the quickening impulse of contact with the outer world. On the other hand, isolation has allowed Burma to build up its own distinctive culture.

Burmans in general[1] have a basis of indonesian or nēsiot blood, mixed with more primitive elements and strongly overlaid with mongoloid

---

[1] Here, and so far as possible subsequently, the term 'Burman' connotes all the indigenous inhabitants of Burma together with permanent residents of alien origin who have come to regard themselves as natives of the country; this leaves 'Burmese' for use as a distinctively racial term.

characters, derived from successive waves of migration from the
north. Until recently the inhabitants of the deltaic plains along the
southern coast were Mons or Talaings, a people with an austronesian
language but a mongoloid physique. Formerly, their northern neighbours were the Pyus, but these were conquered and assimilated by
the Burmese who came down into the plains about A.D. 600–800. By
1100 the Burmese had conquered the whole of Burma. Two hundred
years later the Shans, cousins of the Siamese, broke across the eastern
border, and the subsequent course of Burmese history is largely a tale
of conflict between Burmese, Shans and Mons, punctuated by wars
with Siam and Arakan. In the event the Burmese gained the mastery,
drove the Shans back to the eastern hills to rule petty states as vassals
of their Burmese overlord, and subjugated, and in great part assimilated, the Mons. They also conquered the Arakanese. Of the other
peoples of Burma it will suffice to mention here the Chins and
Kachins, backward hill tribes but in racial stock and language akin to
the Burmese, and the Karens, a mixture of mongoloid peoples with
doubtful affinities, who have gained in importance under British rule
by the conversion of large numbers to Christianity. The Burmese,
Shans and Mons, though of somewhat diverse racial origin and
widely different in language, all partake the common Buddhist culture
that they have absorbed from India.

During the first millennium of the Christian era, though at long
intervals, merchants from India established trading posts and settle-
ments all along the coasts and up some of the larger rivers of the
Tropical Far East. They brought with them their religion and a
higher civilization than had hitherto been known. Some were
Hindus, and some Mahayanist or Hinayanist Buddhists. In Burma,
Hinayanism seems always to have predominated and was the religion
which finally prevailed. Early Chinese sources portray among the
Pyus a social life that in its leading features was still characteristic of
Burma during the nineteenth century. There was little intercourse
with India after the tenth century, but contact with Hinayanism was
maintained by the occasional interchange of missions with Ceylon.
It is Buddhism that has moulded social Burman life and thought, and
to the present day the ordinary Burman regards the terms Burman
and Buddhist as practically equivalent and inseparable. The whole
political and social life of Burma, from the palace to the village,
centred round the Buddhist religion and the monastic order. The
King had his domestic chaplain and every village its monastery.

The Crown regulated clerical affairs through a patriarch who, with the assistance of a council of ecclesiastics, presided over the whole organization and had jurisdiction over the monks and over matters of religion.[1] Within the Order there were sectarian divisions, represented on the central council, and a dignitary of one sect had no authority over monks of a different sect. Although a monk could be unfrocked and excommunicated for heresy or gross sin, obedience to a superior was voluntary and the monasteries were largely autonomous. Each village appointed, or rather 'invited', its own monk, just as the King selected his own chaplain, but a monk once inducted to a monastery was almost independent of control. Another feature of the organization was its democratic character. Anyone of approved life could obtain ordination by taking the prescribed vows, and the great majority of the monks were ordinary villagers. If the monastic discipline and vows of chastity and temperance should prove too rigorous, a monk could at any time return to secular life. But so long as anyone wore the yellow robe, he was the object of superstitious veneration. The King, as head of a Buddhist State, was head also of the Church and had large patronage, but, as an individual, he recognized yesterday's new monk as his superior. This loosely knit religious organization helped greatly to preserve social continuity when civil government collapsed.

One tradition of Buddhism, which has been observed in Burma with great faithfulness, is that every boy should learn at least his letters. Under Burmese rule there was a monastery in every village, with a monastic school, in which all boys, regardless of rank or wealth, learned from the presiding monk the creed and moral precepts of their religion, and gradually absorbed the national traditions of their people. There was a tradition also of female education, though, in fact, not many girls learned to read and write. The freedom and high social status of the women, a feature common to all the peoples of the Tropical Far East, even among those which adopted Hinduism or, later, Islam, has always been especially conspicuous in Burma. Along with their religion the Indians brought the arts of architecture, sculpture, wood-carving, and painting, and these also the Burman peoples made their own in a form distinct from that of India but common to the whole of Burma, so that all the leading peoples, and even those hill tribes which accepted Buddhism, had a common social culture, shared also by Siam. Neither in learning nor the arts

[1] *UBG*, ii, 1 ff.

did their civilization attain a level comparable with that of India, China, or Japan, but it had its own distinctive character and was very generally diffused among the people.

The social and political structure was in the main indigenous. The unit of social life was naturally the agricultural village or settlement, but the higher organization was partly tribal and partly territorial. Groups of ten or twenty villages up to fifty or more were governed by a hereditary local chieftain. But his authority was personal, not strictly local; the political organization was quasi-regimental, and if, within the territory of a local chieftain, there were people of another regiment or group, they were subject to the jurisdiction of their own leader and not to that of the local chieftain. Above the local organization there was a central administrative system; how far this derived from China or India is uncertain. At times the Supreme King ruled the country through subordinate kings or vassals governing large provinces, but from a very early period there was a tradition of a more centralized form of government, and this acquired sharper definition under the dynasty that ruled from the middle of the seventeenth century. The Crown, with an Advisory Council, serving also as a High Court, was the centre from which there radiated an official administrative organization linking up through the hereditary petty chieftains with local affairs. The functioning of the system has not yet been adequately studied, but certain features are clear. One is that there was a dual system, with a purely official central element and an hereditary local element. The next is that it was a product of gradual evolution with the complexity inherent in such a process. Thirdly, it had no firm basis either in law or on military force and was accordingly unstable. There was no regular army beyond the quasi-feudal levies, no regular police, and there were practically no prisons. Thus, although in theory absolute, and in practice often arbitrary, the King had no means to enforce orders that were not regarded as within his customary powers. There were law books regarded as expositions or adaptations of a Buddhist version of the Laws of Manu, and, in addition to the High Court, already mentioned, the provincial governors and their subordinates exercised judicial functions, in addition to their other duties. But they acted as arbitrators rather than as judges, referring to the law books for guidance, but not for rules, and aiming to effect a settlement between the parties rather than to decide on points of law and fact. The officials drew no fixed salary. Some were paid by allotment of the revenue of a particular district, but for the most part their emoluments were derived from a commission on revenue collected, or from fees paid by the parties to a case. One great source of revenue was from local tolls on the transport or sale of goods.

In theory life was minutely regulated. The whole kingdom, according to an eighteenth-century traveller, was governed by the pen. No one could move without permission from one village to another. No one could transfer to another regiment or group, nor could anyone marry outside the regiment or group without paying a fine. No one could build a house, or dress, or even be buried except in a style appropriate to his rank. But the periodical census rolls which illustrate some of these precepts show also that many of them were often disregarded. And anyone of the humblest birth, with few exceptions, could aspire to the highest position, one broad avenue to promotion being the monastery.

This complex social organization, medieval in its character, was based almost entirely on agriculture. External trade was unimportant and subject to severe restrictions, exports being regarded with disfavour. There was little in Burma to tempt the outside world until the eighteenth century, when the teak forests acquired a new value for shipbuilding during the wars in Indian waters between the French and English. At long intervals when, as during the late war, the sea route and main land route to China from the West were blocked, Burma figures in history as a backdoor to China, and it is probable that the early Indian settlements up the Irrawaddy at Prome and Pagan may have been in connection with this trade. But the silks of China, and spices from the Moluccas, ordinarily went straight across Asia or round by sea, and Burma was left in a backwater cut off from the outer world. It had little to attract the outer world, and, on the other hand, it produced at home all the requirements of a simple medieval agricultural civilization; its own food, rice, millet, vegetable oils, fish and salt; its own silk and cotton; its own pottery and tools and weapons. In its agricultural resources it was exceptionally fortunate. Central Burma with its dry climate grew cotton and oil-seeds, while the deltaic plains of Lower Burma, with their regular and heavy rainfall, could yield vast quantities of rice, and an ample supply of fish and salt. At one time the rice plains seem to have been closely peopled, but they were the chief scene of the wars between the Burmese and the Mons and, during the last war leading to the final victory of the Burmese in 1752, they were laid waste so thoroughly that a generation or more later the census rolls report some tracts as almost uninhabited.

A comparatively small area yielded a surplus adequate to meet the
requirements of Upper Burma, and fresh land came under cultivation
only as the population gradually increased and required more food.
In such conditions it is a slow and difficult process to reclaim land
that has once been abandoned to the jungle, and it was not until some
time after the British occupation that, with the opening up of a foreign
market, cultivation spread rapidly. Thus at the time of the first war with
Britain in 1824–6, Upper and Lower Burma presented a striking contrast. In the central dry tract of Upper Burma there was an established
peasantry practising mixed agriculture on dry land, whereas in the
deltaic plains the chief occupations of a scanty people were the cultivation of rice, fishing, and salt-boiling, and (except in the parts
bordering on Upper Burma and supplying it with rice, fish and salt) a
few small market towns and some villages and hamlets were sparsely
scattered among wide areas of swamp and waste. Those conditions
have very largely determined the whole course of the subsequent
economic and social development of Burma.

One other feature must be noted. Although the history of Burma
is so largely made up of war between Burmese, Shans and Mons,
yet during long periods they have been united. From the end of
the eleventh century to the end of the thirteenth, Burmese kings
ruled in Pagan over a region corresponding to the Burma of the
present day. During this period the Burmans absorbed the Mon
civilization, and research indicates that the kings were partly of Mon
blood. In the middle of the sixteenth century a Burmese prince made
himself master of the Mon country and adopted Mon ways, while his
successor on the throne of Pegu, the capital of the Mons, extended his
rule over the Burmese homeland, and reunited under one rule the
whole of the former Burmese Empire of Pagan. After a sudden
collapse in 1600 the whole country was once again brought under a
single rule for a hundred and fifty years. This dynasty fell when the
last king was taken captive by a Mon rebel, but the Burmese immediately rose again under a new leader who reconquered the whole
country, and established a new line which held the throne up to the
time of the British conquest. Thus for the greater part of the time
since 1100 the whole country recognized a common rule. When the
Burmese finally defeated the Mons in 1752 they laid waste the country,
but for the most part re-established the hereditary local chieftains,
and although most of the provincial governors were Burmese and the
official language was Burmese, Mons were eligible for the highest

offices under the Burmese Crown, and their separate national feeling was fast disappearing.[1] The whole country, marked out by nature as a distinct political unit, and with a common religion and a uniform social culture, had a far more national character than one could find anywhere in India. 'The Burmans, in fact, correspond far more closely to the ordinary conception of a nation than the Indians.' They had 'developed what may fairly be called a nation State, and possess a national consciousness';[2] the Mons and even many Karens preferred to be considered Burmans.

In this national society, however, authority was personal. Burmese, Shan, Mon and Karen were all ruled by chieftains of their own people. The Court and the central administrative organization were largely Burmese, but the local administration was racial, not because of the difference of race, but because rule was based on personal relations. The Karens had their own head, but so also had the brokers, and the manufacturers of palm-sugar.[3] Racial differences were not reflected in economic functions and, so far as the people were Buddhist, they had a common civilization and all met and mixed together. This civilization which the people of Burma, despite frequent and prolonged civil and foreign wars, built up through the centuries, had many pleasant features. In every village the monks, in a community singularly free of scandal, imparted to all the boys the elements of letters and practical morality. The monastic order, free to all and spread over the whole country, was influential but not oppressive, and Church and State, instead of dividing the country by their rival claims, lent each other mutual support. The women enjoyed a freedom greater in some ways than in other countries of the Tropical Far East, unparalleled elsewhere in Asia and, until recently, exceptional in Europe. And if one aim of the State be the organization of happiness, then, by common consent, few people have been more light-hearted than the Burmese, a happiness that the numerous and severe political catastrophes must have interrupted but did not dispel. This national civilization was held together mainly by two strong links; the monastic order and the hereditary local chieftains. Through intervals of anarchy these survived, and it was round them that society grew up anew, but on the old lines, when order was restored.

The best picture of life in Burma under native rule is that given by

---

[1] Gouger, p. 266; Trant, pp. 117–18; *BBG*, II, 168.
[2] *ISC*, XI, 570; Harvey, *CHI*, V, 566; VI, 447; *BBG*, II, 553.
[3] Harvey, *Burma*, p. 352; *BBG*, I, 483; II, 127, 181.

Gouger, who was a prisoner in Burma during the first war with Britain. He was a merchant who had found it impossible to compete against the agents of the East India Company in Bengal, and came to sell his cotton goods to Burmans. On his arrival in Rangoon he was favourably impressed by 'the absence of all unauthorized exactions',[1] and took his goods to the capital in Upper Burma 'with no annoying exactions or tolls to impede them on their passage'.[2] When he reached it 'no royal or municipal dues were demanded; no troublesome official appeared to obstruct the course of business, and he found himself comfortably established in his new quarters with less vexation and annoyance than he would have encountered in any town in Europe'.[3] British envoys had always complained of vexatious delays before they could secure a reception, but 'nothing of the kind was experienced by the foreigner who had no State dignity to uphold'. There was, he remarks, far less difficulty in gaining an audience with the King than he would have had in interviewing the Secretary of State in Downing Street; 'a few questions were asked at the *Byadike* (secretariat), and in less than an hour I was in the presence of the King'. Like the others present he squatted on the floor, half sitting and half kneeling, but the King, noticing his discomfort, desired him to be at ease, and before long he 'had the audacity to sit upright and stare His Majesty in the face'.[4]

His next visit, when he brought samples of his goods, gave him 'a pleasant impression of the freedom allowed to the inmates of the Palace. The hilarity, good humour, and cheerfulness exhibited by the ladies of the Royal household, were sufficient evidence that no excessive strictness of discipline was exerted to mar their happiness.' The girls dressed up in his wares 'and no effort was made to restrain the laughter and fun'. Even when the Queen entered, 'her presence did not serve to impress more than a salutary restraint'. The King himself saw that all the girls paid for what they took, and 'entered into the spirit of the trafficking, laughing heartily at every dispute'.[5] A like cheerfulness prevailed among the common people, and he was greatly struck by 'the free-and-easy bearing of the natives, contrasting so harshly with the obsequiousness and the polished insincerity to which he had been accustomed in Hindostan'. On the other hand, towards their own rulers there was 'certainly no lack of servility'. Every one in authority was despotic, and the people were submissive.[6]

---

[1] Gouger, p. 15.   [2] *Ib*. p. 24.   [3] *Ib*. p. 27.
[4] *Ib*. pp. 29, 33.   [5] *Ib*. p. 43.   [6] *Ib*. p. 10.

As customers he found them very satisfactory. To some he had to grant credit, and was astonished at their very loose manner of committing engagements to writing, with merely a record of the transaction, and the witnesses, written in pencil and unsigned. He was assured that this was their custom, and that the debt could be established by the witnesses, and 'it spoke well for the people that none of them failed in their payments'.[1]

In view of his freedom from unauthorized exactions when landing his goods and taking them up-country, it is rather strange to read that 'bribery is the mainspring by which all manner of business is moved throughout the country'. But this was brought home to him when he wished to go back to India with his profits, as the law allowed him to take neither money nor goods. Restrictions were so numerous, and regulated life so closely, that it was inconvenient and almost impossible to live within them; but it was always possible to get round them. When he wanted to get round the regulations, he 'became as expert a briber as the rest'.[2] In other respects, however, his account of the conduct of official business is favourable. He gives a very interesting description of the disposal of affairs in the Privy Council, which was also the High Court. This was presided over by the King, and met every day at sunrise. 'Nothing could exceed the order and solemnity with which business was transacted, for although I very imperfectly understood what was going forward, and although bribery and corruption might be at the root of every subject discussed, yet it was evident that there *was* a discussion, that rival interests were represented, and that the semblance at least of a certain amount of freedom of opinion was preserved. The usual form of introducing a topic was by a written document, which was read, or rather sung, or intoned, by an officer of the Court...and before the Royal order was given on it, those present were permitted to express themselves....The sight was altogether an imposing one, calculated to inspire confidence in a stranger by the strict order and apparent deliberation that prevailed in the assembly.'[3]

Thus, although social life in Burma had a very limited horizon, and its political institutions, lacking any secure foundation in law, were unstable, yet the country when first brought into contact with the West provided a good example, both in its virtues and defects, of a medieval eastern society embodying a system resting on personal authority, custom and religion.

[1] Gouger, p. 63.   [2] *Ib.* p. 50.   [3] *Ib.* p. 56; cf. Trant, pp. 241 ff.

5. NETHERLANDS INDIA

If we turn over the pages of the atlas from Burma to Netherlands
India, we find a map suggesting conditions very different from those
of Burma. In place of a comparatively small country shut in by sea
and mountain there is an open archipelago, comprising numerous
islands, large and small. Yet, as is apparent in the British Empire,
to a seafaring people the sea is a bond and not a barrier. Man learned
the art of sailing earlier than the art of making roads, and in early
times, indeed until quite recently, the waterways were the main
highways. The peoples of Netherlands India have in general a
common racial stock, similar to that of Burma, though less strongly
mongoloid and more profoundly nēsiot, and they speak indonesian
languages, distantly akin to that spoken by the Mons. Now they are
commonly termed Indonesians and their common home is often called
Indonesia. Three times the whole region, or the greater part of it, has
been united under a common rule: during the ninth century under
Shri-Vijaya in Sumatra; in the fourteenth century under Majapahit
in Java, and then under the Dutch. Shri-Vijaya and Majapahit were
respectively Mahayanist and Hindu, and had their origin in the
Indian settlements of the first millennium. Civilization in the archipelago, as in Burma, has an Indian basis and, although from about
1300 Islam has spread gradually and has become the dominant creed,
it was India that moulded social life.

The attraction of Indonesia for these Indian merchants, as for later
merchants from the West, was presumably the trade of China and,
more especially, the spices of the Moluccas. It was only along the
coasts on the main routes to China and the Moluccas that they founded
settlements and spread civilization. Their chief settlements were on
the mainland in the Malay Peninsula and Indo-China, and in the
archipelago on Sumatra and Java. The other islands, even Borneo and
Celebes, show little trace of direct Indian influence. In Java there
evolved an agricultural civilization similar in many ways to that of
Burma. The diet of the people consisted of rice, vegetable oils and
fish, and they grew and wove their own cotton. As in Burma the
women enjoyed great freedom, and the conditions of land tenure were
very similar in Burma and Java. The social and political organization
also was very much the same. In Java there were three distinct
peoples, the Sundanese, Javanese and Madurese, sometimes independent and sometimes under a common overlord, but all had a dual

administrative system in which provincial officers of the central Government ruled the people through hereditary chieftains.

Within the archipelago Sumatra and Java have always been rivals for supremacy. Sumatra commands the gateway and the trade, but Java is the main granary. When the Dutch came East, they found the Portuguese, strongly entrenched in Malacca, guarding the northern seacoast of Sumatra, and they established themselves in Java, where they gradually extended their rule over the whole island. They also held the Spice Islands, but elsewhere they had only garrisons and trading posts. Up to about the beginning of the present century regular administration hardly extended beyond Java (including the adjacent small island of Madura) and the Spice Islands; the whole region outside Java and Madura was known collectively as the Outer Possessions or, later, Provinces. It was in Java that the Dutch system of administration took shape, and subsequent references to Dutch rule disregard the Outer Provinces unless otherwise indicated by the context.

Dutch rule in Java dates from the occupation of Batavia and the surrounding territory in 1619. Their chief concern was to obtain rice and other requirements, including products for export, among which coffee and sugar came to be the most important. They recognized those native chieftains who would undertake to supply them with what they wanted, and for long they abstained so far as possible from further interference with native life. These native chieftains came in general to be known as Regents. A European official was posted at suitable headquarters to see that the Regent fulfilled his obligations; this officer became known as a Resident. In order to obtain produce, and especially coffee, subordinates were charged with the duty of supervising cultivation, and eventually special officers for that purpose were appointed as *Controleurs* (inspectors) who had no authority but served merely as the eyes and ears of the Resident. That, in brief, was the origin of the Dutch system of indirect rule. There was a dual system comprising a European responsible for the business of the Company, and a native responsible to the Resident for the supply of produce, and with the Controleur as a link between the two. On this plan the Resident was regarded as the overlord, or 'elder brother', of the Regent who held the position of a largely autonomous vassal chieftain. On no other plan could the Dutch obtain the coffee and other things they wanted, as they had nothing to exchange for them.

This system, which arose by a process of gradual evolution, survived until the fall of the Company, largely as a result of the wars arising out of the French Revolution. In 1800 its possessions were taken over by the State. An acute controversy then arose as to the manner in which the country should be administered. Reformers wished to introduce a system somewhat resembling that of direct rule, then recently adopted in British India. Finally, it was decided to retain the system of indirect rule, but the Resident, as 'elder brother', was expected to prevent the abuses that the people had formerly suffered from the Regents. Before the new system could be introduced, Java passed by the fortune of war into the hands first of the French and then of the English. From 1811 to 1816 it was governed by Raffles on behalf of the East India Company. Raffles was conspicuous among the many leading servants of the Company at that time who believed fervently in the new Liberal faith. He set aside the Regents and introduced direct rule through officials, with the village under an elected headman as the unit of administration; in place of compulsory cultivation and services, he substituted taxes in money, thereby encouraging the people to sell their produce and buy imported British manufactures. At the end of the Napoleonic wars, however, the Dutch regained their territories. By this time Liberal doctrines were held by all enlightened men, and the Dutch came back to Java with the intention of ruling it on new Liberal principles, only to find that Raffles had applied these principles far more thoroughly than the Dutch had ever contemplated. That was the general position at the beginning of the modern period of Dutch rule in Netherlands India.

CHAPTER II

BURMA, 1826–1870: LAISSEZ-FAIRE

1. THE WARS OF 1824–6 AND 1852

(a) *1824–6.* Up to the beginning of the nineteenth century Burmans were still living in the Middle Ages, and in their medieval world they had good reason for complacency. In 1759 they conquered Pegu, and shortly afterwards their troops overran Siam and repelled an invasion from China, the traditional great power of the Tropical Far East. In 1785 they conquered Arakan and, with the new century, carried their arms still further, defeating Manipur in 1813 and Assam in 1816. This brought them into political contact along a common frontier with the expanding British power in India. At the same time they were making contact with the British on a common economic frontier. The long struggle between England and France during the eighteenth century created a demand for Burma teak, and, when the Continental System of Napoleon made British manufacturers look outside Europe to dispose of the cheap cotton goods produced by the recent Industrial Revolution, Burma offered a potential market. Thus quite suddenly, within a few years, the rulers and peoples of Burma were faced with a new challenge. Burma was brought into political and economic relations with the modern world; its whole political, economic and social organization needed readjustment to these new conditions and, failing reformation from within, forces that would not be denied were working for foreign intervention.

The rulers of Burma, secluded in the centre of their kingdom, were incapable alike of recognizing their danger and of imagining reforms, and they refused intercourse with the outer world except on their own terms. But, in standing out against the current of world progress, they were challenged by moral and material forces that they were wholly unable to resist; subjugation by some outside power was inevitable, and that Burma became involved with British India was merely the accident of propinquity. The two countries faced one another on the frontier of two different civilizations, and naturally there was a succession of difficult incidents culminating in the war of 1824–6, which showed that the power to determine the frontier between Burma and the modern world lay with Britain.

When hostilities began the British expected help from the Arakanese and the Talaings. These expectations were largely disappointed.[1] In 1785 Arakanese chieftains, in rebellion against their own King, had called on the King of Burma for assistance, but turned against him on finding that he treated their country as a conquered province. When their repeated insurrections failed, the rebels found refuge across the border in British territory which they used as a base for new attacks. This kept the spirit of resistance alive among the Arakanese and gave them a juster estimate of British power, so that, on the outbreak of war, the British were able to recruit an Arakanese levy. In Pegu the situation was different. Many, if not most, of the local chieftains were Talaings, whose ancestors had held the same position under their own kings; even the Governor of the important charge of Syriam, commanding the entrance to Rangoon, was a Talaing, with a sister married to the Burmese King.[2] They had accepted Burmese rule and, believing the Burmese to be invincible, made no attempt to rise until after the Burman power had been broken. The Burman forces, though no match for modern troops in armaments or military skill and discipline, made a brave but ineffectual resistance and, after operations in which the invaders suffered heavy losses from disease but few in battle, the Burmese Government was compelled in 1826 to accept the Treaty of Yandabo, including among its terms the cession of the two maritime provinces, Arakan and Tenasserim. These gave the British a bridgehead on each side of Burma in the event of further strife; Arakan marched with Chittagong and had formerly been the centre of a flourishing trade in rice; Tenasserim had valuable teak and was expected to open up a channel of trade with China and Siam.

For several years conditions were unsettled. Arakan gave most trouble. The chieftains, who had welcomed British aid against Burmese rule, were equally impatient of British rule. After a succession of petty risings, a widespread rebellion which had long been smouldering came to a head in 1836.[3] This was promptly suppressed, and there was no further serious disturbance. Tenasserim was quieter, but here also the men who had sided with the British turned against them. Under Burmese rule Tavoy and Mergui had been the seats of provincial governments. In 1830, insurgents captured Tavoy and in Mergui the British garrison, either panic-struck or misled by false rumours, withdrew, leaving the town in the hands of the rebels.[4]

[1] *BBG*, II, 553; Gouger, p. 266; Hall, *Europe and Burma* (1945), p. 114.
[2] *BBG*, II, 675.   [3] *BBG*, I, 480; II, 290, 623.   [4] *BBG*, I, 483; II, 382, 691.

Order was restored and subsequently British power remained unchallenged.

(*b*) *1852*. Relations with the Burmese Government, however, grew no better. Burma was unfortunate in its kings; two in succession became insane and the third was at best unstable. King and people alike bitterly resented their defeat and the loss of territory, and failed to profit by the sharp lesson of the first war. The Treaty of Yandabo provided that each Government should be represented at the other's capital, but the Burmese had no wish to be represented at Calcutta and regarded the British representative in Ava as a spy. Successive Residents found the position so difficult that in 1840 the Residency was withdrawn. This was the more unfortunate because one result of the extension of British power over the maritime provinces was a growth of trade with the Burmese. But more trade meant greater friction. British merchants in Tenasserim complained of the restrictions on trade, and were supported by local officials in pressing for a forward policy and for the extension of British rule over the interior. The grievances of traders in Rangoon were partly their own fault, as 'the unruly conduct of some of them tended to invite oppression rather than inspire respect'.[1] Many complaints against the Burmese Government had no better foundation than similar complaints in Tenasserim, where the merchants grumbled that after fourteen years of British rule no one had yet been able to engage in their trade without loss.[2] The Indian Government, mindful of the great cost of the first war and apprehensive lest a further contest should be 'ruinously embarrassing', was reluctant to support even legitimate grievances. Moreover, the possession of Tenasserim proved unprofitable, and for some years there were suggestions that it should be restored to the Burmese or even sold to Siam.[3] The Indian Government was more inclined to cut its losses than to extend its liabilities.

The appointment of Dalhousie as Governor-General brought a change of policy. He regarded the expansion of the British Empire as a law of nature, and was acutely sensitive on matters of prestige. Complaints from two ship's captains of unfair treatment in Burmese courts gave him an occasion to intervene. His demand for redress soon took the form of an ultimatum backed by an expeditionary force, and in 1852 the Burmese Court found itself at war almost before it was aware that negotiations had begun.

[1] Gouger, p. 76.   [2] *SL*, p. 268.
[3] Desai, pp. 57, 132-7.

Dalhousie anticipated that the Talaings of Pegu would be actively friendly[1] but, apart from furnishing supplies in regions occupied by the British troops, they gave little help. In the earlier stages of the operations, according to the despatches of the general commanding the expedition, the Burmans showed themselves better armed and bolder than in the first war; they displayed skill in defending Rangoon, put up an obstinate resistance in Bassein, made a formidable attack on Martaban, and stood their ground with great resolution in Pegu; their fortifications were carefully and substantially built in a manner that would have done no discredit to a European engineer; and they were no less brave than in the former war and would fight until the enemy reached the muzzle of their guns. Other witnesses and the British casualties suggest that this account of the resistance was exaggerated. The Burmans were 'morally beaten'; most of their troops had little training in the use of their weapons; their fire was ineffective, and they were no better able than in the first war to make any prolonged stand against western military science and discipline. The British expedition was much better organized than in 1824, and could rest on advanced bases in Arakan and Tenasserim instead of depending on the long communications with Calcutta and Madras. By the end of June the British were masters of Lower Burma. The Burmese however were holding out in Upper Burma, and Dalhousie feared that, even after further victories, the King would still 'oppose to our advance the passive resistance of a retreat beyond our reach'. He decided, therefore, merely to stand fast, and on 20 December 1852 issued a proclamation annexing the Burmese provinces of Pegu and Martaban, thereby linking up Arakan with Tenasserim and giving the British effective control over the trade of the whole country by cutting off Upper Burma from the sea. Thus the second war decided that Burma could no longer hold aloof from the modern world. The British provinces came to be known collectively as British Burma, and the independent Burmese kingdom was usually distinguished as Ava, after its capital.

The annexation of Pegu synchronized with a palace revolution. This strengthened the British hold on Lower Burma, as the troops were called back to the capital to suppress it;[2] it also proved helpful to the British by placing on the throne the King's brother, Mindon, who was pacifically inclined and more enlightened than most members of his family. But Dalhousie was soon compelled to realize that he had

[1] 1852-53, Cmd. 1608, pp. 48-9.   [2] *BBG*, II, 665.

been optimistic in expecting a general welcome.[1] The Talaings were 'cowards, if not worse', and the Karens, apart from the Christians, were unhelpful; for three years the British had to conduct minor operations against guerilla bands. Those who still held out were treated for the most part as dacoits, liable to summary execution on capture. Some, however, earned respect for their prowess, as, for example, one of the most famous, Myat Htoon. 'A man', wrote Dalhousie, 'who has 4000 men under him, who repulses three British attacks and after a very stout defence is routed only by a Brigadier-General after a month's operations and with severe loss to us, must be regarded as a Chief and a Soldier—and a good one too.'[2] After about three years, serious military operations ceased, but disorder still required firm handling. In 1857 a rising under a Karen pretender in Martaban spread to the Delta of the Irrawaddy and Bassein,[3] and eight years elapsed from the first annexation before Pegu could be regarded as finally pacified.

2. ADMINISTRATIVE POLICY

(a) *1826*. When Arakan and Tenasserim were first added to the Indian Empire British policy in India was in a stage of transition. The transformation of the East India Company from a body of merchants into a sovereign state was still quite recent, and, indeed, not yet complete. In early days the Company had been content with trading privileges but, with the dissolution of the Mogul Empire, it began to trade in kingdoms, seeking a profit in tribute rather than in commerce. Most of the profit, however, went to its servants in bribes and booty, and their corruption and misrule were disastrous both to the Company and to its subjects. Within a few years it was threatened with bankruptcy and had to seek aid from Parliament. Meanwhile its servants were using their huge gains to corrupt home politics, and party jealousy impelled the British Government to use the financial difficulties of the Company as a lever for insisting on its responsibility for good administration. At the same time the Company, in the interest of the shareholders, was aiming at reforms.

The authority of the native princes was almost unlimited, but they would not and could not govern along western lines. A solution was sought in direct administration through the Company's officials.

---

[1] *BBG*, I, 487; Hall, p. 48.
[2] Hall, p. 57; 1887, Cmd. 4962, pp. 104, 247.   [3] *BBG*, I, 488.

Hastings was sent out as Governor-General (1772–85) to organize the collection of the revenue, and Cornwallis (1786–93) carried the process a stage further by converting the writers and merchants of the Company into civil servants exercising criminal jurisdiction. In pursuance of these reforms the territories of the Company were divided into districts, each under a European officer, who was both magistrate and collector, and drew a fixed salary from funds derived mainly from land revenue, a charge on land collected either through the holders of large estates (*zemindars*) or from peasants (*ryots*) through their village headman.

This novel experiment of direct rule not only helped to prevent corruption and extortion, but also furthered the commercial interests of Britain, and it was in line with the current political philosophy. Through the Industrial Revolution Manchester was able to send its earliest samples of cotton goods to India in 1786,[1] and the closure of the European market during the Napoleonic wars encouraged merchants to extend their trade in Asia. Manufacturers and merchants had a strong interest in promoting Indian welfare, and in encouraging the use of money, the extension of free trade, and the observance of the western law of contract. Thus colonial policy reflected the Liberal doctrines of economic freedom: freedom of trade, enterprise and property, and equality before the law. But Liberalism was not merely a sordid philosophy of self-interest. Although claiming that everyone should be allowed to pursue private interest in any way that was not forbidden by the law, it held that such restrictions on the activities of Government would best serve economic progress, and that economic progress was a sufficient guarantee of general welfare, both material and moral. It assumed, what many then denied, that the oriental would respond to economic motives and that, in this respect at least, he was 'a man and a brother'. Liberalism was not merely a policy but a faith.

It was a faith that was not held by the elder servants of the Company, who inherited the former policy of ruling indirectly along native lines through native chieftains and the tradition of 'shaking the pagoda tree'. But the new doctrines were eagerly discussed in correspondence between Raffles in Malaya, Munro in Madras, Elphinstone in Bombay and others of the remarkable group of scholar-statesmen who then gave lustre to the service of the Company. They prevailed also in the India House, where from 1819 James Mill was a leading figure, and

[1] Parshad, I. D., *Some Aspects of Indian Foreign Trade*, 1757–1893 (1932), p. 93.

they were being taught by Sir James Mackenzie at Haileybury to the probationers for the Indian service. In India the new policy found its staunchest protagonist in Bentinck, whose rule as Governor-General (1828–35) coincided with the establishment of British rule in Burma: 'I am going to India', he said to Bentham on his departure for the East, 'but it is you who will be Governor-General.'[1] Commercial interest and Liberal philosophy, no less than the conquest of oppression and corruption, required a system of direct rule on western lines under the immediate supervision of British officials. Regard for native custom still survived as a tradition, but in practice, from the earliest days of British rule in Burma, Liberal doctrines prevailed.

(b) *1852*. These principles were held even more firmly at the time of the second war in 1852. Although at home conditions in the factories were already throwing doubts on *laissez-faire* as a complete panacea for all social ills, the Great Exhibition of 1851 was an effective illustration of the prosperity that it had brought to England. In India the rapid growth of the population, cultivation, revenue and trade seemed to justify a belief in Liberal principles, and encouraged a belief in the inherent superiority of British rule and a confidence in British power that found expression in Dalhousie's policy of annexation. Naturally in these circumstances the machinery of Liberal administration was set up, without hesitation and with practised skill, in the new province of Pegu.

3. The Foundations of Administrative Practice[2]

When the maritime provinces were first taken over, they were separately administered under the direct supervision of the Governor-General of India. Arakan was soon transferred to the Government of Bengal, and in 1828 the Superintendent of Arakan was subordinated to the Commissioner of Chittagong. 'By 1831 the administrative system was complete. It was imposed ready-made from above, not built up from below',[3] and naturally it was modelled on the pattern recently introduced by Hastings and Cornwallis. Tenasserim, however, remained under the Governor-General until 1834, when the judicial and revenue branches of the administration were made over to Bengal. Thus for nearly ten years it could develop along its own lines, and up to 1843 the officers in charge of it were men from Penang with no personal experience of administration in India.

---

[1] Bell and Morell, p. xxx.
[2] Furnivall, *Leviathan*, passim.   [3] Harvey, *CHI*, v, 563.

Mr Maingy, the first civil officer appointed to Tenasserim, took over charge from the military in September 1825, before the conclusion of hostilities. His instructions illustrate the transitional character of contemporary policy; for they required him to govern according to local laws and customs, but at the same time to introduce a system in accordance with Liberal ideas. The double aim appears in the Proclamation that he issued on his first arrival. In this he undertook to provide 'a Civil and Political administration on the most liberal and equitable principles'; to defend the people 'against all foreign and domestic enemies', and to administer justice 'according to their own established laws'; in regard to revenue and all other matters, 'their own customs and local usages would be taken into consideration, but the most free and unrestricted internal and external commerce would be established and promoted'.[1] He promised in effect to reconcile Liberal policy with Burmese practice. But it was no easy matter to ascertain Burmese practice. Every vestige of the Burmese records, together with every paper in any way connected with the late Government, had disappeared; those officials who had not fled or been taken prisoner were hostile, and either would not or could not explain the Burmese system, which, as the product of a long and gradual evolution, was illogical and complex and, when described through interpreters by men who did not understand it very well to a foreigner who did not understand it at all, appeared still more complicated. Moreover, the Burmese system and Liberal principles were fundamentally opposed. Maingy had to choose between them, and naturally chose the Liberal system that he understood. It is, indeed, striking to observe the close parallel between the system adopted in Burma and that which Raffles had introduced on avowedly Liberal principles some ten years earlier in Java.

Judicial System. The instructions to Mr Maingy directed him to re-establish the Court of Justice as formerly constituted. Enquiries showed that judicial administration had been one function of the general government, comprising the Governor, three high revenue officials, and six officials of lower rank, including two officers of police, two scribes and two reporters. In a full court all these took their seats on three tiers of benches, 'the Governor on the most elevated, the three next on the second and the last six on the lowest seat'.[2] All these might hear suits in court jointly or separately, but attendance in court

[1] *SL*, pp. 15, 16.   [2] *SL*, pp. 9, 10, 27.

was optional, and each might try cases in his own house, either in person or through a privately appointed deputy. From every decision, whether of a bench or a single judge, there was an appeal to the Governor, but the Governor might refer the appeal to his own deputy, and the decision, whether given by Governor or deputy, was final.

All this was very puzzling, and it was a further puzzle to find out what the people regarded as 'their own established laws'.[1] At first Mr Maingy inclined to the view that there had been 'no fixed Code of Laws', and that all the decisions were arbitrary. Subsequent inquiries showed that this view was mistaken; there were two kinds of law books, 'a Pali version of the Laws of Manu, and a collection of precedents and rules and regulations established by different kings of Ava'. These, however, seemed 'too vague and indefinite to prove of any service', and Mr Maingy thought (conveniently perhaps) that the people had 'little veneration for them'.

Mr Maingy was quite unable to fathom the Burmese judicial system. In his view legal proceedings were meant to ascertain disputed facts and arrive at a logical decision on them according to fixed legal principles; he failed to understand that Burmans went to court to find a man of wisdom and authority who could help them in arriving at an amicable settlement of their disputes; that the various officials who tried cases, jointly or separately, in person or by deputy, in court or in their private house, were (according to English notions) arbitrators, and that the so-called codes were compilations by jurists,[2] used for guidance but not for literal application. He found the whole 'so complicated' that he drew up a new code, providing in its first clause that in every court 'the Commissioner, his Deputy or Assistant shall preside as the sole judge'. In order to safeguard Burmese custom he directed that there should 'always be in attendance a person skilled in the Burman laws and usages, and well acquainted with the decisions that would have been given by the late judges'.[3] But the whole idea of giving judgment in accordance with fixed legal principles was contrary to Burmese custom, and the decisions on this plan were as foreign as the court. For Burmese custom Mr Maingy substituted the rule of law.

Another innovation was the jury system, which Raffles had formerly introduced in Java. This gave a human touch to legal procedure, and

[1] SL, pp. 10, 53, 105.
[2] Furnivall, JBRS, Aug. 1940, p. 351. [3] SL, pp. 10, 11.

for some years the law courts in Tenasserim were perhaps all-too-human. When they were placed under Bengal, the Honourable Judges were scandalized and perplexed by some of their proceedings. In one case both complainant and accused were sentenced to be tom-tomed round the town; the Commissioner explained that they were husband and wife who had repeatedly troubled the court with frivolous complaints until neither he nor the jury wanted to see any more of them. In another case the complainant had been punished instead of the accused: a woman who had brought a charge of rape was convicted of seducing the accused to commit adultery with her. An absconding husband was sentenced to be forcibly employed on Government work and part of his wages made over to his wife. Similarly, a thief was set to work until he should have made good money that he had stolen. Another man was sentenced to 'exposure': he had been made to stand up in the public bazaar with a placard showing his offence. The Commissioner was given to understand that these sentences were irregular; a sense of humour was banished from the courts, and the majesty and machinery of law replaced the native jury.[1]

One Burmese custom that Mr Maingy retained was the levying of court fees. Under Burmese rule the unsuccessful party to a law-suit had to pay 10 % of the amount in issue, and fees were charged for the issue of summons to a defendant or a witness. Such charges contravened the Liberal principle of cheap law. The Board of Directors 'disapproved in principle of all such taxes, and were only prepared to countenance them if sanctioned by long custom or essentially important as a source of revenue'.[2] The judges in Calcutta also regarded such charges as objectionable. In general, however, the judges stood for the formality of law, and the Commissioner, apprehensive lest they might 'have it in contemplation to introduce a closer analogy to the system of the Courts in Bengal', urged that this would cause 'delay and the introduction of peculiar forms adapted to a higher and more refined state of society', and would prove unwelcome.[3] He would have preferred to make the procedure even less formal by restricting the administration of an oath, which seemed unnecessary owing to 'the happy infrequency of Perjury in this Country'.[4] In other ways also there was increasing friction with the judges in Calcutta. One trouble was the employment of advocates. It was a source

---

[1] Corr.TD, p. 44.   [2] SL, pp. 11, 106, 249.
[3] SL, p. 139.   [4] Corr.TD, p. 55.

of pride to the Commissioners that no *vakeels* or advocates were recognized; time and again they refer to this as a most valuable feature in their judicial administration, but with an ominous absence of any expression of approval from Calcutta. When at length the growing mercantile community petitioned the Government of Bengal that they might be permitted to engage advocates, the Commissioner objected that this would 'raise up a set of low adventurers seeking a livelihood by conducting cases on speculative terms'.[1] But he was overruled. The matter had, in effect, already been decided when Mr Maingy introduced the rule of law.

Revenue System. It was no easier to reconcile Liberal principles with the Burmese revenue system. The export of rice and other products had been prohibited; there were oppressive and, it seemed, arbitrary duties on exports and imports; fees had been levied on traders large and small, and even on pedlars; almost every form of productive activity was taxed: the cultivation of rice land and gardens, sugar-boiling, fishing, the manufacture of torches and the collection of forest produce.[2] The Karens in the hills of the interior paid a household tax consisting of beeswax, cardamoms, sesamum oil and cloth; and the Sea-gypsies, or Salons, a village tax in beeswax and mats. Ordinarily the taxes were collected in kind; so much as was required for the local officials was retained, and the balance remitted to Ava only once in three years. Judicial and other officers had derived the major part of their emoluments from fees and commission. In addition to the regular revenue the people had been liable to compulsory services, as, for example, on the construction of war-boats, paid for at half the market rate.

The whole system conflicted both with Liberal canons of taxation and with practical convenience. Burmese officials lived on the produce of the country, rice and sesamum oil and fish; but British and Indian troops wanted beef and flour and butter. These things had to be purchased, and, for other reasons also, the collection of revenue in kind, though useful in the barter economy of Burma, was unsuited to a commercial economy using money as the medium of exchange. Under the Burmese system of spreading the burden of taxation as widely as possible, some taxes had brought in very little, and some were injurious to trade, while the practice of remunerating officials by fees and commission facilitated extortion and embezzlement. The use of compulsory services, underpaid or unpaid, reduced the supply

[1] *SL*, p. 106; *Corr.TD*, p. 100.   [2] *SL*, p. 12.

of labour available for private employers, and restricted the market for imported goods. Mr Maingy preferred orthodox fiscal methods; the collection of revenue in cash, the abolition of taxes which were unproductive or a burden on trade, and the payment of fixed salaries to officials in lieu of fees or commission. For the bulk of his revenue, like Raffles in Java, and in accordance with the general fiscal system of India, he looked to a tax on the produce of land, supplemented by the farming-out of gaming houses and of opium and liquor shops, for which, as for a tax on land, the authority of Adam Smith could be invoked.

The land tax which, under Burmese rule, had recently purported to represent 6 % of the produce, was at first fixed at 10 %.[1] For each village the produce was estimated on such information as was available, including crop measurement on selected fields, and from 1827–8 onwards it was valued at a price taken to represent the market rate; the total amount due was distributed by the villagers among themselves, and a list posted in the village showed the contribution of each cultivator.[2] The tax collectors were paid a fixed salary, but this was found too costly; the Burmese custom of paying them a commission was revived, and subsequently the largest taxpayer (*kyedangyi*) in each village was charged with the collection. The yield, however, was inadequate to meet the cost of administration, and the share taken by Government was raised gradually to 25 % of the gross produce, while, in order to avoid inconvenient fluctuations, it became the practice to settle for a period of years the amount due annually. This system formed the basis of the procedure for the 'settlement' of land revenue now in force. But, even at the enhanced rate, the revenue was inadequate, and most of the other Burmese methods of raising money for the State were retained or gradually reintroduced. For some years it was still found necessary to employ 'compulsive labour', until a substitute was found in the importation of convict labour, and subsequently of free coolies, from India.

Thus, in 1834, when the revenue administration of Tenasserim was placed under the Government of Bengal, the fiscal system was very similar to that previously obtaining under Burmese rule, and was open to much the same objections from the standpoint of orthodox finance. The Board of Revenue not unnaturally regarded it as in various ways 'inimical to the general welfare of the Province'.[3] It recommended the abolition of the tax on salt as 'peculiarly liable to

---

[1] *SL*, pp. 12, 28, 43–4.   [2] *SL*, pp. 74, 100, 170.   [3] *SL*, pp. 82, 192–4.

the objection of harassing the people, salt being a necessary of life and a condiment essentially conducive to health'; the bazaar tax was 'objectionable in principle' as a restraint on trade and, if continued, should be limited to the amount necessary for the upkeep of the buildings; the duty on teak might prejudice exports; and the charges on mineral and forest produce, on the manufacture of pots, of chewing lime and of torches were unremunerative and oppressive; the poll taxes on Karens and Salons were excessive and should be reduced, or, better, abolished. But Tenasserim was still unprofitable. The Government had to raise money as best it could; like Mr Maingy the Board pocketed its scruples, and things went on much as before. Liberal principles are admirable in theory, but when they cost money, one must be prudent in applying them.

In 1839, of a total revenue of Rs. 4 lakhs, land revenue produced over one-third, and together with the excise on liquor and opium, over one-half. These taxes were consistent with Liberal doctrine, but the Government had to scrape together money where it could. The bazaar tax, and the poll tax on Karens and Salons, although condemned by India, came next in importance, closely followed by the proceeds of hiring out convicts to private individuals. On teak, the chief item of export, the duty, which fell on European merchants, amounted to Rs. 21,814, rather less than was derived from the hire of convicts.[1]

4. ADMINISTRATIVE MACHINERY

(a) 1826–52. On the introduction of civil rule Arakan, as already mentioned, was placed under Bengal, but the earliest civil officers in Tenasserim, Maingy (1825–33) and Blundell (1833–43) were appointed from Penang. Penang at that time belonged to the East India Company, and naturally the system of direct rule that Cornwallis had recently established in Bengal, provided a model for the machinery of administration in Tenasserim. One of the first problems was the re-employment of the former Burmese officials. As usual under Burmese rule, these were in two grades: superior officials belonging to the central administrative system and appointed by the Crown; and subordinate local officials, of whom the most important was the *Thugyi*, the hereditary chieftain of a small district. Under British rule these two grades were treated differently.

[1] *Corr.TD*, p. 98.

The superior officials had enjoyed 'unbounded influence' and were 'viewed as troublesome and disaffected characters'; from all he saw and heard Mr Maingy was 'well convinced that the natives would put much more confidence in an English judge'; their retention would destroy the Burmese expectation of obtaining under British rule 'a just and impartial administration without the fear of oppressive exactions', and, moreover, it would nullify the introduction of Liberal principles, as 'no vigilance could prevent their following the old system'.[1] Government on western lines required direct rule on the model recently adopted in Bengal, and Tenasserim was accordingly divided into three Districts, with a European Deputy or Assistant Commissioner in each District as judge, magistrate and collector of revenue. For some years, under the easy rule of the Governor-General, officials in Tenasserim were left to dispense justice and collect revenue according to their own ideas of equity and common sense with very little interference from above. All this was changed in 1834, when they were placed under the Government of Bengal. They were called on to furnish explanations, submit periodical returns and fill up forms, which were so foreign that they could not even understand the headings. Gradually the administrative machinery became standardized on Indian lines, and, after the departure of Mr Blundell, the process was expedited under four officers from India who held the appointment of Commissioner in rapid succession during the next ten years. These were at home in the routine of Indian machinery and knew nothing of the province, the people or the language, and the administrative system was worn into the routine grooves of the Indian mechanism. All this, however, was implicit in the first decision to replace the superior officials by Europeans, and the subsequent development was one of gradual centralization, bringing Tenasserim under the impersonal rule of law, and allowing little scope for initiative on the part of local officers. The result has been described as 'an undeveloped copy of the non-regulation model' of Indian administration; in fact, however, it was the germ of the non-regulation system, subsequently adopted in the Punjab.[2]

Meanwhile, and partly for the same reason, local administration was developing in a contrary direction towards a restoration of the Burmese system. Mr Maingy decided to retain the services of the hereditary local headmen, the *thugyis*, and to hold them responsible for the maintenance of law and order, the collection of revenue, and

[1] *SL*, pp. 10, 27.   [2] Harvey, *CHI*, v, 569; Durand, I, 104.

general administration within their charges. But he tried to convert them from hereditary chieftains into government officials. The local organization in Tenasserim was much the same as in the rest of Burma.[1] The normal and stable unit of administration was a tract known almost indifferently as the *myo* or *taik*, which may conveniently be rendered in English as the Circle. The circle, under its *thugyi*, or headman, often comprised smaller units, villages and hamlets, under a *gaung*, or head, appointed by the *thugyi*. But the circle headman was not necessarily the overlord of all the people in his circle; authority was based on personal relations, and some of the inhabitants might belong to a separate overlord. Mr Maingy preferred a more uniform, rational, arrangement.[2] He graded the headmen in three classes according as they had charge over several districts, over one district containing several villages, or over one or more villages. On this system of 'gradationary control' every headman was to receive a fixed salary, and to be responsible for all the people within the circle instead of merely for those of his own group or class. The headman was given the general charge of his circle, and made responsible both for police duties and for the collection of revenue. But it was soon found expedient to form a village police; each police officer or *gaung* had charge of a group of villages in which he had to investigate cases reported by the circle headman. Similarly the actual collection of revenue for payment to the circle headman was allotted to a villager, who was nominally the largest taxpayer (*kyedangyi*), but, in practice, a village servant of the headman. This system, so far as it was put in force, changed the whole character of local administration. It encroached on the autonomy of the circle by interfering with its internal administration; it converted the hereditary chieftain into a salaried official; and, for the rule of authority, based on personal relations, it substituted a territorial system based on law, placing all the people regardless of race or class under the legal authority of the circle headman.

But the plan worked out very differently in practice. One district alone was 'nearly as large as the whole province of Oudh, and unlike Oudh, mountainous and covered with dense forests'.[3] There were no means of communication with the interior except by country boats on tidal rivers, and the circle headmen had to be left practically unsupervised, to run their charges in their own way. The payment

---

[1] Mya Sein, *Administration of Burma* (Rangoon, 1938), pp. 34, 44, 47, 83.
[2] *SL*, pp. 36, 51, 54, 59; *Corr.TD*, p. 11.   [3] *RAB*, 1868-9, p. 61.

of salaries soon proved too costly, and the Burmese system of payment by a commission on revenue collections was revived.[1] The circle
headman, though nominally liable to transfer, ordinarily remained in
one charge for life and, as in Burmese times, was succeeded by a
member of his family, while the *gaung* or village policeman and
kyedangyi or village head were merely retainers of the headman. A
more striking instance of reversion to the Burmese system is that
twenty years after the introduction of British rule it was discovered
that, within the same tract, two or three different circle headmen
might still be exercising a personal criminal and revenue jurisdiction
over their own people, regardless of the territorial system nominally
in force since the beginning of British rule.[2] Thus, while the European
branch of the administration was becoming more centralized and
mechanical, the local or Burmese branch was reverting to type, and
the people were still managing their own affairs much as under their
own rulers.

For some years the European and native branches of the administration continued to function separately, the chief link between them
being a Head Native (*gaung-gyok* or *sitke*) in each district.[3] No native
of the country could legally exercise judicial or magisterial powers, as
these were reserved to Europeans. But Bentinck believed on utilitarian grounds in the employment of 'native agency', and in 1835 the
Commissioner was asked to report how far it could be adopted in
Tenasserim. Mr Blundell, like his predecessor, held that 'the feelings
of the people generally were adverse to seeing judges in the courts
selected from themselves', because 'their thoughts would immediately revert to the days when bribery and corruption held unlimited
sway'; he doubted if the men to be entrusted with judicial powers
would exercise them to the best advantage, but thought that, nevertheless, they might in fact be granted rather extensive powers, as they
would be working immediately under his own eyes.[4] The numerous
misappropriations and irregularities discovered among the European
officials shortly after Mr Blundell's departure suggest that his eyes
may sometimes have been closed,[5] but it was the accepted policy in
India to employ natives so far as possible, and the Head Natives were
accordingly promoted to be magistrates and judges. Henceforward,
alongside the circle headmen exercising personal authority through

---

[1] *Corr.TD*, p. 26.   [2] *BBG*, I, 483; II, 127, 215, 220.
[3] *SL*, pp. 107, 126.   [4] *SL*, pp. 125, 148–50, 248.
[5] Harvey, *CHI*, v, 569; Durand, I, 90.

hereditary influence, Burman judicial officers were appointed to dispense western law according to western ideas. But so late as 1870 practically none of them knew English or had been to a western school, and even ten years later some courts had no copy of the laws which they were supposed to administer.[1] It may be presumed then that in the subordinate courts eastern ideas carried more weight than western laws. Moreover, the people continued to settle their disputes by private arbitration rather than in the courts.

(b) *1852–70*. When Pegu and Martaban came under British rule after the second war, the former was placed under a separate Commissioner, directly responsible to the Governor-General, and the latter was allotted as a separate province to the Commissioner of Tenasserim. In 1858 the British possessions in Burma passed, with the rest of India, from the East India Company to the Crown. Within a small and largely homogeneous area there were four distinct provinces, governed separately, but on much the same system. This was costly and inconvenient, and in 1862 they were amalgamated as the Province of British Burma, under a Chief Commissioner with headquarters in Rangoon. Then, in 1868, there was a modest step in the direction of provincial autonomy. Until then the 'Local Government' for Burma was technically the Governor-General in Council, but by Act I of 1868 the term was so defined as to include the Chief Commissioner. This gave him the legal power to extend Indian Acts to Burma of his own mere motion, but in fact there was little change, 'because the Indian system was one of strict subordination and the Chief Commissioner would not extend an Act without the prior approval of the Supreme Government'.[2]

The officer appointed as Commissioner of Pegu, and subsequently as Chief Commissioner, was Major (later, Sir Arthur) Phayre, who had been in Burma for close on twenty years and was outstanding in his knowledge of the people, their language and their history. Naturally he adopted in Pegu the system which had grown up in Tenasserim under the direction of the Bengal Government, and 'Indian ideas of administration prevailed in the British reorganization of the conquered Province'.[3] Pegu was divided into five Districts, each under a Deputy Commissioner, who was at once magistrate, civil judge and collector. The Districts were divided into Townships, in which the Township Officer (*myo-ok*) discharged the same varied functions as the

---

[1] *RAB*, 1868–9, p. 61; 1881–2, p. 23.
[2] *BBG*, I, 496.　　　　[3] Hall, p. lxii; *BBG*, I, 485.

Deputy Commissioner, but with smaller powers. The township comprised a number of circles, each under a Circle Headman (*taik-thugyi*) with police and revenue powers, and responsible for the general order and welfare of his charge. Subordinate to the circle headmen were rural police officers (*gaungs*), responsible to the circle headman for matters of police within a small group of villages but also assisting him in the collection of revenue; and in each village (which might comprise several hamlets) a village officer (*kyedangyi*) charged with revenue collection and with some police duties. Thus at the outset the administrative system of Pegu and British Burma closely resembled that of Tenasserim, both in the superior or central, and subordinate or local grades. There was a further parallel with Tenasserim in the chief direction of affairs. The two earliest Chief Commissioners, Phayre (1862–7) and Fytche (1867–71), were both, like the two earliest Commissioners of Tenasserim, officers who served almost their whole life in Burma, and their successors, the seven heads of the province between 1871 and 1897, were all men from India and looking to go back to India on promotion. As in Tenasserim between 1843 and 1852, the administrative convenience of a mechanical conformity with Indian routine carried greater weight than a regard for the organic growth of local institutions. In other respects, however, administrative development contrasted with that of Tenasserim in earlier days; in Tenasserim the machinery grew less efficient, and in Pegu more efficient.

The constitution of the province of British Burma in 1862, while allowing a reduction in the administrative staff, required greater uniformity in administrative methods, and this was met by a gradual reorganization of the machinery along departmental lines. The weary and uncongenial task of pacification compelled attention to the inadequacy of the police. Phayre believed firmly in village autonomy in the maintenance of order.[1] But the village police, though sufficient for the needs of Tenasserim in quiet times, could not cope with the disorder that troubled Pegu for many years after the second war; an Inspector-General was appointed in 1861 to organize a police force in Pegu, and his charge was extended to the whole of British Burma on its formation in 1862. Formerly the Deputy Commissioner had himself been head of the police; under the new system he still remained generally responsible for the maintenance of law and order, but was given the assistance of a Superintendent of Police who in

[1] Hall, pp. 101, 107.

departmental affairs was directly under the Inspector-General. The Deputy Commissioner had also been in charge of the local jail, with the assistance of an army surgeon, or in outlying districts an assistant apothecary. In 1864 the jails were placed under an Inspector-General, who was also Inspector-General of Civil Hospitals, Sanitary Commissioner and Superintendent of Vaccination. Public works likewise had been directly under the Deputy Commissioner, though in military stations he could obtain technical advice from the garrison engineer. On the constitution of British Burma a chief engineer was appointed, though extensive public works still received little attention until 1869. In Tenasserim the destruction of the teak forests had necessitated the appointment of a special conservator, and a second was appointed for Pegu. Although this new departmental organization may appear considerable, actually it reflected the contemporary opinion that, beyond the maintenance of law and order, Government should do no more than seemed unavoidable; but the creation in 1866, at the instance of the Indian Government, of a Department of Public Instruction foreshadowed a change that will come under examination in the next chapter. Thus, during the sixties, within the narrow limits of contemporary views, there were laid down the functions of the modern departmental organization. The central administration was becoming more efficient, or at least more elaborate, than before the second war.

This tendency was still more strongly marked in the subordinate or local administration within the district. We have seen that the scheme of local administration devised by Mr Maingy declined into a system more on Burman lines; after the second war this tendency was reversed. The general character of the Burmese system in Pegu resembled that in Tenasserim. There were hereditary circle headmen, exercising a personal authority 'more tribal than territorial'; some threw in their lot with the Burmans, or were killed during the war, but most of the others were retained, and Deputy Commissioners had some difficulty in making them understand that they were responsible for all the residents within their charge. But the organization in Pegu was vastly more complex than in Tenasserim. There was a great diversity in the status of the circle headmen: some were subordinate to the local Governor, others were in direct relations with the Crown. There was a similar diversity in the area of circles: some were large and fairly populous and others comprised only one or two villages. In the early days of British rule this diversity became more intricate, as many who had been no more than village officers managed to gain recognition as hereditary circle headmen. But when 'these hereditary officials began to find that their position was no longer what it had been...[and that]...they were nothing but underpaid and hard-worked underlings, many of them came to the conclusion that their appointments were not worth holding'.[1] As time went on, circles were amalgamated or divided for the sake of administrative convenience, and an artificial and mechanical uniformity replaced the rich diversity natural to the gradual evolution of a living organism. In Tenasserim the project of uniformity in village rule had failed; in Pegu, and later in British Burma, it was enforced, but the appearance of greater efficiency concealed a loss of vitality.

For many years, however, this new trend had no great effect on social life. District officers still attempted little beyond the maintenance of law and order and the collection of the revenue. Although districts and circles were subdivided or remodelled as population grew and cultivation expanded, they remained unwieldy, and communications were so defective that the people in general continued to live their own life in their own way, hardly conscious of any authority higher than the circle headman. The circle headman, though appointed by the Deputy Commissioner and liable to transfer like any other official, still usually remained in one charge for life and was succeeded by a son; the village taxes were collected by a fellow-villager, the *kyedangyi*, who was a servant of the circle headman rather than a Government official; civil and petty criminal disputes were ordinarily settled by private arbitration, and villagers, unless required to attend court in connection with criminal proceedings, saw nothing of the Government. The system, though in theory one of direct rule, was in effect a system of indirect rule through the circle headman.

5. ECONOMIC PROGRESS, 1826–52

When Mr Maingy first arrived in Tenasserim he conjured up a glowing vision of its economic prospects, needing for their realization nothing but the sound political economy that he thought to introduce. 'Its central position, both with regard to the Burman and Siamese territories, point it out in every respect as a depot for Commercial Emporium, and with an increased population, combined with the

---

[1] *BBG*, II, 766.

industry and enterprise of British and Chinese merchants, it may reasonably be expected that the ancient commerce formerly carried on with Siam will again be revived, and that by this means the manufactures of England and British India will be widely dispersed.'[1] He proposed accordingly to establish and promote the most free and unrestricted internal and external commerce. It soon appeared, however, that free trade had its disadvantages. The people 'received such a spur from the large and unknown profits of a free foreign export that the love of gain was in danger of running away with a due regard for their own wants'; they exported not only their surplus but their seed grain and their food. 'In the balance of good and evil he preferred a deviation from Political Maxim to the misery of a starving population',[2] and imposed a temporary embargo on the export of grain. But this 'deviation from Political Maxim' was merely an exception to his general policy of encouraging freedom of enterprise.

Communications. Good communications are the first condition of economic progress and, both in Arakan and Tenasserim, the new Government set to work with enthusiasm on making roads. But road-making needs labour, and this was scarce. Mr Maingy was compelled therefore to revive the Burmese system of 'compulsive labour', and on a more extensive scale. Under a Government less zealous for progress the use of forced labour had been exceptional, but under British rule the villagers were called out to work for about two months in the year. These forced services were not only contrary to Liberal doctrine and 'most irksome to the people', but they interfered with cultivation; it was unprofitable to make roads to carry rice if road-making left no rice to carry. Arrangements were made therefore to import convicts from India. By these means the old Burmese trunk road from Mergui to Amherst was reopened and extended to Moulmein. Before Mr Maingy left the country he could report that this had been effected by the inhabitants themselves, who had been 'taught the value of good roads, and had cheerfully constructed them or borne the expense of having them constructed'.[3]

But private individuals also wanted cheap labour, and it was found simpler and more lucrative to hire out the convicts than to provide them with work. Thus after fifteen years of British rule the whole Public Works establishment in Tenasserim consisted of 'one Native Superintendent on Rs. 20 a month', and this meagre establishment was regarded as sufficient because there were 'no roads, canals, tanks,

---

[1] *SL*, p. 4.   [2] *SL*, p. 48.   [3] *SL*, pp. 44, 63, 65, 105.

or other public works in the interior'.[1] In Arakan the course of events
was much the same. At first a road was built down to the mouth of
the river at Negrais, and the old roads across the passes into Burma
were patched up; but there was little traffic and they all relapsed
into jungle.[2]

Population. The chief obstacle to progress was the scanty population. At first hopes were entertained of a great influx from Pegu,
especially of Talaings. These seemed likely to be justified when the
former Talaing Governor of Syriam, after the failure of an attempt
to rebel against the Burmese, fled across the border with followers
estimated at 10,000. But some of these returned, and few came afterwards.[3] It was thought also that the 40,000 Talaings, said to have
emigrated formerly from Burma to Siam, would return to their ancestral home to enjoy the benefits of British rule, but the few who
visited Tenasserim annually seemed to come as spies.[4] Attempts were
made therefore to recruit foreigners. Malays were encouraged because 'the dread which all Burmans and Talaings entertained of
them' should make it possible 'to dispense with a portion of the
Military force'.[5] Suggestions were made that the Company's super-
cargoes should 'quietly inform' the Chinese of 'the salubrious air
and fertile soil in Tenasserim', and money was advanced to a Chinese
contractor to import miners from Penang, but, although he was 'very
respectable', the advance had to be written off as irrecoverable.[6] Only
from India did settlers arrive in any numbers. The troops at Moulmein were chiefly from Madras, and these were accompanied by a
numerous crowd of moneylenders, shopkeepers, washermen, tailors
and barbers. Nothing seems to have come of a proposal to offer a
free passage and a grant of land to 'the destitute and half-starving
population on the coast of Coromandel', but from 1838 labour was
imported from India for the commissariat, and more came after 1843
when convicts were withdrawn from private employ and debtor-
slavery was abolished. Almost all the Indians, however, settled in
Moulmein. In 1826 this was a mere fishing village, but it grew
rapidly owing to its selection as the civil and military headquarters,
and within a few years one finds frequent references to its 'motley
population'. By 1852 the inhabitants numbered about 40,000, of
whom perhaps one-third were natives of India.

[1] *SL*, p. 195.   [2] *BBG*, I, 514; II, 299, 607, 623.
[3] *SL*, pp. 60, 74; Desai, p. 57; *BBG*, II, 15, 50.
[4] *SL*, pp. 102, 104.   [5] *SL*, pp. 95, 101.   [6] *SL*, pp. 38, 102; *Corr.TD*, p. 26.

Despite the failure of attempts to attract immigrants, the favourable conditions of life under British rule stimulated a rapid growth of the home population. This cannot be exactly measured, as the estimates based on the revenue returns were far from accurate and, during the early years of the British occupation, can have had little relation with the facts. According to these estimates the population of Tenasserim was originally 70,000 and that of Arakan 100,000 but the correct figure for the two was probably not less than 300,000. In 1852 it was estimated at 543,824.[1]

Production and Trade. British merchants were less enterprising than Mr Maingy had anticipated. Grants of land were offered on easy terms; but few responded, and those who did so failed. The timber trade was more attractive. Teak was the chief product of Tenasserim, and at first the Government proposed to reserve this for the Navy. From 1828, however, licenses were issued to private traders. These were mostly adventurers of little substance, who did not visit the forests but obtained timber through indiscriminate felling by Burmese agents, and the licensees did no more than pay duty, when they could not dodge it, at the rate of 15 % *ad valorem* on logs arriving in Moulmein. For many years their operations were practically unsupervised and, through fraud and neglect, three-quarters of the timber escaped duty, while competition among the licensees bred confusion in the forests. In 1841 the Executive Engineer was appointed as Conservator, apparently in addition to his other duties, and was given an establishment of one headman and three peons to supervise extraction over thousands of square miles of virgin jungle.[2] Teak accounted for about half the total value of the local products exported, but up to 1841 yielded only some Rs. 20,000 in revenue;[3] under the system then introduced the revenue rose to Rs. 71,630 by 1852, but by this time the forests, it is said, were ruined.[4]

In connection with the timber trade sawmills were erected, and there was a considerable development of shipbuilding. Between 1830 and the second war more than a hundred ships, with a gross burden of over 30,000 tons, were built in Moulmein.[5] In all branches of the timber industry Burmans found employment, and in 1852 Burmese carpenters from Moulmein helped to construct the barracks in Rangoon.[6] But Indian convict labour, hired from the Government, was

---

[1] See p. 59, Growth of Population.   [2] *SL*, pp. 208, 279.
[3] *Corr.TD*, p. 98.   [4] Harvey, *CHI*, v, 567.
[5] *BBG*, II, 368.   [6] 1852–53, Cmd. 1608, p. 113.

cheaper and more docile than free Burmese labour. From one report it appears that 88 convicts were hired as private servants, 64 as day labourers, 60 as sawyers, 220 as brick and tile makers, and others as weavers, potters, blacksmiths and brass founders.[1] In 1839 more revenue was obtained from the hire of convicts than from the forests. Convict labour was not always cheap, as when a man 'in whom his master placed every confidence' bolted across the frontier with cash and valuables worth Rs. 4000. If convicts had not been available, Europeans and Burmans would have learned to work together in these various employments, and the people of the country would have been developed at the same time as its material resources. The importation of convicts failed even as regards its professed object, the construction of roads, and it erected a barrier between Burmans and the modern world that has never been broken down. When the hiring out of convict labour ceased, the importation of Indian coolies raised an even more formidable barrier against the economic education of the Burman. The officers of the medical and engineering departments were accustomed to working with Indians; the subordinates in those departments were Indian and, when more were needed, it was cheaper or less trouble to import Indians than to train Burmans. The camp-followers of the garrison, the moneylenders, shopkeepers, tailors, barbers and washermen were all Indian. Modern India had grown up with modern Europe; western banks and merchants were accustomed to dealing with Indians and knew their language, while Indian moneylenders and traders had long experience of western ways of business; naturally in Burma Indians came to function as middlemen between the British and Burmese. Thus from the very earliest days of British rule there evolved a mixed community with a racial differentiation of functions.

In this community the function of the ordinary Burman was agriculture, and especially the cultivation of rice. In this the Indian immigrant, an unskilled labourer accustomed to a different soil and climate, was no match for him. The same process that drove the Burman from the town drew him to the country, and under British rule he found new opportunities for disposing of his produce. The proximity of Arakan to India provided a market for the local rice crop, and, with the removal of the restrictions formerly imposed by the Burmese Government on the export of rice, British merchants entered the rice trade. By 1846 the export rose to 74,203 tons, though

[1] *Corr.TD*, p. 48.

little over 6000 went direct to Europe.[1] Tenasserim produced little
more rice than it required for home consumption, and the larger
output under British rule was absorbed by the growing population
of Moulmein; only during the forties did a small export trade
develop, mostly with the Straits.[2] At that time, however, there were
wide annual fluctuations in the demand for rice in India and China,
and cultivators were under no temptation to cultivate primarily for
the market; they worked small holdings for domestic consumption
and merely sold the surplus if the market were favourable.

   Trade with Ava. Apart from timber Tenasserim found its best
market in Ava.[3] In 1833, out of European piece goods to the value of
Rs. 6 lakhs imported, about two-thirds were re-exported, mainly to
Ava, and this item alone constituted half the total value of the exports,
including timber. Subsequently the import of European piece goods
declined; in 1839 not merely had re-exports almost disappeared, but
less were imported for local use. The import of woollens also declined. It would seem that, despite the complaints of merchants in
Rangoon, more trade was passing direct by that port instead of
through Moulmein. For, during the same period, Moulmein was
importing more goods from Ava; the value of Burmese piece goods
rose from Rs. 11,000 to Rs. 85,000, and Burmese 'sundries' from
Rs. 15,000 to over Rs. 200,000.[4] Tenasserim was an unprofitable
possession to the British, and it might almost be claimed that the
chief benefit of the British occupation of Tenasserim went to Ava.

6. ECONOMIC PROGRESS, 1852–70

   Communications. Although Tenasserim had failed to pay its way,
Dalhousie anticipated that the acquisition of Pegu would establish
British interests in Burma on a more profitable footing. 'It could be
held easily and cheaply. Its ports, tidal rivers, fertile soil, products
and forests held out a fair promise of commerce and wealth.'[5] Both
on military and commercial grounds he stressed the importance of
road-making and, as in the early days after the first war, ambitious
schemes were projected. One road was to be built from Rangoon to
Prome and another from Rangoon to Pegu, whence the frontier at
Toungoo could be reached by water. Toungoo was to be linked up
with Prome, and Prome with India by a great highway through

[1] *BBG*, I, 460.   [2] *BBG*, I, 461.
[3] *SL*, p. 103.   [4] *Corr.TD*, pp. 49, 99.   [5] Hall, pp. xxiv, xxviii, 114.

Chittagong to Calcutta. Pegu was likewise to be the starting point of
another main road by way of Moulmein, Amherst and Mergui to
Malaya. Most of these were old Burmese routes, and the stretches
within the former British territory had been repaired and afterwards
abandoned during earlier years. The road from Chittagong to Akyab
was reported as almost finished within six months of its commence-
ment, and by 1854 the section from Arakan to Prome was 'traversible
by a horseman at full gallop'.[1] A start was made on other roads. But
road-making needs money and labour, and neither was available. For
eight years the enforcement of order was the primary concern of
Government. The roads were neglected and most of them abandoned,
and in 1869 the Chief Commissioner reported that in the whole of
British Burma there was not a single completed road. 'Arakan', he
said, 'has been under British rule for more than forty years, Tenasserim for the same period, Pegu fifteen years, and in these periods but
five incomplete roads gave evidence of our possession of a country
covering an area of 90,000 square miles.'[2]

Roads, in fact, were a luxury; for most purposes the waterways
were good enough. The only important place really difficult of access
was Toungoo, which was a journey of six weeks from Rangoon. This
was reduced to a fortnight or three weeks by the construction of a
canal to join the Pegu and Sittang rivers. All over the Delta and as
far as Thayetmyo the mails were carried in Government steamers, but
these very rarely went beyond the frontier. Steamboats of the King
of Burma sometimes visited Rangoon, but the only other form of
transport was in country boats. In pursuance of the policy of encouraging private enterprise all the Government steamers and plant
were sold to a private company about 1863, but in 1867 only four
British steamers had ever taken merchandise to Mandalay and none
went farther.[3]

The maritime provinces were even more isolated. Apart from
irregular visits by a Government steamer they long depended on
small sailing craft that could not face the monsoon. A pathetic report
of 1856 reveals the condition of Mergui. 'I beg', writes the Deputy
Commissioner, 'with all the earnestness that may become me, to
report the miserable state of this station from the irregularity with
which it has been visited. We have run short of all the common
necessaries of life. Bread, meat, flour, candles, potatoes, wine, beer,

[1] *BBG*, II, 607.   [2] *RAB*, 1868-9, p. vi.
[3] *BBG*, I, 515; II, 829; Fytche, II, 323.

brandy all are done.'[1] Ten years later, the annual shipping entering Kyaukpyu, the second port in Arakan, was some half a dozen small sailing vessels with a total burden of 651 tons.[2] Not until the late sixties, when private enterprise at last woke up to the possibilities of steam transport in eastern waters, did these conditions change.

Thus, to keep in touch with the interior, the frontier and the outside world, the Government was dependent on the telegraph service. Lines were opened to the frontier at Thayetmyo and Toungoo in 1858, to Akyab and Calcutta in 1862, and to Moulmein in 1863. The cable between Akyab and Calcutta broke down, and in 1865 they were linked up by a land line. Only in 1870 did it become possible to communicate with England by a direct and independent cable from India.

The Chief Commissioner, then, had good grounds for complaining in the annual report for 1869, cited above, that 'beyond the mere fact of our military possession of the country, beyond the existence of a police, most inadequately paid, there is hardly anything in the length and breadth of the Province to testify the presence of any rule superior to the one from which it has been wrested.... Of barracks, of gaols, of court-houses we have not a few, but as for Public Works in the true sense of the word, they are only now being called into existence.' Cobden opposed the annexation of Pegu, but it would be difficult to find a better application of the principles for which he stood than in the conduct of its administration. By the canons of Liberal orthodoxy the Government deserved credit for its fiscal policy; although part of the revenue from Burma went to India, and there were complaints that India took more than its fair share, the general aim of policy was to keep down expenses and to raise no more revenue than was necessary for the maintenance of law and order, leaving economic development to free private enterprise. But the real reason why no more was done was that the system of Indian government was 'one of strict subordination', and nothing beyond the maintenance of law and order could be attempted without sanction from the Government of India.

Population. During the 1852 war large numbers of the people fled to Upper Burma, or were evacuated in accordance with the 'scorched earth' policy adopted by the Burmese Government, and after the annexation of Pegu there was a further exodus. According to the revenue returns the remaining population was only about 700,000,

[1] Butler, p. 9.   [2] *RTC*, 1867–8, p. 90.

but this estimate was far too low.[1] In 1857-9 the Indian Mutiny created a demand for Burmese rice, and there began a steady flow of immigration from Burmese territory, partly of people returning to their homes and partly of newcomers.[2] In 1861 Indians and Chinese in Pegu were still few in comparison with Tenasserim and Arakan, and, although they increased in number during the following decade, they did not venture beyond the towns.[3] From 1867 the Government renewed attempts to import labour from India, but these met with so little success that in 1876 they were finally abandoned.[4] Probably the original population of Pegu and Martaban was rather less than 900,000 and the subsequent increase was mainly due to natural fertility under favourable conditions.

Production. For many years after the occupation of Pegu European enterprise was as slow to take advantage of its new opportunities as in the maritime provinces in former days. Attempts to attract planters by the grant or lease of lands on easy terms had a discouraging reception, and those Europeans who settled in Rangoon mostly had their eye on the new teak forests now made accessible. But one result of the occupation of Pegu was to establish rice instead of teak as the staple export of Burma. Even before the war the price of paddy had been rising, and between 1852 and 1856 it rose from Rs. 35 to Rs. 53 per hundred baskets. As yet, however, the Europeans were only merchants and not millers. The first steam mill was erected in 1861; apparently it was unprofitable, as no more were built for many years. Rice was in fact a risky business, as the precarious harvests in India and China were the chief factor in the demand. The quantity exported, after reaching a maximum of 470,000 tons in 1864-5, fell to 248,000 two years later, and the average export for the three years 1863-6 was 420,000 as against only 340,000 for the years 1867-70. The price of paddy was the same in 1872 as in 1855,[5] and the area under cultivation between 1861 and 1870 rose only from 1·61 to 1·96 million acres. This was considerably below the increase in the population, and it is evident that the people still cultivated primarily for home consumption rather than for export. Before the opening of the Suez Canal the results of leaving economic progress to private enterprise were disappointing.

[1] See p. 59,   Growth of Population.
[2] *RAB*, 1861-2, p. 32.
[3] *RAB*, 1861-2, pp. 7, 32, App. A.   [4] *RAB*, 1877-8, p. 13.   [5] *BBG*, II, 588.

7. WELFARE

(a) *Individual*. Yet there is good reason to believe that the cultivators, as individuals, were vastly better off from a material standpoint
under British than under Burmese rule. Formerly they had been
liable to compulsory service, debarred from the free disposal of their
produce, and subject to restrictions on freedom of movement and
of marriage, and on their clothing, housing, and other items of
personal expenditure. Under British rule they were relieved of all
these disabilities. However little they may have resented such restraints so long as they could imagine nothing different, their readiness
to take advantage of the boon of economic freedom showed that it was
welcome. Quite apart from positive and customary restrictions, the
Burmese economic system had discouraged the production and
accumulation of wealth. The frequent references to the comfort and
prosperity of the older villages are sufficient to discount as exaggerated, if not wholly without substance, the common allegation that
under Burmese rule the people dared not gather riches for fear of
being victimized by unscrupulous officials, but with a barter economy
there was little incentive to increase production or accumulate
wealth. Under British rule money became the medium of exchange,
and its use was encouraged by the collection of revenue in money
and, still more effectively though indirectly, by the importation
of goods that the people liked to buy. Formerly there had been
little incentive to make money because there was little to spend it
on; now they had to make money to pay their taxes, and wanted to
make it in order to provide themselves with various exciting and
attractive novelties. Also, with the rapid rise of prices during the
first years of British rule, it was much easier to make money; when
the cultivator obtained two or three times as much money as before
for the same quantity of produce, he had more to spend and was
readier to spend it.

As mentioned above, cultivation expanded less rapidly than the
population, and the people had not yet taken to cultivation for export.
Although they gained higher prices for their paddy, they did not
make much more per head. But, on the other hand, there was little
to tempt them into debt, and we shall see below that, even ten years
after the opening of the Suez Canal, when cultivation for export had
already made some progress, few were in debt and practically none
in difficulties. It was not only cultivators who were more prosperous.

Salt-boiling, fishing, pottery and boating were almost as important as rice cultivation, and in some parts more important. All these industries prospered. Until 1867, when foreign salt was first imported, the manufacture of salt and of dried fish continued to expand. So little foreign pottery was used that in 1869 the value of pottery imported from abroad was still less than the value of lacquer ware (used for plates and cups) from Upper Burma. There were practically no steamboats on the river, and the increase of traffic under British rule brought new wealth to boatmen, and stimulated boat-building. Foreign cloth was beginning to compete with local cloth, but the import of yarn was still high in relation to the import of cloth; most of the clothing was still home-woven, and the imported yarn furnished the weavers with new and cheaper materials. Up to the opening of the Suez Canal, and for some years later, everyone enjoyed under British rule freedom and a degree of material prosperity formerly unimagined.

Taxation was heavy; its incidence was about double that of any British possession in the East, and, so far as any comparison is possible, heavier than under Burmese rule. The marginal table gives the figures for Pegu. Formerly dues to Government had been rendered mostly in personal service or in produce, and the officials had lived on what they could make out of the people. The customary payments to the central Government in produce or in money were on record in official documents, and were ordinarily light or even nominal. The demands of local officials

Taxation in Pegu*

	Rs.
Burmese	1,469,160
1852–3	2,977,538
1861–2	5,700,216

* *BBG*, I, 450–1.

were limited by custom though not by law, and could easily be evaded by migration if excessive; various estimates by British officers suggest that they averaged about two-thirds of the amount taken by the Crown.[1] So long as the demands were not excessive, this suited the people better than taxation in money. The British Government, with a more elaborate administration, and paying salaries in money, needed a much larger revenue, imposed heavier taxes and could enforce its demands more stringently. But higher prices enabled the people to bear a heavier burden, and the taxes did not prevent the growth of population or the spread of cultivation.

Moreover, there was this difference between the two systems of taxation. Under Burmese rule arbitrary demands had been recog-

[1] *BBG*, I, 450; II, 434, 560, 622.

nized as part of the ordinary machinery of government. It cannot be claimed that British rule put an end to oppression, and extortion by subordinate officials did not cease under British rule, but they became illegal. That was one benefit conferred on the people by the rule of law. Again, under Burmese rule, bandits could try their strength against the Government on almost equal terms, and if a capable and energetic official tried to suppress them, they could take refuge elsewhere; under British rule, with its formidable apparatus of magistrates and police and prisons, and its immense reserve of military strength, there was much greater security for life and property.

(b) *Social Welfare*. But, despite the great increase in individual prosperity, there were already signs of the activity of forces adverse to social welfare. We have noticed that from the earliest days of British rule the towns became largely Indian. After the second war this process continued more rapidly. The increase in the native population was accompanied by a wholly disproportionate increase in the foreign population. The earliest figures that can be accepted as approximately correct are those in the Administration Report for 1861–2.

Population of British Burma, 1861

Class	Pegu	Tenasserim	Arakan	British Burma
Indigenous	1,111,809	330,096	344,809	1,786,714
Indian	17,907	28,731	26,841	73,479
Chinese	2,001	8,118	135	10,254
European	1,252	1,146	164	2,562
Unclassified	17,220	3,311	4,357	24,888
Total	1,150,189	371,402	376,306	1,897,897

Already in 1861 the town police were chiefly Indians, 'as being more likely to understand those with whom they are brought into contact'.[1] Between 1861 and 1872 the number of Indians was nearly doubled, rising to 131,000. The labour on the wharves was still Burmese,[2] but unskilled labour in the towns was Indian, and so was most of the skilled or semi-skilled labour. With the exhaustion of the forests of Tenasserim and the substitution of steam for sail, the ship-building industry declined, and with it the employment of Burmese as carpenters. In 1852 Burmese carpenters from Moulmein were

[1] *RAB*, 1861–2, p. 7.　　　[2] *RCLI*, x; Pt II, 163.

mentioned among those employed on building barracks in Rangoon, but soon they ceased to find employment on Government buildings. The change was noted with regret. In former times Burmese and Karen carpenters had 'executed excellent work in pagodas and monasteries; in outlying towns and villages capital wooden houses, belonging to well-to-do cultivators, were to be seen with close-fitting joists and ornamental well-designed staircases. The American Baptist Mission had built, through the agency of Karen and Burman carpenters, fine school houses and churches in many parts of the country.'[1] But regrets were ineffectual to hinder the economic forces ousting them from employment on Government work.

Under Burmese rule there were native schools of medicine, and the King accorded special recognition to skilled practitioners. Europeans who knew the country recognized that Burmese treatment might effect cures where western medicine failed,[2] but there was no place for Burmans in the Government medical service. 'The entire staff of the several dispensaries was composed of natives of India and with a difference of caste, creed and language it was impossible to expect that the benefits of scientific medicine would be brought home to the people in the way that they would be if administered by native agency.'[3] 'Even the menial establishments of the dispensaries were almost entirely composed of foreigners.' The European doctors were ignorant of Burmese, and the Government found it necessary to protest against the appointment from India of subordinates who were ignorant not only of Burmese but also of English; such men 'could be of little use in Burma'.[4] But it was easier and less expensive to employ Indians than to train Burmans. Under a system dominated by the idea that Government activity should extend no further than necessary beyond the maintenance of law and order, expenditure on medical attention was jealously scrutinized. 'The buildings were of the simplest and cheapest kinds and everything was done to diminish expense; thus for instance the hospital at Prome was a mat building inside the gaol walls and served for a prison hospital as well—an arrangement conducive neither to the encouragement of applications for medical relief nor to the discipline of the prison.'[5]

The fact that the engineering and medical departments could be staffed at little expense from India reacted prejudicially on education. About 1800 the Burmans compiled histories of China and Portugal;

---

[1] *RAB*, 1880–1, Intr. p. 33.   [2] *CISM*, pp. 9, 13; Forbes, pp. 156, 234.
[3] *RAB*, 1868–9, p. 117.   [4] *RAB*, 1880–1, p. 123.   [5] *BBG*, I, 527.

Burney notes an attempt to translate an English encyclopaedia into Burmese; Mindon sent Burmans for education in Calcutta, and at the time of the Annexation of Upper Burma in 1886 some Burmese officials knew English and a few were proficient in French. But under British rule until close on 1870 education languished. Thanks to the monastic schools practically all elderly Burmans and Talaings could read and write, but before very long the monks lost much of their prestige, and the Commissioner, Mr Maingy, was apprehensive lest the rising generation should grow up almost wholly uneducated. Missionaries were already at work in Burma, but were making 'far more progress among the simple-minded Karen than amongst the more astute Burmese'.[1] Mr Maingy therefore sanctioned a grant to a missionary school which would take Burmese pupils. This experiment failed, because the missionaries wanted to teach Christianity and the boys merely wanted to learn English. The Government wanted English-speaking clerks and Burmans wanted clerkships, and between 1834 and 1844 a Government school was opened in each of the three chief towns. A return for 1852 shows that just before the second war there were 316 pupils in Government schools, of whom about two-thirds were natives of the country.[2]

On the occupation of Pegu another Government school was opened in Rangoon, and missionaries began to extend their activities to the new province. But the Government could get along without Burman engineers or doctors, and even in general administration it needed few English-speaking subordinates. For clerical and administrative appointments, the education given in monastic schools sufficed; Burmans could get jobs without attending western schools, and even the judges still had 'little other education than that which they had received as boys in some Buddhist monastery'.[3] When the Province of British Burma was constituted in 1862, out of some 5000 children in western schools only about 1000 were Burmese; the others were mostly Christian Karens. Of the four Government schools, that in Moulmein, the oldest, was recommended for abolition, and the school in Rangoon had only twenty-nine scholars and shortly afterwards was closed.[4] Education in Burma was left almost entirely to private agency; western education to the missionaries, and Burmese education to the monks. Formerly the mental horizon of the Burman

---

[1] *RAB*, 1868–9, p. 123.   [2] 1852, Cmd. 361.
[3] *RAB*, 1868–9, p. 61.   [4] *RAB*, 1861–2, pp. 19–21.

had been restricted to the narrow world of medieval Burma, but was commensurate with its boundaries; now in a wider world his outlook was still narrower. But as yet few Burmans were conscious of their social impoverishment; most of them had always been cultivators with little interest in the world beyond their village, the Europeans and Indians and other foreigners resided in the towns, and the cultivator in the village was conscious of little change under British rule except that in many ways he was better off.

Every picture of Burma under native rule and in the early days of British rule brings out the charm and cheerfulness of Burmese social life. Captain Forbes[1] gives a good description of the country in the early seventies, dwelling on the Burman's 'love of sport and social amusement as well as his intense appreciation of the ridiculous.... The Burmans are a lively people, fond of amusement. Horse and boat racing and dramatic performances are the greatest attractions. The young men and boys may often be seen of an evening playing football in the street, and the elders engaged at chess in the verandahs.... The great national sport of the Peguans is boat-racing.... The boats belong to certain towns or villages, and are rowed, or rather paddled, by the men belonging to them; and sometimes, when a match occurs between two localities that have long been rivals, the enthusiasms, the wild excitement, is almost incredible, and certainly indescribable.... One of the characteristics of the Burman race is their intense love of dramatic performances.... No festival, public ceremony or private rejoicing is complete without a performance of this kind... which with him is always a gratuitous exhibition by the hirer of the troupe.... In some large villages the youths and maidens form an amateur company. In the ordinary performances the dancing or, as we should say, the incidental ballet form a principal attraction. (But) the legitimate drama or high Art is the puppet show.... No festive gathering is complete without a band. Almost every important event in a Burman's life is made an occasion for a festival or a feast.' The chief were those at the beginning and end of the Buddhist Lent, and he describes a typical carnival where pasteboard hobby-horses, turtles and gigantic figures revelled in all the fun and freedom of a carnival in southern Europe. These festivals were all part of the common village life, and almost all of them centred round religion.

Yet, even in the village, life was not quite the same as under Burmese rule. The monastery was, as it still is, the centre of village

---

[1] Forbes, pp. 135 ff, 186.

life in Burma, and one natural and almost inevitable result of British rule was to undermine monastic influence. Under Burmese rule the monks, in addition to conducting the whole education of the country, from the Court down to the village, had played a considerable part in political affairs, holding a balance between the Government and the people. At first they sought to play a like part under British rule.[1] It was at the instance of the monks that a monastic building used by the troops for an armoury was restored to religious purposes; and at their instance also the Commissioner of Tenasserim obtained permission from the Government of India to abolish gaming houses. But so early as 1833 we find a report that the monks were no longer regarded with the former veneration. Although this report was probably exaggerated, the monastic order naturally lost cohesion when cut off from the regular establishment with its headquarters at the Burmese capital. The second war struck it a further blow. When the people fled from Pegu to Upper Burma they were accompanied by the monks, and the substantial wooden monasteries fell quickly into disrepair. From 1857 onwards the refugees returned, but often they could not afford to build a monastery or maintain a monk, and many of the monks remained behind in the more congenial environment of Buddhist rule in Upper Burma; instead of a monastery to every village, in Pegu there was only one to every three or four villages.[2] Moreover the monks in British territory were exempt from all ecclesiastical supervision, and before long there were complaints of indiscipline and insubordination.

Such conditions hindered the revival of common social life within the villages, which the troubles incidental on the Annexation had disturbed. This was most evident in Thayetmyo, where the comparatively scanty rainfall necessitated common action among the villagers for the irrigation of their rice lands. As the result of the British occupation harmonious co-operation was no longer possible and the village irrigation systems decayed.[3] In general, however, village life went on much the same as before. Anyone who went to law might find the law and procedure unfamiliar and uncongenial, but very few people went to law until the conditions of life were changed by the opening of the Suez Canal in 1869. In a report for this year, we are told that 'in a large number of disputes, the people prefer to have their differences settled in their own village by their own village elders....(They) have been accustomed for

[1] *SL*, pp. 62, 77.   .[2] Census, 1891, p. 66.   [3] *BBG*, II, 755.

ages to have their differences settled by arbitrators—who receive a fee—and consequently they are content with such an award and hardly ever dream of disputing it; for them it is as binding as any Civil Court could make it.'[1] If they wanted an arbitrator with greater authority they could resort to the circle headman, and very few ever encountered any official higher than the circle headman. If finally they obstinately took the matter into court, they would find that it tended to support the decision of the circle headman, and that the law administered was still based on Burmese custom as expounded in the first Civil Code of 1860.

In practice it was only in some criminal matter that people ever had to come into contact with the law. And there was very little crime, and among all sections of the community the Burmese section was the most law-abiding. In this matter there was an astonishing contrast between Burma then and now. In 1826 the British occupation was followed by a period of unrest both in Arakan and Tenasserim. But after the country had been effectively pacified, the annual reports testify repeatedly to 'the generally peaceable and orderly habits of the people...' and to 'their highly flourishing circumstances with consequent diminished temptation of crime'. Moulmein with its 'motley mixture of people of all countries and castes' was a partial exception, but this was attributed to bad characters from Martaban across the border, and to 'the constant influx of strangers from all parts of India'. 'The country districts and villages continued to be very generally free from offences of all descriptions, although none of them have any Police Establishment.'[2]

The course of events was very similar later on in Pegu. At first the country was disturbed and there were numerous local risings, some on a considerable scale, until about 1860, but then, for nearly twenty years, there was little crime, and those chiefly responsible were Karens or Toungthus from the hills or Shans and Upper Burmans from beyond the frontier.[3] The Burmese and Talaings were conspicuously law-abiding; in 1879, 0·74 % of the Hindu population was in jail, 0·28 % of the Moslem population, 0·20 % of the Christian population, and only 0·12 % of the Buddhist population.[4] In the light of future development these figures are of great significance. The British Government relieved the people from the abuses to which they were subject under Burmese rule, and beyond that left them free to prosper

[1] *RAB*, 1868–9, p. 60.   [2] *SL*, pp. 159, 161, 176–7.
[3] *BBG*, II, 57.   [4] *BBG*, I, 514.

according to their own devices and in their own way. Despite the slow rate of economic progress, or because of it, there was a general diffusion of greater material welfare, and it is probably correct that, as reported in 1879, although there was no enthusiasm for British rule, the majority of the respectable classes were content with it and would be unwilling to see it disturbed.[1]

Note on Growth of Population, 1826–72.

The first regular census in British Burma was held in 1872; previously there had been annual estimates based on revenue returns. In the census of 1872 the population was given as 2·75 million. From subsequent enumerations it appears that the record in rural areas was very defective, and that the correct figure should have been about 3·11 million.[2] In the revenue returns for 1872 the population was given as 2·63 million. In earlier years, when conditions were still unsettled, they must have been much less accurate.

In 1852 the population of Arakan was estimated at 352,348, of Tenasserim at 191,476 and of Pegu and Martaban at 718,464. For Pegu and Martaban the estimate was certainly far too low.[3] From about 1858 there began a steady flow of immigration from Burmese territory, partly of people returning to their homes and partly of newcomers. The earliest figures for British Burma as a whole are those of 1861, which gave a population of 1·90 million. Until that year, pacification was not complete, and between 1861 and 1870 the country was quieter and cultivation more profitable, so it would seem likely that the increase, whether from natural causes or immigration, would be slower between 1852 and 1860. The returns show an increase from 1·90 million in 1861 to 2·50 million in 1870; even if it increased at the same rate in the earlier decade the population in 1852 would have been 1·44 million and of Pegu and Martaban about 890,000 instead of only 718,000.

Similar difficulties hinder attempts to gauge the increase of population in Tenasserim and Arakan between 1826 and 1852. According to the official returns the population in Tenasserim grew from 70,000 to 191,000 and in Arakan from 100,000 to over 350,000. On the basis of these figures Fytche calculated the immigration from Pegu and other native Burman states up to 1855 as 257,000

---

[1] *RAB*, 1880–1, Intr. p. 4.   [2] Census, 1891, p. 21.
[3] *BBG*, I, 443; II, 553.

and this figure, which was followed in the official Gazette has frequently been quoted.[1] But it is demonstrably absurd. Harvey puts the immigrants into Tenasserim in 1827 at 30,000, and the Gazette says that 20,000 arrived in the first four years. Both these estimates seem to be based on the Annual Administration Report for 1868–9. Desai, apparently following reports from Burney, the Resident in Ava, mentions 12,000.[2] But the original records are practically silent as to immigration from Burma except for 10,000 who came with the Governor of Syriam on the failure of his rebellion in 1827, and some of these returned.[3] Attempts to encourage immigration from Siam, Malaya and China were unsuccessful. The only immigrants were Indians, and these remained in Moulmein, where in 1852 there were about 25,000. Thus the increase in population in Tenasserim must have been almost entirely due to natural causes.

Arakan was annexed to Burma in 1784, and there followed numerous reports of emigration into Bengal, where it seems that two Arakanese settlements, each of some 10,000, were established at Harbang and Cox's Bazar about 1798, though within a few years many returned to Arakan.[4] The Burmese Census figures, however, though in most cases rather low, give the population in 1802 as 248,604. The apparent decline to 100,000 in 1826 is usually ascribed to further emigration consequent on Burmese oppression, and the subsequent increase to the return of the emigrants after Arakan had come under British rule. But, according to the official Gazette, a great trade was carried on between Arakan and Ava before the war of 1826, employing annually, it was said, forty thousand people; and a road laid down in 1816 to carry the traffic was maintained in excellent order.[5] This is hardly consistent with the references to widespread devastation. The alleged influx after 1826 is also contradicted by the evidence. In 1840 Phayre reported that emigrants were 'gradually returning'.[6] At that time it was believed that many had returned before 1833, although no figures were available. Yet, according to a report of 1835, unfavourable rumours as to conditions in Arakan had deterred emigrants from returning for some years after 1826, and it was not until recently that a better opinion

---

[1] Fytche, II, 291; *BBG*, II, 50.
[2] Harvey, *CHI*, v, 567; *BBG*, II, 50; *RAB*, 1868–9, p. 1; Desai, p. 57.
[3] *SL*, pp. 60, 74.   [4] Banerjee, *Eastern Frontier*, p. 192 n.
[5] Banerjee, *Eastern Frontier*, p. 46 and n.   [6] *BBG*, II, 15.

had been 'gradually spreading and bringing with it a return of the original inhabitants and their descendants to the country of their forefathers'.[1] It seems, moreover, that this flow was checked again in 1838.[2] Doubtless some returned, but if British rule in Tenasserim did not induce emigrants to return from Siam, one would not expect many to return from Bengal, where they already enjoyed its benefits. The early records refer also to the immigration of Indians, but even in 1861 there were less than 27,000 Indians in Arakan out of a population of 376,000. There were also reports of immigration from Ava and Pegu, but in fact this was negligible; so late as 1872 there were less than 5000 Burmese and not a single Talaing in Arakan.[3] It would seem, therefore, that the revenue returns were no more accurate in Arakan than in Tenasserim, and that the increase of population was mainly due to natural causes. Thus with a population of over 500,000 for the two provinces in 1852, the population in 1826 cannot well have been less than 300,000.

[1] *Letters Issued, Arakan* (unpublished) 1835, p. 100; 1841, p. 142.
[2] *BBG*, II, 15.   [3] *BBG*, II, 15.

CHAPTER III

BURMA, 1870–1923: EFFICIENCY AND SOCIAL JUSTICE

(a) PROGRESS

1. ADMINISTRATIVE POLICY

IN reviewing the background of colonial policy, we have noticed that 1870 may be regarded as a turning point in the transition from a policy of *laissez-faire* to one of active participation in the economic development of the tropics. During the first three-quarters of the nineteenth century industrial progress in Europe was building up a supply of capital available for investment overseas, and the demands of industry for raw materials from the tropics were rapidly increasing. Among the earlier manifestations of western enterprise were the construction of railways and, from about 1860, the growth of steam traffic in eastern waters. In this process, gradual but steadily accelerating, the opening of the Suez Canal at the end of 1869 may be taken to mark the dawn of a new era in the economic, social and political relations of Europe with the East and with the tropics in general.

The new age required a new social philosophy. In Liberalism there was a double strand combining the practical common sense of Adam Smith and Bentham with the humanitarian ideals of Rousseau and the French Revolution. The new philosophy also had a dual origin; from Darwin's principle of the survival of the fittest it derived a justification of efficiency, and, from St-Simon, Robert Owen and other Socialists of various schools, the doctrine of social justice. These ideas, applied to colonial policy in the new environment, gave birth to modern imperialism. Liberals could view with detachment the prospect of an independent India that would still provide a market for European goods; but capitalists, engaged in western enterprise in the tropics and concerned for their supplies of raw materials, demanded a more active and intensive colonial policy. Accordingly, during the closing decades of the century, we see the European powers engaged in 'the struggle for Africa', and jockeying for position with a view to the prospective 'break-up of China'. At the same time the growing sense of social justice encouraged a more sympathetic attitude towards native welfare, fostered by the Labour movement, and also by the natural tendency of rival powers to justify their colonial pretensions on moral grounds as promoting the general welfare of the world and of their tropical subjects. By the end of the century both these aspects of colonial rule found expression in British policy as the doctrine of 'the White Man's Burden'.

In Burma the outstanding illustration of the new turn in colonial policy was the annexation of Upper Burma in 1886. Until then, the only form of economic activity to attract Europeans, apart from the exploitation of the teak forests, was the export of rice, grown by the natives. The opening of the Suez Canal gave a tremendous impulse to the cultivation and export of rice, but this still remained wholly a product of native enterprise, though the rapid multiplication of steam rice-mills gave Europeans a larger share in preparing it for the market. From 1886 onwards, however, European capitalists began to engage in productive enterprise, first in the ruby mines, then in the winning of oil and other minerals, and a little later in developing rubber plantations. The earlier reactions of this course of events on administrative policy may be found in the elaboration of departmental machinery with a view to greater efficiency; this led in 1897 to the recognition of Burma as a Provincial Government, with a Legislative Council mainly representing capitalist interests. The further development of the Council is described below.

For some time, however, the elaboration of administrative machinery was not accompanied by any noteworthy change in the general colour of administrative policy. On the annexation of Upper Burma in 1886 it was conceived in much the same terms as at the annexation of the maritime provinces sixty years earlier, and was directed to the provision of a suitable code of laws, the enforcement of a moderate system of taxation, the recognition of religious and personal freedom as a fundamental principle of rule, the freedom of trade and abolition of oppressive duties, and the improvement of roads and other means of communication.[1] Except for the final item this policy was merely negative, a policy of *laissez-faire*. Only with the new century did it assume a more constructive aspect, with a corresponding elaboration of administrative machinery for the more efficient development of material resources and the promotion of social services in respect of agricultural indebtedness, sanitation, primary instruction, and other matters bearing on the material welfare of the people. Administrative

[1] 1887, Cmd. 4692, p. 113.

policy was no longer content to leave economic forces uncontrolled, but aimed to protect the people against their deleterious effects. This involved a new attitude towards western enterprise; it required that Government should maintain an impartial balance between the interests of western enterprise and of the people. 'The standard that the Services have tried to follow', said one of their most distinguished representatives, 'has been the standard of "Justice, Equity and Good Conscience", involving a just balance of the claims and interests of all classes of men.'[1] Under the new conditions, the due adjustment of conflicting claims and interests raised difficult problems of justice, equity and conscience. In disputes between Hindus and Moslems a British Government could, in the words of Burke, observe 'the cold neutrality of an impartial judge'. But the chill is taken off neutrality when a western Government holds the balance between western enterprise and native subjects; both interest and sympathy falsify the scales, and the problem of holding a balance becomes difficult if not impossible, while it is impossible to convince outside observers that sympathy has provided an adequate equipoise to interest. It was, however, the conception of Government as a benevolent but impartial umpire that dominated policy during the period inaugurated by the opening of the Suez Canal. The earlier policy of *laissez-faire* was gradually transformed into a policy of actively promoting economic progress, and this was slowly permeated by ideas of social justice and concern for the welfare of the people. Only with the political reforms of 1923 did policy take a new turn in the direction of autonomy.

2. UPPER BURMA AND THE THIRD WAR

King Mindon, who came to the throne by a palace revolution arising out of the war of 1852, was probably the best sovereign of his line, and under his fostering care his people grew in numbers and prosperity. He introduced a coinage, remodelled the system of taxation, aimed at abolishing taxation by State enterprise and commerce, and built up a fleet of river steamers.[2] He despatched missions to Europe, sent lads abroad to study English and French, and had others trained in telegraphy in Rangoon, subsequently introducing a telegraph system based on the Morse Code adapted to the Burmese alphabet.[3] He encouraged

---

[1] Craddock, p. vii; Garratt, G. T., *Europe's Dance of Death* (1940), p. 39.
[2] *RTC*, 1867–8, p. 155.   [3] *RAB*, 1868–9, p. 121.

industry by erecting factories, with European machinery and in some cases under European management, for the manufacture of lac, cutch, sugar, and of cotton and silk piece goods;[1] with a view to making Upper Burma less dependent on British Burma he stimulated the cultivation of rice, apparently with no little success.[2] These experiments were costly, and he was 'induced under the stress of financial difficulties to obtain all the cotton he could to meet the requirements of certain European houses to whom he was in debt, and to pay the cost of machinery and steamers he was persuaded to order from Europe'.[3] This, however, was in line with his general fiscal policy of reducing taxation by deriving revenue from trade. He entered the market both for home and foreign produce, purchasing for export cotton, wheat and palm-sugar produced in Upper Burma, and employing agents to buy rice and British cotton goods in Lower Burma. He 'did everything possible to foster trade with Yunnan', sent embassies to India and Persia, and tried to open up commercial and political relations with Spain, Italy and France. During his reign there was a great increase in the value of the trade between British territory and independent Burma.

After some years of steady progress a commercial treaty was arranged in 1867, with the result that during the next two years the exports averaged rather more than Rs. 135 lakhs and the imports close on Rs. 100 lakhs. Ten years later, on the death of King Mindon in 1878, the value of exports had risen by a third, and the value of imports had doubled.

Trade with British Burma

(Rs. lakhs)*

Year	Exports to Ava	Imports from Ava
1858–59	39·8	31·9
1865–66	83·4	72·5
1877–78	177·6	200·1
1884–85	200·1	196·0

* Lakh = 100,000, usually of rupees.

The imports of cotton and silk piece goods, the item of chief interest to the common man, rose not only in volume but in value, suggesting that 'the people of Upper Burma, like those within British territory, were in a position to buy more expensive articles of apparel than formerly'.[4] His successor, King Thibaw, continued and in some ways extended the same policy, and the figures for 1884–5, the last complete year before

[1] Lac, RTC, 1874–5, p. 24; Cutch, RAB, 1877–8, p. 54; Sugar, RAB, 1879–80, p. 68; Cotton, RTC, 1871–2, p. 44; RAB, 1877–8, p. 51; 1879–80, p. 66; Silk, RAB, 1877–8, p. 51.
[2] RTC, 1874–5, p. 40.
[3] RTC, 1871–2, p. 47.　　　　　　　[4] RTC, 1875–6, p. 49.

the annexation, show that trade continued to prosper. Cheap English crockery was rapidly replacing lacquer ware, and tinned provisions, glass lamps, safety matches and fuzees, were prominent among the articles of petty luxury that found their way across the border.[1] It would seem that, as formerly after the occupation of the maritime provinces, the extension of British dominion over Pegu was profitable to Burmans still living under native rule.

The growth of trade with Upper Burma was certainly profitable to the European mercantile community in Rangoon. But they expected more trade and greater profit if Upper Burma could be brought under the British flag. The King exercised a strict control over the export of the more important products by restricting the right of export to his own agents or to licensees; this system was applied to cotton, wheat, palm-sugar, pickled tea, cutch and ivory. The merchants could obtain earth-oil at Rs. 2·5 in the open market, but the King held out for Rs. 5. In a good cotton year the price might have fallen to Rs. 25, but the King demanded Rs. 35. Purchasers could get palm-sugar at Rs. 100 a ton, but next year the King bought up the whole output and, for a rather larger crop, charged Rs. 125 a ton; he is said to have made a 100 % on the transaction. He paid Rs. 7 for lead and sold it to British merchants at Rs. 15.[2] Even if the people received no more, the profits remained in the country instead of going abroad. This 'vicious system of monopolies'[3] was a sore point with the European merchants of Rangoon. Strictly speaking, however, the system was not one of monopoly. 'The trade was free, but under the pressure placed upon him by European firms, the King was obliged to obtain all the produce he could to meet his liabilities.'[4] The people could grow what crops they liked and were free to dispose of the produce in the home market; the only restriction was that certain goods, if sent across the frontier, had to be sent through a Crown agent, or a licensee, to whom the concession had been granted. 'The monopolist', it was admitted, 'cannot interfere with the trade in Upper Burma itself; but all the goods of which he holds the monopoly must, before being exported to other countries, pass through his hands.'[5] Still, whether monopoly or not, it was a grievance, except to European firms fortunate or astute enough to obtain such a concession—then,

---

[1] Crockery, *RTC*, 1874–5, p. 31; 1875–6, p. 16; 1876–7, p. 31; 1882–3, p. 28; Tinned provisions, *RTC*, 1882–3, p. 98; 1884–5, p. 24; Glass lamps, *RTC*, 1883–4, p. 29; Matches, *RTC*, 1876–7, p. 28.

[2] Hall, pp. 163, 173, 399.   [3] *RAB*, 1877–8, p. 49.

[4] *RTC*, 1871–2, p. 47; 1883, Cmd. 3501, pp. 4, 11.   [5] *RAB*, 1881–2, p. 80.

as happened with cutch, they could use it to drive the Chinese off the market.[1]

Importers of piece goods also had their grievances. They could fix their own price when dealing with individual traders in British Burma, but all such goods for Upper Burma were bought through agents of the King who could insist on lower prices and extended credit,[2] and, if Rangoon prices were too high, could deal directly with Calcutta. Similarly, 'legitimate private traders'[3] could not sell rice to Upper Burma because the King's agents dealt directly with the Delta cultivators. This was especially annoying when there was a famine in Madras, and merchants could have found a profitable market in India for all the rice in Burma, if the royal agents had not purchased a quantity sufficient to meet the requirements of Upper Burma. In respect of the rice trade especially Government was sympathetic, for rice to Ava paid no duty and 'withdrew from the revenue of British Burma a large sum annually which would otherwise be secured to Government were the rice sent seaward,'[4] and both Government and shippers felt aggrieved when 'a large amount of rice which would otherwise have been conveyed to Rangoon for shipment, went inland instead'.[5]

The King's speculations were not always profitable, nor even governed solely by ideas of profit.[6] His purchases of paddy were for the army, and also to relieve distress in tracts liable to scarcity. But it was just in these tracts that a year of good rainfall might yield abundant crops, as in 1872 when paddy was selling in Upper Burma at Rs. 15 to Rs. 25, half the price in Rangoon, while the royal granaries were overflowing with grain bought in the previous year at Rs. 60 to Rs. 70.[7] Such miscalculations exposed his policy to criticism as conflicting with a sound political economy. Not only did his policy touch the pockets of the merchants, but it stirred them to sympathy with his downtrodden subjects. The King, they said, 'forced advances' on the cultivator to secure a lien on the produce[8]—a practice not unknown in the rice trade of Lower Burma. They complained also that the concessionnaire oppressed the cultivator by 'fixing the price sufficiently low to enable him to realise a profit by sale at the rates which he can obtain in the country to which

[1] *RAB*, 1880–1, Intr. p. 43; 1881–2, p. 73.
[2] *RTC*, 1876–7, p. 7; 1877–8, p. 6.   [3] *RAB*, 1877–8, p. 51.
[4] *RAB*, 1877–8, p. 51; *RTC*, 1877–8, p. 2.   [5] *RAB*, 1879–80, p. 67.
[6] *RTC*, 1875–6, p. 50.
[7] *RTC*, 1871–2, p. 45; *RAB*, 1880–1, p. 84.   [8] *RAB*, 1877–8, p. 55.

he exports'; so that the cultivator 'had to sell as much of his product as possible in the home market and leave as little as possible for export'.[1] It is unlikely, however, that foreign merchants would have bought produce at rates which they did not expect to leave a profit.

The advantages anticipated from annexation were not limited, however, to the prospect of freer trade in Upper Burma; the merchants looked across the border to China.[2] 'The teeming cities of China', it was said, 'remain to be reached, and the vast inland trade of that province directed down the Irrawaddy rather than through the tempestuous seas which wash the southern coasts of Asia.' Like the merchants of Tenasserim in earlier days they found allies among the local officials in urging a forward policy. Everyone 'confidently believed' that after annexation Burma would become one of the best fields for British energy and capital; communications would rapidly be opened up and the great resources of the interior and the neighbouring territory of China 'developed'. It was urged that 'if we do not annex Burma America will', and one of the main objects of solicitude was the 'hot haste' of America to secure if possible the command of the Chinese market; it was thought therefore 'highly prudent on Imperial grounds that we should be in a position to substitute a western ingress to China for the present seaboard approach, destined to be disproportionately shared, if not entirely absorbed by America'.[3]

But the Government of India refused to be scared by the bogey of American imperialism. Apprehensions of French imperialism had more substance. From 1867 political relations between Burma and the Indian Government deteriorated. The rift had its origin in the treaty of that year which allowed the King to import arms and ammunition subject to the sanction of the Chief Commissioner, who undertook, in a note appended to the treaty, that this would ordinarily be granted. Repeatedly, however, applications to import rifles were refused, and this never ceased to rankle.[4] Another continual source of friction was the claim of Burma to suzerainty over Karenni, a cluster of hill tribes on the eastern hills, where there were valuable teak forests. Then in 1876, Lord Lytton, newly appointed Viceroy,

[1] RAB, 1881–2, p. 80.   [2] RTC, 1867–8, p. 30.
[3] Fytche, II, 120, 127; Gordon, C. A., Our Trip to Burma (n.d. [1874]), p. 159; Durand, II, 185; Laurie, W. F. B., Our Burmese Wars (1880), p. 355; Thomas, E., Gladstone of Hawarden (1936), p. 66.
[4] Banerjee, Annexation of Burma, p. 243; Macaulay, p. 143; 1868–9, Cmd. 251; 1883, Cmd. 3501, p. 25.

insisted that the British Agent in Mandalay should abandon the practice of removing his shoes in the presence of the King, with the result that he was no longer received in audience and British influence declined. On the accession of Thibaw in 1878, Lytton urged the home Government to press matters to an issue even at the risk of hostilities, and sent troops to Burma. He followed the same course in 1879, when Thibaw, fearing an insurrection, sanctioned the massacre of a large number, variously estimated at 32 to 80, of members of the royal family. A few months later the British Agent was withdrawn on the ground that his life was in danger, though British merchants, visiting Mandalay just afterwards, received a friendly welcome from the King.[1]

The Burmese feared that the Indian Government was stirring up trouble with a view to annexation, and their fears were not wholly unjustifiable. In 1867, the Myingun Prince, who had taken refuge in British territory after an unsuccessful rebellion, escaped from internment and made another attempt upon the throne. There were similar incidents in 1881 and 1882.[2] Mercantile interests had long pressed for intervention and in 1884, when renewed fears of danger from the Myingun Prince occasioned the 'liquidation' of his prominent adherents on the excuse of suppressing a jail outbreak, merchants and missionaries alike clamoured for annexation.

Meanwhile the Burmese Government was cultivating relations with other European powers, and chiefly with France. This was the direct consequence of the refusal to abide by the agreement regarding the import of arms. But the situation did not become serious until January 1885, when the French Government, in pursuance of Ferry's forward policy in south-east Asia, signed a treaty with Burma. At first the danger of French influence was regarded as potential rather than imminent, and the Indian Government, reporting on the mercantile demand for intervention, remarked that the treaties with Burma had been on the whole respected, British commerce protected, and friendly relations maintained between officials on the frontier. The Home Government agreed that, despite the French treaty, annexation would not be justified. In July, however, it transpired that the arrangements with France seriously threatened British interests, and the Chief Commissioner suggested that, unless the

---

[1] 1886, Cmd. 4614, pp. 2, 11, 18, 54; Macaulay, p. 141.
[2] 1886, Cmd. 4614, p. 40; *UBG*, I, i, 104; *RAB*, 1868–9, pp. 15, 21; Macaulay, p. 141.

proposed concessions were abandoned, there would be no alternative to annexation.[1] The occasion was propitious because of a new turn of events in France, where reverses in Tonkin had caused the fall of Ferry and inspired a revulsion against colonial adventures. This gave Britain a free hand in Burma, and there was soon a chance to use it. A British company was working the teak forests and the French wanted to take over their concession. In August the Burmese Government imposed a heavy penalty on the company, which it accused, not entirely it would seem without some grounds,[2] of defrauding the revenue. This furnished a pretext for intervention with a view to clarifying the general situation. The Burmese, still hoping for French support, stood firm, and, shortly before the French Senate was due to ratify the treaty signed in January, the Indian Government addressed an ultimatum to the King, allowing him a week for submission to its terms, and backed the ultimatum with the despatch of troops. It was known that the Burmese did not expect immediate invasion and were not ready for it,[3] but their reply was interpreted as a final rejection of the terms, and the army was ordered to advance. After a short and almost bloodless campaign, the King was induced by one of his ministers to surrender, and on the first day of 1886 Ava was annexed to the Indian Empire. Although it is true that Burma forfeited its independence because the Government was unable and unwilling to accept the conditions of independence in the modern world, the annexation may be regarded from a wider standpoint as an episode in the rivalry of Britain and France for supremacy in South-east Asia, and can best be justified as removing at an opportune moment a potential cause of a European war.

The Burmese army, however, was still undefeated. 'They refused to obey the order to surrender which had come from Mandalay...[and]...waged a guerilla warfare against the invaders.' As in 1826 and 1852 the British expected a welcome. The Viceroy reported that the people would generally regard with pleasure 'the prospects of the substitution of a strong and orderly Government for the incompetent and cruel tyranny of their former rulers'. But, as on former occasions, this optimistic view was an illusion. In Upper Burma 'the resistance was more widespread and obstinate than anyone had foreseen', and the people of Lower Burma,

---

[1] 1886, Cmd. 4614, pp. 125, 160, 173.
[2] UBG, I, i, 108.   [3] 1886, Cmd. 4614, p. 256.

after thirty-five years of British rule, seized the opportunity to rebel. When the larger units of the regular army were broken up, scattered bands under local chieftains all over the country carried on guerilla warfare, 'euphemistically termed dacoity', into which it gradually, degenerated. But, even when suffering from the depredations of the dacoits, the people refused to help the British troops, and were zealous in giving aid and information to their countrymen. 'The only course open to us was to make them fear us more than the dacoits.'[1] Pacification required an army, numbering at one time 32,000 under the Commander-in-Chief in India, and in the course of five years, by rigorous administration, supported where necessary by armed force, the country was effectively subjugated.

3. ADMINISTRATIVE PRACTICE

The administrative machinery of the central Government remained almost unchanged from 1870 until the end of the century. In 1872 a Judicial Commissioner was appointed to relieve the Chief Commissioner of judicial work and, in 1881, arrangements were made for the Judicial Commissioner and the Recorders of Moulmein and Rangoon to sit together on occasion as a single Chief Court; in 1890 a Judicial Commissioner was appointed for Upper Burma. Immediate control over the revenue was delegated to a Financial Commissioner in 1888. Otherwise the Commissioners, Deputy Commissioners, Subdivisional Officers and Township Officers continued to discharge civil and criminal judicial functions, and to be responsible for all aspects of revenue and general administration within their charges.[2] But the growth of trade and the trend of opinion towards a more active administration demanded a more elaborate mechanism, and from about the end of the century the whole system was gradually reorganized. Changes were made both in the constitution of the central Government and in the machinery through which it worked.

The transformation of the system of *laissez-faire* into one inspired by the doctrine of efficiency may be dated from 1897 when the Chief Commissioner was promoted to be a Lieutenant-Governor and was given a Legislative Council of nine nominated members including five non-officials. This measure 'was one of decentralization for administrative convenience rather than of constitutional progress'.[3] In

---

[1] Crosthwaite, pp. 2, 13, 14, 104; Smeaton, pp. 2, 3; Churchill, Rt Hon. Winston, *Life of Lord Randolph Churchill* (1906), I, 524.
[2] *RAB*, 1882-3, p. 7; 1901-2, p. 11.   [3] Leach, p. 15.

1909 the membership was enlarged to fifteen, and of the nine non-official members one was elected by the Rangoon Chamber of Commerce, representing European business interests. A further revision in 1920 increased the membership to thirty, with two elected representatives of the European mercantile community and twenty-eight nominated members, of whom twelve might be officials, and two experts. The nominated members always included native non-officials. In 1920 these numbered thirteen (ten Burmans, two Indians, one Chinese); nearly half were lawyers and the rest belonged to the land-owning, trading and money-lending classes.[1] Thus the reforms tended to increase the preponderance of capitalist interests in the direction of affairs, and reflected their growing importance in the economic life of Burma. The changes symbolized a greater efficiency in economic development; only with the subsequent constitutional reforms of 1923 did the main interest shift to political development.

Up to the end of the nineteenth century district officers were struggling ineffectually with the new tasks imposed on them as the local government, under pressure from the Government of India, gradually and almost reluctantly accepted new responsibilities. From about 1900, however, and largely under the impulse to efficiency given by Lord Curzon, the Government of Burma began to provide for the discharge of these new functions through special officers and departments. Notable changes were the appointment of two separate officers to the charge of jails and hospitals (1899), of a Commissioner to deal with the settlement of land revenue and the machinery of land records (1900), of an Excise Commissioner (1906) and, more important, the constitution of an enlarged Chief Court (1900), followed by the creation (1905–6) of a Judicial Service, to relieve district officers of civil, and of some criminal, work. These innovations aimed chiefly at increasing administrative efficiency. Others were directed towards making the Government more efficient as an instrument of economic progress. Among these were the appointment of a Chief Conservator of Forests (1905), of a Director of Agriculture (1906) and the constitution of distinct Agricultural, Veterinary and Fishery Departments; another innovation under the same head was the constitution of an Advisory Board for Communications in 1916, due mainly to the growth of motor traffic. A third series of reforms aimed to promote welfare. A growing concern for education appeared in the assumption of closer control in

[1] *RAB*, 1911–12, p. 11; *ISC*, XI, 7.

1900 over public instruction, and the subsequent extension of state provision for instruction, leading in 1920 to the creation of Rangoon University. Other developments of welfare administration were the constitution of a Co-operative Credit Department (1904), and the appointment of a Sanitary Commissioner (1908) followed by the creation of a Public Health Department distinct from the medical service. All these departments dealt separately with isolated aspects of social life and had to be linked up with one another and with the Government and district officers. The link was provided when, in place of the single secretary who had sufficed for the Chief Commissioner up to 1886, there came into existence an elaborate and many-sided secretariat; but it was only a mechanical link, for the secretariat dealt with cases according to rule and precedent, devoid of human interest, and, though the administration might appear more efficient, it became more rigid and less human. One result of the process was that the simple machinery which, up to the end of the nineteenth century, sufficed for the maintenance of law and order, almost disappeared from outside view beneath an imposing western superstructure, designed for the furtherance of economic progress and the enhancement of human welfare.

But the machinery of law was far more obvious than ever before to those beneath the harrow with whom the administration had to deal, for the new departments touched their life on all sides, imposing on them new regulations which they had to obey under the sanction of a legal penalty. It was, indeed, in local affairs, both urban and rural, that the doctrine of efficiency was first manifested, long before the end of the nineteenth century. From the earliest days of British rule funds were raised to meet local requirements, and in 1874, at the instance of the Government of India, municipal institutions were introduced in certain towns in order to provide more efficiently for public requirements under the conditions of the modern world. The working of these institutions will be examined in connection with self-government; here it may suffice to mention that by 1923 there were about fifty municipal committees charged with certain responsibilities in connection with roads, lighting, water, public health and schools. The motive force on these committees was the local officer of the central Government. In rural areas there were no corresponding bodies, and the care for all such matters rested solely with the local officer in person.

But it was in rural areas that the transformation of the administrative system in the interest of efficiency was carried furthest. As we have noticed, the Burmese system of local administration was based on the circle under a hereditary circle headman, exercising a personal authority over his own people but not necessarily the overlord of all the inhabitants of the circle. Although the British authorities changed the character of this system by the partial transformation of the circle headman into an official, and by the frequent subdivision, amalgamation or abolition of circles for administrative convenience and without regard for local sentiment, there was no intentional departure from the Burmese model. In practice local administration still centred round the circle headman, who retained much of his former authority as an instrument of local autonomy within his charge. In 1883 Mr (later Sir Charles) Crosthwaite, an official from India acting temporarily as Chief Commissioner, commented on the absence of village communities with recognized heads, and on the importance of the circle headman. These features, distinguishing the administrative system of Burma from that of other Indian provinces, appeared to him defects, and, on returning to India, he drew up a project of village administration more in accordance with Indian ideas.[1] Shortly after the annexation of Upper Burma he was appointed Chief Commissioner, and brought with him a draft of his new plan.

Conditions in Burma provided an occasion to introduce it. In Upper Burma many circle headmen led the resistance to British rule, and in Lower Burma they failed to suppress, if they did not sympathize with, the rebellion. Sir Charles Crosthwaite accordingly introduced his new system of breaking up the circles into villages, and a Village Act, passed as an instrument of martial law, imposed on both headmen and villagers duties under penal sanction without conferring on them any rights. This abolished self-government over any unit larger than the village and, by converting the village from a social and residential unit into an administrative unit, cut at the roots of organic social life within the village. Just as formerly the circles had been cut up and reshaped in the interest of administrative uniformity, so now were the villages. They were regarded merely as units of administration and 'consequently many considerations irrelevant to the life of the community enter into the formation of a village. It may contain one or more hamlets within its borders, or its boundaries may cut with seeming irrelevance through the heart of some large residential unit. The general principles determining its formation are that its

---

[1] Crosthwaite, p. 23.

area must not be too great for the control of a headman, and the revenues must be sufficient to afford by the commission on their collection an adequate remuneration for his various responsibilities.'[1] At first the tendency was towards greater subdivision. Later it was thought that better-paid headmen would be more efficient, and the amalgamation of charges gained favour. With a view 'to achieve the happy mean, the combination of adequate emoluments and efficient administration', a systematic scheme for amalgamation was drawn up in each district. Between 1909 and 1919 the number of headmen declined by over 2000, mostly in the later years, when 'the vigorous continuance of the policy of amalgamation' led to the abolition of 593 charges in a single year. Yet at the same time the remaining circles of Burmese rule were being abolished. Thus, while organic ties were broken down, new artificial units were constituted. 'The policy was naturally unpopular with the villagers who almost invariably resented the extinction of their villages as a separate entity.' A year after the policy of amalgamation had reached the stage of 'a systematic scheme' it was suddenly reversed;[2] rather perhaps because a new Governor had different ideas than because of its unpopularity with the people. From the first introduction of the village system the village was in fact little more than a cog-wheel in the machinery for maintaining order and collecting revenue, and it was under the head of 'police administration' that a paragraph on village affairs was published annually. The results are perhaps best summarized in the Administration Report for 1931–2, which states that the village head-men had performed their difficult tasks satisfactorily 'in face of the apathy or opposition of the villagers'.[3] As will appear below, the greater efficiency of the machinery for dealing with crime was in-effective to prevent the growth of crime.

With the substitution of the Village System for the Circle System, local administration, like the central administration, became more mechanical and, by undermining common social life, it allowed, and indeed encouraged, individual villagers to encroach on customary common rights. The process of abolishing the circle headman was gradual, but, even where he still survived, the new policy reacted to the prejudice of his authority. Formerly, the more serious disputes between adjacent villages were settled by the circle headman, and in 1883 the Courts still tended to confirm his orders. But by 1891 a

---

[1] Census, 1911, p. 24.
[2] *RAB*, 1919–20, p. 51; 1920–1, p. 51. [3] *RAB*, 1931–2, p. 77.

decision by a circle headman, based on Burmese custom and ratified
by a Burmese judge, was set aside by the Judicial Commissioner as
contrary to 'Burmese' law.[1] That signified the passing of the habit
of referring disputes to a local arbitrator with a view to arriving at a
compromise according to known custom; the search for greater
efficiency substituted the mechanical logic of the law courts, applying
laws which the people, and not infrequently the judges, did not
understand.

In course of time, however, the multiplication of petty units under
the village system was found to occasion administrative inconvenience
and a project of grouping village headmen was contemplated.[2] The
original object of grouping them was to obtain joint security for the
revenue which they collected. Then in 'the very criminal district of
Tharrawaddy' the groups were given new functions 'in the interests
of law and order'. 'The primary functions of the group were to secure
co-operation in the maintenance of order, any inefficient member
being reported with a view to replacement.' The work of the group
included 'surveillance of bad characters and suspicious strangers,
the maintenance of fences, and of village guards at night, drills in
defensive tactics against dacoits, and the prevention of offences'.
They were allowed, however, to submit recommendations with
regard to sanitation and other village interests, and were expected to
submit monthly reports for the information of the Deputy Commissioner. But this system of grouping headmen had no organic
basis and, so far as it was adopted, served merely to make them more
efficient instruments of Government. As was remarked in connection
with the political reforms of 1917–23, the headman in Burma was
'far more an executive officer of Government than under any similar
system in any other province'.[3] The village system was no organic
growth but a mechanical contrivance, and, in the pursuit of administrative efficiency, the native political and social organization was
broken down; there remained no organic unit higher than the village,
and even the village became very largely an artificial administrative
unit. The general effect was that the popular self-government of
Burmese times was replaced by a foreign legal system unable to
control the anti-social forces which it liberated, and favouring the
decay rather than the growth of local autonomy.

In 1870 the system of administration, so far as it impinged upon

[1] *Ru.SJ*, 1883, p. 233; 1891, p. 607.
[2] *RAB*, 1920–1, p. 53.   [3] 1920, Cmd. 746, p. 13.

the people, was still one of indirect rule through the local circle headman, normally hereditary and remaining in one charge throughout his life. Even up to 1900 the people saw little of any Government officials, and very few ever caught more than a passing glimpse of a European official. By 1923 the Government was no longer remote from the people but, through various departmental subordinates, touched on almost every aspect of private life. The people were no longer unconscious of foreign rule, but were continually reminded that they were subject to a foreign government actuated by alien ideas. Moreover, the contact between Government and the people had taken on a new character. In 1870, if ever they met an official, he was a human being able to take a comprehensive view of their affairs. In 1923 they had to deal with departmental subordinates, each concerned solely with his special functions: the school inspector looked at the children, the agriculturalist at the crops, the veterinary inspector at the cattle and the sanitary inspector at the latrines. None of these officials saw life whole and, by reason of frequent transfers, none of them saw it steadily. But life cannot be cut up into departments, nor can any problem be treated without reference to the past and future. Most of the subordinate officials, even, and perhaps specially, those charged with welfare activities, were regarded as agents of oppression, to be propitiated by petty bribes.[1] Again, the multiplication of departmental specialists deprived administrative officials of their more congenial functions, and presented them to the people merely as magistrates and tax collectors, so that their relations with the people became both more distant and less kindly.

4. Economic Progress

Communications. The opening of the Suez Canal gave a new stimulus to trade and to the improvement of communications. There was a spasm of interest in road-making and many old projects were revived, only to be forgotten before the roads were built. By 1918, in a country covering twice the area of the British Isles, there were 'still barely 2000 miles of metalled road, less than in a London suburb'.[2] Roads were not really needed. When the crops were off the ground, the villager could drive to market across the open fields; for longer journeys the rivers, which hindered the building of roads, rendered them unnecessary. Until the advent of the motor-car the country could manage without roads.

[1] *CBC*, p. 8.   [2] Harvey, *CHI*, VI, 444

But the relations with Ava were such as to render war almost inevitable, and the Indian Mutiny had demonstrated the need of railways for military operations. Private enterprise was not forthcoming, and the project of a State railway to the frontier at Prome was adopted in 1868, though nothing was done until 1874 when construction was put in hand to provide relief for the famine-stricken peasants of Bengal.[1] The line to Prome was completed in 1877, and in 1885, just in time for the third war, a line to the frontier at Toungoo reduced the journey from twenty-five days to less than half as many hours. In 1889 it was carried on to Mandalay, and then to the Chinese frontier at Myitkyina in 1898 and at Lashio in 1902. These last extensions were laid down by the Burma Railway Company, to which the line was leased in 1896. It also opened lines to Bassein in 1902 and to Moulmein in 1907, when, for the first time in history, one could travel across Lower Burma from east to west by land without having to force a way by footpaths and ford innumerable creeks.

During the same period there was a corresponding improvement in communications by water.[2] The small company which took over the Government steamers in 1863 was reorganized in 1868 as the Irrawaddy Flotilla Company. At that time the King of Burma was adding to his fleet, and another private firm in Rangoon was running occasional steamers up the Irrawaddy. But it was rarely that any boat went beyond the frontier. After the treaty of 1867, trade with Upper Burma increased so rapidly that, two years later, the Government was able by the grant of a subsidy to induce the Irrawaddy Flotilla Company to run a weekly service to Mandalay and a monthly service to the Chinese frontier at Bhamo. For a few years the company made cautious headway, but in 1875 it embarked on a bolder policy by importing five large steamers and six flats or houseboats to be attached to the steamers as travelling bazaars. The activities of France in Burma in 1885 aroused some apprehension lest a French company should take over the King's vessels and enter into competition for the river traffic, but, fortunately for the Irrawaddy Flotilla Company, these fears were dispelled by the Annexation, and by 1900 it had secured a practical monopoly of steam transport over all the inland waters of Burma.

External communications also made rapid progress. The minor

[1] *BBG*, I, 516; *RAB*, 1884–5, p. 46.
[2] Fytche, II, 323; *RAB*, 1868–9, p. 14; 1880–1, Intr. p. 34; *RTC*, 1867–8, p. 155; 1871–2, p. 13; 1875–6, p. 12.

ports, formerly almost cut off from the outer world, were linked up with Rangoon in 1871 by a fortnightly service of the British India Steam Navigation Company, and from 1873 there were regular services to Penang and Singapore. A local European firm had three small steamers on the same run; the Chinese began to replace their junks by steamers, and the King of Siam sent an occasional vessel to Rangoon. Direct steam communication with Europe began in 1871–2, when three steamers from Glasgow arrived in Rangoon by way of the Suez Canal. This experiment was so successful that in the following year a regular line of cargo steamers began to run between these ports. Not until 1883, however, did they carry passengers. In that year, although 70 % of the imports came through the canal, only a quarter of the export trade took that route. By the end of the century, however, practically the whole trade, both export and import, used the canal, and 95 % of the tonnage entering Rangoon from foreign ports was steam. Meanwhile, in 1889, another line had opened a regular service between Liverpool and Rangoon.

At the end of the century there was a new development. Up to then practically the whole trade of Burma was in the hands of British shipowners, with headquarters either in Britain or India. But the British policy of the 'open door' gave free access to all. Between 1899 and 1902 three German lines began to call at Rangoon. Direct trade between Burma and Japan also began in 1899, and direct communications were opened with the Philippines in 1902, and with Netherlands India, chiefly for the exchange of rice and sugar, in 1905. Japan, however, proved the most formidable competitor. In 1911 a Japanese line opened a direct service to Tokyo, and also cut into the trade between Rangoon and Calcutta. Just before the war of 1914 Japan headed the list of foreign ships entering Rangoon.

Population. The economic progress after 1870, indicated by the improved communications, was reflected also in the growth of the population.[1] In the first regular census, held in 1872, the population of British Burma was returned as 2·75 million, though actually, it would seem, about 3·11 million. By 1901 the population of the same area was 5·58 million, and by 1921 7·05 million. The population of Ava in 1872, apart from its dependencies, may be put at 3 million. By

[1] Census, 1931, p. 8; 1886, Cmd. 4614, p. 72. As part of Ava was transferred to Lower Burma the census figures of 1901 for Lower and Upper Burma are 5·65 million and 3·61 million.

1901 the population of the same area, according to the census figures, was 3·68 million, but actually about 3·70 million. Thus between 1870 and 1900 the population of Burma, excluding the Shan States, rose from about 6·11 million to about 9·28. The total population, including some hill tracts, rose from 10·5 million in 1901 to 13·2 at the census of 1921. In regard to the population two matters deserve special notice. One is the growth of the large foreign element, concentrated chiefly in the towns, especially the larger towns. The other is that, in the lowlands, the wealthiest districts are the most thinly populated in proportion to the cultivated areas. It is a remarkable fact that the richest districts of the delta, the centre of rice production, come lowest in the scale with less than 500 per thousand cultivated acres. One would expect to find a scantier population in the far less productive districts of the Dry Zone, but here the lowest figure is 621. Among purely agricultural districts the most closely populated, in relation to cultivated areas, are those where, as in the delta, rice is the sole crop, but agriculture is least commercialized, and has spread slowly from the earliest days of British rule.

These matters will be further examined in connection with the welfare of the people.

Population per 1000 acres cultivated *

Delta	
Pegu	442
Pyapon	448
Hanthawaddy	456
Myaungmya	473
Dry Zone	
Sagaing	621
Myingyan	656
L. Chindwin	706
Meiktila	715
Kyaukse	760
Maritime	
Kyaukpyu	1076
Sandoway	1179

* Census, 1931, p. 36; Subsidiary Table I b.

Trade. The best measure, however, of the economic progress between the opening of the Suez Canal and the introduction of political reforms is given by the figures for the growth of trade. In this one may discern three stages. The first ended with the nineteenth century. Until near the close of the century even direct trade between Burma and the continent of Europe was carried in British vessels, and exports were registered as destined for the port at which the vessel called for orders instead of according to their final destination. With a view to elucidating the actual British share in trade, the returns for 1903–4 aimed for the first time at showing the countries to which goods were actually sent. It is convenient, therefore, to take this year as the end of the first period. The second stage ends with 1913–14, the last complete year before the war. When the period of executive rule came to an end in 1923, the violent oscillations set up by the war had not yet subsided, and it is preferable to take the end of the third stage as 1926–7, when trade relations had become relatively stable. The selection of this year allows, moreover, of comparison over a complete decade with the conditions at the time of Burma's separation from India.[1]

The period as a whole was one of astounding economic progress. Between the opening of the Suez Canal and the end of the century the value of imports rose fourfold; by the outbreak of war it was ten times and by 1926–7 more than fifteen times as great as in 1870. The value of exports rose even more steeply; it showed a five-fold rise by the end of the century and by 1926–7 was well over twenty times as great as in 1870. The crude figures need correction to allow for changes in the value of money, but the bare comparison just given sufficiently indicates their general dimensions. The actual figures, with the necessary corrections, are given in the table on p. 187. If British rule be tested by its effect in enhancing the contribution made by Burma to economic progress, to the welfare of the world, one may fairly claim that it has been abundantly justified by the results.

Yet to ascertain their bearing on local welfare the figures need somewhat closer analysis. The exports of Burma may be classed under two main heads: *Rural Produce* due to native enterprise, mainly in rice cultivation; and *Capitalist Produce*, due to western enterprise in the forests, oilfields, mines and plantations. Up to 1900 rural produce, and especially rice, formed an increasing proportion of the exports, rising from rather less than three-quarters in 1870 to as much as 85 % in 1900; after that date, the products of native enterprise, while continuing generally to increase in volume and value, did not keep pace with capitalist produce. In 1870 capitalist produce was confined to timber, and furnished about one-fifth of the total exports. By 1900 the oilfields were beginning to come under production, but timber was still the chief item in capitalist produce. But by 1923 capitalist enterprise was furnishing a third of the total exports, with oil as the chief item and minerals almost on a level with timber. Thus one outstanding feature of this half century was the increasing part played by foreign capital in the production of wealth in Burma.

The greater importance of foreign capital appears likewise in the figures for import trade. Here one may distinguish *consumption goods*, mainly for the native market, and *capital goods*, mainly for production by western enterprise. The import of capital goods rose from 19·6 %

[1] For details of trade during this period see the tables, pp. 187, 191 and Appendices I and II.

in 1872–3 to 23·1 % in 1903–4, and to 24·3 % by the outbreak of war; then it grew more rapidly and by 1926–7, in little more than ten years, it rose by as much as during the previous forty years, to 30·3 %. It is only natural that with increasing wealth a larger proportion should be devoted to capital goods, but in Burma, as in other tropical dependencies, the capitalists are Europeans or, to some extent, foreign orientals working on capitalist lines, and the growth of capitalist imports indicates the increasing hold of foreign capital on economic activities. In this connection it is instructive to notice the parallel and contemporaneous change in the character of the imports for consumption. Burma can produce its own food, but depends on the outer world for certain luxuries. At the opening of the Suez Canal the imports of food constituted one-fifth of the total imports, but they comprised mainly luxuries (15·6 %) and only a small proportion of necessities (4·9 %). By the end of the century food imports constituted 32·6 % including 13·5 % of necessities. In 1926–7 necessities accounted for 11·2 %. A larger proportion of the imports went to provide the necessities of life. Imports of clothing show the same trend even more clearly. Cotton goods may be taken to represent necessities and silk goods and European apparel luxuries. In 1872–3 clothing accounted for 51·3 % of the total value of imports, and included 19·7 % of luxuries. At each of the turning-points selected for examination we find a declining proportion of luxuries and by 1926–7 it had fallen to 6·6 %.

Changes in the geographical distribution of trade also show features of interest. It is rather strange that, before the opening of the Suez Canal, two-thirds of the exports of Burma went to Europe, and that when Europe was brought nearer by the canal, its share of the exports dropped by the end of the century to one-third. The new century, however, coincided with a growing demand in Europe for tropical produce, and until the war of 1914 the proportion of exports to Europe showed a rising tendency. Imports from Europe, on the other hand, rose with the opening of the canal, because previously European merchandise had been imported through India. There was a still more marked rise during the early years of the present century; due presumably to the increasing share of foreign shipping. The European share of the trade reached a peak in 1913–14; this was followed by a decline both in exports and imports. The distribution of the trade by countries has some interesting features which we shall examine later.

Production. The figures for trade indicate both the general course of production, and the need to distinguish the parts played in production by native and western enterprise. In general, rice, cotton and other agricultural commodities are produced by native enterprise, and purchased by non-natives, European or Oriental, for treatment, if necessary, and export. Timber is extracted by natives employed by, or under the direction of, large European firms; plantation crops are grown by capitalists, mostly European, using imported labour. Oil and other minerals are worked by capitalists, who for long employed, chiefly or solely, imported labour, though of recent years there has been an increasing tendency to use native labour on the oilfields. Transport and industry are also in European hands, employing immigrant labour, though here also native labour has of late years made some headway.

Western Enterprise. Up to 1900 western enterprise was confined mainly to transport, the Irrawaddy Flotilla Company and the railway; and to the old-established rice and timber industries. Under native rule the extensive deposits of 'excellent iron ore' were worked by Burmans until iron could be imported more cheaply from abroad.[1] Salt was an important item in native production until the seventies. Ships carried it at low rates to avoid sailing in ballast, and this reduced the homeward freight on rice; thus foreign salt gradually replaced the native article, at first in domestic use, and then in curing fish. Burmans worked the oilfields, and in Tenasserim Chinese miners washed for tin. But the tin mines were worked by primitive and wasteful methods, and by 1880 American kerosene was competing successfully with the native product even in the neighbourhood of the oilfields. Among other native industries, weaving, pottery, and lacquer ware were gradually displaced by imported goods.

During the present century Europeans have taken a wider interest in agricultural produce, especially cotton, groundnut and beans. The first factory for ginning cotton was erected in 1898 and the first cotton-seed mill in 1900; a few years later groundnut mills were established. Apart from isolated and usually unsuccessful experiments, capitalist methods were not applied to agricultural production until the early years of this century, when a demand arose for plantation rubber. But the chief advance of western enterprise has been in mineral production.

[1] Iron, *BBG*, I, 44, 62; Salt, *RTC*, 1868–9, pp. 3, 25; 1871–2, p. 36; 1875–6, pp. 19, 50; 1876–7, p. 36; *RAB*, 1877–8, p. 52.

The mineral resources of Upper Burma, and especially the ruby mines, were its chief attraction to European capitalists.[1] At a notorious public meeting in 1884, urging the annexation of Upper Burma, the chairman was the local representative of a firm which had its eye on the ruby mines. But the concession (granted to a rival firm) proved of no great value. Rice and oil were more precious than rubies. Before the annexation the wells were worked on very crude lines by their owners. Some wells belonging to the Crown were taken over by the British Government. A Rangoon firm, which had formerly been dealing in the native produce, formed the Burma Oil Company to lease the Government wells and also some of the wells in private ownership. With modern machinery, American drillers and Indian labour it soon drove American kerosene off the Burma market. In 1890 it began to export oil to India and in 1895 to Penang. By 1898 the production exceeded 20 million gallons, and by 1923 270 million. The capitalist development of oil was followed by an extension of western enterprise to other minerals. In 1891 Europeans began exploring the mineral resources of the Shan States and various concessions to work lead, silver and other minerals were granted, though progress was slow until they were taken over by the Burma Corporation in 1920. About 1909 the Tenasserim tin mines began to attract interest through the discovery that they yielded wolfram, but it was only during the war of 1914–18 that scientific methods under European management were introduced on any considerable scale.[2] Thus western enterprise, almost negligible in 1870, had come by 1923 to play an important part in the economy of Burma.

Native Enterprise. At the same time, native production also grew rapidly. 'The greatest achievement in the history of the Province, the colonization of Lower Burma, has been almost entirely the work of the Burmese.'[3] Despite the growing value of cotton and the introduction of groundnut and other new crops, rice contributed more largely to the total value of native exports in 1923 than fifty years earlier. But rice cultivation took on a new character; it was no longer cultivated mainly for subsistence but for export. Up to 1870 the population increased faster than the area under cultivation; from 1861 to 1870, while the population of Lower Burma, the main rice centre, grew by 595,000, the area under cultivation rose by only 354,000 acres. But between 1890 and 1900, the population grew by

---

[1] 1886, Cmd. 4614, pp. 126, 130.
[2] Chhibber, pp. 140, 202.   [3] *RAB*, 1916–17, p. 1.

987,000, and the acreage by 2,295,000. Thereafter the rate of expansion declined, but remained higher than the increase of population. During this period the agricultural economy definitely assumed a new character that is discussed below; here it is enough to notice that large-scale production for export yielded a larger surplus, as fewer hands were needed to cultivate the same area and fewer mouths had to be fed. This partly explains the fact, already noticed, that the wealthier districts are the less populous. During the first few years after the opening of the canal the export of rice and paddy remained fairly steady, averaging 425,000 tons, but in 1872–3 there was a sudden rise to 720,000 tons. By the end of the century the export, expressed in terms of paddy, had risen to $2\frac{1}{2}$ million tons, and twenty years later to $3\frac{1}{2}$ million.

Some aspects of native enterprise deserve closer examination, and especially rice cultivation, not only because of its importance in the economy of Burma, but because the course of development is probably without any close parallel, and yet presents in an extreme degree the working of unrestricted competition in a tropical society. Lower Burma when first occupied, and still even at the opening of the Suez Canal, was a vast deltaic plain of swamp and jungle, with a secure rainfall; when the opening of the canal created a market for rice, this wide expanse of land was rapidly reclaimed by small cultivators, with easy access to capital and an abundant supply of seasonal labour, producing a single crop for the export market. Some of these conditions obtained in Siam and Indo-China, but it is the combination of all these factors in the delta of Lower Burma that has produced a type of agricultural organization which would seem to be unique. Formerly, the villager in Lower Burma, like peasants in general, cultivated primarily for home consumption, and it has always been the express policy of the Government to encourage peasant proprietorship. Land in the delta was abundant, and the people would ordinarily cultivate rather more than was sufficient for their needs. If scarcity in Upper Burma, India or China created a market for rice, they would sell the surplus, but in years when there was little demand for paddy, much of the crop might often be left unreaped. The opening of the canal provided a certain and profitable market for as much rice as people could grow. Everyone took up as much land as he could, and men from Upper Burma crowded down to join in the scramble for land. In two or three years a labourer could save out of his wages enough money to buy cattle and make a start on a modest scale as landowner. But a man who did not stake out a claim over as much land as he thought that he could work was liable to find himself forestalled. The land had to be cleared rapidly and hired labour was needed to fell the heavy jungle. In these circumstances newly reclaimed land did not pay the cost of cultivation, and there was a general demand for capital. Burmans, however, lacked the necessary funds, and had no access to capital. They did not know English or English banking methods, and English bankers knew nothing of Burmans or cultivation. Even up to 1880 there were few Burmans outside the large ports who could raise £500 (Rs. 5,000) at a fortnight's notice.[1] But in the ports there were Indian moneylenders of the *chettyar* caste, amply provided with capital and long accustomed to dealing with European banks in India. About 1880 they began to send out agents into the villages, and supplied the people with all the necessary capital, usually at reasonable rates and, with some qualifications, on sound business principles. At that time very few cultivators were in debt, and none seriously in debt, even near Rangoon, though the position was not quite so satisfactory in Arakan, where the rice trade was of longer standing. But now the *chettyars* readily supplied the cultivators with all the money that they needed, and with more than all they needed. On business principles the moneylender preferred large transactions, and would advance not merely what the cultivator might require but as much as the security would stand. Naturally, the cultivator took all that he could get, and spent the surplus on imported goods. The working of economic forces pressed money on the cultivator; to his own discomfiture, but to the profit of the moneylenders, of European exporters who could ensure supplies by giving out advances, of European importers whose cotton goods and other wares the cultivator could purchase with the surplus of his borrowings, and of the banks which financed the whole economic structure. But at the first reverse, with any failure of the crop, the death of cattle, the illness of the cultivator, or a fall of prices, due either to fluctuations in world prices or to manipulation of the market by the merchants, the cultivator was sold up, and the land passed to the moneylender, who found some other thrifty labourer to take it, leaving part of the purchase price on mortgage, and within two or three years the process was repeated. Thus the land was continually changing hands, and already in 1895 a Financial Commissioner remarked that land in Lower Burma was

[1] *RAB*, 1880–1, Intr. p. 3.

transferred as readily as shares on the London Stock Exchange.[1] The moneylenders in general, and notably the *chettyars*, a purely money-lending and non-agricultural caste, did not want the land. But they could always find a purchaser to take it off their hands; in early days the buyer was usually a cultivator, but, as time went on, the pur-chasers came more and more to be men who looked to making a liveli-hood from rent, or who wished to make certain of supplies of paddy for their business. In the rice districts 'the ownership of land was to a large extent a branch of the rice-export industry, traders and brokers buying it in order to control supplies of paddy'.[2] Others also, mer-chants and shopkeepers, bought land, because they had no other investment for their profits. These trading classes were mainly towns-folk, and for the most part Indians or Chinese. Thus there was a steady growth of absentee ownership, with the land passing into the hands of foreigners. Usually, however, as soon as one cultivator went bankrupt, his land was taken over by another cultivator, who in turn lost within two or three years his land and cattle and all that he had saved. Thus on the revenue records a considerable, though steadily decreasing, proportion of the land was still registered as held by cultivators, and in 1930 only 27 % of the occupied land in Lower Burma was recorded as in the ownership of non-agriculturalists. Then the depression of the thirties prevented moneylenders from finding purchasers at prices approximating to the value of their loans, and the land registers began to reveal the true proportions of the problem. It appeared that practically half the land in Lower Burma was owned by absentees, and in the chief rice-producing districts from two-thirds to nearly three-quarters. But for the past sixty years the land had continually been passing to and fro between the money-lenders and a succession of transitory occupants and, if one looks at the facts beneath the forms, it may be said that most land in the rice tract has been held by absentee moneylenders since its first reclama-tion. The policy of conserving a peasant proprietary was of no avail against the hard reality of economic forces, and the picture given by official records was misleading.

The process had other interesting reactions upon land tenure. In a country with an old-established peasantry, one finds the land fairly evenly distributed between the villagers in holdings that are sufficient to provide a subsistence for the family. That was formerly, and is still very largely, the position in Upper Burma. When such a tract comes

[1] Smeaton, quoted in *Agriculture in Burma* (1927), p. 21.   [2] *RAB*, 1914-15, p. 17.

into contact with the market, there is a tendency to the parcelment or minute subdivision of holdings. One can see this state of affairs very clearly along the Arakan coast of Burma, where the rice trade developed gradually in the first days of British rule, and the holdings nowadays average an acre or so. But in the delta, as holdings have continually changed hands, they have tended, by the natural working of economic forces, towards the size that gives the maximum net produce and not, as with peasant cultivation, the maximum gross produce. According to local circumstances the separate units of occupancy may require two to four or more yokes of oxen, but the area has been determined by close reference to the rent obtainable. In some parts 30 acres may yield the maximum surplus of yield over cost, in others 60 or 80 acres; but only in the districts that were under cultivation before the opening of the Suez Canal does one, generally speaking, find any traces of a peasantry. The units of occupancy, however, are by no means identical with the units of ownership. The gradual transfer of land to absentee landlords has built up large estates of some hundreds, or even thousands of acres, not continuous but scattered over a wide area. These landowners have little know-ledge of agriculture or interest in cultivation, and there evolved a kind of annual auction with the land 'let out to the highest bidder, the tenant of the previous year being replaced by any one willing to offer a slightly higher rental'.[1] On this system good cultivation was im-possible, as a man holding land for no longer than a year, especially rice land where so much depends on a skilful use of water, cannot make the best of it. Indeed, the system encouraged bad cultivation, because an inferior cultivator would bid higher than a man who could earn good wages as a labourer, and many tenants were worse off than their labourers. It likewise expedited the substitution of Indian for Burman tenants, for Indians, though they got less out of the land than Burmans, could offer a higher rent on account of their lower standard of living. It also fostered improvidence and dishonesty, for prudent and honest cultivators would not bid so much as those who were reckless or dishonest. The landlord usually financed his tenants, and, as these grew poorer, they had to borrow more. It mattered little to the landlord whether he took his profits under the name of rent or interest, and the problems of rack-renting and debt became inextricably entangled. The labourers lived on advances from

---

[1] *Hanthawaddy Settlement Report*, 1911, p. 19; *Myaungmya Settlement Report*, 1920, p. 29; *RAB*, 1909–10, p. 11.

the tenants, the tenants on advances from the landowners; the smaller landowners were continually losing their land through debt to money-lenders, and even the larger landowners mortgaged their land as security for funds required in their main occupation as brokers and paddy merchants. By 1930 the agricultural indebtedness of Burma (excluding seasonal advances, short-period loans to be repaid at harvest), was estimated at £40 million.[1]

Possibly, however, the feature of chief interest in the rice economy of Burma is the evolution of what has been described as 'industrial agriculture'. While economic forces were working to the prejudice of landowners and tenants, they were also reacting adversely on the labourers. So long as people cultivated for the home they hired little outside labour, and those without land found their chief employment in other occupations; in boating, salt-boiling, the manufacture of salt fish and fish-paste, in pottery, or in the towns in milling rice by hand, in shipbuilding and as coolies on the wharves. With the multiplication of steam rice-mills during the seventies there arose a strong demand for cheap coolie labour during the milling season, from about January to May. The volume of immigrant labour from India, though considerable, was no longer adequate to the demand. The Government attempts to import Indian labour failed,[2] and in 1876 recruitment was left to private enterprise. The system of private recruitment had been criticized so far back as 1840, but, when objections were revived in 1880, the Government held that private enterprise 'got over more labourers, provided for them better, met the demands of the labour market more regularly, and generally managed the business more cheaply than Government could do'.[3]

At that time some 16,000 coolies arrived annually from Madras, but a new shipping company cut passage rates, and the number of immigrants rose sharply to 40,000. The Government decided therefore to subsidize immigration. Within three years the number of immigrants had nearly doubled, and a subsidy was no longer required.[4] The conditions under which these coolies lived were so insanitary that the death-rate was enormous. Burmans would not live in conditions under which the Indian coolies died, and were driven from the towns out into the jungle. By the end of the century it was remarked that in four out of the chief six towns, despite a much larger total population, there were actually fewer Burmans than at the previous census, while

[1] CLA, III, 77.   [2] RAB, 1877–8, Intr. p. 13; p. 77.
[3] RAB, 1880–1, Intr. p. 52.   [4] RAB, 1880–1, Intr. p. 52; 1882–3, p. 140.

in the other two the increase of Burmans, in comparison with that of Indians, was negligible.[1] At the same time Burmans were losing other forms of employment. The hand rice-mills worked by Burmans gave place to steam-mills employing Indian coolies. The substitution of steam for sail on sea and river compelled the boating population to look for work on land, and cheap Indian labour drove the Burmans from the wharves. The introduction of foreign salt and the tax on local manufacture ruined the salt-boilers and the salt-fish industry, to the prejudice also of the potters who specialized in making the large pans for boiling salt. From 1900 onwards Upper Burma became involved in the same process, and between 1900 and 1910 the number of people employed on spinning and weaving fell by a half.[2] All these people, driven out of the towns and out of other occupations, had to look for employment on the land, and especially in rice cultivation, the only form of agriculture requiring much hired labour.

Thanks to the rapid spread of cultivation, this large influx of labour had little direct effect on wages; the results were chiefly apparent in the consequent reorganization of production on rice lands, and this reacted on wages indirectly. Up to 1870 those few cultivators who employed outside labour hired it by the agricultural year of ten months. This system continued during the earlier years of cultivation for export. In 1880 a labourer usually earned 150 baskets of paddy, together with his board and lodging for the year; he lived with his employer and became a member of the family.[3] But men from Upper Burma were already beginning to come down, not for the year, but merely for the harvest 'to reap, thresh, store and cart the paddy'. At about the same time the Indian coolies in the rice-mills found that, by coming to Burma rather earlier, they could obtain employment on reaping.[4] These immigrants from Upper Burma and India introduced an agricultural revolution in the delta. 'Cultivation to meet local requirements gradually changed into the system of industrialized agriculture organized for the export market which prevails to-day.... In the more developed areas the earthwork, ploughing, planting, reaping, threshing, etc., are all separate operations performed by different people, and the division of function has been pushed almost as far as is possible in agriculture.'[5] The deltaic plain became in effect a factory without chimneys. This was possible only because of the large area in which a single crop was cultivated under almost uniform

[1] Census, 1901, p. 27.   [2] RAB, 1911–12, p. 72.
[3] BBG, II, 551.   [4] RAB, 1884–5, p. 63.   [5] ISC, XI, 18.

conditions, and because an abundant supply of seasonal labour was available to undertake such operations as did not require special skill. One result was to reduce the cost of agricultural production, because the cultivator no longer had to maintain and pay his men throughout the year. But it impoverished the agricultural labourer and left him without work, wages or maintenance for a great part of the year, and compelled him to be continually on the move in search of work. 'An important feature in agriculture in Burma is the large proportion of labour which is migratory.'[1]

These conditions were developing gradually from the eighties onwards. A settlement officer then remarked that 'the immense wealth of the Burmese cultivator is as much a myth as the unbounded fertility of the soil. In some parts the cultivator is in easy circumstances but in others he is in a state of chronic indebtedness and as miserable as a Burman can be.'[2] Not, however, until the end of the century did Government come to recognize that these conditions were general, and that for some years the land had been passing to moneylenders whose tenants enjoyed no fixity of occupancy and had no protection, legal or customary against excessive rents.[3] From that time onwards there are frequent references to the subject in the annual reports. By 1911 we read that land was being transferred to absentee owners and 'a large proportion of the non-resident owners were of non-Burman nationality and had thus no interest in their land or tenants save the extortion of as large an income as possible from them'; most of the lessees were 'tenants one year and labourers the next, working their lands as tenants only for a single year and generally dependent on their landlords for advances to meet the cost of cultivation and living'; and 'a very considerable proportion of the agricultural population, particularly among the tenants and labourers were dependent for their subsistence during the working season on loans at high rates of interest, which were barely covered by the produce obtained by them at harvest'.[4]

A graphic picture of conditions in a tract newly brought under cultivation is given in a report of 1926.[5]

'Immigration has been, in fact, a scramble for land...the immigrants came from various localities and various races. Rich men, poor men, Burmans, Karens, Chittagonians, Indians were all animated by the sole

[1] ISC, XI, 19.   [2] Bassein Settlement Report, 1880-1, p. 35.
[3] RAB, 1901-2, pp. 13, 28; RRA, 1895-6, Resolution, p. 5; 1901-2, p. 29.
[4] RAB, 1911-12, pp. 15, 34.   [5] Myaungmya Settlement Report, 1926, ch. IV.

idea of each man doing the best for himself regardless of every other consideration.... Government indeed appointed headmen and ten house gangs, but in practice these commanded practically no respect or obedience. There was thus no local authority or public opinion making for reasonable compromise and equitable settlement on the spot between disputing parties, but a dispute became forthwith a lawsuit or a fight.'

Anyone who could obtain possession of land long enough to start clearing the jungle could obtain a loan of about Rs. 100 an acre even before he had sown paddy, and the prospects of material gain held out an attractive bait to immigrants. But 'the inducements presented to what we may call the capitalist were greater still'. Much of the land was uncultivable except by the construction of large dykes to prevent floods and promote drainage. That was a costly business.

'It was an inevitable economic process that the land should pass into the hand of the capitalist. The capitalist could clear more extensively and more rapidly than his poorer competitor. Where his occupation was forestalled he could often buy out the smaller squatter. Moreover, whether from illness, misfortune, or pure reckless management, the squatter is always tempted by the offer of ready money, and plunges into mortgages and other commitments which usually culminate in a transference of possession.'

'Not a little sharp practice attended the transference of land to the capitalist.' Usually the borrower was required to execute a registered deed of sale and was given a written or oral undertaking that, in accordance with Burmese custom, the transaction would be treated as a mortgage. This was an old practice, already general in 1900.[1] But only the registered deed was legally valid, and the creditor thus secured the outright possession of the land at its mortgage value. 'The rapid absorption of waste land by the capitalist, together with the legal and barely legal transference of possession to the capitalist naturally embittered the relations between the capitalist and the squatter.' The professional moneylender, the *chettyar*, was not yet prominent in this tract, but there were numerous Indian and Chinese capitalists who had accumulated large estates. Some lived on their lands, but most were absentees.

'Many wealthy men, it is true, were content to amass land as quietly as possible, but others more aggressive were constantly intent on forcing the pace. The practice of maintaining a body of retainers became prevalent. These retainers were usually men of bad character, and their function was to overawe, and override, by violence if necessary, those who in any way opposed the interests of their employers.... There can be no doubt that

[1] *RRA*, 1901–2, p. 28.

the squatter has in many cases been bullied off his land by brute force. If he had been so unfortunate as to settle on a section of jungle required to round off an estate, he would probably be visited at planting or at harvest by these retainers. At planting his work would be harrowed over, and he would be compelled to stand aside while the area was planted on the capitalist's behalf. Or the visit might be postponed until the harvest; then a man might see the fruit of his year's work disappearing in sampans and his field hut burnt into the bargain.'

But the most violent conflicts were between rival capitalists:

'There were at least three organized bands of retainers. Two were led by Burmese ex-headmen, who found it more profitable to exercise their activities in this area and acquire land by fair means or foul. They possessed motor boats and operated like veritable flying columns, directing and organizing their nefarious schemes in different parts of the area.... Their exploits...are too numerous to mention, but one worthy of notice was a pitched battle between Chittagonians and Burmans in 1921....About fifty to eighty persons on each side took part in the fight, the Burmans being armed with crossbows while the Indians defended themselves with sticks and dahs. In the end the Burmans took to flight, leaving several of their members on the field, badly disabled.'

But the capitalist did not always have matters his own way. Although in fact the process of evolution has created a capitalist class of landlords, it has always been the policy of Government to encourage smallholders. The land regulations accordingly direct that extensions made by a tenant shall be registered as his own property and not that of his landlord; but this assumes a high standard of diligence and integrity in the surveyors. In this tract large bodies of tenants not infrequently combined to induce the revenue subordinate to register as their own property not merely the extensions but all the land that they had taken on lease, and 'the large landlords were brought to a standstill by the mass of litigation in which they were involved to sue recalcitrant tenants all over the country'. By way of protection 'it became customary for a landlord to insist on a tenant's signing a blank stamped document. Tenants are thus compelled to deliver themselves over to the mercies of the Landlord, since the latter can at any time adjust the terms of the document to a pitch of severity calculated to daunt the slightest symptoms of insubordination.' Moreover, the whole situation was aggravated by the defects of the original survey. 'Untouched jungle has frequently been shown as cultivated, presumably for the benefit of some client of the revenue surveyor wishing to establish title in advance of occupation; similarly

cultivation has been wiped off the map'.... 'Reports were also forthcoming of a trade union of land dacoits...this association apparently
mobilized its forces at planting and harvest to establish spurious
evidence of occupation.'

A former Governor of Burma has suggested that one needs experience and skill to read between the lines of published official
documents.[1] But it would need penetrating vision to detect any ap-
proximation to the facts in the statement, in almost the last administration report published under his rule, that 'cordial relations are said to
have prevailed between landlord and tenant'.[2] This has been a stock
remark, often expressed less cautiously, in such reports throughout the
present century, apparently because 'the tenant is so completely in
the hands of his landlord that he is unable to assert himself in any effective way'.[3] Unfortunately it sometimes deceives the writers, who picture
complacently a golden age when 'at the hush of the Pax Britannica...
the people gradually settled down to a life of peace, leisure and amusement, tempered now and then by a little toil'.[4] The committee dealing with the report from which the above passages are taken suggested
that it 'would furnish an ideal example for any philosopher desirous
of expounding the *homo homini lupus* theory of mankind'. Such conditions were not distinctively characteristic of that particular time or
that locality; they have accompanied the spread of cultivation over the
whole of Lower Burma. The technique of land-grabbing has gradually
been perfected, but conditions essentially similar have prevailed in
newly opened areas from the beginning of the century and earlier. As
appears from an earlier report from the same district, land-grabbing was
not confined to agricultural land. New residential settlements were
usually formed on a narrow strip of high land beside a stream. The area
occupied as house sites paid no revenue, and was ordinarily shown as
vacant on the maps. 'Quite frequently', either by carelessness or for
a consideration, the revenue surveyor included the house sites in an
adjacent holding. After paying revenue on the land for a few years, the
man shown as owner evicted the people from the residential area, and,
if they ventured on appealing to the courts, the map was taken as
conclusive evidence against their claim. Few however dare to go to
court 'because the hope of successful resistance is so weak'.[5]

[1] Craddock, p. 211.   [2] *RAB*, 1920–1, p. 31.   [3] *CLA*, I, 12.   [4] Craddock, p. 111.
[5] *Myaungmya Settlement Report*, 1920, pp. 21, 222. It should perhaps be mentioned that if any single individual was responsible for these conditions, it was the
present writer, who was in charge of the district from 1915–19, and had observed
similar conditions elsewhere, almost from the beginning of his service.

The Rice Trade. The evolution of the paddy market also presents many features of interest as illustrating the course of events where economic freedom is subject to no restriction but the rule of law. Up to 1870 rice was still grown on small holdings by peasant cultivators for their families, and the surplus was sold to merchants for shipment, either to India, mostly as paddy (unhusked rice), or to the East or Europe, as 'cargo rice' (one-fifth paddy and four-fifths roughly cleaned in hand-mills), because white rice would not stand the long passage in sailing vessels round the Cape. From about 1870, with the opening of the Suez Canal, the substitution of steam for sail and the erection of steam rice-mills, conditions gradually changed.[1] During the course of development six distinct parties were competing for the profits of the rice trade: the Burman cultivators, the Indian money-lenders who financed them, the middlemen who bought the rice, the millers in the ports of Burma, the shipowners, and the fine-millers in London who cleaned the cargo rice. The substitution of steam for sail gave the local millers a stronger position in the outside market. The quicker journey, by allowing the shipment of cleaned rice, eliminated the London fine-miller. At the same time shipment became possible throughout the year instead of depending on the monsoons, and shipowners had to compete for cargo instead of millers for cargo-space. The greater security of the millers in the outside market enabled them to combine and obtain control over the local market.

Until about 1880 the advantage rested with the cultivators. They grew rice mainly for food and kept a reserve until the next harvest; they could sell their surplus if the price was good enough, but were under no compulsion to dispose of it. The millers, on the other hand, were forced to buy under the penalty of paying demurrage, or even of missing the ships, which had to sail before the monsoon, and thus breaking their European contracts. So far back as 1867 there was a preliminary skirmish. The merchants, hard pressed by the ship-owners, 'tried to force a reduction of price on sellers'. A few years later a strong demand from Europe coincided with famine in Bengal. In Akyab the millers had some success in keeping down prices because they could call in their advances, but in the delta the people were still free of debt and, 'as demurrage days drew near' they got their price. Next year a shortage of shipping enabled the millers to suspend buying. In Akyab they seemed likely to repeat their former victory, but one firm broke the ring and swept the market; in the delta, as

[1] *RTC*, 1868-9, pp. 3, 25; 1871-2, pp. 9, 13; 1875-6, p. 27.

'tonnage had to be filled...necessity compelled the demands of the sellers'. The cultivators got their price, but the 'one redeeming feature' (according to the official report) was that, owing to the fall of the rupee, merchants could well afford to pay it.[1] Thus, during the seventies, millers and cultivators competed on almost equal terms.

The change dates from about 1880. Indian moneylenders began to penetrate the interior and furnished the capital required for the speedy reclamation of the waste, and cultivators, who had to pay their debts, could not hold back their stocks. Moreover, cultivation for export discouraged the practice of reserving a supply for the coming year. Already in 1877 high prices, consequent on a famine in Madras, 'drained Burma of its stocks of rice'.[2] The millers were not slow to press their advantage, and their first great victory was in 1882. This year they were once more 'obliged to combine', and kept down prices 'to an extent which brought distress in some instances to the native agriculturalists'. But officials looked for a remedy to political economy. Values would 'sooner or later adjust themselves in accordance with the laws of supply and demand', and, if people were 'taught by their present experience to erect mills of their own, they would defeat the European combination and a further step would be taken towards an equitable adjustment of prices in their favour'.[3] Next year the fall of the rupee, and the conjunction of a short crop with Indian competition and the ties of forward contracts, hindered combination among the millers. In Akyab a combine was attempted but 'unfortunately for the shippers' a new firm broke the ring; in Bassein, remarks the official report regretfully, the European firms 'might have saved some £80,000 to £90,000 if they had entered into a combination as last year'.[4]

One weak point of the millers was in their forward contracts. In 1884, with another short crop, they tried to cancel their charters and buy back their contracts. But 'the shipowners, perceiving the straits to which they were reduced, exacted the utmost penalty for cancelment'.[5] Moreover the Indian and Chinese moneylenders and traders were not only middlemen, but were also potential rivals of the millers, as they bought rice for India and the Straits. This aroused a new sympathy for the cultivator. The *chettyars*, it was said, 'had done much to destroy the independence of large numbers of Burmese

[1] *RTC*, 1867–8, p. 144; 1874–5, pp. 17ff.; 1875–6, pp. 27ff.
[2] *RTC*, 1876–7, p. 39.   [3] *RTC*, 1881–2, p. 38.
[4] *RTC*, 1882–3, p. 34   [5] *RTC*, 1884–5, p. 14

cultivators, to whom they make advances on ruinous terms. When harvest time comes round, it usually turns out that to satisfy the moneylender's claims, the debtor's whole crop of paddy has to be made over to him', and the *chettyar*, instead of selling it at a low rate to the European miller, shipped it to Madras.[1] Sometimes the Chinese were pictured as the villains. In 1886 some wealthy Chinese combined 'to purchase all the paddy coming in and hold it up against the millers'. But the disorder consequent on the third Anglo-Burmese War broke out anew; 'the dacoit scare came in very handy about this time to bring down prices, for alarm was taken by these would-be controllers of the local market and they gave up purchasing'. The European millers, however, were not to be intimidated by attacks upon their brokers. Although Lower Burma was aflame with rebellion, a combination of millers was fairly successful in 'keeping down prices and receiving good weight and quality'. Not unnaturally 'a great deal of discontent prevailed among the cultivators at the persistence of merchants in keeping down prices',[2] and their action must have enhanced the difficulty of restoring order. But, with the replacement of sail by steam, there was no longer the same need for millers to make forward contracts and to charter vessels in advance, and this weak spot in the armour of the millers ceased to be vulnerable.

Meanwhile the annexation of Upper Burma had stopped competition from the King. But European merchants still had little contact with the Upper Burma market; their interest lay in export by sea. In 1889 there were rumours of a famine in Upper Burma and, 'had not steps been taken officially to suppress these rumours, and thus bring down prices a great deal of mischief would have been most probably caused';[3] millers would have lost their profits and Government the revenue accruing from rice sent to Europe. Another weakness of the merchants was the lack of common action between those in different ports. In 1893, however, the Rangoon millers managed to gain control over all the rice-mills in the country, and were thereby able to obtain paddy at an average rate of Rs. 77 as against Rs. 127 in 1892. There was a stubborn fight, and demurrage had to be paid on nearly all the vessels in port. It was to be hoped, said the official report on trade, that 'the cultivators will give in'. Eventually they did give in, and the ring held until halfway through 1894.[4] The conflict set back economic progress for two years, damaged the revenue

[1] *RTC*, 1884–5, p. 55.   [2] *RTC*, 1886–7, pp. 17, 21.   [3] *RTC*, 1888–9, p. 22.
[4] *RTC*, 1892–3, pp. 21, 22; 1893–4, pp. 1, 22; 1894–5, p. 1.

and the importers and bankers, and ruined thousands of cultivators, stimulating the rapid transfer of land that, as mentioned above, shortly afterwards engaged the attention of the Financial Commissioner.

In other ways also the combination on this scale had reactions on the organization of the rice trade. It encouraged Indians and Chinese, and later Burmans, to erect godowns and small rice-mills in the interior. Partly because of the improved facilities for storing paddy up-country, and partly it may be because of the injury sustained by European import houses and banks, subsequent combinations were for many years less comprehensive and less successful. But in 1912–13 matters came once more to a head. On this occasion millers resorted to the device of importing paddy from Bengal. Shippers complained that the millers could not legally sell Bengal paddy as Burma rice, but 'their complaints were overruled as the millers were completely masters of the situation in Rangoon'.[1] Of the six parties who had competed in 1870 for the profits of the Burma rice trade, it was the millers who had gained the victory. But the detached observer may perhaps offer the comment that for an illustration of the *homo homini lupus* theory of mankind, it was unnecessary to travel to the backwoods. The further development of the rice trade must be reserved for a later chapter.

The process of economic development that we have just been examining was chiefly active in Pegu, the territory occupied after the second war. It was less active in the maritime provinces, where by 1870 conditions were more or less stabilised. In Upper Burma it came into operation later and more gradually. Here the open country was closely peopled, the social system was stronger, there was no mass immigration, Indians and Chinese were less numerous, there was less to attract the moneylender, land was of lower value and less tempting to the speculator, and the change from a subsistence to a commercial economy was less rapid and less complete. The chief items of rural produce exported from Upper Burma just before the Annexation were palm-sugar, cutch, cotton, wheat and hides. Under British rule the restrictions on export were abolished; from about 1905 groundnut was introduced and spread rapidly, a new market was opened for the innumerable variety of pulses, and improved irrigation raised the output of rice to such an extent that in good years there was a surplus available for export. At the same time, in the mines of Upper Burma and especially in the oilfields, western enterprise tapped resources previously almost neglected.

[1] *RTC*, 1912–13, p. 13.

CHAPTER IV

BURMA, 1870–1923: EFFICIENCY AND SOCIAL JUSTICE

(b) WELFARE

1. INDIVIDUAL WELFARE

On the liberal theory that economic progress guarantees the general diffusion of welfare, the rapid development of Burma after the opening of the Suez Canal should have multiplied prosperity. One might expect to find the people far better off in 1900 than in 1870, and again during the present century achieving a still higher standard of comfort through the greater activity in welfare measures. That, on the whole, was the official view, as expressed in successive annual reports, though not always without qualification. We read of 'the advance of the people towards a higher standard of living', and that 'the increasing wealth and prosperity of the country are undeniable, and are reflected in the material condition of the people'.[1] If in one year 'doubts were expressed whether after all successive years of good crops and high prices had effected any permanent improvement in the position of the ordinary agriculturist', the report for the following year notes 'a further rise in the prosperity, intelligence and comfort of the community'.[2] Consecutive reports often pronounce conflicting verdicts, the one suggesting optimistically that the condition of the people 'attains a high level of prosperity throughout the country generally', the other stating that high prices are prejudicial to a considerable proportion of the agricultural population.[3] Again, on the eve of political reforms, after fifty years of rapid economic progress under executive rule, we are told that 'the general rise of prices benefits only a comparatively small proportion, mostly of the wealthier classes'.[4] But these sudden fluctuations of opinion may possibly reflect little more than the passing mood of the official writing the report.

The more optimistic view derived support from the growth of the population, revenue, exports and imports. The rapid increase of the

---

[1] RAB, 1904–5, p. 5; 1906–7, p. 6.   [2] RAB, 1908–9, p. 11; 1909–10, p. 11.
[3] RAB, 1911–12, p. 34; 1912–13, p. 7.   [4] RAB, 1919–20, p. 18.

revenue naturally coloured the vision of the officials who collected it, and the ample profits which accrued to merchants who exported rice or imported cotton goods, encouraged them to believe that all was for the best in the best of all possible worlds. Yet the burden of agricultural debt was growing, cultivators were losing their land to moneylenders, and in general making no more than a bare subsistence.[1] Although the statistics of imports suggested that the people were spending more money, the conditions of agriculture showed that they had less money to spend. A closer examination of the trade statistics helps to explain the apparent anomaly.

Imports. At a first glance the trade statistics support the view that the cultivator was generally better off. For, while he was getting better value when he sold his rice, the cotton goods that he bought were getting cheaper. At the end of the century Burma was exporting more than twice as much rice as when the Suez Canal was opened and at about double the price; and it was importing nearly four times the volume of piece goods at a rather lower price. The higher value of rice was partly due to the fall of the rupee, and one would expect a corresponding increase in the price of imports; but the actual rupee price of cotton goods declined. It would seem then that the cultivator

Imports of Cotton Goods

(a) Million yards; (b) Value (Rs. lakhs);
(c) Price index (1872–3 = 100)

Year	(a)	(b)	(c)
1872–3	29·85	61·19	100
1903–4	103·60	190·67	90
1913–14	182·75	445·96	118

was buying much more cloth, and for the same quantity of paddy was obtaining about twice as much cloth; and this was of a more expensive quality, as the imports comprised a larger proportion of coloured cloth. In 1876, however, the cultivator had worn cloth woven in Burma, and by 1900 this, 'notwithstanding its better and richer quality'[2] had been driven out by the novelty and cheapness of imported cloth. It was not so much that the people were better clad, as that they were differently clad, with foreign instead of local cloth. Moreover, although the total value of imported piece goods was impressive, it represented an annual expenditure of less than Rs. 2 per head of the population.

From 1900 imports continued to increase in volume, value and variety. The war of 1914 and the subsequent boom and slump enhance

---

[1] *RAB*, 1920–1, p. 38; *CLA*, i, 10.
[2] *BBG*, i, 402.

the difficulty of arriving at a statistical basis for a comparison of welfare between 1900 and 1923. But the general trend is clear enough from the figures for 1913–14 when, apart from a general rise of prices, conditions were still fairly stable. Between 1900 and the outbreak of war, while the population was increasing by about 15–20 % the value of the imports, even allowing for the rise in prices, was nearly doubled. There was again a great rise in the import of cotton goods, but these were more and more replacing goods woven in Upper Burma, as formerly they had replaced the home-woven goods of Lower Burma. As already mentioned, the census of 1911 revealed that the number of people employed on spinning and weaving had fallen during the decade by one-half. Imports of food included wheat and pulse for the rapidly growing Indian population, and there were now imported large quantities of salt and fish, formerly produced in Burma. Similarly local pottery and lacquer ware were being ousted by imported crockery. Thus the growth of imports was not wholly a net gain, but replaced a drop in home production. There was also a notable increase in the value of capital goods imported for use in western enterprise.

One feature supporting the more optimistic point of view was that many of the goods were petty luxuries: boots and shoes, cigarettes, and European provisions, such as biscuits, sardines and condensed milk. It was remarked in 1912 that the import of such goods into Rangoon to supply a population of 12 million was practically equal to the import of corresponding goods into Calcutta for a population of 87 million.[1] At the beginning of the century the people smoked native cheroots; by 1913–14 the import of cigarettes exceeded 600,000 lb., a remarkable development, but only equivalent to about half a pound annually per head. The import of boots and shoes rose from less than 200,000 pairs in 1900 to nearly a million in 1913–14; but this was less than one pair for every ten people. The use of cigarettes and European footwear did not extend beyond the towns and larger villages, and this was generally the case with European provisions. Thus Europeans in the towns, who saw their clerks and servants gay in imported silks and cottons, and wearing boots and smoking cigarettes, gathered an impression of prosperity and of a rising standard of living that conditions in rural areas, outside the places where rich men congregated, did not justify. In comparison with most parts of India the people were still well fed, well clothed and well housed, but how far the great

[1] *RTC*, 1911–12, p. 5.

mass of the people were better or worse off than formerly it is very difficult to say.

One reason why it is difficult to say whether the people were more or less prosperous is that there was no longer a people, but a mixture of peoples. Even in 1872 it was remarked that 'there is possibly no country in the world where the inhabitants are more varied in race, custom and language than those of Burma'.[1] To this question we must return later; here we are dealing solely with Burmans, the indigenous peoples. Among these also there was a wide range of variation in respect of welfare from one race to another, and from one place to another, between Burmese, Karens and the more backward peoples, between Lower and Upper Burma, and between urban and rural areas.

In the maritime provinces the people had come slowly into contact with the West for about half a century before the opening of the Suez Canal and the change in their economic environment had been gradual. In Tenasserim, the capital, Moulmein, was largely an Indian town, and in the immediate vicinity there were wholly Indian villages, but the people as a whole retained the character of a typical agricultural community of peasants. Not until 1907 was it linked up with Rangoon by rail, and internal communications were still primitive; in the narrow valleys between the hills the people were settled on the soil, living much as they had always done but enjoying the greater security of British rule, and problems of debt and land alienation were comparatively insignificant. Arakan was similarly cut off from the rest of the country, but even more effectively. Here, however, cultivation for export had been prominent from the earliest days of British rule, and a flood of immigration from Bengal drove the natives into the more distant villages, where, as in Tenasserim, they lived their customary life. Until well into the present century the people pounded their own rice, and one could hear in the villages the clatter of the loom. Most of the people were peasants cultivating small holdings, and the distinctive feature of the agricultural economy of Arakan was that here, as in no other part of Burma, except in small patches, the growth of population led to a minute subdivision of the land into tiny parcels.

Conditions were very different in Pegu, and those parts of Tenasserim which, as the Province of Martaban, came under British rule in 1852. This large expanse of almost uniformly level plain was by far the greater part of Lower Burma. In 1852 it had been for the most

[1] Census, 1872, p. 27.

part a waste of swamp and jungle,[1] and 'the conversion of such land into fertile paddy land was an epic of bravery and endurance on the part of the Burmese cultivator, who was then generally a settler from Upper Burma'.[2] In the older villages and towns, which dated from Burmese times or which had grown up along the river-side during the earlier years of British rule, the Burman could enjoy all his customary amenities of life, together with such imported goods as he could afford to buy. In the newer towns, and especially those along the railway, there was more wealth, but less comfort; and the richest people were largely foreigners, Indians and Chinese, while many of the Burmans were little better off than the crowd of Indian labourers who dragged out a brief and miserable existence in coolie barracks. The inhabitants of the towns and larger villages, however, formed a very small proportion of the total population; the bulk of the people lived in small hamlets, often little better than rural slums. The centre of village life in Burma is the monastery, but, as already mentioned, it was remarked in 1891 that, whereas in Upper Burma there was a monastery for almost every village, in Lower Burma about three-quarters of the villages had no monastery. The villagers were tenants and agricultural labourers, continually shifting from one village to another in search of land or work. Rents were continually rising and, with the development of industrial agriculture, labourers were unemployed for half the year or more, while there was no clear line of distinction between tenant and labourer, with people moving from one class to the other in successive years. It is difficult to resist the conclusion that over Lower Burma as a whole the great mass of the people were steadily growing poorer, and there is further evidence of this in the increasing difficulty in the collection of the capitation tax. Despite the rising price of paddy, the people were earning less money. And they were also worse off in other ways:

'In the old days of farming for subsistence, the cultivators could get free grass for thatching free bamboos and free firewood from the public waste lands. They could get fish free in the neighbouring pools or streams, and they could weave their own clothes in their own homes. As the public waste lands became converted into cultivation, as fisheries were declared the property of Government and as home weaving became unprofitable, the small proprietors, like the tenants, were increasingly obliged to find money for needs which they could formerly supply themselves.'[3]

[1] Furnivall, *Economic Journal*, 1909, p. 554.   [2] *CLA*, II, 37.
[3] *CLA*, II, 51.

Moreover the labourer in early days had been supported by the hope of saving enough money to become a landowner. As his wages fell and more land came under cultivation this hope disappeared. The myth of the immense wealth of the Burman cultivator and of the unbounded fertility of the soil survived, but over Lower Burma as a whole, as had been noticed locally in the earliest stages of development, the cultivator was 'in a state of chronic indebtedness and as miserable as a Burman can be'. To this general statement a partial exception may be made in respect of the Karens. Under the guidance of American Baptist missionaries the Karens made great progress, and the Karen village, with its church and school, was more prosperous than most Burmese settlements; but even the Karens were not exempt from the influence of the environment. Thus, in Lower Burma generally, the conditions of living in 1920 contrasted very unfavourably with the general diffusion of a modest standard of welfare that had characterized the country fifty years earlier.

In Upper Burma, however, for some years after the Annexation, economic freedom, as formerly in Lower Burma, brought new prosperity, especially in those tracts which had previously been least flourishing. The introduction and rapid spread of groundnut brought unimagined wealth to villages which formerly had barely had sufficient food in good years, and about once in every ten years had been liable to scarcity, amounting at long intervals, after a succession of bad years, to famine. With a wider market for their crops the people could buy more rice from Lower Burma, and, with the improvement of irrigation, even the poorest were enabled to substitute rice for the less palatable, though possibly more nutritious, food grains of former years. Up to about 1910, as in Lower Burma up to about 1870 or 1880, the people were better off than under their own rulers. But in successive annual reports and elsewhere one can trace economic forces acting in the same direction as in Lower Burma. From the beginning of the present century there are references to the growing pitch of rents in some localities, and to the activities of Indian moneylenders. The market for the chief export crops, cotton and groundnut, was dominated by the European millers, and these, being comparatively few in number, were better able to manipulate prices than the more numerous and more widely spread rice-millers of Lower Burma. Owing to defects in the methods of compiling agricultural statistics, which ignored the forms of mortgage and tenancy customary in Upper Burma, the course of economic development cannot be traced so

clearly as in Lower Burma; but export crops were comparatively insignificant and the people clung jealously to their ancestral holdings,
so that economic forces were less powerful and were more strongly
resisted, and it would seem probable that in Upper Burma as a whole
the people enjoyed greater individual welfare in 1910 than under
Burmese rule. But from about 1910 there were increasing signs of
the decay of social life.

2. SOCIAL WELFARE

We have seen that in the maritime provinces, and also in Lower
Burma generally for some twenty years after the occupation of Pegu,
there was little change in village life. In the towns the population
was more mixed, and the monastic order was losing its hold on education and, in this and other ways, much of its influence; but, in the
villages, life went on very much as before. There was in effect a system
of indirect rule through the circle headman, and the village was a
residential and agricultural unit, managing its own affairs in its own
way, but not an administrative unit. Then in 1886 the Village Act
broke up the circle into villages, which became administrative units
to the detriment of their former organic unity. Economic forces,
reinforced by administrative regulations, carried disintegration a stage
further by breaking up the village into individuals.

Over the greater part of Lower Burma, newly occupied by immigrants, there never had been any social life, and, in the economic
conditions that prevailed, with the land passing backwards and forwards every two or three years between moneylenders and a succession
of transitory occupants, or held on annual lease from absentee landowners who knew nothing either of the land or of their tenants, and
with people, whether cultivators, tenants or labourers continually on
the move, it was impossible that any communal feeling should develop;
often there was not even a monastery to serve as a nucleus of social
life.

In Upper Burma things were different. Before the Annexation and
for some years afterwards, there was a strong communal feeling in the
villages. Under British rule this faded. The people were much freer
under British rule; freer to make money and to spend it, but freer
also to disregard customary social obligations. In most villages
custom had set aside certain lands for grazing or fuel, or for sanitary
convenience. Under Burmese rule no one thought of encroaching on
them, and would have gained little by doing so; while any trespass

would have been prevented by public opinion and the authority of the headman. But under British rule there was money to be made by encroaching on common land and no law to prevent it, while the headman no longer wielded the authority given by popular support. Before long someone would brave public opinion; there was no effective remedy and others followed his example, with the result that common land tended to disappear, to the detriment of social life. Most of the rice land in large parts of Upper Burma depends on local irrigation systems. We have noticed that in Thayetmyo in Lower Burma such systems were already breaking down by 1880.[1] The same thing happened in Upper Burma. Under Burmese rule every one wanted to grow rice. Under British rule someone might think, say, onions more profitable, and, by cultivating onions, which make different demands on the supply of water, throw the whole system out of gear. He would make a profit, but the gross production of the village would decline, and the village as a whole would suffer by the collapse of the irrigation system, while communal feeling would decay.

Rules for the protection of common village rights and interests were included in the instructions for assessing land. But in practice communal interests were disregarded. When the modern system of assessment was first introduced in 1879, the officers charged with this function were recruited from India and brought over their own establishments. Much inconvenience and delay was occasioned by the inability of the subordinates to talk Burmese and, despite protests from officers 'with a distrust of Burmans as workmen',[2] it was found expedient to train Burmans in this work. The experiment was soon justified by its success, but for the preliminary survey, however, it was possible, and still seemed cheaper and less trouble, to employ Indians. One result of their inability to speak Burmese was that the demarcation of common lands was neglected; there was a tendency 'to make the record of customs stereotyped and, after a few facts had been ascertained, to assume a community of usages all over the tract'.[3] In the newly reclaimed and recently settled parts of Lower Burma this disregard of common rights was of small importance, for there were few to place on record; though, as already noticed, the omission to demarcate and map residential areas often led to illegal evictions and oppression. But in Upper Burma there was an infinite variety of local

[1] See p. 57 above.
[2] *RAB*, 1879–80, pp. 6, 8.   [3] *RAB*, 1879–80, p. 10.

custom, and social welfare was closely dependent on the preservation of common rights. Not merely on irrigated land but also on dry land, cultivation depended on water from the adjacent catchment area; so likewise did the supply of water for drinking and bathing and for the cattle. Village welfare was closely bound up with rights of pasturage, and fuel, and with the maintenance of rights of way across the fields. But when officers from Lower Burma came to assess land in Upper Burma, they brought with them the tradition of disregarding all such rights.

By this time, moreover, waste land in the delta was becoming valuable and people were 'land-grabbing', putting forward unfounded claims to waste land. In Upper Burma the British Government found that land in private ownership had been exempt from revenue. By Indian tradition land revenue was the main source of income to the State, and the Government hurried through a Land Regulation to make all future extensions liable to revenue. One result was to exclude from the maps land not actually under cultivation. But in Upper Burma the poorer soils require long periods of fallow; much of the land omitted from the maps had long been private property, and much of the land shown on the maps soon passed out of cultivation. That, however, was not the most serious defect of the revenue survey. In Lower Burma the land was newly occupied and belonged solely to the occupants, man and wife; in Upper Burma the land was a family affair in which all members of the family had complicated interests but, in accordance with the Lower Burma practice, it was usually registered as the property of the actual occupants at the time of survey. Much confusion also was caused by definitions of tenures in terms that had little relation to the facts. All this multiplied disputes and litigation to the further prejudice of common village life.

In still another way the British revenue system was a potent factor in the disintegration of the village. The Burmese Government derived most of its revenue from a tax on *property* under the name of *thathameda*. This was assessed on villages at a fixed rate per household and distributed among the people according to their means by village assessors. Under British rule agricultural income was assessed to land revenue, and a separate tax imposed on non-agricultural *income*.[1] For the tax on non-agricultural income the name of *thathameda* was retained; it was calculated at a fixed rate per household and its total amount due was distributed by village assessors. But a tax on property

[1] *Burma Settlement Instructions* (1911), p. 91.

differs fundamentally from a tax on income. Everyone in the village knows whether a man lives in a large or small house, has much or little land or none, and has many or few cattle, and whether his wife wears gold and jewellery or cheap cotton cloth. But enquiries into income are invidious; it is unpleasant to disclose one's income to an official, but far worse to have to discuss it with one's neighbour. No more effective method of destroying village harmony could well have been devised. In practice, however, this was mitigated, because the assessors disregarded the rules and often levied the tax at a uniform rate on rich and poor alike. Sometimes district officers made a further encroachment on village autonomy by intervening to obtain what they regarded as a more equitable distribution. In one district an attempt by a Deputy Commissioner to distribute the tax, as he thought, more equitably, led to something like mass civil disobedience.[1]

One system of social disorganization was the increasing dreariness and drabness of ordinary village life. At the beginning of the present century it was still possible to attend cattle races between prize bullocks, gay in ornamental head-gear and many-coloured harness, drawing small racing chariots. But the cattle races and the traditional village rivalry in boat races were condemned by the iron hand of efficiency as promoting gambling and a cause of crime; and so also were the pony races—except on European courses. In Upper Burma one could still watch village theatrical performances, and troops of village dancers; but these disappeared with the decay of village life. The dances have been forgotten, and one of the most charming and entertaining, an elaborate ballet called a sword dance, is hardly, if at all, known to modern Burmans. The theatre has been commercialized, and the old puppet show, which in 1900 as in 1870, Burmans preferred to live-shows, seems quite to have died out, even before the introduction of the cinema. The water festival and festival of lights are less spontaneous and general, and the carnival processions are no longer a feature of ordinary village life, if they have not wholly disappeared. Burmese football still flourishes, and the introduction of English football must be placed to the credit of British rule, possibly the chief item on the credit side. But this has hardly reached the village and, as we have noticed, by 1920 the 'decay or suppression of the old-fashioned amusements' was suggested as a partial explanation of the growth of crime, and (for a short time) an officer was placed on special duty to revive them. But the decline of village amusements

---

[1] *RAB*, 1920–1, p. 22.

was part of the same process as the growth of crime, and both were symptomatic of the decay of village communal life and the disintegration of society.

Thus, chiefly through attrition by economic forces, active everywhere and always, and partly through regulations devised with greater regard for administrative convenience than for the protection of social welfare, the village community, even in Upper Burma, broke down into individuals. Now it has become a catchword that 'individualism', a disregard of common welfare and a reluctance or inability to combine for common ends, is a Burmese characteristic, often attributed to the influence of Buddhism.[1] Of the modern Burman this is probably not untrue, especially in Lower Burma, where the wild beasts that roamed the forests have passed with the felling of the jungle, but man has preyed on man as a condition of survival in the new jungle growth of unrestricted competition. Individualism, so far as it finds expression in free enterprise, is beneficial, but it can be turned to good account only in a suitable environment; and the rule of law alone is powerless to hinder it from sapping the foundations of society. The Government seems never to have realised this; it tried, not perhaps very vigorously or continuously, to provide remedies for land alienation, rack-renting and indebtedness, but it approached these as separate problems, without recognizing that they were related, and with little or no appreciation of the fact that they were merely different economic symptoms of a common social problem.

3. AGRARIAN CONDITIONS

In its essence the native system of land tenure was simple and closely resembled the Indonesian system of land tenure, from which it may possibly derive. The village, or other social unit, was regarded as having the disposal of the land in the neighbourhood. Anyone who was recognized as a member of the community could clear a patch of waste and, as the first to clear it, *dama-u-kya*, was allowed to continue in occupation. Shifting cultivation was usual, but it was only with the consent of the former occupant, express or implicit, that another could enter on land by the right of *thu-win, nga-htwet* ('he comes in, I go out'); customarily, if a man left land unoccupied for twelve years, another might take it up. Where the same man continued in occupation, it passed on to his descendants and became *bo-ba-baing*

[1] *ISC*, xi, 22.

(ancestral property). Possession, however, was never absolute against the community; cultivated land could be taken up for house sites, and house sites for a monastery (*yua-lok, ya-hsok*; *kyaung-la, yua-sha—* village-make, field-goes; monastery-comes, village-withdraws). In practice *bobabaing* land could be alienated, but alienation was never final; any member of the family could at any time redeem it, but seven generations were usually regarded as the limit of kinship.

Under British rule anyone was allowed to take up land as a squatter on condition of paying the revenue; after paying revenue for twelve years it became his private property in the western sense of property. When land grew in value many began to stake out claims to land and pay revenue on it for twelve years without cultivating it. With a view to encouraging cultivation the Government also introduced a system of making small grants of land, up to 50 acres, known as *pattas*, free of revenue for a period of years, supposed to represent the time required for clearing the jungle. Now and then attempts were made to induce capitalists to take up large tracts of waste land on grant or lease, but these attempts met with little success and were soon abandoned. With very few exceptions the land in Burma has been brought under cultivation by squatters, or by men holding a *patta*. The *patta* system proved unworkable. Ordinarily there were several applicants for the same plot of land, and by the time that their claims had been surveyed and adjudicated, someone else was found to be in occupation as a squatter; the *patta* system facilitated the transfer of land to wealthy landowners and moneylenders, and between 1905 and 1910 it was abandoned.

In practice, under either the squatter system or the *patta* system, anyone who could get his name on the revenue records could raise money on the land, even while yet uncleared. Only in very favourable circumstances will new land provide a living for the first year or two, and most of those who cleared it had to borrow money. A man had to stake out a claim over a considerable area, more than he could immediately bring under cultivation, in order to prevent others from settling on land that he would need to employ his cattle profitably. Much of the land was under heavy jungle, or required strong embankments to keep out salt water. The settlers had to borrow money, and usually lost their land to the moneylender by the time they had cleared it. 'The official policy of Government had always been to discourage the growth of a landlord class and to make Burma a country of small landowners. It would appear however that Govern-

ment has not in the past regarded its declared policy as imposing
on it any obligation to action, since very little has been done to
make the policy effective.' In practice there was 'free trade in
land'.[1] The dangers of land alienation were pressed on the Government of Burma by the Indian Government from the nineties of
the last century, but, after desultory consideration at infrequent
intervals, a draft Bill to deal with the matter was finally abandoned in
1912, in circumstances leading the Government of India to remark
that the opposition to the Bill was 'not based on the interests of the
peasant proprietor but of those from whom it is desired to protect
him'.[2] Nothing more was attempted until it appeared that the serious
rebellion in 1931 was partly due to agrarian distress. The subsequent
agricultural depression revealed something of the gravity of the situation. The revenue records for the
thirteen chief rice districts of
Lower Burma showed that half
the land was held by non-agriculturists, and that the chief
moneylending caste, the Indian
chettyars, alone held a quarter of
it. In fact, however, there was
nothing new in this. The only
difference was that the money-

Occupancy in Lower Burma*
(acres 000)

(a) Total area occupied; (b) Area held by
(i) Non-agriculturists, (ii) *Chettyars*

	(a)	(b) (i)	(b) (ii)
1930	9249	2943	570
1937	9650	4929	2446

* *CLA*, II, 39.

lenders, *chettyars* and others, could no longer find anyone to take the
land off their hands; for over fifty years most of the land, as it gradually
came under cultivation, had been passing backwards and forwards
between the moneylenders and a succession of transitory cultivators.

The history of the tenancy problem is very similar.[3] 'In the early
eighties of the last century the Government of India put the Government of Burma on its guard against the growth of a tenant class and
advised it to be prepared to impede this growth.' The matter received
more attention than land alienation, and a succession of abortive
drafts from 1892 led up in 1908 to 'the first Bill of its kind in Burma
to be placed before the public. It encountered opposition in the
Legislative Council [then representing capitalist interests] and among
the public from the landlord class, the *chettyar* community and
the European merchants in Rangoon engaged in the rice and
piece-goods trade.' The Bill was based on Indian precedents, and

---

[1] *RRA*, 1901-2, p. 29; *CLA*, I, 2.   [2] *CLA*, II, 44 ff., 50, 52.
[3] *RRA*, 1895-6, p. 5; *CLA*, I, 3, 5, 6.

displayed a singular ignorance of local conditions in confining protection to tenants with a record of continuous cultivation, whereas in
Lower Burma few tenants held the same land for longer than a year,
and in the rice plains of the delta even men registered as owners held
their land for only two or three years before having to abandon it to
the moneylender. But that was not the ground of the violent opposition which it encountered. Free trade in land was profitable to
commercial and capitalist interests, and 'the discussions went on
intermittently and half-heartedly until 1914' when the project was
abandoned. Another draft Bill in 1927 'raised such a storm of protest from landowners that Government decided not to proceed with
it'. So the problem of tenancy, like the problem of land alienation,
was left as a heritage to the Government established under the new
constitution of 1937, when a committee, appointed to examine the
matter, found, as had long been apparent in settlement reports, that
the rents throughout Lower Burma and in some parts of Upper
Burma were too high and that, after subtracting rent, debt charges
and costs of cultivation, 'the balance remaining was in many, perhaps
even in the majority of cases, insufficient to provide the tenant and
his family until the next harvest with a bare subsistence'.[1]

The committee suggested that the unsatisfactory economic condition of the tenant might possibly be attributed to his indebtedness
rather than to the level of rents. Yet the problem of debt had long
received attention, though only in isolation, apart from other
agrarian problems with which it is closely entangled. The opening
of the Suez Canal, which revealed the potential value of the Burma
rice trade, coincided with the transition from a policy of *laissez-
faire* to one of efficiency, and it appeared to Government that
the rapid spread of cultivation was hindered by the lack of labour
and the lack of capital. As already mentioned, during the early
eighties it took action to increase the labour supply by subsidizing immigration. At the same time it began to assist the cultivator
with loans under the Land Improvements Loans Act of 1883 and the
Agricultural Loans Act of 1884. Originally both these Acts were
designed to promote efficiency rather than welfare. For various
reasons the former Act has always remained practically inoperative.
But the latter proved useful in helping cultivators who could not
readily obtain loans from other sources. Although the interest
charged by Government was below the market rate, the cultivators

[1] *CLA*, I, 10.

could not obtain loans without considerable trouble and expense. The village headman was required to stand security and naturally expected a commission, a practice that was regarded as both general and legitimate.[1] The clerks expected a small percentage, and in some districts it was common for the officer disbursing the loans to take from 5 % to as much as 25–30 % of the capital advanced.[2] For these and other reasons the loans, which from 1919 to 1929 averaged about £125,000 annually, did little to relieve indebtedness, though they were often useful to alleviate exceptional distress and were in practice generally confined to such occasions.

The co-operative credit movement, started at the beginning of the present century, was more directly inspired by solicitude for the welfare of the cultivator. As with the discussions regarding land alienation and tenancy, the original suggestion came from India, having been put forward in the report of the Indian Famine Commission of 1901. For some years official returns showed rapid progress, and hopes were entertained that co-operative credit would solve the problem of agricultural debt in Burma. But conditions in Burma were unfavourable to the provision of credit on co-operative principles. Debt was heaviest in the districts with a migratory population, where transitory occupants, living in small scattered hamlets, with no social cohesion, were cultivating large holdings. In such conditions co-operation was impossible, and the movement never made much progress. In Upper Burma, on the other hand, where the villages still enjoyed a common social life, the formation of societies among certain of the villagers for economic ends tended to weaken rather than to strengthen social life among the village community as a whole. The system of co-operative credit requires that the members of a society shall understand, accept and apply the principles on which the system rests. Their education in such principles is necessarily a slow process, and, while the people are slowly learning the principles of sound co-operative credit, they must obtain from other sources such capital as they require. These considerations were disregarded. The education of members in co-operative principles was neglected, and an elaborate and costly departmental superstructure served chiefly to make borrowing easier than before, with little regard to any necessity for borrowing. By 1925 there were some 4000 agricultural societies, lending £1½ million to their members. But in 1929 the Provincial Bank, the apex of the whole movement, was found to be insolvent, and the

[1] *RAB*, 1906–7, p. 34.   [2] *CBC*, p. 19.

position of many societies was unsound. Most of them succumbed to the subsequent depression, and by 1935 only 1387 societies survived; the loans due by cultivators to these societies totalled about £450,000, of which some £400,000 was overdue.[1] As against a total volume of permanent indebtedness amounting to some £40 million, with another £5 to £10 million of seasonal indebtedness,[2] the advances from Government and from co-operative societies were inconsiderable.

It was necessary that the cultivator should have capital to live on while bringing the jungle under cultivation. If the land was to be reclaimed rapidly, it was necessary that he should borrow large sums. In the interest of the rice trade and of the outside world it was desirable that the plains of Lower Burma should be brought under rice as rapidly as possible. But it was only in the interest of alien moneylenders and business men that he should be encouraged to borrow as much as possible. That, however, is what happened.

Under Burmese rule there was no foreign market for most produce, and, if a cultivator grew more than was sufficient for his household, the surplus might not be worth gathering. He had little money, because a barter economy prevailed; he did not need much money, because he could himself provide for most of his requirements, and there were not many things on which he could spend money. No one need save for his old age, because of the tradition, deeply rooted in Burman social life, that children should support their aged parents. Men did not borrow to gain wealth, and it might even be dangerous to appear too rich. Those who borrowed through poverty were protected by custom against excessive interest and the loss of land; interest could not accrue beyond an amount equal to that borrowed, and land was a family possession that individual members of the family could not alienate. Under British rule the cultivator was encouraged to borrow and to spend money, and deprived of the customary protection against borrowing and spending it unwisely. The principle of economic freedom stimulated cultivation for export. Formerly the cultivator had been content with as much land as he could live upon; now he wanted all that he could work. The moneylender could supply the cultivator with as much money as he needed, but made greater profit by supplying him with all that the security would stand. The substitution of money for barter provided cultivators with cash to spend, and attractive foreign novelties tempted them to spend it. By the end of the century they had less money to

[1] *CLA*, III, 85, 86, 102.   [2] *CBE*, p. 53.

spend, but there were many things on which they had to spend money. Formerly, during the two months' interval between harvest and ploughing, the people obtained from the adjacent jungle the material for repairing their houses and agricultural implements; now, with the spread of cultivation, they had to buy these things. They could no longer earn money in the dry weather by making salt and fishing, but had to buy their salt and fish. Instead of earning money as boatmen they had to pay steamer fares for their necessary journeys. In place of home-made clothes they had to buy foreign cloth. By their own standards the people were still well fed and well clad, and in some ways better fed and better clad. Imported salt was better than local salt; imported cloth, if less durable than local cloth, had a much greater variety of patterns. But those who could not afford to buy these things felt poorer than before; their wants expanded as their income declined. Naturally men borrowed recklessly, and took full advantage of the new facilities for borrowing. Western law fixed no limit to the accumulation of interest, and gradually defined and restricted family property in land, making it freely and finally transferable by the occupant, while the courts supported creditors in treating as sales transactions that in the intention of the borrower were mortgages.

When the extent of agricultural indebtedness came to be realized it was regarded, not without some justification, as a sign of wealth rather than of poverty, or was attributed to 'the characteristic thriftlessness of the Burman', his 'want of foresight and tendency to extravagance and speculation'; he 'squandered his money on unproductive luxuries'.[1] Investigation showed that these charges were largely untrue, 'that thrift and saving were not alien to his character',[2] and that indebtedness was due in great measure to his new environment. In 1880 it was reported that 'as a rule Burmans of all classes invest their savings in gold and silver ornaments'.[3] Now many find it difficult to make both ends meet, but the bolts and bars on the doors and windows of the richer people show that their houses are their banks. Many, all but the really poor, store in their house posts, or bury in the ground, a few rupees to meet emergencies. In a year when much damage had been caused by floods a woman dug up the savings of many years to pay the family poll tax of Rs. 30, and was greatly distressed because the Treasury refused the money as no longer

---

[1] *RAB*, 1901–2, p. 28; 1908–9, p. 11.
[2] *RAB*, 1909–10, p. 11.   [3] *RAB*, 1880–1, Intr. p. 46.

current; it consisted wholly of William IV rupees. The savings in these little hoards must be considerable. Until quite recently cultivators used to set aside enough rice to provide for all their needs until the next crop should ripen. In Upper Burma the usual form of tenancy is a system by which the poor man saves up enough money to take land on mortgage from the rich. But the outstanding example of thrift among the cultivators appears in Lower Burma, where the burden of debt is most severe and the people are often regarded as conspicuously thriftless. Practically the whole of the ten million acres now under rice has been reclaimed by men who started life as field labourers, and saved enough money to buy cattle and to clear or buy some land. Out of his wages the cultivator saved up money to obtain land, and then, within two or three years, he lost the land, his cattle and his savings. These facts refute the easy explanation that the burden of debt is due to thriftlessness or any excessive tendency to extravagance and speculation; it has come about through the working of economic forces restrained solely by the rule of law, and was the outcome of a process over which the people could exercise no control. Thus 'the epic of bravery and endurance' relating 'the greatest achievement in the history of Burma', the reclamation by Burmese enterprise of ten million acres of swamp and jungle, ends with a picture of imposing Government offices and business houses in Rangoon, and gilded *chettyar* temples in Tanjore, while in the rice districts, the source of almost all this wealth, nearly half the land is owned by foreigners, and a landless people can show little for their labour but their debts, and, for about half the year, most of them are unable to find work or wages.

4. SOCIAL EVOLUTION

The large foreign element has long been the most obvious aspect of social life in modern Burma. This has special features due to the incorporation of Burma in the Indian Empire.

'In India the British administration had to employ Indian agency for all posts, major and minor, which were not filled by Europeans. Indian commerce and Indian professions were gradually built up by the people themselves. All that was not European was Indian....But in Burma the people were in no position to compete with the influx of Indians who flooded in to exploit the resources of the country and to take up posts for which no trained Burmans were available.'[1]

[1] 1920, Cmd. 746, p. 60.

In the administration, commerce and industry, it was less trouble and usually cheaper to recruit Indians than to train Burmans; and Indians, once they had gained a footing, naturally tended to build up an almost insurmountable barrier against the admission of Burmans. In 1872 aliens were 5·50 % of the total population; by the end of the century, although the annexation of Upper Burma had meanwhile brought in a large and almost entirely indigenous accession, the foreign element rose to 6·97 %, and by 1931 to 9·74 %. The table below shows the details at decennial intervals.

Racial Constitution, 1901–31 *

Year	Total population (ooo omitted)	Percentage (a) Foreign (b) Indian		Percentage of Non-Buddhists (a) Large towns (b) Other towns	
		(a)	(b)	(a)	(b)
1901	10,491	6·97	5·84	—	—
1911	12,115	8·02	6·15	62·8	22·3
1921	13,212	8·98	6·69	63·5	25·3
1931	14,667	9·74	6·95	62·7	28·1

* Census, 1931, p. 224.

So large a proportion of foreigners differing in creed, custom and language is sufficiently indigestible; but the gravity of the situation lay in the fact that the foreign element was concentrated mainly in the towns, and controlled almost the entire commercial and industrial sides of economic life. Unfortunately figures for the urban population by race are not available until 1931, but the foreign element may be roughly equated with the non-Buddhist element, although it is really larger, because many Chinese return themselves as Buddhists. Accepting this assumption, however, it appears that from the beginning of the century about two-thirds of the population of the six large industrial towns have been foreigners. Taking the urban population as a whole, the foreign element has been steadily increasing and, as shown on p. 118, at the latest census in 1931 it exceeded 40 %.

In 1872, although in the ports, and especially the older ports, Moulmein and Akyab, the population was largely Indian, numerous urban occupations were still open to Burmans, and they were employed even in the heaviest labour. In Rangoon the ships were still

Racial Constitution, Urban and Rural, 1931 *

Race	Racial population (a) Large towns (b) Other towns		Racial percentage in			
			Large towns	Other towns	All towns	Rural areas
	(a)	(b)				
Indigenous	210,796	679,170	36·0	72·7	58·5	93·9
Indian	290,124	173,090	49·6	18·5	30·5	4·2
Chinese	39,262	32,871	6·7	3·5	4·7	0·9
Indo-Burmese	24,497	39,708	4·2	4·2	4·2	0·9
Others	20,555	9,964	3·5	1·1	2·0	—

* Census, 1931, p. 50.

handled by Burmese labour, and 'there was no port in the world where timber was stored as well as it was in Moulmein, and they were all Burmese workers'.[1] All this was changed by the rapid influx of cheap Indian labour, encouraged by a Government subsidy, and the Administration Report for 1884–5 shows that by then the social economy of Burma was beginning to acquire its modern features:

'A large number of natives of India are permanently settled in the sea-ports and large villages, and they have driven the more apathetic Burman out of the more profitable fields of employment. The moneylending busi-ness of the country is in the hands of the Madrassi banking caste of Chetties; the retail piece-goods trade is chiefly in the hands of Suratis, natives of India, and Chinamen; the retail liquor trade is almost ex-clusively in the hands of Chinamen. The natives of India have also driven the Burman out of the field where hard manual labour is required; the coolies employed by the Public Works Department are almost exclusively Indian, the gharry drivers everywhere are chiefly Madrassis, the coolies on the wharves and at the railway stations are also natives of India, and natives of India are here and there settling down to permanent rice cultivation.'[2]

The whole trend of development illustrated the economic process of natural selection by the survival of the cheapest, justified in con-temporary thought, and especially in the eyes of those who paid for labour, as the survival of the fittest.

The working of this process in rural areas has already been de-picted. In the towns it can perhaps best be illustrated from the history of coolie labour in the rice trade. Old reports tell of the clatter of thousands of Burman rice-mills all along the river-side at Rangoon. In 1861 the first steam-mill was erected, but machinery was not yet cheaper than men, and no more were put up until 1867. In that year

[1] RCLI, x, 163.   [2] RAB, 1884–5, p. 64.

there were three mills, but by 1872 the number had risen to twenty-six. The mills employed Indian coolies, and overcrowding among them was already attracting notice. The danger to the health of the whole country arising out of such conditions was frequently admitted, but they continued to deteriorate as the supply of cheap labour grew with the demand. The influx rose by 1918 to 300,000 coolies a year and made Rangoon second only to New York as a port for immigration;[1] but they spread disease, raised the death-rate, and, by driving Burmans out of the towns, deprived them of contact with the stimulating influence of modern industry.

If Burmans could no longer get a footing on even the lowest rung of the industrial ladder, still less could they aspire to enter the higher ranks of industry and commerce. In finance Indians had long done business with European banks; and naturally came to function as middlemen between them and the people. In commerce Indians had learned to deal with European merchants before ever the British came to Burma. Importers did not speak Burmese; Burmans did not understand European methods of business; they could obtain credit or capital only on ruinous terms; and they had at the same time to compete against the lower standard of living of the Indian. When local cloth was driven off the market by the flood of imported cloth, the retail trade in clothing passed largely into Indian hands. With the growth of an import trade in dried and salted fish from Singapore and Indo-China as a result of the tax on local salt, this trade, for similar reasons, became largely a Chinese monopoly. The same thing happened throughout the whole sphere of economic life. All the large European firms had previous connections with India or China, and naturally found it cheaper and less trouble to import Indian or Chinese employees than to learn Burmese and train Burmans in western methods of business. The most comfortable explanation was Burman apathy and incompetence; yet in goods which were both produced and consumed in Burma, the trade, wholesale and retail, still remained in Burman hands. The exclusion of the Burman from modern economic life was not deliberate, was indeed frequently deplored; it just happened.

It happened likewise in the professions which, outside the European or westernized community, were branches of the administration. In the early hospitals, as already remarked, 'everything was done to diminish expense', and they were staffed from India, even down to the menial staff. Larger funds allowed more liberal expenditure on buildings,

[1] Harvey, *CHI*, VI, 446.

and a new hospital in Rangoon in 1910 was proudly claimed as 'one of the most imposing buildings in the East'.[1] But the new buildings were still staffed with Indian hospital assistants, Eurasian nurses and Indian menials, and were little patronized by Burmans, except those brought in as police cases or involuntarily detained as suspected of infectious disease. Burmans and Europeans had different ideas of welfare in respect of medical assistance. Up to the end of the century and later there were still no facilities in Burma for training the people in western medicine. A few scholarships to medical schools in India, though nominally open to all in Burma, mostly went to Anglo-Indians and Indians, who would find themselves at home in India.[2] Some of the Indian doctors were excellent men, whose wards were always overcrowded, but many were content to draw their pay, and such fees as they could pocket from false evidence in cases of assault.[3] There were not even sufficient Indian doctors, as these did not wish to serve in Burma, and the establishment was always below strength. Among the Burman population less than $\frac{1}{2}$% attended hospital, and in 1908, as in 1868, their reluctance was attributed 'to the fact that so large a proportion of the subordinate medical staff are not natives of the Province'.[4] The provision of a Medical School in 1907 was intended to promote the recruitment of Burmans. But it was easier to open a school than to change the conditions of service. The hospitals still remained Indian institutions. It was almost impossible for a Burman to get a training even as a compounder; and still more difficult for a Burman compounder or ward-servant to find employment in a hospital where, by long tradition, the whole staff and atmosphere were Indian. Naturally in such conditions the recruitment of Burmans to the medical profession was a slow process, and the spread of western medical science among the people even slower. Meanwhile the native tradition of medicine was declining, and the traditional drugs formerly gathered and compounded by the practitioner were being ousted by the free competition of adulterated or imported substitutes such as cheap quinine tabloids with coatings that defied the strongest gastric juices, and 'white oil' kerosene to adulterate the vegetable or animal oil of the local dietary.[5]

The outbreak of plague in 1905 raised a new problem. But it was solved on the old lines. Gangs of Indian coolies were employed to

[1] *RAB*, 1910–11, p. xii.   [2] *RAB*, 1901–2, p. 95.
[3] *CBC*, p. 31.   [4] *RAB*, 1868–9, p. 117; 1907–8, p. xiii.
[5] *RTC*, 1910–11, p. 10; 1911–12, p. 9.

clean out the houses of the Burmese, causing no little discontent and, incidentally, tending to spread rather than suppress the disease. These worked under a staff of Indian sanitary inspectors and, when a Sanitary Commissioner was appointed in 1908, his usefulness was limited by his ignorance of the country and the people. Experience suggested that 'properly trained Burmese Inspectors would be a valuable asset to the Province' but 'shortage of funds' made this impossible.[1] In matters of public health as of medicine, policy was conditioned by economic factors, though the experience of nearly a hundred years had demonstrated that this was false economy.

Burmans had to face the same obstacle in the other professions. King Mindon had trained telegraphists and adapted the Morse code to Burmese.[2] But the postal and telegraph departments in British Burma were managed from India, and it was cheaper and less trouble to employ Indians than to teach Burmans, so that the telegraph department became, and even after the annexation of Upper Burma remained, an Indian preserve. So likewise did the telephone system, and up to 1930 or later one could not use the telephone in Burma without a knowledge of Hindustani. The postal department also was staffed by Indians, though sometimes the Indian postmen had to get Burmese villagers to read the addresses on the letters. All branches of engineering remained Indian for the same reason. Burmans and Karens could build schools and churches for missionaries and fine houses for wealthy cultivators. Engineers admired the skill and resource with which in 1871 Burmans raised to the top of the Shwe Dagon pagoda, a height of over 300 feet, a massive finial weighing $1\frac{1}{4}$ tons, 47 feet high with a diameter at the base of $13\frac{1}{2}$ feet.[3] This was achieved successfully and at little cost; all were only too anxious to lend a hand or supply the workmen with provisions. But that was not the way of conducting public works under a foreign government, believing in individual profit and apprehensive of religious zeal, and it was cheaper and less trouble to employ Indians. With the rapid growth of cultivation after the opening of the Suez Canal, some interest began to be displayed in the introduction of labour-saving machinery, until Indian immigration relieved the shortage and there was no more need to save labour.[4] On the construction of the first railway, arrangements were made to train apprentices in the railway workshops, and for a time

[1] *RAB*, 1905–6, p. 26; 1909–10, pp. 104, 107; 1910–11, p. xvi.
[2] *RAB*, 1868–9, p. 121.   [3] *BBG*, II, 637.
[4] *RAB*, 1880–1, Intr. p. 51; 1885–6, p. 26.

lads were sent with scholarships to India but, as with the medical scholarships and for similar reasons, few Burmans took advantage of them.[1] In 1895 an engineering school was opened to train men for subordinate positions in the Public Works Department, but here again most of the students were Anglo-Indians or Indians.[2] In all branches of the public works, on the railway and on the river steamers, Indians had a monopoly of employment; the Burman could not get a job unless he took to wearing trousers and passed himself off as a Eurasian. In all these various activities there was no demand for Burmans, but Indian lads came over from India to study in the technical schools of Burma. Only when the School of Engineering was closed to non-domiciled Indians, coming from India to attend it, did the number of Burman students rise from six to twenty-two;[3] this enabled about 2 per million of the Burman population to obtain sufficient technical instruction for subordinate appointments in the Government services. Outside Government service, even fifty years after the opening of the Suez Canal had brought Burma into economic contact with the West, there was still no opening for Burmans as technicians, though European and Anglo-Indian apprentices, for whom stipends were provided by Government, were taken in the workshops of the Burma Railways, the Irrawaddy Flotilla Company, the Dockyards, Tramways and other important corporations and private firms connected with technical work.[4] It was not the policy of Government to exclude Burmans from these various careers; on the contrary it wished to help them, but this remained no more than a pious aspiration, because the Government, like the Burman, was the victim of circumstances.

There is one striking exception to this monopoly of urban occupations by non-Burmans. Thanks to the monastic schools almost every Burman learned to read and write. When the British introduced printing, it was less trouble to teach Burmans how to set up type than to teach Indians the Burmese alphabet; hence Burmans secured, and managed to retain, a position in the printing trade, though in the Government press they were ousted subsequently by cheaper Indians. Thus, apart from employment under Government in general administration, Burmans had to look to agriculture for a living. Europeans directed or controlled all large-scale enterprise; Indians or Chinese manned the urban occupations and acted as middlemen

---

[1] *RAB*, 1880–1, Intr. p. 33; p. 130; 1892–3, p. 124.   [2] *RAB*, 1901–2, p. 94.
[3] *RAB*, 1913–14, p. 86.   [4] *RAB*, 1915–16, p. 106.

between the Europeans and the Burman cultivator. There was a
racial division of labour. All the various peoples met in the economic
sphere, the market place; but they lived apart and continually tended
to fall apart unless held together by the British Government.

5. EDUCATION

For the backwardness of Burmans in non-agricultural activities education was commonly regarded as the remedy. In this as in other matters,
policy in Burma was directed from India, and to understand the course
of educational progress in Burma one must have some acquaintance
with the Indian background. The encouragement of education by the
State dated from long before the emergence of the idea that the State
should actively promote welfare; it had the sanction of Adam Smith
and derived its inspiration from sentiments, liberal, humanitarian and
Christian, transcending the material plane. In 1793, when Wilberforce opened his campaign for modernizing education in India, it was
the conversion of the people that he had in mind. Again, in 1836
Macaulay firmly believed that if his plan of education were adopted
there would not be a single idolater among the respectable classes in
the next generation. One argument for the annexation of Pegu was
that it would have 'a blessed effect by spreading civilization and the
Gospel'.[1] The education of the general public was expected to remove
superstitious prejudices and to attach them more closely to British
rule. Accordingly from the first conception of a policy of systematic
education in 1854, the leading item was the spread of primary instruction among the masses of the people.

But education had a more practical side. It furnished Government
with cheap subordinates and the people with well-paid jobs. Government wanted schools to train clerks, and the people wanted schools
to obtain clerkships. There was an economic demand for schools.
The demand became more urgent when the Suez Canal gave a new
stimulus to commerce, and consequently to administrative expansion.
Educational progress was dominated by the economic laws of demand
and supply. This tendency was accentuated when, in accordance with
liberal doctrine, the Indian Education Commission of 1882 recommended that education should be left so far as possible to private

[1] Durand, II, 185.

enterprise. The principle of spreading primary vernacular instruction among the masses was still put forward as the chief aim of policy, but in practice the system provided secondary anglo-vernacular instruction for the middle classes. When there was a surplus of lads from the fourth standard, they would try to secure a job by working up to the seventh standard; when that was no longer sufficient qualification they went on to matriculation, and then a few years later to a university degree, either locally or, if they could afford it, in England. Thus in India, by the end of the century, merely under the pressure of economic forces, at every stage there was a growing surplus of university and school graduates, who were a focus of discontent and disaffection. The educational system did not foster attachment to British rule or conversion to Christianity, but a reaction against western civilization and the British Government. It was generally said that the system of instruction was 'too literary in character' and had 'stimulated tendencies unfavourable to discipline', while the ignorant superstition of the masses was 'a source of administrative difficulty and political danger'. Lord Curzon accordingly formulated a new policy.[1] Government was to be more active in providing educational facilities; the encouragement of elementary vernacular instruction was to be a primary obligation and a leading charge on provincial revenues; technical instruction was to be promoted, especially in agriculture; female education was to receive special attention, and discipline was to be strengthened by 'moral text-books and primers of personal ethics' and by a stricter departmental supervision over schools and pupils.

As already explained, up to close on 1870 little progress had been made in Burma in education along western lines. The demand for educated men was very limited, and was met chiefly by the monastic schools. Under early British rule, as formerly under Burmese rule, these gave the brighter lads a chance to rise in the world. But their primary object was to teach the boys how to live and not merely how to make a living, so that there was no possibility of the over-production of school graduates, and the more who went to school the better. Then, during the sixties, when the Government of India was concerned to promote education, Sir Arthur Phayre was directed to submit a plan of public instruction for Burma. In 1866 he introduced a system based on the monastic school. The moral discipline of the monastic training had always been highly esteemed and he hoped

[1] *RPI* (India), 1897-1902, App., pp. 457 ff.

that by the exercise of 'very great tact, judgment and discretion' the technique of monastic teaching might be improved and the curriculum extended. As Director of Public Instruction he selected a man with thirty years' experience as a schoolmaster in Burma. Unfortunately ill health compelled the Director to retire within a few months, and his place was taken by an educational expert from Bengal, who knew nothing of Burma. Phayre's plan languished, and in 1868 there was a proposal to abandon it and substitute the establishment of village lay schools. By 1871 only 46 monastic schools had adopted the plan. A new Chief Commissioner, just appointed from India, considered this unsatisfactory and started lay schools. Had he known more of Burma he might have had more patience, and even a little more patience might have justified Phayre's hopes, for by 1873 the number of recognized monastic schools had risen to 801 as against 112 lay schools.[1]

By this time the effect of the Suez Canal was beginning to be felt. Trade was growing rapidly; the policy of Government was turning in the direction of efficiency; and there was an increasing demand for English-speaking clerks, and for opportunities to learn English. 'As an agency for moral training', it was said, 'the value of the monastic schools is incalculable, viewed as an agency for secular education their value seems to have been over-rated...much more is to be expected from lay schools.'[2] It was believed also that the monastic schools, instead of improving, had been deteriorating. A proposal to encourage the teaching of English in the monastic schools was vetoed on the ground that the boys would not acquire a correct accent,[3] and the attention of the Education Department came to be concentrated on anglo-vernacular schools. For the most part these were conducted by missionaries of various denominations, chiefly American Baptists and French Roman Catholics; officials of the Education Department inspected the schools, conducted public examinations, and awarded grants. When the standard of instruction was sufficiently advanced, the schools were affiliated to Calcutta University, but by 1880 only nine Burmans had been able to matriculate.[4] One reason for the slow progress was that few Burmans or Karens could teach English, mathematics or history, 'The masters of the middle and higher schools', it was said, 'are chiefly Englishmen or Natives of India, who can not make Burmese the vehicle of

---

[1] *BBG*, i, 529; *CVV*, pp. 130, 132, 136.   [2] *RAB*, 1877–8, p. 80.
[3] *RPI*, 1928–9, p. 11.
[4] *RAB*, 1880–1, Intr. p. 36.

instruction; and so the boys do not really grasp what they are taught'. Up to 1918 Burma had produced only 400 graduates, including many non-Burmans.[1] But until 1900 or later the seventh standard was a sufficient qualification for well-paid employment.

Thus, when Lord Curzon formulated a new educational policy, conditions in Burma were very different from those in India. The proportion of literate males was three times and of literate females five times the corresponding proportion in the most advanced province in India; there was as yet no local university; the output from western schools was still inadequate to the demand; industrial development had not yet begun; and Burma was considered to 'stand high in respect of discipline and moral training'. In Burma the new educational programme could be drawn up on a blank sheet. Yet in Burma, under the new policy, educational progress followed much the same course as formerly in India under the old policy. Under economic pressure contrary policies gave identical results. Let us then trace briefly the course of development in respect of secondary and vocational instruction, of female education and of cultural and moral values.

One principle of the new policy was that the Government 'should devote proportionally more money to primary instruction and less to secondary instruction'. But economic progress during the present century multiplied the demand for clerks, and, with the supply outpacing the demand, secondary schools were multiplied and standards rose until, in 1920, it was deemed expedient to constitute a university in Rangoon. All this entailed a much greater proportional expenditure on the higher standards. Meanwhile two-thirds to three-quarters of the villages still had no provision for learning except in the monastic school, if any; and the monastic schools were no more closely in touch with the modern world, and were losing their hold on the people, because the wealthier and brighter lads were forsaking them for schools which paved a quicker way to better jobs.

Economic factors also dominated professional and vocational instruction. The medical school, opened in 1907, provided for the training of medical subordinates, and the closure of the engineering school to non-domiciled students in 1913 encouraged Burmans to train for subordinate appointments in the Public Works Department, but up to the end of executive rule in 1923 men still had to go to India to become a doctor or an engineer,[2] and for neither was there an effective

[1] *RAB*, 1880–1, Intr. p. 36; Harvey, *CHI*, VI, 445–7.   [2] *RAB*, 1921–2, p. 154.

demand. Long experience of western medicine as practised by Indian medical subordinates failed to wean Burmans from their own medical system and practitioners, and few could afford the fees that a modern doctor with a long and costly training had to charge. Europeans preferred European doctors, and there was no opening for a Burman doctor except in government service, where the conditions and standards of pay had been adapted to Indian requirements. There was no demand for Burman doctors trained on western lines. Similarly there was little demand for Burman engineers. European firms preferred European engineers for the higher posts, and were accustomed to Indian subordinates, who were also cheaper than Burmans. In village life there was no scope for men trained in western engineering science. The steam engine came to Burma with Indians trained to use it; only later, with the advent of the petrol engine, was there any demand for Burman mechanics. The promotion of technical instruction in agriculture was a matter on which Curzon laid great emphasis, and he commented on the absence of an agricultural school in Burma. But, although the influx of Indian labour revolutionized agricultural organization in the delta, agricultural technique remained unchanged, and there was no demand for technical skill beyond that common to all cultivators in their inherited tradition. Thus in 1923, as when Curzon formulated the new policy, there was still no school of agriculture.

The legal profession furnished a striking contrast. In the law there was no need, as in medicine and engineering, to encourage students. There was a demand for lawyers. Doctors and engineers could not find employment except in Government service or in the western sphere of social life. Burmans, Indians, Chinese and Europeans all wanted their own doctors; but all had to employ lawyers trained in western law; the Government had only to regulate by examination the right to appear before the courts. With the spread of Indian moneylenders and of modern business methods, the practice of settling disputes by arbitration declined. Even in 1875 an experimental law class failed to attract students, and a decade later litigation among Burmans was still infrequent. But the abolition of the circle headmen, and the encroachment of the courts on custom, gave a further blow to arbitration. Burmans increasingly resorted to the courts; there was a demand for lawyers and the demand created a supply. At first, as in other lines, the lawyers were Indians. But men who struggled through the schools and failed to find employment, had no resource except the law. Burman lawyers multiplied rapidly in competition with the ever-growing number of Indian lawyers, and the excess of the supply over the demand encouraged litigation and a decline of ethical standards.[1] The gloomy prognostication of the Commissioner of Tenasserim in 1840 was fulfilled, and 'the system has helped to create a class of denationalized native lawyer who shows little skill save in raising obstructions and procuring perjury'.[2]

There was, however, a notable advance in the number of girls attending school. Under Burmese rule there was an old tradition of female education. In Ava in 1826 Trant reports that women 'for the most part know how to read and write' and 'entered with the greatest warmth into the news and politics of the day'. The first census report of 1872 states, with very considerable exaggeration, that female education 'was a fact in Burma before Oxford was founded'. In practice however, literacy among women was exceptional, though, according to the same report, 10 % of the female convicts could read and write.[3] It was a defect of the Burmese system of education that it made no provision for the girls; parents welcomed the opportunities given by the lay schools, and the new facilities were valued as helping the women in their business as petty traders in the bazaars. The advocates of female education stressed its cultural value in domestic life, but an acquaintance with the rudiments of arithmetic made little difference in the home, and the progress of female education in contrast with the stagnation of vocational instruction is significant chiefly of the difference in their market value.

In his review of education Curzon remarked that in India it had a commercial rather than a cultural value. With no openings for doctors and engineers there was no incentive to study the elements of natural science, or to acquire the mental discipline on which the modern world is based. Natural science was not taught in any of the schools and, though the few who struggled on to the university standard could take chemistry and, from 1915, physics, there was no provision for the teaching of biology. The chief attraction of the science course was that it was reputed less difficult than the arts course. What the students wanted was a job, and for this science and art degrees were of equal value. Similarly there were no openings in which they could turn to account a knowledge of economics, and no provision was made for them to study the economic aspect of

[1] *RAB*, 1877–8, p. 83; 1880–1, p. 130; 1887, Cmd. 4962, p. 119.
[2] Harvey, *CHI*, VI, 443.
[3] Census, 1872, p. 25; Trant, pp. 209, 259.

the modern world. Arts graduates from the university colleges had a competent knowledge of English, but on leaving the university they had nothing to read; even in Rangoon there were no bookshops. There was no museum, no art gallery, no theatre or concert hall, nothing to represent the cultural aspect of the modern West.

Meanwhile Burman culture was decaying. It is true that successive census reports indicate an advance in literacy. Formerly almost all the boys learned to read and write, but few had occasion to practise what they learned and many forgot what they had been taught in school. Under British rule the introduction of printing and other developments, that will call for notice later, helped them to remember their alphabet, but although they did not so readily forget how to read and write their language, foreign rule narrowed the range of intellectual interest which it provided. Under their own kings they knew little of the outer world but within their native medieval world the language was co-extensive with their national life. After the conquest English became the medium of discussion for all the higher social activities, and Burmese degenerated into a language for the cultivator and the home. In a wider world the people led a narrower life. This process was aggravated by the decline of the monastic school and was reflected not only, as already noticed, in the deterioration of native medicine but in all the native arts. In these matters no British governor could replace a Burmese king. No one could expect him to patronize Burmese medical practitioners or to be a connoisseur of Burmese art. The Government did what it could to stay the decline of native arts and crafts. From the eighties onwards art was 'sedulously fostered'. One artist was 'said to be the best. He finishes work fairly to time, keeps regular accounts, completes his orders in rotation, and has apprenticed pupils.'[1] Yet art continued to languish. One reason was the wide difference between Burmese and European standards of artistic values. Still more potent was 'the severe competition of cheap jewellery and fancy articles of European or cognate make', and attempts 'to stem the competition by combining art and utility in the articles produced'[2] only too often produced articles that were neither beautiful nor useful. In fostering cultural values the new educational policy was no more successful than the old, and economic values still remained supreme.

Yet the most conspicuous failure of the new policy was probably in its attempt to improve moral standards. Curzon had thought to

[1] *RAB*, 1885–6, p. 32.   [2] *RAB*, 1911–12, p. 91.

effect this by closer supervision over the schools and by extending Government enterprise in education. In Burma, 'under private enterprise, education had not spread to the extent necessary for the needs of the Province'.[1] There was a reaction against '*laissez-faire* principles which preferred to leave the guidance and practical management of education to private bodies and persons, more or less irresponsible and with very varying views on the needs of the educated and the ends of education',[2] and Government schools were expected to educate more children more efficiently. But the Government could not provide enough schools without the contributions of the faithful in America and elsewhere. More than twenty years later, among 6000 institutions providing general instruction there were only 79 Government schools, and of these 47 were anglo-vernacular schools.[3]

Official and non-official schools alike were expected to inculcate morality and discipline by moral text-books and primers of personal ethics, but all had in common one feature which vitiated moral teaching. Many lads passed from one school to another. As small boys in the monastery they would be taught the vanity of desire; then in a Roman school they would be exhorted to abhor the heresies of Wycliff and Huss; if they went on to a Protestant school they would start the day with a prayer for success in the next examination; and they would probably seek a final polish in a Government school where success in the examination was the only thing that mattered. That was the one thing that all schools, other than the monastery, had in common. Few parents cared for anything except success in the examinations. 'Moral text-books and primers of personal ethics' had no examination value, and stricter discipline and closer supervision over the schools were of no avail in an environment where the sole end of education was to get a job. Discipline, praised as satisfactory in 1900, deteriorated so rapidly that in 1915 there was a strike in the chief Government school, and in 1920 the foundation of Rangoon University was the occasion for a general school strike. It was followed by many similar incidents and for some years the morals of the schoolboys were continually under discussion.[4] And the Director of Education noted regretfully that districts with the best record for education had the worst record for crime.[5]

---

[1] *RAB*, 1901–2, p. 93; *RPI*, 1897–1902, Intr. p. 4.
[2] *CVV*, p. 133.   [3] *RPI*, 1928–9, App. I, p. v.
[4] *RAB*, 1915–16, p. 103; *RPI*, 1927–32, p. 37.
[5] *RPI*, 1927–32, p. 36.

6. LITIGATION AND CRIME

Litigation. The growth of crime was one aspect of a general growth of litigation. The significance of this cannot be appreciated without an understanding of the difference between British and Burmese ideas on legal procedure and law.

We have noticed that Mr Maingy was quite unable to make sense of Burmese legal procedure. Even an observer so sympathetic and competent as Burney commented on the absurdity of going to law to reach a compromise.[1] The ten judges in the Court of Mergui, whether hearing cases individually or as a bench, did not try to arrive at strict legal decisions on proved facts but to settle disputes. They were arbitrators rather than judges. That continued to be the Burmese system. In 1878 the British representative on the Mixed Court at Mandalay noted that 'in deciding civil suits the principal aim of the judges was, if possible, to satisfy both parties, the usual result being in almost all cases a compromise'. It was still the practice for judges to hear causes through a deputy, and no decision was regarded as final unless both parties signified their acceptance of it by the ceremony of 'eating tea together'.[2] This difference of principle between Burmese and western legal procedure seems to have been overlooked in British Burma until, about 1880, Jardine, as Judicial Commissioner, made a close study of Burmese law. He then suggested that 'the Native system of settling disputes was not by a decree of original jurisdiction, which a Court could enforce irrespective of the will of the parties, but by conciliators, whose duty, expressly stated in cases of matrimony, was to soothe and advise the parties to make a compromise agreeable to both'.[3] In early days of British rule matrimonial disputes, in which the parties obtained a divorce and then shortly afterwards came together again, were a nuisance to British judges until they drove them from the judgment seat by punishing both man and wife. Jardine stated his view more explicitly in a judgment. 'I am convinced that in the Burmese family system the reasonable is to precede the legal, not under the system of the English courts by undeviating arithmetical rules and compulsory decrees, but by contracts and compromises obtained by argument, expostulation among themselves, all parties appealing more or less to what is right (i.e. the *dhammathats*) and more or less allowing

---

[1] Desai, p. 103 n.   [2] Jardine, Note ii, Circular, p. 15.
[3] Jardine, Note iv, p. 4.

themselves to be governed by these considerations.'[1] But this procedure was quite inconsistent with a system based on the rule of law,
and upholding the sanctity of contract in the interest of economic
freedom. In British courts the judges, whether British or Burman,
applied western principles of law, and preferred what was legal, or
what the judge regarded as legal, over what Burmans regarded as
reasonable.

British and Burmans differed not only in their systems of legal procedure but also in their conception of law. Burmese law was founded on
'the *Dhammathat*, a Pali version of the Hindoo laws of Menu, and the
Yazathat, a collection of precedents and of rules and regulations
established by different Kings of Ava'.[2] Burmans drew their idea of
law from the *dhamma*, the Moral Law. To the Buddhist this is not a
divine law, a law of God, a commandment; it lacks the element of
'command' which Austin took to be an essential element of law, and
Burmans regard law rather as a statement of cause and effect, like
the laws of nature. Every act or omission entails certain consequences
in this world or the next. Some consequences are beyond the jurisdiction of the courts, but they fall within the subject-matter of
their law books; thus anyone guilty of striking a monk is liable
to a fine of Rs. 100 and to innumerable existences in various stages
of hell. The function of the judge was subordinate to that of the
jurist whose aim was to discover the law, much as a scientist aims at
discovering natural law. The men who wrote the *dhammathats* were
mostly clerics wishing to advance religion, jurists looking for promotion, scholars demonstrating their erudition or ingenuity, or men
of letters showing their skill in prose or verse; of the better-known
dhammathats about one-third are in verse.[3] The extant *yazathats*
purport mainly to record the decision of wise men on knotty points,
and in fact are largely folklore of Indian Buddhist origin.

[1] *Ru.SJ*, p. 197. The Burmese idea of law still apparently persists in Japan. 'There is
not in the Japanese mind that clear-cut distinction between, say, justice and injustice,
pure and impure, legal and illegal, that there is in the Anglo-Saxon.... For example,
take a law case. There is a law suit about a sum of 10,000 yen. This has been
borrowed on terms, and has not been returned to the lender according to the agreement. There is no dispute about the terms. All that is clear and agreed. The leader
seeks the authority of the court to compel the borrower to keep the letter of the
agreement. There is no need to ask what a British court would decide; the agreement,
the whole of the agreement and all its implications would be implemented. Not so
in Japan. Judgment would probably (I have known such cases) take the form—
9000 yen to the lender, 1000 to the borrower.' Rt Rev. Bishop Heaslett, *Spectator*,
13 April 1945.
[2] *SL*, p. 105.   [3] Furnivall, *JBRS*, Aug. 1940, p. 351.

British judges were puzzled by the apparent disregard of Burmans for their own law, and thought at first that they treated the *dhammathats* with little veneration. This idea was quite mistaken. Both in Lower and Upper Burma, elders called in to arbitrate professed to be following the *dhammathats*, while giving decisions that ran counter to them.[1] The British judge on the Mixed Court remarked that the Burmese judges 'used the Laws of Menu to some extent as a Civil Code'. In the official digest of Burmese-Buddhist law, published for the British Government in 1893-6, the compiler, a judge of the former Burmese High Court, defines a *dhammathat* as 'a collection of rules, which are in accordance with custom and usage and which are referred to in the settlement of disputes';[2] they had no claim to authority except as representing the views of learned men. They were venerated, as the Bible was venerated by the British, but they were applied only so far as the judges thought expedient. As was remarked by a judge of the Chief Court, who had long previous experience as an administrative official, 'The law to which Burmans were subject was not the law of the *dhammathats*, but the customary law to which the *dhammathats* were a very important but not the only guide.'[3] To the Burman a code of law furnished 'rules of conduct'; to the British judge the law was a command.[4] Under British rule the *dhammathats* came to be treated like western codes of law and, so far as possible, were literally interpreted and strictly enforced.

Of necessity the new idea of law changed the law. But the change was gradual, as for many years the *dhammathats* were neglected in the British courts; until 1847 none had been translated. By that time the tradition of disregarding them had been established, and the first Civil Code, compiled by Major Sparks in 1860, was based on current practice, including only a few phrases from the *dhammathats* that had become proverbial as expressing general custom. With the appointment of a Judicial Commissioner in 1872 legal administration began to pass into the hands of professional lawyers, who tended to give the *dhammathats* an authority and rigidity which they had never possessed under Burmese rule, and tried to interpret and apply them strictly like statutory law. For example, the general Burmese custom on the inheritance of an estate is for all the children to obtain an equal share; but the *dhammathats* can be held to support the view that the first-born child should be regarded as an *orasa* child entitled to a larger

[1] *Ru. 2 UB*, p. 102; *Ru. 5 LB*, p. 8.   [2] *Digest*, p. 2.
[3] *Ru. 3 LB*, p. 187.   [4] *Ru. SJ*, p. 197.

share. In Sparks' Code all the children shared alike, and the right of
the eldest to special treatment was wholly ignored. Not until 1882
does the term *orasa* appear in a judgment. Jardine then remarked
that, according to the *dhammathats*, the eldest son or *orasa* held a
superior position,[1] but in his Note on the subject in the following year
he states that, although Burmans who know the *dhammathats* say
that under their codes the eldest son has special rights, these are
seldom exacted.[2] No claim to such special rights was put forward
until 1899, when it was asserted by a man who knew something of
the British interpretation of Burmese law.[3] Now, anyone who can
make good his position as *orasa* can obtain a special share through the
courts, but among the people in general the old custom of equal
division still survives.

Thus, even where professing to apply Burmese law, the courts have
substituted the *dhammathats* for Burmese custom; they apply them
as rules of law instead of as principles of conduct; and they try to lay
down the law instead of aiming at a reasonable compromise. But they
have gone beyond this, by disregarding both Burmese law and custom,
and substituting western law. Burmans regarded land as a family
possession over which all members of the family had rights; no one
could alienate it without the consent, express or tacit, of all parties
interested. The British courts defined and restricted family rights,
and made land subject to the western law of property. Under Burmese
rule the outright sale of land was unknown; if a man 'sold' his land,
it was always understood that he or any member of the family might
at any time redeem it. The British courts came to treat such conditional sales as final. According to Burmese custom the interest on a
debt could not accumulate beyond the sum originally borrowed, but
the British courts recognized no limit. The Burmese held that all who
had taken part in cultivation were entitled to a first claim upon the
produce, but this was disregarded in the British courts. In all these
matters Burmese custom, in the interest of social welfare, formed a
barrier to economic progress. Moneylenders would not grant loans
on land if the title was uncertain, or if they could not sell it to realize
their claims, or if they could not recover more than the original loan
as interest, or if labourers had a prior claim upon the produce.
Economic progress took precedence of social welfare; western ideas
of individual property in land were substituted for the Burmese
custom of family possession; transactions which the Burman regarded

---

[1] *Ru.SJ*, p. 115.   [2] Jardine, Note iv, p. 22.   [3] *Ru.PJ*, p. 585.

as a mortgage were construed as sales; debts were allowed to accumulate; and labourers lost their security of payment for their labour. But all these changes were implicit in the introduction of the rule of law, and this was necessary for the conduct of business on modern lines.

Although the courts were supposed to apply western law on western lines, most courts of original jurisdiction, from almost the beginning of British rule, have been presided over by Burman officers. Up to 1870 and later few were acquainted either with English or the law. For the more efficient administration of justice they were then required to pass examinations in law. This gave an advantage to candidates who 'had received some smattering of education in a government or mission school to the exclusion of the old class of hereditary and highly influential men'; but even ten years later some courts still had no copies of the Acts which the judges were expected to administer. As they 'did not understand what they learned and had little or no power of applying it',[1] these changes tended to produce uncertainty rather than efficiency; though in practice they probably had little effect in either direction and, in the courts, as in native custom, the reasonable continued to have preference over the legal.

That was well enough so long as the courts were dealing merely with Burmans. But from about 1880 Indian moneylenders, attracted into the interior by the profits of paddy cultivation, looked to the courts for the enforcement of their contracts, and judges had to pay more attention to law, and to the view that would be taken on appeal. At the same time the constitution of a provisional Chief Court of three judges in 1881, 'to the great satisfaction of the mercantile community',[2] marked a step in the direction of efficiency, carried still further by the constitution of a formal Chief Court in 1900 and the creation of a separate judicial service in 1905–6. But the judicial system became more and more the apparatus of a foreign government. In the great majority of courts in Burma the law was administered by Burmese judges and magistrates, but on the bench they were living in a different world from that in which they lived at home. It was no longer true that the judges could not apply the law, but, as the law had no roots in the community, they applied it literally, mechanically. The British lawyers on the Chief Court also applied the law mechanically because they did not know the people. It has been alleged that

[1] *RAB*, 1868–9, p. 61; 1881–2, p. 23.
[2] *RAB*, 1881–2, Intr. p. 9.

'there were no High Courts in the British Empire where the atmosphere was so unreal'.[1]

The cleavage between law and life has had many unfortunate results. One result, further noticed below, was to encourage corruption. Another result was the growth of litigation. Up to about 1870, as already noted, the people preferred to settle their disputes by arbitration, and in difficult matters would accept the decision of the circle headman. The demand for lawyers was confined to the mercantile community, European, Indian and, to a less extent, Chinese. These classes wanted lawyers who could speak English and appear in western courts. In India law was the only profession outside Government service for the unemployable surplus of the schools, and large numbers of Indian lawyers, naturally not the ablest, flocked over to Burma, giving the courts a still more alien aspect. Even in 1880 there were no facilities in Burma for the study of law and, though every little court throughout the country had a few licensed pleaders, none of them, except possibly one or two Indians, had any legal training.[2]

But conditions were already changing. The Indian moneylenders employed lawyers to conduct their cases, and Burmans had to employ lawyers in self-defence. The growth of litigation was beginning to attract attention. In 1862 the total number of cases before the courts was less than 20,000. During the next ten years it rose by only 2000; but in the following six years by more than 6000. By 1886 even in the remote hill tracts of Arakan 'the large increase of litigation' was attributed to 'the disuse of the custom of referring disputes for arbitration to the local chiefs'.[3] For many years the law remained the prerogative of Indians; as there were few Burmans with a general education sufficiently advanced to study western law, there were still no law classes and naturally few Burman lawyers. Moreover, in cases before European judges, Burman litigants preferred Indian lawyers who could speak the same language as the judge. Gradually, however, Burman lawyers swelled the crowded ranks of the profession, and the instigation of lawsuits and the employment of touts grew until legal practice became synonymous with sharp practice, while the courts and judges, though increasing in numbers almost every year, were still unable to cope with the accumulating mass of litigation. The growth of commerce stimulated the demand for lawyers, the supply

[1] Harvey, *CHI*, VI, 443.   [2] *RAB*, 1880–1, Intr. p. 12; p. 130.
[3] *RAB*, 1881–2, Intr. p. 9; 1886–7, p. 16; *BBG*, I, 500.

of lawyers stimulated the demand for lawsuits, and the supply of law-suits stimulated the demand for courts. Litigation hastened the decay of custom, the decay of custom encouraged litigation, and the courts, intended to promote efficiency and welfare, served chiefly to break down the social order that was the best guarantee of welfare and the strongest bulwark against crime.

Crime. The growth of crime during the past sixty years is one of the outstanding characters of modern Burma. We have seen that in Tenasserim the Commissioner was impressed by 'the generally peaceable and orderly habits of the people'. Again in Pegu, after the suppression of disorder consequent on the British occupation, crime diminished and the people settled down to a quiet life; dacoity became less frequent, and its former accompaniments of torture and cold-blooded murder almost entirely disappeared.[1] Gang-robbery, though not entirely unknown, was rarely committed by British subjects, and the proportion of Burmans in jail was far lower than that of any other people. In some years, as in 1872, there were waves of crime, but such years were exceptional. Then, from about 1880, there was a change for the worse.

The change may best be illustrated from Tharrawaddy which, during the present century, has been proverbially the most criminal district in Burma. Yet in 1860 it had less crime in proportion to population than any other district, and was so peaceful that a separate district magistrate was thought unnecessary. From 1861 to 1876 dacoity was regarded as practically impossible, because a gang would find no sympathy among the people.[2] For some twenty years the district, now regarded as conspicuously criminal, was just as con-spicuously peaceful. Then, in Tharrawaddy as in the rest of British Burma, something went wrong. The problem of crime in Burma seems first to have attracted attention in 1878 when, 'during the past few years there had been a large and continuous increase of crime'.[3] By 1884 this had assumed such dimensions as to call for comment by the Government of India, and the criminals were no longer from outside British territory but were local men. Dacoity was rife even in the vicinity of Rangoon. The rebellion that broke out at the time

---

[1] *BBG*, I, 509, 514; II, 57, 564.   [2] *Tharrawaddy Gazetteer*, pp. 33, 74.
[3] *RAB*, 1877–8, Intr. p. 4; *BBG*, II, 564–5. It should, however, be noted that the annual reports are inconsistent. In 1880–1, there is reported a gradual *reduction* since 1870 when violent crimes were twice as numerous (pp. 12, 22), whereas in 1881–2 there was '*again* an increase in violent crime in Rangoon and the districts around' (Summary, p. 8), and there was also 'a serious increase' in 1882–3.

of the third war gave a new impulse to disorder,[1] and from 1900 onwards the growth of crime is noticed in almost every annual report.

Crime in Upper Burma followed a like course. For some five years after the Annexation conditions were disturbed, but from 1890 Upper Burma 'enjoyed greater freedom from crime than the Province formerly known as British Burma'.[2] In 1906 there were only 16 dacoities in Upper Burma as against 84 in Lower Burma, and, including all violent crime, there were 201 cases in Upper Burma as against 729 in Lower Burma. The annual report for 1910 re-echoes that of 1890. But in 1911 Upper Burma went the same way as Lower Burma,[3] and the number of cases under the more serious heads rose by 1080 in Upper Burma as against 280 in Lower Burma. The sudden rise was probably due to a failure of the crops, but within a few years there was little to choose between them, and sometimes an increase in Upper Burma coincided with a decrease in Lower Burma. The marginal table illustrates the incidence of the most serious crime per million people.

*Murder and dacoity per million people**

(a) Lower Burma only; (b) Whole Province

Period	Murder	Dacoity
1876–80	26·5	11·6 (a)
1886–90	War and Rebellion	
1896–1900	24·8	9·5
1906–10	32·0	9·4 ⎫ (b)
1916–20	42·9	17·9 ⎬
1926–30	59·7	31·9 ⎭

* Harvey, *British Rule in Burma* (1946), p. 40.

The prevalence of crime in Burma is the more impressive if contrasted with conditions elsewhere.[4] By 1913 it was remarked that, in proportion to the population, the number of people sentenced to rigorous imprisonment in Burma was three or four times as great as in any other province of India; the jails were continually being enlarged and continually over-crowded. New jails were built, but the jail population outgrew the new accommodation. In 1910, with accommodation for rather less than 15,000 convicts, there was a jail

[1] Crosthwaite, pp. 23, 50, 54.   [2] *RAB*, 1901–2, p. 8; 1906–7, p. 16; 1911–12, p. 9.
[3] *RAB*, 1911–12, p. 43; 1918–19, p. 27.
[4] In England and Scotland, with a population of over 40 million, there are on an average about 150 murders a year; in two districts of Burma, with a combined population of less than 1 million, the murders in 1927 numbered 139. In the United States, where social ties are looser than in England, the number of cases of murder and deliberate manslaughter even in the largest cities, taken as a group, is no more than 33 per million, whereas over the whole of Burma, including the most remote and peaceful areas, there are close on 40 per million. One district alone, about the size of Devonshire and with a population of only half a million, had 87 murders in 1927, as many as there are in Chicago with 3½ million and world-wide notoriety for gangsters. *ISC*, XI, 24; *The Times*, 28 Dec., 1935.

population of over 16,000. Whipping was substituted so far as possible for imprisonment; convicts were employed on extra-mural labour on the roads and other public works and in the mines; every opportunity was taken to release well-behaved convicts on occasions of ceremonial importance and, during the war of 1914–18, many were drafted into a Labour Corps. But in 1920 'the old trouble of overcrowding, for which during the war several palliatives presented themselves, had now once more to be faced'.[1]

The growth of crime was not due to lack of efforts to suppress it. When it was first noticed in 1878 the immediate reaction of Government was to strengthen and improve the police; the police force was frequently reorganized and repeatedly enlarged. But all in vain. The population was growing rapidly, but crime grew more rapidly. Between 1900 and the outbreak of war in 1914 the population increased by about 15 %, the number of police rose from 1 for every 789 people to 1 for every 744, but crime increased by 26 %.[2] Police training schools were opened and a special detective branch was formed, but crime still increased. In 1921 it was noted that during the preceding decade the population had risen by about 9 %, but the percentage of increase in the more important forms of crime 'ranged from 31 % in the case of murder to 109 % in the case of robbery and dacoity'.[3] In the more criminal tracts the ordinary police was reinforced from time to time by 'punitive police', an addition to the local establishment of which the local residents had to bear the charges. Heavy sentences were imposed, and for certain offences rigorous imprisonment for two to seven years became almost a matter of obligation. Magistrates were multiplied and magisterial powers steadily enhanced. Ordinarily only the district magistrate had been vested with special powers to impose sentences of seven years' rigorous imprisonment, and when in 1903 these special powers were given to selected European officers, it was with some hesitation and only 'to relieve over-burdened Deputy Commissioners in the most hardworked districts';[4] thirty years later the same abnormal powers had been conferred on some 200 officers, including even some Burmese township officers, the lowest grade in general administration. Again, the ordinary law has always allowed preventive action by the taking of security or

---

[1] *RAB*, 1910–11, p. vi; 1911–12, p. 50; 1912–13, p. 26; 1920–1, p. xi.
[2] *RAB*, 1877–8, Intr. p. 4; 1910–11, p. vi; 1914–15, p. 23.
[3] *RAB*, 1920–1, pp. xi, 38.   [4] *RAB*, 1903–4, p. iii.

imprisonment in respect of reputed criminals who cannot be convicted of a specific offence. Magistrates were continually exhorted to make full use of these preventive sections, but eventually they had to be supplemented by an Habitual Offenders' Restriction Act and a Criminal Tribes Act, which rendered any portion of the general public liable to be treated as a criminal tribe.[1]

These measures under the penal law were supported by forceful executive action under the Village Act. This Act, as we have noticed, was introduced on the annexation of Upper Burma as an instrument of martial law, and reports on village administration were made annually under the head of 'police'; the village was regarded as an instrument of law and order rather than as a social unit. Under the Village Act collective penalties may be imposed on villages which fail to resist or to report on criminals; relatives and friends of suspected criminals may be deported, and villages are expected to maintain fences and to report on the movements of strangers. These powers were vigorously employed. In some years upwards of 300 villages were fined up to a total amount exceeding a lakh of rupees. Deportation was not infrequent, and in exceptional cases a whole village was removed. Headmen were required to fine villagers for omitting to maintain the village fence or to report strangers, and they were themselves fined for derelictions of duty. It may fairly be claimed that Government did everything possible to suppress crime. But it did not succeed in preventing the growth of crime.

From time to time various explanations were suggested.[2] It was often attributed to 'the passionate nature of the Burman', which might explain the prevalence of crime, but not its growth. Another suggestion was 'improved detection', though one might have thought that this would check it. A more plausible explanation was found in the greater indulgence in alcohol. The use of alcoholic liquor had been prohibited under Burmese rule, but this was impossible under British rule, as provision had to be made for the requirements of Europeans, Chinese, and Indian coolies. Another theory, which certainly cannot be accepted, was that suggested to the Simon Commission in 1931, that it was due to 'unrest following the war'. Clearly the cause lies much deeper. The abnormal criminality is a feature of British rule, which did not appear until some years after the British occupation. Up to 1880, as we have seen, the people in Lower Burma

[1] *RAB*, 1918–19, pp. ii, 24.
[2] *RAB*, 1910–11, pp. 17, 22; 1920–1, p. 38; 1887, Cmd. 4962, p. 122; *ISC*, xi, 24.

were law-abiding, and the jail population contained a remarkably small proportion of Burmans. Again, in Upper Burma there was very little crime for twenty-five years after the Annexation. In Lower Burma the growth of crime first attracted notice a few years after the opening of the Suez Canal, and it spread to Upper Burma when similar conditions began to prevail there after 1910. In Lower Burma it synchronized with a steadily increasing difficulty in the collection of the poll tax, despite measures that in some districts amounted to 'undue harshness'.[1] A review of the problem in 1921 suggested that

'in certain portions of Lower Burma, the root of the trouble is probably agrarian...the slow but steady passing of the land into the hands of non-agriculturists, especially non-resident members of this class. Agricultural instability induces a want of ballast which reacts disastrously upon the communal life. With no incentive to improve another's land and no guarantee of fixity of tenure a man is apt to find a life of crime more profitable and exciting than a bare subsistence on the balance of the profits of his labour after the non-cultivating landlord or moneylender has been satisfied.'[2]

Other factors noticed were the 'loosening of civil and religious authority and the decay or suppression of the old-fashioned amusements'. Here we would seem to be nearer to a true explanation of the growth of crime during the last thirty years in Upper Burma and sixty years in Lower Burma. In view of the fact that social disintegration, unemployment and impoverishment were all features of the same period, and all alike due to the abnormal predominance of economic forces, it seems unnecessary to look further for a cause, or to expect a cure except by the reintegration of society on a new basis.

[1] *RAB*, 1885–6, p. 54; 1911–12, p. 85.   [2] *RAB*, 1920–1, p. 38.

CHAPTER V

BURMA, 1923–1940: POLITICAL DEMOCRACY

(a) POLICY AND PRACTICE

1. ADMINISTRATIVE POLICY

DURING the early years of the present century few Europeans questioned either the benevolence or beneficence of British rule in India. Although European peoples 'rightly struggling to be free', whether in Ireland, the Balkan States or South Africa attracted Liberal sympathies, for Asia good government was thought better than self-government, and that Indians should govern themselves was only less absurd than that they should govern Europeans. But the suppression of nationalism in India gradually became more formidable, and, when Indian troops rendered good service in 1914–18, the moral fervour for the liberation of subject peoples, which from the first had been proclaimed as a major purpose of the democratic powers, found new scope in Asia. In 1917 the Government announced that the goal of British policy in India was the gradual realization of responsible government within the British Empire. At the same time forces, brought into action by the war, began to change the economic relations between East and West, leading up to the economic crisis of 1929, which signalized the end of the period dating from the Suez Canal, and the dawn of a new age in world affairs, more favourable to the autonomy of dependent peoples in the tropics.

2. BURMESE NATIONALISM

Nationalism of the modern type was a late development in Burma, not for lack of national sentiment but from ignorance of the modern world. As elsewhere in the Tropical Far East its source of inspiration was the victory of Japan over Russia, which taught the East that it might use western science to defeat the West. The stir of a new spirit was first evident in the enthusiasm aroused by the sermons and publications of a Buddhist monk who conducted a revivalist movement throughout the country from 1906 onwards, and in the foundation of numerous Young Men's Buddhist Associations (Y.M.B.A.).[1] One outcome of

[1] *RAB*, 1907–8, p. 88; 1909–10, p. xviii.

the movement was a revival of interest in the past of Burma, and a society then founded to study art, science and literature in relation to Burma and the neighbouring countries attracted a considerable Burman membership. That some Burmans were beginning to look towards Japan was manifested by the visit to Japan in 1910 of a young monk, U Ottama, who subsequently played a leading part in Burmese politics, and by the publication of an account of the Russo-Japanese War, and of an illustrated description of Japan.[1] But it was to India rather than Japan that Burmans looked for their ideas, and their current political literature came largely from India. The Y.M.B.A. movement soon developed political activities, and Government servants were warned against taking part in them. One feature of this new development was a protest against the use of footwear in the precincts of pagodas and monasteries; this protest gained such general support that Europeans had to comply with it.

Yet in 1919 the Government still regarded the political ferment as an alien importation due to 'consistent efforts by Indian agitators to capture Burman opinion'.[2] But national sentiment had never lain far below the surface, and when Burmans studied the Indian press, or sometimes listened to Indian agitators, it was only because they hoped by copying their methods to convert national sentiment into an effective political force. In 1920, when the proposals for a reformed constitution in Burma seemed less advanced than those proposed for India, the Y.M.B.A., 'which had become the principal political organization in the country' began to advocate the Indian device of non-co-operation with the Government. When the Y.M.B.A. was succeeded in 1921 by the General Council of Buddhist Associations (G.C.B.A.), the aim of Nationalist policy was formulated as Home Rule, some favouring complete independence, and non-co-operation was adopted as the most effective line of action. On the publication of the Reform scheme the more moderate members of the association decided to co-operate with Government, so far as this did not prejudice the speedy attainment of Home Rule, and formed a separate party, known from the number of those who signed its programme as the Twenty-one Party. This marked a definite stage in the progress of nationalism: the severance, if only formal, of politics from religion. Hitherto Nationalists had been linked together, nominally at least, on the basis of their common Buddhism, but the manifesto of the Twenty-one Party was Nationalist, not Buddhist; political, not

[1] *RAB*, 1914–15, p. 101.   [2] *RAB*, 1918–19, p. 39.

religious. In the more extreme nationalist party some Buddhist monks were prominent; there remained a close tie between Nationalism and Religion, and Nationalism still drew much of its strength from Buddhist sentiment; but the new policy made a wider appeal, potentially embracing all peoples in the country instead of only Buddhists. Since then there has been no division of principle between the various groups of Nationalists; all have been agreed on Home Rule, which has ordinarily been identified with independence from foreign control, and, apart from personal rivalries, they have differed only as to the method by which it may soonest be attained.[1]

3. LOCAL SELF-GOVERNMENT

We have seen that although under Burmese rule the circle was practically autonomous, under British rule it first lost its autonomy and was then broken up into villages, which were converted into instruments of rule without regard to organic social ties. Under British rule the popular self-government of Burmese times decayed, and was replaced by the machinery of a foreign legal system, unable to control the anti-social forces which it liberated, and favouring the decline rather than the growth of local self-government. But the development of commerce gradually raised new problems of urban administration. For many years the towns, left to the care of local officers, were left to look after themselves. At length sanitation began to compel attention. Even in Rangoon the people still resorted for their necessary occasions to the surrounding waste. With the felling of scrub for fuel this practice became so unpleasant that public latrines were contemplated;[2] those using them were to be taxed, and those not using them were to be taxed more heavily, while the sweepers were to make strangers use them at a fee of one pie a head. But this plan was too costly, and it was thought sufficient to forbid the people to clear jungle round the town. In Moulmein, after fifty years of British rule, 'attempts to introduce efficient conservancy and other measures for the health of the town had only recently been made'. In Akyab, ten years later, there was still 'no system of removing the night soil'.[3] In Pegu, thirty years after it had been conquered, only in two towns, Rangoon and Bassein, had there been any attempt at scavenging and water supply, and only two, Rangoon

---

[1] *ISC*, xi, 25, 267, 273.
[2] *Syriam Gazetteer*, p. 171.   [3] *RAB*, 1877–8, p. 77; 1884–5, p. 66.

and Toungoo, were lit at night. Meanwhile, with the clearing of the scrub jungle round Rangoon, the streets became the only public convenience, and 'the back drainage spaces had long been a disgrace to the town'.[1]

Under purely official rule these matters were neglected and, apparently, unrecognized. Not until municipal institutions were introduced in 1874, at the instance of the Government of India, did the state of affairs attract notice. The formation of municipal committees, including members nominated to represent the people, stimulated interest in local administration, enabled Government officials to avail themselves of local knowledge, and provided them with local funds to do what they thought necessary. But it did not help the people to get what they might want. In 1882, again at the instance of the Government of India, arrangements were made to increase the number of municipalities, and to introduce the principle of election. Hopes were expressed that in Rangoon sanitary needs would 'receive constant and careful attention at the hands of the elected committee'. The prospect of managing their own affairs seems to have been generally welcome in the towns where this privilege was conceded, and 'for the most part the townspeople, especially the Burmese, took a hearty interest in the elections'.[2]

Yet it is now the general opinion that local self-government in Burma has proved a failure. In 1915, 'in view of the lack of success of the elective system...committees were ordinarily nominated, and only 13 of the 46 included elected members'. The elections 'evoked no interest' and 'such work as was accomplished was almost wholly due to the efforts of the official Presidents, Vice-Presidents, and Members'. In Moulmein, the headquarters of Tenasserim, after eighty years of British rule, the elective committee was suspended for incompetence. In 1921, by way of preparing for constitutional reforms, officials were withdrawn from municipal committees, and subsequent reports show a progressive increase in expenditure and decline in efficiency; by 1927 expenditure had risen from Rs. 58 lakhs to Rs. 70 lakhs, and the number of committees classed as unsatisfactory or worse had risen from 43 to 95 %. Rural self-government on modern lines dates only from 1921 and has given as little satisfaction. How is it that, with so promising a start, municipal government fifty years later could be pronounced a failure? The official view

---

[1] *RAB*, 1880–1, Intr. p. 27; 1881–2, p. 127.
[2] *RAB*, 1881–2, p. 127; 1884–5, p. 17.

was that 'the principle of self-government is an exotic plant, and the character and temperament of the people are not favourable to its speedy growth'.[1]

But if we look into the matter more closely, this explanation seems inadequate. We have seen that under British rule the organic structure of Burmese local administration was broken down; for many years, under a system that attempted little beyond the maintenance of law and order, local affairs were neglected, and municipal institutions and the elective principle were adopted as devices for repairing this neglect. The committees were expected to do and pay for things they did not want, and they represented sectional communities which had little in common except a dislike of taxation; naturally they preferred to do nothing. The only people who wanted most of the things that municipal committees were expected to provide were the official members, and these rarely stayed long enough in any one place to undertake and carry through reforms. But economic forces were active all the time in all aspects of social life. These conditions were not confined to municipalities; they obtained also in small towns and rural areas under executive rule, and with similar results. On the other hand, popular self-government in the villages, so far as it was possible, was reasonably successful in giving the people what they wanted. Let us examine these points severally.

Municipal Self-government. The failure of municipal administration might have been prophesied when the elective principle was first introduced. Projects of forming new municipal institutions with nominated members had already met with opposition. One town, Shwaydoung, protested that 'if we had a municipality we should be obliged to pay grievous taxes like people in Rangoon and Prome, and we would be prevented from tying up goats under our houses'. (The reference to goats suggests that the protest was raised by Indians rather than Burmans.) The case of Yandoon is even more instructive.[2] Yandoon was the chief purely Burmese market town in British Burma, and organic social life survived. Here, without municipal institutions and at a time when, under government officials, sanitation was neglected, the people 'combined among themselves to carry out a regular system of night conservancy'. But they objected to a municipal committee and, significantly, Government yielded to their protest.

Rights along the river front were disputed between Government

---

[1] *ISC*, XI, 422, 442, 454, 466, 487.
[2] *RAB*, 1880–1, p. 32; 1881–2, p. 127.

and the people; local opinion was so strong that even a nominated committee might have outvoted the official President, and Government thought better not to run the risk. 'Subsequent experience showed that...local interests would have benefited if the action of the local magistrate had been controlled by an intelligent committee of the townsfolk.' Here the people of Yandoon were managing their own affairs in their own way better than local affairs in other towns were being managed by officials; they objected to municipal institutions lest these should put an end to self-government, and Government acquiesced for fear that such institutions, even with a nominated committee, might allow too much self-government, and 'perhaps end in the committee's outvoting the resident magistrate'. And on the matters in dispute the people were right and the local official wrong. It is not strange that people welcomed the promise of electing representatives to manage their affairs, and that they became apathetic on finding that election gave them no greater power of self-government than nomination.

The Government displayed its zeal for self-government by calling on the Government Advocate, who knew nothing of the country, to draw up 'a complete set of by-laws, applicable so far as possible to all municipalities'.[1] These machine-made rules were translated into Burmese, largely unintelligible, and at that time few except European officials knew enough English to understand them. They provided mainly for things that the people did not want, and often in a manner least likely to commend them. One or two illustrations must suffice. Vaccination was introduced into Burma within a year or two of the occupation of Tenasserim. The practice of inoculation against smallpox had already been introduced about 1800 and had spread rapidly.[2] Presumably the people would have taken just as kindly to vaccination if it had proved more effective. But, after fifty years, one explanation for its slow progress was 'the frequent failure of the lymph supplied'. Another reason was that the inoculators were Burmese and the vaccinators Indians—it was cheaper and less trouble to employ Indians than to train Burmans. 'Few medical officers understood Burmese well enough to explain the superior advantages of vaccination.' Naturally the people 'preferred to adhere to the practice to which they were accustomed and in which they had most faith'.[3] Even in Rangoon the honorary magistrates petitioned that vaccination

---

[1] *RAB*, 1880–1, p. 37. [2] *BBG*, I, 526.
[3] *RAB*, 1877–8, Intr. p. 13; 1881–2, p. 128; 1886–7, p. 59.

should not be made compulsory. Until well into the present century the lymph still gave unsatisfactory results and the people had greater faith in inoculation;[1] but the committees had to pay the cost of the Indian vaccinators.

Again, as already noticed, the Government needed hospitals for prisoners and police cases, but did not try to make them attractive to the public. A report of 1869 explains that 'at present the entire staff of the several Dispensaries is composed of Natives of India and, with a difference of caste, creed and language, it is impossible to expect that the benefits of scientific medicine will be brought home to the people'. They continued to believe in their own medical system, as they do to the present day;[2] but the committees had to pay for the upkeep of the hospitals.

Not infrequently, as in Yandoon, the local officials made mistakes, wasting money, for example, on laying out markets in unsuitable localities, or on buildings of an unsuitable type.[3] By-laws require that meat stalls in bazaars shall have fly-proof doors and windows. These are costly and, on the approved pattern, dark, damp and hot. The butcher wants to attract custom, the purchasers want to see what they are buying, and the fly-proof doors and windows are kept permanently open. The shop with open doors and windows attracts more custom, and, against economic forces, official regulations unsupported by public opinion are of no avail. Quite possibly the meat keeps better with more light and air. Certainly the people do not want these things; but the committees must spend money on them. 'Self-government' after this fashion does not give the people what they want.

Again, though more people now know English, and the Burmese version of the by-laws may possibly be less incomprehensible, the whole western machinery of self-government, with formal agenda and resolutions and legal regulations, does not work in a way that the public understands; even if some of the members appreciate what they are doing, they do not carry the people with them. The East has its own democratic machinery which one can see at work in Karen Christian conventions. In the Burma volume of evidence before the Royal Commission on Labour of 1931 there is an instructive account of the manner in which a public meeting of Telugu coolies achieved an

---

[1] *RAB*, 1904–5, p. 65; 1907–8, pp. xiv, 76; 1912–13, p. 85.
[2] *RAB*, 1868–9, p. 117; *CISM*, Resolution, and p. 22.
[3] See e.g. *Ru.SJ*, 1880, p. 94.

unanimous decision.[1] Official municipalities do not work on the lines of oriental democracy. If 'such work as was accomplished was almost wholly due to the efforts of the official members', it is because only the officials wanted such work done, and because they alone understood how to manipulate the machinery. To the people in general the municipal committee was a western device for doing what Government wanted.

Moreover, taking the whole community in any town, there was very little that it did want. By the time that municipal institutions were adopted, the urban population was already divided into separate Burmese, Indian, Chinese and European communities, with very different and often conflicting interests, different ideas of welfare, and few wants in common. There was indeed little that all wanted, except to avoid taxation, and on this point all the non-officials would usually (and vainly) oppose the official members. Self-government was impossible because there was no self to govern itself. Inevitably in such circumstances, the non-official members were for the most part men who on various grounds wanted to stand well with the officials, or saw a chance of making money.

The pressure of economic forces may perhaps be demonstrated most easily in Rangoon, where municipal institutions worked under the most favourable conditions and with most success. Here there was a considerable European community, well represented on the committee, together with the most enlightened and westernized Burmese, Indians and Chinese, under the chairmanship of a high Government official, who held the post as a whole-time job and usually for some years. One of the most urgent problems was to safeguard the health of the town, and the whole country, from the dangers consequent on a large floating coolie population. This was an old problem. In 1872 there were barracks capable of accommodating 500 coolies. In 1881 the density of the population over the bulk of the business portion of the city was double that of Liverpool, the most crowded town in the United Kingdom. In 1891 the Census Report notices the fearfully high mortality among the Indian immigrants; 'crowded together in insanitary lodging houses, they swell the death rate of our chief town'. Thousands lived 'in the veriest hovels in the suburban swamps, with the most disgusting filth piled up in heaps or fermenting in pools at their very doors'. Rangoon, it was said, owes most of its high death rate to the imported coolies. Yet in 1931

[1] Smeaton, p. 205; RCLI, x, Pt I, p. 25.

the Royal Commission on Labour found things even worse. In a room without windows, ventilation passages, or sanitary arrangements, licensed for nine coolies, there would be forty to fifty men with one or two women. Many others slept in the streets, so tightly packed that there was barely room for a wheelbarrow to pass.[1] These were the conditions under the eyes, or one might say, under the nose of the officials busy in the Secretariat, drafting model by-laws and designing plans for sanitary meat stalls. The methods of importing coolies had been criticised in 1841; in 1880 the Government had declined to intervene, remarking that it could not import coolies 'more cheaply', though taking steps to make the cost of importation cheaper still. In the absence of any common social will, economic progress took precedence of social welfare, and in 1931 the firms chiefly concerned could not imagine any better system, representing that any change would not only 'increase the miller's difficulties but also the cost of his labour bill, and he cannot afford to do anything that will make it more difficult than it is at present to meet the competition of other rice-producing countries'.[2]

Outside Rangoon municipal administration was still less efficient, but its defects remained for the most part unnoticed. Even as regards overcrowding, the abuses, as suggested in the Census Report for 1911,[3] were not so bad in Rangoon as in some towns and even in some villages in the surrounding districts. People will not of their own volition do or pay for what they do not want, and the local officials who managed municipal affairs rarely stayed long enough in any one place to know what it needed, or how to do what it needed, and never stayed long enough to carry through constructive measures that would bring economic forces under control. Despite efforts to limit transfers and changes of officers[4] it was impossible to achieve continuity of tenure, and transient officials were unable to keep pace with economic changes; they could not know what was happening. The law was always at the service of private interest, but there was no one to set it in motion in the public interest, and it helped to promote and not to prevent the working of economic forces. Popular representation on local bodies increased the efficiency of local government, but 'self-government', despite the liberal ideas by which it was inspired, served merely to induce a mixed community

[1] *RCLI*, Report, p. 434; Census, 1872, p. 13; Census, 1891, p. 177.
[2] *RCLI*, x, Pt I, p. 173.   [3] Census, 1911, p. 21.
[4] *RAB*, 1880–1, p. 8.

which had no common wants, to acquiesce in raising money for things that the Government wanted and the people did not want, and it was imposed on them often, if not usually, against their will. Self-government did not fail because it was an 'exotic plant'; it came to be regarded as a failure, but it never failed because it was never tried.

Rural Self-government. But matters were no better under the direct rule of Government officials in small towns and rural areas outside the jurisdiction of municipal committees. Rural District Councils were set up in 1884 at the instance of the Government of India, but executive rule was regarded by the Burma Government as more efficient, and this experiment in rural self-government on western lines ended with an epidemic of infantile mortality among the new-born councils. The district officer remained solely responsible for rural welfare. From early days district officers had at their disposal various local funds, and in 1865, at the instance of the Government of India, a cess of 5 % (raised subsequently to 10 %) on the land revenue in Lower Burma was levied to provide amenities in rural areas. But, as in the municipalities, the money was spent on what the Government or the local official thought the people ought to want and not on what they wanted. With the development of trade there sprang up numerous small towns which could not afford municipal institutions. Most of the local officer's work lay in these towns, which naturally got most of the money; though raised in the villages it was spent in the towns. As in municipal areas, and for the same reasons, much of the money was spent in ways that the people disapproved, and much of it was wasted.

Control over lands and buildings is a first condition of urban sanitation, and a few remarks on this matter will serve to indicate the degree of efficiency attained under purely official rule. In 1883 rights over town lands and the mode of their acquisition had for several years engaged the attention of the local Government.[1] The matter continued to engage attention, and this prolonged gestation eventually gave birth to the Town and Village Lands Act of 1898. The present writer spent the first two years of his service as subdivisional officer in Toungoo District, where thirteen places were notified as 'railway towns' under this Act, and no one could build in them without previous approval of the site and building. In 1903 there were piles of applications from each town; some of the stacks, containing hundreds of applications, stood higher than the office table. It had

[1] *RRA*, 1882–3, Resolution, para. 6; *RAB*, 1892–3, p. 5; 1897–8, p. 30.

been impossible to dispose of them for lack of instructions. Some towns had been notified without any boundary on the north and south and, to judge by the notifications in the official *Gazette*, ran parallel to the railway line the whole way from Rangoon to Mandalay. During two years five different Deputy Commissioners held charge of the district. Although they got the notifications rectified, their attempts to obtain orders as to procedure were in vain. Meanwhile the wiser and bolder people were building houses without sanction, presumably paying the local surveyor a small fee to keep silent. The last Deputy Commissioner decided to deal with the matter by the light of common sense, without waiting further for instructions; but apparently the proceedings were set aside as irregular, as the cases were said to be still pending two years later.

The matter of town lands came to my attention again as Deputy Commissioner of Myaungmya, one of the busy districts in the delta, from 1915 to 1919. Meanwhile in 1908 a Sanitary Commissioner had been appointed and, possibly at his instance, town plans had been prepared. Some of these plans showed nothing but the main roads, leaving large blocks that would inevitably become congested. Subsequently all plans had to be passed by the Sanitary Commissioner; one could not hope to obtain his sanction within two years and if, as usual, he wanted changes, the matter would take four or five years—if it was not forgotten. The Sanitary Commissioner knew nothing of the people or, as a rule, of local circumstances, and often wished to impose conditions that were quite impracticable and would have led to worse congestion; he would require large vacant spaces on land round the market worth hundreds or perhaps thousands of rupees for a few square feet. His ideal, the Divisional Commissioner suggested, was 'a wilderness of latrines'. A little later in another district, Pegu, there was a set of town plans that the Sanitary Commissioner had approved. But they had been drawn up in the local record office according to a model plan in the *Manual*, and without relation to conditions on the ground, so that they were of no use except as a source of income to revenue subordinates, who could threaten proceedings where the house sites were not in accordance with the plans.

At the same time the Government was losing revenue through defects in the system of assessment. In 1927 a special officer was appointed to deal with the revision of town land taxation, 'long overdue because district officers had neither the necessary time nor expert knowledge'.[1] But that was merely one of the simpler problems of urban administration; it is much simpler to raise revenue than to provide for welfare. Control over land and buildings is a first condition of urban sanitation; the towns were the centre of interest in local administration, and sanitation one of the most urgent problems. But while plans were being drawn and redrawn, and regulations elaborated and multiplied, the land was daily growing more valuable, buildings were being erected, new vested interests were accumulating, sanitary conditions were deteriorating, and improvements were becoming more difficult and costly. Necessarily the whole process created new opportunities for subordinates to make money, and allowed the haphazard oppression of those who did not pay enough. Only in one matter was there any notable difference between administration by local officials and municipal committees; under official rule the accounts complied better with the Accounts Rules. An official had practical experience in complying with regulations as part of his everyday routine and, unlike the non-official Commissioners, was liable to make good defalcations. In one district the Commissioners were called on to show cause against recouping certain losses. 'We would resign', they said, 'and you would get no one else to take our place.' But book-keeping is no cure for corruption. In Myaungmya one of the most respectable inhabitants was a retired district cess fund overseer, whose pay had never exceeded £60 a year, but who had managed to maintain a son at Cambridge.

Thus municipal committees were not exceptional in respect of maladministration. Both under municipal and official rule, welfare measures on western lines, applied by western methods with no other sanction than the penalties imposed by law, and with no one to apply them but a rapid succession of district officials, were in general ineffective and unwelcome; they were regarded, not without reason, as oppressive, and tended to excite discontent and disaffection. An official was no better able as Deputy Commissioner than as president of a local municipal committee, to give effect to western ideas of welfare, or to hinder the unceasing activity of anti-social forces.

Village Self-government. The ill-success of municipal administration along western lines is the more striking in contrast with the comparative success of self-government in village life. All the time the people were in fact managing their own affairs, so far as circumstances allowed, with reasonable honesty, efficiency and economy.

[1] *ISC*, xi, 177.

Their opportunities were limited. In some things a village cannot act alone, but any combined action between villages became impossible with the break up of the circle. The village contributions to the district cess fund were intended to provide material amenities, such as in riverine villages a landing stage, sheltered from rain and sun. But the villages had no say in the spending of the money; much of it went to build and maintain rest houses for inspecting officers on tour and, if the people wanted landing stages, they had to build their own or go without. Many villages, as already noticed, were unable to provide a site for a monastery as a centre of their social life, or even adequate living space for the inhabitants. Where, as over large parts of Lower Burma, the population was migratory, a crowd of strangers could not act together; and in villages with Indian or Chinese moneylenders as shopkeepers or landowners, the division of interests on racial lines prevented common action. Yet villages more happily circumstanced provided for their own requirements in their own way with little or no help from district officers.

The anti-social effect of economic forces in mixed communities was very strikingly illustrated in Toungoo District. Under Burmese rule, and also under British rule until the opening of the railway in 1885, the river had been the main high road, and along the banks there was a succession of small towns and large villages which had long enjoyed organic social life. They had their monasteries and schools, rest houses, open spaces, wells, tanks, paths, bridges and so on; there was a community with a life of its own governing itself in its own way, like the community in Yandoon which attracted notice as a pioneer in modernizing its conservancy arrangements. But trade shifted from the river to the railway, and the new railway towns, with a mixture of Indians, Chinese and Burmans were far richer. Yet in the two richest towns, although the roads were reported as newly completed by the Public Works Department in 1901,[1] it was impossible a year later to get from the district bungalow to the bazaar during the rains except along the railway line; in the more important of the two, shortly afterwards constituted a subdivisional headquarters, the mud along the road was almost knee-deep within twenty yards of the bungalow. One finds everywhere a similar contrast between the provision of local amenities by official and by local agency. Officials try to provide western amenities that Government approves, and often fail; the people try to provide the amenities that they appreciate, and often with success.

[1] *RAB*, 1900–1, p. 48.

Some villages run their own bazaar. In the delta a few small towns have been lighted by electricity without official help or supervision; the people wanted to light up the pagoda and incidentally provided electric light for private houses—that is not the way district officers or municipal committees go to work. Where there is an organic community capable of common wants, it will try to meet those wants. That is self-government, and it is no exotic plant in Burma. But to try and make people do of their own accord what they do not want to do, is neither self-government nor common sense.

Popular Control. It is not strange then that, even after fifty years, municipal institutions failed to take root in Burma. But the *Report on Indian Constitutional Reforms* recommended that as part of the project of introducing responsible government 'there should be as far as possible complete popular control in local bodies and the largest possible independence for them of outside control'. By way of complying with this direction the official presidents and members were withdrawn. Of thirty-seven presidents in 1921 only one remained in 1923, and the number of *ex officio* members was reduced from 172 to 6. Thus the committees were left to do what the Government expected of them with no one on the committee who wanted to do it. At the same time arrangements were made 'for more frequent and comprehensive inspections of the accounts' and 'for greater scrutiny and more efficient audit'. There was also 'an important change in the efficiency and standard of audit', which was no longer to be confined 'to the formal examination of authorities and of rules', but to be conducted with a view to ascertaining whether rate-payers were 'getting the best value for their money'. The officials who had formerly been members of the committees were now required to supervise their work, and were perhaps rather more critical of defects than when they had been responsible for the work themselves.[1] Doubtless municipal administration was less efficient than before, but the recommendation by the Royal Commission on Labour that Government should exercise greater control over it[2] would have been justified at any time since municipal institutions were first introduced.

In accordance with the policy of extending popular control in local bodies, the Rural Self-Government Act of 1921 created district councils.[3] But these were as artificial as the municipal committees and at least as ineffective, and for the same reasons. Despite all

[1] *ISC*, XI, 245, 454, 459, 470.　　[2] *RCLI*, Report, p. 436.
[3] *ISC*, XI, 424, 431, 441.

experience the village was neglected. Provision was made for circle boards and village committees; but the circle boards remained inoperative, and the village committee had no powers or functions. The chief matters delegated to the district councils comprised vernacular education, public health, sanitation and vaccination, and the maintenance of dispensaries for men and cattle. 'It was not unjustly claimed', we are told, 'that these local bodies either have had, or may have, transferred to them almost every aspect of administration affecting the people in their daily lives.' But the councils had no organic unity; the members could not understand the elaborate western regulations by which their activities were controlled; even in matters that interested them, such as education, their freedom of action was restricted; in some matters, such as public works, the necessary machinery was lacking; and in matters of sanitation and public health 'their apathy was a reflection of the attitude of the general public'. 'The only chance of improvement', it is suggested, 'is to have an efficient executive'. But an 'efficient executive' doing what the people do not want to do, is hardly 'self-government'.

How far was there in fact any real transfer of local administration to the people? How far will people, who mistrust western medicine and other foreign welfare measures, do or pay for what they do not want? How far can any system on that basis be termed self-government? And how far will self-government on such lines counteract the ceaseless pressure of economic forces? The answer to all these questions may be found in the history of the coolie barracks in Rangoon. In Rangoon the Royal Commission on Labour was 'struck by the contrast presented between the thought and foresight devoted to technical and commercial aspects of industry, and the comparative neglect of the labour aspects'.[1] But that is merely one instance of the contrast between economic progress and social welfare in modern Burma. The village, so far as circumstances allow, still manages its own affairs in its own way. But, in general, economic forces have prevailed over social interests, and it is only by bringing them under control in the interest of social welfare that self-government can be adapted to the requirements of the modern world. And this implies nothing less than the reintegration of society.

[1] *RCLI*, Report, p. 442.

4. NATIONAL SELF-GOVERNMENT

The problems of national self-government were essentially the same as those of local self-government, but more difficult and complex. The four main sections Europeans, Indians, Chinese and Burmans had nothing in common but the economic motive, the desire for material advantage. In some economic matters the foreign sections had conflicting interests, but they all had a common interest in economic progress and in the promotion of commerce and industry, and they were content that the Government should maintain law and order and leave everything else to the play of economic forces. The leaders of this group were the heads of the large business concerns, whose shareholders knew nothing of Burma except as the place where they had invested capital, and cared nothing so long as their investments were secure and profitable. Some few among the mercantile community might have a wider vision and a more sympathetic view, but very few knew anything of Burma outside the mainly Indian city of Rangoon, and in any case they were the agents of shareholders whose attitude to Burma was purely economic. That was the attitude also of the Indian and Chinese sojourners, down to the humblest coolie who came to Burma for a few months to earn higher wages than he could get at home. All these interests may be summed up as capitalist. For Burmans, on the other hand, the country was the home of their national traditions and aspirations. There were cross-currents, racial, political and economic, but the main issue in political affairs was the conflict between Capitalism and Nationalism, with European business men and Burmans as the protagonists on either side, and with the Indian and Chinese sections generally in loose alliance with the Europeans.

Thus in 1917, when Parliament accepted the principle that in India government should be made responsible to the people, there was in Burma no homogeneous people to which it could be made responsible. Among the various groups the Europeans alone possessed a working knowledge of western institutions, and not only were these few in number but their common organs, the Chamber of Commerce and the Trades' Association, representing western capitalist production, 'regarded themselves as charged with special commercial interests only'.[1] As such they were necessarily anti-social, because not related to the welfare of society as a whole but merely to the economic

[1] 1920, Cmd. 746, p. 17; Craddock, p. 123.

interests of a single section. On the other hand the Burmans with their large numerical majority lacked both experience and education. The then Governor has vividly depicted the Burman share in modern Burma. 'Her military forces, her military police, are not Burmans, her prison warders, her clerks, her post office, her labour force are largely manned by the Indian races. In her capital, Rangoon, there are 190,000 Indians, or nearly 60 %. Her captains of industry and her richest men are almost entirely non-Burmese.'[1] Their education stopped short at the threshold of the modern world. Although a hundred years had elapsed since the death of Ricardo and the birth of Darwin, it did not include economics or biology. Practically no one had read any history; in the leading Government school it was not taught.[2] Hitherto the political energy latent in the common religious and national sentiment had found its chief outlet in waste and destruction, extravagant festivities and futile insurrections; now, at a word, it was expected to take a major part in constructing the political machinery of a new social order. With good reason the Government of Burma expressed doubts whether the country was fit for responsible government.

Two alternatives were possible. One was to make a bold stand on the principle of Nationalism as the only means available for dominating economic forces; to provide Burma with a national system of defence, to build up Burmese enterprise in industry and commerce, as had formerly been attempted by King Mindon, and to bring the people into cultural relations with the modern world, as was the policy in the neighbouring kingdom of Siam under its own rulers. Along those lines the Government of Burma might have looked to achieve more than native rulers because of its better understanding of the modern world. It would have seemed possible to capture the imagination of the people and to create a new environment, a common society to which a modern government might be responsible. The other alternative was to introduce the forms and machinery of western government, with such precautions as would leave economic forces supreme. The latter alternative was chosen.

In the *Report on Indian Constitutional Reforms*, 'the problem of Burma's evolution was set aside for separate and future consideration'.[3] The Burma Government believed that the people had always been 'content to pursue their private callings and leave affairs of State alone, secure in the sincerity and impartiality of their British officers'.

---

[1] Craddock, p. 128.   [2] *CII*, p. 61.   [3] *ISC*, XI, 7.

Political strife was deprecated as 'so foreign to the nature of the people, and so inimical to their true interests'.[1] 'Never', the Governor wrote subsequently, 'was a country and its people more untimely ripped from the womb of political future progress than Burma and the Burmese, when Mr Montague with his magic midwifery from across the Bay of Bengal started to disturb them from their placid contentment.'[2] The Government accordingly submitted proposals in line with its views on political advance. The discussion on the proposals caused delay and, under the guidance of a few leaders, Burmans advanced from the extreme of acquiescence to the extreme of self-assertion. Their national sentiment, long perverted and suppressed, broke out in a violent attack of Nationalism, and there was 'a rapid development of political activity among the people which few, if any, of those most conversant with the psychology of the people ever predicted, or could have predicted'. 'Great dissatisfaction was caused in Burma by the delay, and by the belief that a smaller measure of advance was to be granted than was already in force in India in the shape of Dyarchy. Two deputations were sent to England, political agitation was intensified, organized boycott was freely used, and the demands of the extremists rose from Dyarchy to Dominion Home Rule.'[3] These demonstrations were accepted as proof that Burma was no less fit for responsible government than India, and an 'analogous constitution' was promised. The Burma Government thereupon took the line that 'there was nothing further to do than to make the best of a bad business, and go through all the processes for a new constitution'.[4] Burma was fitted up with the machinery of responsible government on the fashionable model of western democracy as applied under the system of Dyarchy in India; this however was restricted to Burma proper, excluding the Shan States, Karenni and the Tribal Hills, long politically associated with Burma though ethnologically distinct, and, incidentally, containing valuable mineral resources.

On this plan the Governor was given an Executive Council comprising two Members nominated by the Governor, and two Ministers selected from among the members of the Legislative Council, which was enlarged and transformed. The functions of government were divided into two categories: Reserved and Transferred. The reserved subjects, comprising defence, law and order, finance and revenue were administered by the two Members; the other functions, sometimes

[1] *RAB*, 1918–19, p. vii; 1920, Cmd. 746, p. 30.   [2] Craddock, p. 109.
[3] *RAB*, 1920–1, p. xxv; *ISC*, xi, 7.   [4] Craddock, p. 118.

comprehensively described as 'nation-building' were administered
by the two Ministers. The Legislative Council in its new form consisted of 103 members (79 elected, 2 *ex officio* and 22 nominated,
including 13 officials and 8 non-officials).[1] A system of communal and
special constituencies was adopted, so as to provide for the representation of interests that might otherwise have been excluded. Rural areas
were given a substantial majority among the elected members lest
the interests of the country at large should be 'subordinated to the
interests of a vocal minority which though representing the views of
an advanced section, mostly young politicians, would not voice the
sentiments of the conservative element among the people'. The
adoption of the village as the primary electoral unit was rejected on
the ground that the headman must remain an executive officer of
Government.[2] The franchise was based on household suffrage at the
age of eighteen; sex was no disqualification.

Thus, in a country where few had ever voted even for a local
council, where the urban councils were regarded as 'an experiment
not justified by success' and self-government as an exotic plant
unsuited to the character and temperament of the people, the first
tentative measure in the direction of responsible government bestowed
the franchise on boys who in England, or anywhere in Europe, were
regarded as still too immature to vote, and on a considerable proportion of the women. Various reasons were assigned for this astounding venture. The official explanation was that no qualifications by age,
property or education could be devised; simplicity welcomed it as
evidence of faith in liberal ideals; cynics ascribed it to petulance,
'making the best of a bad job' or to astuteness—if the people do not
like bureaucracy, let them have democracy in full measure to disillusion them. The kindest explanation is that the Government
trusted, as it believed, the well-merited affection of the 'conservative
element' against the disaffection of a few pernicious agitators. It is
a comfortable and flattering belief that the people like foreign rule,
and apparently invincible. In Tenasserim in 1826 'every one hailed
with delight the certainty of being considered and protected as
British subjects' and 'received with horror the possibility of being
again made subject to the authority of their old masters'. In
Arakan we were greeted as allies until the people gathered that we
meant to stay. But in both provinces we soon had to suppress

---

[1] *ISC*, XI, 249 ff.
[2] 1920, Cmd. 746, pp. 13, 35, 36.

formidable insurrections.[1] In 1852 Dalhousie believed that Lower Burma would 'hail the substitution of any dominion for the savage oppression of the Burmese Government', but pacification was not completed until 1860.[2] Again in 1886 the Viceroy reported that the British force was welcomed as a deliverance from past and existing evils, and as a prelude to the establishment of British rule for which the people evinced a genuine desire. This view was based on reports from civil officers accompanying the expedition who had no doubt that the people would 'soon be as peaceful and loyal subjects as those in Lower Burma'.[3] But within a few months 'it had become evident that a considerable minority of the people, to say the least, did not want us', and this was emphasized by a rebellion in Lower Burma.[4]

'The Mandalay campaign', said a prominent civilian, 'was undertaken with a light heart in the belief that the people of Upper Burma would welcome us with open arms. Events have proved how ill-founded the belief was. While our army was far away north, on the Irrawaddy, a real campaign was being prepared for us in the low country. The people do not want us any more than they did thirty years ago. They rose to throw off the yoke, now they are still carrying on a guerilla warfare against us.'[5]

Finally, however, the people came to acquiesce in British rule, and for some years their natural dislike of foreign ways was tempered by increasing material prosperity. But it remained latent, and during the present century there have been petty local risings every few years. Their sympathies were clearly apparent to anyone whose official position allowed him to move inconspicuously among the people and overhear their remarks. In Upper Burma, for some twenty years, the people were about as well content as is possible under foreign rule. Men of middle age still bore the tattoo mark indicating the regiment or group in which they had been liable to compulsory service, and the irksome customs and various abuses swept away by British rule were a living memory; the new market for cotton and other produce and the introduction of groundnut put money in the pockets of the people, and their social system had not yet been seriously corroded by economic forces. As formerly in the older province, men welcomed their new freedom and the protection against arbitrary authority given by the rule of law. Yet so far back as 1907, long before they had come into contact with modern nationalism, one could hear complaints that they had to work so much harder than

[1] *SL*, p. 4; *BBG*, i, 481, 483; ii, 14, 382, 691.
[2] 1852–3, Cmd. 1608, pp. 48, 49.   [3] 1886, Cmd. 4614, p. 265; 4887, p. 15.
[4] Crosthwaite, pp. 13, 14, 103, 104.   [5] Smeaton, p. 3.

before; they pitied 'the little king whom the foreigners had carried off into captivity'; and a boy, tending cattle in the jungle, would chant, 'It is not fit, it is not fit, that foreigners should rule the royal Golden Land'. In Lower Burma also, even before the dawn of Nationalism, an old man at the pagoda would regret that the people were 'stifled with *kalas* (foreigners)'; younger men would tell how they had to dress as half-castes in European trousers in order to secure a job; a knot of villagers discussing the comparative merits of British and Burmese rule would admit that 'it is cooler now, but, like the soil under that water-stand, rotten'. The people valued their national customs, traditions and religion, and, when things went wrong, felt they would have gone better under Burmese rule. In their eyes things were going wrong. There was increasing resentment of Indian moneylenders and landlords, and of Indian competition as tenants and agricultural labourers; vaccination, plague precautions, veterinary regulations and other welfare measures stimulated discontent, and the townsfolk at least saw only too clearly that the 'richest men were almost entirely non-Burmese'. That was the 'placid contentment' among the major element of the public, when a Government, committed to the maintenance of British rule, was nominally made to share its responsibilities with the numerical majority including lads of eighteen. People did not even have the trouble of getting registered, for all were entered automatically on the roll, and the vote was no more highly valued for being made so cheap.

The new constitution undermined village administration,[1] the basis of executive authority, without providing any substitute, and those few (including the present writer) who protested that it would be necessary to restore order with machine-guns were amply justified when, within less than ten years, the most serious rebellion since 1886 broke out, involving military operations over a great part of the country, together with internment camps for thousands of prisoners. But Government had the guns, the Europeans had the money, and it was thought safe to let the people have the vote. The plan, like the municipal institutions, tried to get the people of their own accord to do what they did not want to do, while leaving undone what they wanted. Naturally the results were very much the same as in local self-government. From the outset the Government was faced 'with an opposition almost altogether Burmese in race and completely Burmese in sympathy'.[2] The desire of the opposition was 'that ample facilities

[1] *RAB*, 1930-1, p. 26.   [2] *ISC*, xi, 268.

should be afforded for the education of Burmans so as to fit them for advance in all spheres; that the public services and public bodies should be manned by Burmans; that indigenous economic and industrial development should be fostered, and the economic condition of the masses improved; that foreign exploitation should be curtailed, and posts in the services for which Burmans were not yet fitted should be reduced; that funds should be diverted from "law and order" departments to "nation-building" departments, and that money should be spent in providing credit facilities for agriculturalists, rather than on buildings and roads'. The contrary policy of the ministerial parties may be summarized as a colourless and comprehensive negative; 'they were not actuated in common by any definite forward policy. Their general attitude was one of support for law and order, the maintenance of administrative, educational and economic principles and standards, and opposition to extravagance.'[1]

In mere numbers, the Government was in 'a perpetual and hopeless minority'. But political inexperience and personal rivalries hindered the opposition from using its numerical strength to the best advantage, and the Government could always recruit ministers, even from among the nationalists. The ministers were highly paid, even by European standards; very few Burmans could earn a tenth, and few even a hundredth part of the salary of a minister, and on these terms there was no lack of candidates and it was possible to witness 'the somewhat unusual spectacle of opposition by a party to a Government on which its own leaders were ministers'. Apart from groups or individuals detached from the opposition, the Government could rely on the official block, the nominated members, the representatives of capitalist and foreign interests, and occasionally the indigenous minorities. The non-official supporters were liable to vote against the Government on matters affecting their particular interests, but the members of the official block were allowed to speak and vote only in support of official policy, and 'it is not too much to say that only the existence of the official block enabled the Government to carry on without serious difficulty.' Thus, except on very contentious matters, it was possible to outvote the opposition.[2]

The public in general took little interest in the proceedings in the Council. The tie between the members and the constituencies, especially in rural areas, was very weak. The old hereditary aristocracy had been reduced to the dead level of the people by the abolition of

[1] *ISC*, XI, 273–4.   [2] *ISC*, XI, 273, 577–9.

the circles. Its place had been taken, though not filled, by the money-lenders, predominantly Indian, and lawyers, now mostly Burmese though little if at all acquainted with village life. In the Council there was a high proportion of lawyers, not always of the best standing in the courts, and many of these became professional politicians. The electorate in general was apathetic. In 1925 only 17 % of the voters went to the poll in contested constituencies, and 20 % in 1928.[1] The total circulation of Burmese newspapers was only a few thousand copies and their circulation was roughly proportional to their Nationalist zeal.[2] Thus the electorate could always be 'swayed by suggestions that religion was in danger, that foreign rule is burdensome, that taxation is heavy, and that therefore the proper course is to vote for the candidate whose programme is to oppose the Government'.[3] In the country as in the Council, there was an opposition almost altogether Burmese in race and completely Burmese in sympathy. The well-disposed 'conservative element' was an illusion.

In general and departmental administration, however, the political reforms made little difference. The executive framework of Commissioner, Deputy Commissioner and so on stood firm. Nationalist ministers, dependent on the support of officials for their salary, 'were cautious in their application to the administration of the policy of their party' and 'adopted the current policy of the Department as substantially suitable'. The transfer of certain services to the nominal control of the ministers led to increased expenditure under those heads, but 'for the most part they were carried on as in pre-Reform days'.[4] It was frequently alleged that the services were dispirited, and that there was a general lowering of the tone of the administration. Officials were harassed by the demands which the new constitution made upon their time, overburdened with the growing complexity of administration, and felt that their responsibility had in some measure been transferred to the Council. But much was done to improve the material condition of the services, and the protection of their interests was entrusted to the immediate care of the Governor. In the newer services designed for 'nation-building', liberal terms were sanctioned, due provision was made for the recruitment of Englishmen, and precautions were taken against the introduction of the 'Spoils System'.[5]

The chief failure of the reforms was in the direction of affairs. The tangible rewards of office naturally stimulated intrigue and cor-

---

[1] *ISC*, XI, 580–1.   [2] *ISC*, XI, 272, 338, 581.
[3] *ISC*, XI, 581.   [4] *ISC*, XI, 274, 577.   [5] *ISC*, XI, 577–8.

ruption in the Council, and encouraged divisions among Nationalists. Unfortunately for the prestige of Government and for the cause of purity in public life, the Chinese leader of its few Burman supporters, who was understood to furnish his party with the funds necessary to secure votes, ended his political career in the law courts on the charge of fraudulently obtaining many lakhs of rupees from European banks.[1] Moreover, the representatives of special interests and communities were always looking to their special interests and defending them when they appeared to be attacked, so that racial and communal feeling tended to become exacerbated; there were violent explosions of anti-Indian feeling in 1924 and again in 1931; the rebellion of 1931 was regarded as partly due to anti-Indian sentiment. In 1931 there was a serious affray between Burmans and Chinese. As the European business men were the ablest and most active exponents of official policy, Burman feeling, which in 1920 had been directed largely against Indians, came to be directed against Europeans. In this atmosphere of mutual suspicion, 'for obvious practical reasons it was necessary to refrain from difficult and contentious legislation'.[2]

The intention of Parliament had been that the Government should gradually be made accountable to the people of the country, as represented on an elected Council. But the Council had no root among the people, and it could not exercise effective control over the Government even within the limits contemplated in the project of Dyarchy; in reality it represented only the western superstructure divorced from national life. Thus, during the first stage of responsible government, the most urgent problems of the country were neglected, and the sores that had broken out during the past fifty years were left to fester; the condition of the cultivators deteriorated, racial tension became more acute, crime increased and disaffection spread. The old fallacy of expecting functions to develop out of forms had vitiated local self-government, and it had a like result in national self-government.

5. SEPARATION FROM INDIA

It must be recognized then that, despite the adoption of responsible government as the goal of policy, there was little indication of any advance beyond a mechanical conception of the problem. The new forms of responsibility were patched on to the old garment of

---

[1] *ISC*, XI, 270–1; Craddock, p. 121. [2] *ISC*, XI, 579.

executive rule, and in practice the direction of affairs was still left to the guidance of economic forces. Administration was necessarily less efficient, because the new forms had no meaning in a purely economic system; it was as if a Board of Directors had suddenly been charged with caring for the employees instead of the shareholders, and yet still tried to carry on as before. When, by the inherent logic of events, the time came for a further advance towards responsible government in India, the question whether Burma should be separated from India became the dominant issue in local politics.[1]

Separation had been advocated intermittently for fifty years or more by British business interests, chiefly because they expected to have greater influence under the Colonial Office than under the Indian Government. Many British officials also, largely through local patriotism, had recently come to favour separation. Others, though content with Burma's position in the old constitution under a British Viceroy, held that 'the Burmese could not, would not and should not consent to become a vassal state of a Nehru's commonwealth'.[2] Burmans had never felt that their country was part of India, and thought that to treat it merely as an Indian province was derogatory to their national status. The Indian with his caste system was in some ways more foreign than the European, and Indian competition and the employment of Indians in the administration and in private enterprise were resented. It was believed accordingly that Burmans would welcome separation.

But when the question came up for decision in 1932, Burmans were growing suspicious of the proposal and its effects. These suspicions were stimulated by the unanimity with which the Government of Burma, Big Business and the European Press declared in favour of it. Yet at the same time the Government was frowning on patriotic groups, such as the *Do Bama* (We Burman) Association, which had 'started a movement against foreign cigarettes, the English style of hair-cut and the wearing of foreign clothes'.[3] It is true that such activities tended to encourage boycotts, picketing and agitation, but the use of home-spun clothing and of home-made cigarettes would have reduced the unemployment, then prevalent in Burma as elsewhere, and would have opened up new avenues to the modern economic world. Burman enterprise was discouraged even when it had no political significance, as when the manufacture of cheap lighters was made illegal lest it should prejudice the revenue

[1] *ISC*, XI, 565.   [2] Craddock, p. 128.   [3] *RAB*, 1930–1, p. x.

from a tax newly imposed on matches. A national government would have encouraged such activities, and it was difficult to believe that the Government had suddenly been converted to nationalism.

Moreover the relations between Burmans and Indians had taken a new turn. Although on the one hand, with the increasing pressure of Indian competition, the former attitude of half contemptuous tolerance had been transformed into a growing antipathy, on the other hand the politically active Burmans were turning to Indians for guidance and support in their common opposition to the British Government, and Burmans and Indians had sometimes joined forces in the Legislative Council. Thus, as Government and the capitalist interests became more insistent on separation, Burmese opinion, partly under the influence of Indian politicians, hardened against it. As an experienced Rangoon journalist has said, the fact that the Government and especially the Governor were believed to be strongly in favour of separation was a good enough reason for voting against it.[1] That is perhaps the most significant aspect of the opposition to separation. One outcome of the political reforms had been to replace dislike of Indians by distrust of Europeans, and the opposition to separation marks a further stage in this process, for the view rapidly gained ground that the real object was to rescue Burma from 'the Lost Dominion' and to make it 'Safe for Capital'.

There were indeed more solid grounds against any sudden and final breach with India. Although the Indian connection had been in many ways unfortunate, it was not without some advantages. The fact that British firms had wished for the transfer of Burma to the Colonial Office suggests that the Indian Government had to some extent acted as a brake on capitalist activities. And we have frequently had occasion to note that measures to promote the welfare of the people usually, if not invariably, emanated from India. This was largely because the Burma Government was merely part of the machinery for maintaining law and order, whereas the Viceroy, to some extent, stood outside the machine, and was not only the source of all initiative, but from time to time inspired the Indian administration with new ideas from England. Also it is not improbable that the link with India helped to protect Burma from being overrun by the Chinese, like Malaya.

These considerations however carried little weight with the opponents of separation, who were mainly actuated by the fear that it

[1] Collis, pp. 56, 59; J. J. Nolan, *Asiatic Review*, 1934, p. 207.

would be an obstacle to further political progress.[1] Although opposed
to immediate separation they wished 'that Burma should be allowed
to enter the Federation on a strictly temporary basis, with the right
reserved to her to secede at will'. It would have seemed possible
to devise some form of association with India which would have
promoted the autonomous development of Burma, while easing the
stresses of transition. But this was rejected and Burma had 'to choose
between two alternatives; either she could separate and pursue her
own political destiny apart from India, or she could enter the Federation unconditionally on the same terms as any other province'.[2] It
was a case of all or nothing, now or never. In view of the hesitation
to accept unconditional admission the issue was decided in favour
of separation, but, as a concession to agitation, separation was accompanied by the promise of a 'more advanced' constitution.

6. THE CONSTITUTION OF 1937

Under the constitution framed on the separation of Burma from India,
which took effect from 1 April 1937, the Burma Government became
directly responsible to Parliament, and the Secretary of State for
India became the Secretary of State for India and Burma, with a
separate Under-Secretary for Burma at the head of the Burma Office.
The Government of Burma consisted of a Governor, appointed by
the Crown; a Council of Ministers, restricted to ten members, responsible to the Legislature for all matters within the scope of its
authority; and a Legislature with two Houses, the Senate and the
House of Representatives. The Governor was allowed to appoint three
personal Councillors, who could attend and speak, but not vote, in the
Legislature. The authority of the Legislature did not extend to the
Shan States, Karenni, or the Tribal Hills. Within Burma proper the
Governor remained solely responsible for defence, external and internal; monetary policy, currency and coinage; and external affairs,
other than those connected with the relations between Burma and
other British territories. In other matters the Governor was bound
by the advice of his ministers, save in a certain range of matters
defined in the statute as those in which he exercised a special responsibility. These included the prevention of grave menace to
internal peace, the safeguarding of financial stability, the protection
of the legitimate interests of minorities, the position of officers in the

---

[1] *ISC*, XI, 567.   [2] Sir Charles Innes, *Asiatic Review*, 1934, p. 203.

services, and the prevention of discrimination against British subjects domiciled in the United Kingdom or British India or against goods of United Kingdom or Indian origin. In such matters he could refuse to accept the advice of his ministers. In practice, however, his reserve powers proved inadequate. As will appear below, there were frequent complaints that officials were exposed to political pressure, and, despite his special responsibility for minorities, there were prolonged anti-Indian outbreaks in 1938–9.

The Senate consisted of 36 members, half elected by the House of Representatives and half nominated by the Governor. Of the 132 seats in the House of Representatives 92 were given to territorial units and were non-communal; the remainder represented communal or other special interests. The franchise was enlarged to about one-third of the total adult male population, and one-tenth of the female.

In the new Legislature there was no official block. But it suffered, even in an exaggerated degree, from the other defects of the former Legislative Assembly. There was no organic connection between the people and their representatives; villagers did not look beyond their village or care twopence who represented them, so that votes went for less than two a penny, paid in promissory notes. The system of special and communal representation still aggravated racial tension. 'The minorities—Karens, Indians, Chinese, Anglo-Indians and Europeans—had between them 37 seats out of the 132, so that any Burmese leader who wanted to depend entirely on a Burmese majority had to command at least 67 out of the 95 Burmese seats. It never appeared likely that this would be the case.' After prolonged negotiations a coalition was formed under Dr Ba Maw 'who had been the most prominent anti-separationist, had expressed his determination to wreck the constitution, and had preached doctrines of advanced socialism'. His coalition included the Indians and Karens, about 12 each, but even so it commanded the barest majority and 'depended largely on the support of the Europeans, who maintained an independent position'.[1] This aggravated discontent with British rule, because the leading representative of British commercial interests was commonly regarded as the effective head of the government, even with a Nationalist premier. It was also a defect of the new system, as compared with the former, that there were now ten ministers and these could appoint members as salaried assistants. The salaries were still extravagantly high as compared with normal

[1] F. B. Leach, *Asiatic Review*, 1939, p. 631.

Burmese incomes. To hold office it was in practice necessary to command the anti-Nationalist vote, and this tended to split the Nationalist camp and multiplied intrigues to obtain the lucrative appointment of minister.

Yet the new Government made an impressive start, and showed a readiness to deal with long-neglected problems. Committees were appointed to examine agrarian distress, and their enquiries were followed by legislation. It formulated proposals to abolish 'the obnoxious capitation tax', regarded since the seventies as 'a very important reform in the fiscal system'.[1] Village administration was examined. And for the first time there was a public enquiry into the prevalence of corruption.

7. CORRUPTION

It has long been frequently asserted among all sections of the community that corruption prevailed in every branch of Government service. According to the official view it was a survival from Burmese rule that would gradually be remedied with the spread of education. Prevention was left to the ordinary processes of law. Those who gained their ends by bribery naturally made no complaint, and complaints from those who suffered were suspect as malicious. Such evidence as was available mostly came from people who had given bribes and, as accomplices, their evidence, even if admissible, was doubtful. It was difficult and dangerous for any private individual to set the law in motion, and in practice this was hardly possible except by some local or departmental superior of the man suspected of corruption. But officials rarely stayed long enough in any one place to collect the necessary evidence, make all the necessary preliminary enquiries and carry through a prosecution; or long enough even to find out what was going on, and who should be prosecuted. In 1941 the current lists of officials dismissed between 1896 and 1939, which presumably showed all those still believed to be alive, contained only sixty-five persons found guilty of corruption.[2] Under executive rule the Government sometimes deplored the prevalence of corruption, sometimes minimized it, but did nothing to stop it, and did not even hold any formal enquiry to ascertain its extent and propound remedies.

The association of Burmans with the Government under the reforms of 1923, however, changed the situation. Members of the

[1] 1886, Cmd. 4614, p. 72.　　　[2] CBC, p. 44.

Legislature knew the facts better than officials; some had a personal interest in preventing corruption, and many welcomed the chance to attack Government in one of the weaker places in its armour. They repeatedly drew attention to the subject and 'the leader of the Home Rule party introduced a motion in regard to the prevalence of bribery and corruption'.[1] But this was one of the many contentious subjects which Government thought it prudent to avoid, and nothing was done.

A further change came, however, with the separation of Burma from India. Burman ministers had greater patronage, and charges of graft and nepotism were freely vented, and taken up with zest by those Europeans who disliked the political reforms.[2] Once again there was a motion for an enquiry into corruption; this time it came from a member of the Karen group. Although the Government persuaded him to withdraw his motion, it was pressed and carried by the Nationalist opposition, and a Committee of Enquiry was constituted. The interest of Nationalist politicians would seem to have been largely factitious as, although members of the Legislature were invited to give evidence, 'with a few distinguished exceptions they not only did not attend, but did not even reply'. Among those who responded, however, were some members of the legal profession and adherents of the *thakin* (extremist) party, and it is interesting to note that it was the extremist party, most keenly opposed to foreign government, which was most solicitous for pure administration. Moreover, an appeal to the general public evoked many replies, 'clearly inspired by the conviction that corruption in the public services is a great evil and by a desire to help the Government to eradicate it'; evidently there was a fund of constructive good will on which a government secure in the affections of the people could rely.[3]

The report of the committee touched on the tradition of corruption under Burmese rule. As already noticed there was then no salaried civil service. Judges were entitled to take fees from the parties according to the value of the matter in dispute; revenue officials drew a commission on collections; everyone in authority could make such demands for fees or personal services as custom allowed or as he could manage to exact. Shortly after the occupation of Pegu, the demands of local authorities were estimated at about two-thirds of the amount due to the Crown, but there is nothing to show how far these estimates

---

[1] *ISC*, XI, 325, 329
[2] Craddock, pp. 122–3; Leach, *Asiatic Review*, 1939, p. 634.   [3] *CBC*, p. 5.

were reliable. It may be well to recall the experience of Mr Gouger. He landed in Burma with valuable merchandise from Calcutta, ignorant of the language or customs. He comments on 'the absence of all unauthorized exactions', and it seems that neither he nor others had to pay anything beyond the prescribed duties. On his way up the river there were 'no annoying exactions or tolls to impede them on their passage', and on arrival at the capital he took up his residence 'with less vexatious annoyance' than he would have encountered in any town in Europe. All that was necessary in importing goods was to comply with the easy regulations. But, when he wished to export produce, he was contravening regulations imposed by a mistaken economic policy, and he had to get round the regulations by bribery.[1] His experience suggests that the view generally accepted as to the corruptness of Burmese administration is exaggerated. That was the view taken by the committee.

'There can be no doubt', says the *Report*, 'that the fees and presents paid to Burmese Judges were to a great extent prescribed by custom, and that honest Judges took no more than the customary amount.... The testimony of European traders and diplomatic agents that they had to bribe Ministers and local officials is largely irrelevant. They were imperfectly acquainted with the scale of customary fees, and in any case...foreigners are fair game.'[2]

But the Burmese system of remunerating officials was radically unsound. The officials had no fixed salaries, there was no fixed rule of law to which aggrieved parties could appeal, and, although under British rule officials might still exact more than their legal due, they could no longer depend on the support of Government in doing so. But 'even to this day the rural public frequently draws no distinction between payments to government officers which go into the Treasury, and those which do not'; and this confusion is by no means restricted to the villager or the uneducated. 'The British annexation placed at the head of things a group of officials who by tradition were inaccessible to bribes; this was an inestimable advantage in that it gave Burma for the first time the idea that an incorruptible Civil Service was a possibility.' But 'the actual advantage to the individual citizen may easily be exaggerated'. The European officers were strange and far away, and the villager was 'exposed to contact with an ever-increasing variety of functionaries—Township Officers,

[1] Above, p. 18.   [2] *CBC*, p. 7.

administering three separate legal systems—all of which were equally
strange to him; Police, Vaccinators, Veterinary Assistants, Cadastral
Surveyors, Road Overseers, Irrigation Overseers, Epidemic Sub-
Assistant Surgeons, Sub-Inspectors of Excise, Forest Rangers, and
superior officers who controlled all these; persons of whose duties
he had only a vague idea, who had to administer regulations with
which he was almost unacquainted, and many of whom administered
them mainly with a view to extortion'.[1]

The *Report* of the committee is melancholy reading. In most services
there are three grades of officers: 'Higher', 'Burma', and 'Subordinate'. In the two lower grades of the general and judicial services the
majority of the committee doubted whether more than 30 % were
honest; estimates of the number corrupt varied from 20 to 99·9 %.
Among the Police it was suggested that 'not less than two-thirds of
the Inspectors were corrupt, and the proportion among Deputy
Superintendents was perhaps less'. The Excise Department was 'by
general consent the most universally corrupt'; honest officers, if any,
were very rare. In the jails 'a prisoner could have anything he wanted
except women; some said he could even have women'.

In the Medical Department there was no point on which the
witnesses were more unanimous than that subordinate medical
officers could be bribed to make false reports or give false evidence in
hurt cases; hospital assistants had to be bribed to give better attendance, and almost everywhere it was reported that the ward servants
and dressers, if not paid, would purposely treat wounds roughly so
as to cause pain; 'that the story should be so widely believed is a
measure of the fear and mistrust which the public feel towards the
hospitals'. Vaccinators had formerly taken bribes to disregard breaches
of the regulations, but 'malpractices had declined with the increasing
popularity of vaccination' (coinciding with improvement in the
lymph and the substitution of Burman for Indian vaccinators).
Formerly extortion by veterinary assistants was extremely common,
and 'the visits of these officers were dreaded in the villages', but
this was no longer generally true and the public was learning to
appreciate the benefit of their services. In the schools there were
many deputy inspectors who did not take bribes, and there were no
complaints against inspectors, but for years the Ministry of Education had acquiesced in 'an elaborate and long-continued system of
corruption' by which school managers furnished false certificates

[1] *CBC*, p. 8.

about the salaries paid so as to obtain larger grants than they had earned. (That was a common practice long before the Reforms of 1923.) In the Public Works Department the public generally thinks that corruption is extensive and serious, but the committee believed that a majority of the executive engineers (officials of the 'higher' class) were honest, and that 'by no means all Sub-divisional Officers were corrupt'; in the Irrigation Branch corruption was less frequent and extensive. The Postal Department had a good reputation among the public, but internal corruption seemed to stop short only at the Director-General, and postmen and clerks paid to get their appointments. In the Agricultural Department, officials were often bribed by would-be tenants of Government farms. In the Land Records Department, corrupt superintendents were believed now to be rare, though inspectors often demanded a share of the illicit gains of their subordinates. Viewing conditions as a whole the committee believed that many officers were led into corruption by the evil influence of corrupt seniors and that 'to put it plainly, if justice were done, a very large proportion of all the public servants of the country would be in jail'. Not infrequently the prevalence of corruption is suggested as a reason for not entrusting Burmans with self-government. Yet it should be remembered that in some of these departments few Burmans were employed, and that the tradition of corruptness dates from a time when practically no Burmans were employed in Government service except as magistrates and clerks; on the other hand there is least corruption in the departments where Burmans are chiefly employed, and the people understand and value their activities.

The published report does not deal with the allegations of ministerial corruption, but there can be little doubt that, even if exaggerated by scandal and by racial discord, they were only too well founded. The official who presided over the enquiry subsequently published his impressions on this aspect of the problem. He was careful to explain that he had known some ministers who were incorrupt and several others whose activities were at least not directed by the motive of putting money in their pockets. But many of their proceedings 'went far beyond the normal bounds of graft', and some ministers 'chose to scrabble in the mud for petty bribes, and to squeeze money out of aspirants to appointments, promotions or transfer in the public service—money which the public servant would usually recoup by extortion from the public, preferably from the poor, for the rich are not such easy subjects for intimidation'. But extortion of the same kind, recouped in the same manner, was an old story. Formerly most of the patronage was reserved to high officials who were above all reasonable suspicion of corruption, and the opportunities of office superintendents and clerks for taking bribes were limited, yet it was commonly reported that there was a recognized tariff for transfer to the more lucrative or otherwise desirable stations. The difference was that those responsible for suppressing the evil would now sometimes share the loot. Also the ministers were more exposed to temptation, and were less fortified to resist it. Officials stood outside party politics, were trained as public servants, and inherited the modern western tradition of integrity in public life. The ministers who took their place were party men, with no special training and the heirs of a very different tradition. It is a tradition in Burma that every one should provide for his dependents, and should use his influence for that purpose (like Sir Thomas Bertram in *Mansfield Park*) 'from a general wish of doing right'. And the conditions were much the same as in Lincoln's Cabinet, where the Secretary of State 'would steal anything but a red-hot stove'. The professional politician incurred heavy expenses, legitimate and illegitimate, and expected to reimburse himself from the prizes of a profession in which his chances of office were uncertain and his tenure insecure. In the general atmosphere of intrigue, it is not strange that some grabbed with both hands all that they could get, and their example and influence must certainly have encouraged corruption in the services. But the main cause of corruption in the services was the cleavage between law and custom and the contradiction between administrative policy and public sentiment.

Corruption may conveniently be classified as either *judicial* or *administrative*; judicial corruption relates to the conduct of the courts, and administrative corruption on the other hand covers all those matters not directly concerned with the administration of justice. Our government is based on the western principle of the rule of law, and in that respect may justly be claimed as superior to the Burmese system. But in England, though not in Burma, law is based on public opinion and on what the people want; in Burma the law and procedure of the British courts conflict with Burmese sentiment, and the rule of law often seems to differ little from caprice. Every one knew more or less what was customary, but even the judges themselves, below the Privy Council, cannot be certain of the law. If a legal decision purports to be based on custom, every one knows more or less whether it is correct, because every one knows local custom. But when, following some obscure *dhammathat*, a court decides that in law an eldest child has certain privileges, the people do not know whether it is good law, but only that it is contrary to custom. If a court decides that a transaction is a sale, or that labourers have no lien on the crop, people do not know whether the decision is technically correct, they know only that it contradicts what they have always believed. Judges no longer have to justify their decisions to public opinion but to the court of appeal, and parties cannot tell whether an adverse decision is due to corruption or to the vagaries of western law. It is much easier, therefore, for judges to take bribes. Moreover, aggrieved litigants will usually attribute an adverse decision to corruption, and this view is encouraged by the fact that the decision usually goes in favour of the longer purse, which can better afford to fight the case and can engage the more skilful advocate. As the general belief in judicial corruption grows, the people are more ready to offer bribes, and judges are less fortified to resist them.

Administrative corruption is largely due to the multiplication of unwelcome 'welfare' measures. These require a host of subordinates on low pay, among whom many, according to the committee, use them 'mainly with a view to extortion'. Ordinarily, however, welfare measures promote corruption in a more insidious manner. The surveyor who omits to notice encroachment on Government land, or infractions of the building rules, the sanitary inspector who is not too active in nosing out nuisances, the vaccinator who overlooks unvaccinated children, the veterinary assistant who does not insist on the slaughter or burial of diseased cattle, all earn the public gratitude, which naturally finds expression in a trifling present; they are regarded as kindly rather than corrupt. Corruption grows together with the elaboration of western administrative machinery, and is at least a by-product if not the main product of 'efficiency'. It is probable that judicial officers are, on the whole, less corrupt than fifty years ago, but, as western rule has reached out further into every department of social life, it has brought new occasions for corruption and, only too often, very little else.

Naturally, corruption grows most rapidly where it is most secure. Local bodies, composed of members who share the general opinion about western welfare, are more likely to give and take bribes than to prosecute offenders. Probably their own houses contravene the building and sanitary by-laws, their own children may be unvaccinated; their own cattle may under the rules be liable to segregation or slaughter; almost certainly some of them are more or less distantly related to the departmental subordinates who take bribes. Self-interest and apathy make them reluctant to suppress corruption and, under their rule, those who take bribes are safe. Again, the notorious corruption in the Public Works Department is largely due to its divorce from Burman life. Through economic forces it has come about that work is given to Indian or Chinese contractors employing Indian labour and working on western lines under the inspection of officials, largely alien, and under European direction. In 1931, of 170 contractors for the Railway, only 12 were Burmans, 140 were Indians and the rest Chinese or European.[1] Such control as is exercised by the law and the Accounts Department is no substitute for public interest, and the corruption and waste of public money are naturally far greater in Government or municipal works than in village works undertaken by the people for themselves; we have already noted the alleged completion of town roads in Toungoo. It is significant that in the Irrigation Department, where the people understand and sympathize with the work done, and where the staff is largely Burman, corruption seems to be less prevalent. Most vaccinators and veterinary assistants are now Burmans and are said to be growing less corrupt as western methods become more effective and, accordingly, better appreciated by the people.

For both judicial and administrative corruption the remedy is essentially the same. We cannot depart from the rule of law, and although, as suggested recently in a ruling of the Chief Justice, much might be done to reconcile law and custom, no one would revive old customs that sufficed for the medieval society of Burmese rule. It should be possible to reduce litigation and to encourage arbitration, but the only effective remedy for judicial corruption is to build up a new society in effective contact with the western world, and able by its inherent vitality to restrain anti-social economic forces instead of leaving control over them to a legal system that encourages rather than prevents corruption. Similarly, we cannot neglect western welfare measures merely because the people have not yet learned to appreciate them; the suppression of disease and epidemics in Burma among men and crops and cattle is not merely of local interest but a matter of world welfare. The remedy lies not in multiplying

[1] Census, 1931, p. 153.

regulations and establishments, and measuring efficiency by expenditure, but in devising some means to enlist public support for western welfare and the law.

8. DEFENCE

Before the separation of Burma from India the military forces stationed in Burma consisted of two battalions of British Infantry, three battalions of Indian infantry, the Burma Rifles (a regiment of four battalions recruited in Burma, but containing no Burmese), a company of Sappers and Miners, and ten battalions of Military Police, acting as an armed reserve for the Indian Army and for dealing with frontier raids and internal disturbances. 'They are, in fact, soldiers as well as police.'[1] There were no Burmese in the regular army and, until shortly before the separation of Burma, none in the Military Police. For this there were two main reasons.

In early days in India the East India Company enrolled guards for the protection of its factories, but for show rather than for military service. Gradually they assumed a more military character, and from about 1750 the Company began also to entertain irregular troops armed with swords and targets, lances and matchlocks, bows and arrows. Clive shaped this material into a battalion of sepoys, drilled, disciplined and clothed on western lines. By the time of the first war with Burma in 1826, there was an Indian army accustomed to European discipline, under European officers accustomed to Indian ways.[2] The Burmese, however, in military as in civil matters, were still living in the Middle Ages; their forces resembled those which Clive had used as the raw material for his levies. The East India Company did not need their services, and had no officers acquainted with their ways to train them; moreover, they needed higher pay than Indians because they were not so poor. It would have been difficult, troublesome and costly to recruit Burmese for the army, and, from the standpoint of economy and common sense, it was unnecessary to recruit them.

It was not only unnecessary but imprudent to recruit Burmese. There could be little reliance on troops raised from among a people with no divisions of caste but united in religion, race and national sentiment with the king and their kinsfolk just across the border, still waiting an opportunity to wipe out defeat in another trial of strength. Obviously security required that the Burmese should be disarmed and debarred from military service. The Karens and other

---

[1] *IG*, IV, 375; *ISC*, XI, 206.   [2] *IG*, IV, 326.

minor tribes, however, might be expected to side with the British, and these have been recruited, even when an initial reluctance had to be dispelled, but it has always been easy to find reasons for withholding military training, even as volunteer cadets, from the great mass of the people.

In this matter there was a difference between the situation in Tenasserim and Arakan. The Arakanese had called in the Burmese for help in ousting an oppressive ruler, but the Burmese who came to help them stayed to rule them. The Arakanese never acquiesced in Burmese rule, and, from across the British frontier, continued to resist. On the outbreak of the war in 1824, it was thought expedient to raise an Arakanese levy to assist in driving the Burmese out of Arakan, and this levy was retained after the end of the war. In Tenasserim, however, the Talaings had in great measure been assimilated by the Burmese, and could hardly be distinguished from them. For many years no attempt was made to recruit Talaings. In 1833, however, the Commissioner urged that the Burmese and Talaings were 'superior in physical strength and in all points calculated to make good soldiers to most of the sepoys of western India', and suggested that, if the experiment of a Talaing Corps should prove as successful as he anticipated, 'the whole of the external defence of these Provinces might be undertaken a few years hence by the Talaings'. But he insisted that care should be taken to select suitable officers. His proposals were approved and the preliminary steps were taken. But the officers, instead of being men with local knowledge, were sent over from India, and the Government of India hoped to save money on the pay. Madras troops in Burma drew pay at Indian rates together with an allowance for foreign service, and the Talaings were expected to serve at Indian rates with no allowance. The Commissioner protested that one could not attract respectable men on inferior pay, and the project was abandoned.

Shortly afterwards war with Ava seemed imminent, and the Commissioner again urged that, to give confidence to the people by putting arms in their hands and by entrusting their defence in some measure to themselves, would be eminently useful 'in Political and Military points of view'; he thought, moreover, that in the long run the measure would 'decidedly prove economical' by making it possible to dispense with Indian troops.[1] The Indian Government again yielded to these arguments, and a Talaing Levy was formed in

[1] *SL*, pp. 140, 165.

1839. But the crisis passed and, under a succession of Commissioners appointed from India and less infected with local patriotism, imponderable sentiment was outweighed by common sense, convenience and economy, and the Talaing Levy languished and was disbanded in 1849.

When the second war broke out in 1852, the question of recruiting local forces was reopened.[1] The Arakanese Levy rendered useful service, and Phayre wished to raise a force in Pegu, partly of Burmans and partly of Malays. A nucleus already existed in Bassein, where Fytche had hit on the idea of using dacoits against dacoits. He 'enlisted no man into the corps unless it was shown that he had been a bad and dangerous character'. 'They were brave enough in all conscience, and required no European officer to lead them into action.' But, inevitably, severe discipline was needed to maintain order among a band of criminals, and neither the character of the men nor the stringent discipline encouraged respectable men to accept military service so long as cultivation was more profitable. However, a regiment was raised as the Pegu Light Infantry. But in 1861 there seemed no longer any near danger of war with Ava, and both the Arakan Levy and the Pegu Light Infantry were converted into civil police.

Besides these two regiments there was also a Karen Levy of some two hundred men.[2] The Karen tribes were small and divided, and could never endanger British rule; formerly a wild jungle folk oppressed by the Burmese, large numbers had accepted Christianity, with a rise in status and prosperity that attached them to the British. Some, however, were Buddhist and regarded themselves as Burmans, and in 1857 considerable trouble was caused by a Karen rising. Regular troops could not operate in their wild country and a special force of two companies, each of a hundred men, was raised. 'It was intended that this should be composed of Karens, but it was found impossible to make soldiers of them, and Shan and Toungthoo were to a great extent enlisted instead.' But the Government persisted in the effort to recruit Karens, and by 1880 these formed about three-quarters of the total. However, they would not serve for long and, as soon as they had made enough money to take a wife, they resigned; or deserted if the resignation was not promptly accepted.

The recruitment of Karens received a new stimulus in 1886.[3] The

[1] Fytche, I, 145; *BBG*, ii, 108.
[2] *BBG*, II, 553, 605.   [3] Smeaton, pp. 7 ff.

Burmese were in rebellion throughout British Burma, and American missionaries were active in rallying Karens to the British cause. Under this stimulus the Karens proved useful auxiliaries and in 1891 a Karen battalion of Military Police was formed; this is said to have proved a failure, and in 1896 the Karens were distributed among Indian battalions. There were still difficulties in filling the ranks, but these were partly overcome by the appointment of a European from the police as a special Karen recruiting officer. Even during the present century, one of these remarked, not wholly in jest, that he reckoned it a good season if three recruits joined up and only one recruiting sergeant deserted. But, as a result of this continual encouragement, the Karens became accustomed to military discipline, securing a place in the Military Police, and later in the army.

The case was different with the Burmese. During the early days of the occupation of Upper Burma, when the people were believed to welcome British rule, some were recruited for the Military Police. But the Chief Commissioner, newly arrived from India and out of touch with Burmese sentiment, found himself opposed by a generally hostile population and a Burmese army still conducting guerilla operations. He was easily persuaded that the recruitment of Burmese involved a 'gross waste of money', and the men were forthwith disbanded. At the same time he determined to disarm all Burmese as rigorously as possible while leaving arms with the Karens; he therefore imposed conditions for bearing arms which, though ostensibly impartial, could be accepted by the Karens but not by the Burmese.[1]

Thus, when war broke out in 1914, Burmese for two generations or more had been given no opportunity of a military career, except in one Company of Sappers and Miners, and the Government congratulated them on the privilege of exemption from military service. But there was 'evinced throughout the Province an unmistakable desire that the Burmese should be allowed to enlist as soldiers' and later, when the problem of manpower became serious 'a vigorous recruiting campaign'[2] was set in hand, mainly through the local magistrates, and the people were congratulated on being granted the privilege to serve. The Sappers and Miners were expanded to three companies and a depot, a regiment of Burma Rifles was formed, and several Mechanical Transport Companies and two Labour Corps.

[1] Crosthwaite, pp. 64, 80, 131.
[2] *RAB*, 1916–17, p. 10; 1917–18, p. i; *ISC*, XI, 23.

These units served in Mesopotamia, Palestine and France. The Sappers and Miners 'did excellent work in Mesopotamia and on the North-west Frontier of India', and the Burma Rifles, 'though a very new formation, with no old soldiers to give it a stiffening, received excellent reports' and 'showed no lack of actual fighting qualities'.[1]

But at the end of the war the forces had to be reduced to a peace establishment, and most of the new units were disembodied. In 1925 it was decided to recruit only Karens, Kachins and Chins for the Burma Rifles, and shortly afterwards the Sappers and Miners were disbanded for reasons of economy. 'The discharge of all the Burmese members of the Burma Rifles and the disbandment of the Burma Sappers and Miners was a great blow to the national pride of the Burmese', but defence was one of the reserved subjects over which the people had no control, and the Government, although expressing sympathy with Burmese sentiment, made no effective protest against the decision.

During the war the Burmese were admitted also to the Military Police. After the war recruitment was suspended and there were numerous desertions, over half of them among Karens and Kachins. Two years later, when recruitment was reopened, Karens, Kachins and Chins were admitted, but not Burmese.[2]

In addition to the regular forces there was also a volunteer force in Burma. This comprised various units dating originally from 1877 at a time of tension with Upper Burma. For this volunteer force only men of European descent on the father's side were eligible, though in fact Indians and Karens were admitted, and some Burmese found admission by adopting European names and costumes. Burmans had long urged their claims to admission, and in 1917, when patriotism was in the air, a committee appointed to promote 'the Imperial Idea' recommended that Burmans from approved schools should be admitted to cadet corps as boys (though not to volunteer corps as men).[3] This recommendation was disregarded, and Burmans remained ineligible for any form of military training either as boys or men.

Thus, between the introduction of the earlier reforms in 1923 and the separation of Burma from India in 1937, Burma became less and not more capable of self-defence. It has been commonly held that

---

[1] *RAB*, 1919–20, p. 46; Leach, *Asiatic Review*, 1940, p. 747.
[2] *RAB*, 1919–20, p. 48; 1921–2, pp. 72–3; *ISC*, XI, pp. 23, 206.
[3] *CII*, p. 29.

the Burmese are not a martial people,[1] and not unnaturally a view
so congenial to our interest has found ready acceptance. It is true
of course that a people deprived of weapons and excluded from
military experience for fifty to a hundred years loses the tradition of
defending itself in arms, but the Burmese do not forget so readily as
we are apt to do their former record of frequent, and on the whole,
successful war, when they were masters of the minor races which
we have recruited for the army. It is true also that, with the growing distrust and dislike of British rule during the present century,
there was little desire for service in an army which might be called
on to support the British Government against their fellow countrymen, and that the pay and conditions of service were less attractive
to the Burmese than to the tribal peoples of the infertile hills.
But those who served with them in the war of 1914 knew that 'the
recruits included some first-rate material and, with care in recruitment and the avoidance of undue haste, there was no reason why
the Burmese should not make excellent soldiers and be able in time
to undertake the defence of their own country'.[2]

If the problem of responsible government had been conceived in
terms of creating a united people to which the Government might be
made responsible, the question of building up an army would have been
recognized as a matter of primary importance, but it was conceived
in terms of constitutional mechanics, of constructing machinery that,
if it could not do much good, could do no serious damage; the military
aspect of the problem was disregarded, and indeed, with an executive
government in 'a perpetual and hopeless minority' in the Legislative
Council, the existence of a Burmese army might have multiplied
embarrassments. When, however, it was decided in 1934 that Burma
should be separated from India, something had to be done about
defence. The problem was solved by converting the units of the
Indian army serving in Burma, together with the Military Police, into
a Burma Defence Force, and placing it under the Governor as Commander-in-Chief. Thus the army still remained non-Burmese, entirely distinct from the people, and an instrument for the maintenance
of internal security rather than for defence against aggression. It was
recognized that the demand for the admission of Burmese to the
Burma Defence Force could no longer be resisted, but there was little
activity in meeting it. At the outbreak of war in 1939 a question in

[1] Sir C. Innes, *Asiatic Review*, 1937, p. 185.
[2] Leach, *Asiatic Review*, 1940, p. 747.

the Council elicited the figures in the marginal table showing the number of men locally recruited according to race, together with the percentage of the total population which each race constituted at the census of 1931. The figures for Burmese include Talaings and Shans. Only on the eve of war, on 31 August 1939, did the Government announce that indigenous peoples would no longer be excluded from the Burma Auxiliary Force which had replaced the former volunteers. Thus, when the Japanese invaded Burma, the people had no means of taking part in its defence. Within four months of the invasion 4000 Burmese were under arms on the Japanese side, and before long the Burma Independence Army reached a strength of 30,000.[1]

Racial constitution of the Burma Army

| (a) Race |
| (b) Per cent of population |
| (c) No. in the army |

(a)	(b)	(c)
Burmese	75·11	472
Karen	9·34	1448
Chin	2·38	868
Kachin	1·05	881
Others		
Native	2·38⎫	168
Foreign	9·74⎭	

[1] T. L. Hughes, *JRCAS*, 1943, p. 91.

CHAPTER VI

BURMA, 1923–40: POLITICAL DEMOCRACY

(b) PROGRESS AND WELFARE

1. Economic Progress

Communications. The main lines of communication by rail had already been laid down under executive rule, and since 1923 the extensions have consisted merely of feeder lines. Projects of linking up the system with India encountered opposition, as this would have encouraged immigration to the detriment of the Burman labourer, and also of the steamship companies which handled the coolie traffic. By 1936 the total mileage worked was 2060. In 1929, however, there was a change in the management of the railway; the lease granted to a private company in 1896 expired, and the system was taken over by the Indian Government. It passed to the Government of Burma in 1937.

The Irrawaddy Flotilla Company maintained its monopoly over the waterways; the new lines of railway did not tap the river, and it could disregard or suppress local competition from a few small private steamers, mostly owned by Indians. The rapid development of motor traffic, however, led to a considerable extension of the road system, and by 1940 there were 17,000 miles open to wheeled traffic, of which some 12,500 miles were available for motors, though only 5000 were metalled. One feature of this new development was the multiplication of bus services and taxis owned by Burmans. But Burma was still cut off from the outer world by land, chiefly because the traffic across the frontiers with India, China and Siam was too small to justify expenditure on roads. The Burma Road lies in China (except for about 120 miles from the frontier to the railhead), and was built by the Chinese in 1938 when the Japanese invasion cut off China from the sea. As throughout the course of its past history, Burma became a channel of world trade only when the normal routes were blocked.

In respect of communications by sea the most noteworthy feature was the development of trade with Asia, and especially with India and

Japan, at the expense of Europe. Wholly new was the emergence of Burma as an important centre on the air routes linking Europe and India with Australia and the Far East. A project of building up an internal air service in Burma, however, proved a failure and was abandoned.

Population. Between 1921 and 1941 the population rose from 13·2 million to 16·9 million, an increase of 24·6 % as against an increase of 25·8 % between 1901 and 1921. As at each census enumeration has extended over a wider area in the tribal hills, the figures are not exactly comparable, but they show that the rate of increase was much about the same. For the census of 1941, figures by race are not available, but the returns for 1931 show that Indians constituted rather more than 6·9 % of the total as against less than 5·9 % in 1901, and Chinese 1·32 % as against 0·59 %. Europeans also were more numerous. Urban occupations, commerce and industry still remained almost entirely in foreign hands.

Trade. We have seen that under executive rule the half century from the opening of the Suez Canal was a period of rapid economic progress, but that the productive apparatus passed increasingly under the control of foreign capital, while as regards imports a smaller proportion went to the natives, and of the imports for native consumption the proportion of luxuries declined. As the constitutional reforms of 1923 were to give the people greater control over their national life, one might expect the trend of the previous fifty years to be reversed, with foreign capital diminishing in importance in the national economy. Again, the reforms led eventually to the separation of Burma from India, and one might expect to find the economic ties with India growing looser, as during the earlier years of the present century. In both these matters the actual course of development followed other lines.

From 1922–3 onwards trade flourished, the exports reaching a maximum of Rs. 777·3 million in 1925–6 and the imports a maximum of Rs. 429·1 million in 1927–8. During the following decade the world depression dominated both exports and imports, the former touching a low point at Rs. 362·8 million in 1932–3, and the latter falling to Rs. 178·7 million in 1933–4. To understand the significance of these figures it is necessary to eliminate changes in the value of money. The marginal table (p. 187) accordingly gives the nominal values of imports and exports at turning-points in economic development, together with corrected figures showing the equivalent values at the prices of 1898–1901. The corrected figures indicate that in 1933–4, on the basis of the prices of 1898–1901, Burma was exporting goods to the value of Rs. 466·1 million and receiving in exchange goods to the value of only Rs. 162·9 million; since the beginning of the century the volume of imports had risen by over 60% and the volume of exports by close on 200%. Thus Burma was receiving very much less for its exports than before.

The increasing discrepancy between imports and exports has indeed been a constant feature of the trade returns since the opening of the Suez Canal. It is often attributed to invisible imports representing payments for services rendered, but to some extent the imports are invisible because they do not exist, and the surplus includes profits for which no services are rendered. At the same time there has been a change in the character of the exports, as is illustrated below.

Trade values (Rs. mill.) *

(a) Imports; (b) Exports

Year	Nominal		Corrected	
	(a)	(b)	(a)	(b)
1868–72	25·4	30·7	19·5	51·0
1898–1901	100·8	159·6	100·8	159·6
1913–14	254·0	389·0	190·6	305·1
1926–27	386·9	659·5	208·3	346·6
1933–34	178·7	389·2	162·9	466·1

* For Index numbers, see *RTC*, 1910–11, p. 2; 1911–12, p. 2. No index numbers were published after 1933–4.

Average Export Surplus (Rs. mill.)

1868–70	3·95	1901–10	90·73
1871–80	13·11	1911–20	War
1881–90	War	1921–30	279·48
1891–1900	39·59	1931–40	268·70

Classified Exports, 1869–1937 *

Class of exports	1868–9	1872–3	1903–4	1913–14	1926–7	1936–7
Native produce						
Rice products	63·7	65·2	72·8	68·5	59·8	39·3
Other agricultural products	2·8	7·8	3·4	6·2	5·1	6·5
Other rural products	9·3	10·0	3·5	2·8	1·8	0·8
Total	75·8	83·0	79·7	77·5	66·7	46·6
Capitalist produce						
Forest products	21·3	15·5	8·2	5·8	7·6	7·1
Plantation products	—	—	0·1	0·4	1·8	1·3
Oil-well products	—	—	10·6	14·1	16·8	34·9
Mineral products	—	—	0·5	1·5	6·4	9·3
Total	21·3	15·5	19·4	21·8	32·6	52·6
Unclassed	2·9	1·5	0·9	0·7	0·7	0·8
Total	100·0	100·0	100·0	100·0	100·0	100·0

* For details, see Appendix, p. 551.

From this table it is clear that, despite the political reforms purporting to endow the people with self-government in respect of 'nation-building' activities, foreign capital continued to strengthen its hold over the economic resources of the country and, by the time that Burma was separated from India, the exports of capitalist produce had come to exceed in value the exports of native produce. We shall see below that, during the same period, capitalist enterprise took a growing share of the imports, and that among the imports for consumption the proportion of luxuries continued to decline. Thus the political reforms were of no avail to promote native enterprise or welfare.

Another feature of the trade from 1923 onwards was the development of closer ties with India. We have noticed that during the present century up to 1914, the European share of the trade was increasing in respect both of imports and exports. After that it fell rapidly under both heads. In 1913–14 the West supplied over half the imports, 51 %; by 1926–7 its share had dropped to 44·9 %, and by 1936–7 to 30·7 %. Thus by 1936–7 Asia was supplying over two-thirds of the imports, and India alone just over half, 50·1 %. It is a coincidence that the Indian share of the imports was almost the same as in 1868–9; but at the earlier date they were largely British goods imported through India, and in 1936–7 these had been replaced by Indian manufactures. As regards exports, Europe took two-fifths, 40·3 % in 1913–14; by 1926–7 its share had dropped to 30·1 % and by 1936–7 still further to 24·5 %. Asia was taking three-quarters of the exports, and India alone nearly three-fifths. Thus, just at the time when Burma was separated from India, the economic ties between the two countries were closer than ever before.

Percentage Distribution of Trade

(*a*) Europe, Africa, America; (*b*) Asia, Australasia

Year	Exports		Imports	
	(*a*)	(*b*)	(*a*)	(*b*)
1868–9	69·0	31·0	38·7	61·3
1903–4	37·2	62·8	44·9	55·1
1913–14	40·3	59·7	51·0	49·0
1926–7	30·1	69·9	44·9	55·1
1936–7	24·5	75·5	30·7	69·3

Production. The growth of capitalist production was, as shown above, mainly under the heads of plantation, oil and mineral products.

The value of plantation products rose from Rs. 1·24 lakhs in 1903–4 to Rs. 74·32 lakhs in 1936–7. During the same period oil products rose from Rs. 216·16 lakhs to Rs. 1936·46 lakhs, and minerals from Rs. 3·27 lakhs to Rs. 512·88 lakhs. In the oil industry Burman labour was to some extent substituted for Indian labour, but otherwise industry and commerce were still characterized by foreign labour and management. Another notable feature of industrial development was the increase in the number of small rice-mills in the interior. In 1900, apart from a few mills in the immediate vicinity of Rangoon, all the mills were concentrated in the ports. But the victory of the millers in the great combine of 1892–4 stimulated the Indians and Chinese to erect godowns and mills in the interior, and subsequently Burmans began to follow their example. The number of small mills in the interior rose from 27 in 1900, all but one close to Rangoon, to 151 in 1914, 260 in 1920, and 528 in 1930. During the same period the mills in the ports increased from 72 to 94. The mills in the interior had a milling capacity of only 10 to 75 tons a day, while the mills in the ports could deal with 200 to 500 tons a day.[1] To a large extent, however, the small mills worked for local consumption, replacing the rice hand-milled in the villages. When steam-mills became locally available, people began to take their rice to them instead of pounding it themselves or with local labour, with a consequent increase in seasonal unemployment. Of the rice from these mills only a small proportion was normally available for export. So far as the small mills competed in the export market with the large mills, they were handicapped by the rates charged by the railway company for transport, which favoured the carriage of paddy rather than rice. Thus the bulk of the rice for export continued to pass through the hands of the millers in the ports, and these exercised a further control over the industry by financing small mills and purchasing their produce. Many of the small mills were erected with capital borrowed at high rates of interest, and, with the onset of the depression, a large number had to close down. This, however, did not prevent the erection of new mills wherever the prospects seemed favourable, and between 1930 and 1939 the total number of mills rose from 622 to 692, of which Europeans owned 27, Chinese 164, Indians 190 and Burmans 311. Over 80 % of the mills employed less than 100 workers. The extent of Burman labour was correlated with the size and ownership of the mills; in the smaller mills, taken as a whole, 34 % of the

[1] Grant, J. W., *The Rice Crop in Burma* (1933), p. 29.

employees were Burman, but in the larger mills at the ports the proportion of Burmans employed was negligible. Thus, from about 1920 onwards, Burmans were making some little headway in the rice industry, in addition to cultivation of the crop; but they were still excluded from the export trade, and their share was confined to the local business, which was very speculative, many mills changing hands frequently or closing down from time to time. The rice industry therefore constituted no exception to the general division of labour along racial lines.

As we have frequently had occasion to notice, the economic progress of Burma, though based in the main on Burman enterprise in cultivation, has been stimulated by foreign capital. Agriculture and small-scale enterprise is financed mainly by the Indian *chettyars*, whose capital in 1929 was estimated at rather more than £50 million (Rs. 750 million).[1] But direction and control of the capital invested in large-scale enterprise, estimated at another £50 million,[2] rests with the European population of less than 10,000, representing only about 0·07 % of the total population. About nine-tenths of the European population is British, and of the foreign investments about the same proportion is in British ownership or control, though there are some Dutch, Danish, American and Japanese holdings, especially in banking and trade. Concessions for oilfields are held only by British concerns, and some of the large corporations restrict voting powers to British subjects, including of course Asiatics. In general however the policy of the 'open door' characterizes both investment and trade, and the large British interest is a natural consequence of the long British connection. Many of the larger corporations have an intricate ramification of interests.[3] The Irrawaddy Flotilla and Airways Co. for example not only controls steam navigation on the inland waters, but owns dockyards, warehouses, rice- and saw-mills, steelworks and a foundry. It is also linked up with one of the two chief shipping companies operating between Burma and the United Kingdom. All the more important mercantile firms act as importers, exporters, millers, estate and shipowners, and some of them also have considerable interests outside Burma. These firms all remit most of their profits abroad. Exact figures are not available. It has been estimated that, with a capital of £50 million, the European firms make an annual profit of £10–12 million, more than half of it from oil and minerals. The estimate may be excessive, and the capital is certainly much larger as the share capital is augmented by the periodical appropriation of

[1] *CBE*, p. 211.   [2] Callis, p. 106.   [3] *Ib.* pp. 101, 104.

some of the profits to capital expenditure. Nevertheless the profits
are undoubtedly high, some of the firms paying up to 20 % and still
retaining a large balance of undistributed profits for new investments in Burma. But these reinvestments remain in European hands
and, since the distributed profits are sent abroad, the export surplus
tends continually to increase, and of recent years has averaged about
£21 million, which is about four times as large as that of Siam.[1]

2. INDIVIDUAL WELFARE

If we turn to examine what Burma was receiving in exchange for its
produce we find that the value of imports rose from an average of
100·8 million rupees in 1898–1901 to 386·9 in 1926–7, and then
declined to 178·7 in 1933–4. Thus for some years the value of imports grew much faster than the population, and, even at the lowest
point of the depression, the value of imports per head was greater
than at the beginning of the century. These figures, like those for
exports, need readjustment owing to the fluctuations of prices, but
if we correct them by valuing the imports for the later years at the
average prices of 1898–1901, they still amounted to 208·3 million
rupees in 1926–7 and to 162·9 in 1933–4, and show therefore a rise
in the actual volume of imports per head from about Rs. 10 to
Rs. 12·3. But there has been a remarkable change in the character
of the imports, as can be seen in the following table:

Classified Imports, 1869–1937 *

Class of imports	1868–9	1872–3	1903–4	1913–14	1926–7	1936–7
Consumption goods						
Food: Staples	5·1	4·9	13·5	9·7	11·2	10·8
Luxuries	18·9	15·6	19·1	18·9	18·2	17·0
Total	24·0	20·5	32·6	28·6	29·4	27·8
Clothing: Staples	35·7	31·6	21·2	24·5	21·8	20·9
Luxuries	17·2	19·7	10·4	8·6	6·6	4·9
Total	52·9	51·3	31·6	33·1	28·4	25·8
Household goods	2·7	3·4	7·0	6·7	5·7	4·2
Total for consumption	79·6	75·2	71·2	68·4	63·5	57·8
Capital goods						
For transport	1·6	3·6	4·9	5·2	6·9	8·3
For industry	12·1	16·0	18·2	19·1	23·4	25·2
Total for production	13·7	19·6	23·1	24·3	30·3	33·5
Unclassed	6·7	5·2	5·7	7·3	6·2	8·7
Total	100·0	100·0	100·0	100·0	100·0	100·0

* For details, see Appendix, p. 552.

[1] Callis, pp. 76, 104.

At the opening of the present century the value of capital imports was less than a third of the value of imports for consumption: by 1936–7 the proportion had risen to three-fifths. With an increase of production one would expect more imports for production. But for their own use the people were importing less per head than thirty years earlier. In 1903–4 the value of imports for consumption was Rs. 103·5 million; in 1936–7, with a population that had grown by close on one-half, the value of imports for consumption had risen by less than a quarter, to Rs. 125·9 million. Moreover, the imports included a larger proportion of necessities, and a smaller proportion of luxuries. Thus in 1903–4 the import of cotton goods was Rs. 30·7 million, rather less than 30 % of the imports for consumption, and in 1936–7 it was Rs. 45·5 million or just over 35 %; although the imports nearly kept pace with the growth of population, the people cannot have been so well supplied with cotton goods because, as we have already noticed, local production had declined. On the other hand, during the same period the import of silks and other luxuries continued to drop, not only in proportion but absolutely; it fell from Rs. 15·1 million, about 15 % of the imports for consumption, to Rs. 10·7 million, or just over 8 %. For silk goods alone, the fall is even more striking, as the value dropped from Rs. 7 million to less than half a million. And for the cotton goods imported they had to give more rice than before. In 1933–4 the index number for rice, based on the prices for 1898–1901, was 73·8, whereas the index numbers for cotton goods were 122·8 for greys, 153·4 for whites and 109·8 for coloured goods. If, at the beginning of the century, a man sold a hundred measures of paddy for Rs. 100 and purchased with the proceeds 100 measures of cloth, in 1935–6 he would receive only Rs. 73·8 for his paddy, and have to pay about Rs. 140 for the same quantity of cloth. He had to give about twice as much as before for what he got. Thus in 1936–7 the cultivators were importing less per head than before, and paying more for what they imported.

This tallies with such information as is available regarding the production and domestic consumption of rice. It has been estimated[1] that during the thirties the consumption of rice in Burma fell by nearly 25 % a head; this estimate rests partly on estimates of production which are very unreliable, and it is difficult to believe that in 1940 the people consumed only about three-quarters as much rice as twenty years earlier. Nevertheless there is good reason to hold that

[1] Wickizer and Bennett, p. 216.

the quantity of rice exported has grown at the expense of that retained for food. With the great fall in the value of rice consequent on
the depression of the thirties, there was a corresponding fall in land
values. Men who received half the price that they expected for their
produce were unable to pay their debts, and had to make over their
land to the moneylenders. As already explained, that was no new thing.
From 1870 onwards landholders in the chief rice districts had been
losing their land for debt. But what happened now was that the moneylenders could no longer find cultivators to take the land off their hands
at a price that they would accept. Thus over half the land in these
districts was now admittedly owned by non-agriculturists. This
naturally tended to reduce *gross* production while increasing *net* production, the surplus available for export. The tenant, on a system of
annual leases, could not get so much out of the land as a man who held
the land for a longer period. Landlords preferred poor cultivators
who would give a high rent, over better cultivators who would not pay
so much rent. Moreover, production on a large scale allowed of
economies in working. A holding of a hundred acres worked with
seasonal labour will produce less than the same area cultivated by half
a dozen smallholders, but will yield a larger surplus for the market.
We have already noticed that, taking the lowlands as a whole, the
richest districts are the least populous. It is quite likely then that the
increase of exports per head synchronized with a decrease in production per head, and likely also that the people were consuming less
rice per head than before, but it is perhaps improbable that the decline in consumption per head fell by more than 10 %. Even that,
however, suggests a considerable decline in material individual
welfare, and it is of particular interest as accompanying the introduction of political machinery supposed to give the people a larger
say in the management of their own affairs.

Under the Constitution of 1923 nothing could be done, because the
Government was unable to take action on controversial issues. The
Constitution of 1937 seemed to give more power to the people, and
the premier, Dr Ba Maw, must be credited with valiant endeavours
to repair past neglect. Besides investigating corruption he appointed
a committee to study agrarian distress. He was in a difficult position
because he depended on the support of capitalist interests which had
opposed agrarian legislation in the past, and his expert advisers had
learned their art under the system of executive rule, when these
problems were evaded. The agrarian legislation was not very

wisely conceived. Instead of harnessing to the task of economic reconstruction the forces of individual interest and nationalist sentiment, it attempted to control economic forces by regulations that
disregarded them; by multiplying work and jobs, it increased the cost
and burden of administration, creating much confusion and some
hardship, and achieving little for the public welfare. Thus, up to the
time of the Japanese invasion, the forms and machinery of self-
government had been no more effective than executive rule in staying
the decline of individual welfare consequent on the abnormal predominance of economic forces.

3. SOCIAL WELFARE

Village Communities. Another matter into which Dr Ba Maw
directed enquiry was village administration. The village system in
Burma, as already explained, was invented by the British Government
in 1886 to facilitate the pacification of Upper Burma and the suppression of rebellion and disorder in Lower Burma. 'This system
was based on the village headman on whom numerous administrative
duties were imposed, who exercised petty powers of civil and criminal
justice, was authorized to punish his villagers for failure to assist him
in the execution of his public duties, and was remunerated by commission on the revenue he collected.' From time to time suggestions
were put forward that village councils should be formed, but 'had not
been accepted by the Local Government on the grounds that they would
be an innovation foreign to the customs and spirit of the people, would
diminish the authority of the village headman and so weaken the
system of village administration'.[1]

One of the earliest symptoms of unrest in rural areas was the constitution by the people themselves of village associations. These were
discouraged or suppressed as political in character and centres of
disaffection. Partly to counter these unofficial associations and partly
to cope better with the growth of crime, the Village Act was amended
in 1924. The new law provided for the constitution of village committees to administer civil and criminal justice and to advise the
headman, while maintaining the individual responsibility and powers
of the headman, who was to be the chairman of the committee. Among
the various defects of the former system were the fact that the headman 'was looked upon by the villagers more as an official than as

[1] *ISC*, XI, 447.

their representative and that unsuitable applicants were at times appointed'.[1] The formation of village committees did nothing to remedy these defects, and was merely another device for getting the people of their own accord to do what they did not want to do. So far then as village committees were appointed, they existed 'not for the exercise of the functions of local self-government, but solely for the trial of petty civil and criminal cases, and to act as an advisory body to the village headman in the performance of his duties concerning the general welfare of the tract'. In practice they made little difference and, as before, village administration centred round the headmen, though it became increasingly inefficient as his authority declined.

The Village Amendment Act of 1924 was in fact a political move on the part of Government. It 'anticipated the introduction of proposals to amend the Village Act by the Nationalist Party at the instigation of the G.C.B.A., which had found village administration, and especially the authority of the headman, an obstacle to the political activity of village associations'.[2] Naturally the creation of officially sponsored committees to counteract non-official associations failed to restore harmony within the village or to revitalize village social life. The committee appointed in 1937 to enquire into village administration did not rise to any conception of the village as an organic social unit, but was content to regard it from the administrative standpoint. Although Nationalists, and some officials, had long urged the substitution of popular for executive control, it reported, rather surprisingly, that there was 'no public demand for any radical reconstruction of the village system'.[3] Despite the known unpopularity of amalgamating villages, it thought this 'a necessary step in the process of gradually providing adequate remuneration' for the headman. It noted that villagers did not generally take a keen interest in the election of the official village committees, but made no proposals to use for constructive ends the numerous non-official village associations. It recommended the enforcement of the numerous regulations, universally unpopular, often unwise, and generally disregarded, for village sanitation, the construction of houses, and the prevention of infectious and contagious diseases among men, cattle and crops. It also urged the stricter observance of the rules for reporting the arrival and departure of visitors, and the retention of powers to impose collective penalties and to deport undesirable characters. Thus

[1] *ISC*, XI, 447.   [2] *ISC*, XI, 314.   [3] *ISC*, XI, 274; *CVS*, p. 2.

it suggested no departure from the policy of treating the village as a unit of administration for the maintenance of law and order, and the village headman as an executive official instead of as a leader of the people, and it quite disregarded the possibility of rebuilding society on the basis of common social life within the village.

Communal Discord. Meanwhile the political reforms were aggravating communal discord, while hindering the provision of remedies. At the beginning of the century it was a commonplace to describe the Burman as tolerant of foreigners, though indifference was a more accurate description of his attitude. At that time such racial or class feeling as may have existed was limited to Europeans, who found Indians less attractive than Burmans, had little sympathy with Indian Nationalism, and to some extent were already apprehensive of Indian competition. But twenty years later Burmans were held to feel a 'natural antipathy' to Indians, and one could trace the main lines of cleavage between capitalist interests, primarily concerned with economic progress, and national interests aiming to promote social welfare.[1] The reforms ranged the groups in opposing camps, and in each camp there were divided counsels.

The various capitalist groups, despite their common interest in economic progress, were competitors in the economic sphere; the Europeans looked to the interests of the big rice-mills, while Chinese and Indians were interested in the smaller mills; Chinese were chiefly concerned with the Eastern trade and Indians in the trade with India. Europeans in general favoured the separation of Burma from India, which would tend to diminish competition, whereas Indians wished to retain the connection. So far as measures touched on Indian nationalist policy and interests, Indians were apt to diverge from the purely capitalist standpoint, and might line up with Burman Nationalists. In the opposite camp were the Burmans. In this camp the chief division was due to the imperfect sympathy between Burmese and Karens, especially the Christian Karens, where religious differences accentuated racial particularity.

During the ten years after the introduction of the reforms there were serious communal riots between Burmans and Indians, and Burmans and Chinese, and the most formidable rebellion since 1886. This broke out at the end of 1930 in Tharrawaddy, from about 1860 to 1880 the most peaceful district in Burma but, during the present century, conspicuous for crime. It spread rapidly over

[1] *ISC*, xi, 21, 268; 1920, Cmd. 746, p. 31; *RAB*, 1930–1, p. ix.

the greater part of the delta so far north as Thayetmyo, and up the railway line to Yamethin. The rebels, styling themselves *Galons*, assumed a distinctive uniform and attempted a military organization. In addition to the local forces, one British and five Indian battalions were called in from India. In August 1931 the rebel leader was captured, but an amnesty offered to his followers met for some time with little response. By March 1932, however, some 9000 had surrendered, and the rebellion was over. The casualties included 102 Government servants killed and 114 wounded; the known casualties among the rebels amounted to about 2000.[1] The Burman who appeared for Government in the subsequent prosecution was promoted to the High Court; Dr Ba Maw, who conducted the defence, and U Saw, who subsequently identified himself with the rebel cause by assuming the style Galon U Saw, were rewarded in due course by election successively as Premier. The rebellion was explained as due in part to anti-Indian feeling, but there were Indians in the rebel army and one, at least, among the leaders. So far as it was directed against Indians, this was due to their association with agrarian grievances as landowners and moneylenders. The movement spread rapidly and widely because executive authority had been undermined by the political reforms, but it had only a very remote connection with modern nationalism. Educated Burmans did not conceal their natural sympathy with the rebels, but were too wise or prudent to take part in the rebellion. It showed indeed how little progress modern Nationalism had made among the people, and was chiefly significant perhaps as demonstrating that time had done little to reconcile them to foreign rule. The rebellion was anti-Government and anti-European, rather than anti-Indian.

We have noticed the growing distrust of Europeans in connection with Separation. Another notable illustration appeared in the case of 'the Bullinger Pool'. Between Burmans as producers of rice and European millers as the chief buyers there is a natural conflict of interest. As already noticed, up to the nineties there was little attempt to conceal the sympathy of the Government with the millers. After the disastrous results of the great combine of 1893–4, the millers were less aggressive and the attitude of Government towards similar combines less sympathetic. With the growth of rice-mills in the interior the position of the large European millers in the ports grew weaker, and in 1920–1 an attempt by the big millers to keep

[1] *MMR*, 1930–1, p. 130; 1931–2, p. 36.

down prices failed because they had to obtain supplies to meet their forward sales.[1] An immediate sequel in 1921 was the formation by the four chief European firms of the Bullinger Pool to observe a common policy in buying and selling rice. This combination was generally believed to exercise a powerful influence in lowering the prices received by cultivators for their paddy, and to use its influence in inducing the railway company to fix rates on rice and paddy prejudicial to the rice-mills in the interior. In February 1929, at the instance of the Nationalist members, the Legislature recommended an enquiry 'into the rice and paddy trade generally, and, in particular, [into railway] freights and combinations to control prices'. The committee charged with the enquiry took the view that the Pool was 'an organization devised in the need for self-preservation in the fight with the too numerous small mills'; 'it does not seem right', says the report, 'to scrutinize too closely the tactics in a fight for existence. The Pool enjoys no legal advantage. It has no monopoly. It rests on its commercial reputation, its business skill and its financial backing. It is our opinion that in all the circumstances no case has been made out for government interference.'[2] This account of the matter is not quite correct, as the Pool was created in 1921 with a view to controlling prices, and at that time the small mills were still comparatively few. When the report of the committee reached the Government in May 1931, Burma had recently become involved in the general collapse of world prices, consequent on the Wall Street crisis of September 1929. The Government, in reviewing the report, disregarded both the terms of reference and the recommendations of the committee. It stated that the main reason why the committee was appointed was in order to enquire into the causes of the fall in prices. Overlooking the fact that the enquiry originated in a recommendation by the Legislative Council in February 1929, it held that the collapse of prices in 1931, being a world-wide phenomenon, could not be due to any purely local cause in Burma, and that accordingly there was no need to take action on the report. Not unnaturally the report, and the Government resolution on the report, failed to remove Nationalist suspicions that, even without any legal advantage and depending merely on business skill, financial backing and tactics which should not be too closely scrutinized, the Pool was detrimental to Burman interests. But the chief importance of the agitation against the activities of the Pool was to demonstrate that the Nationalist attack was no longer directed

[1] RTC, 1912–13, p. 13; RAB, 1920–1, p. 104.   [2] CRT, p. 27.

mainly against Indian moneylenders and landowners but against European capitalists, and against the Government as supporting them.

This change of direction is the more significant because at the same time capitalist activities were tending to promote communal discord between Burmans and Indians. The use of cheap Indian labour has long been justified on the ground that 'Burmans dislike hard work'. But in 1924 a strike among the Indian dockyard coolies was broken by calling in Burman labour.[1] As soon as the Indians had been brought to terms, the Burman labour was dismissed. The same expedient was adopted on the occasion of another dockyard strike in March 1930. On this occasion, when the Indians submitted, the Burmans refused to acquiesce in their dismissal; for a few days there were serious riots, causing much damage to life and property, but securing for Burmans 'a foothold ... in the Rangoon labour market'.[2] Again, in May 1931, Burmans were called in to break a strike of the Rangoon Conservancy staff.[3] These incidents not merely aggravated communal tension between Burmans and Indians, but aroused ill-feeling against the European employers of the Indians. Further evidence of increasing communal tension was apparent in 'a serious riot, between the Burmese and Chinese communities which resulted in considerable loss of life'. Thus, by the time that Burma was separated from India sectional discord and racial antipathy prevailed, and there was urgent need for a strong Government capable of restoring harmony. This the new constitution of 1937 failed to provide.

4. CLERICAL DISORDER

A further symptom of social disintegration was the growing turbulence of the monastic Order. Clerical intervention in political activities is often regarded as wholly new. But monks were among the leaders of resistance to British rule in 1886 and 1852, and have been prominent in numerous petty insurrections back to 1831.[4] The rebellion of 1886 was everywhere headed by the monks; some actually took part in the fighting, and Karens brought in numerous decapitated shaven heads to claim rewards.[5] The Order inherits a political tradition; under Burmese rule clerics played an important part in local and national affairs, and the monastery was an avenue to promotion

[1] *RCLI*, x, Pt II, p. 163.   [2] *RAB*, 1930–1, p. x.   [3] *RAB*, 1930–1, pp. x, 37.
[4] *BBG*, I, 481, 487; II, 290; *Tharrawaddy Gazetteer*, p. 34; *UBG*, ii, 7.
[5] Smeaton, p. 14.

in the State. The Order, which 'theoretically had nothing to do with politics or things of this world, was really a political power, the only permanent power'.[1] Under British rule all that was changed.

But that was not the only ground for disaffection. In Burmese times the whole Order was knit together in a complex system under a central committee with a single head, and it was very largely autonomous. The piecemeal occupation of Burma by the British cut off the monasteries within British territory from the central committee and thus left each monastery an isolated unit. Just as the native political organization was broken up into villages, so also was the ecclesiastical organization. This allowed the machinery of discipline to decay, and the growth of 'laxity and insubordination'[2] already attracted notice in 1870. Despite this, on the occupation of Upper Burma in 1886, the central authority in Mandalay, still recognized throughout the newly conquered territory, was set aside as of no concern to the British Government. For some years ecclesiastical causes were left for decision by the Order, but judicial decisions gradually brought them within the jurisdiction of the civil courts. In ecclesiastical as in lay affairs, British law supplanted Burmese custom, the last vestiges of monastic autonomy disappeared, and with them the only effective machinery for regulating admission to the Order and expelling disreputable members.

In other ways also the monks lost much of their influence and prestige. We have noticed that there were reports to this effect so far back as 1833, that at least since 1852 many villages in Lower Burma have been unable to build a monastery or maintain a monk, and that from 1870, if not earlier, there have been complaints as to the deterioration of monastic schools. Nowadays the monk can no longer be so helpful to the village, and in particular the Order has lost its hold on education. Formerly the monastic school provided a training in democracy, as boys of all classes worked and played together, sharing alike in the menial duties of the monastery. To-day the children of the wealthier and urban classes are sent to lay schools to pass examinations. Pali, the classical language of the monastic curriculum, now has no market value, and the suggestion made in 1870 to encourage the demand, then finding expression, for the teaching of English in monastic schools was rejected,[3] so that the monks in general are now among the most unenlightened of the people instead of, as formerly,

---

[1] *UBG*, II, I.   [2] Fytche, II, 334.
[3] *RPI*, 1871–2, cited *RPI*, 1928–9, p. 10.

their leaders in cultural development. Moreover, Buddhism, as ordinarily understood by the Burmese monk, is wholly incompatible with western individualism, and even the strictest monk, though he may hold aloof from anti-British agitation, tends to sympathize with it and condone it.

But the monks are still regarded, at least among the lower orders and generally in rural districts, with a superstitious veneration that gives them power without responsibility. Anyone may become a monk at any time, but as soon as he assumes the yellow robe, he becomes sacred. The small boy in the monastic school, who yesterday hardly dared venture into the presence of a European official, will address him on terms of equality immediately on becoming a novice. In any attempt by Government to take action against a monk, popular sympathy and support are always, whatever the merits of the case, in favour of the monk and against the Government. Hesitating to act firmly, even in notorious cases, lest this should further alienate the people and multiply unrest, the Government takes refuge in pious platitudes or vague aspersions, thereby advertising its weakness, and furnishing new cause for disaffection among both clerics and laymen.

There is nothing new either in the power exercised by the monastic Order, or in its disintegration or its antipathy to western rule. What is new is that recently men have taken the yellow robe as a cloak for political activities, because they can rely on general sympathy among the monkhood for their political aspirations, and because the monastery affords the best shelter for attacking a foreign government. From a very early stage in the modern nationalist movement monks have been active, forming an association which 'threw in its lot with the extremists and ere long dominated their activities'. This militant section plays a conspicuous part in annual conferences and in meetings to discuss political or other grievances, and their speeches, though decried by Government as 'not of a high order as regards accuracy or reason',[1] are effective in inflaming sentiments of disaffection. Thus the vacuum caused by the decay of the force which held society together has been filled by an instrument of disruption, and the only organized body among the clergy now serves for disseminating malice instead of fostering goodwill.

[1] *ISC*, XI, 24–5.

5. EDUCATION

The introduction in 1923 of a constitution based on the principle of responsible government implied the need for a more active encouragement of education, so as to bring the people into closer touch with the modern world, and to provide both an instructed electorate and leaders. Until then, as we have seen, the schools produced clerks and lawyers, but practically no doctors, engineers or men of business; there were no facilities for the study of economics and practically none for the study of natural science. Burma had been thrown open to the world, but the world had not been opened up to Burma. In 1923, as in 1869, it might have been said without much exaggeration that of barracks, of jails and court-houses there were not a few, but hardly anything in the province to testify the presence of any rule higher than that from which it had been wrested. There were many more barracks, jails and courts, and the public offices and business houses in Rangoon were now built of brick or concrete instead of native timber; there were also many more schools, but these, like the courts, were instruments of British rule. Just as the village had been adapted from social to administrative ends, so had the schools been adapted from cultural to economic ends.

All were agreed that Burma needed better education to equip it for the modern world. But opinions differed as to how this should be done. The Government favoured the spread of primary instruction; Burmans set more store on higher instruction that would enable them the sooner to take over the government. Both parties, however, tended to identify education with instruction, and both looked to attain their ends by multiplying schools. And both parties alike ignored the fact that education is conditioned by environment. The Government tried to extend primary instruction by providing more schools and teachers, but without taking measures to stimulate the demand for learning; Burmans wanted men trained for industry and commerce without regard to the demand for their employment. Thus efforts to promote education had very little effect, and in 1940 Burma was still almost as remote from the modern world as in 1923. We have discussed the state of education in 1923 under the heads of primary instruction, secondary and higher instruction, technical and vocational instruction, and the education of women. Let us examine now the further progress under these several heads.

Primary Instruction. Looking merely at the numbers attending school, a comparison of the figures of 1900 with those of 1940 suggests a considerable advance. The total number at school rose from 307,000, or 3·34 % of the population, in 1900 to 827,000, or 4·90 % in 1940. But the increase was largely due to the remarkable progress in female education, as the number of girls at school rose during the same period from 36,000 to about 220,000, so that, in proportion to the population, there was a very small increase in the number of boys at school.[1]

Some would even question whether the progress in instruction represented progress in education, for at the same time the per-centage of the population in unregistered schools, almost all monastic, is shown as having declined from 1·61 to 1·26, though the figures for these schools must be accepted with caution. Up to about 1900 it was the custom to recite the praises of the monastic schools, but, when Government adopted a policy of closer supervision over instruction, advocates of the official system became more critical of the monks, describing them as 'very ignorant, or very bigoted or both',[2] and condemning monastic schools as inefficient. Yet, even thirty years later, of the pupils in the registered schools 75 % did not go beyond Standard I, and 88 % failed to complete Standard IV, which is regarded as the minimum for permanent literacy.[3] Lay schools were claimed as more efficient than the ordinary monastic schools because they taught the children their alphabet in shorter time. But time was a consideration only for children who were meant to press on to higher standards, so as to qualify for a job at an early age; as regards children who would never go beyond the alphabet it mattered little whether they took a year more or a year less to learn their letters. In fact not many got beyond 'the unwieldy infant class in which the majority of the pupils had barely passed the crawling stage'. An onlooker, it has been said, 'would no longer wonder why children left school so soon, but why they were ever sent at all'.[4] There was a simple explanation. 'People for the most part send their children to school to get them out of the way.' The lay school, which took girls as well as boys, was more useful as a crèche. It would seem, then, that only a small proportion of the lay schools teach more than the unregistered monastic schools while, on the other hand, some monastic schools are still capable of educating lads who, with no other schooling, could, at least until quite recently,

---

[1] *RPI*, 1899–1900, p. 57; 1897–1902, p. 4; 1932–7, p. xx.
[2] *RPI*, 1897–1902, p. 41. [3] *CVV*, pp. 147, 151, 153. [4] *ISC*, XI, 497.

rise to become magistrates. After the official policy of concentrating on primary instruction had been in operation for nearly forty years, a committee, appointed to report progress, found that it presented a picture of 'almost unrelieved gloom'.[1] Under Burmese rule all the boys were sent to monastic schools because there was a social demand for education; but primary vernacular instruction provided little opportunity for material advancement, and when, under British rule, education came to be valued solely as an economic asset, 'the difficulty was to create a demand for the school',[2] and primary instruction languished.

Secondary Instruction. For the same reason that primary instruction languished, secondary and higher instruction flourished. While the number of boys in the primary standards did little more than keep pace with the growth of the population, the number of pupils in the middle standards (V–VII) was eight times as many in 1937 as in 1900; in the higher standards (VIII–X) twenty-five times as many; and in the colleges fifteen times as many. These figures provide an instructive comment on the official policy of regarding the extension of elementary instruction as 'a primary obligation'. The secondary schools led to jobs, and the higher standards to better jobs; soon, as formerly in India, lads from the middle schools could no longer find employment, and a little later, when the market for higher standard qualifications was glutted, they went on to college.

They went on to college because there was no opening for them in industry or commerce, and the only avenue to a well-paid job was through 'academic' studies. Lads from Burma had to take a Calcutta degree, and their choice of subjects was limited by the curriculum which was adjusted to the conditions of employment. Scientific studies especially were backward and in 1922, when Burma was officially recognized as fit for an instalment of responsible government, only eight men took a degree in science; despite the mineral wealth of Burma, there were no facilities for the study of geology. But, just as the period of executive rule was drawing to a close, the output of the schools was thought sufficient to require a local university. The University of Rangoon, established in 1920, comprised two colleges, one a Government institution, the other managed by the American Baptist Mission; a Training College for Teachers, and a Medical College were added in 1930–1. With the growth of the university the course of studies was widened both in

[1] *CVV*, p. 156.   [2] *RPI*, 1928–9, p. 13.

arts and science. In 1923 provision was made for taking economics in the arts course, but, as the teachers from India knew nothing of Burma, their lectures were very remote from the life and surroundings of the students. At about the same time the curriculum was expanded to include all the usual scientific studies. But there are still comparatively few science students. As there is little demand for Burmans in the scientific professions, little science is taught in the schools. In 1937 ten anglo-vernacular high schools provided courses in chemistry and physics, but only one—a girls' school—taught botany and zoology; eleven vernacular high schools professed to teach 'general science', but the course included no practical work. In these circumstances not many take science in the university and, in 1937, of 108 male graduates only 25 took a science degree.

The latest report notes 'the universal desire of parents to provide opportunities for their children to enter the superior services and the "professions" to which the road lies through the University'.[1] But, for various reasons, the proportion of Anglo-Indians and Indians at the university is high in relation to their numerical strength in the population; the former are 0·2 % of the population, but 8·3 % of university students, and for the latter the corresponding figures are 6·9 and 33·8 %. One reason for this is that the universities represent the urban population, in which most of the Anglo-Indians and Indians are concentrated, and Burmans are comparatively few. In 1937 out of 1744 students receiving university or intermediate education, only 155 were classed as coming from rural areas. But secondary instruction as a whole is very largely urban, and one-third of the pupils are concentrated in Rangoon.[2] Thus there is a cleavage in society not only along racial lines but between the educated and uneducated classes, and the educated who have spent all their life in towns are astonishingly ignorant of rural Burma, and the life of the people. They cannot even write the language well, and it has been said, with much truth, that those who know English do not know Burmese, while those who know Burmese know nothing else. Nowhere are the relations between Europeans and Burmans so human and friendly as in the University where an able and enthusiastic staff, English and American, tries to persuade the students that, despite their experience and environment, life in the modern world is not solely concerned with making money. But most of them on graduating are caught up into the machinery of general administration, where cultural

[1] *RPI*, 1932–7, p. 7.   [2] *RPI*, 1932–7, Tables iv a, b; *CVV*, p. 181.

values are at a discount, and, in an atmosphere devoid of books or other instruments of humane life, such impression as the university may have made upon them fades. Moreover, even within the university politics are rife; to the Government it is a hot-bed of dangerous thoughts, to the Burman an instrument for inculcating 'slave-mentality', and both sides are suspicious of the staff.

Vocational Instruction. One feature of Curzon's policy was the encouragement of technical and vocational rather than academic instruction. In Burma this problem was less urgent, because the rapid growth of the administration provided adequately for the output of the schools. But gradually a surplus of school graduates led, as earlier in India, to a greater interest in technical and vocational courses, and the problems arising in this connection were examined by special committees in 1927 and again in 1936.[1] During a discussion of the subject in the Legislature it was suggested that 'only criminals and detectives could obtain technical education in Burma'. The Director accepted the criticism as not without foundation for the schools, but thought the provision outside the schools not inconsiderable 'for an agricultural country'.[2]

There is in fact provision for instruction in medicine, law, forestry, veterinary science, teaching, engineering, industry, commerce and art. But the total under all these heads in 1937 was only 2488, and of these 1269 were training as teachers and 613 were studying commerce, leaving only 616 under all the other heads to meet the requirements of a population of 16 millions in the modern world. Of the students in the highest or university grade, Burmese numbered 32 out of the 79 law students, 55 out of 141 in education, and in engineering only

Technical Students, 1937*
(*a*) University; (*b*) Collegiate

	(*a*)	(*b*)
Law	79	—
Medicine	147	103
Education	141	1128
Engineering	54	75
Industrial	—	39
Veterinary	—	17
Forestry	—	47
Commerce	—	613
Art	—	45

* *RPI*, 1932–7, Tables v a, b.

16 out of 54, in medicine 23 out of 147. The usual explanation is that the Burman dislikes a professional career because the work is too arduous and poorly paid; yet in the courses for subordinate professional appointments, certainly no less arduous and much worse paid, the proportion of Burmans was much higher. In education there were 880 out of 1128; in engineering 52 (mostly training as

[1] *RPI*, 1927–32, p. 2; *CVV*, pp. 389ff.   [2] *RPI*, 1927–32, p. 28.

revenue surveyors) out of 75, in medicine 42 out of 103, in forestry 28 out of 47, and in commerce 344 out of 613. As Burmans form over 80 % of the population, these figures are not very satisfactory to National- ists. It is remarkable that one subject is conspicuously absent from this list, and that the most important—agriculture. But there was no demand for such agricultural instruction as western institutions could impart. An Agricultural College on ambitious lines, opened for teaching in 1924, was not very successful, because of 'the reluctance of educated Burmans to adopt an agricultural career'. An Agricultural School of a more elementary character, founded by American missionaries, is said to have demonstrated the value of its methods. But teaching in such schools demanded 'Burmans with high technical qualifications, and a flame of zeal and energy'[1]—a pious aspiration rather than a practical suggestion. It seems that both college and school succumbed to the depression of the thirties, as there is no reference to either in the latest quinquennial review of education. The only schools under the head of Vocational and Special Education in which Burmans pre- ponderated were the reformatories, where they numbered 308 out of 342—still less satisfactory, and pointing the gibe in the Legislature that technical instruction was reserved for the criminals and police. Under executive rule the lack of a demand for Burmans with technical qualifications prevented the growth of technical instruction, and the machinery of western democracy, when introduced in 1923, was of no avail to change the social and economic environment, and failed consequently to attract lads to technical institutions.

Morals and Discipline. Under the new system of government, school morals and discipline received even more attention than under execu- tive rule. In addition to primers of personal ethics, recommended in 1904 by Lord Curzon, Burmans advocated, partly on political grounds, the provision of systematic instruction in the Buddhist religion, though educational officials had greater faith in football.[2] But during the last five years before the separation of Burma from India, there were more than thirty school strikes, and, though freedom and preparation for free citizenship received fuller recognition in the theory and practice of education, the boys in the upper standards reacted by showing less temperance and less tolerance of the ordinary rules of school life. For over a hundred years the monastic schools had been criticized as un- practical; the schools that had replaced them were severely practical:

---

[1] *ISC*, XI, 115, 137; *CVV*, p. 399.
[2] *RPI*, 1927–32, p. 37.

'How to spiritualize education', writes the Director, 'is the real problem.'[1]

Female Instruction. On the other hand, as already noticed, female education continued to make great headway. The provision for teaching girls has been the great contribution of British rule to the system of instruction. Except in the number at school, however, the progress of female education was disappointing. Curzon looked to the women to improve 'the educational and moral tone of the people'. But even fewer girls than boys get beyond 'the unwieldy infant class'. The lay schools in towns, however, gave them better opportunities to learn enough reading, writing and arithmetic for retail trade in the bazaar; they had an economic value. The few girls who went further looked on instruction, like the boys, merely as a means of livelihood. 'What beacon of light', asked an inspectress, 'can we hold up to induce girls to seek education in the higher departments',[2] if it gives them no opening to a profession? There was a demand for schools as crèches, a demand for elementary instruction for use in retail trade, and a very small demand for higher instruction so far as this was an economic asset. But there were few signs that girls regarded western education as having a cultural value. To Christians, whether Burman or Karen, the education of the girls was a matter of religious obligation, like the education of boys among Buddhists, and many girls went back from the high school to the home; but the Burmese girl in the university looked for a job, or, possibly (if not preferably), a wealthy husband. Even among the women education served economic and not social ends.

Literacy. We have already noticed that under British rule the proportion returned as literate has risen, not merely, as one might expect, among females but also among males. The first census after the annexation of Upper Burma showed that the newly conquered province had a greater proportion of male literates than British Burma, with 46·2 % learning and literate as against 44·3, though Lower Burma was ahead in female literacy with 3·8 against 1·5. The lower proportion of literate males in Lower Burma was largely due to the influx of illiterate Indians, and was in fact lower than ten years earlier. Between 1900 and 1940 the percentage of literate males rose from 37·6 to 56·0 and of females from 6·1 to 16·5. It would seem difficult to reconcile the rise in male literacy and its high proportion with the small increase in the number at school, and with the fact that so small a proportion remain at school

[1] *RPI*, 1932–7, p. 45.   [2] *RPI*, 1927–32, p. 25.

long enough to acquire permanent literacy. Figures for literacy must needs be somewhat arbitrary; they are obtained by enumerations at the census by subordinate officials who have no time for detailed enquiries and, moreover, the standard of literacy varies from one census to another. Even in the earliest census probably a much larger number, if pressed, could at least have signed their names. Here we may find an explanation of the apparent anomaly. Under Burmese rule practically every Buddhist boy learned his letters, but subsequently lapsed into illiteracy for lack of practice. Printing was unknown and manuscripts were costly, and letters were of little use except to monks, traders and officials. But under British rule there arose a social demand for literacy; every railway station and every railway ticket gives a reading lesson; the public notices, the courts, still more the moneylender, and most of all the post office prevent people from forgetting what they learned. It is the environment and not the school that has promoted literacy. In 1860 few but Europeans and Indians used the post office, and up to 1880 there were few postal facilities for towns and villages in the interior.[1] About that time, however, the rural police began to be useful as postmen. The people soon took advantage of this privilege, and gradually the regular service was extended. It is perhaps not too much to say that the postal system, introduced originally for the benefit of the foreign community, did more to promote literacy than all the lay schools; it fostered a latent demand for *adult* literacy, and the ability to read and write ceased to be merely an ornament that one discarded on leaving school.

This consideration applies much more widely. If the number of children at school has not increased more rapidly in Burma, it is because there was little demand for primary instruction; formerly the people *wanted* to send their children to the monastic school, and for this and other purposes maintained at their own charge the monastery and its inmates; there was a social demand for education. If there is to be any great increase in primary instruction, it is not sufficient to supply schools and teachers; it is essential to cultivate a demand for them. Similarly, if Burmans are to be held responsible for the conduct of their national affairs, it is necessary to cultivate a demand for the type of education that will help them to discharge their responsibilities. The machinery of democratic government is a dangerous implement to place in the hands of uneducated people but, when introducing a modern constitution with household suffrage, the Government did

[1] *RAB*, 1861–2, p. 25; 1880–1, Intr. p. 38; pp. 17, 90; 1882–3, p. 117.

little to train leaders in a knowledge of the modern world, or to fit the people for the franchise. A private association for the encouragement of reading, though regarded with suspicion by some administrative officials, enjoyed the patronage of the Governor and the support of the Education Department. Successive Directors also devised plans for supplying the public with books, though none was carried very far, as each new Director had a new plan. By these means subscription libraries were established by some municipal committees, but in 1940 as in 1923 there was still only one public library, which in some years, as a Director of Public Instruction noted, with an income of nearly £1000 managed to spend about £10 on the actual purchase of books.[1] There was still no museum, art gallery or theatre. For a long time nothing was attempted in broadcasting and then only in a very small way, while the cheapest wireless set cost over £30. The cinema was left to private enterprise and the only glimpse of Burmans on the outer world was from the angle of Hollywood.

But the great need of the country was a modern vernacular litera-ture. According to the official returns less than 200 books were published annually, only about half of them in Burmese and almost all of them still medieval in their outlook. There were one or two monthly magazines of some merit, but the total circulation of Burmese newspapers was still negligible. The first vernacular newspaper was started in the seventies. There were two in 1877, and by 1879, when they had grown to five, we are told that 'the tone was gentlemanly and on the whole loyal to the British Government, though traces of a decided national feeling were occasionally visible'.[2] Their circulation was only 150-300 copies. By 1930, among the newspapers in Burmese, four, with a circulation of 3500, were subsidized by the Sino-Burmese supporters of Government; four, mainly non-political, had a circula-tion of 4600 (chiefly due to the 'Burmese Cinema' with 2500); six nationalist, with a circulation of 11,350 and six extremist, with a circulation of 12,500.[3] Thus the circulation varied with the violence of opposition to the Government. But there were no modern books in Burmese, and no attempt had been made to solve the difficult problem of translating western literature, apart from some half-dozen adaptations of popular novels. From the earliest days of the reforms the encouragement of a modern literature and the translation and adaptation of western books was a main item in the nationalist pro-

[1] *RPI*, 1928-9, p. 23.   [2] *RAB*, 1879-80, p. 104.   [3] *ISC*, XI, 272.

gramme, but a motion to this effect was opposed by Government on the ground that 'there was no demand for translated books as there was no reading public for such literature',[1] though at the same time a private organization was demonstrating that it was quite possible to organize such a demand on a paying basis.

Educational Progress. The progress of education under all its forms in Burma during the period between 1923 and 1940 shows a notable contrast with that achieved in neighbouring countries. The figures for Burma in the marginal table omit the Shan States. Sixty years ago Upper Burma, under native rule, had far more children at school than any country outside Burma in the tropical Far East; in 1900 Burma as a whole still held the lead, but by 1940 it had sunk to the fifth place, and, in respect of institutions managed or helped by Government, was little ahead of Netherlands India, where general public instruction dates only from 1907. Moreover, many children never attended any school. The number of children of school-going age (6–11) in 1936 was estimated at 1·6 million of whom 0·4 million attended recognized schools and 0·2 million other schools, leaving a million with no schooling.[2]

*Percentage of population at recognized schools,** 1936–9*

Formosa	11·16
Philippines	10·75
Thailand	9·69
Malaya	6·02
Burma	3·92
Netherlands India	3·35
Indo-China	2·06

* Furnivall, *Educational Progress in S.E. Asia* (1943), p. 111.

But the picture is darker than these figures indicate. It might be claimed sixty years ago that Burma was the best educated country in the tropical Far East, with the possible exception of the Philippines. It would be difficult to repel the charge that at the time of its separation from India it was the worst educated. In the Philippines there were hundreds, and in Siam scores of people, who had seen something of the modern world; in Burma only about eight students were sent abroad annually, and for three successive years during the depression none were sent. Both in the Philippines and Siam many men have a long experience of practical administration along modern lines in responsible positions; in Burma the corresponding posts were held by Europeans. In Malaya many Chinese are citizens of the modern world, and even the Malays, though still backward in higher education, almost all receive primary instruction. In Java, comparatively few have been to Europe, though some members of the upper classes

[1] *ISC*, XI, 296, 366. [2] *CVV*, p. 148.

have been brought up in Dutch families and Dutch schools for three or more generations; all Dutch-vernacular students above the primary grade learn three European languages; and some have made original contributions to knowledge. In Indo-China, though little has been done for primary vernacular instruction, not a few natives have had brilliant academic careers in France. In Burma it would be difficult to name more than half a dozen works in English by Burmans that are worth reading, and only one or two of these look outside Burma. In the Philippines, Siam and Malaya there are many-sided adult education movements, and much has been done for adult education in Netherlands India. In technical instruction Burma seems to stand at the bottom of the list, except for Indo-China.

Burmans demanded, justly, a greater part in industry and commerce, and urged accordingly that technical and vocational instruction should be provided to train them for such careers. Government replied, truly, that one cannot create an industry by training men to practise it. But the whole situation arose out of the fact, which neither party recognized, that education is governed by demand, and when social demand is ineffective, it is governed by economic demand. The solution lay in creating a demand for Burmans in industry and commerce. A policy of social reintegration would have aimed at fostering such a demand, but the forms of political democracy served only to expose and irritate this sore in the social body, without contributing towards a remedy.

6. REVIEW OF PROGRESS AND WELFARE

In the early nineteenth century Burma was cut off from the world, as it had been from the beginning of time. It was almost inaccessible except by sea, and lay along no high road, either by sea or land, except as a difficult back entrance to China, when at infrequent intervals both the main routes between West and East by land and sea were closed. It contributed almost nothing to the world except a little teak, and, though Burmans were quite willing to take from the outer world what they could get, they could get nothing because they had little to offer, and what they had they would not sell. Under British rule all this was changed. Restrictions on trade were abolished; the people were encouraged, and provided with the money, to purchase foreign goods; the opening of the Suez Canal created a steady market for rice, and by the end of the century British capital was beginning to develop the mineral resources of the country. Just before the great depression Burma was exporting a wide variety of native and capitalist produce, and, as shown in the marginal table, ten years later, when the depression was first lifting, the value of oil and mineral exports had risen. The total value of local merchandise exported in 1926–7 was Rs. 654·7 million, and in 1936–7 it was Rs. 555·27 million. That is an index to the contribution to the world which Burma has made under British rule. Regarded as a business concern, it was good business.

Chief Products of Burma (Rs. million)*

Class	1926–7	1936–7
Native produce		
Rice products	391·49	218·42
Other field crops	33·48	35·87
Other rural produce	11·85	4·63
Capitalist produce		
Oil products	110·00	193·64
Other minerals	41·86	51·41
Timber	49·87	39·73
Plantations	12·04	7·43

* For details, see App. I.

Naturally it was especially good business for the British. About 90 % of the foreign capital invested in Burma was British,[1] and practically the whole direction of industry and commerce within the country was in British hands. But, until the Ottawa agreement of 1932, all peoples could trade on equal terms with Burma. In 1903–4, the first year for which approximately correct figures as to the distribution of trade are available, Europe took about one-third of the total exports, with Britain taking 12·3 % and Germany 8·4 %. Ten years later, just before the war, the British share had dropped to 9·3 %, and Germany with 8·9 % was almost on a par with Britain. By 1926–7 the British share had declined still further to 8·4 % and Germany with 7·9 % had almost recovered its pre-war level. Subsequent developments, economic and political, raised the British share in 1936–7 to 12·4 % and reduced the German share to 2·3 %. The course of trade with India has already been noticed; as regards other Asiatic countries, Japan, since developing its own sources of rice, has been a very moderate customer of Burma. Britain has always had a larger share of imports. In 1903–4 it supplied 33·3 %, the nearest competitor in Europe being Germany with 3·3 %. Ten years later their shares had risen to 35·1 % and 4·5 % respectively. By 1926–7 the British share had fallen to 27 %, though Germany, with 3·8 %, was still supplying a larger proportion than at the beginning of the century. Even the Ottawa agreement could not stay the

[1] Callis, p. 105.

decline of the British share, which dropped to 18·9 % in 1936–7. The benefit of the Ottawa agreement went mainly to India, yet the Japanese share of the trade, only 3·4 % in 1903–4, rose from 6·9 % in 1926–7 to 10·9 % ten years later. Whatever the destination of exports or the source of imports, the handling of the business in Rangoon is very largely in the hands of British subjects, European or Indian with some Chinese, nevertheless it is true that under British rule Burma was thrown open freely to the world, and made great and rapid economic progress.

Regarded from the standpoint of welfare, however, Burma presents a very different picture. The effect of British rule was to remove the abuses of the Burmese political and social system, and endow the people with the privileges of economic freedom and the rule of equal law. But, as we have seen, this undermined all the stable elements in social life; it reduced the hereditary leaders of the people to the common rank, broke up the political organization into villages, transformed the village from a social unit into a unit of administration, and the village community into a crowd of individuals; it cut at the roots of the national religion and converted education from a social force into an instrument of individual ambition. These changes, however, were gradual, and the people, while quick to profit by their new freedom, were slow to recognize what they had lost.

For economic freedom and equality before the law may be doubtful privileges. As Blake said in one of his Memorable Fancies, 'One law for the lion and the ox is oppression.' The people were freed from servitude to their hereditary chieftains only to find themselves bound to foreign moneylenders in chains firmly riveted by western law. Economic forces, subject to no restraint but law, upset the balance of native economy, sapped the foundations of religious life and institutions, ousted native arts, crafts and industries, and killed the social pastimes and recreations. Welfare is a social good, and the dissolution of society led to a decline in individual welfare. The growth of debt, the loss of land, the seasonal unemployment, the smaller proportion of luxuries among the imports, the reduced consumption of rice all indicate growing impoverishment among the great mass of the people, the Burmans in general, while the growth of foreign elements in numbers and wealth was creating a mixture of peoples with nothing in common but the desire of gain.

British rule only opened up Burma to the world and not the world to Burma. It could neither stay the decline of Burman culture nor replace it by a new western culture. Despite increasing cause for discontent the people remained acquiescent; they did not venture or even think to question British rule. Those who saw it most closely were the least inclined to question it, for they saw its power and it was the only power they saw. The victory of Japan over Russia came as a revelation. Burmans saw an eastern nation able to challenge the West by using western science. Hitherto the natural but latent dislike of foreign rule had been manifested only in sporadic futile risings among the most ignorant and superstitious; now some of those from western schools began to look on education as a path, not merely to higher pay, but to a national revival. But they hoped to pluck the fruit of western learning without planting the tree of moral discipline on which it grew, and this hope was, inevitably, frustrated.

Meanwhile the machinery of government rolled on, regardless of new hopes and new ideas. Nationalism was politics, and in the government of dependencies, as Count Smorltork said, 'The word polteek surprises by himself.' Moreover Nationalism was bound up with religion, which was even more dangerous. Even if the Burma Government had been gifted with the imagination to lead the new movement, it could do nothing because it was only part of the machinery of Indian rule, and the power to direct the machinery lay not in Burma, nor even in India, but in London, where Parliament knew little of India and still less of Burma. Thus the direction of affairs was still left to the unceasing activity of economic forces, uncontrolled by human will.

But in 1917 the decision of Parliament to grant responsible government in India opened a new prospect of rebuilding Burma on the basis of a common nationalism. Here was a chance for leadership. 'It is not enough to give good laws, or even good courts', said Elphinstone in the early days of British rule in India, 'you must take the people along with you, and give them a share in your feelings which can only be done by sharing theirs.' But the Government of Burma, grown old in the grooves of mechanical routine, had lost the art of leading. The Government made no attempt to capture the imagination of the people, and was content to 'go through all the processes for a new constitution'. Burmans now hoped to get from political reforms what they had failed to get from education; they had a large numerical majority and looked to win freedom through the franchise. Again, inevitably, this hope was frustrated.

The reformed system aggravated the tension between the several communities, and the conflict, active everywhere in all human affairs, between social will and economic forces took shape as a conflict between Burmese nationalism and western capitalism supported by the British Government. Despite the quasi-democratic constitution, the hold of capitalism grew stronger, as is demonstrated in the greater share of capitalist enterprise in both the export and import trade. Among Burmans the national religious sentiment gave place to a religion of nationalism, as yet blind and leaderless. The growth of crime, corruption and clerical unrest are, like the growth of debt and loss of land and the widespread agrarian distress, merely symptoms of a social order, or rather disorder, in which economic forces have been held down only by law and not by social will.

All this happened despite the best intentions of the British Government. Good intentions paved the way to evil and one may almost say that the ill results were the direct consequence of its good intentions. For the greater part of the nineteenth century everyone believed in *laissez-faire* and economic freedom as the key to progress and welfare, and British rule conferred on Burma the boon of economic freedom. Everyone likewise believed in equal law, and in Burma all were made equal before the law. Everyone believed in education and the Government tried to foster monastic schools, and supplemented them with lay schools on a western model. When the doctrine of *laissez-faire* gave place in England to ideas of efficiency and social justice, the British Government in Burma multiplied its administrative activities in order to enhance production and welfare. During the present century, with the general acceptance of the principles of democracy and self-determination, the Government constructed democratic machinery on an up-to-date model, and distributed the franchise with a liberality that would have been thought rash in England. Yet economic freedom merely allowed the people to pile up debt and lose their land; law multiplied litigation, even at the expense of justice; education lost its spiritual content and became a means of livelihood; the departments charged with enhancing production and welfare became vehicles of oppression and corruption; democratic machinery fostered civil strife and political discontent. All these things that worked so well in Britain went awry in Burma.

It should be instructive, therefore, to study the course of events in Netherlands India, where the administration was conducted with a different objective and on a different plan.

CHAPTER VII

NETHERLANDS INDIA

1. Administrative Divisions

NETHERLANDS India, often termed the Dutch East Indies, has been examined in some detail by the present writer in another work, which follows the same general plan as that adopted here for Burma. It may suffice here, then, to attempt merely a general survey with a view to illustrating the more notable points of similarity and contrast in respect of colonial policy and practice in Netherlands India and Burma.

Netherlands India is a great empire comprising many diverse regions. In popular usage two major divisions are recognized: Java, together with the adjacent small island of Madura, which will not subsequently be distinguished from Java unless this is indicated by the context; and the remaining territories, known collectively as the Outer Provinces but, since 1934, grouped in three Governments, Sumatra, Borneo and the Great East. Until the present century the Outer Provinces received little attention, and the following account of Dutch policy and practice relates especially to Java, which has been under Dutch control for nearly three hundred years; it does not deal with administration in the comparatively small part of Java where native states survive.

Between Java and Burma there is much in common. Under native rule their social and political institutions were fundamentally similar, despite the fact that Burma professes Buddhism and Java Islam. Now, in both countries there is a tropical people, mainly agricultural, under the rule of a western power; and in both there is a mixed community of natives, Chinese, Indians and Europeans, who have little in common outside the economic sphere. At a first glance there would seem also to be a close resemblance between their respective systems of administration. Java is divided into provinces, rather like the divisions of Burma; these comprise residencies, corresponding roughly to the Burma district; in a residency there are *afdeelingen* (subdivisions) that seem to resemble the Burma subdivision, and in the *afdeeling* there are usually two regencies, which may roughly be equated with the Burma township. The general administration is

conducted by civil servants, European and native, and these are
assisted in matters requiring expert knowledge by specialist officers
of various departments. The smallest unit is the village under an
elective headman. As in Burma, representative government on
western lines has been introduced. The people are represented in
Regency, Urban and Provincial Councils, and in a National or
Peoples' Council, the *Volksraad*, which includes delegates from the
whole of Netherlands India. At the head of the administration is the
Governor-General, responsible to the home Government, but sharing
the task of government in Indian affairs with the Volksraad; he also
has a small official council, the 'Raad van Indië' to advise him. But
the general similarity between the administrative machinery of Java
and Burma is superficial, and covers a profound contrast; the form
and functions of the machinery in the two countries, and the principles on which it works, are quite different. It is hardly possible,
however, to appreciate the nature and extent of this difference without
some knowlege of the past history of Java under Dutch rule.

2. NETHERLANDS INDIA UP TO 1830

We have already touched on the earlier history of Netherlands India,
but it may be convenient to recall the main facts before tracing its
later course. The Dutch East India Company was founded in 1602
to trade in eastern produce, and especially the spices of the Moluccas.
In order to carry on trade it had to assume sovereign powers, and it was
thereby enabled to obtain produce not only by trade but as tribute. In
1619 it conquered the small kingdom of Jacatra, and founded Batavia,
from which it gradually extended its rule over the whole island. In Java
there were hereditary local officials, corresponding to the circle headmen of Burma. Many of these officials were confirmed in their charges
with the title of Regent on condition of providing the produce and
services that the Company might require; otherwise they were left
a free hand in governing their people. A European was appointed at
suitable stations to see that the Regent fulfilled his obligations, and
this officer came to be known as a Resident. Thus, solely on economic
grounds, and with a view to administrative convenience and commercial profit, the Dutch from the earliest days adopted a system of
Indirect Rule, with a native chieftain in charge of native affairs, and
a European agent to look after the business of the Company. The
Company introduced coffee, and, to see that the people cultivated it

properly and in accordance with the requirements of the Company, some of the subordinate European officials were charged with supervising its cultivation. These officials, later styled Controleurs (inspectors), formed a link between the European and native branches of the administration.

For many years the Company, obtaining produce for little or nothing as tribute, flourished exceedingly; but in the course of time it suffered losses through the corruption of its servants. The Dutch Company, like the English, and at about the same time, tried to reform the administration but, largely because the States-General had less power than the British Parliament, these attempts failed. At the end of the eighteenth century, by reason of the war with England and the French Revolution, the Company went bankrupt, and in 1800 its possessions were taken over by the State.

A sharp controversy followed as to the policy to be adopted. One party, led by an official who had been in touch with the reforms recently adopted in British India, advocated the introduction of a similar system of direct rule based on liberal principles. The conservative majority, however, prevailed, and the principle of indirect rule through native chieftains under European supervision was reasserted; the relations between the European officials and native chieftains were to be those of an elder and younger brother, the term used in Java, as formerly in Burma, to describe the relations of suzerain and vassal. It was recognized, however, that under the Company the people had been subject to oppression by their chieftains, and European officials were enjoined 'to protect the common man against all arbitrary treatment' and to act towards him 'more like a father studying to promote the welfare of his family than a ruler governing his subjects'. One conspicuous abuse under the Company had been the tendency of Regents to alienate large tracts to wealthy Chinese; the occupants went with the land, or rather the land went with the people, whose services were lost to the Regent and consequently to the Company, while they were more oppressed than by their native rulers. It was decided, therefore, to prohibit the alienation of native land to foreigners. From that time on Dutch colonial policy has always recognized three basic principles: indirect rule; the protection of the people against oppression; and the retention of native land in native hands.

Apart from the formulation of principles, however, the controversy had little practical result, as, during the Napoleonic Wars, Java was taken over by foreign powers, first by the French and then, 1811–16, by the British. Raffles, who was appointed Lieutenant-Governor, was a fervent disciple of the new political economy with its doctrines of economic freedom and equal law. The English, like the Dutch, wanted tropical produce, but, whereas the Dutch had to obtain it as tribute because they had no goods to sell, the English wanted to sell western goods, the cheap cottons of Manchester, which, by the recent industrial revolution, could now be sold in Asia at lower rates than native cloth. For the English, trade was more profitable than tribute. As a humanitarian Raffles aimed at liberating the people from the oppression of their native rulers, and as a practical man he wanted to put money in their pockets so that they might buy English cottons. The measures that he adopted were almost identical with those adopted a few years later in Tenasserim. For the Regents he substituted European magistrates and judges, trying cases with the assistance of a jury; for the regency as the unit of administration he substituted the village; and, for compulsory contributions and services, he substituted land revenue collected in money through the village headman. His great contribution to Dutch colonial practice was the village system, which he claimed to be in line with native custom, though it more nearly resembled the British system of administration in South India.

3. THE CULTURE SYSTEM, 1830–70

When the Dutch recovered their possessions in 1816–18, they found that Raffles had gone further in the Liberal direction than their own most advanced reformers had ever thought possible. By this time Liberalism was in the air, and the new Dutch Government attempted a compromise between their old traditions and the new policy of Raffles. Among the features of his rule that they retained were the village system and land revenue. But the Dutch, after twenty years of French domination, had no merchants, no manufactures, no shipping, no capital—and no enterprise. Under a system of economic freedom the English monopolized the trade of Java, while the Dutch had to bear the cost of government. The King induced them to found a large commercial firm, the Netherlands Trading Company, providing out of his own purse a great part of the capital and guaranteeing a profit, in the hope that it would be able to compete with English merchants. This plan was ineffectual; the Dutch preferred an easy-going, un-adventurous life of petty retail trade at home. Then he took up a scheme for colonizing Java 'with capital rather than with men', and created the Java Bank, of which practically the whole capital was furnished by the Government and the Netherlands Trading Company in equal shares. These measures established another tradition of Dutch rule, the active participation of the Government in economic development. But they failed to restore financial equilibrium or to ensure peace and quiet (*rust en orde*). The colonial debt accumulated and disorder grew more serious. The Governor-General was forced to mortgage all the Dutch possessions in the East to a British firm in Calcutta, and the disorder culminated in a dangerous rebellion, the Java War, 1825–30.

A saviour was found in Van den Bosch, who had served under the Company and, in 1830, returned to Java as Governor-General. He attributed the financial breakdown and the general unrest to the system introduced by Raffles, based on the principles of economic freedom and the rule of law. Raffles, he said, had made Java profitable to England by remodelling its institutions on the Indian pattern, with the result that Chinese and Arab moneylenders and middlemen had replaced the hereditary leaders; and the collapse of authority and social order, and growing impoverishment had then brought into existence 'a numerous class of proletarians who go about and steal', against whom judicial forms were useless. His description of Java in 1830 reads in fact very like an account of modern Burma. His remedy was to revive the methods of the Company on a new plan, known as the Culture System.

The essence of the Culture system was that the people, instead of paying land revenue in cash, should furnish an equivalent amount of such produce, ordinarily export crops, as the Government might want; they were also encouraged to sell the Government additional produce at a low rate. On this plan it was necessary to restore authority to the Regents, who could use their influence to make the people grow these crops and perform such services as might be required for public works. Van den Bosch recognized that the village would be useful as a unit of communal production, and therefore retained the village system introduced by Raffles. So long as the requisite produce and labour were forthcoming, he abstained as far as possible from interfering in native affairs, which he left to the Regents and the villages, 'the little republics'. The chief duty of the Resident was to look after the interest of Government in connection with the Culture system, while the controleur, as under the Company, formed a link between the European and native branches of the administration. The Culture system, however, was only one aspect of a comprehensive plan to encourage Dutch manufactures, banking, shipping and enterprise. Dutch firms, financed by Dutch banks, exported Dutch cotton goods in Dutch ships in exchange for tropical produce to be sold to the rest of Europe at auctions held in Amsterdam. The Government assisted manufacturers of cotton goods; the Netherlands Trading Company had a monopoly of the trade and shipping, and provided funds for the Government at home; while the Java Bank, on behalf of Government, financed the scheme in Java. Under the Culture system the whole of Java became 'one huge State enterprise'. For twenty years this system was consistently and vigorously applied by two men, Van den Bosch and his successor Baud, either as Governor-General or Colonial Minister.

The main object of Van den Bosch was to stimulate Dutch enterprise which, in 1815, had been killed by twenty years of foreign rule. In this he was successful, beyond his hopes, and even perhaps beyond his wishes. The profits of the Culture system enriched the Dutch Treasury, but it also enriched manufacturers and others, who began to look with a jealous eye on the profit that Government was making out of the plantations, and to sympathize with the Liberal doctrine that Government should leave business to private individuals. The revolutionary movement of 1848 brought the Liberal party into power, and led in 1854 to the enactment of a new Indian Constitution bringing India under parliamentary control. For the next twenty years colonial policy was a central issue in home politics, with considerations of economic progress and the welfare of the people vehemently debated in a tangle of argument based on practical and moral grounds. Meanwhile the course of events in Java strengthened the Liberal contentions. Van den Bosch had claimed that his plan would diffuse prosperity by enabling the people to produce more, and therefore to earn more. For some years his claim was justified by the results, and all classes became more prosperous. But, with money pouring into the Dutch Treasury so easily, the Government always found some new occasion for expense, and wanted still more money. The system encouraged this, for it was radically vicious in combining political and economic control in the same hands. All the officials, European and native, from the Resident down to the village headman, shared in the profits of the Dutch Treasury by drawing a commission on produce. Naturally they used their authority to enhance production, and were stimulated to do so by the Home Government. On the plan, as originally conceived by Van den Bosch, officials were expected to supervise and encourage the production of subsistence crops alongside export crops. But attention was concentrated on export crops, and a succession of famines during the forties strengthened the liberal appeal to humanitarian sentiment. Baron van Hoëvell, formerly a pastor in Java, impressed on the States-General that the Culture system handed over the people of Java to oppression by their own chieftains; Dekker, an ex-official, under the pseudonym of *Multatuli* spread the news abroad in a novel, *Max Havelaar*, which 'sent a thrill throughout the land'; and Van de Putte, a planter, convinced Holland that the Culture system was unprofitable business. In 1870 it was decided to replace this system 'rooted in unrighteousness', by one 'which preferred freedom and justice above profit-seeking'; or, in other words, based on the principle that profits should go to private individuals rather than to the public.

4. THE LIBERAL SYSTEM, 1870–1900

Liberalism gave a new impulse to economic progress and, for a time, to welfare. But within a few years welfare declined, and progress gradually slackened to stagnation. On the new system, private planters took over the plantations formerly managed by Government, and used the influence of the village headmen to secure labour and produce, as the Government agents had done formerly. Business, it has been said, went on much as before, 'but with many shareholders instead of only one'. Private enterprise tended to be more oppressive than State enterprise. But three things protected the people.

Foremost among these perhaps was the tradition of Dutch rule that Government should protect the people against oppression by their chieftains. Liberalism had a double aspect, practical and humanitarian, and practical men and humanitarians had joined forces to defeat the Culture system. The planters represented in the main the practical aspect of Liberalism; they were interested in economic progress. But the new generation of officials, inspired by Liberal humanitarian ideas, showed a more lively interest than their predecessors in the welfare of the people. They no longer drew a commission on the produce, and their transformation from quasi-mercantile agents into a regular civil service was a step towards the separation of political from economic control. Similarly in the central Government political and economic control were divorced. Formerly the Government had been blinded to the abuses of the Culture system by the profits; now, with the Indies under the control of the States-General, there was a division between the planting interest, profiting by low wages, and the manufacturing interest, which could find a better market with high wages; and both parties, in appealing to neutrals in Parliament and elsewhere, urged their case so far as possible on moral grounds. Thus under the new system officials regarded it as one of their main functions to protect the people from oppression by their native chieftains acting as agents of the planters, and in this they had the support of Government; the demi-official manual for controleurs directed them to encourage, though without actively instigating, complaints.

The second form of protection was the long-established principle of Dutch rule that native land should not be alienated to foreigners. Under French rule, and even more under Raffles, financial stringency had been relieved by the sale of large estates, often comprising many villages, to be held with almost full sovereign rights over the occupants. On these estates the Government lost its revenue and the services of the people, and oppression by the owners frequently caused unrest. The Government feared that, if the people were allowed to dispose of their land to foreigners, large areas would be transferred to planters and Chinese moneylenders. It accordingly resisted all attempts by Liberals to apply western ideas of property to native land. Planters could obtain waste land on long lease from the Government, or they could rent land on an annual lease from villagers; but they were not allowed to buy village land, and the village retained full control over the disposal of its land in accordance with village custom.

The third protection of the people was the village system. This was not wholly to their advantage, for the planters obtained labour through the village headman, and sometimes enrolled him on the list of their establishment. To this extent they were interested in the maintenance of the village system, and they upheld the tradition of abstaining from interference in the 'holy hamlet'. On the other hand, the village system kept up the rate of wages by reducing the supply of labour available. The Government still required the people to give their services instead of paying taxes in money. Compulsory service was burdensome and wasteful, but men called out to work for Government or the village reduced the labour available for private enterprise. The planters, and liberal interests in general, were zealous for the principle of free labour, which would give them command over a much larger supply, but they did not gain their point until the Liberal period was passing.

Like the Culture system, the Liberal system did not fulfil its early promise; in both cases progress was followed by stagnation and collapse, and 'to many who expected great things from the noble sentiments and shrewd forecasts of Liberal prophets the results were a bitter disappointment'.[1] The practical Dutch idealists who instituted the reforms of 1870, though certainly mindful of potentialities for Holland itself, were quite sincere in their conviction that in giving its chance to private initiative in the Indies, they would be acting in the best interests both of that country and of its inhabitants: free labour in a frame of world free trade would bring to the Indies prosperity and development and to an eager and avid world a great increase of resources. The new system actually had some of these results and they could hardly foresee its other consequences whereby 'free enterprise eventually became from a social and economic ideal to be almost a byword for capitalistic exploitation'.[2]

The Liberal period gave a new turn to the policy of indirect rule. The European officials had always been expected to protect the culti-vator from oppression by his native rulers; under the Liberal system it became necessary also to protect him from oppression by Europeans engaged in western enterprise. That was not the only change. Euro-pean officials had always been required to look after European affairs; this was in accordance with the basic principle of Dutch rule that the rule of 'like over like is welcome'. There were native Regents to ad-minister native affairs; Chinese and Indian 'captains' to look after the affairs respectively of Chinese and Indians, and similarly European officials for European affairs. But until 1850, and even until 1870, there was little in Java that was European except the Government. With the growth of private enterprise, European officials had more work in connection with European business, and this emphasized the dual aspect of the administrative system, with Europeans for the rapidly increasing European business, and Regents for the native business, and with the Controleur still acting as a link between these two distinct elements in the administration.

During the Liberal period also, the simple administrative machinery which had sufficed for Van den Bosch grew far more elaborate. The development of trade and private enterprise made it necessary to cut up the residency into *afdeelingen* (subdivisions). But there was a

[1] Rengers, cited *Netherlands India*, p. 223.   [2] Hart, p. 40.

characteristic difference of principle between the manner of constituting subdivisions of the residency in Java and of the district in
Burma. In Burma, the principle of Government is one of 'strict subordination'; the subdivisional officer is a subordinate of the Deputy
Commissioner, and naturally there is one in charge of the headquarters
subdivision as well as at out-stations. In Java the officer in charge
of an *afdeeling*, known as the Assistant Resident, is an agent rather
than a subordinate of the Resident, and accordingly there is no
Assistant Resident at residency headquarters. The controleurs grew
in number and their functions were multiplied, but they were still
regarded as merely the eyes and ears of the Resident or his assistant,
and they remained without administrative powers. In the native
branch of the administration the changes were so great as to give it
a new character. Partly for greater efficiency, and partly to serve as
a check upon misuse by the Regents of their authority, each regency
was divided into three or four districts, and each district into three
or four sub-districts, comprising about twenty villages, and a native
civil service was created to administer these charges. The Regent
and his assistants constitute the Native Administration (*Inlandsch
Bestuur*), alongside but not directly subordinate to the European
Administration (*Binnenlandsch Bestuur*). The native officials of lower
rank are not hereditary, like the Regent, but ordinary civil servants
and, although nominally at the service of the Regent, they are more
amenable than the hereditary Regent to suggestions by the European
Controleur. A comparison of this organization with that of Burma
suggests the far greater intensity of Dutch rule. In Burma the lowest
grade in general administration is the Township of about a hundred
villages; in Java the smallest unit of general administration is the
sub-district of about twenty villages.

5. The Ethical System and Political Democracy

The earlier hopes of Liberalism were dispelled by a severe economic
crisis, 1883–5, and individual enterprise began to yield place to
combination; the economic structure was no longer individualist,
but definitely capitalist. Again, from about 1895, the Indies encountered another depression. Meanwhile new interests were exerting
an influence on Dutch colonial policy. Low wages were profitable to
the planters and to those concerned in the export of tropical produce;
but they were bad for the Dutch cotton trade, and chambers of com-

merce began to press the view that native welfare was declining. In 1902 the Queen promised an enquiry into 'the Diminishing Welfare of the People of Java'. This may be taken to mark the transition from the Liberal policy to what the Dutch call the Ethical policy, based on ideas similar to those which at about the same time in England inspired the doctrine of the White Man's Burden.

The Ethical policy had a two-fold aspect, economic and social. On the economic side it aimed at promoting development by western enterprise with a view to providing funds for the enhancement of welfare. On the social side it aimed at promoting social welfare through the village. Van den Bosch, believing that the Liberal experiment inaugurated by Raffles had multiplied unrest and impoverished the people, used the village as an instrument for maintaining peace and order, and as a lever for increasing material production. Similarly the Ethical reformers, holding that under Liberal rule economic freedom had weakened village solidarity, aimed to strengthen the village and use it as a lever, not for increasing material production, but for enhancing social welfare, and for promoting democratic self-government, an idea which they inherited from the Liberal tradition. These views found expression in the Village Act of 1906, intended to convert the village into a petty municipality on western lines, endowed with power to administer village affairs, property and land in the interest of the people, and functioning under the control of the general body of villagers. It was thought that this would train the people in political democracy, and at the same time would furnish European officials with a 'practical apparatus' for enhancing village welfare, and thereby individual welfare. Thus the Dutch welfare movement and the welfare movement that took shape at about the same time in Burma were based on different principles. In Burma the Government aimed at promoting individual welfare through the elaboration of administrative machinery; the Dutch aimed at promoting it through the growth of social welfare. It was common to both policies, however, that they required a great expansion of official machinery, the western superstructure over native life.

In practice the new machinery was used in the interest of efficiency rather than of political education; village meetings were held, and the records showed that they were attended by the prescribed quorum and that resolutions were adopted by the prescribed majority. But this procedure, so far as it was observed, was largely formal; the resolutions usually originated in suggestions from the Controleur.

At the same time councils on western lines were constituted for larger rural areas, for urban areas and ultimately for the whole territory in the Volksraad, or People's Council. Representative institutions are examined separately below. Here it is sufficient to notice that the original local councils proved lacking in inherent vitality, and subsequent reforms were directed to linking up the whole system of self-government, from village to Volksraad, in one organic system. As a part of this development the residencies were grouped between 1926 and 1928 into three Provinces under civil servants as Governors.

In respect of administration the chief outcome of the new policy was to change the character of indirect rule. During the Liberal period the Regent was regarded with some suspicion as a survival from the days of arbitrary oppression, and lost some of his authority. Under the Ethical system this tendency was carried further. Many Regents were impatient of new-fangled notions, and the Controleurs, zealous for promoting welfare, came to work more and more through the subordinate ranks of the Native Civil Service, who were readier to interpret suggestions as commands; thus the Regent tended to sink into the background. With the extension of Government activities, specialist officers were recruited to promote education, agriculture, medical and veterinary care and so on, and, alongside the general administrative services, there came into being large departments charged with these special functions. At first the specialist officers worked through the Assistant Residents and Controleurs, but gradually they became more independent, working in direct relation with the native subordinates, and turning to the European civil servants only for assistance in enforcing measures that the people were reluctant to adopt. This was directly contrary to the traditional Dutch policy of ruling through the Regents, with the European civil servants emerging from the background only in the light of benevolent protectors.

Another aspect of the Ethical policy was, in fact, a heritage from the Liberal doctrine of equal law for all. The Dutch rule of 'like over like' recognized a dual system of administration, with Europeans and natives under their respective laws and customs. Many Ethical leaders advocated a unified system of administration, with Europeans and natives all in one combined service administering uniform law. One application of this policy was an experiment in liberating the Regents from the tutelage of the Controleur (*ontvoogdij*). But the chief function of the Controleur had been to look after the Regent, and the new plan left the Regent to look after himself and the Controleur with nothing to do. The experiment was never popular either with Dutch or natives, and the first Regent to be emancipated declared afterwards that he never noticed any difference. In 1931 it was abandoned.

From the financial standpoint, the Ethical policy looked to the development of the country by western enterprise with a view to providing funds for social services. Like the doctrine of the White Man's Burden, it originated at a time of imperialist expansion, when a rapidly growing demand for tropical produce was attracting western capital and large-scale enterprise. Capitalist enterprise provided much of the revenue expended on social services, but experience suggested that these welfare services were of little benefit to the people. The head of the Credit Service, afterwards Professor of Tropical Economy in Leiden gave a depressing picture of the results. 'I really cannot assure you that the people are any better off for the millions which they have borrowed from the State Banks.' Similarly, he continues, irrigation, emigration, colonization, are catchwords that have lost their lustre; other catchwords—the promotion of export crops, the improvement of hygiene, the relief of taxation—have their ups and downs in the current of policy, as, for example, the cry for industrialization rising and falling with the economic conjuncture. 'But the only popular response to all these nostrums is an increase in numbers, while foreign capitalists and foreign energy take out of native hands a rapidly increasing share of native activities.'[1] Another high official said, 'The welfare of the native population has not been noticeably raised, for higher production is counterbalanced by increase of population.'[2] The policy was attacked from another side also as purely artificial. One of the foremost advocates of the Ethical system, disillusioned by long experience, exclaimed, 'As soon as we withdraw our hands, everything sinks back into the marsh.' And after a consistent endeavour for over twenty years to strengthen the village community, and use it for promoting welfare, a survey of the results led to the conclusion that 'deplorably little village autonomy remains'.[3]

Meanwhile a Nationalist movement had been gaining strength. Growing unrest culminated at the end of 1926 in a serious rising in Java and Sumatra. An enquiry into unrest in Bantam supported the

---

[1] Boeke, cited *Netherlands India*, p. 403.
[2] de Wilde, Dr A. Nietzel, *Asiatic Review*, 1934, p. 232.
[3] Adam, cited *Netherlands India*, p. 404.

view that one source of trouble was the tendency under the Ethical
policy to displace the Regent. Thus the Ethical policy was subjected
to an increasing volume of criticism on all sides, as a departure from
the traditional principle of ruling the people through their own leaders,
and as an attempt to westernize the East too rapidly. Opinion turned
towards restoring the Regent to the centre of the picture, and thereby
bringing the people into contact with the modern world by methods
less artificial and more congenial to their ideas. That was the position
when suddenly the whole situation was changed by the depression
of the thirties.

6. ECONOMIC DEMOCRACY AND NATION-BUILDING

From 1800 it has been the express principle of Dutch policy that its
officials should protect the common man against oppression. This
principle has become a tradition among the European officials. They
protested against some aspects of the Culture system so forcibly as to
call from Baud the remark that 'the tender feelings of a few young
gentlemen Controleurs' could not be allowed to affect the profits
drawn by Government. From 1870, inspired with the new Liberal
humanitarianism, they sought to protect the people not only against
the native chieftains but against the planters. After 1900 they were
zealous in pursuing the new Ethical policy of not merely protecting
the people but of actively promoting their welfare. Their training and
their duties fostered a sympathetic attitude towards the people.
During a long course at Leiden University an enthusiastic staff aimed
at enabling them to understand the East. For their first ten or twelve
years they moved intimately among the people, with no executive or
magisterial functions to produce estrangement. Accordingly, when
the welfare movement seemed to favour western capitalists rather than
the people, they were among the earliest to react against it. At the
onset of the depression 'the younger civil servants...had long been
dissatisfied with the shape and tempo of the Indies community
socially and economically: with its crippling dualism; with the out-
flow of profits to shareholders outside the country; with the limited
chances for Indonesians of establishing enterprise of their own or of
obtaining higher positions in western concerns; with inadequate
Government control of wages and land rents'. 'It happened that,
in the early thirties when the depression broke, these men were just
stepping into key positions in the central and local government.' Even
those who had not been so keenly sensible of Indonesian disabilities

began 'to realize clearly that this crisis was not a passing phase in a trade cycle, but the initial stage of fundamental social and economic changes which would develop into a major disaster to humanity if they were not met by new conceptions and new methods'.[1]

At the same time the depression changed the relative position of western enterprise and the Government. Many held that, among other defects of the former system, was the fact that western enterprise 'had grown too powerful in the country and that it wielded that power in order to retard progress in the political, economic and social fields, lining up for that purpose with other political groups...there was at one time certainly more activity lobbying and browbeating by private interests on political issues, both in Batavia and the Hague, than is consistent with the proper place of business'.[2] Formerly Government had been largely dependent on the goodwill of western enterprise; the depression made western enterprise dependent on the goodwill of Government. Also Japan, flooding the country with cheap cottons, threatened not only Dutch manufacturers but the young local weaving industry. Western enterprise called on Government for help, and 'Government intervention never seemed to stop just where the business interests would like it to stop'.

Thus, just when the Government was adopting a new outlook, it acquired greater power, and adopted a policy of directed economy, aiming at the development of economic democracy as the basis of political democracy which if 'not based on or closely related to economic democracy...could never really flourish among the Indonesians...(but)...would remain a bewildering and dubious blessing'. The apparently easy way of promoting native welfare by encouraging development through western enterprise had proved fallacious. Now, says Dr Hart,

'we had to learn directed economy, the hard way, because we could not afford the easy way; very little public money went into any of the schemes, because there was very little money available in those depression years. There were no large-scale credits, no so-called "money injections", no expensive organizations, paid out of public revenues. Persuasion and legislation were the principal instruments and the inevitable costs of running the new machinery were met by levies from the interest involved.'[3]

The result, it is claimed, was 'the birth of a nation'.

'An Indonesian nation was being born, not made, born by the will and the efforts of the best of the Indonesians themselves.... The European and

[1] Hart, p. 53.   [2] *Ib.* p. 48.   [3] *Ib.* pp. 60, 62.

Chinese elements were becoming conscious of their integration into this new community while the Administration felt that for the first time in history, it was becoming, slowly, but quite perceptibly, from a benevolent and progressive western superstructure, the natural and true Government of the Indies.'[1]

7. NATIONALISM

The Ethical system, as we have seen, took shape at the beginning of the present century. No sooner, however, had Government set the helm along an Ethical course than it ran into a new and unsuspected current of Nationalism. As Dr Colijn, the colonial statesman and Prime Minister, remarked, national consciousness in Java, probably always latent, suddenly emerged above the surface. The victory of Japan over Russia inspired the educated classes with new hope of a national revival, and this spread rapidly to the other classes and the other islands. The changed attitude of the Javanese towards those who for three centuries had been their masters was suspect, yet it was not wholly unwelcome, as it seemed to promise favourable results for the Ethical movement; and, even when further developments brought disillusionment to many well-wishers, and the current of opposition to native claims grew stronger, the principle of autonomous political democracy gradually replaced welfare as the main end of policy.

The nationalist movement in the Indies has tended to follow the same lines as the somewhat earlier movement in British India, but certain features of society have given it a special character, though with some resemblance to the course of events in Burma. Among the native population in general there is greater social unity than in India for, as in Burma, they are free of caste, accord a high status to women, are largely of one religion and, at least in Java, culturally homogeneous. There is a resemblance to Burma also in the relations of the foreign elements, European and oriental, with the natives. The Chinese, like the Indian in Burma, acts as a middleman between European and native, tending to be a focus for the animosity of both, and yet at the same time a buffer, averting the direct collision of their conflicting interests. In political developments the Chinese have played a part very similar to that of the Indians in Burma. Signs of new life first appeared among the Chinese, and the success of Chinese agitation encouraged the Javanese to adopt like methods. But Chinese interests are capitalist rather than nationalist, and the introduction of representative institutions tended to draw them into alliance with

[1] Hart, p. 21; Vlekke, pp. 369, 371.

Europeans against the numerical superiority and separate interests of the natives. Peculiar to Netherlands India is the large Indo-European (Eurasian) community. An even more outstanding character is the presence of a large European population of very diverse composition, not merely as a ruling class but all down the social scale, and actively engaged in various economic activities. It is chiefly this European element that has given a distinctive course to the nationalist movement in Java.

As in Burma one can trace national sentiments in the earliest publications of the native press. Modern Nationalism was clearly foreshadowed in the work of a remarkable woman, Miss Kartini. Under the sympathetic encouragement of Dutch officials she developed, about 1900, a project of female education as an instrument of national welfare. Thus Nationalism was already present as in a saturated solution, ready to crystallize out at the first shock. Although the shock came from outside with the victory of Japan over Russia, the vital force of Nationalism came from the people themselves; the Japanese victory merely transformed national sentiment into modern Nationalism, inspired by the idea of using western science and western education to counter the supremacy of the West. As in Burma, it first became manifest among the educated classes. In 1906 a retired medical subordinate began to tour the country with the advancement of Java as his text. In 1908 he founded the first nationalist society, *Boedi Oetomo*, the Glorious Endeavour. This organization did useful work, but chiefly among those from western schools; it never became a popular movement and on the whole exercised a moderating influence in politics. The next development had a very different character; it was popular and primarily economic. In 1911 some Javanese traders in cloth, resenting the sharp practices of the Chinese, took their religion as a symbol of social unity, and formed a society under a title subsequently abbreviated to *Sarikat Islam*. This grew rapidly and became the spear-point of the nationalist movement.

The movement took on a new and more aggressive character when it was joined by recruits from among the Indo-Europeans, popularly known as Indos. Although Dutch policy has always been to assimilate Indo-Europeans with Europeans of pure blood, there is in fact a cleavage of interest between permanent and temporary residents. With the influx of Europeans consequent on the growth of western enterprise during the present century, the cleft grew wider, and in 1912 an Indo journalist, Douwes Dekker, nephew of the author of *Max*

Havelaar, created a great stir by an article claiming 'India for the Indians', including under one head domiciled Europeans, Indos and Indonesians. Together with some native leaders he formed an 'Indian Party', aiming avowedly at independence.

The intervention of the Indos in nationalist policy was soon followed by European intervention, but in circumstances that were wholly new. The outbreak of war in 1914 cut off Java from its usual markets and supplies, and there was a move to develop local markets and local manufactures. Before long the war stopped the supply of new assistants, and western enterprise had to recruit and train a local staff. At the same time the problem of defence assumed a new importance and, under the influence of a struggle, represented on all sides as being waged for human freedom, other colonial problems were transformed. 'In 1915 autonomy was in the air.' The European population began to take a new interest in local politics, and the creation of the Volksraad gave them a new opportunity to participate in the direction of colonial affairs. Many Europeans were of humble social origin and were employed in the lower grades of economic life. In Europe they had belonged to democratic political associations and to trade unions, and they brought their politics and trade unionism with them to the East. In 1914 they formed the Indian Social Democratic Union (I.S.D.V.), corresponding to the Social Democratic Labour Party in the Netherlands. This was soon countered by the Liberal Bond (N.I.V.B.), which aimed to unite moderate Progressives of all races. In opposition to these secularist parties there were formed the Christian Ethical Party and the Indian Roman Catholic Party, representing the two main branches of the Dutch Clerical Party. At about the same time the I.S.D.V. developed revolutionary tendencies, and the moderate element split off to form the Indian Social Democratic Party (I.S.D.P.) leaving the original I.S.D.V. an extremist party with Communist views. In all these parties, from Right to Left, the different races were associated.

At the opening of the Volksraad in 1918 every 'non-clerical' European was Liberal and progressive, aiming at the development of Java as a province of Europe in the East. Then a nationalist colour visible in the policy of the Governor-General led to a reaction. Big Business scented danger and said so, forcibly. Others followed with more discretion and the more conservative elements of the N.I.V.B. founded the Political Economy Bond (P.E.B.), corresponding to the *Vrijheidsbond* at home. Like the other political groups this was an 'association-party' comprising members of all races. Under European influence the nationalist movement developed in the direction of Socialism and then of Communism. Although the Indonesian labourer cared little for Karl Marx, and the great bulk of the party cared only for Nationalism, with Islam as its symbol, the leaders succumbed to the prestige of their European allies, and to their greater organizing capacity and better understanding of political tactics. In this new line, however, they were heading for a split. The fourth Nationalist Congress in 1919 purported to represent two and a half million members, but two years later the revolutionary section broke away from the main body. The post-war depression bred industrial disputes, and the vigorous suppression of strikes under a new Governor-General encouraged the spread of revolutionary views, fostered by Chinese Communists under Russian influence. Despite the appointment in 1926 of a new and more sympathetic Governor-General, the movement ran its course leading up to 'carefully planned and widely extended revolutionary operations, which indicated that the conspirators were able to reckon on at least the connivance of a large part of the native population'.[1]

The rising was suppressed, and the failure of the revolutionary movement allowed the older organization, Sarikat Islam, to resume the lead. But once again extremism made headway, and by 1930 there were three main parties, all however aiming to break loose from the Netherlands and differing only as to the best line of action. On the other hand among Europeans also an extremist, or diehard, movement was gathering strength. Irritated by the succession of strikes and alarmed by the rising of 1926, they formed in 1929 the Vaderlandsche Club as a reaction against Indian Nationalism. In the elections of 1931 strictly racial parties came to the front, while those based on the association of all races for the common welfare collapsed; even the Christian religious parties were organized on racial lines, and Muhammadan parties appeared racial rather than religious. In 1934 the *Stuw* group of Europeans, mainly officials, who had most sympathy with native aspirations, was no longer able to publish its journal, and the organ of the civil service remarked that it had suffered the natural fate of idealists;' whereas many Europeans, more realist in temperament, who found the Vaderlandsche Club too moderate, formed a Fascist organization. On the opposite side the Women's Movement, and still more the Youth's Movement, tended to become aggressively nationalist. Thus the course of political development,

---

[1] *Indisch Verslag*, cited *Netherlands India*, pp. 253, 254.

among Europeans and natives alike, appeared to show a steady trend in the direction of extremes.

But common distress inspired a community of sentiment. As in 1900 and 1870 and 1850, realists found that idealism had roots in common sense, and practical men and humanitarians joined hands. The *Stuw* group, as already noticed, acquired more influence in the direction of affairs. The membership of Fascist organizations was declared illegal. Strong action by the Government, in controlling western capitalism and vigorously promoting Indonesian economic activities, did much to attract native support, so that, when the test came, all sections of the community seem to have presented a common front against Japanese aggression. Since 1916 Nationalists have been demanding a larger part in military defence, and in July 1941, when it was clear that war with Japan was inevitable, the Volksraad passed a bill for a native militia, by a majority of 43 to 4, the only dissentients being the representatives of the extremist *Parindra* party, who asked that political reforms should have priority over military service; these abandoned their opposition when in December the bombing of Pearl Harbour was immediately followed by a declaration of war on Japan.[1] Although the number of the native militia was limited to 18,000, upwards of 100,000 volunteers presented themselves for enrolment. On the Japanese invasion 'the Government ordered everyone, Indonesian and Dutch, civil servant and private individual to remain at his post: there should be no quitting in the hour of direst need'. 'Dutch men and women', it was said, 'belong in the Indies and to the Indies; they are part of the Indies; it is their country as much as it is that of the Indonesians themselves, for better or for worse.'[2] In Netherlands India, as elsewhere, the Japanese found men of some standing to co-operate with them, and it seems that those who joined the Japanese have not forfeited the respect and sympathy of other Indonesians;[3] it is therefore still uncertain how far the war will tend to weld together as one people with a common Nationalism the various sections in the social structure of the recent past.

8. Administrative Practice

(a) *District Administration.* The foregoing account of the evolution of the administrative system of Java has shown that, despite a superficial resemblance to the system of Burma, it is in fact quite different.

---

[1] Vlekke, pp. 390, 394.   [2] Hart, p. 13; Vlekke, p. 404.
[3] *Vrij Nederland*, 27 Nov. and 11 Dec., 1943.

There is indeed hardly anything in common between the character and functions of the civil servants of the two countries. In Burma there is one service divided into three grades, there are no Europeans in the lowest grade but even the highest grade is open to natives, and all, from top to bottom, so far as they are engaged in general administration, do the same kind of work. In Burma the Deputy Commissioner, the head of the district, is primarily magistrate and collector; he is a servant of the law, and is directly responsible for the collection of revenue, but in every capacity he must observe legal procedure and act strictly according to law. His subordinates, the subdivisional and township officer have the same functions, and must work under the same limitations. The European civil servant, within a year or so of his arrival in the country, becomes a magistrate of the first class, empowered to impose a sentence of rigorous imprisonment for two years; some four or five years later he becomes a district magistrate, empowered to impose a sentence of transportation for seven years. Subdivisional and township officers are likewise magistrates, with judicial powers varying according to their experience and capacity. The Deputy Commissioner and township officer are personally responsible for the collection and safe custody of the revenue, and are liable to make good defalcations; the Deputy Commissioner must himself count the money in the treasury once a month.

In Java, instead of a single service, there are two separate services, one European and one native, each with its own functions, and in neither service does any officer perform either of the two main functions of the civil servant in Burma. There is a separate judicial service and a separate treasury service, and the administration of justice and collection of revenue form no part of the duties of the ordinary administrative civil service. The European civil servant starts as a Cadet (*adspirant-controleur*) and, even when confirmed as a Controleur, has no magisterial or judicial powers, and no administrative responsibilities of any kind: his function is to keep Government in touch with the people, and to watch over and help the native civil servants. After ten or twelve years he rises to be an Assistant Resident. In the less important charges the Assistant Resident has magisterial powers, corresponding roughly to those of a third-class magistrate in Burma, and tries petty cases on one or two days a week; but he is being relieved even of this work. The Resident does no judicial work. In the native civil service the lowest grade is that of the Subdistrict officer in charge of general administration over a small tract of some twenty villages. Above him comes the District officer,[1] and at the head of the native civil service is the Regent. The sub-district and district officers are purely official in character, but the Regent holds his appointment by an hereditary tenure, though he qualifies for it by service in the lower grades or in the police. The Regent has petty judicial powers such as might be specially conferred on a village headman in Burma, and the district officer has much the same judicial powers as an ordinary village headman; but such few cases as they try are disposed of in a very informal manner. No European or native civil servant is a magistrate as the term is understood in Burma. No civil servant, European or native, ever has charge of a treasury or any direct responsibility for the collection or safe custody of revenue.

In Java the administrative officials are not servants of the law but officers of police or policy and, in rural areas, until quite recently there was no organized police force apart from the civil servants and their orderlies. As agents of policy they are expected to maintain, not law and order, but peace and quiet (*rust en orde*), and to see that revenue collections are proceeding smoothly; but these are only incidental to their main function which is, as it has always been, to see that effect is given to the policy of Government: under the Culture system they saw to the encouragement of export crops: under the Liberal system to helping the planters and protecting the peasants: under the Ethical system to promoting village uplift. In the machinery for giving effect to the policy of Government three features deserve special notice: the *Vergadering*; the Subdistrict officer and the Regent.

The *Vergadering* (Gathering or Assembly) is an application to modern administrative practice of the oriental institution which in India has survived as the formal durbar, or has languished as the *panchayat*; in Dutch practice it is a meeting in which an official discusses affairs with representatives of the people, and, as in oriental usage, it has both an educative and a democratic character. From the restoration of Dutch rule in 1816 the Resident was expected to hold once a month a *vergadering* of his subordinates for the discussion of current affairs; the Regent held a similar meeting of his subordinates. The practice seems to have been developed by Van den Bosch, and

---

[1] It is important not to confuse the district officer of Java with the high official, often known as the District Officer, in British tropical administration. In Java the district is merely a subdivision of the Regency, and the Regency itself is a subdivision of the Residency, which corresponds more closely with a British District.

was useful under the Culture system as a means by which the Resident could explain what produce and how much was required, and could ascertain how much was likely to be forthcoming and discuss measures for obtaining more.

During the present century the mechanism has become more or less standardized. The subdistrict officer holds a gathering of his ten or twenty village headmen once a week; the district officer holds a gathering of subdistrict officers and others so many times a month; the Regent holds a gathering of district officers and others once a month, and the Resident, or at out-stations the Assistant Resident, likewise holds a gathering once a month. The Controleur holds no gathering, but attends that of the Resident or Assistant Resident, and is at liberty to attend the gatherings of the Regent or his subordinates. Attendance is not restricted to administrative officers and village headmen. At every meeting, from that of the subdistrict officer upwards, departmental officers of the appropriate rank may ask or be invited to attend for the discussion of affairs concerning their department. Forest officers, public health officers, education officers, and officers of the agricultural, veterinary or credit services may attend as necessary to explain policy or smooth out difficulties. Similarly, at the gathering of the subdistrict or district officers, the village officials, the village policeman, schoolmaster, or the man in charge of irrigation may accompany the village headman. Ordinarily only one or two services will be represented in any one meeting, and there is no need for specialist officers to attend unless there is some matter within their sphere of interest to discuss. The Controleur may be present at any of these meetings to represent the views of Government, and to help in clearing up misunderstandings and removing difficulties. Thus, on the one hand, the procedure goes far to cure the evils of departmentalism, as specialist officers are compelled to recognize that their work is not an end in itself, but only one aspect of social life; and on the other hand it seems admirably designed to secure the willing and intelligent acceptance of official policy by presenting it as fully, forcibly and reasonably as possible to those who carry weight among the people, and will have to obtain the co-operation of the people in making it effective. The whole system is indeed one of practical adult education; it is a form of government through social education.

At the same time the *vergadering* has a democratic character. It does not work on western lines with agenda, motions, amendments, numerical majorities and resolutions, but allows an informal discussion in which the presiding officer can gather from representatives of the people, the general sense of the meeting, and can take such steps as may best give effect to it or, if some measure proposed by Government does not sufficiently command approval, can make provision accordingly. Both as an institution in line with oriental democracy and as a means of adult education it is a powerful instrument of official policy, and helps to build up a strong Government based on popular support.

Another valuable feature of Dutch administrative machinery is the Subdistrict officer. In Burma the smallest unit of general administration is the township comprising about a hundred villages. The township officer is a busy man, chiefly concerned with trying cases and collecting revenue. More often than not he is transferred to another appointment within a few months. Education, sanitation, irrigation and so on, so far as they receive attention, are the concern of departmental subordinates who look at them from a departmental standpoint, knowing and caring little for their reactions on other aspects of life. The Government is impersonal; it never comes into human contact with the people as living individuals with a hundred and one different interests. But in Java the Subdistrict officer within his tiny charge can get to know the leading people as human beings, and in his own person coordinates all aspects of administrative activity.

Still more valuable is the Regent. He is a permanent institution; through all the divagations of official policy he remains a link between the past, the present and the future. He can see what is going wrong, because he knows what went before; he can use his personal inherited influence to set it right; and he remains permanently to see that his advice is followed. For example, a Regent showed the present writer a clump of trees on a hillside. Shortage of fuel had led the people to cut down a small copse. He noticed that erosion was damaging the cultivation on the slope, explained matters to the people, and encouraged them, used 'gentle pressure' as the Dutch say, to plant the trees. In Burma no one would stay long enough in one place to notice the erosion until simple remedies were no longer possible; the matter would go from one department to another while the erosion was getting worse, and in the end probably nothing would be done, because a remedy would need the co-operation of several different departments, and no one in any department would stay long enough to see the matter through and, for lack of a few trees, land would go out of cultivation and village harmony would be endangered. Welfare measures do not take root without prolonged encouragement and supervision, and unless recommended by someone with personal influence. The Regent satisfies all these requirements. He is permanent and enjoys general respect. Most of the younger Regents are well-educated, and some have been to Europe; they can recommend western welfare measures in a way congenial to the people. In the Ethical period, when enthusiastic Controleurs tried to push reforms through subordinate native officials, they did not understand so well as the Regent the way to make reforms acceptable, and when they were transferred 'everything sank back into the marsh'. Frequent transfers of officials are unavoidable, but, in working through the Regent, transfers may even be a source of strength by bringing the Regent into touch with a succession of new ideas. Many suggestions may fall on barren ground; but some, one here, another there, take root and yield a rich harvest. Thus the Regent has once again become, as in the days of Van den Bosch, the hub on which the administration turns. It is a Regent of a new type, using, as will appear below, the new machinery of representative institutions, but he still embodies the Dutch tradition of ruling the people through their own leaders, and the welcome principle of 'like over like'.

(b) *Village Administration*. The Regent, however, still works through the village. Perhaps the most interesting and instructive aspect of Dutch rule in Java is the consistent effort to conserve village solidarity. There have, it is true, been frequent encroachments on village autonomy. Under the Culture system the village was used to promote cultivation for the State; under the Liberal system it was adapted to the requirements of the planters; under the Ethical system it was used to promote welfare along western lines. But the Dutch have never abandoned the principle that, so far as the interests of Government allowed, the village should be left to manage its own affairs. The Village Act of 1906 was expressly designed both to strengthen the village community and to adapt it to the modern world, 'to stimulate social growth, and enable local officials to cope with their main function, the care of public welfare'. In the manner of its application three points are of especial interest.

In Java, as in Burma, it seemed common sense that to get better headmen one must give them better pay, and the Government adopted the policy of amalgamating villages so that headmen should collect more revenue and draw a larger commission. But it was soon found that the headman remained a stranger within the new village added to his charge; in some cases, it is said, he hardly dared to show his face there. The readjustment of village charges tended to convert the village from a natural social unit into an administrative unit and, although the headman earned a larger income, he had less and not more authority than before. Thus experience brought a reaction towards leaving traditional village boundaries intact.

When the Village Act was first introduced, the villages were given powers similar to those of a western municipality, and were expected to use them similarly: to prepare a budget, pass it in a legally constituted Village Meeting attended by a quorum of villagers duly qualified to vote, to spend their funds accordingly, and to prepare annual accounts. Other matters of general interest, the leasing of village land to sugar planters, and so on, were dealt with in such village meetings. Before long almost every village had its village treasury to provide funds for everything that the Controleur thought the village ought to want: school, village bank, paddy bank, bazaar, stud bull, pedigree goat, and so on. The people were educated in business principles, and numerous registers were prescribed for the headman, clerk and village priest; but, with anxious care lest democracy should be sacrificed to efficiency, everything had to be put before and passed by the village meeting. That at least was the ideal of policy, but in practice very few villages came up to this high standard. Even the 'village clerk' was often illiterate, and for some villages the records and registers had to be maintained in the subdistrict office. The whole machinery was too complicated and western. Some few villages could manage it competently, others not at all. The mistake lay not merely in introducing western machinery, but in treating all the villages alike. Warned by this experience, when measures along somewhat similar lines were adopted for the Outer Provinces, they were applied gradually to selected villages.

A third defect was the experiment of working through the Controleur instead of through the Regent. The Controleur pressed some welfare measure on the people, but his successor would have a different enthusiasm, and strike out along new lines. Some of the reforms, sound enough perhaps in Europe, were so unpopular that the people would not accept them. For example, the veterinary department wished to improve the breed of cattle by castrating unsuitable bulls; but in Madura, the chief cattle breeding centre, the people sold their animals for slaughter rather than allow them to be castrated. The people could be made to build latrines, but were so careful to keep them sanitary that they never used them. Only with a reversion to the principle of working through the Regents did reforms take root.

(c) *Departmental Administration.* For the Culture system a very simple type of organization sufficed, and it was not until 1866–70 that departmental administration was adopted. With the rapid growth of Government activities during the present century numerous special services were constituted, but they were grouped in large departments, and at the latest reorganization in 1934 the functions of general civil administration were distributed between six departments dealing respectively with justice; finance; internal affairs; education and religion; economic affairs; and public works. At the head of each department is a director. The comprehensive character of these departments is a notable feature of Dutch administration, as it minimizes the evils of departmentalism by enabling the director to take a wide view of several related services and thus co-ordinate their activities. Another device to the same end is the appointment of liaison officers between the departments and services. The Director of Education, for example, has two advisers from the European administrative service to help him in respect of native education. There is also a special liaison officer between the agricultural, credit and civil services.

Much use is made of specialist Advisers, charged with studying important problems, but without any responsibility for policy. There have been Advisers on native affairs, on Chinese affairs, on Japanese affairs, on credit institutions, on native education and on decentralization. These Advisers make a continual study of large issues from a broader aspect than is possible for officials immediately concerned with the daily routine of administration. It was largely through the advice of the Adviser on Moslem affairs that the Dutch finally succeeded in pacifying Achin. This device helps in some measure to minimize a difficulty common to all colonial administration, the lack of institutions and periodicals in which large issues can be studied and discussed by an intelligent and instructed public.

(d) *Judicial Administration.* In accordance with the principle of 'like over like', law and procedure are adapted to the several requirements of the various sections of the public. Since 1915, however, there has been one Penal Code applicable to all sections. If civil disputes between natives come into court, they are decided according to native customary law, including thereunder any statutory laws that have been made applicable to natives. Religious matters between Muhammadans come before Moslem clerical tribunals.

Petty offences by natives mostly come before the Regent or district officer, who may hear them in the large open verandah that forms part of his official residence; he has no court and his only office is a small out-house that might easily be mistaken for a garage. Local dignitaries sit on a bench with the presiding officer, but the latter alone gives the decision. The whole procedure is very informal, and the penalties imposed are little more than nominal. Other petty offences and misdemeanours by natives or others are tried in the local police court (*landgerecht*) by a magistrate, who until recently was usually the Assistant Resident; a native official (*fiscaal-griffier*, registrar or bailiff) sits beside him, but the proceedings are conducted by the magistrate. Most of the cases before him would be tried in Burma by honorary magistrates, or be dismissed as insignificant. He rarely seems to impose a fine of more than a quarter or half a guilder (sixpence or a shilling), or imprisonment for longer than three days. The procedure is far more informal than could be imagined in any court in Burma. There is no police officer in court. The accused is shown in and sits upon a bench. There is a short and apparently friendly conversation, and the witnesses, if any, join in the conversation without taking an oath. The magistrate announces his decision, scribbles it in blue pencil on the charge sheet together with his initials and that, together with an abstract by the registrar of the offence charged and the decision, constitutes the whole record. The cases on an average last rather less than two minutes. No appeal lies against the order, but the High Court is entitled to intervene on revision, though apparently it never does.

People, other than Europeans, charged with more serious offences come before the *Landraad*. This consists of a judicial officer as chairman and a bench of local dignitaries. The decision is collective, by a majority of votes, the laymen are not merely assessors. The court is attended by a *djaksa* (judge-advocate) and *griffier* (registrar). The president, *djaksa* and *griffier* are all professional lawyers, holding a university degree in law, and the president achieves his position as a judge, only after some years of experience as *djaksa* and *griffier*. Europeans charged with serious offences are tried by a Court of Justice, consisting of a bench of judges, all of whom are professional lawyers; in Java there are three such courts.

Petty civil disputes between natives may be settled in the regency or district court, which indeed do not always distinguish very carefully between criminal and civil matters. The regular court for the decision of more serious questions is the Landraad, constituted as for criminal cases. But a visitor from Burma is impressed by the fact that even civil disputes of considerable value or importance may be brought for arbitration to the Assistant Resident, although in law he has no judicial powers or functions. He seems to take it as a matter of course that he should give up much of his time to the amicable settlement of such affairs. 'Why', he asks, 'should the poor people waste their money on litigation?' Cases of minor importance between Europeans come before the Residency Court, consisting of the chairman of the Landraad, sitting alone with a *griffier*; more serious matters come before the Court of Justice.

Religious questions between Muhammadan natives are dealt with by a clerical tribunal (*priesterraad*) comprising a high cleric and three to eight Moslem religious officials. It has jurisdiction over all religious disputes, so far as not otherwise prescribed, and it applies Moslem Law.

The ultimate authority in all cases, criminal or civil, is the High Court of Justice in Batavia.

Some features of the judicial system are of outstanding interest. One feature is the type of law applied in civil matters between natives; it is not the written law but the customary law. In Burma the courts have recognized certain legal treatises as codes of law, and try to give the codes a strict legal interpretation. In Java strenuous endeavours have been made to ascertain and enforce those customs which have the force of law. Closely allied to this is the procedure adopted. In Burma, under the rule of law, the tradition of settling disputes by an amicable compromise has died; all differences must be referred for decision to the regular courts, and even matters that are not within the cognizance of courts of law must be dealt with so far as possible according to the processes of law. The informal settlement of disputes by civil servants, native or European, is practically unknown. Again, in Java even the official magistrate disposes of matters as speedily and informally as possible, whereas in Burma even the village headmen are expected and encouraged to observe legal forms. On the other hand the courts in Java are manned by professional lawyers, and cases ordinarily come before a bench; in Burma few magistrates or judges have any legal training, and except in the High Court (and in the courts of honorary magistrates) there is no bench of judges, but the presiding officer sits alone.

9. Representative Institutions

One aspect of the Ethical movement was a new stimulus to the Liberal tradition of representative government on western lines. In 1900 the Government was constituted in much the same manner as under the Company. The Governor-General, from the first appointment in 1610, had been given the assistance of Councillors with, nominally at least, a share in the responsibility for government. In 1836 these councillors were for the first time recognized as a formal Council of India, which functioned merely in an advisory capacity, and consisted of a few senior officials. With the growth of private enterprise after 1870, non-officials chafed at the restrictions imposed on them by the States-General. On Liberal principles they urged that the Indies should be 'free'; in other words they wanted to abolish the restrictions on economic progress which the Hague imposed on the Government in Batavia, and to cut the red tape of bureaucratic rule in the interior. One favourite project was the enlargement of the Council of India by the addition of non-official Europeans, thereby converting it into an instrument of western enterprise, like the Legislative Council established in 1897 in Burma. This was steadily opposed as prejudicial to the welfare of the people, and the principle of representation was first applied in local affairs. Under the Decentralization Act of 1903 certain of the larger towns were constituted municipalities, and, subsequently, Residents were given a Residency Council, and smaller councils were formed for special rural areas.

These measures were intended to serve a double purpose; to promote efficient administration and to develop local autonomy. But the title of the Act emphasized efficiency rather than autonomy and 'those who held the baby to the font, guided its earliest footsteps'. The large towns had a considerable European element, and the urban councils, though, or rather because of, representing European interests, functioned efficiently. But the other councils languished, doing little to promote efficiency and nothing to introduce autonomy. With the growth of Nationalism after 1906, and especially after 1911, policy inclined in the direction of native representation, and the outbreak of war in 1914 brought a change in the climate of opinion; by 1915 autonomy was in the air. In this new atmosphere criticism of the local representative institutions became more audible, and the principle of representation was extended also to the central government by an Act of 1916 constituting a People's Council, or Volksraad, to advise the Governor-General in matters solely concerning the Indies.

Criticism of the local representative institutions was based mainly on two grounds. The residency council was condemned as a mechanical device giving the semblance of autonomy to an artificial unit; and the various councils lacked the organic relationship of local government in the Netherlands, where rural and urban councils form part of the same system as the provincial councils, which link them up in a single chain of popular self-government to the States-General. Attempts were made accordingly to organize local self-government on lines more congenial to Dutch ideas. The Residency Council was abolished and, in place of it, Regency Councils were constituted and given certain powers of supervision over village administration. This system linked together the two traditional units of native society, the regency and the village, under the guidance of the Regent, whom the common man still regarded as his natural leader. The process was carried a stage further with the creation of Provinces.

Just as the regency was the hub of the native branch of the administration so was the residency the hub on which the wheels of European administration turned. In 1921 there were seventeen residencies in Java and twenty corresponding units, mostly termed residencies, in the Outer Provinces. There was no one between the Residents and the Governor-General. The Residents could not, it was held, be entrusted with extensive powers, and the Governor-General was therefore overwhelmed with detail. With the growth of administrative activity during the present century decentralization became urgent, and this led to grouping the residencies into larger Governments. In Java the residencies outside the native states were grouped between 1926 and 1928 into three Governments, roughly coinciding with the three major racial divisions; Sundanese, Javanese and Madurese; with two others, much smaller, for the Native States. Subsequently, in 1934, the charges in the Outer Provinces were grouped into three Governments: Sumatra, Borneo and the Great East. The constitution of these Governments was purely a measure of administrative decentralization; but in Java the opportunity was taken to combine administrative and political reforms. For the administration of local affairs the three Governments in Java were constituted Provinces, in which the Governor conducted local administration with the assistance of a Provincial Council, exercising certain **powers** of supervision over the Regency Councils, and forming a link between the Regency Council and the Volksraad. Thus the Volksraad, the Provincial Council, the Regency Council and the villages were all brought within one system of self-government on the principle obtaining in the Netherlands.

The first Volksraad, opened in 1918, merely had in law the right of being consulted on the budget and on certain legislative measures. But in 1925 a new constitution for the Indies (*Staatsinrichting*) made its assent necessary for the budget and, normally, for other legislation on internal affairs; it was also given power to amend Government measures and to initiate legislation, and was granted the rights of petition and interpellation (i.e. to ask for information),[1] but not the right of 'enquiry' (i.e. to appoint commissions of enquiry with legal powers to obtain evidence). It cannot change the Government; there are no ministers and neither the Governor-General nor departmental heads are responsible to it, but it can influence policy by a vote of non-confidence, indicating its disapproval of men or measures. Its chief function in full assembly is the criticism of the budget; legislation and other functions in respect of administrative routine are mostly assigned to the College of Delegates, a permanent committee of twenty (later sixteen) members elected in the first session for the whole period of four years that forms the life of the Volksraad, and presided over by the chairman of the Volksraad. Any conflict of opinion between the Governor-General and the Volksraad is decided by the Home Legislature; a conflict as to legislation is decided by the Crown, but the Governor-General may take action in matters of urgency.

The Chairman of the Volksraad is appointed by the Crown; of the other members some are elected and the rest nominated by the Governor-General. Representation is based on the communal principle. Only Dutch subjects are eligible for the franchise or for membership. Three communities are recognized: natives, Dutch and 'others' (preponderantly Chinese); until 1927 the two last categories formed one constituency. The constitution of the Volksraad since 1918 is shown on p. 249.

The electorate consists of the members of the rural and urban local councils, and was therefore greatly enlarged when the Residency Councils gave place to Regency Councils. Formerly each community formed a single constituency, but in 1927 the native community was divided into twelve constituencies, with a single constituency or each

---

[1] The right of interpellation did not carry the right to a written answer, leading up to a debate, and a vote of confidence. Visman, I, 98, 106.

Membership of the Volksraad*

(a) Elected; (b) Nominated

	1918–21		1921–7		1927–31		1931–42	
	(a)	(b)	(a)	(b)	(a)	(b)	(a)	(b)
Native	10	5	12	8	20	5	20	10
Dutch	} 9	} 14	} 12	} 16	15	15	15	10
Others					3	2	3	2

* Visman, I, 82 ff.

of the other two groups, then first separated. The total electorate in 1939 numbered 2228, comprising 1817 in Java and 411 in the Outer Provinces. The electorate in Java consisted of 312 members of urban councils, and 1505 members of Regency Councils. The urban members, comprising 98 natives, 177 Dutch and 37 'others', all obtained their seats by election. On the other councils some members are nominated by the local Governor. The membership of the Regency Councils consisted of 774 natives elected, and 334 nominated, together with 231 Dutch and 166 'others', all nominated. In the local councils, constituting the electorate in the Outer Provinces, there were 139 elected members (65 natives, 59 Dutch and 15 'others') and 272 nominated or *ex officio* members (181 natives, 76 Dutch and 15 'others'). Thus out of the total number of 2228 electors, 1003 have obtained the privilege by nomination (515 natives, 307 Dutch and 181 'others'), and only 1225 (937 natives, 236 Dutch and 52 'others') have obtained their seats on local councils by election. In the towns the franchise is restricted to resident males, literate and assessed to not less than f. 300 for income tax. Not many natives have so high an income, and of these some may be barred for illiteracy. As shown above, the Dutch members have a majority over the other two communities together, and in some towns there is even a Dutch majority among the electors. The regency franchise in Java is based on the village, and is granted to all those who by the custom of the village take part in the election of the village headman. Each village chooses one 'elector' for every 500 inhabitants, and these 'electors' constitute the electorate for the native members of the regency council.

One feature of Dutch political life is the multiplicity of parties and, as already indicated, this has spread to India. In the latest Volksraad the twenty-five European members represented eight parties, and one belonged to no party; of the thirty native members, twenty-three represented ten parties and seven had no party affiliation, and even in the small group of 'other' members there were two and at one time three parties. To a certain extent this is due to the system of nomination, as it is an accepted principle that the Governor-General, or other official charged with the duty of nomination, shall aim at providing for the representation of parties which have not obtained adequate representation in the elections; in practice the Government has nominated some of its bitterest opponents, European or native. There is no official block, but a large proportion even of the elected members are classed as officials. Officials, however, are quite free to speak and vote against Government measures, and are often the keenest and, naturally, the best-informed critics; the only limitation on their freedom is an understanding that they shall not disclose matters which are officially 'confidential'.

The Provincial Councils comprise elected and nominated members of all three sections of the community, with the Provincial Governor as chairman. The electorate, as for the Volksraad, consists of the members of the regency and urban councils, and is predominantly official and largely nominated. The full council does little more than consider the budget, and routine work is conducted by a College of Deputies. One function of this college is to pass the budgets for the regency and urban councils, which is a step in the direction of organic local government such as obtains in the Netherlands. The revenues are largely derived from public services, and the functions are such as might be allotted to a local board in British India assisting a Divisional Commissioner in the administration of a divisional fund. Thus the Provincial Council has little resemblance to the Provincial Legislatures of British India.

The Regency Council comprises all three sections of the community, with elected and nominated native members, and nominated members of the other two communities; the figures are given above. In 1932 out of 1583 members, 813 elected and 770 nominated, no less than 651 elected and 186 nominated native members were officials. Only 54 of the members were classed as cultivators, but the 'officials' apparently included village headmen, who are agriculturalists and sometimes large landholders. The system of election has already been explained. The Regency Council meets once a year for the budget, and at other times when necessary, usually three or four times in all. The routine work may be allotted to a College of Commissioners. The

council and the college have a say on the village budgets. The activities
of the Regency Council seem to depend largely on the attitude of the
Regent; a prominent Regent has stated that he found it of great
assistance in the administration of his regency.

The Urban Council, as noticed above, is predominantly Dutch in its
constitution and character. The revenue comes mainly from a cess on
Government taxes, mostly paid by Europeans, and from municipal
services, such as housing, the supply of electricity, water, trams and
buses. The varied range of municipal activities is very striking; even
in a small town one may find a theatre and a swimming bath. It is
hardly too much to say that the towns are run by Europeans for
Europeans, though of course the other communities benefit by the
amenities.

10. Economic Progress

In respect of economic development the progress achieved during the
past century is no less remarkable in Netherlands India than in Burma,
and in some ways even more impressive. At the beginning of the
nineteenth century Java contributed practically nothing to the world
but a little coffee, indigo and tin, and bought nothing but ship's stores,
and a few luxuries for Europeans; the Outer Provinces still yielded
only spices, and of these the value was declining. It was under
Raffles that the foundations of foreign trade were laid. The table
below shows the growth since then for Java and the Outer Provinces,
and brings out the striking progress during the present century,
especially in the Outer Provinces.

Trade of Netherlands India (f. million)*

(a) Java; (b) Outer Provinces; (c) Total

Year	Exports			Imports		
	(a)	(b)	(c)	(a)	(b)	(c)
1825	16	—	16	12	—	12
1873	149	35	184	83	36	119
1894	137	45	182	112	46	158
1904	171	96	267	119	65	184
1914	385	351	736	319	154	473
1924	1002	747	1749	588	316	904
1937	290	661	951	317	173	490

* Visman, 1, 2; *Indisch Verslag*, 1938.

In 1890 the mineral exports, consisting solely of tin, were valued at f. 24 million, and by 1925 the value had risen to f. 94 million, and oil products to the value of f. 173 million also were exported. These come mainly from the Outer Provinces, and are won by western enterprise. Meanwhile the value of agricultural exports had risen from f. 153 million in 1898 to f. 1455 million in 1925, and the native share in these exports from f. 16 million, or 10 %, to f. 530 million, or 36 %. In 1937 the agricultural exports were valued at f. 660 million, to which natives contributed f. 302 million or 45 %.

In the promotion of economic development the Dutch Government has always been far more active than the British Government in Burma. Under the Culture system it had almost a monopoly of production for the western market; during the Liberal period the State was still associated with the cultivation of coffee and managed the chief tin mines; and the present century has seen a renewal and extension of State enterprise. Even in the Liberal period private capitalists were reluctant to risk their money in railways and coal mines, and these were developed by the State. From about 1900 the Government has taken a prominent part in experimental cultivation, and has developed numerous estates under a variety of crops. These are managed on commercial lines and are expected to be self-supporting; the managers and employees are not officials, but derive part of their remuneration from the profits of the business. The Government has also assumed a monopoly of pawnbroking, and has built up an extensive credit service. The forests, formerly leased to private firms, have now mostly been taken over by the State. Raffles introduced a monopoly of salt, and almost all the salt is now manufactured in government factories with a very up-to-date plant.

One interesting development of State enterprise may be found in the mining industry. The first Mines Law of 1899 was framed on the assumption that the exploitation of minerals would normally remain in private hands. The oil fields were then beginning to attract private capital to mining enterprise. A trend in the direction of State control found expression in an amendment of the law in 1910, providing for the exploitation of mineral resources by the State under direct State management or through contractors. For large undertakings direct management was thought expedient, but exploitation through contractors left the control and a large share of the profits to foreign capital. In 1921 therefore the Mines Law was further amended to allow the formation of 'mixed enterprises' conducted by a private company working under State control. Since then there have been four forms of working minerals: (*a*) by the State; (*b*) by a mixed company under State control; (*c*) by a private company on an exploitation contract; and (*d*) by a private company, holding a concession and paying royalties. Experience shows that a mixed company is preferred where prospects are good, and an exploitation contract, where exploration costs are high and the risk great.

The Mixed Company was originally devised for the exploitation of the Djambi Oil Fields. The Colonial Minister was empowered to form a company to work the fields and select a firm to conduct its business. He selected the Batavian Petroleum Company, a branch of the Royal Dutch and Shell group, which was already working oil in the vicinity. Together with this company he formed the 'mixed enterprise' known as the N.-I. Petroleum Company. The success of this plan in the oil business led to its extension to tin. From the time of Raffles the Government had been working the Bangka tin mines. A private firm, the Billiton Tin Company, founded on the initiative of the Crown in 1851, had yielded high profits. On the expiry of its lease in 1924 it was taken over as the Joint Mining Company, Billiton (G.M.B.), with a capital of f. 16 million, of which five-eighths was subscribed by Government. The executive management was entrusted to the former company under a council of five members, including three nominated by Government. In 1933 the G.M.B. bought up the Singkep tin mines, administering them separately but with the council of the G.M.B. as the board of directors. The device of a mixed enterprise has also been applied to the provision of electricity and water power. The Government is also interested in the organization of finance, as it still holds shares in the Java Bank and is represented on the board.

One interesting feature of economic development in Netherlands India is the activity displayed by private enterprise in scientific research. The sugar firms led the way, combining to form the General Syndicate of Sugar Producers. Firms in other lines also formed unions, subsequently amalgamated as the General Agricultural Syndicate; in Sumatra there is a Union of Tobacco Planters. These associations maintained experimental stations, which have been largely responsible for the conspicuous progress of scientific agriculture. All these representative bodies are themselves represented, together with other European interests, on the General Federation of Indian Industry and Commerce (*Indische Ondernemersbond*), with

which the Government maintains a close contact. The Government
has also created, chiefly during the present century, numerous
institutions for the promotion of pure and applied science, and in
1928 the Council of Natural Science was founded as the coping-stone
of a comprehensive organization for scientific research. Until 1906,
though European and native civil servants had always been expected
to encourage and direct native agriculture, their efforts were unorganized and amateurish. In that year the Department of Agriculture was established. With the growth of a wider conception of
state functions, this was merged in 1911 into one of greater scope
dealing also with industry and commerce, which came to function as
the mainspring of economic life, and in 1934 was converted into the
Department of Economic Affairs. The private associations are accepted as the official representatives of their interests; the committees
directing them are advisory in respect of Government but have power
to regulate their respective organizations. Thus, through all these
various institutions, the whole structure of economic life is linked
together in an elaborate economic constitution and, during the present
century, the State has come to have, as it were, a dual framework,
political and economic.

The depression of the thirties brought greater power and a new
place to the State in economic affairs. One of the earliest signs was
the inability of private enterprise to maintain its experimental stations.
In this and many other ways the State had to intervene in support of
western enterprise. 'The business men in the Indies, at least a
sufficient number of them, gradually under-
stood and accepted that Government intervention in economic affairs was indispensable
under the circumstances, and that it could
not in reason be limited or modelled to suit
the purposes of big business',[1] and it has been
suggested that the post-war world will see the
'overall governance of business in the hands
of public spirited business men, co-operating
with business-minded public servants'.

In the development of Netherlands India, as
of Burma, the policy of the 'open door' has been
observed. A recent estimate of capital investments is given in the
margin. These figures do not include reinvestments out of undivided

*Capital Investments
in N.-I. (f. million)**

Dutch	2500
Indonesian	900
Indo-Chinese	320
British	450
U.S.A.	380
Franco-Belgian	160
German	30
Japanese	30
Italian	30

* Sitsen, p. 12; Hart, p. 44.

[1] Hart, p. 61.

profits. Indonesian investments are of especial interest as quite a
new development, mainly due to native rubber, although there are
also native plantations of coconut, coffee and tea. Agricultural production, disregarding annual crops, accounts for f. 700 million out
of the Indonesian total of f. 900.

11. WELFARE

Equally remarkable with the economic development of Netherlands
India has been the growth of the population, especially in Java. At
the beginning of the nineteenth century the density of the population
in Java and Burma seems to have been very much the same. Estimates
suggest that the population of Java doubled between 1815 and 1845
and again during the next thirty years. Returns were made annually
from 1860 onwards, but until 1895 they remained very incomplete
for all except Europeans, and not until the first regular census of
1905 were any useful statistics compiled for the Outer Provinces.
The following table shows the growth in numbers by classes. Figures
for the Outer Provinces in 1905 were still very defective.

Growth of Population, 1880–1940 (*thousands*)

Year	Java				Outer Provinces				N.-I. Total
	Eur.	F. Or.	Nat.	Total	Eur.	F. Or.	Nat.	Total	Total
1880	33·7	219	19,540	19,794	—	—	—	—	—
1890	45·9	259	23,609	23,914	11·9	—	—	—	—
1900	62·4	298	28,384	28,746	13·3	—	—	—	—
1905	64·9	317	29,715	30,098	16·1	298	7,304	7,619	37,717
1920	135·2	415	34,433	34,984	34·4	461	13,871	14,366	49,350
1930	193·2	634	40,889	41,717	48·7	709	18,253	19,011	60,728
1940	(a)		47,456	48,416	—	—	21,176	22,060	70,476

(a) Estimate, Statistical Abstract, 1940; Census of 1940 postponed.

Two things stand out from this table: the rapid growth of the
population of Java; and the still more rapid growth of the foreign
element in the population. Java is the most densely inhabited major
area in the world. In 1930 there were already 800 inhabitants to the
square mile; far more than in the most densely peopled industrial
countries of Europe and nearly twice as many as in Japan. In one
district there are 4100 to the square mile. 'It is no exaggeration to

say that the problem of overpopulation is the central problem of
Java...the vital problem primarily of finding food for more mouths
and secondarily—most desirable, but definitely
secondarily—more food for each mouth.'[1]

The rapid economic development during the
Liberal period created a demand for labour, and
the population responded to the new demand.
With the growth of population there was an increase
in the area under rice, but it seems that the production of rice did not keep pace with the rise in
population and 'the growth of the people gobbled up the larger yield'.[2]
By 1900 the people were producing less food per head, were drawing
lower wages from the planter, and had fewer opportunities to earn
money by odd jobs. The people were liable to various compulsory
services and it was thought that, if relieved of this obligation, they
would be able to earn more in wages by free labour; a capitation tax
was accordingly imposed in lieu of compulsory service. The express
object of the Ethical policy was to help the common man.

Density (1930) per sq. mile*	
Java	800
Belgium	670
Netherlands	578
U.K.	485
Japan	425

* Hart, p. 34.

'Never, perhaps, has any Government set itself so wholeheartedly and
with such zeal and comprehensive thoroughness to building up the welfare
of its subjects as the Government of Netherlands India at the beginning
of the present century. Most of the officials at that time had fallen under
the spell of Multatuli during their studies at Leiden, and came to India as
enthusiastic idealists, filled with ardour to take part in the great civilizing
mission of the Netherlands. On their arrival they found a welfare programme as the official policy of Government; zeal for the well-being of the
people was a condition of promotion, as any who were reluctant to interfere
with native life were regarded with disfavour as "weak and recalcitrant
administrators".'[3]

The new opportunities afforded by the Village Act were seized with
enthusiasm. Yet successive welfare surveys, confirmed by the figures
for the import of goods consumed by natives, suggest that the people
were rather worse off in 1930 than in 1913. In 1926 it was found that
the substitution of capitation tax for compulsory service had done so
little to improve the condition of the people that they could not even
afford to pay the tax.[4] About 1935 the Director of Economic Affairs
remarked that, although for sixty years it had been possible to stave
off the disasters consequent on over-population, new and radical

[1] Hart, p. 36.   [2] Gonggrijp, cited *Netherlands India*, p. 214.
[3] *Netherlands India*, p. 382.   [4] *Ib.* p. 401.

measures were still urgently needed or the position would soon
become critical.[1]

Native rubber planting has done little to relieve it, as this is mostly
on small holdings, except for a comparatively few plantations, almost
all in Sumatra and Borneo. The villager, especially in Java, still culti-
vates rice, and a recent survey suggests that during the past ten
years the consumption of rice per head has fallen by about 8 %.[2]
It is true that to a casual visitor the standard of comfort appears
much the same as in Burma, and is certainly far higher than in
Bengal or Madras, yet it would seem that the rapid economic development of the present century, despite the multiplication of welfare
services which it has made possible, has had little effect on welfare.

One notable feature of welfare activities in Java has been the
attention paid to public health. So far back as 1851 a school was
opened for training medical subordinates; by 1900 there were 103
Europeans and 90 native medical practitioners in Java, and by 1930
the combined number had risen to 667, while the expenditure on
public health rose from f. 2·2 million in 1900 to 20·7 million in 1930.
The chief items of expenditure have been the provision of hospitals
and dispensaries, inoculation, the improvement of housing and, later,
propaganda. The most obvious result of this activity is the large proportion of houses with tiled roofs, which were regarded as conferring
security against plague. From the first it was recognized that hygiene
was very largely a matter of education, and it is a notable instance of
the sympathetic imagination which so often characterizes the administration that the Public Health Service forms a branch of the Education Department. 'Gentle pressure' was freely exercised to improve
rural sanitation. Naturally zeal for sanitary welfare was not always
tempered with discretion. The people often understood the wishes
of the civil officers better than the intentions of the medical service,
and there are numerous stories, some doubtless *ben trovato*, of villages
where the headman proudly led the Resident to his new model
latrine, bearing the banner 'Welcome', and of others where the people
observed so strictly the injunction to keep the latrines clean that they
refrained from using them.

Public instruction, however, until the present century, was comparatively backward. Schools for Europeans, including of course
Indo-Europeans, were maintained from 1816, and, with the influx

[1] Hart, p. 35.
[2] Wickizer and Bennett, pp. 223, 328.

of Europeans from 1870 onwards, educational standards improved. These schools have usually been open to a limited number of natives of good birth. One condition for admission was an adequate knowledge of Dutch, and many natives were accepted in European homes where they could learn the Dutch language and Dutch ways of life. Thus, for over a hundred years, there have been a few among the upper classes who have absorbed western culture from intimate contact with Europeans instead of merely learning about the West from books. Even a hundred years ago some Regents could speak more than one European language.[1]

Under the Culture system western schools were little needed, and the people were left to attend Koran schools. The Liberals of 1848 struck out a new line. They regarded it as 'their task, their duty, to spread light among the Javanese'. Humanitarian ideals were gradually reinforced by practical considerations, because the growth of commerce and the extension of Government activities created a demand for clerks. Indo-Europeans did not suffice to meet the demand, and from about 1870 schools were provided for natives, though on a very modest scale until after 1900, and it was not until 1914 that the Government provided Dutch-vernacular schools leading up to a higher education. Since then the progress of education among the natives has been rapid. In 1930 there were nearly 12,000 children in Mulo standards, corresponding to the High School in Burma, and close on 5000 in the middle standards, corresponding to the Intermediate course in an Indian university. In the Middle School there is a special section for Oriental Letters. Children in the Mulo standards take not only the usual school subjects (including natural science) but also three European languages—Dutch, English and German—as well as two oriental languages. The standard of attainment seems extraordinarily high. There is, as in Burma and for the same reasons, a competition for diplomas, with the natural result that students press on in growing numbers towards diplomas of higher market value. But one factor tends to prevent the devaluation of diplomas. Dutch parents expect their children in the European schools to enter the corresponding classes in Holland; the diploma is of no use to them unless it carries its face value. Similarly pupils in Dutch-vernacular schools must be able at any time to enter the corresponding standard in the local European school. Thus the standards of instruction are protected against deterioration, despite the demand in Java for

[1] *De Zieke Reisiger*, by a Bengal Civilian (1853), p. 75.

diplomas, by the demand in Holland for the qualifications that the diplomas are supposed to represent.

Technical and vocational instruction has also made great progress during recent years, owing to the demand for technical subordinates on western enterprise, and in Government service. Also, as in Burma and in the tropics generally, the petrol engine has stimulated a new demand in the native world for mechanics to drive and repair taxis, buses and lorries. One aspect of vocational education of great interest is the training of civil servants, both European and native. The course for Europeans is designed to give them a wide understanding of native society and covers five years' study of 'Indology' at a Dutch university, where the probationers specialize either in letters or economics, with the alternative branch as a subsidiary. The course for native civil servants is designed to give them a western background for their work; they live in hostels, furnished on European lines with books, pictures, a piano, radio and billiard table, etc., and the course includes tropical economy and hygiene among the subjects. Thus the training of Europeans and Indonesians is complementary; it aims at making Europeans understand the East and Indonesians understand the West, and to equip both as social engineers in a modern tropical environment.

Colleges of university standing date from 1920 to 1926. The leaders of the ethical school held that higher western education could not flourish healthily except in a western background, and advocated that students should finish their course in Europe. The results of experiments along these lines were regarded as unsatisfactory, and not many students were sent. The war of 1914–18, however, created a demand for locally trained engineers, and in 1920 a School of Engineering was founded by some private capitalists. It was taken over by the Government in 1924, and Schools of Law and Medicine were created during the next two years. These gave a university course in their respective faculties. In 1940 Schools of Agriculture and of Humane Letters were constituted, and a bill to merge all the faculties in one University was adopted by the Volksraad.

One matter of great educational and political importance is the encouragement given to what may be termed the adult education of officials and others of like status. In Dutch practice the university course does not confer a degree on the successful student but entitles him to qualify for a degree by writing a thesis. The titles of Doctor and Master are highly valued, and many colonials, officials and others, aspire to them. The thesis usually relates to some aspect of colonial life or administrative policy which has attracted the attention of the student in his daily work, and an able thesis may lead to preferment. By this means colonial problems of importance are studied from an academic standpoint by men with practical experience, and not infrequently the resulting thesis is a useful contribution to colonial policy or administrative practice. Moreover, officials are encouraged to discuss both policy and practice freely in departmental periodicals and also in periodicals for the general public, and, as already mentioned, they are free to criticize Government measures in the Volksraad. This considerable volume of well-informed criticism necessarily has a salutary effect in stimulating an intelligent interest in colonial affairs among officials and non-officials, and presents a notable contrast to the traditional reserve of British administration, which allows the public discussion of affairs only by the ignorant or malicious.

Nevertheless, many serious educational problems still await solution. One of the most difficult arises out of the close connection between western education and economics. In the past there has been no demand outside Government service for highly educated Indonesians, and of necessity there are limits to the number whom the Government can employ. But the supply is limited only by the ability of students to pass the examinations, and the ability of parents to pay the fees and other incidental charges. An enquiry in 1928 showed that a large percentage of school graduates failed to find employment. On an average, since 1900, about half of those passing the clerkship examination had entered Government service; but in 1928 the number obtaining this qualification was 6559 and the annual demand was 447. It was then estimated that, taking public service and private enterprise as a whole, if every post requiring a knowledge of Dutch were filled by men who had passed the clerkship, or some higher examination, the supply would still be about three times the demand.[1] During the subsequent depression fewer pupils could afford to stay the course, and the numbers in the various western institutions declined; but those who remained seem to have studied more diligently, for the number of graduates from all classes of school and college rose, as appears from the table on p. 261.

Another difficulty is the emergence of 'wild schools', private schools which refuse State aid. These arose out of dissatisfaction on

[1] *HIOC*, Eindrapport, pp. 45, 46.

Graduates from Western Schools and Colleges*

(a) 1914-15; (b) 1938-9

Class	Europeans		Natives		F. Or.		Total	
	(a)	(b)	(a)	(b)	(a)	(b)	(a)	(b)
Lower	1598	3743	951	7349	209	2274	2758	13,366
Mulo	107	740	8	1012	5	487	120	2,239
Middle	49	457	4	204	3	116	56	777
Higher†	8	20	—	40	—	21	8	81

* Visman, I, 60ff.

† For 1914-15 read 1924-5, the first year when higher students graduated.

political or economic grounds with the aided schools, which found expression in the *Tamansiswo* movement, aiming to reconcile western education with oriental traditions. Some of these accept State inspection, but few of those inspected are regarded as on the same level of efficiency as the corresponding public schools. When the depression of the thirties restricted government expenditure on education, the wild schools multiplied rapidly, and by 1940 there were 120,000 pupils in the Dutch-vernacular schools of this type as against 66,000 in the corresponding aided schools.[1]

It is in the sphere of vernacular instruction that educational progress during the present century has been greatest. Not until 1907 was there any serious attempt to provide instruction for the masses, but the village schools first established in that year have been remarkably successful. By 1937 the proportion of children at recognized schools was nearly as high as in Burma, and a recent estimate places it at 40 %. A very large proportion fail to remain even for the three years which constitutes the complete course in the village school; but those who persevere may cross the narrow bridge leading to the western schools with their attractive prospect of well-paid employment. The possibility of promotion through the village school into the western world has probably been one factor in making it popular. Another factor has been the adaptation of the school to village life, which has been rendered possible by appointing civil servants to advise the Director with regard to native education. But the chief factor undoubtedly has been the constant exercise of 'gentle pressure' by the subdistrict officer. 'Mild coercion had to be employed to inveigle parents into sending their youngsters to school. And it often

[1] de la Court, p. 39.

happened in primitive regions that a school would be set afire in the hope that this would offer an escape from the painful necessity of education.'[1] One important function of the subdistrict officer is to inspect the school registers, and enquire into the reasons for irregular attendance. The success attained in Java appears to be due in great part to insistence on the value of education as a social asset enabling the Javanese to compete more adequately with the Chinese. In this, as in other matters, the minute attention paid to welfare, is possible only because the charge of the subdistrict officer is so small, and the successful working of gentle pressure through the headman is largely due to the survival of common life within the village.

The Dutch have not been content merely to teach the people how to read, but have provided them with reading matter in the People's Library. There are nearly 3000 recognized libraries; school managers act as local librarians, lending books free to children and at $2\frac{1}{2}$ cents ($\frac{1}{2}d$.) a volume to adults. Motor book vans are also sent out, and some of these sell 2500 books a month. Thus there is readily available to the schools and general public an extensive modern literature comprising popular handbooks on a wide range of subjects, from carpentry and agriculture to hygiene, and translations and adaptations of European literature from Dickens and Dumas to Molière and Kipling. In this manner the Government has succeeded within a single generation in organizing a demand for books that will serve to bring the people into touch with the modern world. As we have noticed above, the Burma Government preferred to leave the supply of modern literature to private enterprise.

12. Social Welfare

We have already remarked that the conservation of village life is an old tradition of Dutch rule, and they pride themselves on its success. Wongso, the typical villager, says a recent account, is a farmer. But he is primarily a member of the closely knit *desa*-community and his landownership comes in the second place because it is altogether tied up in the clan, which is his village. That membership gives him rights and duties, but the duties come first, and they come naturally, self-evidently. He has duties towards the *desa* (village), a whole system of duties which he fulfils as a matter of course, as his ancestors have

[1] Vlekke, p. 323.

done through the ages, without payment or recognition. There is another set of duties to which Wongso adheres no less rigorously; they are the services which he gives, not to the village but to his fellow villagers individually—duties which are summed up as mutual help. The *desa* is primarily a social unit, and 'economic man of individualistic liberalism has never been either loved or understood in the Indonesian village. That is why Government schemes, both large scale and small, to further Indonesian enterprise and initiative, risk failure if they try to appeal to the individual economic instincts, and have a fair chance of being comprehended and accepted, if they are based on a foundation of organic co-operation, which has the *sambatan* touch'.[1] This social sense, it is claimed, has been transferred to village industries organized in 'industrial centrals', 'the co-operating craftsmen have developed the same sense of obligation to make good towards that central as they have always had towards their *desa*'.[2]

It is difficult for anyone of a critical temperament wholly to repress a suspicion that this picture is just a little too good to be true. It is certain that for the past sixty years there has been a trend towards the relaxation of communal ties, and this has been furthered by the policy of encouraging agricultural production for profit instead of for subsistence.[3] On the other hand, the scrupulous care for the preservation of customary law, the restrictions on the alienation of village land to foreigners, and the tradition of abstaining from intervening in village affairs seem on the whole to have been effectual in protecting the village community against the solvent influence of economic forces, and the foregoing picture of the typical Indonesian village which the Dutch have consistently endeavoured to conserve would seem to depict accurately, at least in broad outline, the Javanese village of the present day. Dutch rule has, in great measure, been successful in softening the impact of the modern west on native social life.

Outside and above the village, however, the social structure presents the normal character of modern tropical society. 'The most obvious feature of the community in Netherlands India is the heterogeneous composition of the population.'[4] This complex social structure is dominated by economic values. In the western or westernized element, as Dr Boeke remarks, 'there is materialism, rationalism, individualism and a concentration on economic ends far more complete and absolute than in homogenous western lands; a total absorption in the

[1] Hart, pp. 64, 65.   [2] *Ib.* p. 89.
[3] *Netherlands India*, p. 319; Visman, I, 27.   [4] Visman, I, 53.

Exchange and Market; a capitalist structure, with the business concern as subject, far more typical of Capitalism than one can imagine in the so-called "capitalist lands" which have grown slowly out of the past and are still bound to it by a hundred roots'. He was writing with special reference to the European element, but his remarks apply with equal force to the Chinese element, and to the growing number of natives 'who have adopted a western mentality as their own, and who possess and use those qualities which modern capitalism requires of its representatives'.[1] Dr Boeke and other Dutch economists tend to contrast this rationalist material attitude of western enterprise with the disregard of economic values that they regard as characteristic of the native element. That will need further consideration; here it will suffice to note that during the present century, up to the depression of the thirties, the foreign elements were growing more numerous and more powerful, and that political reforms did nothing to check this process. On these points Netherlands India resembles Burma; what is distinctive of the social order in Netherlands India is that, for good or ill, the native community has largely been cut off from and protected against the working of economic forces, which in other tropical regions, as in Burma, have been allowed free play.

13. NETHERLANDS INDIA AND BURMA

In the foregoing pages we have tried to bring out some of the more important points of similarity and contrast between Java and Burma. In both there has been rapid progress; both countries have been thrown freely open to the modern world under the policy of the 'open door', and both now make a valuable contribution to the material resources of the world. In both alike the process of development under foreign rule has resulted in a racially mixed community in which economic forces are abnormally active, and in both a nationalist movement voices a reaction against foreign rule.

We have seen, however, that in the principles and machinery of administration a superficial resemblance conceals a profound difference. British rule in Burma rests on the principles of economic freedom and equality before the law, and there is a single uniform system of direct rule in which the administrative officers are essentially servants of the law. Dutch rule in Java rests on the principle of 'like over like', and there is a dual administration

[1] Boeke, cited *Netherlands India*, pp. 452, 457.

in which European and native officials have different functions but are both alike agents of a policy directed towards 'the spontaneous and autonomous promotion of the interests of land and people'.[1] In pursuance of this policy the Dutch have aimed at the conservation of the village and of village customary law, and at the retention of native land in native hands; in Burma, on the contrary, under the rule of law, the policy of Government has been to allow the people to pursue their individual interests within the limits of the law. We have seen that the system adopted in Burma has allowed the emergence of certain notorious abuses; self-government is generally regarded as a failure; agricultural debt has assumed vast proportions and is only one symptom of agrarian distress; there has been a formidable growth in litigation and, what is worse, in serious crime, and this has been accompanied by increasing clerical unrest, while the whole administration is riddled with corruption. It may be useful to examine rather more closely how these matters stand in Java.

Self-government. For many reasons it is difficult to make any fair comparison between Java and Burma in respect of self-government on western lines. In Java the problem of westernized self-government is simplified to some extent by the presence of a much larger and more stable European element, especially in the towns and even in small towns in the interior; in Burma, outside the main ports, and, one may say, outside Rangoon, the European element in the population, if any, is negligible. One would naturally expect self-government on western lines to run more smoothly where Europeans take part in running it. Europeans form a stabilizing element both in the Volksraad and provincial councils, and, moreover, these have not been granted such extensive powers as the corresponding organs in Burma. It is significant that, as soon as the Volksraad was entrusted with a share in the Government under the constitution of 1925, the association parties broke up into their racial elements. 'This is the last Association-Volksraad', said the Chairman in his final speech to the first Volksraad under the new constitution. 'Henceforth each group will pursue its own interests, keenly and without reserve.'[2] The Dutch recognize that 'at least in that still comparatively thin upper stratum of the Indonesian community which is conscious of political and other problems' there is 'a desire for further extension of political rights and suffrage, for formal embodiment in the constitution of

---

[1] Van Vollenhoven, cited *Netherlands India*, p. 91.
[2] Visman, I, 88.

[liberal] conventional practice, an ambition to obtain greater influence within the Realm on affairs of the Realm as a whole'.[1] In Burma the constitution formally embodies those rights that the Javanese demand, but, because the form has no substance in political realities, it is a source of discontent rather than of satisfaction, and the people make still further demands.

As regards self-government in local affairs, urban administration in Java is in many ways a model of efficiency, contrasting very favourably with municipal administration in Burma. But it is largely run by Europeans for Europeans and, in the provision of amenities such as houses for the people, it aims at European standards. The Regency Councils, corresponding roughly to District Councils in Burma, seem to reflect in great measure the personality of the Regent, but one does not hear the charges of gross inefficiency and corruption, ordinarily levied against western institutions of local self-government in Burma.

Western self-government however hardly touches the mass of the people, either in Burma or Java. These live in villages. In Burma western self-government has been constructed, in accordance with western ideas, on the basis of individual rights. The Dutch system was built up on the basis of the village, and aimed to bring the village into organic relation with higher units of popular self-government. But the preponderance of local officials among those elected suggests general indifference, due perhaps to the device of indirect election. Yet in Burma we find a similar indifference, and the lack of any local ties between members and their constituencies has often been deplored; politicians can easily secure votes by appealing to the natural dislike of foreign rule, but they know and care little for their constituencies, and the villagers know and care little about what happens in the legislature.

In Burma as in Java local interest does not extend beyond local affairs, but there is a striking difference between them in village administration. In Java the Dutch have tried to conserve both the form and content of traditional self-government while adapting it to the requirements of the modern world; in Burma a contrary policy has been pursued. In Java the intricate complexity of the native political organization has been simplified, but the regency and village have been retained. In Burma the organic unit, the circle, has been replaced by the purely official township, and the country has been broken up into villages, while there is no organ of oriental

[1] Hart, p. 29.

democracy corresponding to the *vergadering* of Java. In Burma the village has become merely an administrative unit, whereas in Java the village still appears to be mainly a social unit. And it would hardly be possible to find a more striking contrast than between the Village Act of Java, designed as an instrument of social uplift, and the Village Act of Burma, designed as an instrument of law and order and 'vigorously enforced' by fines on villages, villagers and headmen. Government schemes in Java, we are told, 'risk failure if they appeal to the individual economic instincts and have a fair chance of being comprehended and accepted, if they are based on a foundation of organic co-operation'.[1]

Indebtedness. Both in Burma and Java agricultural indebtedness has accompanied, and has indeed been a condition of, economic progress. It was through giving out advances that the planter in Java secured his land and labour, and that the miller in Burma made certain of getting an adequate supply of paddy at the lowest possible rate. The Dutch, with their State pawnshops and People's Banks, have done more than has been attempted in Burma to provide credit on sound lines, but they have by no means solved the problem of indebtedness; alongside the state institutions the private moneylender still flourishes. But the application of native customary law to land, and the prohibition against the alienation of land to foreigners have obviated the most pernicious social and political consequences of agricultural indebtedness, and it is not in the same measure as in Burma a cause of agricultural distress and political ill-will.

Litigation and Crime. Until quite recently litigation was as unusual in Burma as it still is in Java. But in Burma the people have been encouraged to settle their disputes by the processes of western law, whereas in Java, customary law and the practice of arbitration and the settlement of disputes by reasonable compromise have survived.

An even greater contrast is presented in respect of crime. In Java the death sentence is almost unknown; for the five years from 1935 to 1939, with a population for the whole of Netherlands India of nearly 70 million, only three persons were sentenced to death; in Burma, with a fifth of the population, the death sentence is passed on some two hundred a year and upwards of a hundred a year are hanged. It is difficult to compare sentences of imprisonment, but the position in Java is very different from that in Burma where, for some thirty years, the accommodation for convicts has failed to keep pace with

[1] Hart, p. 65.

the number sent to prison, and one reads year after year of over-
crowded jails. In Burma whipping is freely used in addition to, or
as a substitute for, imprisonment, and is a regular feature of jail
discipline, whereas in Netherlands India whipping has been abolished
as a judicial penalty and, though still permissible for unruly convicts,
is in practice never used. In Burma, in addition to those convicted
of offences, upwards of two thousand people a year may be placed on
security, imprisoned or restricted under the ordinary Criminal Procedure Code, and another five hundred under the more rigorous provision of the Habitual Offenders Restriction Act.[1] In Netherlands
India action along these lines seems to form no part of the ordinary
processes of law. After the revolutionary outbreak of 1926–7 in Netherlands India, upwards of a thousand people were interned and deported
by executive authority; but this was an exceptional measure to counter
an emergency. In Burma, however, the Village Act provides for deportation as part of the recognized machinery of administration, and
under this Act over twelve hundred were deported in connection with
the rebellion of 1931.[2] In Burma collective penalties are imposed over
large areas under the Police Act by quartering on them punitive
police, of which the inhabitants must defray the cost; collective
penalties may also be imposed on villages under two distinct sections
of the Village Act. In the police courts of Burma a fine of less than
Rs. 5 is unusual; in Java the penalty rarely seems to exceed half a
guilder.

Yet in Burma, despite this vigorous enforcement of the law, crime
continues to increase, whereas in Java the registers of the police
stations seem mostly to be filled with charges as to the use of an
unduly severe bit, riding a horse without a saddle, or something
of that order.[3] In Netherlands India the whole system of administration is directed to preventing crime by removing its causes;
in Burma the Government has been content to aim at maintaining law and order through legal penalties. In Lower Burma up to
1880 the proportion of Burman convicts was far lower than among
other sections of the population, and up to 1910 Upper Burma was
comparatively free of crime. These facts sufficiently dispose of a
general indictment against the people as normally and naturally
criminal, and the only possible conclusion would seem to be that the
principles on which the administration of Burma has been conducted

---

[1] *RAB*, 1930–1, p. 23.   [2] *RAB*, 1931–2, p. 77.
[3] *Netherlands India*, p. 299; Colijn, cited Bousquet, p. 90.

were such as to develop their worse rather than their better qualities. Our methods might have done very well for Europe; they may have been suitable in India, where the people are protected against economic forces by the ties of caste, but they did not suit the Burman. 'It was the best butter', said the Hatter; but it spoiled the watch.

Clerical Unrest. In Burma the turbulence prevalent among the monks is one of the more recent features of social disorder and unrest, but it is merely one aspect of the dissolution of society indicated by the growth of crime. In Java there is nothing of the kind. As already noticed, causes relating to religion are tried in special Moslem courts, instead of, as in Burma, coming before the ordinary lay court; and the law applied is Moslem ecclesiastical law as interpreted by native Moslem judges, whereas in Burma the rule of decision is looked for in the *dhammathats* as interpreted on the principles of western law. The procedure in Java does not weaken but fosters corporate authority in the religious establishment. Moreover, the village clerics are appointed by or with the approval of the Regent, whereas in Burma the Government has held aloof from all concern with promoting the establishment, while actively breaking it down by the transfer of religious causes to the civil courts. The Dutch have with good reason tried to conciliate Moslem sentiment and, even if they have not been wholly successful, there is nothing in Java corresponding to the clerical unrest in Burma.[1]

Corruption. We have had to notice the prevalence of corruption in Burma. By all accounts it is practically unknown in Java. The absence of judicial corruption can easily be understood. Petty cases are settled by arbitration either out of court, or before a bench of notables with a senior and well-paid official as chairman; or they go before a civil servant or judicial officer with long service and on high pay. Moreover, the penalties imposed are so trivial that it is cheaper to be punished than to bribe a policeman or magistrate to escape punishment. Serious matters go before a bench containing at least three high judicial officers as well as laymen of good standing. It would be difficult and dangerous to bribe the whole bench. In civil cases the decision purports to follow customary law, and the people can know whether it is right; the court must justify itself to popular opinion and not to higher judicial authority. In these circumstances there is little scope for bribery.

But that corruption should be unknown in general administration,

---

[1] Bousquet, pp. 51 ff.; *Vrij Nederland*, 27 Nov. 1943.

with a Government intervening so actively in every branch of social life, seems almost incredible. That, however, is certainly the general opinion. For example, the People's Banks, in dealing with applications for loans, depend largely on reports from the village headman as to the character and circumstances of the applicants. This would seem to provide a ready means by which the headman might supplement his income. In Burma it was regarded as natural and not improper that the headman should charge applicants for loans from Government a fee for making his report. In Java a suggestion to this effect met with the response, 'But there would be a complaint!', and that was taken as a sufficient and final answer. So far as the general opinion as to the absence of corruption is well-founded, there would seem to be two explanations: one is the tradition of 'complaints'; the other, the permanence of the Regent.

As already explained, it has been a tradition from the early days of Liberal rule that the Controleur, without actually instigating complaints, should encourage the people to complain of any oppressive act. The Liberals prided themselves on relieving the people from the oppression by their native chieftains that had been one feature of the Culture system, and one chief duty of the Controleur, as he moved among the people, was to detect and bring to light oppression by encouraging them to complain, so that the 'complaint' has become a word of magic. In Burma anyone may petition the local magistrate; but the petition must bear a court fee stamp; in practice it is written by a legal practitioner or by a licensed petition writer; it must be presented in open court, and must disclose some matter in respect of which the law entitles the petitioner to relief. It is an application to an officer of the law for some action according to the law. In Java anyone may complain, orally or in writing, at any time, on any matter; no stamp or court fee is required; there are no licensed petition writers, and anyone may write the complaint. Even diehards recognized one good feature in the nationalist movement: that the nationalist leaders encouraged the people to formulate complaints. The tradition goes back far beyond the Liberal period; it dates from the principle adopted in 1803 that Government should act 'more like a father studying to promote the welfare of his family than a ruler governing his subjects'; the Liberals merely devised machinery for making the tradition more effective. Thus the 'complaint' has come to take a place alongside 'gentle pressure' as a distinctive feature of Dutch colonial practice.

Another safeguard against corruption is the Regent. In Burma no one stays long enough in one place to ascertain in what quarters and to what extent corruption may prevail; still less is it possible to work up and carry through proceedings against those who are corrupt. In Java the Regent is permanent. His position and his high pay protect him against the temptation to accept petty bribes, and concern for his own authority and prestige makes him jealous of the influence of corrupt subordinates. These cannot practise corruption long or effectively without attracting the attention of the Regent, who can see that the offender is brought to account. If, then, the administration is so free from corruption as one is told, the credit is probably due in great part to the Regent.

Authority and Law. It must be admitted then that, in all those matters which stand out conspicuously as abuses under British rule in Burma, Dutch rule in Java presents a favourable contrast. Yet there is another side to the picture. The Government has employed 'gentle pressure' to protect the village community against dissolution, and to promote welfare; yet 'gentle pressure' may be debilitating rather than a stimulant, making the patient less able and not more able to stand alone. And it is difficult to reconcile gentle pressure, however well-intentioned, with the principles of liberty and law. In an address to a Dutch audience interested in colonial problems, the present writer endeavoured to illustrate this point.[1]

'One of your subordinate native officers described his work. "I improved sanitation. I got the people to found schools, and build bazaars, and provide a polyclinic. And I would not allow bamboo bazaars; if they could not afford wooden walls, I took care that the posts were of substantial timber and that the roof was sound. I even planted flower gardens, a thing that practically no one else has done; and it was all my own idea, without pressure from above." I have heard your European officers described as social engineers and your native civil servants as welfare officers, and the terms are justified. As I went round your villages and saw the infinite pains you take to conserve village society and build up social welfare, I found myself humming a tune. It was a hymn tune. Gradually the words came back to me: "Can a mother's tender care, Cease towards the child she bare? Yes, she may forgetful be, Yet will I remember thee." I thought of the hours and days we spend on the Bench, listening to advocates (trying to mislead us), laboriously taking down evidence (much of it false evidence), and sending poor unfortunates to jail, and I was filled with envy and admiration of your officers who have the privilege of giving

[1] Furnivall, *Asiatic Review*, 1935, pp. 655 ff.

their life to constructive social work as missionaries of western civilization. ...Your Regent can look round his Regency and say, "*si monumentum requiris, circumspice.*" Our energetic township officer reviewing his work would take you to his record room and point to Alps and Himalayas of completed cases; here, he would say, "*si monumentum requiris, circumspice*".

'In your offices of equal standing I found no such mountains of proceedings. There would not have been room for them. I remember visiting a native subordinate. A broad drive through a walled park of several acres took us to a roomy house with a spacious audience hall. In one corner of the park were two outhouses. One was a garage; the smaller one I took to be a bicycle shed. But it was not a bicycle shed; it was his office. I do not wish to guarantee the details of this picture, but it represents correctly the general impression that I gathered everywhere....Things are changing, but until within the last few years, you had large houses and little offices; in Burma we have large offices and little houses. Your system is, or has been, personal: ours, mechanical....

'(Yet), by a quasi-natural process, by the play of supply and demand, we arrive at very much the same results as you—with very much less work and worry. But the principle is not the same, the method is not the same, and the results are not quite the same. Your policy is, professedly, ethical; ours, practical. These are not mere catchwords. You try to give the people what they ought to want; we are content to give them what they will pay for. Your method is one of personal influence, *zachte dwang, parentah aloes*; we rely on the economic motive, the desire for gain, working within the limits of the law. The results, I admit, are not quite the same. Our villages compare very badly with yours in respect of hygiene and roads; it is hardly an exaggeration to say that, outside the larger towns, until the coming of the motor-car, we had no roads. People do not want disease, and they would rather go dry-foot than through mud. But no one can make money out of hygiene and roads, and not much can be done by a private individual in respect of either. The want for these, and for many other things, is a social want. On the ethical system you aim at organizing social demand; on the practical system we neglect such wants until they threaten to create a public nuisance. Your system works very differently from ours....

'Let me recapitulate the main points of difference. Our officers are magistrates; yours are policemen and welfare officers. Our methods are repressive; yours are preventive. Our procedure is formal and legal; yours, informal and personal. Our civil service is an administrative machine; yours is an instrument of Government. Our aim is negative—to suppress disorder; yours is positive—to maintain order. Order—it is a word we both use frequently, but with a significant difference of context. We talk of "law and order" and you of "*rust en orde*"; but in the absence of a social conscience it is difficult to distinguish between law and the letter of the law, and between *rust* and the placidity of a good baby in its perambulator. The caricature which depicts your system as a *baboe*, a nursemaid, and ours as a *babu*, a clerk, does emphasize a difference in vital principle. You try to keep a man from going wrong; we make it unpleasant for him if he does go wrong. You believe in protection and welfare; we believe in law—and liberty.'

Burmans, after so many years of British rule, would probably feel stifled in the hot-house atmosphere of Java, and Javanese would shiver in the bleaker, if not bracing, climate of Burma. But it must be admitted that the version of Dutch policy given above did not pass without protest. Everyone readily admits that the people are too fondly coddled. There have long been general complaints that they are treated as children who will never grow up; that 'a villager cannot scratch his head unless a district officer gives him permission and an expert shows him how to do it'. In a powerful article that met with wide approval, the late Professor Van Vollenhoven pressed home the point that, in exercising 'gentle pressure', officials are not hampered by an obsequious deference to law. But not many would accept the suggestion that their colonial practice encroaches on liberty. Possibly their attitude may be due in part to their heritage of Roman law. 'Its influence', remarks Sir Henry Slesser, 'in stimulating a disciplinary outlook in politics and study on the Continent has been incalculable.' Yet even continental students present a rather similar picture of Dutch practice.[1] Whatever criticisms may be levelled at British colonial policy, and whatever defects may be manifest in practice, both policy and practice are based on the principles of equal law and individual freedom. That is why, in the earlier stages, it is both successful and in many ways congenial to the people; it liberates them from arbitrary oppression by native chieftains or Government officials. And it is probably one reason why, in its later stages, it is found irksome and unpopular; it brings them under bondage to economic law.

Another point which our comparison has brought out is that neither Dutch nor English have solved the problem of enhancing native welfare. The Dutch, by strenuous endeavours, have succeeded in maintaining an astonishingly high level of material welfare, far above the level in those parts of India which are comparable in respect of population, and about the same level as in Burma with much fewer mouths to feed. Yet if the Dutch have protected the people against

[1] Slesser, Sir H., *The Judicial Office* (1943), p. 83; Bousquet, pp. 90 ff.; *Netherlands India*, pp. 382, 390.

those factors which have caused agrarian distress and fostered crime, corruption and clerical unrest in Burma, the price has had to be paid in other ways. For the problem of enhancing welfare, says Dr Boeke,

'a real solution can be found only by instilling into the masses of the people a rational view of sex relations and a dynamic view of production. This is the only conclusion that can be reached by those who desire to make actual a general, a mass-welfare policy. And it is striking to note how often writers on welfare policy for Oriental peoples finally come to the conclusion somewhat in the nature of a cry of despair, that the only hope of saving the situation lies in neo-Malthusianism. Unfortunately this has never proved to be a remedy for the very poorest; and Java is a country of the very poor. What is worse, it can never be counted upon as a means of enhancing prosperity in the Indies, because it is in itself a symptom, the sign of the dynamic spirit, of a new frame of mind not yet acquired by the people. This dynamic spirit is the crux of the matter—but how to arouse it?'[1]

Only with diffidence can one venture to question the views of a Dutch economist on the affairs of Java. Yet one cannot suppress the feeling that Dutch writers who do not know Burma and India tend to be over gloomy as to the poverty of the Javanese. And there is evidence that the people do not wholly lack the 'dynamic' spirit, the desire to improve their lot. Throughout the last half of the nineteenth century there was a steady flow of immigration to districts where new public works offered prospects of higher pay; practically all the crops now cultivated by natives are of foreign origin, and one finds now that the areas under cash crops, such as potatoes, rise and fall with prices. So far as it is true that the Javanese are lacking in initiative and that the outstanding problem is to provide food for more mouths, the cause would seem to lie in their past history and present environment. In any case it is difficult to accept the lack of a dynamic spirit as the crux of the matter. In Burma the colonization of the Delta is only one instance of the dynamic spirit of the Burmese, and the people have long taken with avidity to new and more profitable crops. And in the delta there is no pressure of population. On the contrary, although containing the richest agricultural land, it is more lightly populated than other settled tracts of Burma. Yet the great mass of the inhabitants are rack-rented tenants or landless labourers, unable

[1] Boeke, p. 164.

to find work for a great part of the year—except when, as happens too frequently, they are in jail. If the population were denser one might be tempted to regard the numerous murders in modern Burma as nature's way of reducing a surplus population. But neither a dynamic spirit nor a thin population have assured welfare to the Burmese. We would seem then to be faced with the melancholy alternative of economic apathy or crime. Before we acquiesce in accepting one of these alternatives as the inevitable outcome of colonial practice, we would do well to enquire further why the benevolent aspirations of colonial policy are frustrated.

CHAPTER VIII

COLONIAL POLICY

1. THE STUDY OF COLONIAL RELATIONS

FROM this brief outline of the course of events in Burma and Netherlands India some facts stand out clearly. Under native rule they both presented typical and not unfavourable examples of tropical society, held together by religion and personal authority in a complex of customary social obligations. Both achieved an elaborate civilization, with many valuable and pleasant features, but their political organization was unstable, and, when challenged by the superior moral and material forces of the modern West, neither was able to preserve its independence. The British in Burma and the Dutch in Java represented the western principle of social order, resting on reason, impersonal law and individual rights, which Europe inherits from Greece, Rome and Palestine. From the beginning of the nineteenth century their policy has been directed towards furthering economic progress and promoting native welfare, but they have employed different methods. The British in Burma adopted the system of direct rule, and the Dutch in Java the system of indirect rule.

In colonial literature the distinction between direct and indirect rule is familiar, and the choice between these systems is sometimes regarded as determined by the national philosophy of rule accepted in the colonial power; it is suggested that indirect rule will be preferred where the goal of policy is to allow the native to attain independence along his own lines, and direct rule where the objective is to find a place for the native in a society of which the principal institutions are European in character. It is true that, so far as colonial administration is directed towards inducing native opinion to accept innovations which it does not actively demand, indirect rule will be favoured by those who prefer genuine acceptance and slow development, and direct rule by those who prefer mere compliance and rapid development. But the theory that the preference for direct or indirect rule depends on colonial policy in respect of native evolution does not cover all the facts. It cannot, for instance, easily be reconciled with the adoption of direct rule in India and the Philippines. Moreover, there is no sharp line between direct and indirect rule, and we find the same power adopting different systems in the same place at different times, and in different places at the same time. But the chief defect of the theory is that it does not sufficiently recognize the connection between colonial policy and economic circumstances. Colonial policy is only one aspect of national policy, and national policy is not directed solely by economic considerations. Similarly a man's business is only one aspect of his life, and his life is larger than his business; yet his business will suffer if he does not run it on business lines. Colonial relations are primarily economic and, although pronouncements on colonial policy will be framed in terms congenial to national traditions, colonial practice is conditioned by the economic environment, and it is this, rather than any national philosophy of empire, which determines the choice between direct and indirect rule.[1]

When Europeans started trading in the tropics they had to gain the favour of the local rulers. In order to acquire influence at court the usual plan has been to support the weaker among rival claimants to the throne. If the object of policy be merely to prevent border troubles, he may be allowed a nominal independence, but ordinarily such a subordinate alliance leads gradually and naturally to indirect rule. Indirect rule through a local chieftain is the simplest and cheapest way by which a western power can obtain economic control. So long as its main economic objective is to obtain tropical produce at low rates, the local ruler can do most to help it. Similarly, with development by western enterprise, though large-scale transactions must be regulated on western lines, land and labour can be provided most readily and cheaply by the local ruler, governing his people on traditional lines, and there tends to evolve a dual system of administration, half western, half tropical, with the natives governed on the principle of indirect rule. But where the dependency is chiefly valued as a market for the sale of western goods to natives, and is opened up through native enterprise, with natives growing crops for sale, even native transactions must be regulated in the ordinary way of business according to western law and procedure, and a system of direct rule is indicated. Where, however, any considerable area of the dependency is taken up for European settlement, direct rule must be applied within that area, and may also be extended to the natives.

Few regions are developed solely as markets or solely as sources of tropical produce. A dependency which is originally opened up as

---

[1] Hailey, *African Survey*, pp. 130ff., 528ff.

a market may acquire importance as a scene of western enterprise, as has happened recently in Burma with the development of oil, tin and other minerals, and rubber. Similarly a dependency, originally valued as a source of tropical produce, will almost certainly, like Java, become important as a market. The economic character of a dependency gradually changes, and so also, and more or less contemporaneously, does the system of rule. Indirect rule is slowly adapted to western requirements, and the western element in the administration becomes more pronounced; or else direct rule on western lines comes to include a popular element. In either case the distinction between direct and indirect rule tends to lose its sharpness.

It is not suggested that the choice between direct and indirect rule is governed solely by economic conditions. Where there is a strong local chieftain, direct rule may be impossible. Where, on the contrary, there is no outstanding local chieftain with authority over a wide area and able to comply with the requirements of the colonial power, direct rule may be unavoidable and is likely to encounter less opposition. In such cases the traditions of rule in the colonial power will carry weight. At the beginning of the present century the Dutch in Java had a long tradition of succcessful indirect rule. On extending active administration to the Outer Provinces they found some tracts where a multiplicity of petty chieftains was an obstacle to indirect rule, but they tried so far as possible to follow their traditional system by creating artificial units. On the other hand, the British had a long tradition of direct rule in India, and there was a tendency at first to adopt this system also in Africa.[1] But in some parts of Africa conditions necessitated indirect rule, and the success of this system encouraged its adoption even where it might at first appear less suitable. (As explained below, in British administration indirect rule is strongly coloured by the older tradition of direct rule.) Apart from such exceptions, economic considerations prevail and, unless the conditions require or justify the more costly and troublesome system of direct rule, one finds indirect rule, with a dual system where western interests require the application of direct rule to certain regions or races.

The connection between economic circumstances and principles of rule gives a special interest to the comparison between Burma and Java. British rule was extended to Burma when the Industrial Revolution was first impelling British manufacturers to seek new markets

[1] *African Survey*, pp. 133, 536.

in the tropics, and just when Indian administration had been re-organized on a system of direct rule. Naturally this system was extended to the parts of Burma then acquired. At that time, and until the end of the century, western enterprise took no part in exploiting the natural resources of Burma, except, on a comparatively small scale, its teak; Burma was developed as a market, and its pro-gress depended solely on the response of Burman enterprise to the stimulus of economic freedom. This method of development necessitated the introduction of direct rule on western lines, as in India. But the conditions were different in Burma and India. India was protected against the disruptive forces of economic freedom by the institution of caste, and it had long been under, or in touch with, British rule; modern India grew up with modern Europe. Burmans were quite different from Indians in their ideas and ways of life; caste was unknown and their social and economic organization exposed them in an exceptional degree to the impact of economic forces.[1] They knew nothing of the modern world. Yet they were governed from India; no one in India knew anything of Burma, and the local governors were mostly transient officials from India with neither the opportunity, the knowledge or the stimulus to adapt Indian administration and the rule of western law to the requirements of the people. Thus Burma represents in its purest form the process of economic development by native enterprise under a system of direct rule. In Java, on the contrary, the Dutch had nothing to sell, and they valued Java only as a source of tropical produce to be ob-tained as cheaply as possible. This required indirect rule through native chieftains who could furnish the necessary produce and labour. Java accordingly came to represent the purest type of indirect rule. Up to the end of the nineteenth century native enterprise for export was negligible; but western enterprise developed and with it the need, within the western sphere of the social economy, for direct rule on western lines. This led to a dual system of administration, with the natives under indirect rule, and the Europeans under direct rule. Burma and Java, then, are typical examples respectively of direct and indirect rule.

In both countries the policy of Government has had a two-fold objective: economic progress and native welfare. In both countries economic development has made remarkable, astounding, progress; in both there has evolved a social structure comprising distinct racial

[1] Census, 1911, p. 304.

sections with an elaborate western superstructure over native life; in both native welfare has lagged behind economic progress, and, in both, during the present century, a growing impatience of western rule has found expression in a nationalist movement. These features are characteristic of tropical dependencies in general. Since Burma and Java furnish extreme types of direct and indirect rule, and of development by native and by western enterprise, the comparison between them would seem to furnish a useful starting point for a more general enquiry into colonial policy and practice. Such an enquiry is indeed necessary if we are to understand the problems of either Burma or Java or of any tropical dependency, for it is only against a background of general principles that the phenomena of western rule in any region of the tropics assume their due proportions, and that we can reasonably anticipate finding a satisfactory solution for the many weighty problems of colonial policy and practice. The enquiry may well seem, and is indeed, beyond the competence of any single student, whose intimate acquaintance with practical administration must of necessity be limited. But one conclusion to which the following enquiry points is the need for better knowledge of the facts and better understanding of their implications, and to the urgency of international co-operation in the comparative study of colonial affairs.

2. SURVEY OF COLONIAL POLICY

Of late years there has been a growing interest in colonial policy and colonial relations. To this many factors have contributed. Prominent among them are unrest in the tropics, consequent on the rise of modern nationalism, and the jealousy of non-colonial powers. Thus colonial policy has a double aspect, domestic and international. These are interrelated, for, while the advantages accruing to colonial powers from their dependencies arouse envy, and stimulate other powers to assert their claims by force of arms, tropical unrest serves as a pretext and a tool for intervention. The international aspect of colonial relations will require attention in due place, but it is convenient first to discuss the relations between colonial powers and their dependencies.

Discussions of this matter often contrast the high aspirations of modern colonial policy with the selfish exploitation of the past. Thus, according to Lord Hailey, 'the imperialist sentiment which animated much of our public policy in the latter part of the last century led us along paths some of which we should not be inclined to follow to-day'.[1] And a well-known Dutch colonial statesman says, 'He who would maintain that in the best colonial empires this predatory but profitable policy belongs to history will have to admit that it is in several respects not too remote history.'[2] This view hardly does justice to our fathers and grandfathers, who indeed themselves put forward similar pretensions. Dutch writers admit as not without validity the charges levelled against western enterprise in Java at the onset of the great depression of the thirties. But that was the generation of the Ethical leaders who aspired to build a brave new world in 1900. They in turn succeeded the Liberals who had thought to introduce a golden age in 1870 on the principle of freedom. The Liberals condemned, as rooted in unrighteousness, the system by which Van den Bosch had expected to restore prosperity to a country ruined by the reforms that Raffles, a generation earlier, had claimed would bestow liberty and welfare on millions of his fellow human beings. We may, and should be, wiser than our fathers, and should have learned from their mistakes; but it would be wise to bear in mind the parable of the Pharisee and the Publican. Although chartered companies may have disregarded the moral obligations of sovereignty, European powers which have accepted responsibility for dominion in the tropics have always claimed a moral basis for their activities.

Spain and Portugal. The earliest system of colonial rule may indeed be distinguished as the religious system. It has been well said that the colonial adventure of the Portuguese was also the last of the crusades. When Alexander VI in 1493 adjudicated on the rival claims of Spain and Portugal to undiscovered heathen continents and islands, he made it a condition that they should exert all diligence to convert their subjects to Christianity and 'instruct them in the Catholic Faith and good manners'.[3] They both took this injunction seriously. Paraguay under the Jesuits has often been cited as a model of colonial rule; in Manila the Spaniards founded the oldest western university in Asia, and by the end of the nineteenth century western culture was more widely spread in the Philippines than in any part of Asia. In the Moluccas the Portuguese established a Christian seminary within a few years of their arrival, and their claim that, if they did not aim solely at conversion, neither did they aim solely at commerce, is justified by the fact that, long after they have lost their colonies, many of their former subjects still retain their Christian faith.

[1] *Britain and Her Dependencies*, p. 46. [2] Hart, *Asiatic Review*, 1941, p. 629.
[3] Danvers, F. C., *The Portuguese in India* (1894), II, 483.

Chartered Companies. The chartered companies, which mark the next stage of western tropical enterprise, were professedly mercantile associations, and, so long as they prospered, were practically independent of the state. Their object was to pay good dividends to their shareholders, and they subordinated political considerations to economic ends. Yet the Dutch in early days were zealous for the conversion of their subjects, and it was only later, when religious enthusiasm had declined, that they came to disregard everything but profit. Even so, during the eighteenth century, there were aspirations after a more generous conception of colonial rule, and the high official who bequeathed his estate as a permanent heritage for his Christian slaves was not alone in caring for the welfare of the people.[1] Still one must accept the verdict on the Dutch East India Company that 'its polestar was profit and the lodestone greed'; and in the eighteenth century this was notoriously true also of the English Company. It is not without significance that in both cases this concentration on economic ends led to bankruptcy, and at about the same time; the English Company was brought under State control, and the Dutch Company was taken over by the State.

Liberalism. In both countries the assumption of effective state control over tropical administration synchronized with the dawn of modern Liberalism. We have already remarked that Liberalism had a double aspect, material and moral, economic and social. Liberals believed in economic freedom—freedom of person, property and trade—and trusted to economic freedom as a guarantee of progress. When the English Government assumed control over India by Pitt's Act of 1784, the Industrial Revolution was already presaging a revolution in colonial relations. Manchester cotton goods were beginning to compete successfully with Indian calicoes and muslins in England; the first consignment reached India in 1786, and from 1814 onwards they rapidly displaced native products. During the same period the ideas that subsequently came to be termed Liberal were making headway, and the East India Company, after a vain effort to retain its monopoly, adopted them. The doctrine of economic freedom implied the introduction of a money economy, and the encouragement of native enterprise which would enable the people to buy imported goods. In assuming that, equally with western peoples, the oriental was alive to the desire of improving his condition, and in introducing the principle of equality before the

[1] Vlekke, p. 187.

law, Liberalism, even in its economic aspect, was strongly coloured by humanitarian ideals.

These ideals were carried further in its social doctrine that all men were equal and had a natural right to freedom of speech and religion. Liberals believed that men had a right to political freedom, to live their own life in their own way under their own national institutions. They hoped to see India free, and tied to England only by ties of interest and affection. If the maintenance of law and order were the sole functions of the state, it seemed that the replacement of British magistrates by Indians should make India capable of self-government. Moreover, with the introduction of direct rule on western principles, economy demanded the employment of natives as officials. This made rapid progress and was adopted as a principle in 1833 when, on the renewal of the Company's charter, it was laid down that 'no native of the said Indian territories shall, by reason only of his place of birth, descent, colour or any of them be disabled from holding any place, office or employment under the Company'. By the end of the century the subordinate establishment was almost wholly Indian, and many Indians held high judicial and executive appointments. The Liberal faith included also a belief in the virtue of self-governing institutions on the English model. The largely European Presidency towns already enjoyed self-government; from 1842 attempts were made to apply the principle of local self-government in the interior, and it was widely extended from 1881-2. Meanwhile Indians had already been admitted to the Central Legislature from 1861 and at the same time Provincial Legislative Councils were established. This project of self-government reached its logical conclusion in 1917, when the Secretary of State for India announced responsible government as the goal of British policy.

While Liberals believed in economic freedom as good business, and in political freedom as a natural right, they looked on education as the main instrument of freedom. They held that the wide diffusion of western education would inspire the masses with the desire of improving their condition, dispel superstition, substitute Christianity for idolatry, and promote affection towards British rule. So early as 1793 Wilberforce tried to interest Parliament in the education of Indians. In 1815 the Governor-General declared his anxiety to see some system of public instruction established.[1] In 1854 the East India Company, in a despatch which laid the foundations of the

[1] *IG*, IV, 409, 413, 417.

modern system of public instruction, proclaimed the advancement of the people through primary education as its main objective, and in all subsequent pronouncements on the subject this leading principle has been reaffirmed. Thus for about a hundred years from 1813 the lofty sentiments of Liberalism inspired British rule in India.

Meanwhile Britain had been carving out a vast new colonial empire in Africa under conditions very different from those of India. Instead of a populous country with an ancient agricultural civilization, there were empty lands and backward peoples. But the empty lands contained resources needed on a large scale for industry in Europe, and capital was available in Europe for the development of these resources by western enterprise. The Ashanti War of 1874 marked the beginning of British penetration into the interior of Africa. It was closely followed by the flotation of numerous large companies to develop the new territories under a charter from the State, as this 'offered a means of asserting British sovereignty without the expense and responsibility that sovereignty usually entails'.[1] The companies appealed to Parliament and the public for support not merely as commercial projects, but as instruments for spreading light in 'the dark continent' and as a response to Livingstone's appeal for commerce and Christianity. But they lacked the resources of a sovereign power and, in the interest of the shareholders, had to keep down the cost of administration. 'Every Government in Africa has been faced with the initial difficulty of administering an extensive area with a small European staff, frequently ignorant of local native custom and language; in every case it has found itself obliged, in the early days of its rule, to make use of chiefs or other native authorities, and the extent to which it has done so has depended on circumstances rather than on any difference of principle.'[2] It was the economic environment and not national political philosophy that dictated the adoption of the system of indirect rule.

In Nigeria, however, Sir George Goldie found a virtue in necessity.

'Even an imperfect and tyrannical native African administration, if its extreme excesses were controlled by European supervision, would be, in the early stages, productive of far less discomfort to its subjects than well-intentioned but ill-directed efforts of European magistrates, often young and headstrong, and not invariably gifted with sympathy and introspective powers. If the welfare of the native is to be considered, if dangerous revolts

[1] Burns, p. 163.
[2] *African Survey*, p. 527.

are to be obviated, the general principles of ruling on African principles through native rulers must be followed for the present.'[1]

As a corollary it followed that, alongside the native administration, there should be 'colonial' courts to deal according to western law and procedure with 'cases involving non-natives, to exercise jurisdiction over natives in areas where native courts do not exist, and, where native courts exist, to deal with cases involving natives which are held to be unsuitable for these courts'.[2] As in Netherlands India there arose a system of indirect rule and dual administration. But the system is notably different in Dutch and British practice. In Britain there is a stronger tradition of the rule of law than on the continent of Europe, and British colonial administration owes much to pre-conceptions based on direct rule in India. Thus British colonial administration on the system of indirect rule emphasizes the judicial aspect of native authority, encourages greater formality in native courts, and insists on close supervision over native judicial procedure by British officials. On the Dutch system even the European officials are policemen, agents of policy; on the British system even native officials tend to become magistrates and judges, servants of the law.

The adoption of indirect rule in Africa did not, however, involve a departure from the principle of *laissez-faire*; rather it carried this principle still further by abstaining from intervention in native ways of life. But whether under direct or indirect rule, the lofty aspirations of Liberals were disappointing in practice, and, beyond narrow limits, conduced neither to economic progress nor to native welfare. For a time the prospect of easy money that had attracted capital in the first instance was realized, but 'the earliest attempts to develop trade sometimes involved the destructive spoliation of the resources of the colony. Rubber or forest timber was exhausted without proper replacement; accumulations of ivory were for a period obtained by exchange for cheap imports. Such a policy of exploitation could not continue indefinitely. Once the realities of the situation were understood, capital was less easily attracted.'[3] Moreover, the concentration of political and economic power in the same hands had shown 'the difficulties of reconciling the responsibilities of the administration with the interests of shareholders, and of demarcating justifiable administrative compulsion from forced labour for the purpose of profit making'.[4] Thus, during the last quarter of the nineteenth

---

[1] *African Survey*, p. 417.   [2] *Ib.* pp. 286ff.
[3] *Ib.* p. 1314.   [4] *Ib.* p. 1314.

century, initial progress was followed by stagnation, and the aspirations of improving native welfare proved illusive. In India likewise under direct rule, Liberal hopes and forecasts proved illusive. The cultivators, burdened with debt, were losing their land to moneylenders, and public instruction, so far from dispelling the superstition of the masses, did not even reach them, while among the middle classes, who went to school to earn a living, the spread of education, instead of fostering goodwill to Britain and diffusing Christianity, bred growing disaffection and a reaction to an aggressive Hinduism. After the roseate dawn of early Liberalism the sky turned dark and stormy, and the century closed in 'gloom and depression'.[1] Liberals, regarding economic freedom as the key to progress and welfare, released economic forces which for a time furthered economic progress, but, at the same time, preyed on social welfare, setting bounds to progress, leading to stagnation and foreshadowing decline.

Under Dutch rule Liberal principles were differently applied, and colonial practice evolved in a contrary direction, but with similar results. On the restoration of the Dutch possessions in 1816–18, the leading statesmen from the King downwards admired all that was 'brave and liberal' and professed warm sympathy for 'the little man'. The King drafted a constitution along these lines for the Indies, and the commissioners sent to introduce it 'decided at once that the time had come when the Indies should be governed for the sake of its own people and not for that of the Netherlands'.[2] They found that Raffles had introduced, at least on paper, a system of direct rule, applying Liberal individual principles, far more thoroughly than any Dutch statesman had ever contemplated. Brief experience showed that 'measures that if seen at three thousand miles apparently are liberal, here prove to be highly illiberal in their effects' and implied 'the protection of European landowners at the expense of the native population'. Affairs drifted in confusion until the arrival of Van den Bosch in 1830. He also claimed Liberal views, but denounced the 'perverted Liberalism' of Raffles as unsuited to the Javanese, and propounded 'a Liberal policy adapted to their character and institutions'. He reverted to the Dutch system of indirect rule through native chieftains, which the commissioners, though recognizing in policy, had departed from in practice. While repudiating the Liberal principle of individual freedom under western law, he appealed, more

[1] *IG*, II, 526.
[2] Vlekke, pp. 254, 256.

logically, to the principle of *laissez-faire* as justifying non-interference with native institutions. It is, however, no fortuitous coincidence that indirect rule in Java was profitable to the Dutch and direct rule in India profitable to the British.

The Culture system introduced by Van den Bosch gave a temporary stimulus to economic progress, but in the long run proved detrimental to native welfare and led to economic stagnation. Also it was unprofitable to a later generation of more orthodox Liberals, who came into power in the Netherlands in 1848 and during the next twenty years gradually obtained control over colonial policy. They substituted private enterprise for state enterprise, and thereby gave a new impulse to economic progress. Like Liberals in Britain they believed in education 'to spread light in India'. But under indirect rule there was little demand for natives educated on western lines, and, with little to gain from schooling, there was little demand among the natives for schools. Western education made slow progress in Java as compared with India. On the other hand, western enterprise in Java required a large and healthy population and, in respect of medical assistance and a care for hygiene in rural areas, Java was ahead of India. The system of rule through native chieftains, introduced by Van den Bosch, made inadequate provision for the Europeans who crowded in when Java was thrown open to western private enterprise, and the dual character of the administration, with different laws for Europeans and natives, became more prominent. Liberals of all hues wanted an administration along western lines for the European community, and urged the need for decentralization—the delegation of power from the home to the colonial Government, from the colonial Government to departments and local officials, and from the bureaucracy to local bodies. From 1848 onwards various aspects of decentralization were discussed, and every year, with the growth of western enterprise, it became more urgent. Finally, in 1903, western political institutions were introduced in local government, and in 1918 the creation of the Volksraad as an advisory body marked a long stride towards the adoption of Liberal principles in the central government. Thus, whereas in British dependencies the system of administration developed during the nineteenth century from direct towards indirect rule, in Netherlands India the tendency was in the contrary direction.

The Liberalism of Van den Bosch was profitable to the Dutch of 1830 and the later individualist Liberalism profited the Dutch of 1870, but in neither case need one question that the appeal to humanitarian ideals was genuine. The Liberals, like those in England, looked forward, in two senses, to a golden age. But in Java, as in India, the century ended in stagnation and depression, with chambers of commerce in the Netherlands demanding an enquiry into the 'decline of welfare'. Under Dutch rule, as under British rule, the Liberal policy of *laissez-faire* gave place to a constructive policy of efficiency and social justice.

Construction. In 1900 the British Government was less reluctant than in 1870 to accept imperial responsibilities, and Joseph Chamberlain, as an apostle of efficiency and social justice, was trying to put the British Empire on a business footing, with Kipling as the popular exponent of the 'White Man's Burden'. This 'involved a new philosophy of [colonial] politics and an ethical standard, serious and not ignoble'.[1] The failure, economic and political, of the chartered companies in Africa, implied that the State, on taking over charge of the colonies, should intervene actively to promote economic development and to enhance native welfare. This new constructive policy with its double aspect came to be known as 'the dual mandate'. In India, under direct rule, the administration, chiefly at the instance of Lord Curzon, proliferated new economic and welfare services, while in Africa and elsewhere the conception of indirect rule acquired a new character. Formerly indirect rule had been justified as a means of protecting the natives from the impact of the west, now it was conceived as a means 'to graft our higher civilization upon the soundly rooted native stock...moulding it and establishing it into lines consonant with modern ideas and higher standards'.[2] It was no longer a negative system of *laissez-faire*, but an active policy of economic and social construction. Liberals looked to freedom as a key to economic progress, and regarded economic progress as a *cause* of native welfare, leading *automatically* to political independence. Modern colonial theory regards economic progress as a *condition* of native welfare, and native welfare as a *condition* of political advancement, but recognizes the need for state intervention to further economic progress. Liberals thought to promote welfare through freedom; the modern tendency is to promote welfare, even at the expense of freedom.

Simultaneously, with this new trend in British colonial policy, Dutch colonial policy turned from Liberalism to a new constructive

---

[1] Buchan, J., *Memory-Hold-the-Door* (1943), p. 125.
[2] *African Survey*, p. 432.

policy avowedly based on 'ethical' principles. This found its
first practical expression in the Village Act of 1906, intended to
strengthen corporate village life and thereby 'stimulate the process of
social growth and enable local officials to cope with their prime function, the care of public welfare'. Thus both Dutch and English may
fairly claim that, from the beginning of the nineteenth century, their
colonial policy has always been inspired by high ideals, and has kept
in sight the dual aim of increasing the contribution of the tropics to
the welfare of the world, while promoting the welfare of the people.
Yet even the 'ethical' system and the theory of the 'White Man's
Burden' are now disavowed, as illustrating the predatory past when
we followed paths that we should now be reluctant to pursue. How
far this criticism may be justified we shall have to examine more
closely when dealing with modern colonial policy and practice. All
we are now trying to show is that the inspiration of colonial policy
by humanitarian ideals is no modern invention, but as old as western
rule.

'But policy is a matter not only of purpose but performance, and
it must be judged by its operation in practice.' In politics, as in law,
men must be held to intend the natural consequences of their acts,
and the natural consequences of colonial practice have differed widely
from the humanitarian aims set forth in colonial policy. This has often
been attributed to hypocrisy. On the suppression of the slave trade
in 1807, humanitarians advocated the encouragement of commerce
as a means of creating an interest which would have a strong motive
for co-operating with the abolition of slavery. 'Thus at an early date
that intimate connection between idealism and commerce was
established which has exposed African administration to the easy
cynicism of those who see in every declaration of interest in the
African's welfare the veiled intention to secure benefits for the mother
country.' In French colonial policy there is often a note of warm
cordiality, 'qui *parfois* part vraiment du cœur'.[1] Raffles had a sincere
liking for Malays, and claimed 'the happiness to release several
millions of his fellow creatures from a state of bondage and oppression' under the Dutch; but Van den Bosch regarded him as
solely concerned to build up British trade. Van den Bosch was unquestionably a philanthropist who, long before he ruled Java, had
shown practical sympathy with the Socialist experiments of Robert
Owen, yet, according to his Liberal successors, he 'wrapped a gilt

[1] *African Survey*, p. 133; Bousquet, p. 156 (italics *sic*).

coating of philanthropic theory round a bitter pill of practice'. The Liberal leader, Van de Putte, was genuinely convinced that economic individualism would create welfare in Java, but Ethical critics remarked that Liberals 'balanced their love for the natives against regard for their own pockets'. The Ethical reformers in their turn were charged by a later generation with 'hoisting the Cross in place of the Jolly Roger, but without changing the sailing orders'.

Yet charges of conscious hypocrisy cannot be sustained. In almost every generation there have been reformers sincerely zealous for native welfare but, while picturing a golden future in the warm glow of their imagination, they have judged their predecessors in the cold light of actual achievement. In colonial relations a wide gap between policy and practice seems perennial, as if there were some factor in the nature of such relations by which the lofty aims of policy are continually frustrated in their practical application. Let us try to elucidate the cause of this divergence by studying the evolution of tropical economy under the rule of *laissez-faire*, when economic forces were left uncontrolled.

3. TROPICAL ECONOMY

In the study of tropical economy it seems necessary, even at the risk of emphasizing platitudes, to go back to elementary principles of economic activity. The endeavours of all colonial powers to enhance progress and welfare in their tropical dependencies are of necessity conditioned by certain economic laws. One fundamental principle is the economic process of natural selection by the survival of the cheapest, known technically as the Law of Substitution. This does not imply deliberate substitution, but is a natural law operating independently of human volition; it is the economic aspect of the evolutionary principle of natural selection by the survival of the fittest. In times of famine, the man or beast that needs less for subsistence is, other things being equal, most likely to survive. Stronger men may take the food out of his mouth, but the ability to sustain life on a minimum of nourishment has in itself survival value. In Burma some poor flooded areas gave a yield below the margin of subsistence for Burmans, and they are cultivated by Indians who can make a living on them. This process of natural selection is reinforced by reason. Everyone would pay twopence rather than threepence for the same thing; that is rational, a matter of universal common sense. There is an economic process, active everywhere and always, tending in all economic operations to increase the margin between yield and cost. This may conduce to economic progress by favouring more efficient methods of production, but at the same time, unless kept under control, it reduces costs by eliminating all human qualities that are not directly required to maintain life on the lowest level of subsistence, the bare need for daily bread.

A second principle of economic progress is the desire of gain, the economic motive of profit. That also is natural; but only in the sense that it is human nature, *phronema sarkos* 'the fault and corruption of the Nature of every man'. Everyone ordinarily wants threepence rather than twopence for the same thing. That is a principle which all accept as rational, irrespective of their race and creed. It is a condition of economic progress, because it checks the tendency towards the degradation of human life inherent in the principle of the survival of the cheapest. It was indeed a postulate of *laissez-faire* economists that, since everyone aims to get as much as possible while giving as little as possible, free competition will conduce to the greatest benefit of the greatest number. But the easiest way to make large gains is to limit competition, and this ends in economic stagnation through monopoly. Moreover, the desire for gain tends to subordinate all social relations to individual economic interest, and, unless kept under control, leads no less certainly than the process of survival of the cheapest, to general impoverishment.

For man does not live by bread alone, and the life of man solitary is brutish, short and poor. The two basic principles of economic progress are supplemented by a third: that progress is conditional on the observance of certain social obligations. These obligations are not natural, and cannot be justified by universal common sense. They can indeed be justified rationally, but only to members of the same society, or to those who accept in common similar moral standards. Where slavery is reprobated, people may be willing to pay threepence for a thing produced by free labour rather than twopence for the same thing produced by slaves. Or they may consent to pay more for home products than for foreign products, and will forgo the attraction of 'a free breakfast table' with a view to strengthening imperial relations. The Englishman regards it as common sense to breed cattle for the stockyard, but the Burman, at least until recently, would lose money rather than sell his beast for slaughter. The Burman will have no compunction in selling the flesh of cattle that have died of foot-and-mouth disease, but the Englishman voluntarily complies with legislation that forbids it. Men with common standards of social welfare can agree on reasons for reacting against the survival of the cheapest and for disregarding profit, but these reasons, based on moral grounds, differ according to race and creed from one people to another. Among all peoples and in every generation the observance of customary standards is a part of the social heritage and, unless a society accepts certain social standards as of superior validity to individual economic interest, it must collapse.

Thus one may distinguish three principles of economic progress: natural, rational and moral; but the two former, which are strictly economic forces, are anti-social. So far as these economic forces were active in primitive society, it was a condition of survival that they should be held in check by social custom, and it was only through the evolution of social custom that primitive societies were protected against disintegration. But custom implies that man adapts his wants and activities to his environment. In accepting the rule of custom, man surrenders his unique prerogative, the ability to use reason in adapting his environment to his requirements. This ability of man to master his environment is the key to human progress as distinct from social evolution; and in the tropics, although the rule of custom protected the social order, it was at the cost of progress. Western Christendom, however, with the rebirth of reason at the Renaissance, achieved a new synthesis of Greek intellectual freedom and Roman law under the energizing and binding force of Christian ideals of duty to God and man. This laid the foundations of a social order based on law, informed by will, that could allow far greater scope to economic forces without incurring the penalty of collapse; it raised economic potential to a higher level. Their goodly heritage emboldened Europeans to seek their fortunes in the tropics, and enabled them to impose western rule on the inhabitants. The resulting impact of western civilization on the tropics liberated economic forces from the control of custom, feebly at first by gradual permeation from outside, and then, so far as the people were brought under direct rule and western law, actively and from within tropical society itself.

Now it is a matter of general experience that western rule in the tropics, after the initial troubles of pacification, is in its earlier stages not unwelcome. It is true that sometimes western rule has merely substituted new tyrants for old, but in general the West comes to the tropics as a liberator; it liberates the people both from the oppression of arbitrary personal authority, and from the burden of social abuses that the people have tolerated in the name of custom. Soon, however, there succeeds a second stage. So far as the people are released from customary inhibitions, economic forces are subject to no restraint but that of western law. In the West the law is an expression of social will, proceeding from the society itself and reinforcing custom, while adapting old customs to new circumstances. But in the tropics western law is imposed on society from outside, and, because it is not an expression of social will, it is powerless to restrain anti-social economic forces. These forces, liberated from the control of custom by the impact of the West, pursue their natural course, breaking down the social order, disintegrating native organic society into individual atoms, and, by thus depriving man of social protection against natural selfishness, operate more intensively, eliminating social values, and diffusing poverty. Let us then examine more closely the nature of their working; first, where the main object of colonial policy is development by native enterprise under direct rule, and then where it aims primarily at development by western enterprise under indirect rule.

Development by Native Enterprise. The development of native enterprise must be a chief object of policy in any dependency which is valued as a market for the products of the colonial power. If a subsistence economy prevails, it must be converted into a money economy by substituting money taxes for taxation in produce and labour. This compels the cultivator to sell his produce in order to pay his taxes, and he finds the best, and usually the only, market in crops suitable for export. The sale of his produce enables him to buy imported goods, and stimulates the desire for individual gain. Once this has been liberated from the control of custom, he needs little further inducement to concentrate on export crops, and wants more money so as to clear or buy land and hire labour; 'where crops are marketable, the ambition of owners is to plough as much land as possible'.[1] Exporters can best make certain of supplies by encouraging cultivators to borrow on the security of their crops; importers of western goods can sell more if the cultivators enjoy easy credit; and the more that cultivators borrow the greater is the profit of western banks which supply the fluid capital essential to the working of modern economic machinery. Thus exporters, importers and bankers all gain by the entanglement of the cultivator in debt, and, however much they may deplore the consequences, they must as men of business work on

[1] *African Survey*, p. 885.

business lines. Men lose their land for debt and work as tenants, and the tenant who can live most cheaply can pay the highest rent, so that a larger portion of the surplus is available for the purchase of foreign goods. Caste in India has been of no avail to protect the cultivator against this process. Irrigation works, undertaken in the name of welfare, serve merely to expedite insolvency. In the Canal colonies of the Punjab, we are told, there is 'a high standard of rural prosperity', but this has tended to 'increase the mass of debt...moreover the debt is largely unproductive; little of it is incurred for land improvement. The moneylender is not in the least concerned with the purpose of a loan; his policy is to entangle the debtor to an extent that will leave him with just enough of the produce of his labour for the bare subsistence of himself and his family.'[1] But it is nonsense to blame the moneylender. A moneylender who did not work on business lines would soon be in the miserable position of the cultivator. The whole process illustrates the unrestricted working of economic forces, largely impersonal; and exporters, importers and bankers alike are all involved in it. In Lower Burma, as we have seen, the whole agricultural system has been 'industrialized', so as to produce the maximum net yield from land supporting only the minimum population requisite to produce that yield. But Lower Burma is exceptional only as an extreme instance of agricultural development under free competition in a tropical region, newly opened up among a people where custom does not exert the binding force of caste. Agricultural debt and the alienation of land are common to tropical dependencies in general. Even in some of the newer dependencies in Africa, debt has already assumed formidable proportions,[2] and, as conditions there have some resemblance to those of Lower Burma, one may expect future development to follow a like course. Ordinarily, economic development links up the cultivator with exporter, importer and banker through middlemen who absorb a portion of the profits, and the next stage in its working, after the cultivator has been reduced to penury, is the elimination of the middleman. This usually involves some measure of Government control over development, and appears as one of the early stages in the transition from a policy of *laissez-faire* to one of construction.

Economic forces react on individual welfare in yet another way. By stimulating the concentration of production on a few export crops, they enable the people to buy more imported goods. These compete

---

[1] *ISC*, I, 275.   [2] *Britain and Her Dependencies*, p. 25.

more or less directly with local manufactures, and create unemployment among artisans and craftsmen. Some of these find employment in agriculture, and the enlarged supply of labour tends to reduce agricultural wages and to lower the cost of trade crops to the exporter, but to the prejudice of the agricultural labourer. For various reasons many will be unable to turn to agriculture and will be left without employment. Where, as in Lower Burma, agriculture develops along industrial lines, there grows up a mass of part-time labour, unable to find employment for about half of the year and with no other source of livelihood but crime. Thus the free action of economic forces tends to create unemployment and under-employment.

One feature of the encouragement of native enterprise in cultivation for export is the introduction of the rule of law. The rule of law is a foundation stone of western freedom, and should provide a far more secure basis for society than the rule of personal authority. But this is true only where the law is an expression of social will; in a tropical dependency it expresses the will of the colonial power, and is an instrument of economic development. The rule of law becomes in effect the rule of economic law. The ideas embodied in the western law of property and contract are foreign to the tropics. Even attempts to apply local law, or to embody local custom in legal codes, must fail if made in western courts according to western procedure by lawyers who, as was said formerly in Java, 'look on native law as a doctor looks on native medicine'.[1] Unwritten custom changes its character when formalized in law and legal decisions, and we have noticed how 'Buddhist law' has been applied in Burma. In India, Elphinstone remarked that Hindu law was 'as a whole beyond the knowledge of perhaps the most learned pundit, and every part beyond the knowledge of the people who live under it....The uncertainty of decisions obtained from such sources must be obvious, especially when required for the guidance of a foreign judge both to the written law and to the usage which supplies its place.'[2] Indigenous law or custom administered in a foreign court is no less foreign than law proceeding directly from a foreign ruler. In either case one result is the encouragement of disputes and litigation, because people can appeal against the custom that all know to the law which no one knows. Law encroaches on custom, and the decay of custom encourages the resort to litigation. Moreover, as is notorious, for reasons already

[1] *Netherlands India*, p. 218.   [2] Cotton, p. 182.

indicated, education tends to flood the land with lawyers, who foster
litigation for their living. The growth of litigation in India has long
been deplored. In Burma there was little litigation until rapid economic development began in 1870, and so late as 1886 it could still
be said that Burmans were not litigious. That is no longer true. We
find the same plague of lawyers in Indo-China and the Philippines,
and in Africa litigation has been described as the curse of the country.
The law breeds litigation and this, married to poverty by agrarian
distress, breeds crime. Here again Burma is exceptional, but it
appears that of the four countries in the world with the highest pro-
portionate jail population, three are British dependencies.[1] All this
is nothing new. In Burma, as far back as 1883, dacoit bands flourished
just outside the capital. So they did in Java in 1830, when the introduction of western law by Raffles created a 'proletariat who go about
and steal'. Still earlier in Madras, on the introduction of the rule of
law from Bengal at the end of the eighteenth century, 'the same
results', says Munro, 'followed here which had occurred elsewhere;
justice ceased in great measure to be administered and the increase
of crime was appalling'.[2] These words might have been taken from
any report on the administration of Burma from the eighties onwards.

Under native rule disputes are usually settled by arbitration. Under
European rule it is at first only in cases with foreigners that natives
come to court. Naturally Europeans best understand their own laws,
and the middlemen and moneylenders learn it in the course of business,
but the cultivator neither understands the law nor how it works and,
as a rule, is least able to afford a skilful advocate. The decision usually
goes in favour of the longer purse. Men who lose their case against
a wealthier opponent and without understanding that a decision,
apparently arbitrary and in their view unjust, may none the less be
good law, naturally attribute the result to bribery, and this is the
readiest excuse given by their advocate for his failure. Nothing is so
favourable to judicial corruption as a belief that it is general. That is a
principle which works in Africa as in Asia.[3] It seems, indeed, to be
generally true in tropical dependencies that western law encourages
litigation, crime and corruption.

The substitution of the rule of law for the rule of custom naturally
expedites the disintegration of the customary social structure. But
it also reacts more directly on the social structure. The former native

---

[1] Barnes, L., *Skeleton of the Empire* (1937), p. 60.
[2] Gleig, pp. 221–2.   [3] *Colonial Review*, June 1944, p. 170.

authorities, who could maintain order in their own way, are unable to apply western principles of rule and must be replaced by Europeans, or by native officials trained on western lines. We have noticed this in Burma, and also as one outcome of the reforms introduced by Raffles in Java. It had already happened still earlier in India. Formerly, under native rule, there were 'large tracts of country, embracing, according to circumstances, ten, twenty, forty or a hundred villages. At the head of each of these was a Zemindar, Poligar, Tehsildar or Amildar who...was to his district in almost every respect what the potail (headman) was to his village.'[1] He was the natural, organic, representative and leader of his people. By the reforms of Cornwallis all power was withdrawn from these local chieftains and made over to the officials of the central government. Under direct rule the whole organic edifice of native polity collapses, and there remains no unit more comprehensive than the village. The introduction of the rule of law is necessary as an instrument in the liberation of economic forces, but it breaks up the country into villages. On this plan the people are easier to govern, as they have no bond of union, but the same process, as we shall notice later, makes them less capable of self-government. The point immediately relevant, however, is that it constitutes the first, or political, stage in the disintegration of society.

The dissolution of the political structure is only the first stage in social dissolution, and it is completed by the second, or economic, stage, breaking up the village into individuals. In this process two factors are operative: economic forces are released; and the checks controlling their action are relaxed. Where, under native rule, an agricultural economy obtains, and the village has replaced the tribe, the village still retains tribal features and resembles a large family in which, by gradual evolution through long ages, economic relations are adjusted by the growth of custom to the common social welfare. The village conducts its affairs in its own way, and the headman derives his authority from the people. But under the rule of law he becomes a servant of the law, an instrument of government, occupying the same position as before, but hanging from above instead of standing on his own feet. The village survives, but from an organic social unit it is transformed into an administrative unit. In Burma the richest man, as the largest taxpayer, was appointed village headman, but the so-called 'largest taxpayer' soon became 'the village drudge'.

[1] Gleig, p. 217.

Similarly in Africa, leadership passes from the hereditary authorities to men with more money or better education.[1] In such circumstances there remains no embodiment of social will or representative of public welfare to control the economic forces which the impact of the West releases.

So long as communal feeling survives, no one thinks of encroaching on land set apart for village amenities, and villagers cultivating for subsistence have little motive to extend their holdings; if, however, anyone should encroach on public land, he will be turned out by the headman with the support of public opinion. But men who cultivate for the market want more land in order to make more money; the headman and public opinion are no longer able to prevent them; the law, without the support of custom, is ineffective to prevent encroachments, and may even sanction or encourage them because they produce more crops for sale. If anyone encroaches it is easier and more profitable for others to follow his example, and before long the village common land is taken up for private cultivation. The village may produce more than before, but at the expense of social welfare. Not infrequently the total produce of the village is reduced. If a man encroaches on the catchment area left waste for the irrigation of crops depending on it, his gain is at the cost of those who lose their water. Or again, one or two members of a common irrigation system may take to cultivating some new crop that gives them larger profit but disturbs the equitable distribution of the water. In these, and many other ways, the economic motive, the desire of individual gain, reduces the total output of the village, and social will, public opinion embodied in the headman, is no longer able to control it in the public interest. The produce available for export rises, and this is taken as an index of prosperity, but social welfare deteriorates.

Even when there is no decline in material welfare, the village is deprived of these social amenities that money cannot buy. The village community is transformed into a crowd, and social recreations and pastimes disappear with social life. That is the natural sequence of the liberation of economic forces from the control of village custom. In the rice lands of Lower Burma, where the process has been carried to a logical conclusion, the village is no longer a family but a factory. In Indo-China we are told that nothing remains between the Government and twenty-three million individuals. In Africa 'atomization' is a well-known symptom of social disease. So far as economic forces

[1] Read, M., p. 21; Wilson, p. 7.

are allowed free play, the disintegration of society is an inevitable sequel. They work, subject to economic friction, towards giving the maximum net produce of commodities for the market, but most of the profit goes to those engaged in commerce and, even if a few cultivators make more money, they are poorer for the loss of things that are bought without money and without price.

It is not merely village life but the whole of native social life that is deprived of its amenities. In every society successive generations make their contributions to the art of living, and the most congenial survive to enrich the social heritage that builds up its distinctive civilization. The process of civilization may be regarded from the economic standpoint as the gradual evolution of the social demand for better living, and it is through the leaders of the people that this demand acts most effectively. Foreign rule inevitably undermines native social values, for common standards disappear and a foreign Governor can never wield the power behind a throne. In Burma, the King, merely as a Buddhist sovereign, was the Defender of the Faith and the lynchpin of the Buddhist hierarchy; he was the natural patron of religion, learning and the arts. The most learned monks, the most successful doctors, and the most skilful artists and craftsmen looked to the Crown for recognition. Now the monastic order has collapsed, the native practitioners of medicine have degenerated, and the artistic genius of the craftsmen is confused by the flood of cheap foreign manufactures.[1] In all such matters Europeans have their own standards, and so also have other immigrants such as foreign orientals, Indian or Chinese. Contact with the outer world should furnish new sources of inspiration and enrich native social life, art and religion. But the people are not brought into contact with the outer world except in the sphere of economics; they remain imprisoned in a dying civilization and their social life is impoverished and not enriched.

In another way also foreign rule is detrimental to native social life, for by the normal working of the process of the survival of the cheapest, economic forces act, directly, rapidly and effectively to eliminate all non-economic values. In Burma, for example, during the past half-century, the native cargo boat, modelled on the graceful lines of the medieval galleon, with decorative figurehead and an elaborately carved and ornamental castle in the stern, a joy to build, to sail and to behold, has disappeared. It has been

[1] See also *African Survey*, p. 1290.

replaced by squat hulks that have no advantage except as cheaper means of transport. Merely for carrying paddy the modern barges are the more commodious, but they add nothing to the beauty of the river scene or to the delight of the builders and the boatmen in their work, and on any reckoning that includes such items they are worse than useless. Everywhere throughout the tropics, apart from the buildings that advertise imperial power or mercantile prosperity, the process of natural selection by the survival of the cheapest operates to strip life of its amenities and reduce it to a struggle for bare subsistence.

Not only does this process impoverish the social life of the people, it imposes restrictions on their economic activities. For another aspect of the same process is the specialization of function by the division of labour. This was favoured by Adam Smith and his disciples as a corner-stone of the wealth of nations. Liberal economists in England could rightly insist on this principle because they could take the stability of social life for granted, but in a tropical dependency this basic assumption is invalid. The development of a tropical dependency as a market for imported goods leads to the elimination of local manufactures and a corresponding contraction in the range of economic activities and of social interest in the native community. We shall return to this point later; here it requires notice as illustrating how the horizon of the native world is narrowed not only by the elimination of non-economic values, but by restrictions on the content of their economic life.

Development by Western Enterprise. If we turn now to examine the alternative method of development through western enterprise, we find that along different lines it arrives at similar results. The great distinction between development by native and by western enterprise is that, as already noticed, with the former, economic forces dissolve native society by direct action from within, whereas with the latter, though gradually permeating native society, they attack it in the first instance from without.

The primary requirement of western enterprise in the tropics is cheap labour. This can be obtained most easily through native chieftains and accordingly, except where large tracts are set aside for European settlement, indirect rule tends to prevail. Netherlands India provides the classic illustration of tropical development by western enterprise. In Java at the beginning of the nineteenth century the people were unaccustomed to work for wages and, even if they could have been induced to do so, the Netherlands produced nothing that they would buy. 'All wise men' were agreed that the native would not respond to the desire of gain, and that he would work only under compulsion.[1] People were none the less sincere in this belief, because it suited them to believe it. Under the Culture system the Dutch used the authority of the native chieftains to obtain labour both for public works and for export crops for the Government. Subsequently under Liberal rule compulsory labour was still used for public works (despite the protests of Liberals who wanted more labour for private enterprise), and the planters employed the native chieftains as agents for recruiting labour. But paid labour was found more efficient than compulsory labour whether on public works or private enterprise, and the people became accustomed to working for wages. In Africa development by private capitalist enterprise has followed similar lines. 'The introduction of capitalist undertakings in Africa found a population that had little incentive to improve its subsistence by wage-earning, and, since it was inexperienced in the use of money it was slow to react to the stimulus of cash inducements.'[2] Moreover, there was 'a popular belief that the "collectivist" organization of African society implied the absence of those individual ambitions in the material sphere which are the mainspring of European development'. Custom supported the use of unpaid labour for the common purposes of the tribe, and this furnished a precedent for using compulsory labour on public works 'such as the construction of railways or major roads for long distance transport which were outside the range of even an extended definition of communal labour, more especially since they at times involved the absence of labour from their homes for considerable periods'. Here there is a significant contrast with Burma, where the object of policy was trade, and therefore of development by native enterprise; compulsory labour interfered with native enterprise and was soon abolished. But in Africa, although 'the wide use of impressed labour for railway construction...led to many incidents which reflected grave discredit on the administration',[3] it did not wholly cease until railway construction came to an end with the depression of the thirties. Again, in Africa as in Java, the people were accustomed under native rule to render tribute in kind or service to the local chieftains. This interferes with the supply of labour to private enterprise, and in Java measures to restrict it were among the

[1] *Netherlands India*, p. 59.
[2] *African Survey*, pp. 604, 694.　　　　　[3] *Ib.* pp. 613, 615.

earliest fruits of Liberal reforms. In Tanganyika such tribute was commuted for a tax in money in 1926.[1]

Employers, while sympathizing with humanitarian protests against compulsion to obtain labour for Government or native chieftains, are not averse from measures which provide labour for private enterprise. In Africa, as in Java, 'if there is now little use of direct pressure by government in order to secure labour for private employment, this was a marked feature of policy in the past....A complete history of this aspect of labour development would comprise the use of means so various as slavery, direct statutory compulsion, the curtailment of native lands, assistance given by administrative officials to the efforts of private recruiters, and the use of chiefs to recruit their people as labourers.' Now in Africa, as long ago in Java, it is 'generally recognized that, apart from any grounds of equity or humanity, labour done under compulsion is uneconomic';[2] yet the use of compulsory labour appears to save trouble and money, and employers are reluctant to abandon it. With compulsory labour wages tend towards the minimum of bare subsistence for a man without a family. The conditions are worst where no single employer stands to gain by healthy labour, and the death roll in the coolie barracks of Rangoon is typical of the impoverishment which naturally results from the exposure of unskilled labour to the unmitigated action of economic forces.

Even where action is taken to protect the individual labourer, the mass recruitment of unskilled labour, especially if recruited through local chieftains, naturally disintegrates native social life. 'The most characteristic results which have followed from the introduction of capitalist enterprise (are) the depopulation of certain areas or the deterioration of local subsistence conditions owing to the migration of labour, the social evils due to the removal from their families of large numbers of adult males, and the difficult situations created by the aggregation of industrial population divorced from the traditional controls of tribal life.'[3] At the same time the use of native chieftains to provide land for concessions and labour to work the concessions conflicts with native custom, and weakens the authority of the chieftains as it makes them look for support to Government instead of standing on their own feet. Then, in a later stage, when an ample supply of labour is assured and the awakening of the desire of gain

---

[1] *African Survey*, p. 437.
[2] *Ib.* pp. 628, 635, 636.   [3] *Ib.* p. 699.

allows the replacement of compulsion by wages, the effect on native society and welfare is much the same as when development proceeds by private enterprise.

General Course of Development. Thus, whether the method of development be through native enterprise working for the market, or through western enterprise employing native labour, 'the disintegration of social life is an almost inevitable result of the contact of primitive peoples with European civilization'. In either case the liberation of economic forces from the moral restraint imposed by social obligations is detrimental to social and individual welfare. During the first stage there may be, and usually is, a rise in the standard of individual welfare through the removal of the abuses normally inherent in native social life. For a still longer period there is an increase in production, by the exploitation of social welfare for material ends. But, as such forces gain in strength, they tend to restrict and even to reduce production, and thus defeat the hopes of gain which set them working. Forests are laid waste and valuable lodes of ore are buried beneath surface workings. Cultivation, as in the delta of Lower Burma, aims at the maximum net outturn by the smallest number necessary to produce it, instead of at the maximum gross outturn by the largest number that the land will maintain at the customary level of social life. Human resources are wasted by under-employment or by unemployment and, as in the Congo under Leopold, so many people may be killed off that capitalist enterprise is no longer profitable or even possible.[1] Both the two great East India companies went bankrupt, and the modern chartered companies had to surrender their concessions because they could no longer pay their way. Profit, progress and welfare, are all linked together on a single chain, and economic forces, unless controlled by social will, corrode the chain that links them. Man is a social animal, but economic forces tend to convert human society into a business concern. In tropical dependencies the outward and visible sign of this is the evolution of a plural society.

4. THE PLURAL SOCIETY[2]

All tropical dependencies, and indeed all tropical countries, so far as they have been brought within the modern world, have in common certain distinctive characters in their social structure. In Dutch

[1] Frankel, pp. 36, 37.
[2] Furnivall, *Economic Journal*, 1910, pp. 23 ff; *JRCAS*, 1942, p. 195.

colonial literature they are often said to present a dual economy, comprising two distinct economic systems, capitalist and pre-capitalist,
with a western superstructure of business and administration rising
above the native world in which the people, so far as they are left
alone, lead their own life in their own way according to a traditional
scale of values in which economic values rank so low as to be negligible.
It is unquestionably true that there is a wide difference between the
social standards of tropical peoples and those of the modern West,
that the natives are slow to assimilate western values, and that over
native life there is a western superstructure representing an outpost
of Europe and not rooted in the soil. Yet the Dutch picture of a
native world, in which economic values are disregarded, seems, so
far as it is based on facts, to be drawn from Java, where for some two
hundred years employers secured labour through compulsion rather
than by appealing to the desire of gain. In Africa likewise, as we have
just noticed, a popular belief in the native disregard of economic values
has been held to justify compulsion as a means of securing labour.
But everywhere experience has shown that the desire of gain can
easily be stimulated or, rather, liberated from the control of custom.
In British colonies under indirect rule, interpreted according to the
British tradition of the rule of law, economic forces soon permeate
the native world and, in colonies under direct rule, it is just in the
economic world that all men meet, if not on equal, yet on the same
terms. Even in respect of Dutch dependencies some of their own
writers vehemently dispute the theory of a dual economy.[1] Yet in all
tropical dependencies the western superstructure over native life is
a prominent feature in the economic landscape.

But the western superstructure is only one aspect of a distinctive
character, common to all tropical dependencies, that cannot fail to
impress even the most casual observer; the many-coloured pattern
of the population. In Burma, as in Java, probably the first thing that
strikes the visitor is the medley of peoples—European, Chinese,
Indian and native. It is in the strictest sense a medley, for they mix
but do not combine. Each group holds by its own religion, its own
culture and language, its own ideas and ways. As individuals they
meet, but only in the market-place, in buying and selling. There is a
plural society, with different sections of the community living side
by side, but separately, within the same political unit. Even in the
economic sphere there is a division of labour along racial lines.

[1] Meijer Ranneft, J. W., *Koloniale Studiën*, 1928, p. 151.

Natives, Chinese, Indians and Europeans all have different functions, and within each major group subsections have particular occupations. There is, as it were, a caste system, but without the religious basis that incorporates caste in social life in India. One finds similar conditions all over the Tropical Far East—under Spanish, Portuguese, Dutch, British, French or American rule; among Filipinos, Javanese, Malays, Burmans and Annamese; whether the objective of the colonial power has been tribute, trade or material resources; under direct rule and under indirect. The obvious and outstanding result of contact between East and West has been the evolution of a plural society; in the Federated Malay States the indigenous inhabitants number barely a quarter of the total population. The same thing has happened in the South Pacific. The Fiji chieftains invited British protection, and one result has been that half the inhabitants are immigrants from India. In African dependencies there are Indian immigrants in East Africa and Syrians in West Africa, and in some regions the 'coloured', or Eurafrican, population forms a separate caste. Sometimes a section of the native population is westernized: 'there are some territories, of which those in West Africa are perhaps most typical, in which sections of the population most closely in contact with European influences have attained a development out of all relation to the rest of the population...which is often still living in primitive conditions and has interests different from those of an urban or industrial society'.[1] One finds much the same thing in Java, and in all tropical dependencies 'westernized' natives are more or less cut off from the people, and form a separate group or caste. The plural society has a great variety of forms, but in some form or other it is the distinctive character of modern tropical economy.

Outside the tropics society may have plural features, notably in South Africa, Canada and the United States, and also in lands where the Jew has not been fully assimilated into social life; in other countries also there are mixed populations with particularist tendencies. But in general these mixed populations have at least a common tradition of western culture, and, despite a different racial origin, they meet on equal terms and their relations are not confined solely to the economic sphere. There is a society with plural features, but not a plural society. It is significant that, in Canada and the United States, and also in Australia, when the influx of alien elements threatened national life and common social standards, barriers were raised against free

[1] *Britain and Her Dependencies*, pp. 34, 44; Teeling, L. W. B., p. 126.

immigration. In tropical dependencies there was no common social will to set a bar to immigration, which has been left to the play of economic forces. The plural society arises where economic forces are exempt from control by social will. It is general in the modern tropics because everywhere and always the social order seems to have had plural features. In Burma under native rule the people were not organized territorially but on quasi-feudal lines by race and occupation, and that is the normal character of tropical society based on personal authority. But in such lands, apart from minor backward groups, there is a common cultural tradition; there is a society with plural features but not a plural society. Again, in the great fairs held annually in medieval times in ports and market towns, each company of merchants was governed by its own heads according to its own customs. But the concourse did not form a plural society, because it lasted no longer than the fair. All that happened was that, during the fair, the town was transformed into a bazaar. In the modern tropics the bazaar lasts throughout the year, and the whole country is converted into a shop or factory; from a social organism into a business concern. Despite certain plural features, tropical society was distinct from the plural society which has been created by economic forces. This is a modern invention because, only in modern times, have economic forces been set free to remould the social order. The result is a social structure quite distinct in its political and economic properties from the homogeneous unitary society of western lands and, for a solution of colonial problems, it is essential that its properties should be clearly understood. Let us examine it first in its political aspect and then in its economic aspect.

Political Features. On looking at a plural society in its political aspect one can distinguish three characteristic features: the society as a whole comprises separate racial sections; each section is an aggregate of individuals rather than a corporate or organic whole; and as individuals their social life is incomplete.

To Europeans the incompleteness of individual social life is most readily apparent in the European section. The European works in the tropics, but does not live there. His life in the tropics centres round his business, and he looks at social problems, political or economic, not as a citizen but as a capitalist or an employer of labour. Many Europeans spend twenty years or more in the tropics, and, on retiring from work to live at home, they know no more of the country than on the day they landed; nothing of the people or even of the language. Foreign orientals, likewise, are transient; they come merely to make money and their interest in the country is purely economic. The life of the ordinary native is similarly incomplete. He is a cultivator and nothing more. Under native rule the people lived within a little world, but their cultural horizon was co-extensive with its boundaries; under western rule their horizon is contracted to their life as cultivators and their social life is less comprehensive than before.

If we look above the individual to the group in which he forms a unit, we find a similar contrast between the plural society of tropical dependencies and the unitary society that western peoples take for granted. In all accounts of the modern tropics we read of the collapse of corporate tribal or village life and the atomization of society. In the foreign sections the individual stands even more alone; even among Indians caste loses its validity, and in every census in Burma it has been found impossible to compile useful returns of Indian castes. Among the Indian immigrants in South Sea Islands one may even find mixed marriages between Moslims and Hindus. Europeans often deplore the isolation of the individual in their own section. Men are continually on the move; they form business acquaintances but not friends; there are no children in the home; the club and not the home is the centre of social life, and all look more or less eagerly to going 'home' on retirement. Each section in the plural society is a crowd and not a community.

On a wider survey of the plural society as a whole comprising separate groups, we may find the nearest analogy in a confederation of allied states, united by treaty or within the limits of formal constitution merely for certain common ends, but otherwise, in matters outside the terms of union, each living its own life as a separate province. Yet this analogy fails to bring out the full complexity of a plural society. In a confederation each unit is segregated within its own territorial limits; there is contact between the states but not between their members as individuals; the union is voluntary; the terms of union are definite and limited; and any party can at will withdraw from the confederacy. In a plural society the sections are not segregated; the members of the several units are intermingled and meet as individuals; the union is not voluntary but is imposed by the colonial power and by the force of economic circumstances; and the union cannot be dissolved without the whole society relapsing into anarchy.

Like a confederation, a plural society is a business partnership rather than a family concern, and the social will linking the sections does not extend beyond their common business interests. It might seem that common interest should tie them closely, for a dissolution would involve the bankruptcy of all the partners. But the tie is strong only so far as this common interest is recognized. Perhaps the only plural society inherently stable is the Hindu society in India. Here there are separate groups or classes, partly racial, with distinct economic functions. But in India caste has a religious sanction, and in a plural society the only common deity is Mammon. In general, the plural society is built on caste without the cement of a religious sanction. In each section the sectional common social will is feeble, and in the society as a whole there is no common social will. There may be apathy even on such a vital point as defence against aggression. Few recognize that, in fact, all the members of all sections have material interests in common, but most see that on many points their material interests are opposed. The typical plural society is a business partnership in which, to many partners, bankruptcy signifies release rather than disaster.

Economic Features. The political aspect of the plural society is reflected in its economic aspect. A plural society is no ordinary business partnership. In form it is also a political society and is, or should be, organized for 'the good life', the welfare of the people, enabling them to live as well as possible. As a business partnership its function is solely economic, to produce goods as profitably as possible. But as a social institution also it has an economic aspect, and is concerned with both production and consumption, supply and demand. It is in the interest of a society that its members shall get what is best and not merely what is cheapest; by custom or law it must regulate demand. It is also in the interest of society that in the supply of goods, production for profit shall be regulated by custom or law on behalf of social welfare. In a plural society both supply and demand take on a special character.

Let us first consider the matter of demand. In buying goods it is only common sense to pay no more than necessary. But purchasers are not always guided solely by common sense. Some will pay a higher price for home products than for foreign products, or for goods untainted by sweated labour. In such cases there is a social demand for home manufactures, or for a higher standard of wages. In this matter there is a difference between the plural society and the homogeneous society. When the recent depression flooded Java with cheap cottons from Japan, European merchants tried to boycott Japanese goods; but the boycott collapsed because Chinese merchants bought them and seemed likely to capture all the trade. When Britain annexed Upper Burma the British Government contemplated retaining the Burmese prohibition of trade in opium and alcohol, but this was impossible because the demand of the Chinese and Indians had to be met. In a plural society the feebleness of social will is reflected in the weakness of social demand, which is the economic aspect of social will. Economists deal in great detail with problems of aggregate demand but, partly it may be because they take a homogeneous society for granted, they have not given social demand so much attention as it deserves. If any town or village in the western world wants better sanitation, it can spend more on conservancy. There is a collective demand which may conflict with individual demand, and at periodical elections people can choose between better conservancy and having more money in their pockets. Economists can measure this collective demand with their supply and demand curves and schedules, but collective demand is only one form of a social demand that, in general, defies measurement. The monastic schools in Burma were a response to social demand, but no one could estimate their cost, or balance it against their value. In tropical countries social demand usually takes effect through custom. Sometimes a patch of scrub jungle round a village is reserved as a public convenience and is closed to fuel cutting. People could get their fuel with less trouble, more cheaply, by cutting timber there, but social demand, taking effect through village custom, prevails over individual demand. So long as custom retains its force, no one would think of cutting down the scrub. But we have noticed that in Rangoon Indian immigrants saw a way to make easy money, and cleared the scrub to sell fuel in the market. Individual demand for private gain prevailed over the social demand for common welfare, and prevailed the more readily because society was no longer homogeneous. Even in the West social demand is most effective when it requires no stronger support than custom, because no one thinks of encroaching on it. In London rickshaws might be cheaper than taxis, but we would walk rather than use them. The individual demand for cheaper transport is overborne by the social demand for human dignity. And because we resist the temptation of cheapness we finally attain better, and probably cheaper, transport in tubes and motor-buses. During the present century Rangoon, in common with most eastern towns, has been flooded with rickshaws. In Batavia the Dutch refused to sanction them; they disliked seeing Javanese between the shafts and already had too many Chinese. Now motor transport in the towns of Java is probably better and cheaper than in any country in the tropics. Social demand can take effect only through organic social will as embodied in the social structure, and, in default of social will, individual demand prevails over social demand. A villager in Burma may wish to spend money on schooling for his children, but the maintenance of a school is conditional on the existence of social demand and, if there is no village school, he may spend his money on giving them new clothes, or on furniture that he does not use, or even on English books that he cannot read.[1] If he cannot satisfy those wants which he has as a member of society, he will satisfy his individual wants; he must take what he can get.

Here is one of the distinctions between a homogeneous society and a plural society. A plural society is broken up into groups of isolated individuals, and the disintegration of social will is reflected in a corresponding disorganization of social demand. Even in a matter so vital to the whole community as defence against aggression, the people are reluctant to pay the necessary price. In religion and the arts, in the graces and ornaments of social life, there are no standards common to all sections of the community, and standards deteriorate to such a level as all have in common. And because each section is merely an aggregate of individuals, those social wants that men can satisfy only as members of a community remain unsatisfied. Just as the life of an individual in a plural society is incomplete, so his demand tends to be frustrated. Civilization is the process of learning to live a common social life, but in a plural society men are decivilized. All wants that all men want in common are those which they share in common with the animal creation; on a comprehensive survey of mankind from China to Peru these material wants, essential to the sustenance of life, represent the highest common factor of demand. In the plural society the highest common factor is the economic factor, and the only test that all apply in common is the test of cheapness. In such a society the disorganization of social demand allows the economic process of natural selection by the survival of the cheapest to prevail.

If, again, we examine plural economy from the standpoint of production or supply, we find a similar predominance of economic forces.

---

[1] Furnivall, *Economic Review*, 1912, pp. 380 ff.

In selling goods it is common sense to charge as much as one can. All those engaged in production have in common, in greater or less degree, the desire for gain, to get as much as possible while giving as little as possible. But, in a plural society, that is almost all they have in common. Everywhere, in all forms of society, the working of economic forces makes for tension between groups with competing or conflicting interests; between town and country, industry and agriculture, capital and labour. In a homogeneous society the tension is alleviated by their common citizenship, but in a plural society there is a corresponding cleavage along racial lines. The foreign elements live in the towns, the natives in rural areas; commerce and industry are in foreign hands and the natives are mainly occupied in agriculture; foreign capital employs native labour or imported coolies. The various peoples meet only in the market, as competitors or as opponents, as buyers and sellers. In Burma the Indian and Chinese middlemen form combines against both the cultivator and the European miller, and Europeans form combines against both middleman and native. In Java the nationalist movement first assumed a popular character in action against the Chinese, whom Europeans at the same time were describing as worse than ten epidemics. In Indo-China Annamese and Europeans regard the Indian moneylender as a pest. It might seem that, on a long view, all sections have a common interest in the common welfare, but the foreign elements, European or oriental, mostly need not look beyond the day when they will leave the country. In any case, the end is so remote that it is out of sight; so far as the horizon of the business man extends sectional interests are opposed. It is true that big business with large capital investments in the country must take long views, and sees further than the cultivator who does not look beyond the harvest and the coolie who looks only for to-morrow's rice, but it looks on the country as a business enterprise.

Moreover, within the economic sphere there are no common standards of conduct beyond those prescribed by law. The European has his own standard of decency as to what, even in business, 'is not done'; so also have the Chinese, the Indian and the native. All have their own ideas as to what is right and proper, but on this matter they have different ideas, and the only idea common to all members of all sections is the idea of gain. In a homogeneous society the desire of profit is controlled to some extent by social will, and if anyone makes profits by sharp practice he will offend the social conscience and incur moral, and perhaps legal, penalties. If, for example, he employs sweated labour, the social conscience, if sufficiently alert and powerful, may penalize him because aware, either instinctively or by rational conviction, that such conduct cuts at the root of common social life. But in the tropics the European who, from humanitarian motives or through enlightened self-interest, treats his employees well, risks being forced out of business by Indians or Chinese with different standards. The only deterrent to unsocial conduct in production is the legal penalty to which those are liable who can be brought to trial and convicted according to the rules of evidence of infringing some positive law. In supply as in demand, in production as in consumption, the abnormal activity of economic forces, free of social restrictions, is an essential character of a plural society.

In colonial relations then, economic forces both create a plural society and, because unrestrained by social will, continue to prevail. The dictum of Dr Boeke, that we have already noted with reference to Java, applies to tropical economy in general: 'there is materialism, rationalism, individualism, and a concentration on economic ends far more complete and absolute than in homogeneous western lands; a total absorption in the exchange and market; a capitalist structure, with the business concern as subject, far more typical of capitalism than one can imagine in the so-called "capitalist" countries, which have grown up slowly out of the past and are still bound to it by a hundred roots'.[1] In the first half of the nineteenth century economists eulogized economic man; in the last half they said he was a myth. Unfortunately they were mistaken. When cast out of Europe he found refuge in the tropics, and now we see him returning with seven devils worse than himself. These are the devils which devastated the tropics under the rule of *laissez-faire* and which it is the object of modern colonial policy to exorcise.

5. Modern Colonial Policy

The foregoing analysis of the course of social evolution in tropical dependencies under a regime of *laissez-faire* may perhaps appear superfluous, for *laissez-faire* is dead, and modern colonial policy aspires to be constructive. The constructive policy, as originally conceived, reflected popular Darwinism, the survival of the fittest, and looked mainly to efficiency. Gradually however it was permeated by the idea of social justice which gathered force in Europe with the re-

[1] Boeke, cited *Netherlands India*, p. 452.

action against the impoverishment due to unbridled competition. These two ideas, when extended to colonial policy, found expression in the theory of the dual mandate, professing to reconcile economic progress with native welfare and to regard native interests as paramount. The new policy, like the Liberal policy, placed economic development in the foreground, but took a different view of the relations between economic development and welfare. The older Liberal colonial policy, as we have seen, assumed that economic freedom was the key to progress, and economic progress an automatic and sufficient guarantee of welfare, which would in due course lead to political independence; it aimed accordingly at restricting State activities to an unavoidable minimum. The modern constructive policy advocates State intervention in promoting development, so as to provide funds for economic and social services intended to enhance native welfare and thereby lay the foundations of autonomy. Liberals regarded economic development as a cause of welfare and, therefore, a means of political advancement; modern colonial policy regards it as a condition of welfare and a condition, therefore, of political advancement. The decline of faith in the doctrine of *laissez-faire* reacted also on the international aspect of colonial relations, but at present we are concerned solely with the domestic aspect.

Another matter calls for passing notice. *Laissez-faire* is dead, but economic forces still remain active, everywhere, unceasingly. When a colonial power adopts a constructive policy with a view to enhancing welfare, it must first repair the ill-effects of economic forces in the past, and then bring them under control so as to prevent further damage; only when it has succeeded to that extent can it raise the general standard of welfare to a higher level. These matters will need attention when enquiring into colonial practice, but first we must look at statements of policy.

Modern British policy has been restated with all the authority of Acts of Parliament in connection with recent projects of colonial development. Formerly the assistance given to the dependencies went little beyond defraying the initial military expenditure on pacification, and providing or guaranteeing such loans as were required for internal development. Of the £110 millions of interest-bearing loans now standing in the names of dependent Governments, about three-fourths have been expended on railway and port development.[1] It was assumed that in other respects local development would

[1] *Britain and Her Dependencies*, p. 14.

ordinarily be financed by the dependent Governments out of their own resources. The home Government, however, would meet deficits in local budgets, and in the ten years from 1919 to 1929 a total of some £12 million was allotted for this purpose. In 1929 there was a new departure. A Colonial Development Fund was created to allow an expenditure of £1 million annually on colonial development in order to promote commerce with, or industry in, the United Kingdom. Up to 1940 a total of £8·87 million was granted, 30 % going to communications and another 5 % to harbours. The plant and machinery had so far as possible to be of United Kingdom manufacture, and all materials of Empire origin, while all orders for imported materials had to be placed in the United Kingdom. One feature of this project was that it aimed directly at promoting British economic interests, and during the subsequent depression the grants did in fact give a considerable contribution to employment in the United Kingdom.[1] Another feature of this plan was that 'the emphasis was throughout on material development'. It aimed at promoting agriculture and industry, and specified the heads on which expenditure might be incurred, while objects of no less importance from the standpoint of welfare were excluded. For example, education, other than technical instruction, was outside its scope. Moreover, the grants were strictly limited to capital expenditure, and were based on the old principle that a dependency should not be equipped with services unless it could afford to maintain them out of its own resources.

A new plan, embodied in the Colonial Development and Welfare Act of 1940, went much further. It recognized the indirect benefit that might accrue to the United Kingdom from colonial development and made provision up to £5 million annually for *capital* expenditure, not merely under specified heads, but on development in the widest sense, and it also permitted grants for *recurrent* expenditure on certain services, such as agriculture, education, health and housing; beyond this it provided an additional £500,000 for colonial research.[2] The emphasis was no longer, as in the plan of 1929, on material development as an end in itself, but as 'the primary requirement upon which advance in other directions is largely consequential'. It was by economic development that colonies would be placed in a position to devote their resources, to the maximum extent possible, to the provision of those Government and other services which the interests of the people demand. Such assistance was held to be justified as, other-

[1] 1941, Cmd. 6298.   [2] 1940, Cmd. 6175.

wise, 'many colonies would not finance the research work, the schemes of major capital development and the expansion of administrative or technical staffs which are necessary for their full and vigorous development. Nor could they always afford in the absence of such development, an adequate standard of health and education services'.

Here we have in brief the modern constructive policy of encouraging economic development with a view to promoting welfare as a condition of political advancement. It is a policy that has been welcomed with remarkable unanimity by all parties, Conservative, Liberal and Socialist, and among that section of the general public which takes an interest in colonial affairs.

The attitude of Conservatives has been formulated in a recent speech by Col. Oliver Stanley as Colonial Secretary.[1] 'We are pledged', he said, 'to guide colonial peoples along the path to self-government within the British Empire. We are pledged to build up their social and economic institutions, and we are pledged to develop their natural resources.' He looked on 'educational advancement and economic development as the twin pillars upon which any sound scheme of political responsibility must be based', and regarded the measures taken under these heads as the most important test of the sincerity and success of our colonial policy.

In education he stressed the importance of primary instruction. 'The spread of elementary education through the colonies is a necessity for everything we are trying to do. Every social improvement, every economic development in some measure demands an increase of knowledge among the people. Every health measure, every improvement of agricultural methods, new co-operative machinery for production and distribution, the establishment of secondary institutions —all these are going to make increasing demands upon the people, and they will be able to respond only if they have had some educational opportunities.' Higher education also would be needed 'to provide the doctors, the teachers, the veterinary surgeons, the specialists and technicians which the approach to higher standards of life will entail'. Education was, in fact, a fundamental condition of all Government activities in the promotion of material welfare. These various activities would entail heavy expenditure. Something might be done by subventions, but the main cost would have to be met by economic development. For promoting economic development he urged the encouragement of air transport, the fostering of secondary industries

[1] House of Commons, 13 July 1943, quoted *Colonial Review*, Sept. 1943, p. 69.

and the constitution of a Central Advisory Committee on economic affairs. In this development he anticipated that private capital would play a useful part, as the people of Britain were coming to understand that the development of the colonies was a profitable undertaking. As a basis for political development he looked chiefly to education 'by life for life', through trade unions, co-operative societies and similar forms of community effort. In this also, however, as he remarked at greater length on a subsequent occasion, education would play an important part. The goal of British policy is self-government but, 'we have got to be certain that when, in any colony, we hand over the responsibility for government, administration, justice and security, it shall be handed over to the whole of the people, and that they are ready and prepared to receive it'.[1]

The latest pronouncement on Liberal colonial policy may be found in the report of a committee appointed by the Liberal National Council to examine the future of the colonies.[2] The report deals largely with machinery. It insists on the maintenance of British sovereignty in the interest of efficient administration, but recognizes the value of international collaboration. The proposals with regard to machinery comprise the creation of an Advisory Council, an International Colonial Institute and Regional Consultative Councils; constitutional problems are expressly excluded from the competence of the two latter bodies. Colonial policy, it holds, should aim at promoting 'the welfare of native populations in the widest sense'. This welfare must have a sound economic foundation, but the construction of such a foundation 'must be regarded not as a sufficient end in itself, but rather as a condition precedent to native advancement in a wider sense', including political advancement. Economic development should therefore be accompanied by safeguards for native populations.

For an ampler statement of Liberal policy we may perhaps look to Lord Hailey,[3] whose Liberal sympathies are enriched by long experience as an administrator and by a wide study of colonial practice. He recognizes the importance of political development, which earlier Liberals valued so highly, but he comments on their failure sufficiently to recognize that 'we cannot hope to build up political institutions on a foundation of poor material resources, of insufficient health or of undeveloped minds'. He holds accordingly that the first problem of colonial policy is to improve the standard of living in respect both

---

[1] *Colonial Review*, June 1944, p. 165. [2] *The Colonies and their Future* (1944).
[3] *Britain and Her Dependencies*, pp. 7, 8, 10, 29, 30, 33.

of the material conditions necessary to physical well-being, and of the extension of educational and other agencies that make for better social organization. To achieve these ends he looks mainly to the institution of economic and social services by the State, especially with a view to grading up subsistence production by natives, by extending their production for export, and by encouraging every means to give them a larger part in the industrial and commercial activities which have hitherto been mainly in foreign hands. Here he breaks away from the older Liberal tradition by accepting the need for some measure of compulsion. For the great mass of the people in tropical dependencies, the fundamental need is 'the mass extension of a form of popular education which will increase their ability to make use for their own benefit of more scientific processes of cultivation, or will break down anti-social or unhygienic customs impeding the improvement of their physical well-being, or will accelerate the progress made by members of the native communities in undertaking the innumerable services—whether in trade, transport or domestic crafts—which are necessary for their economic and social life'. This he regards as the only sound means of social advance, which 'must be a corollary of economic development, since the possibilities open both to the administration and to the individual depend on the achievement of a progressive measure of economic well-being'. Like the older Liberals, he welcomes the prospect of political advancement, but he gives priority to economic progress as a condition of political advancement; like them also, he believes in economic development through capitalist enterprise, but would supplement private capital by State subventions; and like them he aims at promoting individual welfare, but he is not averse from compulsion, where necessary, to reinforce the desire of gain.

Socialist colonial policy is very similar.[1] According to a well-known writer of this school, 'the intense poverty of colonial areas...is directly due to lack of capital. Through lack of capital the colonial areas have been deprived of the fundamental public services on which all economic progress is based.' As the colonies cannot afford to borrow capital, it must be given freely by the State or supplied at nominal rates of interest; 'they must be given their railways and roads and harbours and water and power supplies; they must be equipped, with schools and hospitals; they must, in short, be endowed, altruistically, with a complete foundation of public services on which to build their economic life'. Moreover, as free enterprise tends to concentrate

[1] Hinden, pp. 187, 194.

on external trade, policy should be directed towards fostering internal trade, and those exports that require development on capitalist lines should be nationalized.

One striking fact about these various programmes of constructive welfare is their unanimity. Formerly Conservatives and Liberals held directly contrary opinions on colonial policy, and Socialists differed from both. Now on the main points all are agreed.[1] Even in the Socialist programme social life is disregarded; it is a project of mass individualism stimulated through the State by foreign capital, and differs little from the Liberal programme except as to the source of capital, while both programmes closely resemble that of the Conservatives as expounded by Col. Stanley. The points of difference are superficial and lie mainly in a diversity of emphasis on matters that all accept. All agree that the maintenance of the imperial connection is to the common advantage of the British people; this solidarity of interest in the Empire is something new. All agree likewise on the need for foreign capital to promote the development of material resources, and thereby provide funds for economic and social services; and all agree that these enhance welfare and make the dependencies capable of responsible government within the Empire. This common agreement is very significant and, as we shall see, has consequences of great interest and importance.

Another striking fact is that this new constructive policy is almost point for point identical with that formulated by the Ethical leaders of Dutch colonial policy forty years ago.[2] The States-General gave practical expression to the Ethical policy by making a free grant of f. 40 million to be expended on colonial development. Western enterprise, public and private, flourished, yielding revenue that was expended on economic and social services. Yet, while economic progress made rapid forward strides, native welfare lagged behind. On the other hand, when the depression of the thirties and trouble with Japan cut off supplies of capital, native prosperity increased. If, then, we wish to promote native welfare, it would seem necessary to scrutinize closely the working of the modern constructive policy in practice.

---

[1] See e.g. Mr Churchill, House of Commons, 21 April 1944; Dr Hinden, *Fabian Quarterly*, April 1945, p. 5.

[2] One difference between the Ethical policy and modern British colonial policy should be noted. The Ethical leaders still held the older Liberal belief in the intrinsic value of western political institutions; but experience has compelled the Dutch to recognize, like all schools of political thought in Britain, that political democracy requires an economic basis.

CHAPTER IX

WELFARE: LAND AND LABOUR

1. THE INSTRUMENTS OF WELFARE

FROM the foregoing survey of colonial policy it should be evident that the promotion of welfare in tropical dependencies is not a new idea; what is new is the recognition that this requires a constructive policy with appropriate instruments of welfare. The instruments devised to promote welfare fall under two heads: economic and social. Measures under the former head aim directly at increasing production, which should enhance welfare indirectly; measures under the latter head aim directly at enhancing welfare, which should increase production indirectly. The machinery for increasing production comprises public works for the development of material resources, *la richesse naturelle*, and economic services for the development of human resources, *la richesse humaine*. The machinery of social welfare comprises services intended to protect the land and labour of tropical peoples against the adverse influence of economic forces, and services to promote health and education. It is often taken for granted that activities under all these various heads are effective in raising the standard of welfare above its native level; the next stage in our enquiry is to examine the validity of this assumption. We must try to ascertain how far public works and economic services do, in fact, increase native production; how far any such increase in production enhances native welfare; to what extent social services are effective in protecting land and labour; and how far the health and education services endow the people with new powers in body and mind. These are the questions that will engage our attention in this chapter and the next.

2. PUBLIC WORKS

Colonial rule is often judged by its achievements in respect of public works, such as ports, railways and irrigation, and colonial powers, in justifying their claim to exercise dominion, point to such things as proof of their beneficent activities. But it is necessary to distinguish between public works as instruments of progress and as instruments of welfare. Railways are the chief item under the head of public works, and in Africa they account for about three-quarters of the total

loans raised by governments of British territories.[1] Some were constructed for strategic ends and some mainly to facilitate administration, but the usual object was to open up the interior to trade. In
dependencies chiefly valued as markets for European goods, the
populous districts usually lie along great rivers, and development
requires little expenditure, because the waterways suffice without
railways or even, as we have seen in Burma, without roads. The case
is different, however, where local products are developed by western
enterprise, as this prefers more sparsely peopled regions; plantations
require large tracts of vacant land, and mineral deposits are mostly
found in barren hilly regions. In such circumstances the cost of
transport by carts or porters to remove the produce of enterprise or to
supply its needs may be so formidable as to preclude development;
in West Africa it was estimated in 1926 that porterage cost 2s. 6d. a
ton-mile as compared with 2d. by rail.[2] In such circumstances, if the
resources of backward regions are to be made available to the outside
world, communications must be improved, and western enterprise
demands the construction of railways. This opens up new and wider
prospects of gain, and provides employment for western capital and
labour in the colonial power. Inevitably there is a tendency to over-
estimate the advantages that improved communications confer upon
dependent peoples, and to overlook the disadvantages. It is usually
assumed that roads and railways act as an instrument of civilization
and promote welfare by bringing the people into contact with the
modern world, but negro slavery was formerly defended on the same
grounds. Whether closer contact is beneficial depends upon its nature
and the results, and where as has happened sometimes on railway construction large numbers die, or where as also has happened, a whole
people fades away, it can be regarded as beneficial to them only on
the ground that they are better dead.

The construction of railways was part of the campaign against
slavery, and against porterage with which slavery was closely linked.
The Uganda Railway, for instance, was approved by Parliament
on the ground that activities against the slave trade must be extended to the interior.[3] Porterage is not only costly, but it is wasteful
of labour, deadly; it is costly both in money and human life, and
modern forms of transport have been acclaimed as an immense
benefit to the peoples whom they free from the scourge of porterage.[4]
But the matter is not quite so simple. Under native conditions, un-

[1] *African Survey*, p. 1657.   [2] *Ib.* p. 1540.   [3] *Ib.* pp. 1538, 1582.   [4] *Ib.* p. 1539.

touched by modern commerce, there was little need for porters, and slavery was in general merely a form of domestic or agricultural service that, under the conditions then obtaining, best provided for the welfare of the labourer.[1] It was the impact of the West, and the consequent liberation of economic forces from the restraining influence of custom, that changed the character of slavery and multiplied the evils of porterage. In Africa 'during the early days of European occupation large demands were made on the population for the supply of porters, with the inevitable result of much suffering and a large loss of life; and it is further clear that the extensive use of human porterage was responsible for the spread of forms of disease which had hitherto been local in their incidence'.[2] So far as economic progress renders slavery and porterage unnecessary, it is removing evils for which in great part it has been responsible. Moreover, it is notorious that road building and railway construction have, at least for the time being, aggravated the abuse of compulsory labour. 'The wide use of impressed labour for railway construction in Africa has, in the past, led to many incidents which have reflected great discredit on the administration', and quite recently the death rate on such work has been 'exceedingly high'. A French writer, commenting on the heavy burden of compulsory labour imposed on the current generation in improving communications, offers the consolation that future generations will be freed from compulsion.[3] But the benefits to future generations are remote and doubtful. As Mr Frankel notes, railway construction 'will be justified on economic grounds only if, after the line has been built, the efforts of the population as a whole, including that of the porters, can be so redirected as to yield sufficient quantities of additional or more valuable goods, of a kind which can enter trade and bear the cost of railway transport'.[4] The completion of a line sets free a large volume of labour for employment on adjacent capitalist enterprises, but there remains a still larger surplus which can no longer find work, even as porters, and this opens up new problems.

Where railways are not needed to replace porters, their advantage to the native population is still more questionable. Liberals had no doubt on this point because they regarded progress as a guarantee of welfare. Now we have come to recognize that railways tend to meet the demand for export products at the expense of subsistence products.

[1] Burns, p. 209. [2] *African Survey*, p. 1538.
[3] *Ib.* pp. 615, 628. [4] Frankel, p. 6.

Of recent years the construction of railways, like other projects of economic development, has usually been advocated on the ground that they would provide funds for welfare services. How far they have promoted welfare indirectly through opening up new fields for commerce and industry we must examine later, but here it is relevant to note that, except where they have served mining enterprise, they have usually been unremunerative and have 'made a serious reduction in the resources available for general expenditure'.[1] Some forms of expenditure on public works are not, like railways, open to the criticism that they deprive people of employment; irrigation, for instance, creates a new and permanent demand for native labour. But general experience shows that, as we have noticed in the Punjab, it tends to increase the mass of debt, leaving the peasant with a bare subsistence and, at best, no wealthier than before.

There is, indeed, no necessary connection for good or ill between public works and native welfare. We have seen that economic development, unless kept under control, is on the balance prejudicial to the welfare of the people; that is one reason for the modern departure from the Liberal doctrine of *laissez-faire*. Public works in general, whether roads, railways, airways, ports or irrigation, serve to expedite development, and thereby enhance the difficulty of protecting natives against its evil consequences. It would, for instance, be difficult to argue that railway construction in the Belgian Congo under Leopold improved the well-being of the natives. In Malaya we are told of a 'once flourishing Sakai village [which] has, since the road touched it, plainly deteriorated, physically and morally.'[2] Even irrigation works must be regarded as a failure from the standpoint of welfare if they merely enable more people to live more miserably. Thus the general belief in the intrinsic value of roads, railways and other forms of public works as instruments of native welfare must be dismissed as an illusion; only too often they do more harm than good to those whom they are supposed to benefit. Public works are instruments of economic progress, of world welfare, not of native welfare; sometimes in some ways they may improve the common lot, but they extend and intensify the action of economic forces and, without protection against these, they do not promote native welfare but enhance the need of measures to protect welfare.

[1] *Britain and Her Dependencies*, p. 23; *African Survey*, pp. 1316, 1606.
[2] Malaya Census, 1931, p. 103.

3. Economic Services and Production

Economic services, intended to improve the human factor in production, have somewhat the same character as public works intended to improve material resources. Like public works, they are primarily instruments of economic progress, world welfare, with native welfare as, potentially, a by-product. Like public works also, they often originate in the need for preventing the spoliation and exploitation characteristic of unregulated economic activities. Humanitarian sentiment condemned porterage, but it was the waste of human life and high cost of labour that stimulated railway construction. Similarly, in Burma as in the tropics generally, it was the devastation of the forests by free capitalist enterprise that created the need for a forestry service. Rich mineral deposits are often buried beneath the refuse of surface workings. In South Africa ostrich farming nearly committed suicide by killing off the ostriches.[1] One natural consequence of the improvement of communications in the process of economic development is the spread of diseases among crops and cattle. In all these and in other ways economic development creates a need for economic services. There is, however, one notable difference between economic service and public works. Whereas public works are mostly intended to promote general economic progress, economic services may be particularly directed towards promoting the economic progress of the natives.

Not infrequently it is assumed that all expenditure on economic services goes to native enterprise. Much of it, however, is incurred solely on behalf of western enterprise, and does not contribute towards increasing native production. Mineral deposits are worked almost exclusively by Europeans, and it is they who profit by the geological survey and mines service. Ordinarily, as in Africa, Europeans hold most of the commercial forests, to which the activities of the forestry service are mainly directed; it may, by reafforestation or in other ways, assist native cultivation, but protective forestry receives less attention, partly because it is less directly remunerative and partly because it lacks the support of native public opinion.[2] The economic services which touch native life most closely are those concerned with agriculture, veterinary care and irrigation, and even in these western enterprise commands a share, and sometimes the chief share, of

[1] *African Survey*, pp. 985, 993, 1313, 1492, 1499, 1528; Frankel, p. 65n.
[2] *African Survey*, p. 987.

their attention. When, therefore, economic development is advocated on the ground that it provides funds for economic services, it is well to enquire how far these services are concerned with native rather than with western enterprise, and how far they do in fact make native enterprise more efficient. Information on such matters is not readily obtainable, but some light is thrown on them by a recent study of Malaya.

Formerly the natives of British Malaya cultivated little but rice. Conditions did not favour the growth of a large export market such as stimulated cultivators in other parts of Indo-China to extend their holdings, and the Government tried to encourage the cultivation of rice by regulations making it compulsory. In the early years of the present century, when the doctrine of efficiency was beginning to replace the principle of *laissez-faire* as the motto of colonial rule, an agricultural service was created. This included a paddy experimental station, but no one was appointed to specialize in rice, and experiments in the improvement of rice cultivation were discontinuous. About the same time plantation rubber was coming into favour, and the agricultural experts 'gave most of their time to the European and Chinese rubber planters'. Malays also found rubber profitable, and tended to substitute rubber for rice. Thus, with the influx of many hundred thousand coolies to the mines and plantations, the country became increasingly dependent on imported rice. When the war of 1914 and post-war developments stopped these imports, the Government had to import rice and lost £42 million on the transaction, while the estates and mines also lost heavily on importing rice for their coolies. 'The result of this experience was the decision that rice cultivation must be increased and more attention paid to native agriculture.'[1]

Accordingly the regulations for compulsory rice cultivation were enforced more stringently, and experiments were undertaken with a view to make it more profitable by improving the yield. Under the latter head progress was slow, as frequent changes in the agricultural staff hindered continuity of policy. By about 1925, however, the agricultural department claimed to have discovered new varieties that would enhance the yield by 30 %. This had little effect on extending cultivation, and in 1930 a committee was appointed to examine the situation. It estimated that the area under rice could be more than doubled by the addition of some 600,000 to 1,000,000 acres of potential rice land, but 'there was no one way of making paddy growing

[1] Mills, pp. 250ff.

profitable and bringing about its extension. The problem must be attacked simultaneously through drainage and irrigation, agricultural betterment and the co-operative department.' One outcome of its recommendations was the reconstitution of the irrigation department in 1932, and the investigations of the new department confirmed the previous impression that 'all over the country padi lands were steadily going out of cultivation.... Even in the fine padi plain of Province Wellesley, ...conditions were steadily deteriorating, the cultivators in debt, and their *kampongs* (villages) often indicating a state verging on poverty.' During the next few years upwards of 40,000 acres were added to the existing irrigation schemes.[1] At the same time, under the influence of the depression there was a fall in the price of rubber, and by 1934 the area under rice had grown by over 100,000 acres.

In the following year, however, with a rise in the price of rubber, the area under rice fell by 35,000 acres. Thus although there was a wide area available for extending the cultivation of rice, and the fall in the price of rubber consequent on the depression encouraged cultivators to prefer rice cultiva-

Area under rice[2]	
(acres, 000)	
1924–5	654
1929–30	657
1933–4	767
1937–8	726

tion, which at the same time was stimulated by compulsion, by extensive new irrigation and by the discovery of more productive strains, yet, with a population that increased between 1926 and 1936 by 29 %, the area under rice expanded by only 11 %.[3]

This brief survey of the attempts to foster and improve rice cultivation in Malaya suggests that neither compulsion nor the efforts of the agricultural service to enhance production met with much success, and it contains many lessons of general application regarding the relation between economic services and the increase of production. The failure of agricultural experts to increase native production is often explained on the ground that it is difficult 'to persuade a conservative and easy-going peasantry to improve their methods',[4] and that the economic motive, the desire of gain, does not appeal to 'natives'. This is the easiest and most comfortable explanation of all failures to enhance native welfare; it is their fault and not ours. But it is inconsistent with the facts. While the Malayan was reluctant to grow more rice, he was taking readily to growing rubber. All over the Tropical Far East, native rubber has expanded rapidly, sometimes in the face of opposition. Similarly in Java the opposition of planters and

---

[1] Mills, pp. 262, 272, 274.   [2] Wickizer and Bennett, p. 314.
[3] *Ib.* p. 195.   [4] Mills, pp. 251, 259.

of some officials could not stop the people from cultivating sugar instead of the less profitable rice.[1] In Africa as in Asia the people are only too ready to substitute commercial crops for food crops, and in parts of the Gold Coast and Tanganyika the farmers are coming to depend on the market for their food.[2] Everywhere the acreage of new crops under native cultivation rises and falls with the demand. The adoption of new crops is nothing new. In Netherlands India, of all the produce now cultivated by natives, only the coconut, soya and the spices are indigenous, and even rice is an immigrant. All the staple crops have come in from abroad over a period of many centuries, and that is true also of Burma. In Africa bananas, rice, wheat and sugar were introduced by the Arabs in the seventh century, and the sweet potato, cassava and maize are attributed to the Portuguese. In the most notable modern developments of native production, agricultural services have played a very minor role. In Burma the two outstanding innovations in agricultural practice, the introduction of hard rice for the European market and, later, of groundnut, both preceded the creation of an agricultural department. So also did the substitution of transplanting for broadcasting in rice cultivation, which became general when the price of paddy rose sufficiently to justify the extra cost. In Africa 'the production of cacao in the Gold Coast and of groundnuts in Northern Nigeria are examples of the development of new industries almost without aid, when the African has been satisfied that production is possible and within his capacity...(and)...this wide adoption of maize and other crops, which are comparatively recent introductions is further evidence of capacity of adaptation'.[3] Where new crops or methods of cultivation are profitable, compulsion and expert assistance are unnecessary; where they are unprofitable, compulsion and expert assistance are of no avail.

General experience shows that even if tropical peoples fail to evince a desire of gain before contact with the West, this is one of the earliest lessons which they learn. For the introduction of new and more profitable crops it is not even necessary that the cultivators themselves should make the profit. Where economic development leads to land alienation and rack-renting, or wherever rents are fixed by competition, the land goes to tenants who can pay the highest rent, and cultivators are compelled therefore to adopt new and more productive crops, or cheaper methods of cultiva-

[1] *Netherlands India*, p. 321.   [2] *African Survey*, pp. 864–7, 961.
[3] *Ib.* pp. 883, 886.

tion, even though the profit goes to the moneylender or the landlord. If an agricultural service can make the cultivation of any crop more profitable either to cultivators or landowners it will increase production; if it does not increase production, the presumption is that it has not enabled cultivators, working under local conditions and with the means at their disposal, to get a better return.

Even in Europe the application of modern science to agriculture is comparatively recent, and practical agriculturists are apt to view the suggestions of experts with suspicion not always unjustified. But the scientific study of tropical agriculture is still in its infancy, and experts must be cautious in their recommendations, for, if they base suggestions on experience in Europe, they are liable to make mistakes. For example, in Europe cultivators prize a warm soil and in the tropics a cool soil, and in other ways conditions are reversed, but specialists are not always capable of adapting to a tropical environment what they have been taught in Europe. In Burma deep ploughing was recommended to rice cultivators, until experience showed that this breaks up the hard pan which holds the water. The early rubber leases in Burma required planters to grow at least 400 trees to the acre, whereas the optimum number was about 80. Western planters condemned the neglect of natives to weed their rubber holdings until the recent depression, by precluding expenditure on the weeding of plantations, taught them that it reduced the yield of sap. Mistakes are accepted as inevitable by western planters, but shake the confidence of native cultivators in western science. There is no doubt that modern science can do much to improve agriculture in the tropics. It has already done much in Netherlands India, where the 'great cultures' have been built up on a scientific basis. But it is European agriculture that chiefly benefits from the modern science of the agricultural service. Naturally agricultural experts can do more for planters who believe in them, seek their help and employ methods of cultivation with which they are familiar, than for peasants who have no faith in modern science and believe, often not unjustly, that they know most about their own job; and just as naturally, where, as formerly in Malaya, there is a choice between helping the planter or the peasant, agricultural officials tend to do the work that is more obviously useful, and prefer to help the planter rather than the peasant.

But the immaturity of scientific agriculture in the tropics, the lack of continuity in policy and experiment, and the prior claims of planters to assistance are matters of comparatively small importance. A far more serious obstacle to the success of agricultural experts is their ignorance of tropical economy. Everywhere production is a social function. In Europe we are apt to overlook this fact because our methods of production grow out of our established social life, and, because we do not notice it in Europe, we tend to disregard it in the tropics. The agricultural official is usually an expert in scientific agriculture, but one cannot expect him to have an expert knowledge of native social life. That is not his business; he is an agriculturist and not an economist. Consequently he tries to adapt native life to scientific principles instead of adapting scientific principles to native life, and, if the people do not accept his suggestions, he regards them as unreasonable. Under experimental conditions some new crop or new method of cultivation may seem profitable, but under the conditions of village life it must fit in with the established rotation of crops and with the available supplies of water and labour. In Malaya, for instance, if the new strain of paddy, said by the agricultural service to increase the yield by 30%, had given corresponding results in practical experience, it is difficult to believe that during the next five years the area under rice would have remained practically constant. In Burma at one time there was a suggestion that sugar palms should be cut down or taxed out of existence, the demand on fuel for sugar boiling was considered uneconomic; fortunately before much harm had been done, it was discovered that palm trees were a stand-by of the cultivator against famine, because drought does not affect the yield until the following year. Similarly, in Africa, 'agricultural experts are becoming more chary of introducing sudden changes in African agricultural technique, for, they say, Europeans lack knowledge of local conditions, and the indiscriminate application of European technique, such as the use of the plough, has in some places had disastrous results'.[1] 'An examination of the present methods used by natives to produce food or cash crops will reveal a planned effort, the balance of which may easily be upset by ill-considered innovations....Such a system is of proved value in native eyes, and is peculiarly adapted to native conditions of life; it needs careful study before improvements can be recommended which are not only sound in themselves but will appeal to the cultivators.'[2] These things lie outside the province of agricultural science, and are not within the competence of experts.

[1] Wilson, p. 118.   [2] *African Survey*, p. 960.

In other matters not only the agricultural expert but the individual cultivator is helpless, and even the whole village, working as a common unit, can do nothing. Production is a social function that extends beyond the village. In Malaya, as we have noticed, it has been recognized that the problem of making rice cultivation profitable requires the co-operation of numerous departments. (This raises the question of departmentalism, which we shall have to examine more generally.) Another illustration of the wide range of what may appear simple agricultural problems may be found in the marketing of crops. In Burma groundnut, and new varieties of beans and onions spread rapidly, without instigation from the agricultural service, because they found a market and were profitable. But attempts by the agricultural service to introduce chickpea, chillies and tomatoes where there was no market, met with failure, and the cultivators lost their time and labour. Tomatoes are widely grown and in one district cultivators were induced to grow a more productive variety. They obtained larger crops but could not sell them, because the flavour did not appeal to the Burman palate, and there was no local European market. Again, millers wanted a special variety of paddy. The agricultural experts produced a variety to meet their wants, and found cultivators to grow it. But it needed a special adaptation of the milling machinery, and this was impracticable unless the new variety was available in quantities requiring the co-operation of many cultivators over a wide area, so that those who grew it had to accept a lower rate and not, as they had been led to expect, a higher rate for their produce. Every such misadventure shakes confidence.

For these and other reasons the possibility of increasing native agricultural production through the assistance of an agricultural service are very limited. Similar obstacles beset the veterinary and other services. In general, economic services can increase production only where they appeal to the desire of gain by enabling the people *as individuals* to make more money; even this, as will appear below, does not always imply greater welfare. Many improvements, however, as we have seen, are profitable to individuals only through co-operative or collective action, and many, though possibly tending to increase the total volume of production, are prejudicial to the peoples as individuals. In such cases it is necessary either to appeal to some motive other than the desire of gain, or to employ compulsion. An appeal to social welfare requires conditions that are not easily fulfilled, and becomes more difficult with the increasing 'atomization' of native social life; ordinarily therefore a remedy is sought in compulsion.

The resort to compulsion for improving output raises new difficulties. Where the expert aims at helping the cultivator to earn more, both have a common object, and the results are readily apparent and can be measured by the standard of profit, which both recognize. If the expert tells the cultivator that some new variety will give a larger yield or fetch a better price, the results soon test the value of his counsel. It is a different matter when experts recommend measures that may possibly improve production in general over a long period, but require time to test their value and, in the first instance, entail trouble or loss to individuals.[1] If they advocate the eradication of dangerous weeds, the use of chemicals for spraying, the destruction of diseased crops, the cutting down of oil palms to protect the market, the inoculation of cattle at the risk of death, the castration of undesirable sires, or the slaughter of cattle to prevent infection, the benefits are distant and uncertain, and the disadvantages immediate and obvious. In such matters they cannot expect the co-operation of the people, but must rely on inspection by a costly staff of numerous subordinates on low pay, ignorant and probably corrupt. Under indirect rule they may enlist the help of native chieftains, but this, like all attempts to employ the chieftains as agents of western policy, tends to undermine traditional authority. Finally, the success of measures of this kind depends not on blind obedience but on genuine acceptance through a recognition of their value. If the regulations intended to promote efficiency are sound, one would expect Europeans to comply with them more readily than natives, yet it seems that in some matters there is least progress on European estates, 'where control is much more difficult to exercise'.[2]

Measures to make production more profitable may gain acceptance if in the long run they show a profit to individuals, even though entailing a temporary loss; it is true also that, so long as a communal sentiment survives, individuals may acquiesce in personal loss for the benefit of the community. In time, if possibly a long time, the value of such measures can be demonstrated, and assessed in terms of money. But it is a different matter to increase the production of unprofitable crops. In such cases the agricultural service and the cultivators have no common standard. If it is difficult and dangerous to interfere in native economy where output and profit, debt and land

---

[1] *African Survey*, pp. 912, 934, 937.   [2] *Ib.* p. 970.

alienation provide comparatively simple tests of the results, the objections are much stronger where experts run counter to the profit motive, and where their recommendations are based, not on agricultural or veterinary science, but on western views as to the nature and purpose of tropical economy. The attempt has often been made and often, perhaps invariably, failed. In Java in the reaction against the Culture system 'officials were so zealous in promoting the cultivation of rice rather than export crops as to insist on the cultivation of long-lived paddy, even where the soil or water supply was unsuitable'.[1] In Malaya, rice land was found to be going out of cultivation although regulations enforcing the cultivation of rice had been imposed for over thirty years. To-day history is repeating itself in Africa. 'The expansion in the growth of marketable crops has seemed to be leading to a dangerous reduction in subsistence crops', and 'there is to-day a much clearer recognition of the need for organizing subsistence production.' Accordingly provisions for the encouragement of subsistence crops have been framed in Northern Rhodesia, Tanganyika and Uganda.[2] Whether they will have greater success in Africa than in Java or Malaya time will show. They are unlikely to strengthen the authority of the native dignitaries enforcing them, or to foster affection towards the western Government responsible for preventing cultivators from turning their labours to the most profitable account; nor are they likely to make the agricultural service popular or to facilitate its work in other matters.

Moreover, in directing economic activities along these lines, it is hard to escape bias, and still harder to escape the suspicion of bias. When Europeans try to 'prevent the unwise extension of the growth of economic crops',[3] they are inevitably exposed to the unpleasant suggestion that they are chiefly considering western interests. We have seen that, in Malaya, it was the loss sustained by Government and the planters through the neglect of subsistence crops, that stimulated activity in promoting rice cultivation. In Africa interest in food crops grew with the need for healthy labour. Measures to encourage subsistence crops may easily be interpreted as meant to discourage unwelcome competition, and the more so because at various times the planting interest has, in fact, opposed the native cultivation of sugar, rubber and coffee. Even with the best intentions

[1] *Netherlands India*, p. 167.
[2] *African Survey*, p. 631; *Britain and Her Dependencies*, p. 23.
[3] *African Survey*, pp. 635, 887, 978.

it is obviously no easy matter to decide whether the extension of cultivation for the market is wise or unwise, and, in view of the generally inadequate acquaintance with native social and economic life and the deficiency and inaccuracy of tropical statistics, the material for a sound decision is unlikely to be available.

The foregoing remarks deal mainly with native agriculture, but this is the chief occupation in the tropics and has received most attention from colonial administrations. Similar considerations apply to other economic services intended to promote native enterprise. Undoubtedly native production grows, and often very rapidly, under western rule. But this is the natural result of greater security of life and property, and of the opening up of new markets, and in the past it has grown rapidly without the help of economic services, as the stimulus given by western rule to the desire of gain has been sufficient. The application of modern scientific methods to native enterprise should make it more efficient. That is the function of economic services. In practice, however, their contribution to the increase of production is confined within narrow limits. They can increase production only by making it more profitable to individuals and for various reasons, some of which we have noticed, this is rarely possible except in such matters as the introduction of new crops, which does not call for expert knowledge. Economic services can and do render much help to western enterprise, and they are useful instruments of progress; but they can do comparatively little to improve native enterprise. Thus the argument that development is necessary to provide funds for economic services in the interest of native enterprise is of doubtful validity and requires closer scrutiny than it usually receives.

4. ECONOMIC SERVICES AND WELFARE

Unless economic services make native production more efficient, they obviously must be ineffective in enhancing welfare. But they may promote efficiency by increasing production or in other ways without contributing to native welfare, and may even have contrary results. In Malaya, so far as the agricultural service enabled cultivators to obtain a larger yield, it did not enable them to make a greater profit. One obstacle was a ring of Chinese mill owners.[1] 'The Malay had no option save to sell at the price offered by the middleman

[1] Mills, pp. 255, 261.

who bought for delivery to the mills.' The Government accordingly built a rice mill in order to break the combine. (One cannot help noticing the contrast between the forceful action taken against a Chinese combine in Malaya and the tolerance of European combines in Burma.) But this touched only the fringe of the problem. From 40 to 90 % of the cultivators were not free to sell their crop in the open market because they were in debt either to Indian moneylenders or to Chinese shopkeepers. Similar conditions obtain generally throughout the tropics wherever the promotion of trade and native enterprise is a main object of policy.

We have seen how, in Africa, throughout the ages tropical peoples have been ready to accept new crops. But 'these early introductions were incorporated with the system of shifting cultivation and the staple diet became a form of rough porridge made from one or other of the grains or from cassava root, ground between stones or pounded into a mortar, and supplemented by a relish of vegetables, meat or milk'. Similarly 'the introduction of cassava and sweet potatoes by the Portuguese conferred an inestimable boon on many tribes by providing them with a famine crop which will flourish under conditions unfavourable to grain crops'.[1] The introduction of these new crops enriched native social life. But where native society has been brought into economic contact with the modern world, the introduction of new crops has a contrary result. In Burma the introduction of groundnut led to the substitution of groundnut oil for sesamum oil because, although less palatable, it is cheaper; cultivators sold their more valuable sesamum and used groundnut oil instead for cooking. Similarly in Java cassava tends to replace rice.[2] Native society has been unable to resist the economic process of natural selection by the survival of the cheapest, and the introduction of new crops has not enriched but has impoverished native life. One finds, of course, the same thing in the West, where potatoes have often displaced more nutritious edibles.

The purpose of economic services is to make production more efficient, and they tend accordingly to concentrate on export crops.[3] On the principle of the local division of function, the production of crops for export contributes to efficiency. Also it encourages trade and provides Government with revenue. But the profits from increased production go mostly to foreign middlemen and merchants; so far

[1] *African Survey*, p. 883.   [2] *Netherlands India*, p. 321.
[3] *Britain and Her Dependencies*, p. 23.

as they remain with the natives, economic development may enrich a few but, unless kept under control, impoverishes the people in general and detracts from welfare by the disintegration of native social life. To seek a remedy by multiplying economic services is like casting out devils in the name of Satan, for they expedite the process, and, like public works, merely enhance the need for social services.

5. SOCIAL SERVICES: PROTECTION

Wherever economic forces have been released by the application of reason to the conduct of social life, it has been found necessary in the general interest to protect those who are adversely affected by the consequences. This is the key note of the long conflict between Capital and Labour. In the West Greece liberated reason from the restraint of custom; Rome substituted the stronger rule of law for the rule of custom; Christianity furnished a moral principle stronger than the rule of law for keeping rational activities within the bounds of social welfare. The happy fusion of these principles in the Renascence allowed a high degree of freedom without disorganizing society. It allowed the freer use of capital in the production of wealth, and there evolved the type of social organization often described as capitalist, or capitalism. But these terms are often loosely used, and it is important to be clear as to their meaning. Human labour applied to natural resources produces a surplus beyond what is needed for sustenance. This surplus, if stored, is wealth. Wealth applied to the production of more wealth is capital. Thus capital may be regarded as disembodied economic energy. Capitalism may be defined as the form of social organization in which economic forces are predominant or, at least, conspicuously prominent. Such a society may be defined as capitalist. But the term capitalist is used also to signify the owner or employer of capital, and is usually confined to those who own or employ capital on a large scale. Thus there may be a capitalist society in which economic forces are predominant without capitalists who are owners or employers of large capital; and there may be capitalists, owners or employers of capital, in a society which is not capitalist in its general character. The neglect of these distinctions often leads to confusion.

In Europe the principle of economic freedom grew out of social life, and a homogeneous society has been able by its inherent vitality, though not without much tribulation, to gain an ever-doubtful victory over the forces of disruption. In the tropics, however, economic freedom was no natural growth but the exotic seed of a plural society, unable to protect itself. Usually the first stage in the transition from a policy of *laissez-faire* to one of constructive effort on behalf of native welfare can be recognized by attempts to protect the people against the economic forces liberated under western rule. As we have noticed, development by native enterprise and by western enterprise react differently on native social life. Each requires its appropriate method of protection. In the former case, with natives cultivating for the market, economic forces attack the native social structure from within, and the problem is to protect them in the produce market and to assure them of the fruits of their labour and suitable conditions of occupancy. In the latter case, with natives employed in capitalist enterprise, economic forces act in the first instance from without, and the problem is to protect them in the labour market and to secure for them sufficient wages and suitable conditions of employment.

6. Native Enterprise and the Land

In the course of development by native enterprise, one conspicuous feature is the growth of agricultural indebtedness; this is indeed a natural and almost inevitable consequence of native cultivation for the market. Rapid development demands that cultivators shall borrow money to take up land and hire labour, but circumstances encourage them to borrow more than they require and more than they can repay.[1] This is often ascribed to the shiftlessness of cultivators, or the wickedness of moneylenders, who deliberately entangle the cultivator in debt so as to leave him with no more than a bare subsistence.[2] It is true that the grant of easy credit to the limit of the security available is profitable to the moneylender, who has least trouble with large loans, but it is profitable also to the exporter, who can obtain steadier supplies at lower prices, to the importer, who can sell more goods to cultivators with more cash than they know how to use, and to the banks which finance the whole series of transactions. Easy credit greases all the wheels of the economic mechanism. We have seen the result in Burma. The indebtedness of cultivators in India is notorious. In the Philippines, Malaya, Fiji, Ceylon, Cyprus, Egypt, Zanzibar and other parts of Africa,[3] everywhere indeed where the people cultivate for sale rather than for the family, the burden

[1] *African Survey*, p. 885. [2] *ISC*, I, 275.
[3] *African Survey*, p. 872; *Britain and Her Dependencies*, p. 25; Mills, p. 276.

of debt lies heavy on them. Indebtedness leads naturally to the transfer of land from peasants to large owners, and then to rack-renting. Protection accordingly takes two forms: one is to protect the people against the loss of land and excessive rents; the other is to protect them against debt.

In the tropics generally the western idea of property in land is a modern innovation. Landlords, so far as they existed, were also quasi-feudal lords over the people, and they were more concerned to multiply the number of their followers than the area of their estates. In western feudalism the people went with the land, but in the tropics the land went with the people, who did not pay rent to their overlord but a customary tribute and services. Where there were no landlords, the peasant might enjoy an hereditary title to individual occupation, subject usually to the interests of his whole family group and to the needs of the village or tribal unit. These conditions are inconsistent with economic development by native enterprise, and cultivation for the market gives land and its produce a new value. Cultivators, inspired by economic motives, borrow money in the hope of earning more, and lose their land to moneylenders and large landowners, often absentees. Landowners, old and new, inspired by economic motives, screw up the pitch of rents. Land alienation and rack-renting attract attention, partly because they are the most obvious symptoms of distress, partly because they foster discontent and political unrest, and, of course, to some extent from humanitarian sentiment. The matter first came prominently to notice in India, where there have been various attempts to restrict mortgage and transfer, 'but these measures are easy neither to frame nor to execute', and they seem to have had little success. Similar attempts have failed in Malaya.[1] Ordinarily they are based on the idea of protecting the cultivator against himself, whereas the real trouble is that he needs protection against the economic forces dominating the whole social life of a plural society. In Netherlands India the cultivator has been saved from the disaster that has overwhelmed his fellow in British India by regulations prohibiting the alienation of native land to foreigners and confirming the rule of native customary law in land transactions. This, however, is possible only where development by western enterprise allows or requires the preservation of native authority and native customs.

Where development by western enterprise is the prime object

[1] *African Survey*, p. 873; Mills, p. 251.

of colonial policy, land alienation need present no problem, except as regards the lands actually taken up for western enterprise, and even debt may not be serious. Thus, in large parts of Africa, 'so far conditions have not favoured the growth of moneylending; the general restrictions imposed on the sale of native land to non-natives, as well as the limitations which some territories have placed on the giving of credit to natives by non-natives have militated against it'.[1] It is sometimes suggested in British publications that there is little indebtedness in Netherlands India. But that is a mistake. The Dutch have protected the native against the worst result of debt, the loss of land, but not against incurring debt. In the development of British India and Burma by native enterprise the merchant gave out advances to secure produce; in Java the planter gave advances to secure labour. The actual moneylender is usually a middleman, in the Tropical Far East mostly Indian or Chinese, who reaps some of the profit that would otherwise be divided between natives and Europeans, with a lion's share to the latter. In such circumstances exporters of produce have a common interest with cultivators. Moreover, as is conspicuously illustrated in Burma, the transfer of land to people whose sole interest is to exact the highest rent, tends to reduce the outturn. Thus everywhere in the Tropical Far East we find sympathy for the cultivators in the clutches of middlemen: in Indo-China 'the chetty is a plague', in the Dutch Indies 'the foreign asiatic is worse than ten epidemics', in Burma the wiles of both *chettyars* and Chinese were denounced so far back as the early eighties. Both practical and humanitarian considerations demand a solution for the problem of indebtedness.

The favourite remedy for debt is the encouragement of co-operative credit societies. But this is no cure for debt, and it may quite possibly aggravate the disease which is the chief cause of debt, the disintegration of society by economic forces. It is no cure for debt, because the success of co-operative credit requires a genuine acceptance of co-operative principles, and this is a slow process, while debt increases daily. It tends to aggravate disintegration, because the principles on which it rests are contrary to those which form the basis of native social life and, indeed, of social life in general. The suggestion that co-operative credit accords with native ideas as being communal in character is mistaken.[2] The village community embraces all the inhabitants of the village in a common bond for all the purposes

---

[1] *African Survey*, p. 872.   [2] *Ib.* p. 1482.

of social life; the co-operative credit society includes only selected individuals who unite for specific economic ends. If a whole village were transformed into a co-operative credit society, it would at the same time be transformed from a village into a business concern. The spread of co-operative principles is much to be desired; it would encourage thrift and train the people in modern business methods, and mark a forward step towards the reintegration of native economy, the economic aspect of their social life. But, unless the limitations of the co-operative movement are appreciated, it is apt to be perverted from an instrument of native welfare into an instrument of economic progress. Ordinarily cultivators can borrow at a lower rate from a co-operative credit society than from a middleman. This should reduce the cost of production of native crops, and increase the margin between cost and yield. But competition in the market transfers the profit from the cultivators to the firms engaged in the export of tropical produce. Co-operative societies provide an attractive investment for banks and private individuals. The elimination of the middleman removes a possible competitor to western firms, and has political reactions by hindering the growth of a politically conscious middle class. In practice the multiplication of co-operative credit machinery usually outruns the spread of co-operative principles, and the co-operative credit service, established in the cause of native welfare, serves chiefly to promote the interests of western enterprise. This is the natural outcome of confounding two distinct problems: the social problem of training the people in modern business methods, and the economic problem of providing a remedy for agricultural debt.

In Netherlands India this distinction has been recognized, though by accident rather than design. One aspect of the Ethical movement was an attempt to foster co-operative credit. This made slow progress. The remedy for debt is to provide the cultivator with as much credit as he requires, and no more than he requires, at the lowest rate that economic conditions allow. The co-operative movement failed to solve this economic problem because the people, though quick to borrow money, were slow to accept new ideas. The Government held the view that the chief need of the cultivators was sound credit, and the co-operative societies were accordingly transformed into State banks of various types. This has been justified on the ground that if the economic problem can be solved, it will then be possible to foster co-operative credit as a social institution. Of recent years, therefore, co-operative societies have been established in addition to the State banks. How far the State banks have been successful in solving the economic problem is a matter of debate. The successful working of such banks demands a restriction on private credit. In Netherlands India this is provided in some measure by the application of native customary law to native lands, which prevents their alienation for debt to foreign moneylenders. But apparently the banks, nominally for agriculturists, find most of their clients among townsfolk; and some critics allege that the people borrow as much from private moneylenders as before, in addition to what is borrowed from the banks. It would appear then that the restrictions on private moneylending in Netherlands India are inadequate, but the banks do at least provide facilities for individuals to obtain credit on sound lines.

The State pawnshops in Netherlands India provide similar facilities for individuals, mainly townsfolk, to obtain temporary accommodation on a small scale. These also were an outcome of the Ethical movement, originating with the same man who started the early co-operative credit movement. Formerly the pawnshops were in the hands of the Chinese, who managed them merely with a view to profit. The pawn-brokers were cunning in sharp practice; the terms for loans were exorbitant, and the arrangements for the safe custody of pledges were unsatisfactory, while the shops were widely believed to be used as opium dens. All this has been changed, and the shops are not only a public benefit but yield a handsome revenue.

Both State banks and pawnshops illustrate the fact that the promotion of welfare does not necessitate the introduction of foreign capital. In fact they require practically no capital as, by beginning on a small scale, they can provide the capital for further development. All they require is a knowledge of the people and their economic situation, the will to promote their welfare and, above all, patience. They differ from co-operative credit societies mainly in three points. They appeal merely to economic motives, common to all men, whereas the co-operative movement urges social ideals easier to preach than to practise. They meet the requirements of individuals as such, whereas co-operative societies only meet the individual requirements of those who are willing to combine for common action. And in meeting individual requirements they fulfil their purpose, whereas the co-operative movement requires common *social* action for common *economic* ends which are prejudicial to common social life and thereby hinder common social action. Credit institutions, like public works, may give the people new opportunities of improving their condition, and, if well managed, may give some protection against economic forces, which public works, even irrigation works for the benefit of native enterprise, do not attempt. For the relation between the co-operative movement and State credit, we may find a parallel in the relation between economic services aiming to increase collective production and those aiming to increase individual production. We have noticed that ordinarily the former fail because it is impracticable to obtain collective action by a sufficient number over a sufficient area, whereas the latter may meet with some success. Yet even individuals who take advantage of the new opportunities to produce more, ordinarily receive no lasting benefit, because they are unable to withstand the economic pressure of the environment. Co-operative credit and State credit are alike intended to strengthen them against this pressure. Experience in Netherlands India suggests that State credit has better chances of success. But it is important to appreciate the conditions of success. The State banks in Netherlands India have achieved useful results because the land policy protects cultivators against the impact of the West, and not because the banks protect them against the natural consequences of this impact. Similarly the pawnshops have been useful because the State monopoly of pawnbroking protects the people against the action of economic forces, and not merely against their natural consequences. State credit has no virtue in itself. It may, as has been charged against State banks in Netherlands India, merely increase the volume of indebtedness, and it is liable to become just an instrument of economic progress instead of helping to promote welfare. As an instrument of welfare it is of value only so far as it is accompanied by other measures in a comprehensive welfare policy.

7. Western Enterprise and Labour

The problems arising out of tropical development by western enterprise have a different character, and are more readily apparent and more urgent. In some cases it may lead to agrarian distress, but this is found chiefly where lands available for native occupation have been curtailed by the grant of large estates for European settlement. Such conditions present special difficulties. Formerly in Burma waste lands were granted or leased for European enterprise, but this resulted in the oppression of the natives, both on the estates and in their neighbourhood, and the concessions remained uncultivated long after the surrounding land had been brought under the plough by natives. That seems to be the general result. In Netherlands India the large estates, created at the beginning of the nineteenth century, were an endless source of trouble and unrest; much of the land long remained unworked, the owners were often absentees, aiming solely at profit and with no personal interest in the welfare of the occupants who were more grievously oppressed than elsewhere. Moreover, the grants tended to pass into the hands of foreign Europeans and orientals, and during the present century this stimulated the Government to adopt a policy of gradually resuming them. In Africa the difficulties arising out of western agricultural settlements are notorious, and European settlers, when faced by even a remote prospect of their eventual displacement by foreign orientals, have carried opposition to the point of threatening armed resistance.[1] The possibility of European settlement in the tropics, however, is confined to particular localities, and it presents, though with special characters, features common to development by western enterprise in general. The outstanding problem in regions developed by western enterprise is not directly concerned with land-holding and debt, but with the relations between western enterprise and native labour.

The first condition of the economic development of backward areas is an adequate supply of labour. Even native enterprise creates a new demand for labour, and we have seen in Burma how this demand has led to a seasonal supply and to the industrialization of agricultural production. But the expansion of native enterprise is gradual, and it can obtain much of its labour from customary sources and dispose of its produce along established routes. Western enterprise, whether in mines or plantations, being usually situated in thinly peopled tracts, requires a large volume of labour quickly, and also requires new and more rapid means of transport; there is a sudden and large demand for labour both on private enterprise and public works. The Government must provide this labour. The provision of labour is no longer necessary when free labour becomes available, but free labour needs protection. Then, as employers gradually realize that healthy and intelligent labour is less costly, attention is directed to improving the conditions of work. Thus in general, labour policy in tropical dependencies passes through three stages: the provision of labour; the protection of labour against abuse; and the promotion of labour welfare.

[1] *African Survey*, p. 165.

The Provision of Labour. The provision of labour by Government might seem to come under the head of economic rather than of social service. But, so long as it is necessary, it is usually regarded, not wholly without justification, as an instrument of welfare. 'To pierce the darkness shrouding entire populations in Africa', said Leopold II in 1876, 'would be a crusade worthy of this century of progress.'[1] At the beginning of the present century Chamberlain was a leading champion of this crusade. The native would not advance in civilization until he had been 'convinced of the necessity and dignity of labour'...'I think it is a good thing' he said, 'for the native to be industrious, and by every means in our power we have to teach them to work.'[2] For a quarter of a century this remained the keynote of British labour policy in the tropics. Even sympathetic officials acquiesced in compulsion, 'in the genuine belief that no advancement was possible unless the native accustomed himself to regular labour', and officers charged with a special care for native welfare have urged the educational value of compulsory labour on European enterprises.[3] It is true that, if tropical peoples are to live in the modern world, they must adapt themselves to the modern world. But it is true also that the use of compulsion to provide labour engenders abuse, and that the labour it provides is inefficient. It is pressed furthest and is most harmful where the Government has an economic interest in production, and in the Belgian Congo, as in the later days of the Culture system in Java, the use of compulsion to obtain labour defeated its own ends by killing off the supply of labourers.[4] General experience has shown that compulsion tends to reduce the labour supply and to furnish incompetent and unwilling labourers, yet employers, accustomed to obtaining labour through the State, prefer this easy though inefficient way of meeting their requirements and, long after the provision of labour has become unnecessary, continue to urge the educational value of labour as an argument for Government assistance in recruiting it. Now, however, that compulsion is no longer needed, it is condemned as generally as it was formerly supported. But the fact that, so long as compulsion was thought expedient, it was justified, like slavery, as an instrument of welfare suggests the need for cautious examination of measures now recommended on the same ground.

---

[1] MacDonell, J. de C., *King Leopold II* (1905), p. 184.
[2] Boulger, D. C., *The Reign of Leopold II* (1925), II, 121.
[3] *African Survey*, pp. 640 ff.   [4] Frankel, p. 37.

Official activity in the provision of labour assumes various forms; it embraces compulsion, direct and indirect, the recruitment of labour by the Government or with official support, and the inclusion of a penal sanction in labour contracts. Under all these heads much may be learned from Netherlands India, where the provision of labour for development by western enterprise dates from the beginning of the nineteenth century.

Direct compulsion has been little used except to provide labour for the State. At various times compulsion has been employed to recruit men for State economic enterprise, for the army and, chiefly, for public works. Where, as in Java under the Culture system and in Africa under the chartered companies, the Government is at once sovereign and merchant, it is naturally tempted to use political control for the advancement of its economic interests, and is not too rigid in restricting compulsory labour to purely administrative purposes.[1] The Culture system in Java is the classic example of compulsion on State enterprise. Van den Bosch justified compulsion on the ground that it would instil habits of industry among the people and, by increasing production, would enable them to earn more. For a time they did in fact make more money, but within a few years a series of famines devastated the tracts that were richest in natural resources, and the people, instead of being inured to industry, acquired the habit of working only under compulsion. Moreover, the system was inefficient because the officials charged with supervising production had not sufficient knowledge either of agriculture or of the people. What killed it, however, was neither its harshness nor its inefficiency, but the growth of private enterprise, and, when private enterprise was ready to take over production, public opinion was quick to appreciate the defects of State enterprise. The system was advocated as an instrument of welfare, it was applied as an instrument of progress, and finally condemned as both pernicious to native welfare and a barrier to progress. The compulsory recruitment of tropical peoples for military service has also been found uneconomic. Only a small proportion can stand the rigour of modern army life, and the withdrawal of large numbers from the labour market conflicts with the demands of private enterprise; 'in view of the shortage of men for internal development such a utilization of man-power would have the effect of economic self-annihilation'.[2]

[1] *African Survey*, p. 1314.   [2] *Ib.* pp. 627, 1121.

Ordinarily then, the main use of compulsory labour has been on public works. Throughout the tropics it was formerly the practice under native rule to obtain such labour as might be required for the common purposes of the tribe or village, or for the chieftains or the State, by calling on the people to supply it. 'It was perhaps natural that the early administrations should see in the use of this "communal" labour an easy method by which to provide for the making of roads or for the transport necessary for official purposes. It became, indeed, the usual method of securing labour for official or public needs.'[1] In Burma and other lands developed by native enterprise, compulsory labour was soon abandoned as interfering too greatly with cultivation. But in Java, as in other countries developed by western enterprise, it has been freely employed. One limitation on its use is the difficulty of securing by compulsion the volume of labour required for large capital works. In Java paid labour was first used on the harbour and defence works in Sourabaya in 1849, when modern Liberal ideas were in the air. It was found so much more efficient and economical that, in 1851, the use of paid labour on all public buildings was enjoined, and in 1857 this order was extended to all public works. In practice, however, it was still used to some extent, especially on irrigation works. Meanwhile Liberal sentiment in favour of free labour was gathering momentum, and was reinforced by the practical consideration that the use of compulsory labour on public works reduced the supply available for the rapidly growing demands of private enterprise. Attempts to restrict labour for the State to seasons when it was not required by private employers proved unsatisfactory, and at the end of the century the system of compulsion was abolished.

Experience during the nineteenth century in Java has been repeated during the present century in Africa. The various administrations used 'communal' labour for local road construction and also needed labour for other purposes, 'such as the construction of railways, or major roads for long distance transport, which were outside the range of even an extended definition of communal labour, more especially since they at times involved the absence of labourers from their homes for considerable periods'.[2] Imported labour was expensive, and the more costly because so many died. Ordinarily, for the improvement of communications, the use of impressed African labour was imperative, and was justified as a moral discipline and a source

[1] *African Survey*, p. 611.   [2] *Ib.* p. 613.

of future welfare. During the present century, under Dutch rule also, compulsory labour, though no longer necessary in Java, was freely used in the Outer Provinces as part of the Ethical policy of promoting native welfare; 'without strong rule, without order and security, no ethical policy'.[1] Compulsion was indeed used so freely as to provoke disorder and unrest. Of recent years, however, throughout tropical regions in general, there has been less need for direct compulsion to procure labour for public works, and now it is generally regarded with disfavour as both prejudicial to social welfare and also un-economic.[2]

Although direct compulsion has been used chiefly for the State, indirect compulsion has frequently been adopted as a means of providing labour for private employment. The usual methods have been by the restriction of natives to reserves and by taxation. Both these expedients tend to reduce the supply of labour. The curtailment of native land discourages the growth of population, and taxation encourages migration. There are technical difficulties in imposing differential rates of taxation and 'the effect of a rigid flat rate is to drive the taxpaying male population to industrial and urban centres, and consequently to disorganize native society to such an extent that, on several occasions, governments have felt obliged to reduce the amount to be paid by men who are without resources other than their labour'. Moreover, men who are compelled to work merely in order to pay the tax, stop work as soon as they have earned enough to pay it, and they fail therefore to acquire efficiency as labourers. Experience shows that 'the shopkeeper probably provides a far greater incentive than the tax-gatherer'.[3] Indirect compulsion tends accordingly to follow direct compulsion into desuetude.

Compulsion, direct or indirect, is however less effective in providing a supply of labour than the employment of a special recruiting agency. In this, as in other problems, Netherlands India has led the way. Labour for private enterprise may be recruited by the State, either directly or through native chieftains, or by unofficial agents, with or without State assistance. Recruitment is often distinguished from compulsion, but 'a State agency for recruitment inevitably involves some degree of pressure', and is open to many of the objections brought against other forms of compulsion.[4] From the standpoint of employers, moreover, State intervention is undesirable as

---

[1] Gonggrijp, cited *Netherlands India*, p. 237.
[3] *Ib.* pp. 596, 648.
[2] *African Survey*, p. 628.
[4] *Ib.* p. 651.

it is usually accompanied by unwelcome restrictions on the terms and conditions of employment. It was on these grounds that the Government of Burma formerly rejected proposals that it should revive the former practice of official recruitment, and fifty years later mill-owners protested against suggestions that the recruitment of labour should be supervised.[1] Even where recruitment is nominally free, private employers may utilize the assistance of native chieftains, and, during the Liberal regime in Java, when officials were no longer allowed to take part in the provision of labour, the planters commonly entered village headmen on the pay roll as servants of the estate in order to secure their influence in recruiting villagers. Usually, however, labour for western enterprise must be imported from some distant region where it is more plentiful, and in such circumstances special arrangements for recruiting are required. Naturally a private agent, dependent for his livelihood on the number of recruits, is less scrupulous than an official in his relations with both employers and labourers; he will supply employers with anyone whom they will take, and entice recruits with advances and specious promises. Although the substitution of private for official recruitment may supply more and cheaper labour, it is in some respects a change for the worse; the supply of labour is doubtful, the men engaged are often immature or weaklings, and the cost per head is high. Moreover, recruitment causes a local shortage in the area of supply; recruitment for South Africa causes a shortage in Rhodesia which has to be made good by recruitment for Rhodesia further inland, and so on.[2] This stimulates opposition among employers to the system of recruitment. Firms with large capital resources can make their own arrangements for obtaining labour, and thereby ensure a more regular supply of better labourers at less expense. Accordingly the strongest firms, best able to influence the policy of Government, add their weight to humanitarian protests against the evil of recruitment, and advocate stringent regulation.

The question of recruitment is closely linked up with the penal sanction, imposing a legal penalty for the breach of labour contracts. This protects the employer against strikes and desertion, and thereby reacts on the demand for labour. In Java such provisions originated in local police regulations dating from 1829, which were designed to ease the transition from servile to free labour in domestic service.

[1] *RAB*, 1880–1, p. 52; *RCLI*, x, Pt 1, p. 173.
[2] *African Survey*, pp. 648 ff.

When similar provisions were embodied in the General Police Regulation of 1872, they attracted the attention of Liberals in the States-General, who obtained their cancellation in 1879. In Java the penal sanction was no longer required as there was by this time an abundant supply of wage labour, but the new tobacco plantations in Sumatra were dependent on labour imported under contract, and their needs were recognized by an Ordinance of 1880, providing for the imposition of penalties. The facilities thus granted were abused, and about 1900 an enquiry, held as the result of Socialist agitation, exposed 'a general collapse of morality'.[1] An attempt to mend conditions by stricter enforcement of the law proved unavailing, as the legal effect of the penal sanction favoured employers. Accordingly labour policy, hitherto directed towards providing labour, turned gradually in the direction of protecting it. The means chiefly favoured were a closer supervision over recruitment, the gradual abolition of the penal sanction, and a more precise regulation of the duties of employers and employees, together with machinery for enforcing the regulations. The change may be dated from 1909 when official agents were appointed to recruit Chinese coolies from abroad, and rules were framed to control professional recruiting in Java. As the Government considered a penal sanction necessary to efficient management even on its own tin mines, its abolition was a slow process. But the closer supervision over private recruiting encouraged employers to take the matter into their own hands, and from 1915 various planters' associations established recruiting agencies. Employers came also to recognize the value of trained and voluntary labour; they tried to induce time-expired coolies to return for a further period of service after recruiting friends and followers in their villages. In this way plantation labour assumed a new character. By 1930 it was no longer mostly alien, temporary and recruited by irresponsible recruiting agents, but much of the labour was Javanese and exempt from penal liabilities, and the relations between employer and employed had become more permanent and human. A new Ordinance of 1931 aimed at encouraging these tendencies, and provided among other matters for a gradually increasing minimum of free labour, engaged on contracts without a penal sanction. Almost at the same time the Blaine amendment to the United States Tariff Law of 1930 prohibited the importation of the products of labour employed under a penal sanction, unless otherwise unobtainable in sufficient quantities. This threatened the

---

[1] *Netherlands India*, p. 354; Vandenbosch, p. 282.

Sumatra tobacco planters with the loss of a valuable market, and they announced their intention of recruiting all labour on a voluntary basis. As a moral gesture this was not very convincing since, owing to the depression, there was a surplus of labour on the estates, but it served the purpose of satisfying the customs regulations of the United States. At the same time, penal provisions were also renounced by Government in respect of the coolies, mostly Chinese, on its tin mines. Thanks to the Blaine amendment and the depression, the results attained under the Ordinance of 1931 were greater than had been contemplated and, when it came up for revision in 1936, a further advance was possible. By 1941, the penal sanction had practically disappeared, and on the revision of the Ordinance in that year it was finally abolished.[1]

In British India, where western enterprise has never been of such predominant importance as in Netherlands India, the Workman's Breach of Contract Act was repealed in 1926. But in most British territories in Africa, western enterprise is influential, and penal sanctions are attached to labour offences; though legislation of this type is less conspicuous in West Africa. The accepted view is that 'the complete disappearance of criminal penalties must await the evolution of social and economic conditions which will replace the sanctions which penalties supply'.[2] Conditions are less favourable for its abolition than in Netherlands India, but possibly a stimulus, such as that applied by the United States tariff to tobacco planters in Sumatra, might expedite the process.

But the abolition of the penal sanction need not, and ordinarily does not, improve the position of the labourer. Just as free recruitment needs regulation if it is not to lead to worse abuses than official recruitment, so free labour, unless protected, may be worse off than contract labour. The social and economic conditions which obviate the need for any legal sanction replace it by a more stringent economic sanction, for the legal sanction becomes unnecessary when the supply of labour is in excess of the demand. Javanese coolies working in Sumatra felt safer under a contract, even when it exposed them to penalties, than when working as free labourers. In Netherlands India it was the Blaine amendment that stimulated the tobacco planters to employ free labour, but their example was followed generally because, owing to the labour surplus resulting from the depression, employers 'were able, easily, and with a certain profit to themselves, to make

[1] *Vrij Nederland*, 22 Nov. 1941.   [2] *African Survey*, pp. 659, 664.

good any deficiency in the coolie force by hiring free labourers, in regard to whom they were much less bound with respect to wages and working conditions than they had been in the case of the indentured coolies'.[1] Women are cheaper than men, and the relation between free labour and the rate of wages is illustrated by the fact that between 1930 and 1938 the proportion of female labour among Javanese coolies rose from one-third to one-half. Thus the conditions that allow the abolition of the penal sanction create a greater need for measures to protect labour.

Protection. Compulsory labour and the penal sanction were opposed to Liberal principles, and were especially repugnant to the humanitarian idealism which gave Liberal principles a moral basis. But *laissez-faire* could not provide the necessary labour or cure the evils that Liberal principles condemned, and humanitarian protests remained ineffective until reinforced by the growing power of Labour in European politics. This gave humanitarians the support of an organized party with a practical material interest in improving the conditions of labour in the tropics, especially in occupations competing with industry in Europe. Still more convincing was the logic of facts. Changes in the social structure made the natives more dependent upon wages, and they grew better accustomed to working for western enterprise.[2] Gradually the more far-sighted employers in the tropics came to recognise 'that an improvement in the efficiency of labour offers a possibility of effecting a reduction in the numbers required, and has an important bearing on the costs of production', and they even went ahead of official activities in the care for welfare.[3] But the original impulse came from Europe. It was the Labour Party in the Netherlands that, at the beginning of the century, demanded an enquiry into conditions in Sumatra, and since 1919 the International Labour Office has taken tropical labour under its wing.

The protection of labour demands suitable regulations and adequate machinery for enforcing them. Paper costs nothing, and in this as in other matters tropical administrations tend to proliferate reforms on paper, but as we have already had occasion to observe, one must scrutinize the extent to which reforms on paper are applied in practice.[4] In Netherlands India the scandals in Sumatra led to the appointment of an Inspector of Labour for that region, and in 1908 he was charged with the supervision of recruiting and the operation of the Coolie

[1] Boeke, p. 151. [2] *African Survey*, pp. 651, 655.
[3] *Ib.* pp. 696, 1194. [4] *Ib.* p. 649.

Ordinances. Meanwhile the increase of factories in Java had led in 1905 to the introduction of a Factories Act. Out of these developments there has grown up an elaborate Labour Service. It is only natural that the need for such a service should first be felt in Netherlands India, where western enterprise has been so long established. In British colonies numerous regulations bear witness to the benevolent aspirations of Government; many of them 'have a common characteristic: they avoid laying down definite standards in regard to diet, housing, or medical attendance, and leave in these matters a considerable discretion to inspecting officers', so that their effect depends on the machinery for supervision. As Lord Hailey remarks, 'the efficacy of social legislation as a whole is dependent on the technical inspectorates which are the most significant creation of modern administrative activity.' Yet 'with the exception of Kenya, inspection for the most part has been left to administrative officers' and 'experience shows that their other duties do not always permit them to exercise that close supervision which is essential when large bodies of labour are employed'; they are liable to frequent transfer and know very little of what happens on the estates and mines; and they have an inadequate acquaintance with labour problems.[1] The regulations may be suitable, but there is no machinery to enforce them. It is instructive that in this, as in other aspects of care for labour, the larger enterprises would welcome closer supervision.

But suitable regulations and adequate machinery are not sufficient in themselves for the protection of labour. They have been useful in the West, but chiefly through the efforts of the labourers, organized in trade unions, either by their influence on legislation or by direct action. It has been generally held that tropical labour has little capacity for organization, and employers have reckoned this a merit. In Netherlands India, however, conditions favoured the growth of trade unions. The policy of segregating the people under their own chieftains and protecting them against the impact of the West, required the importation of Europeans of humble social status and on low pay to perform tasks for which under a different policy natives might have been trained. These men brought with them their labour politics and unionism. That was probably one reason why colonial problems attracted the attention of Socialists earlier in the Netherlands than elsewhere. It was certainly the reason why trade unionism reached the native world in Java. Europeans were linked

[1] *African Survey*, pp. 678–9.

up with the natives through the large body of Indo-Europeans and in 1908 the railway staff, comprising all three groups, formed the first trade union. Before long purely native unions were formed, at first in Government service and from 1915 in private employment. By 1918 there were over twenty unions with upwards of 70,000 members, and by 1931, 106 unions with 111,344 members, including 46 nation unions with over 85,000 members. In Africa 'natives are to a great extent debarred from forming unions to protect their interests, and legislation makes it an offence for contract natives to strike or withhold their services without giving notice of the termination of their contracts'.[1] Experience has shown that some collective means for the ventilation of grievances is desirable, as otherwise they may remain unknown to the authorities until disorders break out, but it has been questioned whether trade unions can serve any useful purpose in territories where the State has assumed a full responsibility for working conditions. The answer to this question depends on the extent to which the State discharges the responsibilities that it has assumed, and, in view of the lack of special machinery to enforce protective regulations, and the general ignorance of administrative officers regarding labour questions and conditions, there would seem to be a wide field in which the organization of labour could be useful.

In the West labour disputes turn chiefly on the point of wages. It may be assumed that better wages will enhance both efficiency and welfare, and that a standard minimum wage will ensure a reasonable level of subsistence. In the tropics the rewards of labour are governed by different considerations. Low wages seem to reduce the cost of production and, until recently, have been regarded as contributing to economic progress. In Burma the Government subsidized the importation of Indian coolies with a view to bringing down the rate of wages.[2] In Java, up to the end of the nineteenth century, low wages were considered one of the chief assets of the country, and a source of its prosperity. In Africa it is only of recent years that employers have tended to question 'the traditional view of the African labourer as crude man-power, which could be suitably remunerated by a low and undifferentiated scale of pay', and the conditions of development and the free use of pressure to provide labour have resulted in artificially low rates, approximating to the amount required for the support of an unmarried man.[3] Low wages attract capital and encourage

---

[1] *African Survey*, p. 698.   [2] *RAB*, 1882–3, p. 141.
[3] *African Survey*, pp. 696, 710; Frankel, pp. 11, 12.

economic development. But experience has shown that they hinder economic progress and destroy welfare. They destroy welfare because they leave the labourer no margin for maintaining his family at home, and thereby contribute in no small measure to the disorganization of social life; they hinder economic progress because they are too low for physical efficiency and discourage the introduction of machinery. Standard minimum rates have been suggested as a remedy. In Netherlands India minimum wages were fixed for the sugar estates of Java so far back as 1898, and for the plantations in Sumatra a few years later. In Malaya standard wages were fixed in certain districts in 1927, as an indirect outcome of the rise of nationalism in India.[1] Britain and other colonial powers have accepted the Geneva Convention of 1928 for the creation of wage-fixing machinery, and in Africa some Governments have been given the necessary powers, though they have been slow to act on them.[2] Regulations can make the best of existing economic conditions, but they cannot in themselves change the conditions. In Netherlands India wage rates have usually been above the standard rates, but in Africa it would probably be difficult to sanction any minimum wage that did not involve a general rise of wages. Moreover, opinion is divided as to the probable result of higher wages. Even in Europe higher wages do not always increase production or enhance welfare. In the tropics many hold that higher wages encourage labourers to do less work, as generally happens where employment is sought merely to pay taxes. There are also complaints that men who make good money tend to waste it on whatever takes their fancy instead of spending it on their food and families. Employers are naturally reluctant to raise wages if the result is that they lose their men, and, when paying good wages, they want the men to spend the money in ways that will make them more productive workers. There is much force in the argument that high wages do little to promote either development or welfare, but are chiefly beneficial to western manufacturers importing goods, often prejudicial to native economy and social life.

Moreover, there are great practical difficulties in raising wages. Far-sighted employers, actuated by enlightened self-interest may wish to pay good wages, but they cannot risk being undercut by employers who are less scrupulous or less intelligent. Also much of the labour is seasonal or casual. No single employer has any interest in raising the wages of the coolies huddled in the coolie barracks of

[1] Mills, pp. 227-9.   [2] *African Survey*, p. 695.

Rangoon on pay that is far below the level of subsistence. The agricultural labourer is in the worst case of all, for except so far as he may be protected by custom, which soon proves ineffective, he is exposed to the full blast of economic forces, and does not even enjoy the support of European labour. These conditions are inherent in the plural character of tropical economy. As Lord Hailey notes, 'the situation presents features essentially different from those of Europe', where economic development implies that 'new centres grow into organized wholes', and imposes responsibilities on the whole community where the labourers reside.[1] In the plural society of the tropics, however, employers and employees, even though living in the same locality, inhabit different worlds with no common social life. The 'iron law' still holds, and wage levels are determined by conditions in the reservoirs from which the labour supply is drawn. In Malaya any very great increase in wages must wait upon a similar rise in the reservoirs of over-abundant and, therefore, cheap labour in India and China.[2] Conditions in Bangkok and Saigon react on the wages of rice-mill coolies in Rangoon. Similar considerations apply to unskilled labour in Africa. Local action is almost impotent to raise the scale of pay, and any attempt in that direction encounters stiff opposition.

It is much easier to improve the conditions of working than to raise wages. Not even the most acute inspector can fathom the implications of a wages bill, but anyone can see housing, hospitals and schools. Good employers may lose their men by raising wages, but they can retain them by providing food and quarters. These things attract labour and make it more docile and contented. Firms which voluntarily provide amenities with a view to increased efficiency naturally support legislation to impose similar conditions on their competitors, and, as the provision of amenities is costly, such legislation favours big business at the expense of less substantial rivals and tends to limit competition. Also capital has often been invested on the assumption that labour would continue to be available at artificially low rates, thus creating vested interests 'likely to demand measures which would, in fact, ensure a supply of labour on these terms'.[3] Such conditions are especially prevalent in urban areas, where industries depend on the existence of a supply of relatively low-priced labour. This allows employers to claim plausibly that 'the contribution which the workers make to industry and through it to the financial prosperity of the

[1] *African Survey*, pp. 709, 1199.   [2] Mills, p. 249.
[3] Frankel, p. 12.

country, carries with it an equivalent obligation for a recognition by the community of its social obligations towards them', or, in other words, that wages should be subsidized out of public revenue.[1] Although enterprises on a large scale with great capital resources can afford to provide amenities, other firms also want healthy, intelligent and efficient labour on low pay, and welcome State assistance in supplying it. Thus there is a general demand that private enterprise shall be subsidized at the public expense, and although, according to the generally accepted theory of colonial policy, economic development must be encouraged to provide funds for welfare, yet, in practice, funds must be provided for welfare in order to encourage economic development. Thus, with a growing demand for more efficient labour, the State has passed on from providing and protecting labour to promoting the welfare of labour, especially in regard to health and education.

[1] *African Survey*, p. 711.

CHAPTER X

WELFARE: HEALTH AND EDUCATION

1. HEALTH AND PROGRESS

GOOD HEALTH is a condition of both human welfare and economic progress. Most people would agree that, if there is one sphere of human life in which the West can promote greater material welfare in the tropics, it is in the conquest of disease. For whereas western medicine rests on modern science and, by applying reason to the cure and prevention of disease, daily performs new miracles, the native medicine of the tropics is pre-scientific. Its practitioners inherit a traditional knowledge of herbs and rules of healing, and probably acquire some skill from clinical experience; even in Africa not all those who practise native medicine can be dismissed as witch-doctors,[1] but native medical practice is empirical, and its sovereign remedy is faith. Not infrequently it cures where western science fails because western medicine still calls, as it has always done, for faith, and the people trust their own doctors rather than Europeans. But if medical treatment in the tropics is to reach a higher standard, the empirical methods of native practitioners must be corrected, supplemented or replaced by methods based on scientific principles. This is the more urgent because economic development, unless kept under control, fosters unhealthy conditions, spreads disease and makes for the deterioration of native medical practice.

Doubtless under native rule the standard of health varied greatly from one place to another according to the climate, soil and native social customs, and the good physique and healthiness of tropical peoples have often attracted favourable comment. In Burma Europeans have been puzzled to reconcile the sparse population with the robust constitution of the Burmese. In Malaya 'the general good health and freedom from tuberculosis'[2] have been attributed to the fact that the villagers usually choose a site where air, light and water are abundant and build their houses in a manner that ensures good ventilation. In Africa 'early European travellers speak of the magnificent physique of the Ngoni warriors and their amazing feats of endurance'.[3] Economic development changes the environment.

[1] *African Survey*, p. 1198.   [2] Mills, p. 320.   [3] Read, p. 21.

Pestiferous slums compel attention in the larger towns, but conditions may be worse in the smaller towns up-country where they escape notice; even the villages often suffer from congestion. Food is less abundant, because cultivation for export reduces the area under subsistence crops, and the greater pressure on this smaller area diminishes the outturn; the demands of western enterprise for labour have a similar effect. Often the people take to cheaper or to more palatable but less nutritious food; thus groundnut oil replaces sesamum oil, cassava replaces rice, polished rice spreads beri-beri; sometimes the food is adulterated with imported products as when for some years large quantities of mineral oil were imported into Burma to mix with native vegetable oils. The natural effect of the economic forces released in the course of development is to lower the standard of health.[1]

Again, with man, as with crops and cattle, there is an intimate link between material development and infection. The improvement of communications and the mass migration of labourers spread old diseases and bring in new diseases. In Africa 'diseases have been introduced to which the African was formerly a stranger, and fresh strains of parasites cause attacks to which he was formerly immune; further, Africans now contract diseases common to temperate zones, and it is possible that the intensity of these is increased owing to the lack of acquired immunity'. The spread of sleeping sickness 'must in many cases be associated with the opening of new communications and the development of trading facilities'. The conditions under which labour is employed foster venereal disease, which in modern Africa seems to have an incidence ranging from 50 to 90 %.[2]

For various reasons also native medical skill deteriorates. The patronage of native rulers encourages the most successful physicians, and helps to maintain traditions, in Burma reminiscent of the Hippocratic oath, that make for professional self-respect. Under western rule the native doctors lose their best and most remunerative clients. Moreover the herbs, formerly gathered in the fields, come to be purchased in the market, and are liable to adulteration, so that the practitioner no longer knows what he prescribes. This applies also to modern substitutes for native drugs, such as cheap brands of quinine tabloids which, if they contain any quinine, are of little use except as marbles owing to the thickness of the coating; prac-

[1] *ISC*, I, 21; Mills, p. 321; *RAB*, 1915–16, p. 30; 1918–19, p. 41.
[2] *African Survey*, pp. 1129, 1144–6, 1199.

titioners and patients do not know the difference and buy the cheapest.[1]

These probably are among the chief reasons why 'the systems of oriental medicine have fallen into decay'. The task of improving the standard of health in the tropics is aggravated by the fact that western medical science usually reaches the people as one aspect of economic penetration, and must first be applied towards repairing and preventing the mischief naturally consequent on the process of development. A solution of the problem has been attempted along two lines: the provision of medical assistance; and the introduction of modern hygiene. It is important to notice the essential difference between these alternatives. Medical assistance aims to promote *individual* welfare, and ordinarily requires the voluntary co-operation of the patient; hygiene aims to promote *social* welfare, and necessarily involves a certain measure of compulsion.

2. MEDICINE

Ordinarily the introduction of western medicine in the tropics originates in the needs of Europeans. From very early days the East India Company arranged with the Apothecaries Company for the supply of barber-surgeons to their ships and settlements. In Africa likewise the various administrations at first confined the provision of medical services to the needs of their own establishments. But administrative establishments are partly native, and non-officials in commerce and industry require medical attention. In Burma the earliest members of the general public to receive the benefits of western medical skill were the convicts in jail, and the expansion of medical services in the interior has been closely bound up with the growth of crime. It is only natural that generally throughout the tropics the provision of medical assistance has developed with the economic demand for doctors, and has been organized so as to cost no more than necessary.

But the spread of western medicine in the tropics has not been due solely to the growing demand for doctors; it has been due in part to the demand for patients. Medical missionaries look for patients. It is true that missionary organizations need doctors to preserve the lives of missionaries. But they have also recognized in western medicine an instrument for extending their influence among the people. To deliver their message they must find some method of

[1] *RPI* (India), 1897–1902, p. 245; *CISM*, pp. 13, 15, 23.

attracting listeners. Where, as under direct rule, the people want education in order to get jobs, missionaries have provided schools. Where, as under indirect rule, education has had less market value, they have provided hospitals. Missionaries have sought patients in the cause of welfare, hoping that by saving life they might rescue souls. Moreover the demand for patients has not been wholly altruistic. On western enterprise employers have come to recognize the economic value of providing medical attention for their labourers, in the hope that by improving health they might save labour. In Java under the Culture system the Government produce depended on the well-being of the plantation coolies and, in the forties, when the pressure on the labour supply led to famine and depopulation, it could no longer be disregarded. Thus, so early as 1851, a start was made in the training of natives in western medicine. In the same year Protestant missionaries were admitted. In Burma, developed by native enterprise under direct rule, missionaries have specialized in education, but in Java, developed by western enterprise under indirect rule, medical work presented a more favourable opening.

It is true, of course, that medical missions have looked on the provision of medical care as a good thing in itself, apart from ulterior motives, and that administrations and employers have been actuated by human sentiment in providing and extending medical facilities. Ordinarily the chief factor in stimulating humanitarian impulse has been the shock occasioned by a sensational outbreak of disease. In Siam the modern medical service dates from an epidemic of cholera in the early eighties; the ravages of sleeping sickness in 1901–2 focussed British attention on Uganda; shortly afterwards the outbreak of plague advertized the need for medical care in India and the Tropical Far East. But humanitarian considerations have been reinforced by the practical requirements of western enterprise, and it is in regions developed by western enterprise that medical work has made most progress. Of the hospitals in Java, other than dispensaries, about two-thirds are private institutions, and in the Outer Provinces nine-tenths.[1] In Malaya, before the late war, the tin and rubber companies were maintaining 232 hospitals. In Ceylon about three times as many were provided by companies managing estates, and there were about an equal number of Government dispensaries together with 93 State hospitals.[2] But Asiatic owners and

---

[1] *Netherlands India*, p. 380.
[2] *Britain and Her Dependencies*, pp. 29, 30.

managers often have little faith in western medicine and are reluctant to incur expenditure that they think of doubtful value, and Europeans, to protect their own interests, demand legislation to bring such estates up to their own levels.[1] On the other hand, some regions, where western enterprise is backward or unprofitable, are very scantily supplied with hospitals.

In these circumstances, though policy may be inspired by humanitarian zeal for human welfare, the spread of western medicine is dominated in practice by economic factors. The Government must provide first for its European staff and for natives in its own service, civil or military, for convicts in jail and for the requirements of criminal administration, and for Europeans engaged in economic development. Efficiency and the numerous other demands on public revenue require that such services should be rendered at as little cost as possible. Often, as in Burma and in parts of Africa, the easiest and cheapest way is to import foreign medical subordinates and menials.[2] These conditions tend to stress the importance of hospital discipline rather than to encourage human sympathy; as Lord Hailey remarks, 'It must need a great deal of skill and personal sympathy on the part of the European staff to overcome the impression left on the African by the discipline and isolation from friends which is the rule in many of the British hospitals.' We have noticed that in Burma the people regard the hospitals 'with fear and mistrust'. In Malaya the cult of efficiency and economy has led to the building of large central hospitals to which patients can easily be brought by ambulance, but where they are cut off from their friends. Similarly in Africa much money has been spent on imposing buildings that alarm rather than attract the people.[3] Even in England hospital discipline is often irksome, but the patient accepts it as necessary; to tropical peoples the need for discipline is less apparent, and it is exercised more rigorously. A tradition of human sympathy is characteristic of the healing art in Europe and also in great measure among native medical practitioners,[4] and a good bedside manner is a valuable asset to the private practitioner, whether of modern western or traditional native medicine. But kindliness is less important to native medical subordinates who regard medicine as one branch, and not the most highly esteemed or best-paid branch, of Government service, and it is easier to teach them

[1] Mills, p. 309.   [2] *African Survey*, p. 1183.
[3] *Ib.* pp. 1195–6; Mills, p. 308; *CBC*, p. 33.
[4] Landon, p. 115.

things required for their examinations than to inspire them with professional traditions.

Medical science, then, serves to further economic progress rather than to promote native welfare. Economy forbids that Government shall spend more on medical assistance than will meet the demand at the least expense, and the demand is limited even more closely by economic factors. Employers who recognize that sickness involves a costly waste of labour can provide medical assistance,[1] and can insist as a condition of employment that their employees shall accept it. Personal interest in the well-being of their staff often induces them to press this doctrine to its farthest limits, but they must submit to the test of annual accounts to shareholders, and they cannot sacrifice efficiency to welfare without risking the loss of business to their competitors. Although missionaries can take more altruistic views, they find most scope for their activities in providing Government and western enterprise with medical facilities for their employees, and Christianity is enlisted in the cause of commerce.

It is not the case, therefore, that economic development is necessary as a condition of providing funds for medical services to the people, but medical services are necessary as a condition of economic development. The progress of medical science *as an instrument of welfare* depends on the organization of a demand for it among the people. How far tropical peoples voluntarily avail themselves of western medical assistance is uncertain; in Burma, as in Africa, they are readier to believe in western surgery which shows results than in western medicine of which the results are slower and less obvious. In general, western medical science has found little favour.[2] Burmans, we are told, 'don't care for English medicine'. In Siam western medicine has been encouraged since 1880, by their own King and not by foreign rulers, but 'in 1939 the old style doctor was still the one to whom the people ordinarily turn in times of sickness'. In Java, where natives have been trained to practise western medicine for nearly a hundred years, the people still have greater confidence in their own system, and in the general hospitals 40 % of the beds are empty because the people do not realize the benefits of western medicine.

---

[1] *African Survey*, p. 1194.
[2] *CISM*, pp. 1, 22; Leeuw, H. de, *Cross Roads of the Java Sea* (1931), p. 109. Fischer, Dr I. A., *Bulletin*, Colonial Institute, Amsterdam, 1939, p. 24; Landon, p. 114; *Rural Hygiene in Indo-China* (1937), pp. 11, 50.

The usual explanation of the general reluctance to accept medical science is ignorance and conservatism. Yet the people readily accept new remedies that they find helpful. They are easily convinced, for example, of the value of quinine, and, as just noticed, will buy cheap imitations that are ineffective. Still more striking is the rapid spread of the new treatment of yaws and venereal diseases by injections.[1] These give speedy and obvious results, and quacks find ready patronage for cheap courses, long enough to cure the symptoms, if not to restore health. We have noticed that Burmans were quick to adopt inoculation as a prophylactic against smallpox, but slow to accept vaccination because inoculation gave results, and vaccination, administered by Indian subordinates with defective lymph, was not infrequently a failure. Natives will not admit the superiority of western medicine unless it effects cures where their own doctors fail, and they often find greater benefit from native treatment.[2] Modern science is no substitute for sympathy and understanding. A French doctor in Indo-China, who accompanied his treatment by tattooing his patients with charms in iodine, is said to have had great success.[3] But ordinarily western medicine is presented to the people as part of the apparatus of foreign rule and western enterprise. In Burma until recently the subordinate medical staff was almost wholly Indian, and the patients in small up-country hospitals were mostly sent there by the police. Yet it was possible to find Indian doctors with a gift of sympathy, whose hospitals, despite the barrier of race and language, were continually overcrowded with voluntary patients. But that was exceptional. The people generally do not want western medicine because they have no faith in it. Economic development multiplies the number of hospitals and doctors, but so far as their only patients are those required by administrative or estate rules to submit to western treatment, they have no bearing on welfare; they merely serve efficiency. If western medicine is to be an instrument of welfare, the people must be induced to want it. It is not enough for them to want it; there must be an economic demand for it. Very few can afford to pay the fees necessary to recompense a western practitioner for his long and costly training. So long as the people do not want and cannot afford western medical attention, the supply of hospitals and doctors is conditioned and limited by the demand arising out of the need for greater efficiency in business and administration.

[1] Mills, p. 315; *African Survey*, p. 1145; Landon, pp. 123, 125, 127.
[2] Teeling, pp. 19–21.   [3] Thompson, V., *French Indo-China* (1937), p. 283.

This hinders the progress of medical science and therefore hinders economic progress. To popularize western medicine 'it is not enough to multiply facilities (however good in themselves) for the treatment of such as apply for relief'.[1] In homogeneous western societies the improvement of medical facilities is a problem of supply; the demand for better medical care is almost unlimited, and the extension of medical relief depends upon the provision of larger funds and a better organization for meeting the demand. But in the plural society of the tropics the problem is one of demand; it is a waste of money to provide medical assistance for which there is no demand. Apart from compulsion, it is first necessary to organize the demand. That is a difficult matter. The appreciation of western medicine, as of co-operative principles, must ordinarily spread slowly, but disease, like debt, spreads daily. The machinery of co-operative credit without the spirit has proved useless or worse than useless, but the machinery of medical attention may seem to offer more scope for compulsion. Tropical diseases are a mass affliction, and their rapid elimination is necessary both to native welfare and to economic progress. Hence it is argued that the treatment 'to be effective must partake to some extent the character of an operation, scientifically planned and humanly conducted, but military in its spirit and in the thoroughness with which it establishes itself in the area which it has occupied'. Thus the provision of medical assistance tends to be transformed from the promotion of *individual* welfare, requiring voluntary co-operation, into the promotion of *social* welfare by compulsion, the method which is characteristic of hygiene.

3. HYGIENE

Even in Europe it was only during the last half of the nineteenth century that men came to regard the state as responsible for public health and for the prevention of disease, and a growing volume of welfare legislation marked the earlier stages of the transition from a policy of *laissez-faire* to one of efficiency and social justice. The new trend of opinion naturally reacted on colonial policy. In India, although the growth of towns consequent on the development of trade had long compelled attention to conservancy, sanitation was not treated seriously until 1863, when a Royal Commission showed that the insanitary condition of urban areas was intimately connected with ill-

[1] *African Survey*, pp. 1115, 1196; *Social Policy in Dependent Territories* (1944), p. 6.

health in the army.[1] Even then the action taken was not every effective, and in rural areas practically nothing was attempted. In Netherlands India the Dutch, with their tradition of civic cleanliness, had been more active from very early days, and the first police regulations, framed for Sourabaya in 1829, required every one to tidy up his compound daily, and twice a day if along a public road. Van den Bosch extended these rules over the whole of Java, and it has been stated that a regular health service existed from the middle of the century.[2] The cleanliness of the villages in Java, as compared with the tropics generally, has often attracted favourable comment from visitors. But under Dutch rule, as elsewhere in the tropics, it is only during the present century that the care for public health has been placed on a scientific basis. Naturally it was in the larger towns with a considerable European population that the new concern for hygiene first took effect. The outbreak of plague in India and the Tropical Far East stimulated greater activity, though for the most part this did not extend beyond the towns. Gradually with the growth of western enterprise a new factor intervened, for the mines and plantations were situated in the interior, and attracted attention to the need for improving rural hygiene.

In Burma the epidemic of plague was the immediate occasion for the appointment of a Sanitary Commissioner and the creation of a Public Health Department, but, as in Java and Africa, the earlier measures to prevent plague tended on the contrary to spread infection. In Burma western enterprise is comparatively insignificant, and the activities of the Department have not been extended to the villages. In Malaya, however, where western enterprise dominates economic life, the public health service made greater progress, and, for various reasons, the course of affairs in Malaya is especially instructive. The Straits Settlements have been business centres for over a hundred years and suffered from the former disregard of public health, so that in Singapore 'immense sums have had to be spent to undo the damage caused by the *laissez-faire* policy of the nineteenth century'.[3] But the Malay States remained almost untouched by western enterprise during the nineteenth century:

'Their economic development and rapid increase of population roughly coincided with the growing realization of the necessity for public health measures. About the same time came the series of discoveries of the cause

---

[1] *IG*, IV, 286, 467. [2] Hydrick, p. 7.
[3] Mills, p. 298.

and prevention of tropical disease which revolutionized or rather created the science of tropical medicine. The Malay States were able to take advantage of this situation without having first to spend large sums in remedying the effects of previous indifference. Tin, and later, rubber provided revenue on a scale which many older colonies lacked; and the administration was generous and far-sighted in its expenditure.'[1]

Moreover, in comparison with many tropical dependencies, the area of the Malay States is small, and the population, though not dense, is mainly concentrated in certain areas, and therefore the people as a whole are readily accessible. The local Sultans are men educated on modern lines, who can appreciate western medicine and can use their influence to recommend it to their people. Probably there is no region in the tropics where conditions are so favourable to the improvement of public health as in the Malay States.

As we have noticed, the rural population is said formerly to have enjoyed general good health. Tuberculosis was almost unknown until fostered by the congestion in the towns consequent on economic development. Similarly venereal diseases have multiplied with the mass importation of male coolies. The rice plains, in which most of the people lived and worked, 'were practically free from malaria'.[2] But when mines and rubber land were opened up to western enterprise, malaria was a formidable obstacle. Klang, the station at the coastal end of the railway to the mines, was very malarious, and the adjacent shipping centre, Port Swettenham, was so deadly that the Government directed its abandonment. But campaigns against malaria proved successful at both these places, and were extended to other towns.[3] At that time rubber plantations were being laid out, and malaria took a heavy toll among both Europeans and coolies, 'as high as one-fifth of the labour force'. Measures for the prevention of malaria were accordingly extended from the towns to rural areas. In 1910 a separate Health Branch of the Medical Departments was established to supervise anti-malarial and other health work in the interior, but its operations were hindered by the lack of adequate control over labour conditions. In 1912 accordingly the numerous separate ordinances for different classes of immigrants were consolidated in a Labour Code, which has since then regulated the conditions of labour on the plantations and mines. 'In earlier years some managers opposed the "interference" of the Health Branch, and failed to realize the

---

[1] Mills, p. 298.
[2] *Ib.* p. 301.
[3] *Ib.* pp. 299ff., 328.

economic value of maintaining their labourers in good health.' The
opposition, however, had some justification, as the measures that had
proved efficacious in preventing malaria in the towns, had a contrary
effect on the plantations, and 'resulted merely in heavy expenditure
and increased mortality'. Patient research discovered and removed
the defects, and by 1935 the protection against malaria was as complete on the larger estates as in the towns.[1] Another disease that has
received special attention is hookworm. This is generally prevalent,
and a special element of contagion exists in the Indian estate labourers,
among whom a high percentage are infected, despite the treatment
given to immigrants at the quarantine stations. It is not serious in
itself, but it causes physical and mental fatigue, and consequently
reduces the efficiency of labour. Strict provisions in the Labour Code
regulated sanitary conditions on the plantations, but they were sometimes disregarded, especially on Indian properties. A campaign against
the disease from 1926 to 1929, partly financed by the Rockefeller
Foundation, effected a temporary improvement, but probably its chief
permanent value was to direct renewed attention to the importance of
rural sanitation. The Government decided accordingly to enlarge the
health service, to enforce the Labour Code more strictly on estates,
to provide sanitary latrines in rural schools and other Government
buildings, and to persuade the villagers to build latrines and wear
shoes.[2]

The beneficent activities of the public health service have gained
the confidence of European employers, who now recognize its value
in improving the health and enhancing the efficiency of their employees, and many provide hospitals and other amenities in excess of official requirements. But 'many Asiatic-owned plantations
frequently evade the regulations, and have to be closely supervised
by the Health Branch. They are a menace to their neighbours who
have obeyed the regulations'. Yet the chief difficulty has been among
the villagers, who 'are the worst offenders against the anti-malarial
and other health measures and require constant supervision'.[3] They
can be compelled or encouraged to build latrines, but, as has been
found also in Java and Ceylon, they cannot be compelled to use them.
In the towns shoes are a sign of higher social status, and every one
wears them who can afford the money, but Government pressure has
met with little success in inducing the villagers to wear shoes, which

[1] Mills, pp. 225, 234, 299, 300.   [2] Ib. 234, 316, 17.
[3] Ib. pp. 234, 316–17; Netherlands India, p. 363.

indeed are hardly suited to the cultivation of rice in mud and water. Much of the expenditure incurred in improving conditions on western enterprise is wasted if the adjacent villages continue to be sources of infection. But 'the Health Branch has to contend against the dead weight of a naturally indifferent and insanitary population' that, perversely, enjoyed 'general good health' without their attentions. Constant inspection is costly, and penalties are apt to raise the pitch of corruption rather than the standard of health. Even in a wealthy dependency with conditions so generally favourable as in Malaya, it has not been possible to do much towards improving the health of the ordinary villager.[1]

Yet one finds Malaya cited as 'one instance where the whole population benefited from medical and health organization assisted by economic development',[2] and it may be well to examine the evidence more closely. According to the Census Report on Malaya for 1931 the death-rate for Malaysians was 22·4 per 1000, for Chinese 24·3 and for Indians 29·8.[3] Since Malaysians receive least attention from the health service, it would seem that its activities play a minor part in reducing the bills of mortality. In Burma for the same year the provincial death-rate was returned as 17·36 and for rural areas, where western medicine and hygiene are practically inoperative, the death-rate, according to the official returns, was only 15·87.[4] But in Burma the apparently low death-rate was explained as due in part to 'slackness in registration', and this probably holds true also of Malaysians. It has been claimed that, in Malaya, 'the fall in infantile mortality is one of the best indications of what has been accomplished'.[5] Of recent years there has indeed been a marked downward trend in the figures, and this has coincided with greater activity in welfare work. In the Federated Malay States, the recorded death-rate for infants under twelve months fell from 218 per 1000 births in 1917 to 147 in 1937, and in the Straits Settlements during the same period it fell from 267 per 1000 to 156. But the first result of greater attention to vital statistics is an improvement in registration, and 'there is unfortunately no doubt that, even in such an area as Singapore Municipality, registration of births has up to quite recent years been very far from complete, and that even to-day it leaves a good deal to be desired'. The failure in registration in Singapore was estimated

---

[1] Mills, pp. 314–16, 320.　　[2] *Social Policy in Dependent Territories* (1944), p. 6.
[3] Malaya Census, 1931, p. 10.
[4] *RAB*, 1931–2, p. 130.　　　　[5] Mills, p. 328.

at 10 % in 1931, over 20 % in 1921 and over 35 % in 1911; yet 'the relevant statistics for Singapore are probably the best available'.[1] Death registration, however, is far more complete than birth registration, and it is certain that no inconsiderable part of the apparent decline of infantile mortality must be ascribed to the more accurate registration of births rather than to the attention to child welfare. Here, again, the figures for Burma are suggestive. In 1931 child welfare work did not extend beyond the towns, but the infantile mortality rate in rural areas was returned as 178 per 1000, whereas the corresponding figure for urban areas was 277. These figures may not prove that most children die where they receive most attention, but they do at least suggest a need for caution in accepting the figures for infantile mortality in Malaya as proof of the benefits accruing from the health service. If those figures are 'the best indication of what has been accomplished', it is unsound, in the face of evidence to the contrary, to conclude that the whole population has benefited.

In Malaya attention was directed to public health by the needs of private enterprise, and by the spread of disease as a result of economic development. European employers often go beyond the official minimum, and expenditure on the enforcement of regulations, as distinct from the provision of amenities, is chiefly incurred on western enterprises managed by non-Europeans, who cannot afford to comply with them or do not believe in them. Experience shows that the problem of improving the standard of health and the efficiency of labour on mines and plantations is ultimately linked up with the improvement of health among the people in general. But an improvement in the general standard of health among the people would seem to require that they shall comply with regulations in which they have no faith, and voluntarily accept rules which they are unable to obey and which the government is equally unable to enforce. In Singapore, as in Rangoon, conditions preclude the enforcement of the housing by-laws.[2] Where ill-health is the direct result of economic circumstances, the remedy lies not in legislation but in changing the environment. To most reforms, however, the chief obstacle is apathy. Without a change of attitude, expenditure on a health service as an instrument of welfare, or even as an instrument of economic progress, is largely wasted; given a change of attitude, most of the urgent reforms could be effected without spending large sums on a public health service, because common sense is sufficient to recommend

[1] Malaya Census, 1931, pp. 106, 108.   [2] Mills, p. 321 n.

them. Where improvements call for more than common sense, experts insufficiently acquainted with tropical hygiene as applied to local conditions are apt to make mistakes, as in the first attempts to prevent malaria in rural areas and to combat plague, and such failures tend to confirm people in their apathy.

Although Malaya has features of special interest, experience in Asia generally points to similar conclusions, and so it does likewise in Africa. The growth of modern views in Europe on the relation between environment and disease, and on the responsibility of the State for public health, 'coincided with the very general recognition that measures which lead to an improvement in health and an increase in population are likely to have a direct influence on African economics'.[1] The larger industrial concerns have in some areas anticipated recognition by the administrations of the need for extending public health measures. 'They have realized that, low paid as the African may be, an ailing and inefficient employee is expensive and wasteful.' 'Experience has shown that efficiency is closely linked with health conditions, and the more important organizations have now adopted, with satisfactory results, the practice of giving a period of "acclimatization" by medical treatment and dieting before the recruit begins active work.' This expenditure could be avoided if the people in general enjoyed better health. Moreover, owing to the generally low standard of health, labour was not only inefficient but deficient. Attention has frequently been drawn to 'the wastage of labour due to ill-health', and a recent committee in Tanganyika suggested that 'with the elimination of waste there is ample man-power for the needs of the territory, both for wage-earning and in the growing of economic crops'.[2] But in most regions much of the labour comes from a long distance, and a solution for the problem of making it more efficient 'lies not merely in attention to the health conditions of employed labour, but in intensive medical work and the promotion of improved standards of subsistence cultivation in the areas from which labour is drawn'. 'In some areas concentration on economic exploitation has resulted in enormous labour migrations which have not only drained the native reserves of the menfolk, needed for subsistence agriculture and a balanced life, but at the other end have brought into existence a dingy, discontented, "atomized" black proletariat which, on any standard of ultimate human values, represents a regression from traditional tribal standards.'[3] In Africa as in Asia, unregulated

[1] *African Survey*, pp. 697, 1194.   [2] *Ib.* pp. 693, 697.   [3] Huxley, p. 121.

economic development tends to spread disease and foster ill-health; the more enlightened employers recognize the need for measures to improve the health of their labourers, and support the Government in taking steps to enforce similar measures on other employers; and attempts to raise the standard of health on western enterprise bring to light the need to raise the standard of health among the great mass of the people.

One aspect of this problem is nutrition. It is now recognized that in lands developed by native enterprise, cultivation for export tends to grow at the expense of cultivation for food, and it seems that during recent years, even where food grains constitute the staple export, less has been available for local consumption.[1] Moreover, the expansion of cultivation deprives the people of spontaneous products of the waste, formerly used to supplement their diet. Naturally problems of nutrition engage most attention where the profits of western enterprise are closely linked with the supply of food. We have noticed that in Malaya the loss to the Government and employers occasioned by the shortage of rice after the war of 1914 led to renewed insistence on the compulsory cultivation of rice. Especially in Africa the inefficiency of native labour is regarded as largely due to inadequate or unsuitable diet, and so 'nutritional problems are now much in the minds of administrations: whether the African eats enough food and, if he does, whether it is the right kind, and whether the attack on nutrition may not be the most important factor in reducing disease'. In the past Africans have adopted new kinds of food, but whether they will be so willing to accept the advice of dieticians would seem doubtful. In Malaya where the polished rice that has recently gained favour is regarded as a cause of beri-beri, attempts to induce the people to revert to roughly husked rice appear to have had little more success than the propaganda for standard bread in England, and it is unlikely that the African will be more responsive. It is unlikely also that the African will be able to afford more nutritious food, if it is more costly; normally, as we have noticed, in the process of economic development, cheap food drives out good food. Moreover, dietetics is a new science, and 'some African tribes seem to maintain physical fitness on food which is, according to nutritionists, wanting in certain constituents essential to health'.[2] Caution would seem necessary, therefore, in introducing innovations, and in any case no one can force the people to eat proper food.

[1] Wickizer and Bennett, p. 188.   [2] *African Survey*, pp. 1122, 1194.

Yet in this matter, as in others, one may notice a growing tendency to use compulsion as a means of promoting welfare. Welfare is an attribute of social life and, for the common welfare, men living in society must accept restrictions on individual freedom. In tropical society they accept such restrictions in the name of custom, but welcome their removal under a policy of *laissez-faire*, allowing them at least the illusion of freedom. Welfare measures limit freedom. Men who value the common good voluntarily accept measures which they think likely to promote it. But in tropical dependencies, economic forces disintegrate society and foster a disregard for social welfare, while the people do not understand the measures that, rightly or wrongly, are expected to promote it. In such circumstances compulsion is attractive because it is easy to issue orders; but it is important to recognize the limits within which they can be enforced.

Compulsion may be *negative*, by penalizing breaches of regulations; that is the method typical of *laissez-faire* and the rule of law. Or compulsion may be *positive*, through pressure exercised to induce the people to adopt new habits, grow certain crops, eat special food and so on; that is the method typical of indirect rule through personal authority. The law, for example, may require that every house shall be provided with a latrine and, with an adequate and honest inspecting staff, and with a sufficient magistracy imposing deterrent penalties, such a law can be enforced. But it is impossible by legal methods to make the people use the latrines. The promotion of welfare through the law multiplies offences and administrative corruption. To make the people use the latrines is possible only by persuasion. And in this comparatively simple matter even the Dutch have failed. With a national tradition of public hygiene, and with the use of 'gentle pressure', on a scale almost beyond belief, through administrative machinery built up on customary authority and far more powerful than may be found in any British dependency, the death-rate in Java has remained almost constant during the last twenty years, 'having fluctuated around 1·9 % annually—about 1 % higher than in the Netherlands'.[1] In a recent brochure Dr Hydrick, of the Netherlands India Health Service, comparing the efficacy of curative medicine with the use of pressure and compulsion for improving hygiene, remarks that the provision of latrines is no more effective as propaganda for hygiene than the hospital as propaganda for western medicine. In a city compulsory hygiene may be possible and necessary, but he insists,

[1] Boeke, p. 163.

with all the emphasis of italics, in rural areas *'the jails are not large enough to make the use of force possible'*. Moreover, coercion cannot give permanent results, and, after a failure due to the use of coercion, it is more difficult to secure the co-operation of the people. It should, he suggests, be used 'only to carry out measures which have already secured the support and the co-operation of at least 90 % of the people of that area'.[1] The use of gentle pressure to improve hygiene was a characteristic of the former Ethical policy in Netherlands India. But experience brought disillusionment. Modern British colonial policy follows the Dutch Ethical policy, in aiming to encourage hygiene by lavish expenditure on social services, and by recourse to legal compulsion or pressure. But compulsion in the interest of public health creates more problems, and more difficult problems, than it solves; the essential factor is human, not mechanical. Hygienic customs in the tropics have grown up slowly as a condition of survival in a tropical environment. Even so far as they suited the environment they reflected the general backwardness of tropical peoples, inviting European intervention which entailed the disintegration of tropical society and the collapse of social customs, good and bad alike. Many customs, indeed, that formerly were useful, now became harmful. Modern conditions require the observance of new restrictions on individual liberty. It is possible to enforce these so far as they are requisite to economic development, and the expenditure of funds on social services has done much to promote economic efficiency, though not to the full extent needed by economic progress. But that is very different from enhancing welfare, in which little can be done until the people themselves or their leaders are conscious of a need for betterment.[2] This change of attitude is usually expected to result from education.

4. EDUCATION: TYPES OF SCHOOLS

In modern colonial policy few subjects have been so voluminously discussed as education. Apologists for colonial rule cite the expenditure on education as proof of its beneficence; critics complain that the expenditure is inadequate and that the methods of education are unsound. There is nothing new in this emphasis on education in tropical dependencies; it is an old tradition dating back to the Papal Bull of 1493. Education has always been regarded as a main instrument

---

[1] Hydrick, pp. 18 ff.   [2] *African Survey*, p. 1206.

of welfare; what is distinctively modern is a new conception of welfare. Formerly attention was concentrated on welfare in the next world, but now few look beyond this world. Education is expected to help the people to produce more, and to teach them thrift and business principles; to improve their health and inculcate modern ways of life, and, finally, to guide them to self-government. On these objectives, despite controversy as to methods, colonial powers in general agree. It seems also that in tropical dependencies in general educational policy has developed along similar lines, has produced similar types of schools, has encountered similar difficulties, and has had similar results. And repeatedly these results have been directly contrary to the ends proposed. At each setback educational enthusiasts elaborate new projects, but with no better success. For the repeated failures there would seem to be one sufficient explanation: they disregard the environment. Educationists frame their projects with reference to conditions in the homogeneous society of the West and attempt to show what education might be and ought to do, but they do not pause to consider what education actually is and does and can do, and accordingly in the plural society of tropical dependencies, their plans miscarry.[1]

The common tradition of western civilization is that education should teach the children how to live as members of the community. This tradition is not merely western but worldwide. It is the tradition of Hindus and Moslems, and was formerly well-illustrated in the monastic schools of Burma, which aimed at teaching the boys how to live as Burman Buddhists. The African likewise has 'his own methods of education in the form of character training and instruction in crafts or, in the case of girls, in the duties of domestic life.... Social obligation forms the core of all teaching given by tribal elders, and the system is directed to fitting the youth to take his place in the traditional life of his group.'[2] But the old systems of education, whether elaborate as in Burma or primitive as in Africa, do not equip the child for life in the modern world, and modern education aims at teaching a new way of life. In the tropics 'education is, and is intended to be, an instrument of change'.

Naturally then the educational activities of colonial powers have depended on their desire to change the outlook of their subjects and to diffuse new ways of life among them. Educational policy accord-

[1] Furnivall, *Economic Review*, 1912; *Proc. Anglo-Netherlands Society*, 1944–5, p. 7.
[2] *African Survey*, pp. 1207, 1279.

ingly reflects both the evolution of political ideas in Europe, and the course of changes in the relations between Europe and the tropics, so that, in broad outline, it has followed much the same course everywhere. Not infrequently missionaries have preceded, and indeed paved the way for foreign intervention, and have included education in their sphere of work. Ordinarily, however, in the earliest stage the Government has made such provision as might seem necessary for educating Europeans and has laid the foundation of modern European schools, but has left native education to the people. Then humanitarians, and especially missionaries, with the support of Liberal opinion, have obtained permission to provide schools for natives. This leads to a third stage in which practical considerations induce colonial powers to encourage native education. All these three stages, though distinct, have a common feature, that the prevailing attitude to education is one of *laissez-faire*: although in the third stage they provide funds and supervise expenditure, they abstain so far as possible from intervention and leave native education to private enterprise. Then, with the transition from a policy of *laissez-faire* to one of active construction, there succeeds a fourth stage in which the colonial administration assumes responsibility for the promotion, direction and control of education.

The process thus briefly summarized may be traced most clearly in the older British and Dutch dependencies; elsewhere the various stages have been telescoped, but we may recognize its operation in the evolution of four different types of schools. For children recognized as Europeans, there are *European schools* which aim at giving an education similar to, if not identical with, the corresponding course in Europe. The schools provided by missionaries have developed along two lines. In some the instruction is based on the appropriate European language, and in others on the vernacular. Both kinds of school are western in type, because directed by Europeans in accordance with western ideas, but it is convenient to distinguish those based on a European language as *Western schools*, and those of the other class as *Vernacular schools*. This classification applies equally to schools maintained wholly or in part from private sources and those managed by the Government. The western schools are intended for the westernized native; sometimes policy has inclined towards making them different from European schools, but the general tendency now is to make the course and conditions in western schools as much like those in European schools as circumstances allow, but with an adaptation to local culture. The vernacular schools are intended for children who will ordinarily remain within the native sphere of life, but in some degree of contact with the western world. The *Native schools*, mostly religious and often confining formal instruction to little more than the elements of religion, are a survival from an older world, and provide for that section of the people which still looks backward to the past. Thus almost everywhere we find these four types of school: European, Western, Vernacular and Native.

The evolution of the same types of school under different colonial powers in widely distant regions of the tropics suggests that the course of progress has been directed by the force of circumstances rather than by deliberate policy, and it is significant that in respect of each type educational policy has been frustrated by the force of circumstances. Until quite recently policy has aimed at marking off the European schools by refusing the admission of natives or restricting it within such narrow limits as not to imperil their predominantly western character. But it has rarely been possible for long wholly to exclude natives, or even to maintain western standards of instruction. Now, at least under British rule, the tendency is to draw the line between European and western schools less sharply. Of still greater interest is the contrast between policy and practice in respect of western and vernacular schools. The policy has been to exercise restraint over the growth of western education and to encourage vernacular education. Yet everywhere western schools are vigorous and have multiplied even to excess, especially under the system of direct rule; one great problem of educational administration has indeed been to keep these schools within limits that the revenue can afford. On the other hand, it has often been easier to provide vernacular schools than to get children to fill them. So far as in some countries vernacular education has made progress, it is for the same reason that has made western education generally popular, namely, that it provides the means to make a living. Similarly, attempts to foster native schools have failed; their curriculum has grown more narrow, and the attendance has declined.

5. EDUCATION AND LAISSEZ-FAIRE

Any examination of educational policy and practice in tropical dependencies must start from India, for this has led the way. We have glanced at education in India when reviewing educational progress in Burma, but it requires closer study. Formerly in India, as in Burma, the native schools aimed at teaching the children how to live, and, where this is the end of education, the more who go to school the better. At the end of the eighteenth century missionaries, aspiring to teach a better way of life, arrived. Despite the sympathy of some liberally-minded men, including the Governor-General, Lord Hastings, who in 1815 expressed a wish for some system of public instruction,[1] they had a long struggle against official discouragement and popular apathy. Their prime object was to elevate the masses, dispel ignorance and superstition, and spread Christianity, and with this object in view they gave instruction both in the vernacular and English. The latter soon proved its utility. So early as 1833 we find an Indian parent instructing his son that, although Sanskrit literature contained all that was really valuable, yet 'for secular purposes, for gaining a livelihood, a knowledge of the English language was absolutely necessary'.[2] These early missionary efforts had a most important influence in fostering the demand for English education. They taught the natives that English was a profitable acquisition, and the Government that English-speaking natives were profitable servants. The four stages of tolerance, approval, and encouragement of private enterprise, and finally of State control over education are marked by four outstanding official pronouncements.

In 1835 a Resolution decided unequivocally on preferring western education over the native system. The foundations of the modern educational system were laid in a dispatch from the Court of Directors in 1854, which recognized it as 'a sacred duty to confer upon the natives of India those vast moral and material blessings which flow from the general diffusion of useful knowledge'. This dispatch stressed the importance of primary instruction for the masses. 'If any portion of the orders can be pronounced characteristic and distinctive, it was education for the great mass of the people.' When a commission was appointed in 1882 to report progress, the instructions required that it 'should specially bear in mind the great importance which the Government attaches to the subject of primary education'. Its report, which guided educational policy for the remainder of the century, was based on the principle of encouraging private enterprise and abstaining so far as possible from official competition. The review by Lord Curzon in his Resolution of 1904 was the fourth of these

[1] *IG*, IV, 409ff.   [2] McCully, p. 44.

landmarks in educational policy, 'the special obligation of the Government towards the vernacular education of the masses, which was declared by the Court of Directors in 1854, was endorsed by the Education Commission of 1882, and has been reaffirmed by the Government of India whenever it has reviewed the progress of education'.[1]

But the masses did not want primary instruction, whereas the middle classes wanted jobs and the Government wanted 'to create a supply of public servants'. There was an economic demand among the public for western schooling, and an economic demand in the administration and in western enterprise for the product of western schools. In these schools missionaries preached the Christian virtues, and educational authorities stressed cultural values, but with the people nothing counted but examination results. Boys crowded the schools, and parents demanded more schools. Missionaries and schoolmasters, zealous in their calling, but not insensible to the lure of larger grants, made room for more and more boys, and educational authorities, also from mixed motives, provided more and more schools. Where schools teach children how to live, the more who go to school the better; but when they teach them merely how to make a living, the more who go to school the less they earn. There was a demand for clerks; and the more clerks, the cheaper. Competition raised the standard of qualification for the various appointments. When the market for school graduates at any standard of attainment became saturated, the boys pressed on to higher standards, and higher education was little more than an euphemism for more valuable qualifications. The results were surveyed by Lord Curzon in his Resolution of 1904. Contrary to the hopes of early enthusiasts, education had become an economic rather than a cultural asset; the desire of Indians 'to realise the manifold advantages as soon and as cheaply as possible, tended to prevent both schools and colleges from filling their proper function as places of liberal education'. There was a keen demand for schools and schooling, but practically none for school graduates except in clerical employment and the law. Thus the schools produced a surplus of unemployable and discontented men, whose intellectual attainments were bounded by the 'literary' syllabus prescribed for their examinations, and whose character had not been strengthened by moral discipline. On the other hand, the primary

[1] Indian Education Commission, 1882, Report, pp. 24, 112, 625; *RPI* (India), 1897–1902, pp. 457 ff; *IG*, iv, p. 417.

instruction of the masses had made practically no progress. The early pioneers of education looked forward to raising the masses, dispelling superstition, spreading Christianity and fostering an attachment to British rule. But a hundred years of educational endeavour left the masses ignorant, stimulated aggressive Hinduism, and provided a focus for seditious agitation. The Resolution of 1904 accordingly marks the turning-point from a policy of *laissez-faire* to one of constructive effort and control.

In Burma and Malaya similar conditions, complicated by the supply of Indian and Chinese candidates for employment, had similar results, though rather later. In Netherlands India educational progress was slower, chiefly because under indirect rule and the Culture system there was a smaller demand for clerks. But the course of development was essentially the same. On the restoration of Dutch rule in 1816 the Government provided schools for Europeans, but in Java it expected the Regents to encourage native education. Missionaries were admitted to the Outer Provinces, though excluded from Java through fear of Moslem sensibilities. With the Liberal reaction against the Culture system, the Government recognized its responsibility 'for spreading light in India'. The adoption of this policy dates, as in British India, from 1854. Missionaries were admitted to Java at about the same time, but, as there was still some fear of Moslem reaction to Christian schools and there was as yet little demand for educated natives, they paid more attention to medical work. The European schools provided the subordinates required for clerical employment, and, except for a very few members of the upper classes who were admitted to the European schools, the natives had no facilities for learning Dutch, though in the towns some attended vernacular schools. From about 1900, however, the rapid economic development created a demand for more subordinates than the European schools supplied; the Ethical leaders emphasized the moral and material value of education and, before long, they found support in the growth of a Nationalist movement. In 1907 Dutch was introduced in some vernacular schools; in 1911 these were converted into western schools, preparing boys for the Clerkship Examination; and in 1914 facilities were given for further study. (The village schools established from 1907 will call for notice in connection with vernacular instruction.) Western education rapidly developed along the same lines as in British India. A junior clerk could earn fifteen to thirty times as much as an ordinary labourer, and the western school became 'the principal gateway to higher social rank and better opportunities of earning money'. Within a little over ten years from 1914, there was a surplus of unemployable school graduates, and diehards were criticizing western education as breeding unemployment, discontent and political agitation.[1] Similarly, under French rule in Indo-China, an educational policy claiming to diffuse the high ideals of French civilization had similar results, and was subjected to the same criticism.

If we turn to Africa we find educational progress following much the same lines. Here, as elsewhere, the pioneers of modern education, western and vernacular, were missionaries, with little support or supervision from the Government. In regions under indirect rule, so long as native chieftains were left to govern on their own lines, there was little demand for men from modern schools and, as in Java, western education made little progress. In Nigeria there was no Government school until 1899 and, when the country was taken over from the Niger Company in 1900, 'the first problem that presented itself to the newly formed administration was the lack of a clerical staff....In these circumstances the various governments, and to a less degree the trading firms, were only too anxious to employ anyone who could read and write, and, as the country developed, the demand increased far more rapidly than the supply.' Education was a profitable economic asset and naturally 'the demand for any form of education was tremendous'.[2] 'At the mines, the trading stores and on European estates, the English speaking native can often command a better position and a higher wage.' The people wanted education 'not only for its use as a medium of approach to the administration and in commerce and industrial relations, but as the symbol of a higher status'. In Africa as in India the competition for well-paid appointments pushed up the standard of qualifications required to secure employment and, for lack of local facilities, natives with sufficient means went on to European or American universities, though 'the resultant efflux was socially and intellectually undesirable'. Thus, within a generation, we find in Africa the same complaints as in India and the Tropical Far East. The curriculum was criticized for 'bookishness', as being 'academic', 'literary'; there was the same 'cult of the certificate' and, although under indirect rule lawyers were not

[1] Creutzberg, Dr K. F., *Asiatic Review*, 1934, p. 119; Freytag, p. 69; Schrieke (*see* Bradley, p. 275).
[2] Burns, pp. 263–4.

so numerous as in India, the superfluity of 'preachers and editors' was criticized from very early days. By about 1925 the conditions which had inspired Curzon to formulate a new educational policy for India in 1904 had arisen also in Africa, and here also education policy took a turn in the direction of control.[1]

6. Constructive Education

When Curzon reviewed education in India the high hopes of early enthusiasts had faded, and the system of public instruction was generally regarded, not only in India but in other British dependencies and under French and Dutch rule, as a horrible example of what not to do. Criticism was chiefly directed against two points. The curriculum was condemned as academic, useless; and the study of English history and of the British constitution was held to be largely responsible for political agitation. Both criticisms were mistaken. The curriculum was, in fact, narrowly utilitarian, adapted to meeting the economic demand for clerks and subordinate officials; and political agitation was far more advanced and effective in the Philippines under Spanish rule than in India where the pupils studied Burke and Mill. Both ideas, however, were shared by Curzon, and he set about providing remedies. He directed that vocational and technical instruction should have a preference over 'academic' subjects; he wished to encourage higher moral standards by ethical teaching, stricter discipline and closer supervision and, especially, by stressing female education; and he reaffirmed the urgent importance of primary vernacular instruction. Through these reforms he expected to further economic progress by enabling cultivators to produce more, and also by providing capitalist enterprise with a larger supply of skilled labour and of more intelligent unskilled labour; he thought also to enhance individual welfare by teaching the people how to earn more, and social welfare by instructing them in modern hygiene; and he hoped to quiet political agitation by providing new openings for the unemployable intelligentsia. 'We have done our part,' he said, 'it rests with the people themselves to make a wise use of the opportunities that are now offered to them, and to realize that education in the true sense means something more than the mere passing of examinations, that it aims at the progressive and orderly development of all the faculties of the mind, that it should form character and teach right conduct—that it is, in fact, a preparation for the business of life.'

[1] *African Survey*, pp. 1219, 1232, 1244, 1258, 1279, 1285.

During the present century the course of economic, social and political evolution has given a similar trend to educational policy throughout the tropics and especially in the direction of giving the system of instruction a more 'practical' character. In Burma, Malaya, Netherlands India, Indo-China and the Philippines, there have been repeated attempts to foster more assiduously vocational and technical instruction; from 1925 a series of pronouncements on policy in Africa almost re-echo the words of Curzon. Advanced education should be 'of a definitely utilitarian type' and mainly directed to 'the improvement of agriculture, animal husbandry and health'. The money spent on it 'would return to primary education in the form of teachers, to health in the form of doctors and to economic production in the form of agricultural, veterinary and forest officers'. It was thought that 'there is little danger of creating a class of educated unemployed as there is a growing need for the services of educated Africans'. There was 'general agreement that education cannot be confined to the few, but must progressively extend to the mass of the people', and there must be 'a drastic improvement in primary education'. At the same time 'the greatest importance was to be attached to religious teaching and moral instruction', and female education was to be encouraged—with such caution as might be necessary in view of Moslem prejudices. Also 'the need for closer inspection and control by government' has been accepted.[1]

That everywhere the current of educational policy should have turned in the same direction at about the same time is remarkable; what is still more striking is that it has been reinforced by the rising tide of nationalism. Between foreign Governments and Nationalist politicians there are many points of acute difference, but all agree on the importance of education and, in general, on the lines that it should take. Official and Nationalist views are not wholly identical. Official policy tends to regard education as an instrument of individual welfare and Nationalists regard it as a means of national advancement.[2] Although Nationalists admit the desirability of general primary instruction, they tend in practice to lay more stress on higher education with a view to political and economic emancipation. Nationalists whole-heartedly endorse the official view as to the importance of technical instruction. There is still another feature common to the educational policy of Nationalists and officials. All alike

---

[1] *African Survey*, pp. 1229, 1233, 1281, 1290.
[2] *Ib.* pp. 1281, 1286.

throughout the tropics recognize the *need* for well-educated natives in all lines of life; but they tend to overlook the fact that there is a very small *demand* for them.

7. EDUCATION AND PROGRESS

It is in the sphere of vocational and technical instruction, bearing directly on economic progress, that one would expect to find the need for education most intimately connected with demand. Throughout the tropics agriculture is the chief, and almost the sole, occupation of the people, and it is conducted on traditional lines without the help of modern science. There should, then, be great scope for improving agricultural methods by instruction. That appeared obvious to Curzon and, in his project of giving a practical bias to education, he assigned the first place to agriculture. In other dependencies the same plausible argument has seemed convincing. Yet in India, Burma, Java and the Philippines attempts to teach the people better cultivation have proved unsuccessful. General experience shows that the courses fail to attract farmers and that the students look for posts under Government or on western enterprise, or else seek non-agricultural employment in the towns. In Malaya, when an agricultural school was opened in 1931, 'there had long been a serious need for it'. There was a serious need but a very small demand. 'A disappointingly high percentage do not intend to manage their own land, but want positions under Government or on estates. Here the experience tallies with that of agricultural schools in Java and the Philippines. The agricultural department is now pretty well staffed, so that the number of vacancies is declining.' The school helped the plantations by turning out cheap overseers, but even these were mostly Chinese, whom the employers preferred to Malays. Although the intention was to promote Malay welfare, the result was chiefly to profit western enterprise.[1] Much the same thing has happened in Africa. In the Transkei agricultural training has been provided since 1904, and there have been special schools since 1914. The men found employment as demonstrators and not as farmers, and in the former capacity their services were in demand so far off as the Belgian Congo. 'There is some fear however that it may not be possible to keep up these schools; the demand for agricultural demonstrators is, for various reasons, already slackening, and shows signs of decreasing still further.'[2]

[1] Mills, pp. 355–6.   [2] *African Survey*, p. 1222.

It is significant that the provision of technical instruction has not been quite so disappointing in forms of production organized on western lines and mainly under western management. Even in this branch of economic life, however, the progress has been unsatisfactory. In most tropical dependencies western enterprise does not extend far beyond primary production and offers little scope for men with technical qualifications. In the Tropical Far East it has been built up on a basis of Eurasian, Chinese or Indian subordinates, thereby obstructing the employment of natives by a barrier which they cannot easily surmount. Even the trade-crafts are largely in foreign hands; the natives encounter similar difficulties in gaining an entrance, and sometimes meet with organized opposition, as when the Chinese master carpenters in Malaya declined to employ trained Malays.[1] In European concerns the higher posts have hitherto been reserved for Europeans, so that natives had no prospect of advancement. Moreover, where technical instruction has been provided, it has often, as for some years in Java, been debarred to natives because their 'academic' curriculum was not sufficiently advanced for them to profit by it. There is a popular belief that 'natives' prefer clerical employment as an easier, softer life, but this has frequently been disproved.[2] In most dependencies the failure of earlier attempts to encourage technical instruction has led to the appointment of committees of enquiry, and their reports have shown that there was little demand for men with technical qualifications. Even in Malaya, where the vast scale of western enterprise would seem especially propitious to the growth of technical instruction, a committee, largely composed of business men, reported in 1926 that 'the number of openings for technically trained men was limited, since the principal need of the country was unskilled manual labour, which was supplied by Chinese and Indian immigrants'.[3] So recently as 1938 a Commission on Higher Education in Malaya reported that the prospects of employment did not justify the establishment of an engineering school at Raffles College, and that training for the limited number of civil engineering posts could be given elsewhere.[4]

The slow progress of technical training in subjects bearing directly on material production is the more striking by its contrast with the

---

[1] Mills, p. 355.
[2] See e.g. Dr Van Mook, *J. Roy. African Society*, Oct. 1943, p. 180.
[3] Mills, p. 353.
[4] *Overseas Education*, 1939–40, April, p. 146.

progress achieved in pedagogy. Ordinarily one finds that most of those receiving vocational instruction are being trained as teachers. Often, as at least formerly in Malaya, the pay and prospects of teachers are inferior to those of a clerk,[1] and the teaching profession is the last refuge of the semi-educated unemployed. Why, then, do so many seek to be trained as teachers? One reason is obvious. The demand for men in western enterprise and in the various specialist departments of Government service is soon met. But there is a general demand for lucrative employment, and consequently for schools to qualify men for employment, and therefore an almost unlimited demand for teachers. The Government can encourage the demand for trained teachers by imposing appropriate conditions on the grant of funds to schools. In agriculture and other special lines it is obviously waste of money to train men in excess of the demand, but there is little danger of an unemployable surplus of trained teachers, because in the teaching profession the Government fixes the demand that it supplies. Not until every school receiving grants from Government is fully staffed with trained teachers can the supply be in excess of the demand.

Whether the money spent on training-schools is well spent is another question. It seems plausible to argue that men will teach more efficiently if instructed in modern principles of teaching. But, in this matter as in others, the concept of efficiency is valid only in relation to the end proposed. Modern teaching methods have evolved out of educational experience in the homogeneous society of the West, where the school and the environment co-operate and teach the children at the same time how to live and how to make a living. But in the plural society of the tropics the children have a choice between attending schools, western or vernacular, where they may learn how to make a living, and native schools that still adhere to the tradition of teaching children how to live. Where children seek education in order 'to realize its manifold advantages as soon and as cheaply as possible',[2] a trained teacher should be better able to help them to qualify for 'a decent job' in the shortest time at the least possible expense. Within these narrow limits the certificated teacher should be more 'efficient'. But, in inculcating a higher, or at least different, point of view, he is no more likely to succeed than the many generations of devoted missionaries and educational enthusiasts in the past;

[1] Mills, p. 335.
[2] *RPI* (India), 1897–1902, p. 459.

and the man who acquires a teaching certificate merely as a condition of employment, or as a qualification for higher pay, is unlikely to recommend a different attitude to those he teaches. Moreover, in vernacular schools the great mass of the children do not remain long enough to acquire permanent literacy or even to get far beyond the alphabet. Often they attend irregularly when they are not wanted at home or in the fields. In such circumstances there is little advantage in scientific teaching, and it seems that teachers, after acquiring their certificates, tend to lapse into traditional methods of instruction; not without excuse, as their chief function is to keep the children out of mischief. In lay schools with certificated teachers, the great majority of the pupils get little if at all farther than in native religious schools such as the monastic schools of Burma, the Koran schools in Moslem lands or the bush schools under missionary auspices in Africa, while they do not enjoy the same moral background, and it may well be questioned whether, from a cultural standpoint, the lay schools are the more efficient. Thus, although the easiest way of spending money on vocational instruction is to multiply training schools for teachers, and such expenditure is less obviously wasteful than on other special types of school, it is not so easy to be certain whether the money is wisely spent, with a proportional return in social welfare or economic progress.

A further instance of the relation between economic demand and vocational education may be found in the contrast between the numbers studying medicine and law. In the dispatch of 1854 one matter thought to demand attention was the provision of special facilities for training lawyers in India. Now, not only in India but in all parts of the tropics where lawyers can find employment, they are even too numerous. Governments no longer need provide facilities for those who want to practise law, but, as with teachers, can insist on adequate qualifications. Yet it is still necessary to encourage the study of medicine. The tropics need more doctors, and generally could do with fewer lawyers. Yet there are many lawyers and few doctors. That is a characteristic feature of plural economy. Every one, European, oriental immigrant or native, who has a case, whether criminal or civil in a western court wants a lawyer trained on western lines. They all want the same kind of lawyer. Demand creates supply and the supply multiplies in excess of the demand, with the result that the lawyers employ touts to seek for clients by fostering disputes, litigation increases, and legal practice forsakes the honourable traditions that mitigate litigation in the West. On the other hand, each group in each community believes in its own system of medicine, and wants its own medical practitioners. There is no demand for western doctors except among Europeans or in Government service, so that natives trained in western medicine can find only a few openings with little prospect of high fees or good appointments. Naturally they prefer the Bar. Even with such un-attractive prospects the supply of doctors is sometimes in excess of the demand and, as in the law, professional standards tend to de-teriorate or, as in the Philippines, a considerable number of doctors and dentists are compelled to seek appointments as clerks.[1] Ordin-arily, however, the training of medical students rests with the Government, which can adjust the supply to the probable demand. The tropics need doctors, but there is a demand for lawyers, and consequently there are many lawyers and few doctors.

Here then we have the key to the slow growth of vocational and technical instruction in the tropics; it is hampered by the economic environment. But that is not a complete explanation. Other factors have contributed, and among them the tendency to regard economic progress as identical with native welfare. Educational policy looks to technical instruction as an instrument of native welfare, but educational practice encourages it as an instrument of progress. In many dependencies there have been repeated enquiries into the pro-motion of technical instruction, but these have been conducted largely from the standpoint of employers. The committee of 1926 in Malaya, for example, said, 'We fear that it is only too true that many of the youth of this country have a genuine distaste for hard and continuous manual labour'.[2] Clearly they regarded the youth of the country as merely so much labour, and this note, less crudely expressed perhaps, dominates most of such reports in most dependencies. Yet the report just cited has exceptional significance. The committee reported that there was little scope for technical instruction. But, just at that time, men were crowding into the motor industry and picking up the requisite technical skill where they could and how they could. That was happening throughout the tropics. One of the most striking develop-ments of recent times is the rapid spread of the petrol engine and the introduction of motor transport in the native world. Men have learned to drive cars and lorries and taxis, and to do running repairs and even more difficult work, without special schools but through some form

[1] Mills, p. 368.   [2] Ib. p. 353.

of apprenticeship or through learning from one another. As with legal training, the demand common to all communities of the plural society has created a supply even without expenditure or encouragement by Government. It is noteworthy also that, so far as the student demands qualifications for employment in the western sphere rather than the ability to exercise his calling in the native sphere, there is the same tendency to the deterioration of standards as in other professions, and the boy claiming to be qualified as an 'engineer' may be employable only as a mechanic's mate or a road ganger.[1] The encouragement of technical instruction without regard to the demand for men with technical qualifications implied that it is possible to create industries by training men to practise them. This idea still survives in nationalist circles, though it has been abandoned by educational authorities. For the encouragement of technical instruction it is not sufficient to found training-schools and institutions or to train men for employment in the western sphere; it is necessary to create and organize a demand for it in the native sphere of tropical economy, by extending the native sphere to comprehend the whole content of modern economic life.

Naturally the cult of the certificate has extended to the domain of commerce. Formerly in Malaya there were great complaints at the salary required by anyone who could read and write a European language, even very imperfectly; 'youths who were neither good clerks *in esse* or *in posse*' could command high pay.[2] With the multiplication of schools employers get better value for their money, and employees find their certificates less valuable. When a child enters the education stakes in the infant class, his parents may look to matriculation as a standard that will insure them a competence in their old age but, by the time that he matriculates, nothing less than a university degree will command an adequate salary. The commercial school provides a less costly alternative, and of late years the number of commercial schools has multiplied rapidly. These are mostly private enterprises run solely for profit, with no encouragement from the State. But of the students receiving vocational or technical instruction, the number in commercial schools usually ranks second only to the number in teachers' training institutes. Yet normal and commercial schools do not give the kind of technical instruction that was contemplated at the beginning of the century, when the authorities were seeking an alternative to an 'academic' and 'literary' curriculum.

---

[1] *African Survey*, p. 1234. [2] 1905, Cmd. 2379, p. 21.

The expectation that technical instruction would provide a substitute for academic instruction has clearly proved fallacious. On the contrary, academic instruction has developed more rapidly than before. For this the insistence on technical instruction is in part responsible. Technical instruction is based on modern science, and requires a higher standard of general education than most pupils in the ordinary western schools attain. In Netherlands India technical instruction dates from 1901, when the growth of western enterprise was creating a demand for locally trained assistants. The technical institutes were open to natives, but were inaccessible because at that time only European schools equipped their pupils to receive technical training. That is still the position in many tropical dependencies. Few pupils study natural science, and only a small proportion reach a stage which equips them to receive technical instruction. Technical instruction does not take the place of general education, but stimulates the further development of general education. But the chief reason for the continued and more rapid growth of ordinary secondary and higher education is the modern expansion of western enterprise and commerce. This has created a greater demand for clerks and for a better knowledge of the appropriate European language. In Burma the growth of private enterprise in teaching English compelled the Government to accede to the teaching of English in vernacular schools. In Java the people insist on learning Dutch, and in Indo-China French. In some parts of Africa 'native life is so closely bound up with a dominant white civilization, that the native is not adequately equipped to meet the conditions with which he has to contend unless he knows a European language'.[1] For nearly half a century colonial education policy everywhere has been directed to giving a technical, utilitarian bent to the system of instruction, but has been unable to prevail against the economic forces creating a demand for (more strictly utilitarian) 'academic' courses. Curzon looked to his new policy to train the people in the business of life, but in practice the new policy, like the old, does no more than train them for a life of business. Under the new constructive policy as under the former policy of *laissez-faire*, education in the plural society of a tropical dependency is an instrument of economic progress, dominated by economic forces, and a powerful factor in converting the social order into a business concern.

[1] *African Survey*, p. 1286.

8. EDUCATION AND WELFARE

Everywhere and always education has an economic aspect, for material welfare is one main concern of human life. The monastic schools in Burma aimed primarily at teaching the boys how to live as Burman Buddhists, but under their own kings they were also the chief means of advancement in Church and State. That was true also of education in medieval Europe. But in the modern world, when the application of rational criteria to social life reached the classroom, the economic aspect of education came into the foreground. In Europe this tendency has hitherto been kept within safe limits by the force of common social tradition but, in the plural society of tropical dependencies, there is no such tradition. It was because experience during the period of *laissez-faire* showed the need for some corrective that Curzon inaugurated the modern policy of providing a substitute for social tradition by teaching hygiene, thrift and morals.

Hygiene, accordingly, is now often taught in schools. The teaching of hygiene can be enforced by attaching suitable conditions to the grant of funds, and teachers can be encouraged to obtain certificates as teachers of hygiene by the lure of better pay. But hygienic principles, as actually taught, are valid only for the examination hall. In Burma, one may find lessons on hygiene being given in a classroom thick with cobwebs. In western schools the teaching of hygiene survives only through compulsion, and in the vernacular schools it 'is a farce'.[1] Similarly in Malaya, as elsewhere, the teachers of hygiene sleep in unventilated rooms and neglect the most elementary precautions as to food and drink that they impress daily on their pupils.[2] In the teaching of hygiene 'success lies not in having the child learn facts about hygiene, but in having him learn hygienic habits'.[3] In this matter the Dutch, as usual, are very thorough. Each child is provided with a form in two parts. Every day on reaching school he must inspect the teeth, hands and nails of the child next him, and enter their condition on that child's form. The other part of the form, concerning his habits during the previous day in washing his hands, using the latrine, cleaning himself after defecation and so on he must fill in for himself. At the end of the month the forms are made over to a sanitary inspector, who visits sample

[1] *RPI*, 1927–32, p. 40; 1932–3, p. 17; 1932–7, p. 26.
[2] *RPI* (Malaya), 1938, p. 89.
[3] Hydrick, p. 59.

homes to check the correctness of the entries. This system would seem unlikely to foster harmony in the classroom or the home, and one would hesitate to recommend it generally; and, except possibly in Java, the entries in the forms, whether made at home or in school, might be inaccurate and incomplete. But, even so, the Dutch recognize that it is useless to teach hygiene in school without raising the standard of hygiene among the parents.[1] In Burma, and probably elsewhere, men who have qualified as sanitary inspectors make a large part of their income by conniving at breaches of the health rules. Children may learn to pass examinations from text-books, but they learn to live from example and experience, and where the text-book teaches one thing and the environment another, it is the latter that prevails.

Again, the modern school is expected to inculcate thrift. In this matter also, in Malaya as elsewhere, teachers exhort the children to be thrifty while themselves notoriously in debt. Another agency for teaching thrift is the co-operative credit movement, but co-operative subordinates are no more solvent than subordinates in other services. The whole economic system of tropical dependencies favours and, one may even say, is based on, indebtedness among the cultivators and labourers; it is through advances to cultivators that exporters get cheap produce, and through advances to coolies that employers get cheap labour. One cannot cure this by teaching thrift in schools. Parents incur debt to provide a western education for their children, and men who have been taught thrift in school from the infant standard to the university do not learn to shun the moneylender. If the schools cannot teach cultivators to make more money, which they do want, they are unlikely to be more successful in teaching them western ideas of welfare which they do not want, and in great measure are precluded by the environment from adopting. Without fundamental changes in the economic environment, and in the climate of popular opinion, the idea that western ideas of material welfare can be taught in school is an illusion.

Very similar conditions apply to education as an instrument of moral welfare. Curzon deplored the lax discipline and low moral standards in the schools, and thought to provide a remedy by introducing moral primers and text-books of personal ethics, and by enforcing stricter supervision and control. We have noticed the sequel in Burma. When the new policy was first adopted, the moral standards

[1] Hydrick, pp. 13, 81.

of the western schools in Burma were considered satisfactory; but religious training, ethical instruction and closer supervision were of no avail to check the decline of school discipline and morals until, within a quarter of a century, they had deteriorated to much the same level as in India. In India itself a tacit admission of the failure of the new policy to attain its end is apparent in the latest report on educational progress, which contains no reference to religion or religious education, and only 'one depressing and colourless paragraph is devoted to moral instruction'.[1] In Africa again, when the need for a constructive educational policy was realized, 'the greatest importance was to be attached to religious teaching and moral instruction'. It seems, however, that the adoption of this formula was partly due to the need for conciliating missionary bodies that provided nine-tenths of the instruction, and in practice moral training fights a losing battle against efficiency. Many of the missionary schools are regarded as unsatisfactory in respect of secular instruction, and Governments, hard-pressed for funds, demand efficiency, with visible and measurable results. Thus 'it may well be felt that the time has come when the state should show greater discrimination in the support it gives to the smaller mission school'. The larger mission schools also feel the strain of reconciling religion and efficiency. As standards of instruction rise with the demand for higher and more valuable certificates, the maintenance of schools becomes more costly, and the missions feel the pinch already, while their prospects of financial expansion are remote.[2] Educational policy pays homage to morals and religion, but economic forces govern practice and oust morals and religion from the schools. As the people want cheap qualifications quickly the Government has their support in cultivating efficiency. 'It is the desire for school-teaching rather than any doubts about his own faith which is often the chief inducement for the native to bring his children to the missionary', and native opinion is beginning to show itself impatient of missionary control.[3] The missionaries themselves recognize the utility of secular instruction and, although there are some 'with whom the impulse to effect conversions has seemed to outweigh all other considerations, it would be far from true to say that this spirit has been characteristic of missionary endeavour as a whole'; many 'would wish to combine a more effective

[1] *Overseas Education*, 1940–1, Oct. p. 75.
[2] *African Survey*, pp. 1229, 1235, 1237, 1242, 1284.
[3] *Ib.* pp. 1216, 1235, 1242.

type of education with their religious teaching did their resources permit'. Some, however, are suspicious of efficiency. '*Education*', wrote Bishop Weston, 'is in danger of killing Africans, soul and body. I view with great alarm the movement for educating Africans as quickly as possible....Education is the right of Africa—but education as practised at present will be Africa's curse.'[1]

The restriction of official support to the more 'efficient' type of missionary school reacts on female education. In Africa since 1925, as in India since the time of Curzon, the importance of female education as a means of promoting social welfare has been emphasized. There was the same apprehension that was felt in Java as to Moslem reactions, but in 1936 experience was held to justify the reaffirmation of this principle with greater confidence, and female instruction went ahead—to the prejudice of female education. In the domestic education of women the missionaries were doing useful work. 'There are few stations where some girls or women are not receiving a valuable if limited training in the domestic sciences or in the care of children, in nursing or midwifery, or as teachers.'[2] This was education—learning a new way of life not from text-books but by example and experience in an appropriate environment; but it could not be tested by examinations, or easily be recognized by grants conditional on any mass criterion of efficiency, and financial limitations and the doctrine of efficiency are causing the withdrawal of official grants from most of such schools. In Burma the American Baptists have done similar work among the Karens, with the indirect result that, among all the native peoples, the Karen Christians show far the highest percentage of female literacy. But that is not all. Many Karen girls after passing through the high schools, or even the university, willingly return to domestic duties in the village and the home. It is different with the Burmese. Despite the tradition of female literacy, there was no systematic provision of instruction for the girls. The women do most of the petty trade and, when the British Government opened schools to them, the girls in towns hastened to take advantage of their new opportunities. But it is only of late years that many have sought more advanced education in western schools, and these seem to be actuated by the same motive as their brothers, the desire to get 'a decent job'.[3] Whether female 'education' among westernized Burmese

---

[1] Maynard Smith, H., *Frank, Bishop of Zanzibar* (1926), p. 257.
[2] *African Survey*, pp. 1229, 1231, 1255.
[3] *RPI*, 1927–32, p. 25.

will produce better mothers, or birth control and cheaper typists, is a question for the future.

9. Vernacular Education

So far we have been dealing in the main with western education, and have seen that the prospect of gain is sufficient to crowd the schools beyond capacity, but only so far, and in such directions, as they lead to a remunerative certificate; and that all values, other than examination values, are at a discount. Primary vernacular education provides the obverse of this picture because, in general, it does not pay; it is merely an instrument of human welfare. Since the beginning of the nineteenth century the diffusion of general enlightenment in India through primary instruction has been a main objective of humanitarian sympathy; this principle was adopted and placed in the forefront of official policy from the middle of the century, and it was reaffirmed by Curzon at its close. Yet the progress achieved 'is shown by statistics admitted by the highest educational authorities to be thoroughly unsatisfactory',[1] and in Burma, which started the nineteenth century under native rule with a literate male population, the picture of primary instruction after a hundred years of British rule is 'one of almost unrelieved gloom'.[2] For over a hundred years there has been general agreement in India that primary instruction is the most effective instrument of material and moral welfare, yet, so far as there has been any progress under either head since the time of Wilberforce and Carey, it certainly cannot be attributed to the spread of primary instruction. This has not spread because there has been no demand for it. Now that it is again proclaimed with new insistence as the chief aim of modern educational policy in the tropics generally, some examination of the grounds on which it has been advocated seems expedient. Apart from humanitarian considerations they fall under two heads, political and economic.

Many have urged the spread of vernacular instruction on grounds of political convenience. Curzon cited with approval the dictum that 'among all sources of administrative difficulty and political danger, few are so serious as the ignorance of the people'.[3] This view is still widely held. Mass education is recommended as a safeguard against explosive temper liable to produce a social upheaval. One is told that 'an increase of literacy makes the people easier to control and govern',

[1] Mayhew, *India*, p. 226.   [2] *CVV*, p. 156.
[3] *RPI* (India), 1897–1902, p. 462; *Mass Education*, p. 7; Mayhew, *India*, p. 226.

and that 'it is pleasanter and cheaper to mould a literate population by appropriate and intelligent methods of education than to suppress an illiterate mob by machine guns'. There is very little evidence for such assertions, and certainly experience in Netherlands India and Burma contradicts them. The Dutch, when ruling an illiterate people through their native chieftains, had less difficulty in preserving *rust en orde*, and in moulding the people to their will, than in recent years when literacy has been making rapid progress. In the serious outbreak of 1926, though few of the rebels were highly educated, many had gone far beyond the common man in schooling. In Burma, with a high proportion of literates, there has been greater difficulty than in Java in maintaining law and order, and in obtaining a ready compliance with Government policy; on the contrary, districts conspicuous for literacy are also conspicuous for crime, and of the rebels in 1931 most would have passed for highly educated men in Africa. The early Liberals believed that education would automatically strengthen the ties between India and Britain; Curzon, finding this belief mistaken, tried to stimulate loyalty by hanging up portraits of the King in schools. In Burma there were attempts during the war of 1914–18 to use the schools for spreading 'the imperial idea', and 'to foster a sense of personal attachment to the King-Emperor'.[1] In French dependencies the schools try to evoke an admiration of France, and in Belgian dependencies an affection for Belgium.[2] But those who learn to read find little reading matter except newspapers, described in Netherlands India as 'cheap and nasty—like other things intended for tropical consumption', and often disaffected towards Government. Both in Burma and Java, long before the rise of modern Nationalism, the earliest native newspapers were critical of foreign rule, and the figures already given show that in Burma the circulation of periodicals varies directly with the violence of their attacks on Government. Under indirect rule the people learn from the newspapers to criticize not only the foreign Government but their own chieftains. There would seem little reason, therefore, to expect that the spread of primary instruction will increase docility, and even if it were true that primary instruction makes a people easier to control and govern, this would not induce illiterate parents who do not value education to send their children to the schools.

Others hold out a more tempting bait. They argue that undeveloped minds are incapable of political activities, and that 'in order to pro-

[1] *CII*, p. 5.   [2] Mayhew, *Colonial Empire*, p. 143.

gress towards self-government in the modern world colonial peoples must learn to read, and to understand, not only their own local affairs but those of wider import'.[1] Primary instruction is advocated as a first step towards 'responsible government', and therefore a condition of autonomy. But in the early nineteenth century, literacy was far more widely diffused in Burma than in Britain, yet this did not secure its independence. Even now the comparatively greater literacy of Burma does not seem to make it apter for western political institutions than Java, whereas Siam, with a smaller proportion of literates, has managed to remain independent. In Netherlands India, despite the spread of primary instruction during the past generation, it has been estimated that 167 years must elapse before the last illiterate is dragged to school, and in the Gold Coast, the most forward dependency in Africa in respect of education, the period has been put at 600 years.[2] Prospects of self-government at so remote a date are unlikely to kindle much enthusiasm for primary instruction, and critics have not unnaturally enquired whether its advocates wish to diffuse enlightenment or to delay self-government.

The recent project of mass education looks to the elimination of illiteracy in Africa within some thirty years.[3] That project, though optimistic, is not impossible if the people can be induced to want primary instruction. The prospect of self-government is an inducement; but it is also an illusion. 'Self-government' suggests that they will be free to do what they may want to do. But unless they want to do what, in the conditions of the modern world they must do, they will not be free, or even able to do it. To change their wants is much harder than to teach them letters and, without that, literacy may help them to express their dissatisfaction at not getting what they want, but it will make government more difficult and will raise a new obstacle to self-government. Literacy in itself is nothing. If it were possible to make the whole of Africa as literate to-morrow as Burma is to-day, it would be no more capable than Burma of managing western democratic institutions. Literacy may be an instrument of good or evil and, if tropical peoples are induced to acquire letters on the ground that this implies self-government, they will use the power of letters to vent their disappointment on those who have deceived them. Their profit will be that they know how to curse. Primary instruction, if recommended as

[1] *Britain and Her Dependencies*, p. 7; *Mass Education*, p. 14.
[2] *African Survey*, p. 1235; *HIOC*, Résumé, p. 76.
[3] *Mass Education*, pp. 10, 11.

a step towards self-government, is more likely to cause than to cure an explosive temper and a social upheaval. It may not be impossible to teach tropical peoples their alphabet within a generation, but 'if means must be found and found quickly whereby the people as a *community* can understand and appreciate the forces which have changed and are changing their lives so radically' and 'to call out the ability and will to share in the direction and control of the social, economic and political forces', this end is more likely to be attained by educating the leaders of the community rather than through the mass education of individuals who, taken in the mass, are chiefly concerned, in Africa as elsewhere, with getting their daily bread, and do not hope or wish to meddle in matters that are too high for them. In this matter nationalist opinion, which insists on the education of leaders, is guided by a sound instinct, and the emphasis of colonial powers on primary instruction, however well intended, makes nationalists suspect that leaders are not wanted.

Among the advocates of primary instruction on economic grounds one can also hear two voices. Those who are chiefly concerned with economic progress urge that it will make the native more profitable as a coolie. 'If he is to work harder, longer and more continuously, education must inculcate the ideas of sanctity of contract and of ordinary honesty to his employers.'[1] This appeal to the sanctity of contract—the only saint in the Calendar of Mammon—suggests that the coincidence between the modern emphasis on primary instruction and the discovery that unintelligent labour is uneconomic is not wholly fortuitous. In Malaya the project of opening special schools for immigrants was formerly regarded as a 'fatal error' creating a plural society by 'tending to keep them aliens and encouraging them in the idea that China or India is their home'. But shortly afterwards, the Government decided to open Tamil schools 'with the object of making the F.M.S. from the point of view of the Indian immigrant, an outlying province of India, like Ceylon'.[2] These schools, though recognized as detrimental to social welfare, were created in the interest of economic progress. Experience has shown that Tamil education 'is of value not only as an incentive to recruiting labour for the rubber estates, but as a means of keeping the Tamil labourer happy and contented',[3] and many plantations now have schools for

[1] Mayhew, *Colonial Empire*, p. 141.
[2] 1905, Cmd. 2379, p. 11, and 11 n.
[3] Sir George Maxwell, quoted Sidney, p. 203; Mills, pp. 340, 348.

coolies. In Africa some western enterprises support schools under the right kind of missionary and although, so far, employers in general have displayed little interest in the matter, it is thought that 'shortage of labour in some African areas may dispose them to offer facilities for education, in addition to provisions for general welfare, as an inducement to workers to stay in one place and become more efficient'.[1] Doubtless human sympathy plays a large part in the establishment of schools on western enterprise, but economic interest stimulates this sympathy, and the substantial contributions from Government and from missionary bodies towards the cost of education help to reduce the cost of wages. Education in the name of welfare becomes an instrument of economic progress even to the detriment of social welfare, as with the fostering of communal separation in Malaya. In any case the diffusion of primary instruction among the general public depends not on the demand of employers for more intelligent labour, but on the demand of parents for more schools, and they will not send their children to school in order that they may 'work harder, longer and more continuously' on western enterprise.

Most advocates of primary instruction, however, state the case, more persuasively, on grounds of native welfare. Curzon held that it would help the cultivator in his transactions with moneylenders, merchants and officials. Many claim that it will not only help the cultivators in their business but will enable officials to teach them better agricultural methods, the principles of co-operative credit and modern hygiene.[2] 'Every health measure, every improvement of agricultural methods, the co-operative machinery for production and distribution, the establishment of secondary industries—all these will make increasing demands upon the people and they will be able to respond only if they have had some educational opportunities.'[3] This sounds plausible, and some hold that it is proved. 'So far in the British Colonies we have acted on the assumption that people would eventually adopt improved methods of agriculture, hygienic surroundings and western medical ideas without learning to read and write....It has been proved that the attainment of literacy makes people aware of the need for social and economic improvements, and therefore they will co-operate more readily with welfare and other agencies working on these lines.'[4] It would be difficult to find another

---

[1] *Mass Education*, p. 27.   [2] Mayhew, *India*, p. 226.
[3] Colonial Secretary, House of Commons, 13 July 1943.
[4] *Mass Education*, p. 14.

example of so many fallacies in so few words. It is not true that we have acted on this assumption, and it is not true that literacy entails better living. On the other hand people take to better living without literacy, for they will take over from the West anything that they find profitable, even education. But education when sought as a means of individual profit is not an instrument of welfare, not even of individual welfare, because it injures social welfare. The assumption is against all probability, and, as will appear below, is contradicted by the facts.

It is certainly not the case that we have tried to improve the condition of the people before teaching them to read and write. In India the diffusion of primary instruction had been a main object of policy for half a century before the promotion of hygiene and other objects of social welfare received serious attention. Since about 1900 it has been advocated as a means of improving hygiene. But the people, in general, have been no more responsive to the efforts to encourage primary instruction than to the efforts to promote hygiene. They did not want to learn to read and write because it would not pay.

Again, the suggestion that literacy leads to better living will not stand the most cursory examination. Doubtless in Singapore the proportion of literacy is higher among the Chinese who live in palaces than among the Chinese of the slums: but the former do not live in palaces because they are literate; they are literate because they can live in palaces. Literacy is often expected to encourage thrift. But if a man wants to borrow money he will sign his name as readily as he will make his mark, though, as a signature is less easy to repudiate, the transaction is really more imprudent. When he sells his crops, literacy will not raise the price fixed by a ring of buyers. In Burma debt is most burdensome in tracts with the highest proportion of literates, and in these tracts co-operative credit was the greatest failure. All over the Tropical Far East literacy under native rule was far more widely diffused than in India or Africa, but it has not kept the people out of debt. Also if so much is expected from vernacular literacy, one would expect more from the higher standard of literacy attained by those acquainted with a European language. Yet in Burma, and probably elsewhere, we find clerks in Government service and commercial firms heavily indebted to illiterate menials. Similarly indebtedness prevails among subordinate officials, including judges and magistrates. In Java one hears of Regents in the clutches of Chinese moneylenders. In the Philippines, for all the efforts of the

American Government to promote literacy, agricultural debt seems worse than in Malaya, and even candidates for the local representative assembly, who are presumably among the more highly educated, readily incur insolvency in their electoral campaigns.[1] For the promotion of thrift and better business methods, the attainment of literacy in itself is nothing, nor has literacy enabled administrations to promote thriftiness. Create an environment that puts a premium on thrift, imbue the people with a spirit of thriftiness, and literacy, though unessential, will be helpful.

But if literacy can do so little in helping the people to improve their economic position and get the things they value, no one can expect it to be more effective in changing their standard of values, in leading them voluntarily to accept the restrictions on personal liberty, involved in modern western hygiene. We have noticed that even the teachers of hygiene do not practise what they preach, and those who give and receive these lessons are all literate. Where a comparatively high degree of literacy has such poor results, universal primary instruction is unlikely to be more effective. If, as is commonly believed, people will not 'adopt improved methods of agriculture, a more nutritious diet, hygienic surroundings and western medical ideas without learning to read and write', they will not adopt them the more readily merely for being taught their alphabet.

In point of fact, however, this common belief is wrong. It is untrue that people must learn to read and write in order to attain greater welfare. We have noticed that throughout the tropics in both Africa and Asia, cultivators, literate or illiterate, have taken to new crops and new kinds of food. In Java, despite illiteracy, the standard of rural hygiene, unsatisfactory as it may seem to the Dutch, has long presented a striking contrast with conditions in most parts of the tropics. If people can be induced to want social and economic improvements they will value literacy, both in itself and as an instrument of other aspects of social advance, but in itself literacy will not inspire them with new wants.

Literacy is one sign of civilization. The Burmese are literate, and stand on a higher plane of civilization than the surrounding hill tribes; but they are more literate because they are more civilized, and not more civilized because they are more literate. Some of these hill tribes are Karens. Missionary work has made great progress among the Karens, and among Christian Karens there is a higher standard

[1] Mills, p. 276; Malcolm, pp. 171, 212, 220.

of literacy, and a far higher standard of female literacy than among the Burmese. But the Karens did not learn to read and write in order to become Christians; they learned to read and write because they had become Christians. Social progress led to economic progress, and both social and economic progress are reflected in their literacy. Similarly the Burmese are not Buddhists because they learn to read and write, but they learn to read and write because they are Buddhists. Literacy is a sign and not a cause of social progress. Inspire tropical peoples with a desire for western standards of social life and they will want, among other things, to read and write; but the ability to read and write will not inspire them with a desire for social or economic progress. It is true that in Russia and China there has recently been great progress both in literacy and in the general standard of living, but that is because a new spirit has descended on them. In Malaya the people remained apathetic in respect of schooling until 'the Malay rulers turned to education to equip their subjects to hold their own against the educated Indian and the intellectual and energetic Chinese'.[1] Similarly in Java the modern growth of literacy has been stimulated by the appeal to patriotism. But, without a complete transformation of the social and economic environment, literacy alone will help the people no better than it has helped the Burmese. 'Even if popular education were made universal and compulsory throughout the dependencies, it would not in itself produce a revolution in social outlook such as seems, for instance to have been effected in Soviet Russia and to some extent in China.'[2]

The easiest way to diffuse primary instruction is to make it pay. That is the way in which western instruction spread. Where, as frequently in urban areas, literacy has an economic value, or where it confers a higher social standing, many lads will pick up reading and writing without special facilities and without encouragement. We can see this in Africa, where 'in some areas a number of them have had a smattering of education, often quite unrelated to their environment and to the possibilities of employment. But this smattering, which includes the three R's, represents the intention of their parents that their children shall have *some* education, and expresses an almost pathetic belief in the inherent value of learning to read and write'.[3] Yet mere literacy has no intrinsic value; it has a scarcity value, and enables those who can read and write to earn more. Parents who

[1] *RPI* (Malaya), 1938, p. 8.
[2] *Britain and Her Dependencies*, p. 33.   [3] *Mass Education*, p. 18.

believe this will send their children to vernacular schools so that they can earn more, just as in the past they have sent their children, often at great sacrifice, to western schools, and with the same result, but on a vastly wider scale, of producing discontent when the supply of those who can read and write is in excess of the demand. If vernacular education be recommended to the people as a means of individual advancement, it may provide more intelligent and more economic labour, but it will be perverted, like western education, from an instrument of welfare into an instrument of progress and its expansion will be governed by the demand for labour. The problem is to find some non-economic motive sufficient to induce parents to send their children to school. If such a motive can be found, then the more who go to school the better.

10. NATIVE EDUCATION

While vernacular instruction has languished, native education has declined. It was formerly the strength of native education that it was based on ideas transcending the economic sphere. It taught them how to live. Now that the world in which it taught them how to live has vanished, the native schools decay. In Burma the monastic schools have lost much of their social value through the drainage of their wealthier and brighter pupils into western schools. In towns they have suffered also from the competition of lay schools, feeding the western schools, providing candidates for subordinate vernacular appointments, and attracting others who for various reasons are content with secular instruction. It has been the policy of the Government to adapt them to the modern world. 'The method of translating the policy into practice varied from time to time, but the variations played on a single theme—the secularization of the curriculum and methods of the monastic school.'[1] The monastic schools sufficed to provide magistrates and judges, so long as no other schools were available, but they did not fit into a scheme based on the assumption that efficiency in education could be tested by the acquisition of certificates qualifying for appointments, and they could not compete with the better lay schools in getting boys quickly through their examinations. Thus they were driven into the backwoods. There was no need to secularize western education, though it was largely in the hands of missionaries, for missionary schools, no less than lay schools, are dominated by the cult of the certificate, and now, as we have noted, the problem is 'how to spiritual-

[1] *CVV*, p. 131.

ize education'. Similarly, in Java, the progress of modern education has led to the decay of native schools. Formerly 'the children were entrusted to some village elder or religious leader for moral and social training, and also to learn simple arithmetic and reading and writing in a local script or in Arabic. These forms of teaching shrank to a simple religious teaching, and this process was quicker at first than the development of the new government education. Paradoxically therefore the creation of modern education increased the number of illiterates'.[1] The introduction of French education in Indo-China seems to have had a similar result. The decay of native education in the Tropical Far East is obvious because these schools, especially in Burma, had attained a comparatively high standard of instruction, but it has happened throughout the tropics from the Pacific Islands to Africa.

In Africa the native system of education was directed to character training and instruction in crafts. But the crafts are dead or dying. 'The African artistic genius has produced objects of singular beauty inspired by religious beliefs and social customs and the necessities of social and domestic life. These sources of inspiration are profoundly modified, if not destroyed by modern conditions, and there is evidence of a decline in artistic taste accelerated by the replacement of indigenous articles by those of European manufacture, the commercial exploitation of so-called native crafts, and lack of encouragement.' Everywhere 'native manufacture is undoubtedly on the decline: the smelting of iron is moribund; the ubiquitous petrol tin has made pottery almost a forgotten art; the handloom has nearly disappeared. It is a regrettable effect of European contacts in Africa that an increase of wealth should thus destroy rather than stimulate local craftsmanship.'[2] In Africa also, as in Burma and the tropics generally, the same process is visible in non-productive arts, in music, dancing and the drama, and also in native pastimes. 'The danger of the present time', it has been said, 'is that undue emphasis will be placed on economic welfare and mechanical progress, and that even leisure will be commercialized so that the true springs of artistic creation and enjoyment may have very little outlet.'[3] But that is nothing new, or peculiar to the present time. Despite benevolent aspirations in colonial policy, it has always been inherent in colonial practice. The decline of native arts and crafts and

[1] C. O. van der Plas, *see* Djajadiningrat, p. 65.
[2] *African Survey*, pp. 1207, 1290, 1420.
[3] *Mass Education*, p. 49.

pastimes is merely one aspect of the elimination of non-economic values in the plural society of a tropical dependency, and native schools and native education decay because the ideas on which they rested lose their meaning.

11. Education and Instruction

Even in England it is often suggested that the ideas on which education has rested in the past are fading and must be recovered. Enthusiasts for education propound large claims as to what education might or ought to be, and what it might, should or must do. But they tend to overlook what education actually is and does, and confound education with instruction. Education is much wider than instruction, and much older. During the long ages of pre-history man survived because he was capable of learning, by example and experience, to adapt his way of life to his environment; succeeding generations learned new lessons in the school of life. Education dates from the emergence of mankind. Instruction, however, was of minor importance before the invention of the art of letters, which gave man a new and more efficient means of transmitting his social heritage and of communicating new ideas. But it was chiefly significant in giving a foremost place in education to mental discipline, the training of the mind. This helped man to understand his environment and made him better able, not merely to adapt his way of life to his environment, but to adapt his environment to his way of life. It gave him a key to progress. In the course of modern progress instruction has come to play a growing part in education. But it is not the whole of education; it is that part of education which consists in the formal training of the mind. Education is much wider; it is the sum of all the processes that equip the child for life in adult society.

The distinction between education and instruction is so obvious that it might seem a platitude if it were not so often overlooked. When advocates of education in the tropics say that 'education is, and is intended to be an instrument of change', or that 'the whole mass of the people must have a real share in education and some understanding of its meaning and purpose',[1] they show that they mistake its meaning, and are regarding it as something grafted on to life. The teacher of a training college in the Philippines tells us to 'think of tropical peoples as organisms having to adjust themselves to a physical and social environment which under modern conditions may embrace

[1] *Mass Education*, p. 4.

more or less of indigenous and alien elements'. That is true. But he goes on to argue that 'education is the process by which they gain the best adaptation',[1] and obviously is thinking merely of instruction. In Burma, 'the major task of education is to help towards the establishment of economic security and the improvement of living conditions in the village'.... 'The task', says an optimistic expert in educational technique, 'can be undertaken *by reconstructing the curricula of the schools.*'[2] Educationalists, in claiming that education should or must promote the good life, or change the social order, or soften the impact of western civilization, overlook the fact that education is not something given in the school or by way of formal instruction, but is the operation of the whole environment. They will readily admit that the school can play only a minor part in education, but underlying the high ideals that find expression in educational policy is the tacit assumption that these lofty aspirations can be realized in practice by instruction for a few years, during a few hours a day in certain subjects as set forth in text-books through teachers who often do not believe in what they teach.

In the West the tendency to identify education with instruction is not unnatural, for the school is the product of and is conditioned by the environment, and the instruction given there is reinforced by and reinforces the social environment outside the school. The education of the child proceeds on the same lines inside and outside the school, and it is convenient to distinguish by the name of education that which is given in the school. But in the tropics 'the school itself is largely exotic in character, and so is often unable really to reflect and interpret the society which it is intended to serve'.[3] The schools are expected to promote welfare, but much of the teaching in school runs counter to and is countered by the social environment outside the school. Europeans are quick to impress on nationalist politicians the folly of trying to create industries by training men to practise them, but the project of creating welfare by training men to teach it is no wiser. Instruction *seems* important, far more important than it is, for whereas we are conscious of instruction, other educational processes are largely unconscious. We know when we are being taught, but often fail to recognize until long afterwards, if ever, that we are learning and, in comparison with the pressure exerted by the environment, school teaching is negligible.

[1] Keesing, p. 43. [2] *CVV*, p. 195 (my italics).
[3] *Mass Education*, p. 6.

The tropics have learned much from Europe; but very little from schools or school-books. Their first lesson is that spears and bows and arrows are no match for bayonets and machine-guns. More is taught by the wrath of the tiger than by the horses of instruction. It is significant that they do not grasp the meaning even of this lesson. They learn from experience the greater efficiency of western arms, but experience does not teach them the secret of moral discipline that has gone to the perfection of western military power. Even the Japanese, whose social tradition was strong enough to provide the necessary moral discipline, overrated the importance of military power and did not fathom the secret of its limitations. Schools, teachers and text-books may try to sow the seed of western civilization, but the pupils are content to pluck the fruit. They see the fruit; they see that export crops are more profitable than food crops; that the motor-car is speedier and more comfortable than the bullock cart; and, among other things, both good and bad, they learn that 'education' is a way to make a living—not from pronouncements on educational policy, but from practical experience both inside and outside the school. From the beginning of the nineteenth century, missionaries and humanitarians have expected education in the tropics to change the character of the environment, but in the event the environment has changed the character of education. The schools meet the demand for officials and subordinates in administration and western enterprise and produce a supply in excess of the demand. In Burma there is 'waste of effort and money on instruction that is making but little, if any, impression on the illiteracy of the masses at one extreme, and adding to the gravity of the already grave problem of the unemployed graduate and product of the secondary schools at the other'.[1] This picture of the results attained in Burma after a hundred years of British rule applies to tropical dependencies in general, but it is a poor return for the labours of so many generations of zealous and devoted teachers, missionaries and laymen.

Western schools produce a surplus of clerical skill, and mass education may produce a surplus of educated unskilled labour. So far as it goes, the instruction given in the schools is good, useful. It enables those, or some of those, who receive it, to earn more money than they would otherwise, and helps western administration and enterprise to function more efficiently and cheaply. Both these things are desirable. But they are not the things that humanitarians have in view

[1] *CVV*, p. 183.

when pleading the cause of education. The advocates of education look on instruction as a key to western civilization and the modern world, and so it is. So long, however, as the people have no books to read, the door is not only locked, but barred and bolted.

Primary instruction teaches the people to read. But if they have no occasion for reading, they tend to forget what they have learned in school and to lapse into illiteracy. A modern environment, with moneylenders, law courts and a postal service, creates a demand for reading as a useful accomplishment; in a literate environment people do not forget their alphabet so readily. But it does not supply them with books or create a habit of reading. If their religion has its scriptures, there will be a demand for religious books, as in Burma, where there has been a demand for such books from the first introduction of printing, though for show rather than for use. Both in Burma and Netherlands India, when the reading public was still very small, it was thought necessary to take action against pornographic literature.[1] That was what the public wanted. Under the stimulus of nationalism, newspapers may achieve a modest circulation, if sufficiently critical of Government. But it is more difficult than it may seem to provide books in the vernacular that open a door into the modern world, and still more difficult to get the people to want to read such books. We have seen that the Dutch have gone some way to solve the problem, and something has been done by private associations in Africa. The crux of the problem is to organize a demand for books, and, if this can be accomplished, it is comparatively easy to supply reading matter.

Western instruction might seem more effective as an instrument of civilization than vernacular instruction, because a European language in itself provides a gateway to the modern world. But the progress of western instruction is conditioned by the economic environment. This places limits on the numbers who receive it, and restricts its scope to attainments with a market value. One distinctive feature of the modern world is the importance of natural science in the affairs of daily life. But in the tropics, so long as the demand for men with a western education is confined to administrative and clerical employment, scientific studies are at a discount. Only when, and so far as, the growth of western enterprise creates a demand for men with technical qualifications, is there a demand for the teaching of natural science. If tropical peoples are to be brought into closer contact with the modern

[1] Freytag, p. 71; *RAB*, 1914–15, p. 101.

world and to contribute as fully as possible to world welfare, it is desirable that colonial administrations should do what they can to foster a demand for western education (including vernacular education on western lines) and for the enlargement of its scope. That is not a problem for educational authorities, though often left to them. How best to meet an actual demand for western studies is an educational problem, but to organize a demand for more men with a western education and for education with a wider scope are matters that lie outside the province of the educational authorities and the schoolmaster.

The people seek western education for its economic value and they wish 'to realize its manifold advantages as soon and as cheaply as possible'. If they are to appreciate its cultural value, and use it as an introduction to the modern world, there must be some inducement sufficient to encourage them to understand the modern world, its material achievements and the spiritual foundations on which its material achievements rest. But just as the western man of business only earns his living in the tropics while his real life is in the West, so likewise the people live in the native world and only earn their living in the western sphere. That is the environment which conditions education, and it is impossible to change the environment through the schools, because the schools supply what the environment demands; if, however, we can change the environment, the schools will reflect the new environment, and it is only thus that we can transform mere instruction into education.

Western education, then, is necessary if the people are to become citizens of the modern world, but the present system of instruction is precluded from performing this function by the environment in which it functions and which it reflects. Among Europeans concerned with education, though some reconcile themselves to a purely utilitarian view of their activities and some lapse into cynical indifference, many and probably most do their best to instil cultural values. But Europeans come into close and direct contact with only a comparatively small number of students, usually in the higher standards. Most of the teachers are natives, often men who have failed to find more lucrative employment, and ordinarily, like the students, they care for little but examination results. Some teachers may inspire some pupils with ideals, but 'idealism is easy in the class-room' and rarely survives contact with the outer world. It is true that western education under British, Dutch and French rule, has produced a few men who are at home in the modern world and some who have achieved an international reputation. But most of these have drunk the waters of modern civilization at the fountain head in Europe, and it is noteworthy that among them the men who believe most fervently in education found schools like the *asrams* of Gandhi and Tagore, or the *Tamansiswo* schools in Java, which repudiate the whole material basis on which public instruction rests. This is in striking contrast with the early native educationists such as Ram Mohur Roy and Miss Kartini, who looked to western education as a means of spreading light in Asia. It is in contrast also with the general attitude among modern nationalists. These have founded Nationalist schools partly with a view to attaining the same results as Government and mission schools, but more rapidly and cheaply, and partly with a view to national advancement by using western learning as a means to rid themselves of western rule. Often such schools are tempted by the lure of grants to succumb to the environment, and become merely inferior imitations of the Government schools, so that nationalists succeed no better than missionaries in transforming instruction into education. Thus humanitarians, missionaries, nationalists and statements of official policy present education as an instrument of culture, according to the common tradition of Europe and the tropics; but in practice, it becomes an instrument of economic development, and even as such is less effective than it would be in a more congenial environment.

CHAPTER XI

PROGRESS, WELFARE AND AUTONOMY

1. Colonial Policy and Autonomy

In the last two chapters we have been examining colonial practice in relation to material and moral welfare. Almost everywhere in the tropics western rule has stimulated rapid economic progress, and that, in itself, is a good thing. It is well that backward regions should contribute as freely as possible to the general welfare of the world; in any case they will be made to do so because, if the inhabitants are unable or unwilling to develop their local resources, they will be too feeble to resist others whom the hope of profit may tempt to undertake this task. But modern colonial policy does not accept economic progress as an end in itself; it regards progress as the means to the material welfare of dependent peoples. That is a heritage from the Liberal tradition. From this tradition also, and from the far older Christian tradition, it inherits the belief that material welfare is not an end in itself. It regards material welfare as a condition of welfare in a wider sense, embracing political welfare and autonomy. In the present chapter we are concerned with the relation between progress and welfare, and with the bearing of colonial practice on political autonomy.

A preliminary survey may help to clear the way. Briefly, then, where economic development fails to promote welfare, the explanation usually propounded is the insufficiency of revenue, and a remedy is sought in more vigorous development so as to produce more revenue. But an enquiry into the relations between revenue and welfare indicates the need to find some other explanation. In seeking it we are hampered by the lack of adequate data for the measurement of welfare. This, although a serious defect in the machinery of welfare, is not the chief defect. The machinery of welfare under direct rule does not comply with the essential conditions of success. Under indirect rule the machinery might prove effective if it were allowed time to work; but it acts slowly, and the modern tendency is to expedite its working by compulsion. Compulsion, however, is worse than useless as an instrument of welfare, and in practice is only one aspect of the constant pressure to expedite development. This leads to the conclusion that the view of progress as a condition of welfare is mistaken, and that, on the contrary, welfare is a condition of progress. If, therefore, colonial powers would enhance welfare in their dependencies, they must aim directly at promoting welfare instead of expecting it as a sequel of economic development.

Here we encounter a preliminary difficulty in defining the concept of welfare. If we define welfare as consisting in harmony between the individual and his environment, colonial policy must aim at reconciling them. They can be reconciled in two ways: by submission to the environment, or by mastering it. The former might be consistent with material welfare if men were no more than cattle, but it fails because men are not merely cattle. It is true that men must accept the facts of their environment if they are to master it, and that tropical peoples, when brought into contact with the modern world, must come to terms with western civilization in order to achieve harmony with their environment, but they alone can promote their own welfare, and whereas modern colonial policy regards welfare as a condition of autonomy, we are led to the conclusion that, on the contrary, autonomy is a condition of welfare.

Colonial autonomy is a heritage from the Liberal tradition. But in the past it has been attempted through mechanical reconstruction by the introduction of a native personnel into the administration, and the imitation of western political institutions in local and central government. Such attempts to adapt tropical society to western forms of self-government are based on the fallacy that form gives birth to function, and they serve merely to facilitate the working of economic forces, destructive both of welfare and autonomy. If we would promote autonomy, and thereby welfare, we must aim at adapting western institutions to tropical society, on the principle that function will devise appropriate forms of government.

These in brief are the considerations that will engage our attention in the present chapter. They lead on to the conclusion that what is needed is not mechanical reconstruction, but a creative impulse, strong enough to solve the problem of restoring unity to a disintegrated social order, and strong enough also to surmount the obstacles arising from considerations of profit and prestige.

2. Welfare and Revenue

Under western rule, tropical dependencies produce more. Because people must grow more in order to eat more, it is natural to assume that they eat more because they grow more. But this assumption is invalid. Public works and economic services increase the productivity of western enterprise. They may also, within limits, increase native production, but without any corresponding enhancement of welfare. Such devices indeed, by allowing freer play to anti-social economic forces, tend to prejudice rather than promote native welfare, and create a need for social services to mitigate their deleterious effects. Yet the services intended to furnish the necessary protection function mainly to make production more efficient, and the services intended to promote welfare directly by improving health and education have a similar result; though designed as instruments of human welfare they are perverted into instruments of economic progress.

When the machinery for enhancing welfare proves ineffective, a remedy is sought in more and more elaborate and costly machinery. For the promotion of welfare, it is argued, economic and social services are needed; these cost money and require larger revenue; larger revenue can come only through economic development, and economic development depends on western enterprise and capital. Therefore western enterprise and capital are needed to provide the revenue for economic and social services that will enhance welfare. This is the proposition that we must now examine.

It is true that western enterprise and capital are effective agents of development; but so also is native enterprise. Both under direct rule and, though less conspicuously, under indirect rule, the maintenance of order and the opening up of new markets have sufficed to call forth native enterprise without the importation of western capital. It is true also that economic development provides more revenue. But at the same time it raises the cost of administration. This rises even with development by native enterprise, because expenditure must be incurred on law and order and on communications. But it rises far more rapidly and further with development by western enterprise. 'The most superficial observer must be struck by the difference which the existence of a resident European community makes in the standards of government expenditure.'[1] The European community demands better provision for its own amenities in respect of health, education and so on, and also demands better provision for natives so that they may furnish more efficient labour or more abundant produce. Some of the services incidental on development become indispensable. But usually the revenue from tropical dependencies barely suffices for urgent expenditure on the maintenance of order and the improvement

African Survey, p. 1463.

of communications. Not infrequently debts incurred to the Home Government have had to be remitted, and in most dependencies the financial position is one of constant stringency, while the inadequacy of the surplus available for economic and social services forms a recurrent burden of complaint both among officials and the representatives of western enterprise.

The argument that western enterprise is needed to provide the funds for social services assumes that the revenue derived from it more than covers the extra cost of administration consequent on economic development. But 'whether the local administrations have yet taken a sufficient share of the profits of foreign enterprise is a matter of some debate....It must be admitted that a number of administrations have shown reluctance to utilise fully their powers to impose taxation on the profits of companies or firms working in their territory, or have done so only in response to pressure from the Home Government'.[1] In practice, there is a deficit, which is met partly by imposing new obligations in services or taxation on the natives, and partly from private contributions, native and foreign.

It is indeed generally recognized that, in the course of economic development, excessive burdens have often been imposed upon the natives, either in taxation or compulsory labour, to meet the charges of general administration and the additional expenditure consequent on economic development, and even for the direct benefit of western enterprise.[2] Especially in the improvement of communications by road and rail, there have been serious abuses. In Africa, moreover, railway construction has mostly been unprofitable, constituting a charge on general revenue and cramping economic and social services so narrowly as to keep them below the standard required even for economic progress.

Another very considerable contribution to the cost of essential services comes from private sources. Among these one may reckon contributions from western enterprise otherwise than through taxation. As already mentioned, the great experimental stations in Netherlands India, which have done so much for the science of tropical agriculture, were until recently maintained by the planters' associations without Government assistance; they were intended to make production more profitable for those who supplied the funds, but their benefit radiated throughout the tropics and beyond, sometimes to the

[1] *Britain and Her Dependencies*, p. 22.
[2] *African Survey*, pp. 613, 635, 1549, 1565.

detriment of local interests as in teaching India and Japan how to grow sugar. In all parts of the tropics, in Asia as well as in Africa, the more enlightened employers provide good quarters, medical attention and schools, and make their employees comply with modern sanitary requirements; such amenities make production more efficient and profitable. Employers will provide such services as they deem profitable, and on humanitarian grounds may carry this principle to the farthest limit or possibly beyond, but they are not disinclined to be relieved of the expense by the Government or private charity.

Private charity, indeed, together with the voluntary contributions and exertions of the inhabitants, seems to bear most of the cost of social service in the tropics. The assistance rendered by missionary organizations to educational and medical services is a matter of common knowledge. We have already noticed their large part in the provision of hospitals and schools. From the accounts of one mission in Uganda it appears that the public revenue furnished only £22,420—less than one-third of its charges—while the natives contributed £13,333 in gifts and £17,667 in school fees, and a grant from Europe provided £17,987.[1] This suggests that educational progress should be ascribed to Christianity rather than to western capital. If the encouragement of western enterprise is necessary to provide funds for economic and social services, one would expect the greatest progress in education where western enterprise penetrates most deeply. This is notoriously contradicted by the facts. As we have seen, during the nineteenth century education made far more rapid progress in Burma with development by native enterprise than in Java with development by western enterprise. Experience in Africa corroborates this view. The total expenditure of Government may be taken as an index to economic progress, and the expenditure on the education of non-natives is an index to the degree of western penetration. Such figures as are available under these heads suggest that the percentage of expenditure on native education is lowest where western enterprise is most conspicuous.[2]

Other facts point in the same direction. The first comprehensive enquiry into African education was financed by the Phelps-Stokes Fund in America, and American funds contributed largely to the foundation of the Jeanes schools that were established as one result of the enquiry. The monumental *African Survey*, conducted by Lord

[1] *African Survey*, p. 1306.
[2] *Ib.* p. 1309, and Table XI.

Hailey, was rendered possible by the munificence of the Carnegie Trust. A substantial contribution towards the cost of a new Burmese dictionary has been made by the Leverhulme Trust. Even so wealthy a dependency as Malaya looked to the Rockefeller Foundation to provide funds for a campaign against hookworm, and to the same generosity it owes two chairs in its Medical School. The Leverhulme Trust makes grants to study economic conditions in Africa, and the Burma Oil Company provided the buildings for an Engineering School in Burma.[1] The two last instances should perhaps be classed with the expenditure incurred by intelligent employers with a view to conducting their affairs more efficiently and profitably.

It appears, then, that doles out of general revenue or by private charity relieve western enterprise of charges that it would otherwise have to incur on amenities in the interest of efficiency and profits, and go to promote economic progress rather than native welfare. In the preceding chapters we have seen that economic and social services, though an important factor in economic progress, do little to enhance welfare, except so far as it is necessary to economic progress. Now it appears that the contribution to public revenue by western enterprise is barely sufficient, and often insufficient, even to cover the additional administrative charges that it involves, and that the public revenue provides only a part, apparently a minor part, of the cost of social services. It is difficult to reconcile these facts with the theory that the provision of funds for greater welfare necessitates the encouragement of western enterprise.

It is equally difficult to reconcile this theory with the state of affairs in dependencies so prosperous as Java, Burma and Malaya. Java, under indirect rule, has been developed by western enterprise employing local labour. During thirty years of Liberal rule, with a rapid expansion of western enterprise, not only did the growing population 'gobble up the greater yield', but there was an actual fall in wages, nominal and real. Again, after another thirty years, with a constructive welfare policy based on ethical principles, and purporting to encourage economic development with a view to enhancing native welfare, economists are unable to assure us that the people are better off. Dr Boeke, whom we have already quoted, returns to the subject in his latest publication. With reference to irrigation, colonization, the clearing of fresh land, the increase of secondary crops and home-grown

[1] *African Survey*, pp. 1228, 1252; Mills, pp. 310, 316; Mayhew, *Colonial Empire*, pp. 120ff.; *Colonial Review*, Sept. 1944, p. 194.

vegetables, he suggests that the race between welfare measures and population cannot be continued indefinitely; he 'cannot escape the conclusion that the standard of living of the masses becomes more and more reduced'.[1] If there is one thing on which all Dutch colonial authorities agree, it is that the cause of poverty in Java is over-population.

In Malaya under indirect rule—though somewhat differently interpreted—western enterprise has developed the country with foreign labour. There is no problem of over-population. But the immigrant coolies draw low wages, because 'any very great increase in the Malayan standard must wait upon a similar rise in the reservoirs of overabundant and therefore cheap labour' in India and China. The Malay, on the other hand, left aside by the main current of economic development, remains stagnating in a backwater, and the progress of the last sixty years has merely changed him 'from a poor man in a poor country to a poor man in a rich country'; relatively at least he is poorer than before.[2]

Burma provides another type of economic development—by native enterprise under direct rule. The population, in comparison with Java is scanty and, in the delta, the chief centre of modern economic activity, the density per acre cultivated is less than in other lowland districts; yet the cultivators have been transformed into a landless rural proletariat and the country as a whole is conspicuous for the growth of crime.

In all these countries, and throughout the Tropical Far East, recent enquiries suggest that the people are less well fed now than twenty years ago, despite the rapid economic progress during the same period.[3] The people grow more but they do not eat more. Java was developed by western enterprise; there was a demand for local labour, and the population has grown up to the limit that the soil will bear. Malaya also was developed by western enterprise; but foreign labour was available and the population adjusted itself to these conditions. Burma was developed by native enterprise. The demand was for cheap produce and not for cheap labour. Holdings, instead of growing smaller grew larger, until they reached the size that would give the maximum net outturn and not, as in Java, the maximum gross outturn; and, under a system of industrial agriculture, the growth of

---

[1] Gonggrijp, quoted *Netherlands India*, p. 214; N. de Wilde, *Asiatic Review*, 1934, p. 232; Boeke, pp. 163, 165.
[2] Mills, pp. 249, 329.   [3] Wickizer and Bennett, pp. 188 ff.

population was checked at the point of diminishing returns. In all these lands the growth of population has reflected the conditions of employment, but whether numerous or scanty, under different systems of rule and with different methods of development, the people remain poor. Economic development has failed to enhance material welfare.

The argument for economic development as an instrument of welfare further assumes that economic and social services are necessary for the provision of welfare. We have already seen that this is not the case. Cultivators adopt new crops and new methods of cultivation without the aid of economic services, and the people take to new foods without encouragement from dieticians. One of the outstanding victories over the tsetse fly in Africa was achieved by ordinary natives, under sympathetic leading, but with no expenditure on welfare services.[1] Most of the reforms most urgently needed in social life in most parts of the tropics need no expert knowledge, and could be introduced without any special staff (though a special staff *should*, of course, facilitate and expedite their introduction). Where the people can be induced to want new amenities they will pay for them, as they do for schooling in Uganda and elsewhere. Thus the inability to promote welfare in tropical dependencies cannot be ascribed to the limitation of economic and social services through lack of revenue or of funds from other sources, and we must seek another explanation.

3. The Measurement of Welfare

If we cannot accept the rapid economic progress of tropical dependencies as sufficient evidence of increasing welfare, we must look elsewhere for a yard-stick by which it may be measured. In social science as in physical science, only beginners and amateurs will conduct experiments without trying so far as possible to measure the results. Some of the older dependencies produce masses of statistics purporting to show the population revenue, and trade, and also matters of social interest, such as litigation, crime and the numbers at school or in jail. The statistics, however, are mostly compiled for administrative purposes and have little meaning or interest for outsiders; many figures are of doubtful accuracy and are frequently misleading, full of traps for the unwary (and even for those who compile them and use them in administration). One might expect at least the trade returns to be intelligible to the public, but anyone who has tried to work on them will endorse the comment of Lord Hailey that 'eccentricity, so in-

[1] Hinden, p. 202.

teresting in social life, loses its charm when applied to trade statistics'.[1] The revenue statistics often seem designed to furnish the least information at the greatest length. The trade and revenue statistics and the figures for population, so far as they are available, accurate and comprehensible, may throw some light on economic progress, but as an index to welfare they are of little or no value.

In India many attempts have been made to arrive at estimates of welfare by calculating the national income, but in the plural society of the tropics the conception of a national income is invalid because there is no homogeneous nation. For the same reason estimates of welfare based on trade returns are meaningless. It has been suggested that in Africa the value of imports retained for consumption provides a basis for measuring economic conditions.[2] But, as a criterion of welfare in a plural society, this has no significance. The import of machinery for constructing mills or factories may increase the profits of western enterprise, but it will not raise the prices paid for raw materials to cultivators. Similarly the export figures tell us nothing about the economic progress of the natives unless they show the native contribution to the exports. Trade statistics do throw some light on the relation between economic progress and native welfare because they usually reveal a large export surplus, often attributed to 'invisible imports' but due in part to quasi-monopolist profits of western enterprise for which no services are rendered. In general, however, statistics afford no criterion of welfare in a plural society unless they furnish information separately for each important section of the community.

That is a matter which has received great attention from the Dutch. The inadequacy of the trade and other statistics came to notice in the 'Enquiry into Diminishing Welfare' held at the beginning of the century; subsequent enquiries of the same kind, official and non-official, have stimulated attempts to give a more precise content to the figures. In some matters the statistics for Netherlands India are less complete and less accurate than those for Burma, but they are notable for the endeavour to differentiate racial sections. There are separate figures according to racial status for production by western and native enterprise, for income-tax assessments, for housing, for the ownership of motor cars and even for the use made of the post office. Moreover, in special enquiries, such as that of Meyer-Ranneft and Huender into the pressure of taxation, and in the 'Little Welfare

[1] *African Survey*, p. 1353.   [2] *Britain and Her Dependencies*, p. 27.

Enquiry' by Wellenstein, a technique has been developed for turning to the best account such statistics as have any bearing on native welfare.[1]

Lord Hailey has remarked that in Africa the existing statistics might be considerably improved without additional expense, and that a comparatively small expenditure would make them much more useful. That remark applies also to Burma and probably to most other tropical dependencies. Unsatisfactory as the statistics for Netherlands India are in some respects, they do at least serve to illuminate many corners that are left dark elsewhere, and the general neglect to provide means for judging how far the benevolent aspirations expressed in statements of colonial policy bear fruit in practice, naturally affords a handle for critics of colonial administration to suggest that it is more keenly interested in economic progress than in native welfare. It is not enough that material should be available for measuring individual welfare. The analysis of welfare demands a suitable technique for measuring social welfare by presenting accurate and intelligible information regarding debt, civil litigation, crime, health, education and other matters that find no place in individual budgets of income and expenditure. There would still remain imponderable elements, those cultural and religious aspects of social life in the tropics which are the first to suffer from the economic struggle for survival of the cheapest consequent on the impact of the West. But this is no reason for neglecting to carry so far as possible the objective scientific measurement of welfare.

4. THE MACHINERY OF WELFARE

The deficiency of statistical material is a notable defect in the machinery of welfare. But it is not the only, and not the chief, defect. It may seem that no special machinery is necessary, that the care for welfare may be left to the local official charged with the maintenance of order. That is very largely true. Any European official can tell the people that dirt breeds disease, or explain the benefit of vaccination, or advise them to destroy mosquitoes and rats, or bring to their knowledge new and more profitable crops, or suggest new breeds of cattle, or inculcate the advantages of thrift and the danger of getting entangled with moneylenders. None of the most urgent reforms in the daily life of tropical peoples calls for special scientific equipment beyond the stock of knowledge common to educated Europeans. Natives have frequently

[1] Furnivall, *Economic Journal of India*, 1934, p. 295.

adopted of their own accord innovations which appeal to them, and it would seem possible for European officials to recommend European standards of hygiene and other reforms with little or no expenditure on welfare services. It is true that modern science has done much and can do more for the welfare of tropical peoples. The connection between rats and plague and between mosquitoes and malaria are recent scientific discoveries, and scientists have traced the origin of hookworm and beri-beri. There is unbounded scope for research, and useful expenditure on it is limited only by the funds available. But it is well to remember that research does not bear fruit until it is applied to daily life; its practical application depends on the efficiency of the machinery of welfare.

It is true also that administrative officials should be better able to promote welfare if they have the assistance of departmental specialists. But departmental specialists will usually need the help of administrative officials if they are to get into touch with the people in their daily life. The departmental specialist is probably an expert in his own line, but one can hardly expect him also to be expert in native economy and customs or to be proficient in native languages. It is useless for the medical officer to advocate shoes for hookworm if the people cannot afford to buy shoes, or for the sanitary department to devise modern latrines which the people will not use, or for the agriculturist to recommend crops which local conditions of labour or water supply do not allow the people to grow. Although the specialist may try to adapt native life to scientific principles, the administrative official should be capable of adapting scientific principles to native life. Thus the welfare specialist must ordinarily work in double harness with the administrative official by his side. But the administrative official can do little to promote welfare unless he knows the locality, and what needs doing; has influence that will lead the people to attend to his advice; and remains among them long enough to make certain that they act on it. All these conditions must be fulfilled if welfare work is to succeed.

The machinery ordinarily employed differs according as the system of rule is direct or indirect. In the adoption of direct rule one object was to promote greater welfare through liberating the people from arbitrary oppression by their own chieftains. On this plan all the administrative officials, European and native, became servants of the law, charged with administering equal law to all. When it became apparent that the law, while liberating the people from arbitrary will, subjected them to mechanical economic forces, attempts were made to protect them against the action of these forces. That is the distinctive character of welfare machinery under direct rule; it allows free play within the law to economic forces, but attempts to mitigate their consequences. This is directly contrary to the method of indirect rule, systematized by Van den Bosch in Java, which tries to soften the impact of economic forces by leaving the people under their own chieftains and their own customs, while aiming to protect them against arbitrary oppression. Direct rule attempts to mitigate the action of economic forces; indirect rule aims at providing a buffer against their action. There is a corresponding difference in the machinery of welfare.

(a) *Direct Rule*. It is often suggested or implied that the promotion of welfare in the tropics requires nothing more than the provision of funds for the services of experts. But this view disregards the conditions limiting their activities. The application of science to the affairs of daily life is quite a novel idea even in Europe; each generation of doctors regards its predecessors as unscientific, and in agriculture, hygiene, dietetics and other studies, what is held for true to-day may be out of date to-morrow. But the tropics are still almost virgin lands in science; experience in Europe may be misleading and conclusions based on it invalid. Conditions are different or even contrary. Cultivation requires a cool soil instead of a warm soil; natives apparently maintain good health on a diet that, according to western science, is defective; plague and malaria were spread by measures intended to prevent them. The application of modern science to tropical problems requires long and patient research, and continuity of experiment. But tropical life is adverse to continuity; men go on leave or are transferred for administrative convenience. Lack of continuity nullified experiments on rice cultivation in Malaya, and official transfers hampered the researches of Ross on malaria. Moreover, any single problem may, and often does, require a whole staff of experts for its solution. In agriculture the investigation of a single crop disease may need the collaboration of agricultural experts, botanists, entomologists and so on. The same principle applies in almost all departments of economic and social life. If the agricultural expert, by patient research breeds a more productive variety of some generally grown crop, the people may be unable to take advantage of it because of difficulties in the supply of labour, water or credit; his work raises new problems for a wide circle of other departmental specialists and it will be wasted without their co-operation.

It is easy, given the funds, to multiply economic and social services. But the multiplication of service tends to defeat its own ends, and greater expenditure gives worse results through excessive departmentalism. Each specialist looks at life through departmental blinkers. The agriculturist sees nothing but the crops, the veterinary expert only the cattle; to the sanitary inspector the latrine is more important than the home, and the policeman would guarantee security more confidently if the whole population were in jail. Often the experts are at issue. The agriculturist advocates grazing reserves to provide fodder, while the veterinary officer wants to close them to prevent infection; the fishery officer advises the people to breed fish, and the medical officer drains the ponds to kill mosquitoes. Everywhere the specialist inclines to a narrow view of life, but in the tropics departmentalism has peculiar dangers; in Europe the expert looks at a familiar world, but in the tropics, owing to his ignorance of native life, the field is out of focus. In Europe the expert understands the public and the public understands the expert, because they have a common background, but in the tropics it is only the European community in the towns and western enterprise that has a mutual understanding with the expert and values his assistance. Thus the natives in towns prefer to live in the native quarter, where they can escape the unwelcome attentions of the sanitary inspector, 'whose unreasonable prejudice against picturesque filth is never understood';[1] and plantation coolies, on returning home, lapse into their old comfortable ways. Moreover in Europe there is an organic community, living its own life, which can decide for itself what it wants most, but in the tropics, where innovations are pressed on the people from outside, there naturally ensues a lack of co-ordination between the competing and often contrary activities of the departmental specialists; too many cooks, as usual, spoil the broth. The confusion may be mitigated on the Dutch plan by grouping allied services in large departments under a single head. But this device alone is insufficient. What an organic community does by the dynamic force of its inherent vitality must in the tropics be entrusted to some official personifying, as it were, the common social will. There must be someone to co-ordinate the activities of departmental specialists and to foster a demand among the people for their services.

Under direct rule the District officer, the local civil servant in charge

[1] Burns, p. 306.

of general administration, is expected to discharge these functions, and to act as a link between the experts and the people. One condition of success is that he should have an intimate acquaintance with tropical economy. So far as he is assisted by native subordinates, they should so far as possible understand these principles of western social life which they are expected to spread among the people. In both these matters Dutch standards are far higher than the British.[1] It seems that training for the British Colonial Service has lagged behind that given by Holland, France and Belgium. Yet the Colonial Service can claim to be ahead of the Sudan and Indian, as well as of the Home Civil Service in this respect. The British system of training administrative officials is a survival from the days of *laissez-faire* when an officer was expected to do little more than try cases and collect the revenue. Tropical administration has never been regarded, like law and medicine, as a profession requiring vocational instruction. European officials while on probation undergo a short course which does not give them any background for their work, and in Burma and probably elsewhere, native subordinates receive no training whatever—a university degree or proficiency as a clerk is regarded as sufficient qualification for administrative work. In Netherlands India, on the contrary, European civil servants are given a five years' course designed to help them to understand the East, and native civil servants a three years' course designed to give them an understanding of the West. Moreover, Dutch officials in Java, for some twelve years after their arrival in the country, have no judicial or executive authority, whereas British officials from their earliest days are primarily magistrates and collectors of revenue; they have neither the training, nor the practical experience, nor the time to acquire the general understanding of native life that is necessary if they are to help departmental specialists to turn their activities to the best account.

But the most thorough preliminary education in tropical economy will avail little without local knowledge, local influence and opportunity to exercise effective supervision. For all these continuity of tenure is essential. Under direct rule, however, there is no permanent element in the administration. In Africa an officer in Kenya was posted to as many as eleven different districts within six years, and the problem of frequent transfers exists possibly in a more acute form in West Africa. This is characteristic of tropical administration in

---

[1] *African Survey*, p. 224; O'Malley, p. 255. Furnivall, *JRCAS*, July 1939 *Koloniaal Tijdschrift*, May 1938, p. 273; 1946, Cmd. Col. 198, p. 22.

general, and is found also in Dutch, French and Belgian dependencies.[1] A contrast is often suggested between modern conditions and the 'good old days'. Yet in Burma, though the numerous transfers were deplored sixty years ago, no remedy has yet been found. In India, in the placid days before the Mutiny, the normal period of service in any one post seems to have been eight or nine months, and that was the case also in Burma under the East India Company, right back to the first years of British rule.[2] Lack of continuity is universal and inveterate.

'Universal experience shows that lack of continuity in the administrative services produces one inevitable result—the decay of the factor of personality and the substitution of a mechanical routine of administration.'[3] One symptom of routine is that everything must be reduced to writing, and as far back as we can go we find this symptom of the disease; and always, so great is the lack of continuity in tropical administration, we find it, as at present, deplored as something new. Eighty years ago in Burma officers were complaining that, if reports continued to multiply, officials might be found to write them, but no one would have time to read them. In 1830 the East India Company framed rules to reduce correspondence. Still earlier Munro complained that 'unless we contrive to reduce the quantity of reading the members of Government will have no time for giving consideration to matters of general importance'.[4] We have no time to think, says the harassed official of the present day, but his predecessors have always made the same complaint, since the time of Sir John Shore (Lord Teignmouth) in 1790: 'The members comprising it (the British Government in India). are in a constant state of fluctuation and the period of their residence often expires before experience can be acquired or reduced to practice. Official forms necessarily occupy a large portion of time, and the constant pressure of business leaves little leisure for study and reflection.'[5] What is new in modern administration is that more is attempted, and the machinery is therefore more elaborate and more obvious. Specialization multiplies departments and concentrates co-ordination in the secretariat, which functions as a clearing house for departmental activities. That is a mark of Dutch administration as much as of British administration, perhaps even more deeply imprinted because the Dutch system is more intensive. Dutch officials, like

---

[1] Bousquet, p. 109; *African Survey*, pp. 231, 237, 243.
[2] *RAB*, 1880-1, p. 8; *RRA*, 1899-1900, p. 53; Bright, I, 101.
[3] *African Survey*, p. 231.
[4] Gleig, p. 321; *Corr. TD*, pp. 2, 85.
[5] *5th Report Select Committee*, 1812, p. 11; O'Malley, p. 193.

their British fellows, deplore the concentration of authority in the secretariat, and complain that they spend the first fortnight of each year reporting what during the past year they have seen, done—and reported. Nowadays there is more machinery, but the administration has always functioned mechanically because there has always been a lack of continuity and it must needs function mechanically unless informed by human will.

Transient officials cannot possibly acquire the local knowledge that is necessary for promoting welfare. The District officer must know the district of which he is in charge. Natural forces, such as erosion, operate continually but gradually. So also do economic forces, leading to indebtedness and land alienation, to the disappearance of communal land in villages and to overcrowding and disease in towns. Sometimes remedial action might be possible in the early stages, but officials come and go, and they notice these things, if at all, only when they can do nothing to cure them.

A knowledge of the district is of little avail without a knowledge of the people. The British tradition of colonial rule may undervalue the study of tropical economy as academic, unpractical, but it recognizes, at least in theory, the importance of an acquaintance with the local inhabitants; it portrays the District officer as 'the father and mother' of his people. Yet where officials follow one another at intervals of a few weeks or months, it takes a wise child to know its father; and the father cannot have any close acquaintance with his family or families, the bewildering succession of adopted foundlings.

Unless the District officer knows the people he cannot exercise personal influence. The need for personal influence was recognized in the recent proposals for mass education:

'Guidance and leadership are clearly of the first importance. The effective guidance given by governments will depend on the vigour and sincerity with which those responsible for government face their task and recognise their responsibility, not only towards the people as a whole, but as inspiring leaders of the agencies which the Governments themselves directly or indirectly control. Of these agencies the district officers have a crucial part to perform. Their close and varied contact with the lives of the people affords unique opportunities for fruitful guidance. In effect they can largely make or mar the efforts of welfare workers and other departmental officers.'[1]

But, as we have seen, although the contact of district officers with the people may be varied, it can hardly be described as close. Under the

[1] *Mass Education*, p. 9.

system of direct rule the only people with whom the ordinary district officer becomes acquainted, outside his court and office, are those who push themselves forward in the hope of a decoration or a job; he may meet people in the villages, but he has no time or leisure to make friends among them, and appears to them as an official rather than as a man.

In order to acquire the personal influence needed for the promotion of welfare among a backward people, sympathy is essential; one must share their feelings. Yet one cannot share the feelings of people whom one does not know, or knows merely in the mass and not as individuals; sympathy requires more than mere acquaintance through official intercourse during a few months. Moreover, under direct rule the official is primarily a magistrate and tax collector, and that has long been recognized as a barrier to sympathy. As Munro observed, a man posted to judicial duties 'learns forms before he learns things. He becomes full of the respect due to the Court but knows nothing of the people. He has little opportunity of seeing them except in court. He sees only the worst of them and under the worst shapes; he sees them only as plaintiffs or defendants or as criminals, and the unfavourable opinion with which he too often enters among them, in place of being removed by experience, is every day strengthened and increased.'[1] It is a common complaint that under indirect rule, in Java or Malaya, officials coddle the people, treat them as children; but under direct rule they are apt to treat them as naughty children.

Without sympathy for the people among officials, there can be no confidence in officials among the people; they will not confide in one unless they know him as a man. In Burma the mistrust of officials is accepted as a fact, and is often ascribed to the native tradition that Government is one of the five enemies of the common man. It is more comfortable to attribute this mistrust to the character of the people rather than to defects in the administrative machinery; but one finds the same mistrust in India, where the people have known British rule for longer even than in the maritime provinces of Lower Burma. While writing these pages an instance comes to hand. 'It is pathetic', remarks an observer of the recent famine in Bengal, 'to see the crowds of destitute lying on the Calcutta pavements rise and scatter when they are approached by anyone who looks like an official'[2]—not neces-

[1] Gleig, p. 279.
[2] *Daily Telegraph*, 2 Nov. 1943.

sarily, of course, a European official. The same report tells of an official who was lynched by the peasants whom he was trying to provide with food. That is not the atmosphere in which a constructive welfare policy can flourish. 'It is significant', says Lord Hailey, 'that a sentiment of alienation or estrangement has rarely shown itself in the earlier days of British administration.'[1] But there must be something wrong with the machinery of welfare if people like it worse as they get to know it better, and one defect certainly is the lack of continuity in the administrative services.

Even if an official can gain sufficient influence to induce the people to accept reforms, his work is incomplete. He must remain long enough to see that they adopt the reforms, not merely because they trust him but because they recognize their value or come to accept them as a habit. Take, for instance, the matter of erosion. An official who knows his district may detect it in an early stage; if he has influence among the people he may induce them to abstain from the cultivation or wood-cutting that is causing the erosion. The cultivators may promise to allow the scrub to grow, but some years must elapse before there is any noticeable difference, and all the time they will be subject to the lure of making a small addition to their income. One or two will succumb, and others will follow their example. If an official who is keen on sanitation tries to enforce housing rules that will improve living conditions but reduce rents, the owners of house property know that they need only bide their time, because he will soon be replaced by some new official with other interests. Successive officials may be zealous for education, for co-operative credit or for sanitation; but, as each one leaves the district, nothing remains of his enthusiasm but a new layer on the dust-heap of abortive projects. Not unnaturally, many lose their early enthusiasm and lapse into cynical indifference, content just to carry on. But, while successive welfare projects fade and are forgotten, anti-social forces, natural and economic, hold the field.

It is comparatively easy for officials to promote economic progress. If an official begins to build a road, although it may and often does relapse into jungle after his departure, a successor, if so minded, can easily go on with it. But in the promotion of welfare, as for example by founding schools or promoting co-operative credit, continued personal influence is indispensable and, as the Dutch remark, when this is withdrawn, everything sinks back into the mire.

[1] *Britain and Her Dependencies*, p. 36.

It is easy likewise to promote reforms that are immediately and demon-strably profitable to individuals; these indeed require little recommen-dation. Good wine needs no bush. But the reforms most urgently needed for promoting welfare impose unwelcome restrictions on the people and offer distant and doubtful benefits; such reforms require close and constant supervision if they are to be adopted into native custom. The District officer, like the departmental specialist, can do something to further economic progress, but the conditions under which he works make it almost impossible for him to promote native welfare.

Under direct rule, which implies the rule of law, the District officer is further hindered in promoting welfare by the fact that all his actions must be kept within the law. In the promotion of welfare as in the collection of revenue, he is as closely bound by legal procedure as in the trial of cases in court when sitting as a magistrate or judge, and he must be prepared to defend his acts against trained advocates who will insist on the letter of the law.[1] The same rule applies to all depart-mental subordinates. They are liable to legal penalties if they exceed their functions, but are exposed to little risk, and, as we have seen in Burma, may add appreciably to their income, if they fall short of them. It is improbable that in this matter Burma is exceptional. Under in-adequate supervision the multiplication of welfare services means the multiplication of corruption, and the subordinate who takes a small gratuity to condone the breach of welfare regulations acquires merit with the public at the same time that he fills his pocket. Hence the ex-penditure of revenue on social services may even promote corruption rather than welfare, and impose new burdens instead of conferring new benefits. Every elaboration of the machinery of welfare calls for closer supervision by the District officer and, at the same time, increases the difficulty of supervision. Unless the District officer knows the district and the people, he can rarely penetrate the conspiracy of silence which conceals such irregularities, and if he hears of them he does not hold charge long enough to punish them. Under the rule of law, suspected offences must be proved according to forms of law, which operate to protect offenders. Moreover, the difficulty of action by the District officer is enhanced because he has little or no authority over depart-mental subordinates, as these are directly responsible to their depart-mental superiors. Thus, although it may seem that specialist services should assist the District officer to promote welfare, they are often, in

[1] O'Malley, p. 96.

fact, of very little use. The most urgent welfare measures require no more than common sense. If the District officer has sufficient local knowledge and influence he can induce the people to accept them and, without this knowledge and influence, the multiplication of subordinates is a hindrance rather than a help. Thus the machinery of direct rule, which served originally to mitigate oppression in the native world, does not fulfil the conditions essential to the promotion of welfare in the modern world.

(b) *Indirect Rule.* Under the system of indirect rule the promotion of welfare is approached from a different angle. This system accepts the position that western rule in the tropics liberates anti-social economic forces from the control of custom, and thereby produces changes that are detrimental to native social life. 'So far as deliberate policy can affect the issue', writes Lord Hailey with reference to Africa, 'it is clear that in the interests of the African himself, it should seek to moderate the pace of change, and allow full scope for the innate characteristics of the people to assert themselves in the conflict of forces that must ensue.'[1] That may be claimed as the principle underlying the policy of indirect rule. The functions and limitations of the departmental specialist are the same under indirect rule as under direct rule, and on both systems the officer in charge of general administration serves to link up departmental specialists with the people. But on the system of indirect rule some native authority, assumed to represent the people, can exercise personal influence among them and is more or less permanent. Indirect rule would seem, therefore, to comply better than direct rule with the conditions for promoting welfare.

As already noticed, there is a wide difference between the Dutch and British interpretations of indirect rule. On the original Dutch model, which still dominates their conception, the 'recognized or appointed heads' were regarded as native chieftains, and, so long as they maintained order and complied with Government requirements for produce and services, they were left to govern the people according to native law and custom with no interference from European officials. Since then western law has been adopted for all classes in criminal proceedings, and taxation along western lines has replaced the customary dues and services, but the officials of the administrative service in Java, whether European or native, try no cases (with insignificant exceptions), and have no formal connection with either magisterial or revenue work. British colonial

[1] *African Survey*, p. 1280.

administration, however, even under indirect rule, derives its inspiration from the tradition of equality before the law that took shape under direct rule in British India. European administrative officials do not, like those in Dutch territories, approximate to the character of the Resident in a Native State, but take an active part in judicial and revenue work, while even the native chieftains tend to be converted into western magistrates and tax-collectors. The system of indirect rule as thus interpreted differs little from direct rule, because the native officials are, in effect, subordinate to Europeans, who supervise the revenue collections and hear cases on appeal from native courts or transfer cases from native courts to their own courts.

Although indirect rule is advocated as an instrument of welfare, the choice between direct or indirect rule has, in practice, been governed by convenience rather than by principle. In general, as we have seen, direct rule has tended to prevail where the colony was regarded primarily as a market to be developed by native enterprise, and indirect rule where it was chiefly valued as a source of raw materials to be developed by western enterprise. This coincidence between the economic interest of the colonial power and the system of rule adopted, suggests a need for caution in accepting the claims advanced for indirect rule as an instrument of welfare. Although now advocated as a means of moderating the pace of change, it won favour originally as a means of expediting change, by facilitating the supply of land and labour through native chieftains. Moreover, few would desire to protect the people wholly from the impact of the West, to segregate them and preserve them as museum pieces in native innocence and ignorance. In order to reconcile progress and welfare, tropical peoples should be brought as rapidly as possible into fertilizing contact with the principles that western civilization derives from Greece, Rome and Christianity, while given protection against the anti-social forces that its impact on the tropics liberates. Indirect rule, however, strictly applied and as originally conceived, has a contrary effect; it cuts the people off from western civilization and keeps them backward without giving them adequate protection against economic forces. It is difficult to resist the conclusion that this is largely responsible for the helplessness of the Javanese which strikes foreign observers[1] so forcibly and is deplored also by the Dutch, and which contrasts so notably with the vigorous enterprise that has impelled Burmans to colonize the delta, even if it also helps to fill the jails.

[1] Bousquet, p. 86.

The older negative conception of indirect rule, however, has given place generally to a positive conception of its value as a means of inducing people to accept innovations intended to raise their standard of living. Here again, one cannot disregard the fact that the acceptance of this new interpretation coincided with the recognition by western enterprise that it required more efficient labour, healthier and more intelligent, and by western labour that its interests were endangered by the competition of cheap tropical labour. These practical considerations added weight to human sympathy, and European officials began to force the pace of welfare, using the native authorities merely as agents to obtain compliance with measures regarded, for the time being, as desirable. Thus the system of indirect rule becomes infected with the disease characteristic of direct rule: the infirmity of will and vacillation of policy consequent on frequent transfers. Moreover, every new use of native authorities to introduce unwelcome reforms strains their authority, on which the system of indirect rule is founded. And unless the native authorities themselves wholeheartedly accept new measures, they will not enforce them when the Government changes its policy, or the officer who recommends them leaves the district, so that compliance is superficial and impermanent. Usually, too, indirect rule is born a weakling. For the native chieftain recognized by the colonial power is the weaker among rival claimants, who seeks or accepts outside support because unable to stand alone. With the help of the colonial power he may be strong enough to place land and labour at its disposal, but this does not strengthen his position among his subjects. More and more, as time goes on, he derives authority from the Government rather than from the people, and it is the form rather than the reality of native institutions that indirect rule preserves.

Even under Dutch rule European officials have in fact interfered in native administration whenever convenient. During the period of the Culture system 'they did not debate whether action would prejudice village autonomy; they acted'. Under the Liberal system they bypassed the Regents in order to protect the people against oppression. Under the Ethical system, intended to strengthen the corporate village, Europeans, zealous for uplift, used the village administration as 'welfare apparatus' until 'precious little autonomy remained'. The conservation of village life and custom has always been a fundamental principle of Dutch administration; departures from this principle have been regarded as unorthodox and have been followed by a reaction to the old tradition, but the temptation to intervene has repeatedly proved irresistible. Under the tradition of direct rule in British India, and with a greater veneration for the rule of law, British officials are less disposed to resist the temptation, so that, in British practice, indirect rule loses its virtue and vitality, and tends to become little better than a sham, differing from direct rule chiefly in the name. The Dutch who tried intervention for some twenty years during the Ethical period were finally disillusioned, and came to recognize that it was mistaken. There seems little reason to anticipate better success under British rule.

Yet the principle underlying indirect rule is valuable. A native authority whom the people accept as representing them personifies their common social will. He has great influence to recommend reforms in which he himself believes, and he remains permanently among the people to supervise their application until they have been adopted into customary social life. But he can do this only so long and so far as he is the prime mover and has the chief direction in affairs. A leading Dutch civilian has suggested that whereas, during the Ethical period and earlier, the European official was the 'elder brother' or overlord of the native official by his side, it has become necessary for the European to accept the position of 'younger brother', as adviser and assistant rather than a chief executive. On this plan the chief defect of colonial administration, lack of continuity, becomes a virtue. The native authority is permanent, but of necessity cannot be in immediate and continual close contact with the modern world, and a succession of European officials can put before him various new points of view and make suggestions among which he can choose those that are congenial and seem feasible. This process, however, works slowly, and requires that the native authority shall be at home in the western world. Some form of pressure or compulsion seems easier and quicker.

5. COMPULSORY WELFARE

It does not require an extensive acquaintance with contemporary colonial literature to note a growing tenderness towards compulsion as an instrument of welfare. There are demands for compulsory education, for the compulsory destruction of diseased crops and cattle, for campaigns against disease by operations, scientifically planned and humanely conducted, but military in spirit and thoroughness. For the common welfare men living in society must accept restrictions on individual freedom. In tropical society the people under their own rulers

accepted such restrictions in the name of custom, but they welcome
their removal. That was the strong point of British rule in former
days; it brought, or seemed to bring, freedom. Now one finds suggestions of regret that compulsion is 'repugnant to the spirit of British
administration', and that 'our traditions have not allowed us to contemplate the general use of regulation for the medical "cleaning-up"
of disease-ridden areas'.[1] This tendency is often justified on the
ground that we ourselves increasingly accept regulations that our
more individualist fathers would have flouted, and that we must 'ask
ourselves whether in dealing with the Dependencies, we are performing the function of a modern State'.[2] But the regulations in
which we acquiesce, not without grumbling, proceed from ideas in
which we share; although we recognize the need for penal sanctions
to enforce them on a recalcitrant minority, public opinion is the
most effective sanction. In tropical dependencies welfare measures
proceed from the foreign Government and find no response among the
great body of the people; on the contrary, they run counter to public
opinion. We have already noted that in such circumstances the
efficacy of compulsion is limited, but the relation between compulsion and welfare is so important that it deserves further examination.

In a city with a large European population it is possible to insist on
modern hygienic precautions, at least within the European quarter.
On western enterprises under European control the management can
require their staff to accept western medical attention, and to comply
with sanitary regulations; they can insist on these things as a condition
of employment, and their hands are strengthened if they have the
backing of the law. But in rural areas one may accept the estimate of
Dr Hydrick, already cited, that compulsory measures are effective only
where they have the support and the co-operation of at least nine-
tenths of the people. No compulsion is required to encourage the
people to attend secondary schools or to seek instruction of any type
that improves their prospects or their status. People readily, too readily,
submit to injections for the cure of venereal disease. But they do not,
in general, believe in primary instruction or in western sanitation or
western medicine. Their apathy is a subject of general complaint,
but compulsion is no cure for apathy; rather it induces a reaction
and transforms apathy into hostility. If the people do not accept
innovations, the remedy is not compulsion but the demonstration

---

[1] Mills, p. 317; *Britain and Her Dependencies*, p. 31.
[2] Hailey, Lord, quoted *Colonial Review*, 1942, p. 155.

of their value by example and experience. Apathy betokens the failure of welfare measures, and the resort to compulsion is not only a sign but a confession of their failure. When measures that would really promote welfare fail, the explanation must be sought in some defect in the machinery of welfare, and as we have seen, this is defective because it works mechanically in response to the will of Government and not as an expression of organic social will. Compulsion can, within limits, be exercised effectively in the interest of economic progress, but to raise the standard of living among people in general it is necessary to organize a demand for welfare. Where an effective majority demands welfare measures, compulsion by penal regulations will give strength to their demand; beyond that, except so far as such measures are needed for the health of Europeans or the efficiency of western enterprise, attempts to promote welfare by compulsion almost certainly do more harm than good.

6. The Relation between Progress and Welfare

Indirect rule as we have noticed, although originally adopted for convenience, has been justified as a means of softening the impact of Europe on the tropics by leaving the people under their own rulers, laws and customs, and thereby moderating the pace of change so that they can adapt themselves to their new environment. Indirect rule does, in fact, provide machinery which should enhance welfare, and we may find cases where it has been effective. But the machinery often fails because the motive principle is unsound; it is applied to further progress rather than welfare. The growing tenderness towards legal compulsion under a penal correction is a tacit confession that, even under the stimulus of gentle pressure, adjustment fails to keep pace with the ever-increasing rate of change. Despite aspirations to moderate the rate of change in the interest of human welfare, there is constant pressure to hasten it for the sake of economic progress. 'A striking feature of most European economic enterprise in Africa has been the constant effort of Governments, companies and individuals to achieve specific developments in particular directions as rapidly as possible.'[1] That is true of modern colonial expansion in general. Governments are expected to bring new territories to a state of financial independence as soon as may be; the numerous departmental heads call for reports on this, that and the other sub-

[1] Frankel, p. 10.

ject, and officials in charge of a district for only a few months must act quickly if they are to do anything and show results; shareholders in private enterprise look for quick returns. 'Means, speedy means', is the motto of tropical development in all its aspects.

The rapid development of tropical resources is not only profitable to the colonial power but helps to justify its position under the 'dual mandate' to the outer world. At the first international conference on colonial affairs held at Berlin in 1884–5, the development of dependencies was laid down as a condition on which their tenure should receive international recognition. The modern world demands access to backward regions, and the pace at which their resources, human and material, are made available for world welfare steadily grows faster. Before the days of steam, the funds derived from the taxation of native enterprise were sufficient to meet the charges of development. With the construction of railways and the growth of western enterprise, the demand for speedier development compelled dependencies to raise loans from or through the colonial power. Now this also is regarded as too slow, and there is general agreement that colonial powers should expedite development by loans free of interest or by outright gifts. The Dutch contribution of f. 40 million to Netherlands India in 1904, for promoting irrigation, emigration and agricultural credit services, was regarded as exceptional and as justified by special circumstances.[1] So likewise was a recent contribution of f. 25 million. But in British colonial policy the grant of financial assistance to dependencies found acceptance as a matter of principle. This is the basis of the Colonial Development Act of 1929, supplemented and extended by the Colonial Development and Welfare Act of 1940.

It is not without significance that, in the title of this Act, development precedes welfare, and that aviation has been recognized as one of the objects having a prior claim on the funds which it provides. Air services have proved useful for the conveyance to Europe of gold and diamonds. They may in future contribute to economy in administration by allowing the concentration of the forces maintained for preserving order, and by reducing the time required for the journeys of officers on furlough, but hitherto the demand for air transport for civil purposes has come from a comparatively small group among the European community.[2] The issue is primarily between transport by air and by sea, but ranged on either side are all those who stand to profit by these

[1] *Netherlands India*, p. 236.   [2] *African Survey*, pp. 1602–3.

respective forms of transport. Even before the present war, a situation was arising which called for measures to prevent wasteful competition between air and rail. It is not improbable that the powerful and vocal interests pressing for air services will obtain for them an undue share of the funds available for economic development, but doubtless all the rival interests will finally reach some form of agreement. Yet whatever agreement may be reached, one thing is certain: that the provision of air services will not 'moderate the pace of change'; on the contrary it will hasten economic development and increase the urgency of social services to mitigate its consequences. Already the subsidy to air transport constitutes a relatively heavy charge on the revenue in some territories, thereby diminishing the funds available for welfare services, and one may assume that, in the conflict of rival interests, the grant of funds for aviation (so far as it is not affected by lobbying) will be determined on purely economic grounds, and that the natives, who are least powerful and least vocal, will not have much influence on the decision.

Although the Act provides for expenditure on welfare services, it is based on the assumption that economic development is a condition of welfare. 'It can hardly be anticipated', says Sir Alan Pim, 'that the tax-payers of the Colonial Powers will, after the war, consent to such an annual levy on them as would meet the colonial needs either free of interest or at a nominal rate.'[1] Although additional expenditure on the development of dependencies does, or should, make them more profitable, it is doubtful how far grants or cheap loans for the purpose of development would benefit the British taxpayer. On the other hand, they would expedite the pace of change, and thereby enhance the difficulty of natives in adjusting themselves to their new environment. Grants made in the name of welfare will have a similar effect. However much may be available from public revenue or private charity for expenditure on social services, its effect on promoting welfare is conditioned by the demand for welfare, which in tropical dependencies, as we have seen, is effective only so far as welfare is necessary to development. Development creates a demand for social services, for the protection of land and labour, for the improvement of health and the multiplication of schools; but these services are transformed from instruments of welfare into instruments of progress. It is not true, as Liberals held, that development is a cause of welfare or, as modern colonial policy holds, a condition of

[1] *Colonial Review*, Sept. 1944, p. 203.

welfare. On the contrary, welfare is a condition of economic progress, and has economic progress as a by-product. We have noticed a striking instance of this principle in Burma, where the people wanted to decorate the local pagoda with electric light. Their interest was primarily in religion and, without any help or subsidy from Government, they illuminated the pagoda. But, incidentally, they also provided electric lighting for the town. It is a matter of general experience that many, probably most, utilitarian reforms have originally been conceived as humanitarian ideals and, indeed, so far as our western civilization has a Christian origin, we may claim that it is based securely on the rock of vision.

Everywhere in the tropics there is abundant scope and need for the enhancement of welfare. But, as Lord Hailey has remarked, little can be done to promote welfare until the people themselves, or at least their leaders, are conscious of their needs.[1] Economic progress under western rule should provide the means for enhancing welfare, but we cannot enhance welfare merely through economic progress. The problem of enhancing welfare has some analogies with the problem of encouraging scientific research. Sir Joseph Thomson made some wise remarks on this matter in connection with the use of Röntgen rays in war. Administrations and employers want research in applied science that will give practical results, and the scientists whom they employ are expected to show results and, indirectly at least, are paid according to results. Research in applied science, starting to find an improved method of locating bullet wounds might, he suggested, have led to the invention of better probes; but the improvement of war surgery was mainly due to the apparently quite useless, unpractical research that led to the discovery of Röntgen rays. He drew the moral that 'research in applied science leads to reform, research in pure science leads to revolutions'.[2] For the enhancement of welfare in the tropics nothing less than such a revolutionary change in our attack upon the problem will suffice. One cannot achieve it by attempting to mitigate the consequences of economic progress. It is necessary both to organize a positive demand for welfare and to control economic development in the interest of welfare. We must go outside the domain of economics to find some dynamic principle, stronger than economic forces, which all accept as of superior validity to the desire of gain. But if we are looking for some principle of welfare, we should have a clear understanding of what we mean by welfare.

[1] *African Survey*, p. 1206.   [2] Rayleigh, Lord, *Life of Sir J. J. Thomson* (1942), p. 199.

7. THE CONCEPT OF WELFARE

Between progress and welfare there is a fundamental difference. Economic progress is a matter of universal common sense. It consists essentially in making two blades of grass grow where one grew previously; in widening the margin between yield and cost. Progress is measurable and, if accurately measured, there is little question as to the degree of progress. But welfare is largely a subjective concept; everyone wants different things. Everyone has a different idea of welfare, and it is differently interpreted by successive generations. All colonial powers have claimed in their contemporary idiom a two-fold objective of colonial policy: progress and welfare. On progress there has been general agreement, but in different ages welfare has been identified with salvation, liberty and comfort. The Portuguese and early Dutch both claimed to open the kingdom of heaven to their subjects, but they opened respectively a Roman heaven and a Protestant heaven. The later Dutch and the English both thought to confer freedom on their subjects; but the Dutch allowed them the freedom of their own custom, and the English gave them the freedom of western law. Modern colonial powers aim at promoting comfort, but different ideas of comfort are reflected in Rangoon, Batavia and Saigon. Welfare has been defined as the possibility to satisfy those needs of which one is aware.[1] This definition is not wholly satisfactory, for welfare depends still more closely on those needs of which one is not conscious until they are frustrated, and it is frustration of this type that is largely responsible for unrest among tropical peoples. The definition does, however, suggest that welfare is not wholly subjective; it contains an objective element because it implies a relation between man and his environment. A bullock cart is good enough for those who do not see others ride in motor-cars, but a poor man in a rich country enjoys less welfare than a poor man in a poor country.

Certain things men generally recognize as good. Peace is a good thing. But the nightly drone of planes and the news of battle in the daily papers reminded us that it can be priced too highly. Order and security are good things, but under foreign rule their value as elements of welfare is debatable. In India it was questioned so far back as 1817 by Munro, who was no idealist but a highly competent administrator, able from his own experience to compare the welfare of Indian peoples

[1] Visman, I, 69.

under their own rulers and under the greater security and order enforced by a paternal British Government. The advantages, he wrote,
'are dearly bought. They are purchased by the sacrifice of independence, of national character and of whatever renders a people respectable....The effect of this state of things is observable in all the
British provinces, where the inhabitants are certainly the most abject
race in India.'[1] (It should be noted that he was not contrasting the
peoples of southern India with what we now regard as the more virile
races of the north, at that time not yet under British rule, but with one
another.) Gouger about the same time was struck by the difference
between the free and easy bearing of the Burmans under their own
king and the cringing humility of the peoples of Bengal. A recent
traveller contrasts the Annamese with the Chinese and Siamese.[2] 'I
must confess', he says, 'that I like my Orientals free.' There was
greater security and order on slave plantations than in Africa, but this
was not regarded by the conscience of mankind as sufficiently justifying
slavery. Peace, security and order usually promote welfare, but, as
may be seen from the *pax Japonica* in Korea, they are not identical
with or even a guarantee of welfare.

Economic progress is still often confused with welfare, and it is
assumed that because a country produces more the people will be
better fed, better clothed and better housed. But, as we have seen
already, this belief is contradicted by the facts. More commonly it is
suggested that the standard of living can be measured by the demand
for European goods, and a rise in imports is taken as an index of
welfare, although they may consist largely of production goods for
western enterprise. The import of foreign cloth is claimed as an
increase of welfare, even when it deprives people of employment,
and is perhaps of inferior quality to native cloth. Rather surprisingly,
the import of tinned foods is said to be a means of 'strengthening
tribal life'.[3] Imports of sewing machines, bicycles, gramophones,
motor cars and other western products for natives show that some
can afford to buy things of which formerly they were unaware, but
at the same time make the general public aware of things that they
cannot afford to buy. The sewing machine, the bicycle and the
petrol engine are probably the greatest boons which modern invention has placed at the disposal of tropical peoples, and an enquiry

[1] Gleig, p. 249.
[2] Gouger, p. 10; Brodrick, A. H., *Little China* (1942), pp. 157, 172.
[3] *African Survey*, p. 690; Mayhew, *Colonial Empire*, p. 82.

into their spread and its effects would be of great interest and also of practical importance. But not infrequently such imports merely show that some people have more money than they know how to use; they indicate superfluity rather than welfare among those who buy them, and at best they do not compensate for the decay of social goods that money cannot buy. Even careful attempts to measure welfare in terms of income and expenditure may be misleading, for they omit all those goods that have no price. Probably in Africa, as in Burma, few people are so well fed or so well housed as the prisoners in jail, but the only people who appreciate the comforts of prison life are the warders. If welfare signifies harmony between man and his environment he may be better fed, better clothed and better housed under foreign rule, and still enjoy less welfare than under native rule.

Perhaps we shall obtain a clearer notion of welfare as an object of colonial policy if we try to look at it from the standpoint of the dependent people. Although between individuals in any land there may be a wide range of preference for one thing rather than another, their general idea of welfare conforms to a common pattern which can be seen by looking at what they themselves make of their own social life under favourable circumstances. The ordinary Burman villager, for example, wants to be well fed and well clad according to Burmese ideas, and to live in a dwelling that is comfortable by Burmese standards. These requirements he can satisfy as an individual, but he has other wants, social wants, that he can realize only as a member of the community. He wants his village, also according to his own standards, to have sufficient house room, good roads and paths, a good water supply for men and cattle, adequate sanitary convenience, shady open spaces for social intercourse, and common land for general village amenities in respect of grazing, fuel and so on. High up on his list of social wants is a monastery, with a monastic school and with pagodas and rest houses in pleasant surroundings. He also values opportunities for recreation and for religious and social festivities and entertainments. This may be taken as an outline sketch of the Burmese idea of welfare, which found material expression in the more prosperous villages under Burmese rule, and was probably diffused more widely in the early days of British rule. The Burman wants these things, and he wants, chiefly, to get them to his own liking and in his own way and, beyond that, to have no more to do with Government than necessary. Production is a social function and welfare is a social attribute; in both his work and leisure he is a member of the village and does not live alone.

Such a conception of welfare is quite different from that which ordinarily finds expression in modern welfare legislation. Much of this is based on western models designed to protect labour against capital and, though less effective in the tropics, does something to prevent a reduction in the standard of living in industrial employment below the minimum essential to efficiency. So far as it aims at more than this, it is for the most part unwelcome. The Burman does not want to eat food that Europeans may regard as more nutritious, to observe sanitary precautions that accord with European ideas, or to cultivate his land in ways that Europeans may think more desirable or profitable. His ideas differ in many ways from ours, and where they differ, he is not always mistaken. Native rule in the tropics gives the people more or less what they want, and allows them in great measure to realize their ideas of welfare. But native authority is liable to abuse, and native custom may unconsciously be irksome. So far as foreign rule, by removing abuses and abolishing irksome customs, confers on the people greater freedom to realize their idea of welfare, they accept it more readily. That was what formerly gave strength to British and Dutch colonial rule. As in Lower Burma until about 1880 and in Upper Burma up to about 1910 the people acquiesce in foreign rule because they are hardly conscious of it. It has always been the set policy of Dutch rule to conserve the native social order, however far they may have departed from this principle in practice. The same principle has found expression in some interpretations of indirect rule in British territories,[1] and apparently is still favoured in parts of Africa. If, then, the earlier days of British administration are the happiest, and it is most successful in dealing with primitive and backward peoples, this is probably because the people have been unaware of a change in their environment, except in some ways for the better.

Yet all the time, and even though they do not notice it, the environment is changing. Gradually these changes impinge on native consciousness; the people no longer feel at home, even in their own homes, and increasingly resent foreign rule and foreign ways. For various reasons, humanitarian and practical, colonial powers endeavour to counteract the ill effect of the forces which they have liberated, and to promote native welfare. But this involves closer and more frequent interference with native life and provides fuel for disaffection. In the homogeneous society of the West reforms which raise the individual standard of living tend also to promote social

[1] *African Survey*, p. 134.

welfare, and it seems not unreasonable to assume that similar results will follow in the tropics. Schools, sanitary regulations, the improvement of agriculture, and so on, appeal to humanitarians as likely to improve individual welfare, and by making for economy in administration and business, they appeal to reason as well as to sentiment. Naturally colonial governments conceive of welfare on western lines, and administrative practice is concentrated on enhancing the welfare of the people as individuals.

These attempts to promote welfare are effective only so far as the people will respond to them. The West may scatter pearls, or what it takes for pearls, about the tropics, but the people will not pick them up unless they appreciate their value. Scientific agriculture, modern schools, western medicine and sanitary regulations may not conduce to, and frequently conflict with, what the people regard as welfare, but if they cannot get what they want they must take what they can get. Agricultural and other economic services may enable them to earn more as individuals; modern schools may provide their youngsters with 'a decent job'; they may adopt some western foods or remedies for illness, and they may, perhaps, go to hospitals to be cured of their complaints. But these are all individual benefits, and have no relation to welfare as a social good. Welfare consists essentially in harmony between the individual and the environment; the environment must allow him to obtain both what he knows he wants and also what he wants without being aware of it. Economic progress enlarges the possibility of welfare by increasing the command of man over material resources, but it profits the native as an individual only so far as he participates in the larger surplus, and it enhances his welfare only so far as it contributes, directly or indirectly, to the enrichment of his social life.

8. Welfare and Autonomy

There is, as we have noticed, a growing recognition of the complexity of welfare problems. 'The problems of development touch upon the work of officers in various departments, such as administrative officers, both at headquarters and in the districts, and the technical officers in the agricultural, veterinary, medical and other services. There is need for machinery to provide complete co-ordination between these separate departmental staffs.'[1] The health officer finds that he must seek assistance from the chemist and entomologist, and the veterinary officer

[1] 1940, Cmd. 6175, p. 7; *African Survey*, p. 1612.

looks to the forest officer to provide grazing for the stock. As experts come more and more to recognize the need for special knowledge outside their own branch of study, there is an increasing demand for the creation of new services, and welfare work is distributed among departmental officials who are unable to see life as a whole. At the same time there is a growing recognition that all aspects of life are closely interrelated. In Malaya the improvement of paddy is found to require coordinated action by the agricultural irrigation, co-operative credit, education and other services.[1] In Nyasaland the Welfare Committee comprises representatives of the Medical, Agricultural and Public Works Department together with non-officials. In Southern Rhodesia there is a Director of Native Development in charge of all native affairs.[2] The Dutch in Netherlands India minimize sectionalism by grouping the various services in large departments and, further, link up some of the departments by liaison officers. All these expedients may improve the co-ordination of the welfare machinery. But it still remains machinery, and acts mechanically on the people taken in the mass as an aggregate of individuals. Each group of specialists takes snapshots of the people from its own angle, but the composite photograph obtained by fitting the results together bears as little relation to the native world as a Hollywood film to life. It shows native life from an alien western standpoint and, however lifelike, it never comes to life. The more elaborate the machinery, the more mechanically it functions, driven by economic forces and not by human will. Improvements in the administrative machinery merely effect reforms which adapt the people better to the economic forces that dominate life in tropical dependencies. Evolution along this line leads to a dead end. It is the type of evolution characteristic of the lower forms of life which have survived by adapting their way of life to their environment; to adapt his environment to his way of life is the prerogative of man, and reforms adapting him to an uncongenial environment produce not harmony but discontent. The impact of the West has liberated forces which were formerly kept under control by custom; for the enhancement of welfare it is necessary that the people shall be enabled to regain control over these forces, that they shall regain their former autonomy. That a higher standard of welfare is a condition of autonomy is alleged as one ground for the elaboration of welfare machinery. But improvements in welfare machinery resemble improvements in applied science. Research in applied science may increase the efficiency of

[1] Mills, pp. 255, 262.   [2] *African Survey*, pp. 1197, 1227, 1230.

current practice, but the great scientific achievements come from research in pure science, which revolutionizes practice by attacking old problems along new lines. Similarly the elaboration of welfare machinery can have no appreciable effect on welfare, and still less can it promote autonomy. It will not give them what they want unless they want what it can give, and the promotion of welfare must be approached from a new angle by a revolution in method. The machinery is not only defective, but is applied on a wrong principle.

But, in the modern world, how is it possible for tropical peoples to get what they want? For the environment has changed, and not the people; they still, if left to themselves, would try to reproduce their old environment. But they have been brought into contact with the modern world and cannot get away from it. All the king's horses and all the king's men cannot set the clock back. They can get what they want only if they want what in the conditions of the modern world they *must* want. A fundamental problem of autonomy is to change the people so that they shall come to want, or at least voluntarily to accept, those conditions which the welfare of the modern world requires. Some light should be thrown upon this problem from an examination of attempts already made to introduce self-government among dependent peoples in various projects of colonial autonomy.

9. AUTONOMY

Colonial autonomy is closely linked with the Liberal tradition, which had two aspects. On the economic side it stood for economic freedom, freedom of person, property and trade; on the political side it stood for freedom of thought, speech and religion. Political freedom was regarded as the natural fruit of economic freedom. In the nineteenth century Liberalism was in the air. British and Dutch colonial statesmen alike claimed Liberal ideals though interpreting them differently; French Liberals recognized their colonial subjects as citizens of France, and Liberalism in Spain, suppressed at home, took refuge in the Spanish territories overseas.

During a great part of the century Liberals in Britain thought colonies a burden, and often cited Turgot's dictum comparing them to fruit that would fall from the parent tree when ripe. Men looked forward to the day when India should be able to stand alone as the proudest day in the story of British rule. Practical administrators like Sir Thomas Munro argued that when Indians were sufficiently enlightened to frame a regular government for themselves, it would 'probably be best for both countries that the British control over India should be gradually withdrawn'.[1] From that time onwards the vision of self-government in India, though often veiled behind the clouds of more immediate problems, has never wholly been obscured. The attainment of virtual independence by the great dominions furnished a succession of encouraging precedents, and the rise of Nationalism in the East transformed the question of self-government from a vague and remote prospect into a live political issue. Indians came to demand variously self-government, dominion status and independence, and their example has been followed in other dependencies. Britain responded by formally accepting self-government within the empire as the professed goal of its colonial policy.

But, as the prospect of self-government grew less remote, its meaning required clearer definition. Mr Curtis, in his book on *Dyarchy*, remarks that on his visit to India in 1916 'self-government was discussed in official as well as in Indian society, as the one conceivable goal of British policy'.[2] But he found no less than four different interpretations, none of them agreeing with his own. To some British officials it meant no more than the emancipation of the Government of India from the control of Parliament and the Secretary of State, coupled with the devolution of specified powers and revenues to the provincial Governments. To others it meant the repartition of India into native states. To some Indians it implied merely the progressive substitution of Indian for British officials. Others thought that executives in India could be left responsible to the Secretary of State, and yet be rendered dependent for the exercise of their powers on Indian electorates and elected legislatures. His own interpretation was that executives should be 'responsible' to elective legislatures. Still another interpretation of self-government is possible; for there is no necessary connection between self-government and the elective principle, and a dependency, recognizing allegiance to the Crown but otherwise independent, would be self-governing, even if the ruler were an autocrat. Shortly after his visit self-government was identified with responsible government in the pronouncement in Parliament in August 1917, and was more exactly defined in the preamble to the Government of India Act, 1919: 'It is the declared policy of Parliament to provide for the increasing association of Indians in every branch of Indian administration, and for the gradual development of self-governing institutions, with a view to the progressive realization of responsible government in

[1] Gleig, p. 316.   [2] Curtis, p. 357.

British India as an integral part of the Empire.' The same doctrine has since been extended to other dependencies; formerly they were regarded as held on trust, but now they are to be admitted to 'partnership'.

In this formula one may distinguish three separate elements: men, machinery and will; a self-governing personnel, self-governing institutions, and self-determination. These are often regarded as necessary and logical successive stages on the road leading to self-government, and they have in fact marked the political advance of Burma, as of the rest of India. This line of advance, however, would seem to be associated particularly with the system of direct rule. Direct rule signifies the acceptance of western principles of rule, and self-government implies therefore the training of men to apply them, the construction of institutions to work them, and the education of the people to adopt them. The approach to self-government along this line assumes that in tropical society western forms of self-government will, at least in time, come to function in the same manner as in the West. It attempts to adapt tropical society to western principles of government, much as the scientific expert in agriculture or hygiene too often tries to adapt native life to scientific principles.

We have noticed that when the Dutch regained their eastern territories in 1816, they were full of enthusiasm for 'all that is brave and liberal'. Van den Bosch claimed to be applying Liberal principles when he left the Regents and villages, 'the little republics', in Java free to govern their people on their own lines. Indirect rule purports to conserve the self-governing personnel and self-governing institutions that are already in existence and, so far as it is used as an instrument of political advancement, implies the adaptation of western principles of government to tropical society. But most Dutch Liberals of 1816 would have ranked with the more backward British 'Tories'; even the more orthodox Liberals of a later generation, when introducing Liberal reforms on a mid-Victorian pattern, expressly disavowed the idea of governing Java on British principles with a view to political emancipation. Yet circumstances compelled the Netherlands to follow the same path as Britain. The expansion of private enterprise under Liberal rule led to the multiplication of administrative activities, and economy dictated the recruitment of a native personnel. With the growth of the western element in the plural society, administrative efficiency required the introduction of western self-governing institutions in local government. Then, during the present century, the convergence of Liberal, Ethical and Nationalist ideas, together with considerations of practical convenience, led in 1918 to the creation of the Volksraad, introducing western institutions in the central government. The new Dutch constitution of 1922 recognized the autonomy of Netherlands India in principle, and, as subsequently formulated in 1942, Dutch policy looked forward to the reconstruction of the kingdom 'on a solid foundation of complete partnership' among all the members.[1] Thus circumstances have dragged the Dutch, for long almost reluctantly, along the track blazed by the British. In Dutch as in British dependencies, colonial policy has sought to make the people capable of self-government by substituting natives for Europeans in the administration and by the construction of western self-governing institutions, and in both alike partnership has come to be recognized as the goal of policy.

10. Personnel

The application of Liberal principles to tropical administration may be dated from the revision of the charter of the East India Company in 1813. Liberal orthodoxy expected Government to confine its activities so far as possible to the maintenance of law and order. On that view it was not illogical to hold that the substitution of Indians for Europeans in the law courts would take India a long way towards self-government. Merely of necessity this process was already making great strides forward. The system of direct rule, inaugurated by Warren Hastings, was completed when Cornwallis took over civil and criminal jurisdiction from native authorities. It soon appeared that the Company could not afford to entertain a sufficient European staff, and Lord Hastings considered various expedients, including the revival of *panchayats*, for dealing with the pressure of business. The easiest and cheapest solution was to train natives as magistrates and judges. They were employed in courts of first instance and, under Lord Amherst, in appellate courts. By 1827 over 90% of the original suits in civil cases were tried by native judicial officers. Thus the employment of Indians was 'rendered imperative by the cost of a purely English administration'. But it was also regarded as 'a great moral duty'.[2] 'With what grace', asked Munro, 'can we talk of our paternal government, if we exclude them from

---

[1] *Netherlands India*, pp. 82, 84, 109, 160; Broek, J. D. M., *Pacific Affairs*, 1943, p. 338.
[2] Ross, p. 202; Boulger, pp. 60, 64, 67; *IG*, IV, 45.

every important office?'[1] The great Liberal reformer, Bentinck, was heartily in favour of the employment of Indians, and, on the renewal of the Company's charter in 1833, this view found expression in the memorable pronouncement that no one should be excluded from any appointment in India by reason only of his colour, creed or race. This principle has always since then been 'adopted by the Government and people of England as a cardinal point in their Indian policy'. It may be claimed that it has been steadily applied. By the end of the century there were Indian judges on various provincial High Courts, while 'the European element in the government was confined within the limits essential for efficiency and guidance', and was employed chiefly where special knowledge or requirements were needed, or where 'as in the case of the Police, a large measure of European control was essential'.[2] But although the administrative personnel was so largely manned by Indians, India was no nearer to self-government. In this matter there was still, says Mr Curtis, 'almost everything to be done. You will not have done it, or begun to do it, merely by substituting Indian for English officials from the Viceroy downwards.' Such a Government might even be further from self-government, because an English Viceroy, merely by the circumstances of his birth and upbringing, is better able to treat with members of the Home Government as one of themselves on equal terms.

Indians were indeed less capable of self-government at the end of the century than at the beginning. In the early years of the nineteenth century India was merely a geographical expression; politically it was a congeries of native states and British territories; the former were self-governing and in the latter the machinery of government was little more complex than in native states. But, with economic progress, the administrative system was unified and centralized at Calcutta, while the machinery of government grew more complex and the art of government more intricate and difficult. As soon as a Government wants to do anything beyond maintaining law and order, it needs experts who can do these things: engineers for the roads and railways, irrigation and drainage; geologists and mining engineers; agricultural and veterinary officials; doctors and schoolmasters. It needs a larger staff, and especially a much larger staff of native subordinates. The multiplication of special services leads to departmentalism. Even in Europe, where the public services have grown up in response to social demand, the delays and obstructions of bureaucracy are a common

[1] Gleig, p. 307.   [2] *IG*, iv, 45.

theme of complaint. But in India and other tropical dependencies, they form the framework of a huge western superstructure over native life, wholly foreign to the people. Not only is there less self-government, but less government than before, because the machinery is too vast and complex to be informed by human will.

The multiplication of native officials is, therefore, no measure of the progress of self-government, but rather the reverse. In Europe the public services provide what the people want, and a comparatively small staff suffices to give them what they want; but in the tropics the much larger staff necessary to obtain the compliance of the people with innovations that they do not want constitutes a hindrance to self-government.

The inverse relation between self-government and the multiplication of native officials is illustrated by the system of indirect rule. Under this system there is a much greater measure of self-government than under direct rule, and one of its advantages is that it does not require so large a staff. During the nineteenth century in Java, when the Regents and villages managed their own affairs, few officials were employed. But, with economic progress, and the influx of foreign elements, there is a demand for the introduction of western law and western amenities, and accordingly far more judges and magistrates and the multiplication of special services. Thus, as native officials become more numerous, native self-government decays. On the other hand, as happened in Siam, an independent country can employ a large number of European officials without ceasing to be self-governing. So long as the Government remains an instrument of foreign rule, the increasing association of natives in every branch of tropical administration is no index to the progress of self-government.

11. Machinery: Local Government

Together with the increasing association of natives in the administration, Liberals placed their faith in the 'gradual development of self-governing institutions'. Local self-government is, of course, no new thing in the tropics. From very early times tropical rulers have allowed foreign traders in the ports to settle their own affairs in their own way according to their own laws. It was in accordance with this principle of 'like over like' that Europeans in India and other parts of the tropics were allowed, and required, to maintain order among their own community. But modern self-government on a western pattern is the child of sanitation. It was owing to trouble over town conservancy that, in 1687, the East India Company obtained from James II a charter constituting a new civil government for Madras on an English model with a mayor, aldermen and burgesses empowered to levy taxes for such matters as seemed 'convenient for the honour, interest, ornaments, security and defence' of the corporation and inhabitants; their powers included the constitution of a court for the trial of both civil and criminal issues.[1] Similar corporations were subsequently established in the other Presidency towns, but the extension of municipal administration to the interior is comparatively recent.

Local self-government in the interior had its origin, as in the city of Madras, in the urgent need to find some more efficient way of dealing with the problem of sanitation. But the situation was very different. In Madras an effective majority of the chief inhabitants wanted better conservancy, and of their own motion they obtained a charter so that they might better be able to do what they wanted to have done. In the interior it was the local officials and not the people who wanted better sanitation. So long as nothing could be done without the sanction of the central Government in India or Europe, local officials could not help themselves; some measure of deconcentration of authority was needed to invest them with the requisite powers and to enable them to raise the necessary funds.[2] Municipal administration provided the machinery. In Madras, as in Europe, western self-governing institutions enabled the townsfolk, or the dominant class among them, to do what they wanted; in the interior Government could provide the machinery of local self-government, but the people did not want to use it.

The outcome of the first essay in municipal legislation was ominous. In 1842 an Act for Bengal enabled 'the inhabitants of any place of public resort or residence to make better provision for purposes connected with health or convenience'. But so far were the people from wanting better provision that in the first town to which it was applied they prosecuted the collector for trespass. This killed the Act, and little more was attempted until the Report of the Royal Army Sanitary Commission in 1863 attributed the bad health of the troops largely to the insanitary condition of the towns. This report may be taken to mark the beginning of both modern sanitation and modern local self-government in India. During the next five years the various Provinces were equipped with municipal legislation. But even so far as the people wanted better sanitation, they did not want, and could not

[1] *IG*, iv, 284.   [2] *ISC*, i, 301.

use, western municipal machinery. We have noticed that in Burma
the townsfolk were beginning to adapt their social life to the new
environment, and could make their own arrangements for conservancy
without western machinery or help from Government. In Madras,
also, there were voluntary associations in some towns for sanitation
and other social ends. Modern sanitation was *needed*, and in some
degree was *wanted*; a social demand for sanitation was emerging. This
might have served as the basis for a gradual organic development, but
it seemed easier and quicker to turn out western municipal machinery
by mass production. Yet the western machinery did not meet the
emerging social demand, and, because it answered no demand, it was
inefficient in providing for the need. The Acts of 1864 to 1868 did
something to improve urban sanitation, but they marked little progress towards self-government. In 1870 the Provinces were for the
first time given some control over their own revenues and were
allowed to raise taxes if the fixed grant from central revenues did not
suffice. The Resolution of 1870, introducing this new system, emphasized the importance of engaging local interest in the management
of funds allotted to education, sanitation, medical charity and local
works, and between 1871 and 1874 a new set of Municipal Acts provided for popular representation on local bodies. Only in the Central
Provinces, one of the most backward territories, was popular representation regarded as successful; possibly because the people were
too backward to question the wisdom and authority of the executive
officers who presided over the committees.

So far, despite Liberal aspirations, efficiency had been the main
theme and object of local self-government, and local organs had been
provided in the towns, where better sanitation was urgently needed in
the new environment consequent on economic progress. But in 1881
the Liberal Viceroy, Lord Ripon, struck a new note by emphasizing
the value of local self-government as a means of political and popular
education. Accordingly, in 1883–4, for the third time within twenty
years, all the provinces were fitted out with new Municipal Acts.[1]
These purported to introduce a more democratic principle. Former
legislation had enabled the Government to get the people to do what
it thought necessary; now the people were given powers to do, of their
own accord, what Government thought necessary.

That was not the only reason for the inefficiency of local self-
government. There was very little that, taken as a whole, the people did

---

[1] *IG*, IV, 164, 286, 287.

want. Even in India, with a comparatively homogeneous population, 'the violent sectional antagonism between Hindus and Mohammedans, or Brahmins and non-Brahmins has certainly impaired the efficiency of local bodies'. In other tropical dependencies, with a more strongly plural character, self-government on western lines is impossible because, as we have noticed in Burma with its mixed population of Burmans, Indians and Chinese, and in the larger towns Europeans, the people lack 'the sense of common citizenship which is the necessary basis for healthy civic life'. It is not only in Burma that the various communities have little common interest except in resisting proposals for enhanced taxation, or that the membership of local bodies largely consists of men who seek official favour or hope to line their pockets. In India the Statutory Commission noticed 'a number of cases of corruption and certain instances where very large sums had been expended in order to obtain seats on local government authorities, suggesting that those who expended such large amounts expected to be able to recoup themselves from illicit gains'.[1]

Most of the functions imposed on local bodies were things that needed doing, and the local bodies helped to get them done. If the inhabitants will not or cannot make the necessary adjustments for themselves, others must perform the task. Ordinarily it has devolved on the local official in charge of general administration. The forms of local self-government help him to discharge his functions more effectively by providing him with funds and by bringing him closer to the people. But form does not give rise to function. He was merely 'carrying out the will of his official superiors. He was just as much the eyes, ears and arms of the provincial Government as when functioning as revenue officer or district magistrate. Local self-government was just one of his many activities.' In India, forty years after the introduction of the forms of self-government through the Liberal enthusiasm of Lord Ripon, it was reported that 'the custom of the country, force of habit, apathy, and lack of desire to assume responsibility among those elected—together with the natural reluctance of an overworked official, desirous of efficiency, to consume much time in getting things done badly which he felt he could himself do well—combined to prevent real and substantial progress being made in political and popular education in the art of self-government'.[2] The view current among officials was that 'certainly Indians of the political class have not shone greatly in the

[1] *ISC*, I, 314.   [2] *ISC*, I, 301.

sphere of local self-government during the last thirty years, although of course they blame everything but themselves'. With wider powers 'many will weary and again blame anything rather than their own lack of perseverance'.[1] These remarks suggest that Indians were not alone in looking beyond themselves to find a scapegoat for the failure of self-government, and they are illuminating as to its effect on causing friction between officials and the people. But such recriminations serve merely to divert attention from the real cause of its failure.

Under indirect rule local self-government follows a like course. With the growth of a western element in social life, it becomes necessary to replace native self-government by western self-governing machinery. In Netherlands India urban self-government on western lines was first introduced under the Decentralization Law of 1903. This was intended to promote efficiency by deconcentrating administrative activity, and also to provide an element of popular co-operation in the task of government. In the large towns self-government proved efficient, partly because it was based on the Dutch rather than the English model with an official *burgomaster* instead of a non-official as Chairman, but chiefly because the large towns contain a stronger European community than in British India, and in effect self-government was government by the European section. Elsewhere, however, it had a different result, and promoted executive efficiency rather than self-government.

Economic progress requires a readjustment of social life to new conditions; most rapidly and urgently in the towns, less obviously but no less inevitably in the villages. Under Lord Ripon the forms of western self-governing machinery were applied to rural areas. Here they were even more unreal than in the towns. For some towns did at least possess economic unity, whereas the districts and their subdivisions were merely artificial units devised for administrative convenience and with no organic cohesion. The natural effect was to expedite the decay of organic self-government in the villages. Under indirect rule, also, the readjustment of social conditions in rural areas comes, if less rapidly than under direct rule, to demand attention. In Netherlands India the Village Act of 1906 was intended to provide western machinery for consolidating village life, and for lifting the community to a higher level. But 'autonomy and progress do not go together', and after twenty years 'precious little autonomy remained', and the western machinery, having no organic relation to

[1] Curtis, p. 33.

native life, ceased to function as soon as the hand of Government was withdrawn. Similarly, in British territories under indirect rule,

'the varied responsibilities now placed on native authorities demand the exercise of close and continuous supervision by the administration.... Many observers have questioned whether the traditional native authorities, or at all events a large number of the weaker units, will not be strained beyond their powers by the tasks now laid on them. Everywhere the supervision now exercised over them must bring home to the people that the sanction for their authority is no longer the good will of their own people, but the recognition accorded to them by the administration.'[1]

And under indirect rule, as under direct rule, native social units are continually readjusted and are often amalgamated for the sake of convenience or economy into large artificial administrative units with no traditional sanction, in which administrative methods can be applied according to a standard plan. Under Dutch rule as under British rule, and under direct rule as under indirect rule, local self-government fights a losing battle against efficiency.

12. MACHINERY: CENTRAL GOVERNMENT

In the machinery of the central government in tropical dependencies, one can trace a similar conflict between the contrary ideals of efficiency and autonomy. From very early days both the British and Dutch East India Companies furnished their representatives in the East with the assistance of a council. In British India, under the rule of law during the nineteenth century, this council took on a new character. From 1833 the Council of the Governor-General was gradually enlarged for the purpose of legislation, and in 1861 the Indian Councils Act provided for the addition to the Central Legislative Councils of non-officials, including Indians, and also for the constitution of Provincial Councils on similar lines. But these councils were merely 'committees by means of which the executive Government obtained advice and assistance in their legislation, and the public derived the advantage of publicity at every stage of the law-making process'.[2] Gradually the councils came to exercise an increasing influence over the conduct of affairs, and there was a growing deference to the opinions of important classes. This became more marked when the Indian Councils Act of 1892 enlarged the Provincial Councils and gave partial recognition to

---

[1] *African Survey*, pp. 538–9; Field, M. J., *Man*, 1943, p. 90.
[2] *ISC*, I, 114–16.

the elective system. Yet there was no change in the constitutional position of the councils; the object of the Act was that 'each important class shall have the opportunity of making its wishes known in Council through the mouth of some member specially acquainted with them'.[1] The Morley-Minto reforms of 1909 were a further advance in the same direction; they created larger councils with numerous non-officials elected either by local authorities, large landowners, trade associations, or universities. But the authors of these reforms expressly repudiated the suggestion that they would lead 'directly or indirectly to the establishment of a parliamentary system in India'.[2] Thus all these successive changes in the form of government were intended to increase its efficiency and not to transfer the responsibility for government from the British Parliament to the Indian people.

On the other hand, however, they went a long way towards local autonomy by strengthening the Provincial Governments against the Central Government, and the Central Government against Whitehall. In all the various councils the predominant influence was that of western industry and commerce. We have noticed that, in Burma, agrarian reforms were pressed on the Provincial Government by the Government of India, and at first not without response. Later, with the enlargement of the Legislative Council, capitalist influence was strong enough to defeat them. In some matters there may be a cleavage of opinion between officials and non-official Europeans, but usually these two classes, from their common origin and upbringing, if for no other reason, tend to adopt the same point of view, and in India from about 1870 onwards, with the growth of western enterprise after the opening of the Suez Canal, there was an increasing tendency towards capitalist autonomy, which became more Indian in colour during the present century, as Indian capital grew more powerful and Nationalism more clamorous and better organized.

Yet, up to the outbreak of the war of 1914–18, the Liberal doctrine of training India for political emancipation had made no impression on the machinery of the Central Government. The Government aimed to promote the welfare of the people, and was amenable to the influence of the Indian public so far as this was vocal. But Nationalists wanted more than influence; they wanted power. The first stirrings of modern Nationalism were directly inherited from the Liberal tradition, but by the end of the nineteenth century it derived most of its strength from a blind reaction, seditious and destructive, against both foreign rule and

[1] *ISC*, I, 183.　　　　　　　　　　[2] *ISC*, I, 119.

western civilization. The Japanese victory over Russia inspired new hopes of freedom and a more constructive attitude. Nationalists came to look on western education, western science and western political institutions as instruments by which India might achieve a place among the nations of the modern world. The Morley-Minto reforms of 1909 aimed to appease rather than to satisfy these new demands, and only when Britain, having drawn the sword to defend the liberty of the small nations of Europe, invited help from India, was the doctrine of self-determination extended to the tropics. Indians demanded self-government and, in reply to their demand, the pronouncement of 1917 held up responsible government within the Empire as the goal of British policy. The substitution of responsible government for self-government is significant. Responsible government was intended to imply a Government accountable to the people, and in England therefore had the whole weight of Liberal tradition to back it. In India it appealed both to those Europeans who held that the strength of British rule lay in the well-merited affection of the masses, who would outweigh the disaffected Nationalists, and also to Indians who looked to the Liberal principle of counting heads as ensuring a majority for Indians in the conduct of Indian affairs.

The reforms that followed this pronouncement 'struck at the essentials of the previous system. Authority, instead of being concentrated at the Centre, was to be in large measure devolved on the provinces; the opportunities of the Central Legislature for influencing the Government of India were to be increased; the control of Parliament over the whole of Indian government was to be modified by marking out a portion of the provincial field in which it would be no longer exercised'.[1] This system came to be known as Dyarchy because the British Parliament remained supreme in certain matters, while transferring control over others to Indian ministers, chosen by the people and responsible to a popular electorate. Forms of parliamentary government were devised in the expectation, or the hope, that they would function in the same manner as in England. But conditions in England and India were very different. In England there was a strongly homogeneous society; in all parts of India (and especially in Burma) there was a much divided plural society. In England the franchise has been extended to new classes as they have gained economic power, and voting power, the numerical majority, is a rough measure of economic and military power; in India generally

[1] *ISC*, I, 122.

(and especially in Burma) the numerical majority lies with that section of the community which has least economic and military power. In England the whole people accept the standards of the modern world; in India only a very small minority lives in the modern world. These conditions, which are general throughout tropical dependencies, are incompatible with parliamentary government in the form which has gradually been worked out in England, and, if attempts be made to introduce western democratic forms, they necessitate the adoption of safeguards to prevent the collapse of government.

In India various safeguards were devised. The executive was empowered to override the legislature, if necessary. Apart from matters expressly transferred to popular control, the executive still remained responsible to the British Parliament. The special representation of particular interests and classes made for a balance of power in the legislatures. The legislatures included an official block, speaking and voting in accordance with the views of the executive. And, possibly the most effective safeguard against unwelcome legislation, the pay and patronage enjoyed by ministers weakened party solidarity among the Nationalist opposition. Responsible government, so far as it makes for better representation, helps Government to know what needs doing, but so far as it involves a system of balance, blocks and bribery, it prevents the Government from doing anything. In India dyarchy failed to gain the approval of the Nationalists, who attributed its shortcomings to the safeguards. But, in fact, it merely brought to light and aggravated the conditions which made India unsuitable to self-government on British lines. The reforms gave new point to Hindu-Moslem competition, and communal tension grew more acute.[1] Similarly in Burma western democratic forms have fostered ill-will and strife between Burmans, Indians, Chinese and Europeans. In Netherlands India likewise the first Volksraad to have an actual share in government was the last 'association-Volksraad', and each racial group began to look to its own interests. Self-government on a popular basis requires the existence of a common social will, but the reforms engendered communal ill-will. In the tropics people in general do not want what the conditions of the modern world necessitate, and self-government consequently does not give them what they want. It does not even give them what they need, for a legislature representing a photographic portrait of a plural society in all its detail of conflicting social and economic interests cannot pass difficult and contentious legislation,

[1] *ISC*, I, 29.

and its composition effectually hinders it from doing what is necessary to counterbalance the play of economic forces; social will is paralysed and anti-social forces become more active than before. Thus in a plural society the forms of responsible government not only prevent self-government but make constructive government impossible, and allow greater freedom to economic forces.

It is not only by intensifying sectional and communal differences that the machinery of responsible government tends to hinder progress towards self-government. In India 'while the experienced member of the Services will admit the benefit of British Raj and realize the difficulties in the way of complete self-government; while the member of a minority community, putting the safety of his community first, will stipulate for safeguards; and while the moderate will look askance at extremist methods which he will denounce; all alike are in sympathy with the demand for equal status with the European and proclaim their belief in self-determination for India'.[1] When nationalist aspirations conflict with capitalist activities, Europeans are usually associated with the latter. In India, where Indians own much of the capital, this is not so marked as in Burma and most other dependencies. In Burma, the Indians and Chinese share with Burmans an inferiority complex; they all want equality of status with Europeans. Yet, at every point of divergence between national interest and economic development, the Indians and Chinese tend to line up behind the Europeans, who stand out in the legislature as the protagonists of capital. But the Government is a European government, and the ill-feeling centring on Europeans is focussed on the Government and accordingly on Britain. A dependency cannot obtain self-government peacefully except by co-operation based on mutual good-will between the people aspiring to autonomy and the colonial power attempting to confer it on them, but this is weakened and not strengthened by the introduction of democratic institutions along western lines.

Thus, although Europeans inheriting the Liberal tradition of democratic government will sympathize with democratic aspirations, both general considerations and practical experience suggest that premature experiments in introducing western institutions hinder rather than help towards the attainment of independence, and prejudice rather than promote the growth of popular government and the ultimate achievement of democracy.

[1] *ISC*, I, 408.

13. Progress, Welfare and Autonomy

It would seem then that the machinery of western democracy, like the machinery of western welfare, operates merely to further economic progress. Idealists pleaded the cause of education, but the effective stimulus was the need for educated officials. Humanitarians denounced the conditions of labour, but with little effect until employers came to recognize that more efficient labour was cheaper. Arguments for the employment of natives in the higher ranks of private enterprise found a hearing only when the recent depression necessitated the substitution of natives for Europeans in order to cut down expenses. In India Liberals urged the employment of Indians in Government service, but this came about through the impossibility of entertaining a sufficient staff of Europeans. Liberals advocated also the principle of self-government, but the machinery of self-government was not introduced until there was a need for better sanitation. Reforms have been conceived in a spirit of idealism, but they have had to wait on occasion for the midwife. It is true that humanitarian ideals have done much to accelerate the adoption of reforms by creating a favourable climate of opinion. And they have done more than that; they have encouraged Liberal experiments. It was hope rather than any confidence in their ability that led to the first employment of Burmans as magistrates.[1] Shortage of labour may have encouraged employers to examine the possibility of improving the efficiency of labour, but human sympathy and faith in native potentialities were needed to justify expenditure on providing costly amenities. It was faith in the Javanese that inspired the reforms of Raffles in Java. He believed that they would respond to the desire of gain, and work harder in order to make more money; the Dutch at that time were firmly convinced that they would not work except under compulsion. But Raffles wanted the Javanese to make more money so that they could buy British goods; the Dutch had no manufactures to sell and wanted the Javanese to provide them with tropical produce as cheaply as possible. Projects of enhancing welfare may be inspired by high ideals, but they are conditioned, and therefore frustrated, by economic circumstances. It is of little avail to attempt social reforms without first creating a suitable environment in which they may achieve their purpose.

This principle applies throughout the whole range of colonial policy.

[1] *SL*, p. 127.

So long as Britain looked on India mainly as a market and enjoyed a natural monopoly of tropical markets, British manufacturers and merchants cared little who should govern India, provided that it was governed well and cheaply and set up no barriers to trade; they looked forward to withdrawing from India and could envisage its independence with equanimity. But, with the growth of overseas investments and of capitalist enterprise in the tropics, there were stronger grounds for retaining political control; at the same time Britain lost its natural monopoly of commerce in the tropics, and had to safeguard the political connection in order to fend off foreign powers with a protective policy. Synchronizing with this change in the economic environment there was a corresponding transformation of opinion, a new pride in imperial responsibilities and a new reluctance to sever colonial relations. The goal of policy was no longer independence but responsible government 'within the empire', or 'partnership'. Dutch colonial policy also reflects changes in the economic environment, but in a contrary direction. Under the Culture system and for some years later the Dutch treasury looked to the produce of Java to maintain financial solvency; the Home Government maintained a strict control over colonial administration, and the British policy of training the people for independence was expressly repudiated. But with the development of Java by private enterprise and the growth of its importance as a market, opinion shifted in the direction of autonomy; Batavia wished to shake off the fetters of The Hague. French colonial policy has fluctuated with each change in the balance of power between industry and agriculture. In the United States the strong tradition against imperialism could achieve nothing for Filipino independence until a combination of dairy farmers, Cuban sugar planters and Labour leaders turned it to account for the furtherance of their economic interests. Whatever lofty sentiments may inspire pronouncements on colonial policy, its practical application is coloured and conditioned by interest. But this interest is not often avowed, and is very largely subconscious. It is important therefore, when examining statements on colonial policy, to scrutinize the means designed to give effect to it.

In Britain all parties, with unanimity if with diversity of emphasis, look forward to making the dependencies capable of independence as 'partners' in the Empire. They agree also that economic development is the means by which this end may be attained; the modern constructive policy regards economic development as leading indirectly through welfare to self-government. Yet we have seen that economic development is, at best, no guarantee of welfare; also that it makes the people less capable of self-government, increases the difficulty of self-government, and makes the colonial power more reluctant to grant self-government. There is no reason to doubt that the policy is stated with all good faith, and there are plausible arguments for regarding it as sound. Yet general considerations suggest that the means usually advocated would defeat the end proposed. Experience confirms this doubt. Let us examine these matters rather more closely.

Economic development, it is said, is a condition of welfare, and welfare a condition of autonomy, because self-governing institutions cannot be built on a foundation of ignorance and ill-health. We have found, however, that there may be great and rapid economic progress with little or no enhancement of welfare; that economic progress is not a condition of greater welfare but, on the contrary, welfare is a condition of economic progress; and that whereas economic progress is ordinarily a by-product of welfare, it may be, and, unless kept under control, is usually if not invariably prejudicial to welfare. So far then as economic progress fails to enhance welfare, the view that it leads through welfare to self-government cannot be sustained.

But, quite apart from its effect on welfare, economic development hinders the attainment of self-government. Everyone now recognizes that it disintegrates and atomizes native society and, obviously, a crowd of individuals is less capable of self-government than an organic social structure. In regions developed by native enterprise, economic development produces a middle class of landlords and moneylenders, possibly native, often or usually foreign orientals. These, in virtue of their economic strength, tend to acquire political importance. But considerations of welfare, and also of political stability, call for measures to protect the peasantry against debt and the loss of land. Such measures hinder the emergence of a middle class, or tend to eliminate it, leaving nothing between the peasant and the western merchants, a situation that is incompatible with popular self-government. On the other hand, in regions developed by western enterprise, there comes into existence a middle class of petty capitalists, possibly native, often or usually foreign orientals. Considerations of welfare call for measures to protect labour against exploitation. But only western men of business apprehend the advantage of welfare measures and have command over sufficient capital to adopt them, and here again the effect of welfare measures is to hinder the emergence of, or to eliminate, the middle class, leaving nothing between the coolie and the representatives of western capital, interested in the dependency solely as a business proposition. Thus economic progress necessitates welfare measures that hinder political advancement. Indeed economic progress makes self-government by the people as a whole impossible, for in place of a whole people it creates a plural society devoid of any common social will and incapable, therefore, of governing itself; in this plural society, moreover, all those sections which are mainly interested in economic progress are in general content that the dependency should be managed as a business proposition, and included among them are some natives, officials and others, who fear to lose the crumbs that fall from the capitalist tables. Economic development creates a plural society not only incapable of self-government, but divided against itself and in part undesirous of self-government.

Again, economic development not only makes a dependency less capable of self-government, but even makes government more difficult. For it builds up above the native world an elaborate superstructure of western economic enterprise in which the people have little or no part; corresponding to this economic superstructure, and as a necessary corollary of its existence, there arises an administrative superstructure wholly foreign to the people, directed and in great part staffed by Europeans. As we have already noticed the administrative machinery finally becomes so elaborate as to be unmanageable, but long before this stage is reached it is beyond popular control. Every new administrative development which does not proceed from the people themselves in response to social will, raises another barrier against self-government. Moreover, the agents of administrative machinery are not merely passive; a steam engine is indifferent whether it enters or leaves its yard, but a horse goes more willingly towards its stable. Similarly officials apply rules in accordance with their inclinations. Under both British and Dutch rule, when officials were converted from mercantile agents into civil servants, it was recognized that, in order to ensure impartial administration, they must be debarred from mercantile transactions. In British dependencies regulations, inherited from the eighteenth century, forbid officials to own land or to engage in trade. This restriction was found essential to uncorrupt administration. But with the growth of joint stock companies it is no longer effective. European officials belong to the same class as men engaged in western enterprise and naturally tend to have similar preconceptions. This natural tendency for them to identify themselves with the cause of economic development is strengthened by material interest where they invest in local companies or can look forward to employment by such companies on retirement from official life. Both environment and interest encourage them to look favourably on economic development, and to be suspicious of entrusting the people with powers that may seem prejudicial to economic progress. While co-operating wholeheartedly with measures to increase production or trade by developing material and human resources, they will tend, even unconsciously, to hamper the transfer of control over development to the natives. Friction of this type is not reduced but rather enhanced by the substitution of native officials for Europeans. Europeans, by their tradition and education, are more likely than natives to oppose measures that they regard as unsound, and by their status can do so with less risk to their careers; for similar reasons there would seem to be especial need for the control over investments by native officials. Thus the personnel of the administrative machinery, whether European or native, hinders smooth progress towards self-government. And in any case, the administrative machinery grows so cumbrous in the course of economic progress that all, together with the leviathan that they seem to guide, are carried along by the current of economic forces. With every forward step in economic progress self-government becomes more difficult.

Again, the ordinary course of economic progress extends the circle of people in the colonial power whose interests would seem to be prejudiced if the dependencies had full control over their own affairs. In Britain comparatively few people used to have any great interest in India. Before the Industrial Revolution the profit derived from the Indian connection went mainly to the directors and shareholders in the East India Company, and to the small class that supplied recruits for mercantile, civil and military appointments. After the Industrial Revolution this small class expanded to include the manufacturers of cotton goods, and to those providing capital and labour to the cotton trade or otherwise benefiting directly or indirectly by its prosperity. With the growth of overseas investment and of capitalist enterprise in the tropics, the development of trade stimulated the growth of shipping, and the multiplication of public and private enterprise was profitable to banks and financiers, so that the circle of those interested in maintaining control over dependencies expanded further to include almost everyone in Britain who was engaged in any form of production or commerce. Tropical education opened up lucrative prospects to the great publishing firms, and a variety of welfare measures provided openings for the professional middle class, and encouraged a sympathetic attitude towards colonial relations in universities and other institutions training men for scientific or social activities in the tropics. If England had lost its tropical possessions at the beginning of the nineteenth century, few people would have felt the loss, but now it would threaten the material interest of almost everyone throughout the British Isles.

Colonies, regarded as a business proposition, need capital for their economic development, and can raise funds in the home money market on more favourable terms than some independent powers. But the financial houses which provide the money allow favourable terms on the strength of the imperial connection, and must naturally view with apprehension any change which weakens their security. Manufacturing interests in the colonial power may seem to be threatened if dependencies are enabled to restrict the import of their manufactures, or to foster industries likely to compete with them. During the recent depression, grants under the Colonial Development Act of 1929 made a considerable contribution to employment in this country. Similar conditions will probably recur, and 'if at any time the existence of an unemployment problem requires the examination of providing work in Great Britain, the possibility of further grants to assist African Governments to purchase railway, bridging or other capital equipment might perhaps be considered'.[1] All parties, Conservative, Liberal, and Socialist, are agreed that such assistance should be provided, and all agree that measures are needed to ensure full employment in Great Britain. If dependencies attain independence, it will not be so easy to control them in the interests of Britain or to fit them into comprehensive projects for ensuring employment in this country. Thus we are in much the same position as the Dutch in Java a hundred years ago when the Dutch people as a whole profited by the Culture system. So far as economic development diffuses in the colonial power a material interest in maintaining colonial relations, it must of necessity increase the reluctance of the colonial power to make its colonies capable of independence. Modern colonial policy advocates economic development as a road to the independence of colonies. But if every step along the road to self-government strengthens and

[1] 1940, Cmd. 6928; *African Survey*, p. 1321.

diffuses those interests in the colonial power which self-government imperils, makes self-government more difficult and dependencies less capable of self-government, there would seem good reason to ask whether it is the right road.

Experience supplies the answer to this question. In few British dependencies, if any, has there been such vast and rapid economic progress as in Malaya during the first quarter of the present century. If economic development leads to self-government, no dependency should be more capable of independence. In the Federated Malay States, however, it has created a plural society in which the natives contribute only 26 % to the general population, and there is no dependency where self-government presents more difficult problems. In Netherlands India economic progress up to 1930 was even more conspicuous. The Government had not disregarded native welfare and, especially from 1900 under Ethical inspiration, it had been zealous in benevolent activities. But the country was run on business principles as a business concern, and it was the huge scale of the western superstructure that made the depression of the thirties so disastrous. For the collapse of the whole edifice seemed imminent, and capital had to seek the aid of Government; it was no longer a master but a mendicant. The Government took this opportunity to impose restrictions on capitalist activities in accordance with a policy of directing economic development in the interest of Netherlands India as a nation. Dutch writers claim that the ten years before the Japanese attack witnessed the 'birth of a nation' in Netherlands India, not merely an alliance of local peoples, creeds and castes agreeing only in a sectional opposition to foreign ways and foreign rule, but the amalgamation of all the distinct constituent elements of a plural society into one society with a common social will. History will test this claim, but the point immediately relevant is that the transformation was effected not by 'injections of western capital', but by restricting capitalist activities in the interest of a common nation.

In other dependencies various new developments during the recent war point in a similar direction:

'In all colonies the restrictions on imports have stimulated the growth of local industries both for making household and other articles of common use and for the processing of local produce. In West and East Africa, for example, among the articles now being made in addition to food products are the following: rope and twine, starch, shingles and tiles for roofing, shoe-leather and shoes, boot polish. These industries have been part of a temporary war time plan to supply local needs as far as possible from local resources.'[1]

In many or most of these new ventures western enterprise has taken a leading part. For the time being, and under the pressure of economic circumstances, capitalists have been transfigured as nationalists. But so far as these enterprises are run by western capitalists, it is doubtful how long they will survive the circumstances to which they owe their birth. During the war of 1914–18 there was a similar expansion of local industry in Netherlands India, but when communications with Europe were restored, western enterprise found other activities more profitable and local industries collapsed.

There is a greater chance for the survival of local industries when they are in native hands. In the Tropical Far East the recent depression which stimulated western enterprise to develop local industries also provided new opportunities for native enterprise. In Burma, for instance, as in Netherlands India, high taxation on matches impelled the natives to manufacture cheap cigarette lighters.[2] The encouragement of native manufactures was an outstanding feature of economic policy in Netherlands India during this period.[3] Between 1930 and 1940 the number of modern handlooms rose from 500 to 49,000, and of mechanical looms from 40 to 9800; the import of cotton thread for weaving rose from 3000 to 28,000 tons and created a spinning industry. By 1936 the local production of *sarongs* had risen to 5·6 million kgs. and imports had fallen to 2·35 million and by 1940 to 0·33 million. The import of caustic soda for soap manufacture rose from 4000 tons in 1930 to 18,000 tons in 1940. The manufacture of native cigarettes and of native straw hats showed similar progress. And a native bank came into existence to finance the various native enterprises. After the war such purely native industries have a much better prospect of survival than local industries in the hands of European capitalists who will find other forms of enterprise more profitable. Moreover, any tendency to restore the conditions that existed before

---

[1] *Mass Education*, p. 48.

[2] The sequel is of some general interest. In both countries the finance department urged that the manufacture of lighters should be prohibited in order to safeguard the revenue from matches. In Netherlands India the Government, though not responsible to the people, resisted the proposal on the ground that in the current depression anything which gave employment was beneficial. In Burma, with nominally a much greater measure of self-government, the proposal was accepted, and the enterprising and ingenious Burman manufacturers of lighters were subjected to heavy penalties by Burman magistrates.

[3] Sitsen, pp. 19, 20n., 47; Mitchell, pp. 197ff.

1930 will encounter formidable resistance because economic power implies political power.

In Netherlands India, then, recent economic circumstances, by imposing restrictions on economic progress, have favoured national solidarity, the enhancement of welfare and economic development on a broader basis, and therefore, in the long run, greater progress. In the first throes of the depression the vision of impatient idealists seemed to be eclipsed. But reality lay below the surface, and even men of shorter vision 'learned that ideals should find their place in practical policy'.[1] As so often in colonial history, humanitarian ideals proved plain common sense. The lesson taught by Netherlands India is reinforced by the course of affairs in China and Russia. Forty years ago European powers were greedily expecting the 'break-up of China' to provide new opportunities for western capital. Twenty years ago Russia seemed to have collapsed. But China and Russia have been restored to greater vigour, not by the medicaments of capital, but by the vivifying tonic of a new idea. The plural society of tropical dependencies is dominated by economic forces, and, as recognized by the Statutory Commission, foreign rule is impotent to counter social and economic evils. Only some force transcending the economic sphere can bring them under control. Christians, Buddhists, Moslems and Hindus accept the principles of their religion as of greater validity than economic forces, but, in religious allegiance as in other matters, the plural society is divided, and there is no principle of social life, transcending merely economic considerations, that all will accept as valid except the principle of nationalism. In Europe at the present time the principle of nationalism is suspect. Men see in it a force stronger than self-interest, but for the same reason they fear it, and seek an alternative in a vague and ineffectual humanitarianism based on Christian tradition but disclaiming Christian doctrine. We may readily grant that 'patriotism is not enough', but one need not reject patriotism in order to rise above it. Economic forces operate everywhere alike, but social and political conditions in the tropics are directly contrary to those prevailing in homogeneous western lands, and in almost all matters it is necessary to apply contrary remedies to get the same results. That is especially true of nationalism as a principle of action. In the West we assume without question that 'defence is more than opulence', and that the individual should subordinate his personal interests to the common weal. In tropical

---

[1] Hart, p. 54.

dependencies the conception of a commonwealth has been destroyed, and only an explicit acceptance of the principle of nationalism can restore it; only by aiming directly to make them capable of independence can we enhance welfare and lay secure foundations for economic progress.

14. THE PROBLEM OF AUTONOMY

If, then, we are to aim at making dependencies capable of independence, how should we set about it? Experience shows that it is futile to proclaim ideals without creating the conditions which make them practicable. If we would make dependencies capable of independence, we must first achieve those conditions which make it possible. The problem of conferring autonomy on a tropical dependency is not merely a problem of mechanical contrivance, of ingeniously constructing political machinery that can be worked by natives, or despite native opposition; it is a problem of creative will. In the colonial power there must be an impulse to create a tropical society capable of political autonomy, and in the dependency a society capable of responding to this impulse, a society with a common social will that accepts the conditions of the modern world. This is so obvious that it would not be worth saying if its implications were not so generally disregarded.

. Self-government implies the existence of a common social will, and a colonial power which aims at making its dependencies self-governing must aim directly at promoting a common social will, and must foster the social, economic and political reintegration of the whole community which economic development disintegrates. Further, self-government in the modern world requires the acceptance of the conditions of the modern world, and implies therefore a process of social education so that the common social will shall be informed with those principles on which modern western civilization is founded. The transformation of the environment through the reintegration of the plural society and through social education represents one aspect of the problem.

But the problem has another aspect. In the colonial power the creative impulse is weakened by considerations of national prestige, and by the economic motive which tempts all to pursue their immediate and obvious economic advantage, and by the rational appeal which economic efficiency makes to universal common sense. We find a law that when we would do good, evil is present with us, and may exclaim, with the apostle, the good that we would we do not: but the evil which we would not, that we do. It is very easy to deceive ourselves, and we have observed that each generation of colonial reformers is apt to accuse its predecessors of hypocrisy. Clearly then, if we aim at making dependencies capable of independence, we must take such measures as are possible to strengthen our good intentions by creating such an environment as is most likely to fortify our will.

Thus the problem of autonomy has two distinct aspects which we consider separately in the following chapters.

CHAPTER XII

REINTEGRATION

1. Conditions of Reintegration

No one who seriously faces the problem of making tropical dependencies capable of independence is likely to under-estimate the obstacles. It is no difficult matter for one people, greatly superior in numbers, wealth, strength and knowledge, to keep another in subjection, just as it is not difficult to keep a criminal in jail. It is easier in proportion as the subject people is divided and ignorant. But those things which make it easier to keep them in subjection, make it difficult to set them free. The problem of endowing a tropical dependency with an instructed social will, so that it can find a place among the comity of nations, has much in common with the problem, simpler though not yet completely solved, of enabling the convict to live as a free citizen. Like the time-expired convict, a people that has known subjection is in need of after care. And a subject people resembles not only a convict but an invalid; it suffers from debility as the result of its confinement. Under foreign rule political and military traditions degenerate, cultural life decays and economic activities, losing their national significance, are distorted to meet the requirements of the colonial power. The social fibre is relaxed, and many will be impatient of restrictions which formerly they accepted without question in the name of custom. If the penal discipline of foreign rule is to give place to the social discipline of freedom, they will need a tonic. Should social welfare require the substitution of food crops for more profitable trade crops, or of local manufactures for imported goods, some will hanker after the fleshpots of foreign rule. They will need leaders to confirm their faith that such unpalatable remedies are necessary to their welfare; but foreign rule deprives them of their natural leaders or deprives their natural leaders of authority. If a foreign ruler is to induce them to accept the necessary restrictions, he must first of all, and above all, capture their imagination.

He must not only capture their imagination but gain their confidence. The wisest doctor cannot cure a patient who doubts whether the doctor wants to cure him, and even regards him as responsible for the disease. It is not strange if the people of a dependency hesitate to trust the colonial power and regard its policy with suspicion. For the doctor is, in fact, not quite certain whether he wants to cure the patient. In Burma, for example, the cutting off of supplies during the war has provided an opportunity to revive the spinning and weaving industry. Yet it has been suggested that the early import of the consumer goods formerly enjoyed would exercise a tranquillizing influence on nationalist aspirations stimulated under Japanese rule,[1] much as a doctor might prescribe an opiate for a sufferer from chronic opium poisoning. That may be the correct prescription, but one's confidence in it would not be strengthened if the doctor himself were in the dope trade.

It may well seem that the difficulties of equipping tropical dependencies for autonomy are insuperable. But if, as there is good reason to believe, this is essential for the survival of western civilization, we must assume that it is possible. How, then, are we to set about it? Are there any general principles to guide us? Some may question the validity of general principles in colonial administration. The English notoriously like to 'muddle through', to deal with situations as they arise. But that in itself is a general principle of action. In the last century the maintenance of peace and quiet could be ensured by the occasional scattering of crumbs beneath the table; this sufficed as a general principle of colonial rule and accorded with the wider general principle of *laissez-faire*. It may be sound to leave well alone so long as things are going well, but few would claim that nowadays colonial relations are improving, and to leave them alone is to go from bad to worse. Some would merely scatter larger crumbs more frequently. But if, as it would seem, this must end in an explosion, only the more violent the longer it is delayed, we must devise some other plan. No plan can apply in detail to all dependencies in all circumstances, but any plan implies the recognition of some general principles, and our analysis of colonial relations would seem to suggest certain general principles bearing on the social, economic and political reintegration of dependencies.

2. SOCIAL REINTEGRATION

So long as the tropics were cut off from the modern world, their rules of behaviour and standards of living were their own concern but, as soon as they come into contact with the modern world, these things are matters of general concern. We cannot pursue our lawful occasions among head-hunters, and we cannot lead healthy lives while dark

[1] *Blue Print for Burma* (1944), p. 8.

corners breed pestilence. In our own interest we must eradicate barbarous customs and raise the standards of living to the minimum that the conditions of the modern world require. The need for higher standards of welfare is obvious, and colonial powers have tried to raise the standard through administrative machinery. From our survey it appears that this solution is impracticable; that the new machinery, though useful as an instrument of progress, is an obstacle to social welfare, and that the enhancement of welfare requires common action by the people, while at the same time contact with the modern world makes them incapable of common action. Here we seem to be faced with a dilemma. But our enquiry suggests that the key to welfare problems lies in the organization of demand, through social reintegration, so that the people can themselves, of their own accord, do what is necessary. It is along this line that we must look to escape from our dilemma.

The problem of enabling the people of a tropical dependency to want what they need, and do what they want, or in other words the problem of self-government, is essentially the same in the village as in the State, but is less complex and on a smaller scale. Let us first, therefore, consider the question of conserving and reintegrating village social life and of adapting the village, as a community, to the modern world. It would seem possible to arrive at certain principles generally applicable to village (or tribal) communities which are predominantly native and homogeneous. Clearly the first object must be to enable them, and help them, to do what they want to do and can do. Colonial powers should be better able to help the people than their own rulers. Under native rule the village community did whatever it wanted to do and could do. But there was much that it could not do; for example, it might be unable, through lack of scientific knowledge, to protect itself against an epidemic of cholera. But, through common life for many generations, sanitary precautions had been adopted into village custom, and public opinion often protected the water supply against encroachment or defilement, thus minimizing the risk of epidemics. Under foreign rule, with the decay of custom, individual interest tends to prevail over social welfare, and common village amenities are sacrificed to the desire of gain, or merely through the growth of population which the colonial environment encourages. The people still want house sites, water for man and beast, grazing facilities and so on, the various amenities formerly supplied by village custom. But they can no longer get what they want, and one condition of local autonomy is that there shall be someone closely and continually in touch with the people who can study and make known their wants.

So far as village social life survives it should be a comparatively simple matter to help the people to get what they want. Where the communal tradition has decayed, reintegration is necessary, and this becomes more difficult at every stage in the process of dissolution. The people still have common needs, but there is no longer a common will. In these circumstances it is no longer sufficient that someone shall be available to study and make known their wants; he must stimulate and foster social wants. This, however, is only a particular aspect of the general problem of *social* education, adapting the village *as a community* to the modern world. It may be comparatively easy to arouse village sentiment against breaches of traditional common amenities as, for example, by encroachment on the catchment area of the village water supply, because this requires no more than, as it were, an appeal to the dormant village conscience. But the problem is essentially the same as that of organizing a demand for modern welfare standards: getting the people to keep the village clean, or to accept vaccination, or to send the children to school. If the traditional local authorities are allowed, encouraged and helped to do what the people want, they will probably accept obligations to do what the people do not, but can be induced to want. In such matters supervision by some external authority is necessary. Moreover some things will strain traditional authority, weakening its virtue, and some are beyond its competence; for such things other provision must be made.

Here, then, we would seem to have certain principles that must be observed if social reintegration within the village is to be successful:

(*a*) The people themselves will do all that they want to do and can do; all such matters should be left to them, but with such help in expert assistance or money as can be given without encroaching on local autonomy;

(*b*) As a condition of being helped to do what they want to do, they may be willing to undertake things that they do not want to do. Such matters also should be left to them, but under the supervision of someone who will see that they are done; this applies not merely to dependencies, but to tropical lands in general, whether dependent or independent.

(*c*) As regards those things which the village or other local authority will not or cannot do, attempts should be made to enlarge their wants and improve their capacity, but, until that has been achieved, such things must be done by some authority outside the village, representing the central government and not the people.

These principles suggest a general design for the machinery of welfare. *There will be a need for specialist services, but equally a need for the co-ordination of these services; the supervision of the welfare machinery requires an element of continuity in the administrative personnel; the administrative units must be adapted as welfare charges to the primary administrative function of promoting welfare through social education; and the whole machinery must be driven by some creative impulse that will ensure the co-operation of the people.* Our comparison of Dutch and British colonial administration would seem to provide material for filling in the details of this general design.

Specialist Services. Although the first condition for the enhancement of welfare in tropical dependencies is to create an environment in which the people can provide for their own welfare, they must be induced to regard as essential to their welfare those conditions in respect of hygiene and education which western experience shows to be essential to the welfare of the modern world. Much may be done with little or no expenditure, yet in any project of enhancing welfare, economic and social services must find a place. If a Government wishes to encourage vaccination, there must be officials to vaccinate the people, and if it wishes to diffuse primary instruction there must be teachers for the children. For the enhancement of welfare, however, specialists in every line must have a double function: executive, to do what the Government requires; and propaganda, to get the people of their own accord to do what the Government requires. From the standpoint of welfare the latter is by far the more important, but the former *seems* more urgent and attention tends to be concentrated (and money to be wasted) on elaborating the machinery of welfare rather than on promoting welfare. Departmental heads can always make out a plausible case for more costly buildings or a larger staff and, because greater expenditure ought to yield better results, there is a tendency to assume that better results will follow greater expenditure. It is easy to spend money, especially other people's money, and welfare is often measured by the money spent. Economic and social services are necessary, but the expenditure under these heads, and especially expenditure on buildings and equipment, needs careful scrutiny if it is to enhance welfare rather than to expedite development. Also, however much or little may be spent on economic and social services, specialist activities can do little or nothing to promote welfare unless they are co-ordinated, and linked up with native life.

Co-ordination. In the co-ordination of specialist activities and in adapting them to tropical conditions, the Dutch system of administration has some advantages over the British system. The difference between the two systems is largely due to history. In England we had no need of an official corresponding to the French prefect and the Dutch burgomaster, 'sent down to a particular locality to carry out part of the work of the Central Government'; this was unnecessary in England because 'local bodies with wills of their own exist'.[1] In India, however, and in other parts of the tropics, circumstances dictated the appointment of such an official, known generally in British colonial literature as the District officer. But, under British rule, on the principle of *laissez-faire*, he was for long solely and is still primarily a magistrate and collector of revenue, trained as such and functioning as such. Under Dutch rule, on the contrary, with a different national tradition, a different conception of administration and a different objective of colonial policy, the local representative of Government was charged with more comprehensive functions and, when the enhancement of welfare came to be accepted as a main object of policy, he developed, as it were naturally, into a social engineer, trained as such and functioning as such. If we wish to promote native welfare it would seem essential to recognize tropical administration as a profession requiring no less special skill than medicine and law, and to incorporate in the administrative machinery a class of social engineers. In British dependencies, however, the constitution of a special service alongside the present administrative service would multiply expense, and its members would lack the prestige attaching by tradition to the District officer. On the other hand the District officer, even if trained in social engineering, cannot do the work of a social engineer, partly for lack of time, and partly because he appears to the people in the unsympathetic capacity of magistrate and 'tax-hunter'. The solution would appear to lie then in converting the District officer into a social engineer by relieving him, as far and as fast as possible, of these repellent functions.

It should be noted that the need for a service of professional social engineers rests not in colonial relations but in tropical conditions. Such a service would still be needed, perhaps with even greater urgency, if the whole administrative staff were native and tropical dependencies were wholly independent. It is needed in Siam no less than in Indo-

[1] *ISC*, I, 301.

China or in Burma. One of the chief causes of the failures and defects of local self-government in India under recent reforms was that when control by the District officer was abolished, no skilled professional administrator was appointed to replace him.[1] In tropical administration a main function of the social engineer is to interpret western ideas to tropical peoples and to adapt modern principles of social life to tropical conditions. In the discharge of that function native officials may have certain advantages in their better knowledge of the people (though town-bred natives may know little more of rural life than Europeans), but in other respects the advantage lies with the European officials through their innate, as it were instinctive, grasp of western principles. An autonomous native government would still need social engineers, native or foreign, just as European lands need their prefects and burgomasters; it would have far greater need of them, in order to instil western ideas of welfare and to induce the people voluntarily to accept the minimum standards consistent with world welfare. Only through the gradual evolution of local bodies with a will of their own, and complying of their own accord with the requirements of the modern world, would it be possible to dispense with supervision; and that is most improbable, for even in Britain, the home of local self-government, its history during the nineteenth century 'might be described from one angle as the steady invasion by the Central Government of a sphere formerly left entirely to local authorities'.[2] In tropical lands generally, whether dependent or independent, some official able to link up the various economic and social services with one another and with native life is likely to remain an indispensable element in the administration.

Continuity. There must also be some machinery for ensuring that modern conditions are so far as possible accepted, and so far as necessary enforced. No one can encourage the acceptance of modern conditions of social welfare, or ensure compliance with them, except through local influence and local knowledge. Under the conditions of tropical administration, representatives of the central authority must needs be transient; they cannot possess these qualifications. In the system of direct rule nothing fills this gap; with indirect rule the local chieftain, hereditary or elective, might fill it. In this, as in other matters, British colonial administration is hampered by its traditions, and especially by the valuable tradition of the rule of law. Under British rule the tendency is to convert native traditional

[1] *ISC*, I, 309.   [2] *ISC*, I, 310.

authorities into magistrates and tax-collectors, administering western law and collecting western taxes, and thereby losing the influence that they derive from native custom. Again, even under Dutch rule, and still more under British rule, there is a tendency to treat native authorities as agents of Government rather than as representatives of the people. No one has the time to do anything; everyone is in a hurry to get things done; native authority seems to offer the speediest means to get things done, and the frequent and extensive drafts on it soon exhaust its credit with the people. Moreover, as the native authorities themselves do not want most of the things that they are expected to get done, their supervision is often ineffective, and perhaps less effective in some cases than the machinery of direct rule.

It is in providing the element of continuity that the Dutch combination of the permanent and hereditary Regent with an official of the central Government seems peculiarly happy. The Regent is, like the representative of the Central Government, primarily a welfare officer; he has little or practically no part in the administration of the law, and no formal responsibility for collecting revenue. So far as the promotion of welfare is the aim of Government, the Regent, with his local knowledge and influence, can lend his help, unhampered by the opprobrium attaching to magistrates and tax-collectors. But he lives up-country in the native world, and must naturally tend to vegetate. Alongside him, however, there is the Dutch equivalent of the District officer, who can help to keep him in touch with the modern world, and the liability of the European official to frequent transfer tends to be an asset rather than a defect. In welfare machinery these two distinct elements would seem indispensable: one representing the modern world, and one, permanent, representing the people. It may seem that the permanent local authority, if really at home in the modern world, might combine both functions. But this is hardly possible. Many Regents in Java are at home in the modern world because for three generations or more the boys have resided with Dutch families in their school-days, but the assistance of a European adviser is still helpful; native chieftains in other parts of the tropics without the same advantages have still greater need of assistance and advice, though it is not necessary that the assistance and advice should be given by a European.

Welfare Charges. But an official in the position of a Regent, with a somewhat extensive charge, despite his local knowledge and influence, cannot be in such close and continual touch with all the people, as is necessary both to protect them against the constant and all-pervasive action of economic forces and to adapt the village communities to the conditions of the modern world. The administrative machinery of Java provides for this requirement by the division of the regency into districts and subdistricts. In each subdistrict comprising some twenty villages there is a subordinate official in charge of general administration. This is a distinctive feature of the Dutch system, contributing greatly to its efficacy as an instrument of welfare. In Burma, also, the villages are grouped together as revenue or police charges, but the units of police and revenue jurisdiction do not always coincide, and there is nothing corresponding to the small unit of *general* administration found in Java, which might be termed a welfare charge. One obvious objection to the Dutch system is the heavy cost of maintaining a large establishment of subordinate officials, but it would not seem necessary that these group leaders should be salaried officials. The village is the natural unit of social welfare. But, as we have noticed in both Java and Burma, there has been a constant tendency to rearrange village boundaries with a view to greater efficiency in administration. Such readjustments of traditional boundaries to administrative convenience can always be supported by common-sense arguments of efficiency and economy. But, if social reintegration be an aim of policy, then it is a matter of fundamental importance to retain natural geographic, historic and economic units even at the cost of administrative convenience, and although the village is the natural unit of social welfare, many welfare projects require the co-operation of groups of villages. Under native rule in Burma, Java and India one could find such groups, but the tendency of foreign rule is to break them up into isolated villages. This tendency should be resisted, and where the traditional organic groups have been broken up, they should as far as possible be reconstituted. Where, as in Burma, each village has its headman, it should be possible to group them in welfare charges under one of the headmen, elected or appointed as their leader and representative. In any case, and by whatever means may be available, it would seem necessary, as already indicated, to collect the villages into organic groups. Economic forces are continually making for social disruption.

Social Education. The machinery of welfare, however, requires more than the conservation of social life; it requires also the adaptation of social life through social education. The construction of welfare machinery and the constitution of welfare charges will have little effect unless the people can be induced to take advantage of their opportunities. Except so far as economic and social services can show immediate results, mere propaganda will mostly be a waste of money. Welfare services can do little for the people in general unless there is a demand for their services, and some form of 'gentle pressure' is needed to stimulate the demand. Here again the Dutch system of social education through periodical and frequent *vergaderingen* at every stage in the administrative organization would seem to provide a useful model.

Motive. Education implies discipline, and social education in the tropics demands the provision of a motive sufficient to induce the people to accept the restrictions on individual liberty that the conditions of the modern world require. Even the most formidable machinery for exercising pressure on the people will prove unequal to constructive work, requiring their willing co-operation, unless it is inspired by some creative impulse. Backward peoples converted to Christianity try to live up to its precepts, and similarly those who adopt Islam or Buddhism accept the imperatives of their new creed. Spain and Portugal owed their success as colonial powers to their zeal for the conversion of their subjects; they found one monk worth a regiment of soldiers. In the modern world nationalism alone can provide the necessary impulse, and it is only by using to the full communal and nationalist sentiment that tropical peoples can be brought voluntarily to accept those conditions that the welfare of the outer world requires. Autonomy is a condition of welfare, and social reintegration requires political reintegration.

3. Economic Reintegration

Social reintegration necessarily has an economic aspect, because the economic, material, sphere is one part, and a very important part, of social life. But measures for social reintegration in their economic aspect aim chiefly to obtain a mastery over economic forces acting on the native social order from *within*; measures for economic reintegration aim rather to master economic forces acting on it from *outside*. These forces take effect through the impact of western capitalist activities, converting the tropical dependency into a business concern. Economic reintegration implies the transformation of this business concern into a human commonwealth, and demands the reintegration not merely of the native social order but of the whole composite plural society.

In this society, as we have seen, the European community usually dominates the entire economic sphere, and has the direction and control of practically the whole industrial and commercial system. Most members of this community are only temporary residents, and its leaders are the local representatives of large enterprises financed by people who know nothing of the dependency except as the place from which they draw, or hope to draw, their dividends. In this they are at one with all foreign elements, Asiatic or African, from the wealthy middleman down to the humblest immigrant coolie. Whatever their race, apart from missionaries, they tend to look on the dependency as a business concern and not as a nation, and their interest is in material progress rather than in national welfare. The whole foreign interest may accordingly be comprehensively described as capitalist, and nationalism represents a struggle against capitalism, the predominance of purely economic values in human affairs. That is a struggle in which we are all engaged, in Europe as in the tropics, and it is our interest, no less than that of dependent peoples, to bring capitalism under control. National welfare should be enhanced by an abundant supply of capital or, in other words, of goods representing the surplus of former economic activity and available to enhance production. But national and capitalist interests are not identical, and frequently diverge, especially where the capital is owned by foreigners. This stimulates nationalist jealousy of capitalist activities and, for the welfare of a country, capitalist interests must be protected—though they can usually look after themselves; but it is through capitalist activities that external economic forces react on social life and, if national welfare is to be paramount, such activities must be controlled. Ultimately, national welfare is the soundest guarantee of economic progress, and is in the interest therefore of foreign capital; but the pressure of economic forces tends continually to sacrifice national welfare to immediate capitalist ends.

Colonial economic relations are fundamentally identical with the economic relations between individuals. It is natural that the colonial power should wish to obtain tropical produce as cheaply as possible, and to find in the dependency a profitable market for its own produce. Even where colonial policy is not deliberately framed to promote the economic interests of the colonial power, it must inevitably be coloured by an unconscious bias in that direction. This is apt to prejudice social and national welfare in the dependency and, if these social interests are not to suffer, some control must be exercised over both exports and imports.

In the tropics production for export illustrates the tendency, found everywhere in the modern world in almost all economic activities, towards working on a large scale. A western enterprise in the tropics needs larger capital than a similar enterprise in Europe, and in other respects also the conditions of production in the tropics are especially favourable to large-scale enterprise. Even in western countries with a constitution on a broad democratic basis, constant vigilance is needed to check the power of anti-social monopolies, but in tropical dependencies there is no such check. Big business reaches out towards a comprehensive monopoly. In Burma we have noted that the more important business houses do not concentrate on trade only but are importers, exporters, millers, estate and ship owners at the same time, and may have considerable interests outside Burma. Similarly a few firms, closely interlinked, have dominated the economic life of Netherlands India. The United Africa Company is a signal illustration of the same tendency in Africa. Merely by its dominant position in economic life, western enterprise exercises a great influence over political and social evolution, and its economic power is ordinarily reinforced by political pressure; as in Netherlands India there is 'more activity, lobbying and browbeating by private interests on political issues...than is consistent with the proper place of business'.[1] If western enterprise, and capitalist interests in general, are to be brought under control, there would seem little prospect of achieving this from inside the dependency; the mainspring of action lies in the larger western world, and it is here that measures must be taken to enforce control.

So far as capitalist enterprise in the tropics succeeds in establishing a monopoly over any kind of produce, the consumer in the West is apt to suffer. In such cases the large wholesale buyers of such produce may combine to resist the monopoly, or it may be possible to form an association to act on behalf of the general body of consumers. Sometimes arrangements have been made for the representation of the consumer (or rather of consumer-business) on organizations to control prices, and in some cases this is said to have been effective. Monopoly is a special danger to the welfare of dependencies where capitalist production competes with native production, as in rubber in the Tropical Far East and in palm-oil in West Africa. In such circumstances western enterprise tries to obtain control over native production, and native interests suffer unless the Governments concerned are resolute to protect them. Yet free competition may be

[1] Hart, p. 48.

more detrimental than monopoly, for then capitalist enterprise is free
from any taint of monopoly, and serves to reduce the cost of tropical
produce, while favouring anti-social conditions of production that the
outer world will tend to disregard, as formerly men condemned slavery
but ate slave-grown sugar and wore clothes of slave-grown cotton.
In these circumstances Labour may join forces with organized
humanitarianism in insisting on welfare legislation, but, as already
explained, this tends to favour big business and not the native world.
In America Labour supported the dairy-farmers and sugar-growers
in its protest against cheap imports, and in France the agricultural
interest has always been suspicious of colonial adventures. But it is
only within narrow limits that external economic interests can be
organized on behalf of native welfare.

On the view that only the principle of nationalism can dominate
economic disintegration, there would seem much to commend the
suggestion, frequently put forward, that in tropical dependencies the
Government should 'nationalize' production, that it should take over
and manage industries which are now in foreign hands because the
natives lack the necessary capital, experience or skill. But one difficulty
is that the direct ownership by Government of properties in rubber,
oil, tin and other products necessary to large-scale industry may
lead to international complications: the Government of Netherlands
India was able to resist the Japanese demands for the supply of war
material on the plea that firms dealing in such products were not under
Government control. The suggestion is also urged plausibly on the
grounds that the State would benefit by the profits that now go to
foreign shareholders; could ensure good conditions of labour and
wages; and could train natives to take over the industries. It is doubtful, however, whether these ends would be achieved, and other methods
of attaining them would probably be more effective.

It is generally recognized that foreign enterprise takes money out of
the country which might otherwise be devoted to the enhancement of
native welfare, and that the quasi-monopolist structure of western
enterprise in the tropics enables it to draw profits out of proportion
with any services that it may render. Nationalization might seem to
provide a remedy but, even if this should transfer the profits to the
State, it might still be undesirable. One objection to private enterprise in tropical dependencies is that it exercises too much influence
over Government policy, that in effect there is a combination of
economic and political control. This would be aggravated under

State control, for a Government engaged in enterprise would try to make, or at least to show, a profit on its undertakings, and the combination of economic and political control would grow still closer. In the past unremunerative State railways have been constructed to serve private interests, and the rates for transport have been adjusted to the advantage of private enterprise. Government would be no less ready to build unremunerative railways for its own enterprises, and to adjust rates so as to make them show a profit; also it would be far better able to draw up flattering accounts than a private firm which has to satisfy the demand of shareholders for dividends. Moreover, if a Government borrows capital to develop an enterprise, the drain in the form of interest may be even more onerous than the outgoing of profits; for a private company pays no dividends unless it makes a profit, but the interest charge would have to be met whether the enterprise succeeded or failed, and in bad years as in good. The Dutch policy is to restrict state enterprise to concerns which promise high profits with small risks, leaving the less attractive projects to private firms and, so far as state enterprise may be desirable, this rule would appear sound. Yet, from the standpoint of deriving revenue from economic development, there would seem to be greater advantage in a system of taxation adjusted so as to take as large a share of the profits of private enterprise as it can bear. If the Government is not strong enough to impose adequate taxation on foreign enterprise, it can hardly be trusted to manage industrial production in the native interest. The nationalization of industrial production in the tropics would seem then liable to confuse business and government to the prejudice of both.

Nor is it certain that the nationalization of industry would lead to better conditions of employment. The Culture system in Netherlands India and the Belgian Congo under Leopold certainly point in the opposite direction. It may be argued that these are old stories, and that the modern world would not tolerate similar oppression. But on a Government enterprise no one would know the conditions until attention was drawn to them by some outbreak of violence. It is well to remember that, even under the Ethical policy, the Government of Netherlands India objected to the abolition of the penal sanction on contract labour for fear of its effect on the profits of the State tin mines. Van den Bosch claimed that the Culture system would benefit the people. 'The field is large enough,' he said, 'there is no need to overwork it'.[1] But the field had boundaries, the limits

[1] *Netherlands India*, p. 137.

were reached, and the system was worked too hard. Now again we see on all sides a tendency to employ compulsion, strictly of course 'to promote native welfare'. But there is little doubt that the field would as before be overworked. A Government is likely to be far more vigilant in its control over business concerns if it is not in business on its own account. It is desirable that Government should exercise control over business, and it may be better able to exercise control if it is itself in business in a small way, as this will enlarge its practical experience of business affairs, but if it looks to enterprise for any considerable portion of its revenue, past experience in connection with alcoholic liquor, intoxicating drugs and gambling suggests that it may sacrifice native welfare to the claims of revenue.

Some degree of Government participation in enterprise would certainly be valuable as a measure of social education by opening up to the natives a wider sphere of economic activity. In the state pawnshops and banks in Netherlands India Indonesians have received a useful introduction to modern business. Probably it is in agricultural finance and in the management of agricultural land that Government enterprise might do most good, just because these are matters about which the people already know something. Government should be able to show them how to manage their own affairs more profitably. But suggestions for nationalization are usually put forward in connection with mines and other forms of enterprise about which the people in general know nothing. If the State is to employ natives in such enterprises it can employ them only so far as, on a long view, their employment is more economical. In the first instance Europeans or other foreigners would have to be employed, and it can hardly be expected that these would show much zeal in training natives to deprive themselves of jobs.

Economic autonomy requires the direction and conduct of private enterprise by natives rather than the employment of natives in state enterprise. It is desirable accordingly that, wherever possible, natives should be substituted for foreigners in the higher ranks of industry and commerce. Economic forces tend in that direction, and the process was hastened during the recent depression, when highly paid Europeans were replaced by non-Europeans on lower pay. For some years past the more far-seeing firms have already made this a feature of their policy. Probably it will be expedited under the conditions obtaining in the post-war world. But steps might well be taken towards ensuring more rapid and more general progress in this direction. One device might be to impose on foreign enterprise a condition that it should furnish annual reports on the progress made in substituting natives for foreigners in the direction, management and staff, and to transmit such reports for review to any international organization established for supervising colonial affairs. Such a measure would be an instrument for converting capitalists into nationalists and nationalists into capitalists. It would create a demand for the employment of natives in western enterprise and, by creating a demand, would stimulate a supply. Here, again, the key to the economic advancement of tropical peoples lies in the organization of demand. Moreover, not a few of the natives employed in western enterprise should prove capable of undertaking industrial and commercial enterprises on their own account, as has in fact happened, on a very small scale, in the past. Thus, although in the first instance the benefit of substituting natives for Europeans would accrue to western enterprise by reducing salary charges, the further result would be a gradual transformation of the colonial economic system.

The approach to economic reintegration through control over imports may seem to present a simpler problem, because tariffs have long been used for the protection of special interests and industries; but the practical difficulties may be no less formidable. Competition is likely to be more open than with exports, though there is a tendency for large export firms to be prominent also in the import trade. And, whereas exporters want to obtain produce as cheaply as possible, and would seem to derive most profit from low wages, or when operating in a primitive economy of barter and compulsory labour, importers and the manufacturers of imported goods gain most where the natives have plenty of money to spend on more, and more costly, foreign goods. We have noticed that the growth of imports is commonly regarded as evidence of welfare, even if only a small proportion of the imports goes to natives; and so far as welfare can be identified with native expenditure on foreign goods, importers have an interest in promoting native welfare. In practice, however, imported goods tend to replace local manufactures, thus limiting the scope of native activities, while the people are thrown on to the labour market to the prejudice of wages, and may be unable to find work. Under-employment is indeed a characteristic feature of the modern tropics, and this is the economic justification for Gandhi's policy of encouraging the people to turn their leisure to account in home-spinning and home-weaving. The encouragement of local manufactures is likely to meet with opposition from competing interests in the colonial power, and these may recruit support from natives who, for various reasons, prefer foreign goods; but if Gandhi's policy were adopted, it would help to restore the balance that cheap imports disturb, and be a notable step in the direction of economic reintegration.

The restoration of this balance is indeed gradually becoming more advantageous to colonial powers. Cheap imports are profitable to a colonial power only so long as it can supply the goods. With the growing industrialization of the tropics, Europe is losing its hold over the cotton trade, the chief item in native imports. If tropical dependencies can buy their cotton goods more cheaply from Japan, India or China, colonial powers stand to gain by encouraging the local manufacture of such goods, so that the dependency shall provide a better market for goods in which Europe still has an advantage. Here then we have a common-sense economic argument for encouraging nationalist sentiment in favour of home products. That a protective policy may assist dependencies has indeed been demonstrated by the success of the Government of Netherlands India in encouraging the native hat, cigarette and fishing industries, while its encouragement of local cotton manufacture was a strong factor in obtaining native support for quota restrictions on the import of Japanese piece goods. Limitations on free trade in respect of home industries are now generally approved, but they imply fiscal autonomy. The control of exports and production in general on nationalist lines also implies economic autonomy. Thus economic reintegration, like social reintegration, is bound up with political reintegration.

4. WESTERN INSTITUTIONS IN TROPICAL DEPENDENCIES

If both social and economic reintegration depend upon political reintegration, then the problem of endowing dependencies with self-government cannot be postponed until they have achieved a higher standard of welfare but, as the older Liberals held, is of primary importance. It is as part of the Liberal tradition that self-government has been adopted as the goal of colonial policy by Britain and the Netherlands, is favoured by some colonial statesmen in France, and is strongly advocated in the United States. It is also part of the Liberal tradition that self-government implies democratic government; government by the people for the people. In British colonial theory this is ordinarily termed responsible government.

But the term responsible government is vague and, in some respects, unsatisfactory, as is apparent in the first authoritative pronouncement on the subject in the Preamble to the Government of India Act 1919. This looks to 'the progressive realisation of responsible government', with the implication that the term signifies a government accountable to the people that it governs. Yet progress is to depend on 'the extent to which it is found that confidence may be reposed in their sense of responsibility'; at every stage the 'responsible' government is accountable, not to the Indian people, but to the British Parliament. Further, the Preamble lays down that Parliament is responsible for the welfare and advancement of the Indian peoples; but this is merely a moral responsibility, and in this matter Parliament is accountable only to the people of Britain. Thus the pronouncement makes no clear distinction between responsibility *to* the people and responsibility *for* the people, between accountability and responsibility, or between legal and moral responsibility.

Every Government has a complex burden of responsibilities. Ultimately it is always responsible, accountable, to its subjects, and they will call it to account, either by peaceful methods or by violence. Only too frequently tropical rulers have been called to account by rebellion or assassination. The British Government in the former American colonies, the Spanish Government in South America and the Philippines were called to account by rebellion. One great contribution of Britain to the art of modern government is the invention of constitutional machinery for calling the Government to account by peaceful methods. That is what is usually understood by responsible government, but the term is really a misnomer, for when a Government is constitutionally accountable to the people, its responsibilities are transferred to them, and it is the people who are responsible and not the Government. Every Government, again, is responsible, accountable, in some measure to the outside world, and must adjust its differences with other Governments either peacefully through diplomacy and arbitration, or by war. It was mainly because tropical rulers failed to realize their responsibilities to the modern world that their peoples lost their independence. The doctrine that colonial powers are responsible to other powers for the administration of their dependencies obtained formal acceptance at the Berlin Conference of 1884–5, was extended by the Mandates System after the war of 1914–18, and forms the basis of recent projects of international supervision over colonial relations. Further, every Government, alongside its responsibility to its subjects and to the outer world, has a moral responsibility for the welfare of its people; it may suppress rebellion and withstand aggression, but it must abide the verdict of praise or blame recorded in the judgment of history.

In statements on colonial policy, self-government is usually identified with some form of democratic government, whether known as responsible government or by some other term. That is only natural, because the colonial powers are democratic powers, whose institutions have evolved as part of the Liberal tradition and who tend accordingly to identify self-government with those forms that they have learned to value for themselves; also it seems easier to export their own machinery of government than to invent new machinery. Moreover, democratic forms of government have proved their stability in two hard-fought wars, and democracy, where and so far as it is possible, would seem the best device for securing a stable government that will permit the adaptation of social institutions to changes in the environment and thereby reconcile economic progress with human welfare. Obviously democratic forms have a very practical appeal. They appeal to Nationalist politicians, who think that the numerical majority of the native group will ensure for them control over the Government. They appeal also to men of Liberal sympathies in the colonial power, who fail to recognize that the difference in kind between homogeneous western society and the plural society of dependencies demands new and appropriate machinery. And they may encounter no more than a show of resistance from the more astute opponents of Liberal ideals, who foresee that democratic machinery will prove the most formidable obstacle to self-government.

We find accordingly that projects of conferring autonomy on dependencies have usually attempted to dress up the colonial type of government in democratic forms. Each colonial power tries to reproduce in its dependencies that type of democratic government with which it is familiar, and in Burma and elsewhere we have tried to introduce parliamentary government on the supposition that what is good for us should be good enough for Burmans. The process of introducing self-governing institutions has indeed been reduced to a set formula: first representative institutions, then a gradual development of partial responsibility, culminating in fiscal autonomy, and finally complete responsibility or dominion status.[1] On this line of approach the first step in political evolution is to give the colonial

[1] Astor, pp. 235, 246; *Britain and Her Dependencies*, p. 42.

Governor a council of nominated officials; then non-officials are included and the principle of election is adopted and extended; this representative body is then transformed into a legislature by entrusting some of its functions to ministers accountable to the people, and in the final stage, not yet attained in any tropical dependency, it is contemplated that the legislature shall have full control over the Government, with the Governor as little more than its chief executive official.

Advocates of political reforms insist with growing urgency that 'we cannot hope to build up political institutions on a foundation of poor material resources, of insufficient health or of undeveloped minds'.[1] They look accordingly to develop natural resources with a view to diffusing welfare in the tropics, so that the people may become fit to exercise the responsibility for control over their Government. We have found, however, that material development does not have these results. Few of those whom it enriches are natives, and it does not diffuse general welfare or enhance social welfare. If, then, autonomy be conditional on welfare, reliance on material development implies that the attainment of autonomy will be indefinitely postponed. We have found also that, quite apart from its effect on welfare, material development hinders the attainment of responsible government, because it converts the social order into a business concern which cannot be run on democratic lines, and it creates a plural society which cannot stand alone but depends on some external force to protect it against disruption. It appears moreover that attempts to introduce the machinery of responsible government in such a society do not help to consolidate it but aggravate the disruptive tendencies by increasing sectional friction. They are detrimental also to that co-operation between the colonial power and the dependency which is essential to the attainment of autonomy. Democratic forms are attractive to nationalist politicians who think they will ensure power for the numerical majority, and fail to realise that voting power without economic power or military power does not confer political power, and the consequent disillusion tends to foster a distrust of democratic principles and, as in the Philippines and Siam, favours the emergence of a one-man, one-party system of government. Thus, in its political as in its economic aspect, modern colonial policy works in a contrary direction to that which it announces as its goal.

That western self-governing institutions in the tropics do not work

[1] *Britain and Her Dependencies*, p. 7.

on western lines is now generally appreciated by those who know most about their working. 'We have encouraged the peoples of the tropics', says Lord Hailey,[1] 'in the faith that self-government can only be obtained through institutions of the parliamentary model with which we ourselves are most familiar. The experience we have gained justifies some doubt whether these institutions can operate to the best purpose in communities which have a tradition and a social organisation so unlike our own, or which are divided by racial differences.' In South America,[2] as in the Philippines and Siam, democracy no longer connotes western political institutions, but has come to signify the type of government that best conduces to national independence. If then we accept the Liberal principles underlying western institutions, 'it is incumbent on us to explore any variation within the general range of these institutions which seems best suited to the conditions of the territories. If we can somehow afford their people practical proof that they can obtain the substance of self-government, they may be willing to agree that the form in which it is embodied is relatively of less importance.'[3] The experiments in introducing western democratic forms in tropical dependencies merely illustrate the old fallacy that form gives rise to function; if we can make dependencies capable of independence the political machinery will automatically assume appropriate forms. In the homogeneous society of western states, the basic problem of applied political science is how best to ascertain and give effect to the common social will; in the plural society of the tropics the basic problem is to create a common social will. The functions of government are different, and there must needs be different machinery.

5. THE FUNCTIONS OF GOVERNMENT

What then are the functions of government in a plural society which is to be made capable of independence? The primary function of any Government is to comply with the requirements of the outer world. This is a general principle which is too often overlooked. The government of village, town and guild had to comply with the requirements of the nation. National Government must respect the comity of nations, and Germany and Japan are now experiencing the con-

---

[1] *Britain and Her Dependencies*, p. 45.
[2] Gunther, J., *Inside Latin America* (1942), p. 12.
[3] *Britain and Her Dependencies*, p. 45.

sequences of transgressing it. If a Government does not provide adequately for economic progress, it will be unable to maintain itself against external economic forces; it will not be permitted to survive. And if it does not attain a reasonable minimum in respect of human well-being, and especially in preventing epidemics of men, cattle and crops, then in the interest of world welfare it must be subjected to some measure of control. Tropical peoples forfeited their independence because, under the guidance of their native rulers, they were unable to qualify as citizens of the modern world by complying with its requirements. The usual type of colonial Government complies with them more adequately than the native tropical rulers whom it has superseded. Doubtless colonial powers, in the management of colonial affairs, look primarily to their own interest, and one source of weakness in colonial rule is the feeling in the outer world that they do not sufficiently regard the interests of non-colonial powers. Still, it is generally true, at least in British and Dutch dependencies, that the Government, though primarily responsible to the colonial power, does on the whole act as a trustee on behalf of the modern world. Throughout the whole course of progress towards the attainment of self-government, it is essential that the new Government shall not fall appreciably below the standard set up in this respect under the colonial type of rule. So far as political progress is on sound lines, the new Government should attain a higher standard, because a Government of the colonial type, though enlightened, is not effectively enlightened; for lack of popular support it cannot spread enlightenment among the people.

Assuming then compliance with the requirements of the modern world as the primary function of government, what other conditions must be fulfilled for the attainment of self-government? No machinery, however ingeniously devised, will confer self-government on a people that is incapable of governing itself. In tropical dependencies there are three formidable obstacles to self-government on the pattern of western democracies. The Government cannot represent the people, because in a plural society there is no 'people' to be represented. It cannot stand alone because of the racial and economic cleavage between the various sections, of which some may not wish for independence. And it cannot be fully responsible to the people because the great mass of them do not accept the requirements of the modern world. It is insufficient therefore merely to construct new machinery; first it is necessary to transform society. The functions of the Government are to create a common social will as the basis for a Government that shall represent the people as a whole; to enable this representative Government to stand alone without support from the colonial power; and by a process of social education ensure that the new Government, while complying adequately with the requirements of the modern world, can be made responsible to the people, and thereby achieve the stability that is derived from popular support.

Until the process is complete, the Government must obviously have a dual character, comprising an element representing the interests of world welfare and an element representing, so far as possible, the people. The colonial type of Government is both unrepresentative, and unable to stand alone, and clearly the first step is to introduce an element of representation. In almost all dependencies of all colonial powers something of this kind has been attempted; there is a *dual government*. A further stage is reached when the element intended to represent the people is, in fact, accepted by them as their representative. The Government has something of this character in territories under indirect rule, where the natives in general recognize the hereditary chieftain as their representative; but it does not represent the people fully until all sections of the community are sufficiently united to accept a common representative. Even then, however, it may be unable to stand alone without external support and is therefore *semi-colonial* in character. The next step is to enable the dependency to stand alone, when it will be much in the position of Siam before the recent revolution. All sections of the community voluntarily recognized the Crown, and it could maintain the national independence. Its independence was *conditional*; it rested on inducing the people to comply with the requirements of the modern world. Economic progress transferred the control of economic life to foreigners, European and Chinese, while the people remained backward. Independence is unstable until the people in general have become citizens of the modern world; only then is a country capable of responsible or *popular* government.

We have noticed that, according to the accepted formula, the stages on the road to independence are representative government, partly responsible government and dominion status. But if we are to set up milestones, the stages, beginning from the purely colonial type, might be: dual government; semi-colonial; conditional independence; and popular government. But in each case the transformation of society is a prerequisite of changes in the form of Government.

Let us then examine these various types of government with a view to ascertaining how the transformation may be most rapidly and smoothly effected.

6. CONTINUITY

In many respects the problem of political reintegration, the equipment of a people for self-government, is fundamentally similar to equipment of a village with the power to manage its own affairs. In both there is a need for dual control, and in both there is need of a definite plan and of someone to devise and supervise the execution of the plan. It is impossible to over-emphasize the need for continuity of person. Perhaps the two most conspicuous examples of the successful conduct of colonial relations on constructive lines are the rule of Van den Bosch in Java and of Cromer in Egypt. Van den Bosch knew Java in his youth, and on coming back to it in 1830 controlled the Government for ten years as Governor-General and Colonial Minister. Cromer devoted the better part of his life to Egypt. In Papua recently Sir Hubert Murray has shown what one man can accomplish who has a lifetime for his work. The modernization of Netherlands India was largely the work of one man, Idenburg, who, when a captain in the Indian Engineers, was elected to the States-General in 1901, held office as Colonial Minister from 1902 to 1905 and in 1908–9, was Governor-General from 1909 to 1918 and again Colonial Minister in 1918–19. It is significant that the most stable democratic governments in the modern world have in general an element of permanence in the Crown, which they value not only as a symbol of national unity, above and outside the conflict of interest and opinion that characterizes democracy, but also in virtue of its permanence, enabling it to accumulate a store of experience and to link up successive administrations representing different or contrary political ideas. Even in the United States, the outstanding exception to the general rule that democracy functions best under a titular monarchy, the need for continuity finds expression in the frequent re-election of the President for a second term, and its urgency in times of stress led to the repeated re-election, against all precedent, of Mr Roosevelt. In tropical dependencies there is far greater need of continuity than in homogeneous western lands with a long tradition of common social life. Any constructive effort, and above all the project of endowing them with independence, demands personal continuity to ensure continuity of policy, but it is very difficult to combine in one person both representation and continuity. Yet, until the course of political evolution is complete, it is necessary to provide for both.

7. Dual Government

In the purest type of colonial Government both representation and continuity are disregarded; a foreign Governor, appointed for a limited period, represents the colonial power and not the people of the dependency. During recent years however there has in general been an advance in the direction of duality by the provision of a representative council to advise and assist the Governor. But it is still the usual practice to appoint a European as Governor for a short period, ordinarily no longer than five years. That is a tradition from the days of *laissez-faire* when little was expected of government. In maintaining order the Governor depends ultimately on the armed force of the colonial power, and must therefore be responsible to the colonial power. This responsibility could most safely be entrusted to a European official of the colonial power and, given normal competence, one man was as good as another, while the short period of office was no serious disadvantage, because the machinery ran of itself. A colonial Government in any form must still be responsible to the colonial power until it is able to stand alone. It might seem then that, at least during this stage, the Governor should be a European. There are other reasons also for preferring a European as Governor. By his origin, upbringing and status a European would seem best able to promote the interests of foreign capital, while restraining its anti-social tendencies. And if the people are to be educated as citizens of the modern world, some may hold that this can best be accomplished by one who, by birth and nurture, is himself at home in the modern world.

Yet it is unlikely, or even impossible, that a European, newly appointed to a colony for a short period of some five years, can adequately discharge the functions of a modern colonial government. For he could hardly escape unconscious bias. In the first instance he would share the outlook of the leading representatives of foreign capital, men of the same origin and traditions as himself, and at first would naturally adopt their point of view. He would be unable to converse with the people in their own tongue freely if at all, and would require some years to understand local conditions, to learn to look at problems from the standpoint of the natives and to appreciate their objections, possibly quite valid, to his well-meant plans. As in the past he would be condemned merely to carry on.

It might seem, however, that a European, gifted in unusual measure with imagination, sympathy, courage and, above all, patience, could, over a long period of years, do something towards building up a unified and enlightened people. But in the meantime all his projects would be exposed to Nationalist criticism as designed in the interest of foreign capital and of perpetuating foreign rule. Take, for example, three measures that, rightly or wrongly, are in great favour among western administrators: primary instruction, peasant proprietorship, and co-operative credit. The ability to read and write may produce more docile subjects and more intelligent coolies—it is often advocated on those grounds; but it does not help the people to run their country or to manage western enterprise, or even to get better prices for their crops or better terms from moneylenders. Peasant proprietors are less able than large landowners to resist combinations among European merchants and are, in general, politically backward. Co-operative credit cuts out the middleman who is potentially the rival of Europeans in political and economic life. Or take the European demand for welfare legislation. We have seen that this favours big business against tropical rivals, and western labour against coolie competition, but tends to hinder the political and economic advancement of the people. Could a foreign Governor be certain that he was wholly free of bias in advocating such measures; and, if so, could he convince Nationalist critics of their soundness? Even if measures under these various heads be sound, a foreign Governor is less well able than a native to make them acceptable. In Burma, as we have seen, one of the most urgent problems is to re-establish monastic discipline and to modernize the monastic schools. In Siam under national rule the monks support the Government, and have allowed their monasteries to be used for lay schools. No foreign Governor could accomplish that in Burma. No policy, however wise, can be above suspicion, and there must always be some opposition to any policy of any Government, for there are two sides to every question. But the critics of a foreign Governor can always rally the people to their side. To accomplish his task he must foster national sentiment, but in doing so he piles up combustible material for his critics and opponents. A foreign Governor can maintain law and order sufficiently to allow of material development, and he can hold the people down, with the support of foreign troops if necessary, but he cannot build it up by converting nationalism from a destructive fever into a creative force. Only in the very earliest stages, and in default of any practicable alternative, can the process of introducing self-government be conducted under the supervision of a foreign Governor, and, if self-government be seriously intended, the first step towards realizing it would seem to be the substitution of a native for a foreigner as Governor.

With a non-European Governor, many difficulties in the task of creating a common social will would be diminished or removed. He might not understand the West so well, and he might need help and guidance in protecting and controlling capitalist interests, but he should understand the people better, and have an instinctive sympathy with their sentiments and aspirations. His measures would be less open to suspicion as actuated by foreign interests, and he would be better able to use personal influence to commend the adoption of necessary but unwelcome welfare measures. The mere fact that the nominal head of the Government was not European would indicate that the European section was not regarded as superior in status; if he were a native of the country, the appeal to national feeling would be stronger. There are, indeed, precedents for such appointments. Non-Europeans have acted as Governor in various provinces of India, including Burma, and the late Governor-General of French Equatorial Africa was a West Indian Negro.

But in any dependency, so long as the plural society remains unresolved, the Governor, whether native or European, must protect and control foreign capitalist interests and cannot dispense with the support of foreign troops. Also he must still be responsible to the colonial power, as this cannot abandon control over the conduct of affairs which might involve it in military operations for the suppression of unrest. The Government, whatever its form, would still retain a dual character, and the best expedient would seem to be the appointment of a European to advise and help a native Governor. At present, on the normal pattern of modern colonial rule, a European Governor acts with the advice and assistance of representatives of the people. There is in fact a dual Government. The position of the Governor resembles that of the Resident in former days in Java, when the Regent, as representative of the people, was expected to treat him as his overlord or 'elder brother'; the introduction of political reforms in Java, it has been said, reversed this position and converted the Resident into the 'younger brother'. The first step in the direction of self-government would seem to be a similar change, giving a different aspect to the dual Government, by nominating a native as Governor, chosen to represent the people so far as possible, but acting with the advice and assistance of an official representing the colonial power and, so far as necessary, in accordance with his directions. The dual Government would then comprise a native Governor and a European official who might suitably be termed a High Commissioner. This new type of dual Government would still be strictly colonial because not effectively representative and not able to stand alone, but it would have the form, and much of the substance, of indirect rather than of direct rule. Doubtless in special cases, where native society is wholly backward or sectional divisions are excessive, such an arrangement is impracticable, but on any system where a colonial Government is expected to justify before some international tribunal the progress made towards self-government, it might well be called on to furnish sufficient reasons against taking the initial step of creating such a dual government with a native head, accepted formally as representing the people.

Under this form of Government, however, there would be no less need for continuity. Permanent representation by one individual, as by the Crown in Siam, is possible only where there is organic unity, and a distinctive character of plural society is lack of organic unity, so that permanent representation is impracticable, and the man chosen to represent the people cannot hold office for more than a limited period of years. The element of continuity must therefore be supplied by the representative of the colonial power, and the arguments against limitation on the period of his office are no less valid when he is transformed from a Governor into a High Commissioner.

8. Semi-Colonial Government

The Government in its new form would be no less competent than a Government of the pure colonial type to discharge its responsibilities to the colonial power and to the outer world, and would be better able to induce the people to accept the responsibilities of modern citizenship. But the appointment of the native Governor by nomination would weaken it. The primary constructive function of the dual government would be to convert formal representation into actual representation. Three essential elements of a representative government in a tropical dependency would seem to be a native President, a National Assembly and an Economic Council.

The President. We may perhaps assume that the native Governor would not be merely a promoted official, but would be a non-official, chosen to represent the people so far as possible. Nomination, however, is clearly an inadequate method of providing for representation. The Government would gain strength if the Governor were chosen by the people, and the next step forward would be the substitution of election for nomination. In countries such as Burma, where the minorities, though possessing great economic power, are numerically almost insignificant, the election of a representative whom all communities would accept should not present great difficulty. Where, as in Malaya, the sections are more equally balanced, the problem, though more difficult, should not be beyond solution. The significance of the change in the character of the Government, implied by the substitution of election for nomination, might suitably be emphasized by styling the elected representative President instead of Governor. The conversion of the Governor into a President should enable the Government to discharge its former functions more adequately but would indicate a change of status rather than any change of function. Until the dependency could stand alone, the Government would still be responsible to the colonial power, and continuity of person in the office of the High Commissioner would be no less important than before.

Representation and Responsibility. How much farther would it be possible to carry the principle of representation? The President would be better able to perform his duties if he were able to consult the particular interests of all important groups in a representative assembly, and such an organ might be valuable both as an instrument of social education and as a means of welding the several groups and interests into a single people. But its usefulness would depend on its composition and functions.

The problem of devising machinery to represent the various peoples and interests is not very difficult. In backward regions where social life has not yet broken down, the people accept the village or tribal authorities as representative. Among more advanced peoples it has usually been found possible and expedient to gather elected representatives of the people in various councils, local, provincial or national. This has added to the strength of the Government, even under foreign rule, and is now a normal feature of colonial administration. But in general, and especially under British rule, the same machinery has been expected to serve both for representation and legislation, on some model based originally on parliamentary institutions. Parliament however discharges a great variety of functions. It brings together those who represent different localities, classes and interests, and allows them to contribute their knowledge to the common stock; it serves for the organization of knowledge. It also provides them with opportunities for discussion and deliberation; it serves for the organization of thought. But it serves also for the organization of the common social will; it enables them to choose someone who shall act on their behalf, and to control his actions. As an organ of knowledge and thought, a representative assembly should cast its net as widely as the diversity of conditions may require. As an organ of will the membership must be limited by two factors: the membership must be restricted to those who accept the convention of democracy that the national interest shall prevail by legal methods over sectional and local interests; and it must be restricted to those who accept the requirements of modern civilization.

Parliamentary government, as understood in Britain, is possible only where one assembly fulfils all these various requirements. Even in Britain it was strained almost to breaking point by the inclusion of a comparatively small body of Irish representatives who did not accept the necessary conventions, and it could not long survive the incursion of any considerable Communist or Fascist element, repudiating the principle of the rule of law. As an organ of will parliamentary government assumes the existence of a united people. But in the plural society of tropical dependencies, each separate section is another Ireland, preferring its sectional interests to common national well-being. Again, parliamentary government implies the acceptance of common welfare standards, but in the tropics the great majority of the people represented, and probably even of the representatives, do not accept the requirements of modern civilization. Yet in tropical dependencies we find the same machinery expected, as in England, to serve both for representation—the organization of knowledge and thought, and for legislation—the expression of the common social will. Under British rule all save the smallest or most primitive territories have a 'legislature'. This system confounds the functions of representation and legislation, and the result is a compromise unsatisfactory in both respects.

In tropical dependencies there is far greater need than in Europe for the organization of knowledge and thought. Europe is both the creator and the child of the modern world, while tropical countries are, at best, adopted children. In European countries there are innumerable societies, institutions and periodicals which diffuse knowledge and promote discussion, but in tropical countries these things are few or wanting. In this respect Netherlands India compares favourably with

British dependencies, even with British India, in the multitude of periodicals to which officials are not merely allowed but encouraged to contribute. But even in Netherlands India the People's Council, the Volksraad, has proved its value in providing new facilities for the discussion of affairs. The benefit of a representative organ will be proportional to its comprehensiveness; it will be most useful if it represents all important communities and interests throughout the land. It should, so far as possible, be a National Assembly. Where, as in the Volksraad, officials are allowed to speak and vote freely without regard to the policy of Government, their position enables them to make conspicuously useful contributions to the debates. But the practical difficulties of allowing them so much freedom are obviously greater if the representative body be vested also with powers of control. As soon as a representative body is given control over the Government as an organ of will, it becomes necessary to limit the membership and, however narrowly limited, the conflict of sectional interests aggravates discord and hinders the attainment of national unity. If, then, the object of policy be to make dependencies capable as soon as possible of independence, it would seem necessary to separate representation and responsibility, and in the first instance to create a National Assembly without legislative powers, deferring the creation of a legislature until there is a united and enlightened people.

The National Assembly. In a National Assembly with advisory powers there is no need to restrict membership to those who are in touch with the modern world or aspire to a common national unity; on the contrary, membership should be as wide as possible. Nomination would serve where election was impracticable. It would seem well, as Lord Hailey suggests, 'to make the fullest possible use of the customary institutions of the people, based on tribal, village or other organizations'.[1] In any case, with a view to the reintegration of social life within the village, it would appear desirable to base the electoral system on the village, as in Java, rather than on the individual as in Burma. Again, since the council should represent all sections of the people, it should provide for the representation of all important sections and communities. It is desirable to foster a common nationalism and get rid of sectionalism. But one cannot suppress sectionalism by disregarding sectional views and interests; such views can find expression only through the section or community as a whole, and it is no less desir-

[1] *Britain and Her Dependencies*, p. 45.

able to promote solidarity in minority communities than in the village. It may seem that the representation of minorities and special interests conflicts with the aim of imbuing all classes with the sentiment of a common nationality; but this is an illusion, for it is only through a recognition of its special claims that a minority will accept common citizenship with the people in general. In a *legislative* assembly, an organ of will, communal representation is a defect because it makes for division of will and weakness; but in a *representative* assembly it makes for strength and promotes community of feeling. In this matter it is of interest to recall the practice in Netherlands India, where the Governor nominates representatives of important minorities which would otherwise be inadequately represented.

Economic Council. In such a National Assembly, based on communal representation, domiciled aliens of whatever origin would, if sufficiently numerous, be represented either by election or nomination. But most of the European community and many foreign orientals are only temporary residents, whose interest in the dependency is in general solely economic. They would be out of place in an assembly purporting to represent national interests and, even if seats were reserved for them, they would have little concern in many aspects of national life, while among the members of the National Assembly in general few would have much interest or competence in many weighty economic problems. It would seem expedient, therefore, to constitute, alongside the National Assembly, an Economic Council, somewhat on the line suggested a few years back by Mr Churchill, and corresponding to the Grand Council of French Indo-China or the Economic Council of Netherlands India. This might be given powers of control over the business concerns that it represented, as is the case with the Federation of Indian Enterprise (*Indische Ondernemersbond*) in Netherlands India, but it would serve chiefly to advise the Government on economic affairs, much as the National Assembly would give advice on national affairs. Various devices might be adopted to co-ordinate their activities, as by establishing joint committees, or by allowing the Economic Council representation in the National Assembly.

Presidential Election. It is not necessary that the constitution of a National Assembly should be postponed until the election of a President or even until the nomination of a native as Governor; there is, indeed, already in most colonies some form of representative body to advise the foreign Governor. On the other hand there might well be a native Governor, or even an elected President, without a National Assembly. It would, for example, be possible to elect the President on some plan similar to that adopted in Presidential elections in the United States. But the National Assembly would seem to be the most convenient instrument for electing a President, and there should be no great difficulty in entrusting the Assembly with this function. Although in the first instance the Governor might tend to represent the majority in the Assembly rather than the people as a whole, one might hope and expect that he would gradually come to adopt the attitude of a representative of the whole people, and that all sections of the community would come to regard him in that light. Such a Government, representing the people though still unable to stand alone without support from the colonial power, would be semi-colonial in character.

9. Conditional Independence

Defence. The essential function of the dual Government in its semi-colonial form would be to enable the dependency to stand alone without external support. For this it would be necessary to create a military and police force on which a representative government could depend without having to call in foreign aid. It is not enough that the troops shall be non-European, as in Burma, where the maintenance of order has rested on the support of Indian troops, or even as in India where the army is recruited from a comparatively small section of the population. How long any national Government could hold India together from Kashmir to Tinnevelly and Bombay to Calcutta, without support from Britain, is a matter that attempts to find a formula for reconciling Moslem and Hindu often disregard. In Burma it would not be enough to recruit soldiers, as on a very small scale in the past, from hill tribes and minor peoples; this fosters and does not conciliate sectional divisions. A national army implies a national militia in which the duty of national defence is incumbent upon all.

Territorial Integrity. This carries two further implications. It implies that one character of the dependency shall be territorial integrity. We have noticed that a plural society resembles a confederation of independent states, and it is this which constitutes the chief barrier to self-government. But the difficulty is aggravated if it also comprises distinct regions that recognize no organic bond and do not wish to hold together, as when Burma was amalgamated with India. The incorporation of Burma in the Indian Empire was solely for administrative convenience, and it has greatly enhanced the difficulty of reconstituting Burma as a national unit. Some of the territorial amalgamations now contemplated in Africa seem to be dictated by administrative convenience or economic efficiency. So far as that is the case, it will be harder in future to make the several constituents capable of independence, and harder also to confer independence on the whole artificially created complex. If after the Mutiny the British Government had accepted the advice of John Bright to constitute five distinct territorial regions in India,[1] the problem of making the people capable of independence would have been greatly simplified. So far then as a dependency comprises distinct territorial units, some kind of federation would seem to be indicated. In Burma, for example, the recognition of the Shan States, the Tribal Hills and possibly Arakan, as separate entities within a comprehensive federation, might promote harmonious co-operation and a real national unity.

Economic Autonomy. The second implication of creating a national militia is that the tension due to the cleavage between numerical and economic power must be resolved. It is no difficult matter to recruit local troops, but it is hazardous to entrust local troops with the defence of foreign capitalist interests. For a country to be capable of independence it must possess economic autonomy, and for this it is essential that the economic system must be largely in native hands. The transformation of the economic system is necessary also as a part of social education. So long as the indigenous inhabitants of a country are restricted to agriculture, and are debarred from gaining experience in modern industry and commerce, they cannot as a people acquire a comprehensive outlook on the modern world.

Thus during the semi-colonial phase of the transition the Government would have a double task: to make the dependency capable of independence in respect of military force, and at the same time to transform the economic system so that the endowment of the people with military strength should not endanger internal security. On the completion of this task the dependency would, like Siam, be capable of independence. It would be able to stand alone and, as the Government would no longer be responsible to the colonial power for the maintenance of order, it would no longer require a dual form of government.

Being able to stand alone it would no longer be tied of necessity to the colonial power, although it might, and probably would, wish to

---

[1] Bright, I, 50.

retain the connection, as the great dominions do at present, and with better reason. For its independence would still be conditional on compliance with the requirements of the modern world in respect of progress and welfare. A representative of the colonial power could do much to help it, no longer however as a High Commissioner directing the control of policy but as a Resident or, better, Agent occupying somewhat the same position as that formerly held by Cromer in Egypt. The change in status might accordingly be recognized by the conversion of the High Commissioner into an Agent; and, if the post of Agent carried a higher status than the post of High Commissioner, the transformation of the form of government would probably be expedited.

10. POPULAR GOVERNMENT

When a dependency had become capable of independence, the Government would be responsible to the people for maintaining their independence. But it is unnecessary that it should be accountable to them for the daily conduct of affairs, and impossible that it can be made accountable to them in such matters until they are, in fact, able and willing to accept the responsibilities of modern citizenship. It is conceivable that there should be a perpetual President occupying a position resembling that held formerly by the Crown in Siam, responsible to the people for maintaining their independence, but not accountable to them for his actions. The people need a leader if it is to make good and maintain its place in the world, but experience shows that leadership only too easily becomes a military dictatorship, and shows also that dictatorship is unstable. Both for stability and as an instrument of social education, it is desirable to create an organ with some responsibility to the people for the conduct of affairs. The National Assembly suggested above would not serve this purpose, as it is expressly devised with a view to organizing knowledge and thought, and not as an instrument of will. Doubtless it would exercise an influence on government, and so also would the Economic Council; experience suggests that they would exercise a strong and increasing influence. In British dependencies the 'legislatures' have little constitutional power, but 'all observers agree that the attitude of the local executive shows a growing measure of response to the influence of their legislatures'.[1] That has been true also of the Volksraad in Netherlands India from its earliest days. Yet representation cannot be accepted as fully adequate

---

[1] *Britain and Her Dependencies*, p. 42.

to the demands of self-government, and everywhere in the modern world the system of monarchy, though embodying the principle of virtual representation in its strongest form, has broken down unless combined with institutions serving to express not merely the general opinion but the general will. For the attainment of independence on a stable basis it would seem necessary, therefore, to devise alongside the National Assembly some organ serving as an instrument of social will. A precedent for the combination of a National Council and a Legislature exists apparently in Fiji.

In a homogeneous society in which the people in general accept the conditions of modern civilization, the same organ can serve both as a means by which they may express their views and as an instrument for doing what they want. It can serve both ends because fundamentally the people are agreed on promoting national welfare, however widely they may differ as to the means by which this may be achieved, and because they all accept the standards and ideas of modern western civilization of which democracy is one expression. In the plural society of a tropical dependency important sections of the community have little or no regard for national well-being; and to some sections, including the great majority of the indigenous inhabitants, the ideas and standards of modern civilization are not only alien but unwelcome, or even repugnant. It follows, then, that the membership of a legislature must be restricted to those who, as permanent inhabitants, have a vital interest in national welfare and at the same time accept the ideas common to the modern world. There is no place in such a body for members who, as foreigners, are primarily interested in the security and rewards of foreign capital. Nor is there any place for members, indigenous or domiciled, who are ignorant of the modern world, or who are dependent for membership on an electorate even more ignorant. This implies that, in the first instance, there shall be educational and property qualifications for the franchise, which may be gradually lowered as an appreciation of the requirements of modern civilization become more generally diffused. Again, communal representation would be precluded because this tends to impair and not to strengthen social will, and makes for sectional division and not for social unity; also it would be unnecessary because, from the conditions of membership, all the members would have a common interest in national welfare and would accept the basic postulates of modern civilization. By excluding on the one hand temporary residents, solely interested in economic progress, and on the other hand those permanent residents who are not at home in the modern world, it would represent the highest common factor of social will and should promote social unification instead of sectional discord.

It is important to distinguish the functions, and therefore the forms of the two separate organs embodying respectively the principles of representation and responsibility. The representative body, the National Assembly, should be as comprehensive as local or sectional diversity might require and would be based on the principle of communal representation; the responsible organ, the Legislature, would, in the first instance, be far more narrowly restricted as regards both membership and franchise and it would exclude communal representation. Such a legislature would not represent economic power, the strong foreign capitalist interest, nor numerical power, the great mass of the people ignorant of the modern world; it would not represent the whole people, and therefore could not be accountable to the people as a whole. The Government, however, must represent the people as a whole and be responsible for them to the outer world and, until the legislature can fulfil both these conditions, it cannot be entrusted with final control over the executive. The main constructive task of Government (beyond the maintenance of order and the care for security against oppression) would be to foster a common social will, but this demands greater continuity of policy than can be expected of a legislature consisting of members electe'l for a comparatively short period. The restriction of the franchise to the educated and wealthier classes should ensure general agreement between the legislature and the Government, but there would certainly remain occasions of difference, and the Government must retain full power to override the legislature and to carry measures on its own initiative.

The irresponsibility of responsible organs in dependencies that are not, in fact, capable of independence has always been a source of difficulty and friction wherever such organs have been constituted, and it has always been necessary to impose safeguards against the dangers of entrusting legislatures with excessive powers. But with a native President the relations between the Government and the legislature, and indeed the character of the Government would take on a new aspect. Differences arise chiefly where the requirements of the outer world demand action that the members of the legislature do not approve. The native President would presumably be one of the most enlightened and intelligent among the people; he would be better able to understand the necessity for such measures than most members of the legislature, and would be better able to recommend them to his people than any foreign Governor. Also a dependency, so long as it is incapable of independence, must needs depend on the support of the colonial power, but the people in general do not recognize the need; a native President would realize that he was dependent on the colonial power for retaining his position, and would listen more attentively to advice from the High Commissioner than would the people as a whole or their representatives in the legislature. In experiments in responsible government under a foreign Governor one frequent cause of friction is that Nationalists urge a wider extension of the franchise with a view to strengthening their hold upon the legislature, and also greater power for the legislature at the risk of weakening the Government, or even in order to make it weaker. If the Government is weak enough to yield to the demand it soon becomes too weak to rule; yet if it resists the demand, it becomes weaker by exciting disaffection. But with a native President or Governor conflicts between the executive and the legislature would lose much if not all their sectional character. The Government would still not infrequently have occasion to override the legislature, but it would be less exposed to the suspicion that it was acting in foreign interests. A native President, aiming to obtain complete autonomy for his country, would appreciate more keenly than the electorate the dangers of transferring control too rapidly to an elected body, and not improbably would even be too jealous of extending the powers of the legislature and of widening the franchise. It is indeed not unusual under indirect rule to find the native ruler reluctant to allow more power to his people, and he does so only under pressure from the colonial power. Similarly, with a dual Government comprising representatives both of the people and of the colonial power, the latter would often be able to take the more Liberal and progressive side congenial to western traditions. As social education brought more of the people more intimately into cultural contact with the modern world, successive extensions of the electorate for the legislature would mark the progress towards popular government. Just as the High Commissioner can be transformed into an Agent when through his help the dependency becomes able to stand alone, so, when the progress of popular government gives sufficient assurance of stability, the Agent could be transformed into a Minister, on a par with the representatives of other powers.

11. POLITICAL REINTEGRATION

Here then we have a project of political reintegration. We have seen that foreign rule in a tropical dependency liberates economic forces, which acting internally produce social disintegration, and acting externally produce economic disintegration, building up a plural society precariously balanced in unstable equilibrium and held in position only by pressure from outside. Our analysis of attempts to promote economic progress and social welfare has shown that these are nullified by the working of economic forces, which can be brought under control only by recognizing the validity of some quasi-religious principle accepted by all concerned as of superior validity to economic motives, and that this can be found only in the principle of Nationalism. We have ventured on suggestions for the reintegration of social and economic life, and have been led to the conclusion that in both respects success can be attained only through political reintegration on a national basis. Political reintegration is not conditional on but a condition of social and economic reintegration. This accords with the Liberal and Christian tradition of the West, which has found expression in attempts at constructing the machinery of western self-governing institutions. The failure of earlier experiments in the construction of such machinery was attributed to the poor foundation of inadequate material resources, insufficient health and undeveloped minds, and a remedy was sought in encouraging economic development in order to raise the standard of welfare to a level at which western institutions would work on western lines. But we have found that economic development promotes efficiency rather than welfare, and enhances the difficulty of political reintegration. It has now come to be recognized that in the plural society of the tropics such institutions cannot work. The fundamental problem is not to create new machinery, but to transform society so that it shall be capable of independence, and thus capable of framing its own institutions in its own way without having the machinery of western political organization imposed upon it by a foreign power. The project here formulated therefore concentrates attention first on building up a common social will, and then on enlightening this common social will, so that the people will gradually be brought to do of its own accord those things which of necessity it must do, for therein alone lies perfect freedom.

12. Independence and Finance

No project of political integration as a condition of self-government would be complete without considering it in relation to finance. Financial control implies political control, and loans have played no less a part than armies in securing the ascendance of the West over the tropics. Every country must pay its way, and the less it has to pay the more likely it is to live within its means. If tropical dependencies are to attain financial independence, it is important that they should economize on administration, both by reducing establishments to the indispensable minimum, and by restricting salary rates to the lowest point compatible with efficiency. It is not only on financial grounds that efforts should be made to simplify administration. We have noticed that lack of co-ordination between the various services is a common defect of tropical administration. This indicates that even under foreign rule the machinery is apt to become unwieldy, and every elaboration of the administrative machinery, by enhancing the difficulty of control over the conduct of affairs, thereby hinders the transference of control from the colonial power to the dependency. Still more effectively does it hamper the transference of responsibility from the Government to an elective body composed of members to whom many of the activities of Government are unwelcome. Both on political and financial grounds it is desirable that the administrative machinery 'should be as simple as possible, and should cost no more than necessary.

A rapid growth of administrative activities is the first result of opening up new regions under colonial rule. It becomes necessary to maintain order at a higher level than under native rule and by more costly methods: capital charges are incurred on communications and other public works necessary to economic development; and various services are constituted in the name of welfare but in the interest of economic progress. These things are essential to economic progress, which is in itself desirable and inevitable, but, as we have seen, prejudicial to self-government. Welfare measures that the people value and demand cost little or nothing to the colonial Government, as in Burma where a high level of literacy has been maintained through the monastic schools. But most of the measures undertaken by western Governments in the name of welfare are unwelcome, and are therefore costly and ineffective. The people, if left to govern themselves, will not of their own accord provide money for measures that they regard as waste of money, and they are therefore incapable of complete self-government until they can be induced to appreciate their value, until they have learned to want what, in the conditions of the modern world, they must want if they are to manage their own affairs. But the organization of demand is a slow process, and in the tropics both government and western enterprise are always in a hurry for speedy results. We have seen, however, that self-government is a condition of welfare and therefore of sound economic progress. If that is so, then it is desirable to restrict all activities purporting to be undertaken in the name of welfare to the minimum required for the sake of economic progress, and so far as possible to relieve the inhabitants of dependencies from charges incurred on that account. That the colonial power should contribute to the cost of development and welfare in dependencies has been recognized by both British and Dutch rule. In Britain this principle finds its latest expression in the Colonial Development and Welfare Act of 1940. But that Act provides for assistance only in respect of such matters as dependent peoples cannot be made to pay for. If economic development is to proceed rapidly it would seem desirable to provide dependencies with funds to the full limit that such expenditure is likely to be profitable. It is on this principle that some Socialists advocate the equipment of dependencies with railways and other capital goods at the expense of Britain. That would doubtless benefit both capital and labour, the manufacturers and labourers employed in Britain in producing the materials, but whether it would be profitable to the general taxpayers who would have to meet the charge is a matter for debate. Also it would tend to expedite economic development in the dependencies to which the gift was made, whereas a slow progress seems more likely to promote their welfare. Whenever economic development requires so-called 'welfare' measures to mitigate its ill-effects, it is important to provide them and to see that they are effective. But the expenditure on such measures should be charged to the enterprises which they make more profitable. Western enterprise in the tropics is advantageous to the colonial power, but its benefit to the country in which it is conducted is, at best, questionable. So far as rapid development is in the interest of the colonial power, there is a sufficient reason to encourage it, as under the Colonial Development and Welfare Act; but it is hardly fair to make the welfare measures that it necessitates a charge on people who do not want them or regard them as promoting welfare; and to claim credit for generosity for such welfare grants is a draft on credulity that is unlikely to be honoured by the people of the dependency to which the grant is made.

The multiplication of welfare services and other Government activities in tropical dependencies involves the entertainment of a large European establishment and the elaboration of the western superstructure over native life. Considerations of economy would tend gradually to replace the Europeans by natives and in the interest of social education it is desirable that they should be replaced by natives so far and so fast as is consistent with efficiency. But experience suggests that the process is likely to be slow, and that one result will be to multiply subordinate officials who will supplement their income by conniving at breaches of the regulations which they are paid to enforce. It is always an easy matter to find plausible arguments for the employment of more welfare officers, and such proposals are likely to engage the sympathy of the colonial power because they expedite development, provide more appointments for Europeans, pacify discontent among the unemployed native intelligentsia by providing more jobs, and enable the foreign Government to display its benevolent aspirations at the expense of its native subjects. There must always, therefore, be a temptation to multiply welfare activities up to the limit that colonial revenues can afford, and colonial powers will find it easier to resist this temptation if they are required to contribute towards the cost.

So far as superior appointments in the various services are transferred to natives, a colonial power will have less interest in adding to their number. But the transfer of such appointments raises an administrative problem of grave practical importance. This matter has been noticed by Lord Hailey:

'Important as it is', he says, 'to expedite the process of opening the superior official cadre to recruitment from the people of the country, there is one danger from which dependencies must be safeguarded. In Great Britain there is a generally accepted ratio between the scale of remuneration given to members of the public services and the average family income. The salaries now given to European members of the services in the dependencies are based roughly on the scale of similar salaries in Great Britain with a necessary addition for the disabilities attending overseas employment. Where natives of the dependencies have been admitted to posts hitherto held by Europeans, there has been a tendency to demand for them either the same salary, or something approaching it, as that formerly paid to Europeans. To concede this demand would involve an unreasonable burden on the finances of the territory, more especially as there will always be pressure on the part of the large body of subordinate services to approximate their pay to that of the smaller number in superior employment.'[1]

[1] *Britain and Her Dependencies*, p. 37.

It is indeed a common defect of administration in the tropics that the scales of pay, even in the lowest grades, are far above what the people could earn in the native world, so that everyone looks to obtain if possible a post under Government or, failing that, in the employ of western enterprise where also rates of pay are based on the standard of living in the western sphere of social life. Lord Hailey suggests that natives employed in Government service 'must be content with salaries based on a scale determined by a ratio to the average income of their own countrymen'. But it is easier to preach contentment than to enforce it. When natives in appointments ordinarily held by Europeans demand equal pay for equal work, it is difficult for a foreign Government to resist the demand without arousing disaffection among just that class which it is most important to conciliate. Men in such positions set the standard of living which those in subordinate appointments try to emulate. These also demand higher pay, and again it is difficult to resist the demand. Like the multiplicity of transfers, the excessive burden of routine, the indigestible masses of reports, it is a defect common to all colonial powers and all dependencies, an inveterate complaint that cannot be charmed away by pious aspirations. Everywhere the administration of dependencies is costly in comparison with their resources, and everywhere, even in wealthy dependencies like Malaya and Netherlands India, one finds complaints that the resources are inadequate to the needs. Yet the example of Japan shows that this high scale of expenditure is unnecessary. When seamen in Netherlands India mutinied for higher pay, it was observed that the men were already drawing higher pay than officers in the Japanese fleet. The modernization of Japan, however, has been effected under its own rulers, and would probably have been far more costly, and less effective, under foreign rule. In India some ministers have accepted low salaries from patriotic motives, but patriotic fervour is unlikely to reconcile the rank and file of native officials to low pay, while they see Europeans drawing greatly higher pay for much the same work.

Yet it would not seem impossible to find a solution of the problem even under foreign rule. The assistance of European officials is necessary both for economic development and for social education, but dependencies with meagre resources cannot always afford to employ as many as is desirable, while colonial powers tend to employ more Europeans than is really necessary. In either case the scale of pay for Europeans must be fixed at a much higher rate than native officials need. It has been suggested, with reference to grants under the

Colonial Development and Welfare Act, 'that it would surely be of far more practical value to the colonies, to relieve them entirely of the cost of European salaries and pensions than to make them isolated grants for development and welfare projects which they would then be able to finance themselves'.[1] From the standpoint of the colonial power this plan, although startling, would probably be advantageous; but it would seem to encourage dependencies to beg for doles while starving them of useful services. If the cost of administration is not to be excessive, the rate of pay in all appointments must be fixed with reference to native standards; but it should be possible to frame a rule that where Europeans are employed the colonial power and the colonial Government shall each pay half the difference between the pay necessary to attract a competent European and the pay fixed for natives in similar positions. This would make it possible for the dependency to employ a larger number of Europeans, and encourage it to recruit Europeans whom it would obtain at little more than half the market rates, while it would discourage the colonial power from multiplying the number of Europeans unnecessarily; at the same time it would tend to keep native scales of pay within the limits that the dependency could afford. The proposal that colonial powers should contribute to colonial expenditures in this manner may appear Utopian. But the principle that dependencies should receive financial aid has already been accepted in the Colonial Development and Welfare Act of 1940. Capital grants tend to promote development rather than welfare, and recurring grants on the above lines in aid of colonial establishments should be more economical than when given merely as windfalls or subsidies, as was abundantly demonstrated by the former practice of doles from the central to provincial governments in India, with alternating periods of extravagance and stringency.

In connection with the remuneration of officials it may be well to recall another matter already mentioned incidentally. Both in British India and Netherlands India Government servants were formerly allowed to trade or to take a commission on produce supplied to Government. This system was incompatible with the encouragement of private enterprise and, on the introduction of the rule of law and the principle of economic freedom, the officials were converted into civil servants and were debarred from trading and from holding land. As civil servants they no longer profited by the exploitation of the natives, and could take a dispassionate view of

---

[1] *Economist*, 30 September 1944, p. 447.

native welfare without the natural bias due to personal interest. But the regulations prohibiting trade and landholding were framed before the modern growth of limited companies. Officials who hold shares in private enterprises operating in the country where they serve, or who may look forward on retirement to highly paid appointments in such enterprises, can hardly remain wholly impartial in questions where capitalist interests conflict with national advancement, and are at least exposed to a suspicion of bias. If, then, the function of government be to promote national advancement, there would seem good reason to place some restriction on the relations between officials and private enterprise. In Netherlands India the Governor-General must abstain from all concern with local private interests, not only during his period of office but for five years subsequently. Some corresponding restriction might well be made more general; at least it would seem expedient that officials should be made to report their holdings in private enterprises operating within the dependency. This precaution is likely to be more necessary with the increasing replacement of Europeans by natives, less fortified by an old and strong tradition of integrity in public life.

CHAPTER XIII

INTERNATIONAL COLLABORATION

1. THE NEED FOR AUTONOMY

IT is obvious, we have said, that in the problem of making dependencies autonomous two parties are concerned, the dependency and the colonial power. A dependency cannot achieve autonomy unless it is capable of independence, but its achievement of autonomy requires also a creative impulse in the colonial power, and almost inevitably this creative impulse is weakened by division of opinion and infirmity of purpose. On the desirability of the economic development of dependencies there will be general agreement; it is a matter of common sense that backward regions should contribute as fully as possible to the resources of the world or, at least, to the resources of the colonial power. Experience shows that their contribution can be made more effective by raising the standard of living among the people and, to this extent, it is a matter of common sense to promote their welfare. But the conferment of autonomy is regarded as a privilege, a concession justifiable only on moral grounds superior to self-interest. Why not, asks common sense, hold what we have?

The answer to this question is usually framed in terms of lofty principles, by no means obvious to common sense, not universally accepted, and of doubtful validity. For instance, in a recent interesting and suggestive essay, Mr Panikkar lays down 'essential principles of colonial administration': that the sovereignty belongs to the people; that the people should be protected against industrial fluctuations; that a progressive policy of education, public health and social consolidation should be adopted; that there should be no racial or colour discrimination; and 'finally' that colonial powers should train dependent peoples for their own defence.[1] Such principles may be admirable as moral sentiments, but who wants these things? Who is going to do them, or to pay to have them done? And in the plural society of a tropical dependency, what is 'the people'? If Mr Panikkar were given a free hand to govern a country of the Tropical Far East on these lines, he would probably find that he needed two hands—to

[1] Panikkar, K. M., *The Future of South-east Asia* (1943), p. 25; Furnivall, *Asiatic Review*, 1944, p. 265.

pull in opposite directions. Humanitarian ideals may point the goal for political reforms, but human nature travels faster with self-interest for its guide. We are probably better judges of our own interest than of the interests of others. We may be, and often are mistaken as to what we want and how best to get it, but at least we think we know what we want, and we can only guess what other people want. It is possible, of course, that having decided where our interest lies, we may, on some ground of higher principle, be willing to forgo it; but we shall at least know where our will needs strengthening. Let us then examine the ideal of colonial autonomy frankly from the stand-point of our interests as citizens of a colonial power and heirs of western civilization. But let us take care also to understand our interests.

Among all tropical dependencies few attract so much attention at the present time as those in the Tropical Far East. The chief reason is that here there is a focus of stresses and tensions which endanger peace. When a recent Colonial Secretary was discussing inter-national co-operation in colonial affairs, he urged that it was needed for security. Security is the keynote of almost every such project. But the word security in this connection savours of 'securities'—investments of foreign capital. We have seen that in the past the whole direction of economic life, and one may say of political life also, lay with foreign capital. After the war foreign capital will again be active in developing the oil, tin, rubber and so on. When we talk of security, are we thinking of security for foreign capital? Capitalist interests will be more concerned in security for capital than in the maintenance of peace. It is true that in any given region capitalist interests are particular and local; not many people in Britain are directly connected, as shareholders or otherwise, with firms operating in Burma; still fewer are those with investments in Netherlands India, Siam or Indo-China. But all capital has a common interest, well-organized and vocal—if need be, clamor-ous—and, for the protection of its interest, it can appeal for general support because we are all capitalists now, all interested, one way or another, directly or indirectly, in the capitalist development of the tropics. Organized capitalist interests demanding security for western enterprise in the tropics are likely to prevail over our silent unorganized general interest as citizens and human beings in the maintenance of peace. But our true interest lies in peace and, if we understand our interest and can get our way, we shall endeavour to promote peace rather than security. Is it indeed economic, or even possible, to ensure security for foreign capital in tropical dependencies? So far as this conflicts with social interests we cannot safely entrust its defence to indigenous native troops. Foreign troops will be more costly, and someone, eventually the consumer, the citizen, must bear the extra charge. Our tropical produce will cost more and, in the long run and not perhaps a very long run, will be cut off by rebellion. Foreign troops may ensure temporary security, but it will be the security promised to Macbeth, 'mortal's chiefest enemy'. If we would maintain peace in the tropics we must enlist the co-operation of tropical peoples and train them in arms, not, as Mr Panikkar suggests, 'finally' and on altruistic grounds, but as a matter of the first importance in our own interests, our true interests as distinct from what may seem at first sight to be our economic interest. This implies, as Lord Hailey remarked at the International Conference in Canada in 1942, that we must try to promote among them 'the status which will give them both the incentive and the means to organize for their defence'. The security of capital is least endangered where the people is divided, as in a plural society; but peace is most secure where the people is united and the tensions and stresses of a plural society have been resolved. Autonomy is needed in the interest of peace.

Again, we are all interested in economic progress; we all want to develop the material resources of the tropics and to open them up as markets for our produce. We are all concerned to promote the activity of economic forces, but experience justifies the social instinct which, in western homogeneous society, keeps their anti-social tendencies within safe bounds. In the tropics these forces, released from the control of custom, disintegrate society, and there is no effective restraint on the conflicting economic interests of capital and labour, industry and agriculture, town and country. In almost all the problems thus arising economic tension is aggravated by racial cleavage. Let us recall merely a few instances from the Tropical Far East. How can one regulate the influx of Indian or Chinese labour with due regard to the respective interests of the natives and foreign capital? Or consider the protection and welfare of labour. Asiatics differ from Europeans in their ideas and standards of welfare. Are we to push up welfare standards to the advantage of European big business in competing with Indian, Chinese or native employers, and of western labour in competition with oriental labour? Economic competition cuts at profits as well as at wages. How far shall western capitalists be allowed to defend their profits against native competition, and thereby hold up the price, say, of rubber, to the detriment of American and other consumers? Or again, what about markets? Are colonial powers, with high standards of living and high wages, to throw open their dependent markets freely to cheap oriental produce? All these, and many other problems, foreshadowed towards the end of the last century with the growth of capitalist enterprise in India, became acute when Japan entered the modern world. But they will not be eliminated even if the war may have put Japan out of business; they will become more acute and difficult with increasing competition from India and China and, if these can support economic with military strength, and can make a common stand, with moral and perhaps material support from Africa, many economic problems will become almost insoluble on peaceful lines or in economic terms because they are not purely economic. The uncontrolled reactions of economic forces will, as in the past, make for the survival of the cheapest, hindered only by the self-interest of competitors for profit. For the solution of such problems we must look outside the sphere of economics for some principle to which we can appeal. We must promote among tropical peoples 'a status which will give them both the incentive and the means to organize for their defence'—not merely military self-defence, but economic self-defence. Our immediate and apparent interest lies in giving free play to economic forces, but our true interest lies in promoting economic autonomy so that these forces may be kept under adequate control.

Moreover, we all want to promote welfare, or what we regard as welfare, not merely on humanitarian grounds but in our own economic interest. In our own interest we want to prevent disease among men, crops and cattle; we want good sanitation in commercial centres and an ample supply of healthy and intelligent labour for western enterprise. Experience shows that attempts to gain these ends by administrative machinery are costly and ineffective; the promotion of welfare requires the voluntary co-operation of the people. Also we want tropical people to be well off so that they may buy our goods, and, in order to earn more, they must produce more. But experience shows that production is a social function just as welfare is a social attribute. Our interest in capitalist development seems to lie in promoting individual welfare so as to increase the efficiency of production, but individual welfare is a by-product of social welfare. In our own interest we must promote among the people a status which will give them the incentive and the means to organize their own welfare. Colonial autonomy is not merely a humanitarian ideal, a privilege to be graciously or grudgingly conceded, but an end that we should pursue in our own interest, and press on dependent peoples who may be reluctant or too ignorant to accept responsibility for conducting their own affairs.

Yet it will seem risky to abandon control over profitable markets and fields for investment. If dependencies should become autonomous they might prefer to buy goods from other sources, to place restrictions on foreign enterprise, and to employ Europeans other than subjects of the colonial power. If Britain after the war should be faced with unemployment, one remedy would be the increase of exports to countries within the Empire; but the dominions might be unable or unwilling to take them, whereas the colonies would have to accept whatever might be thrust on them in the name of 'colonial development and welfare'. However strongly humanitarian ideals and practical, though remote, considerations of our own interest may support arguments for making dependencies capable of independence, we are apparently and more immediately interested in making certain of the profits that accrue from our established relations with tropical dependencies, and this tends to weaken the creative impulse that the task of fostering autonomy demands. It is common sense that 'every effort should be made to increase the contributions which each dependency can make to the economic or military resources of the Empire', and although in pronouncements on colonial policy this may be formally subordinated to local interests, yet in actual practice 'for many years to come the African colonial dependencies of Great Britain, France and Belgium are unlikely to give active encouragement to industries of a type which will compete with their home manufactures'.[1] It is a matter of common knowledge that men prefer higher wages rather than a reduction of the cost of living which would really be more beneficial, they prefer the glitter to the gold. Similarly we have a direct interest on business grounds in retaining our control over dependencies, and only a remote, less obvious though more substantial, interest in promoting their independence. We can, moreover, support our reluctance by the plausible argument that, if they are granted nominal independence before they are in fact capable of independence, they will be unable to maintain it. For sound

[1] *African Survey*, pp. 247, 979.

reasons then as well as for selfish reasons we are divided and infirm of purpose in facing the problem of colonial autonomy.

This is apparent in the accepted formula that the goal of policy should be self-government 'within the Empire'. Strictly construed this formula is meaningless, for it implies that dependencies shall be free to do what they want, so long as they do what we want. Also, as we have found already in the case of India, it cannot be enforced, for effective self-government must carry with it ability to secede from the Empire. There are two guarantees against secession. One is the inability to stand alone, a defect that, if we aim at colonial autonomy, we should endeavour to remove. The other, more durable, is the tie of interest and affection. The advantages of the connection with Britain are, or should be, so great that no dependency, once capable of independence, should wish to secede. Yet we endeavour to impose as an obligation what they should welcome as a privilege, and thereby foster disaffection, and enhance the already difficult task of making them capable of independence. Until a national sentiment develops, a dependency is incapable of autonomy; but where such a sentiment exists, every delay will be regarded with suspicion as dictated by the interest of the colonial power and will promote ill-feeling. If in such circumstances the connection be violently ruptured, there will probably remain a legacy of ill-will, such as still complicates the relations between Britain and the United States. Our true interest lies in the promotion of colonial autonomy; but our natural selfish inclination is not to look beyond the short period within which (at least apparently) it is more profitable to keep dependencies in subjection. It is necessary then to strengthen colonial powers in the resolve to make dependencies capable of independence, and to minimize suspicion among dependent peoples, anxious, perhaps unduly, to expedite the process.

2. POLITICAL AND ECONOMIC CONTROL

It would appear then that the project of making dependencies capable of independence implies a revolution, if not in colonial policy yet in its practical application. It is a striking fact that, probably without exception, all the great revolutions in colonial policy have followed the same general plan. Under all forms of colonial rule there is a constant tendency towards the unification of economic and political control. 'Where the Ruler is at the same time Merchant, compulsion knows no bounds',[1] and revolutions in colonial policy have been

[1] *Netherlands India*, p. 116.

effected by separating economic and political control. In the first period of modern colonial history we find both the Dutch and British East India Companies seeking trade as merchants and then, by force of circumstances, acquiring political control and using this to make their economic control more effective. In Britain the corruption of home politics by the vast fortunes of the nabobs stimulated those whose political interests were thus endangered to deprive the East India Company of political control over India, and the financial difficulties of the Company gave an occasion to attempt this in the Regulating Act of 1784. This partial separation of political and economic control was formal rather than effective, and for a generation the Company remained almost as powerful in India as before, though exercising control through Parliament rather than of its own unquestionable motion. Then the Industrial Revolution changed the environment, and the company, when challenged by the cotton manufacturers of Manchester in the cause of free trade, had to surrender its monopoly. Political and economic control, however, were both transferred to Manchester, which for fifty years dictated colonial policy on the principle of economic freedom under the direct rule of law. The next transformation in colonial policy came through the accumulation of capital available for overseas investment and the needs of large-scale industry for raw materials which native enterprise could not furnish in sufficient quantities, if at all. Birmingham and the City favoured the active development of colonial resources by western enterprise under indirect rule through chartered companies. Later, when these proved unremunerative, Government was induced to take up 'the White Man's Burden'. About the same time colonial policy took a new turn with the rise of the Labour Party which, fearing the competition of cheap tropical labour, urged measures to promote the material welfare of native subjects, especially those engaged in western enterprise and industrial employment. At the same time also other powers challenged British supremacy in colonial affairs, and their demand for freer access to colonial resources gave birth to the doctrine of the dual mandate, according to which colonies are held in trust for world welfare and the welfare of the natives.

What, however, is most significant in these successive transformations of colonial policy, lies below the surface. For the undercurrent of western Christian tradition has flowed steadily below the surface throughout all the various phases of colonial relations. 'Where the ruler is at the same time merchant', there is no criterion of policy but profit. Under company rule, with economic and political control held firmly in the same hands we find in the direction of affairs, as was said of the Dutch East India Company, 'the pole-star profit, and the lodestone, greed'. Parliamentary rule not only allows but necessitates the emergence of other considerations. It allows economic interest to dictate the course of policy, but it also allows newly emerging economic interests to challenge the established order, and in no case is there a clear ring for the contending rivals. Each party must appeal for support to the indifferent majority of normal men who 'would fain see the world go well, so it be not along of them'. Both sides must base their claims on an appeal to national interest and morality. When Manchester denounced the monopoly of the East India Company in the name of free trade and Liberal humanitarianism, the Company called in the aged and venerated Warren Hastings to expose the evils likely to attend the free admission of the private trader. Always since then, practical men with a material interest in colonial reform have had to enlist humanitarian support to win their cause, and their opponents have responded by a similar appeal to moral principles. Although both parties have urged moral considerations, the advocates of the established order have been able to cite facts and figures showing its material advantage, whereas reformers have had to base their arguments on the evidence of things as yet unseen. Faith has been justified by its fruits in material advantage, but after each victory the indifferent majority has lapsed into indifference, and economic factors have resumed their sway.

These conditions are not the peculiar character of British colonial policy, but obtain wherever a democratic legislature exercises supreme control over colonial affairs. When the Dutch East India Company went bankrupt the Home Government, as in Britain, assumed control. But it was the Crown and not the Parliament which took over the territories of the Company, and it administered them as a State enterprise, retaining complete and unquestionable political and economic control of their affairs. On this system the only criterion of policy was the tribute that Java yielded to the Treasury, and despite good intentions, economic development in the interest of profit followed the normal course of oppression and demoralization. When the Revolution of 1848 transferred political control over the States-General there was, as in Britain after 1784, no immediate change in colonial practice.[1] But parliamentary rule allowed the emergence of

[1] *Netherlands India*, pp. 159, 175, 227.

a 'Colonial Opposition', and both parties appealed to moral principles. Steam transport worked in favour of the Liberals and their crowning victory in 1870 synchronized with the opening of the Suez Canal. The sequel justified Liberal claims as to the effect of the new policy on economic progress and Conservative apprehensions as to its effect on native welfare. Economic development in the interest of profit again followed the normal course, leading to 'diminishing welfare' in Java and 'moral collapse' on the plantations of Sumatra. Meanwhile Conservatives were attracting humanitarian support by their doctrine of moral responsibility for colonial welfare and, when the Chambers of Commerce protested in 1900 that, under Liberal rule, the Javan had less to spend on clothes, Conservatives found material support for their appeal to the indifferent majority, powerful in numbers and therefore powerful in a democracy, which inclines in favour of any good cause that does not touch its pocket. Colonial policy turned in an 'ethical' direction.

Similarly, in France, industrialists and agriculturists have appealed to the generous traditions of French culture in support of their conflicting interests in colonial problems, and the close balance of agricultural and industrial interests in France goes far to explain the vacillations of French colonial policy. But the most conspicuous illustration of the connection between economic and political control comes from the United States. Americans had practically no economic interest in the Philippines before taking them over from Spain, and there was a strong prejudice against imperialist adventures. From the earliest days of American rule, its policy was directed toward enabling the Filipinos to manage their own affairs more efficiently and with greater regard for economic progress than under Spanish rule. But American capital and trade found profit in the Philippines, and a current of opinion adverse to Filipino independence grew stronger, submerging the general distrust of imperialism, though, as in France, it remained suspect to agriculturists. Dairy farmers and sugar producers and refiners feared the competition of cheap Filipino products, and organized Labour demanded the restriction of Filipino immigration. For some years there were vain attempts to keep out Filipino goods by differential duties, and Filipino labour by new immigration laws. In 1929, however, it became clear that these attempts were bound to fail so long as the Philippines were legally American territory, and the groups whose interests were affected organized humanitarian sentiment so efficiently that in 1934 the Tydings-McDuffie Act was passed to arrange for Filipino independence within ten years from 1936.[1]

Everywhere, then, experience shows that economic interests seek political control over tropical dependencies with a view to strengthening their economic control, and that this combination of economic and political control is fatal to native welfare. Political control has been surrendered only at the challenge of newly emerging economic interests and, under democratic forms of government, this raises the question of colonial relations to a moral plane. Rival interests bid for the support of the indifferent majority, and must appeal to faith in moral values transcending the economic sphere of human life. These considerations suggest that the key to success in colonial administration lies in the separation of economic and political control which parliamentary institutions facilitate, and they go far to explain why Governments on a broad democratic basis have managed colonial relations most successfully. They tend to the general conclusion that only democratic powers should be entrusted with dependencies.

But the same considerations lead still further to a conclusion of immediate importance. Parliamentary institutions favour good colonial administration because they allow the emergence of new interests, and compel the public discussion of colonial issues in terms of right and wrong. In the past colonial policy has come into the foreground only with the emergence of some new claimants to a share in the profits of colonial rule, and only at such times has the moral aspect of colonial rule attracted widespread interest and been vehemently debated. But, in the ordinary course of democratic evolution, Parliament comes to represent a people with a single solid interest in the management of colonial affairs, so that economic and political control are once again concentrated in the same hands, and Parliament can no longer function effectively to keep economic interests within due bounds. Notwithstanding the vast extent of the British Empire and the tremendous responsibilities of Parliament 'in the period between 1934 and 1939 the House of Commons debated colonial affairs on (only) nine occasions, of which four were devoted to Palestine'.[2] Burma may attract the attention of Parliament once in ten years, or not so often. It is true that, under the stress of war, as during the war of 1914, there has been a revival of interest in colonial affairs; as the

[1] Porter, C., *Pacific Affairs*, Sept. 1943, p. 270; Pelzer, K. J., *Economic Survey of the Pacific Area* (1941), p. 41.

[2] King-Hall, S., *Britain's Third Chance* (1943), p. 142; *Colonial Review*, 1944, p. 198; *Hansard*, 12 Dec. 1944, p. 1086; *Netherlands India*, p. 229.

Colonial Secretary remarked, with no cynical intention, Colonial Governors 'are only too anxious...to "cash in" on the present good will'. It is significant that among all parties there is general agreement on the main lines of colonial policy. Not infrequently, one may notice suggestions that colonial affairs, like foreign affairs, should be outside party strife as matters of common national concern. All parties look forward to the attainment of colonial autonomy on the basis of responsible government; all regard the multiplication of welfare services as the key to responsible government; and all assume that the provision of capital is a condition of tropical welfare. Yet the provision of capital favours economic progress rather than welfare; the multiplication of welfare services hinders the growth of responsible government, and the insistence on welfare as a condition of responsible government implies the indefinite postponement of autonomy. Parliament represents a solid national interest in the management of colonial affairs and, by ceasing to be an impartial tribunal in which rival claimants to the profits of colonial rule can refer their case to an indifferent majority, it can no longer discharge the function of dissociating economic and political control. Only before some supernational tribunal can the moral aspects of colonial rule be sifted, and only by constructing international machinery to supervise colonial relations can we fortify ourselves against temptation to maintain practical control over dependent peoples even when announcing that the goal of policy is to set them free.

3. International Collaboration

It would appear then that the logic of history requires some form of international supervision over colonial relations. Under native rule, custom preserved social order in the tropics, but insecurely and at the cost of progress. Clerical rule allowed a higher standard of welfare, but finally collapsed because it identified welfare with the Church and failed to provide adequately for economic progress. Under Company rule the subordination of political control to economic interest confined both progress and welfare within narrow limits. The transfer of political control to parliamentary government encouraged a more rapid exploitation of the material resources of the tropics and also the exploitation, the *mise en valeur*, of their human resources so far as economic development required; but the enhancement of native welfare was still conditioned by economic factors, and these set limits to economic progress. Ultimately, under parliamentary control, the whole people of the colonial power comes to occupy a position similar to that of the shareholders in a chartered company, and this sets up a new and more formidable barrier to progress and welfare in the tropics. Just as formerly the personal interest of the shareholders in chartered companies came into conflict with national welfare, so now does the national interest of colonial powers come into conflict with world welfare. Precedent and analogy suggest that the barrier will eventually be broken down, if not by peaceful means then by revolution or war. But barriers of interest do not collapse merely by the operation of logic. Some new contending interest must be brought up to force a breach. In the United States the dairy farmers in their own interest led the assault. In Britain all the ranks of economic life, the cotton trade, shipping, heavy industry, finance, labour and the professional classes have been called up successively to man the citadel of private interest, and no one remains to lead the forces of humanitarianism. That is even truer of the Netherlands. The chartered companies of the late nineteenth century surrendered control over their possessions, because they were no longer profitable and yielded no dividends to the shareholders. It might seem that colonial powers would similarly relinquish their hold voluntarily on unprofitable dependencies. But national interests cannot be audited by methods of accountancy, and colonial powers are naturally reluctant to hazard the profit and prestige that accrue from colonial possessions, and even if these are a doubtful asset to the nation as a whole, they may still be profitable to particular interests, which will vehemently oppose any relaxation of control. Yet the defects of existing colonial relations in respect of progress, prosperity and peace, increasingly compel attention.

That national interest may hinder the material progress of dependencies was recognized at the first great international conference on colonial affairs held at Berlin in 1884-5, when the powers laid down the principle that colonial rule must be justified by economic development. This decision was one factor stimulating the Dutch to extend effective administration to the Outer Provinces of Netherlands India, then still neglected. At the same time, from about 1870 and especially after 1900, capitalist activities showed a rapidly increasing disregard of political boundaries; private individuals invested more freely in foreign enterprises, local enterprises reached out to even wider regions, and large enterprises linked up with one another in world-wide trusts and combines. One instance was the expansion of British tea-planting from Assam to Sumatra. Dutch prospectors in the nineties obtained British capital in London for exploiting the oilfields of Netherlands India. In the new century a rate war between British and Dutch oil interests led to an agreement delimiting their spheres. These are merely illustrations of a general trend. A more ambitious project took shape during the inter-war period in the Stevenson Rubber Restriction scheme. But these developments were economic rather than political, extranational rather than international. Though capitalists may know most about the dependencies of their own country, capital knows no country and follows the line of least resistance; trade follows the flag, but only so far as the national flag offers greater security or other advantages. Capital and commerce are impatient of political authority. The depression of the thirties changed the situation. Extranational control gave place to international control, and the production of numerous tropical products, such as tin, tea and rubber, was brought under control through the national Governments concerned. International collaboration was found necessary for the security of profits.

Western labour naturally responded to extranational capitalist activities by seeking to protect its interests against the competition of cheap tropical labour. The consolidation of the labour front, however, was more difficult than the consolidation of capitalist interests and necessitated action through the state, international collaboration, political and not merely economic. This first became effective with the foundation of the International Labour Office in 1919. It soon appeared that the regulation of tropical labour was in the interest of large-scale European enterprise as against non-European capitalist interests, and western capital joined hands with labour to secure international co-operation in support of welfare. Epidemics among men, crops and cattle have no more respect than capital for national flags and boundaries, and the regulation of such matters was also recognized as needing international co-operation. Thus the decade following the creation of the International Labour Office saw a very active multiplication of international agreements in the name of welfare and the cause of progress. But in this matter also the depression of the thirties marked a new stage. For the international combinations to regulate production and marketing were so successful from the standpoint of producers that they aroused protests from capital interests representing the standpoint of consumers. The American motor business, for example, could not disregard attempts to maintain rubber prices at an artificially high rate. This introduced a new element in international collaboration: the adoption of devices to represent large consumers on the international committees established to regulate production. Thus practical men of affairs were increasingly insistent on international collaboration not only for safeguarding profits, but also for promoting welfare as a concomitant and condition of progress; and tropical conditions in respect of employment, and the regulation of epidemics and other matters came to be recognized as of importance to the West.

This new development reacted on colonial administration in a way that is often overlooked. World welfare requires higher standards of hygiene and public instruction in the tropics than tropical peoples themselves regard as necessary. Hence one of the leading notes of modern colonial policy is a growing tenderness towards compulsion, ostensibly in the interest of native welfare: compulsion to improve native agriculture, to grow export or subsistence crops as the economic conjuncture may require, to eat such food as current expert opinion deems nutritious, to build and use latrines, to take such precautions against disease as are fashionable in the West, to send their children to the elementary school, and so on. Most of these things were originally humanitarian visions; most of them are desirable and are still supported by humanitarian sentiment; but the driving force is western interest. For these and many other things that western opinion thinks beneficial, colonial powers are increasingly held responsible. So far as the measures are effective the benefit accrues to the outside world in general; but the odium of enforcing welfare legislation and of raising taxes to provide the necessary funds, falls on the colonial power immediately responsible. Except so far as mitigated by corruption, welfare regulations foster disaffection and unrest, which on occasion has had to be repressed by force of arms. Prudence requires that the colonial power responsible for enforcing welfare measures shall be able to appeal for international support, and the common interest of the western world requires that the necessary support, moral and if necessary material, shall be accorded. Welfare, no less than progress, or rather, because it is a condition of progress, requires international collaboration in colonial affairs.

The dominant consideration however in arousing international concern for colonial affairs has been security. So long as colonial powers gain, or are believed to gain, peculiar advantages from their dependencies, other powers will envy these advantages, and the colonial powers must hold what they have in the manner of the strong man armed. Colonial rule endangers peace. It was the danger to peace that brought about the Berlin Conference in 1884. The development of industry in Europe during the nineteenth century caused a demand for larger supplies of tropical produce, and for tropical markets as a vent for home manufactures. Hence arose from 1870 onwards the 'scramble for Africa', and the Berlin Conference sought to prevent war over colonial issues by confining international rivalry in Africa to 'the peaceful competition of trade and industry'. But competition in trade and industry does not make for mutual good will between the competitors. Colonial rivalry grew keener with the anticipated 'break-up of China'. One source of contention was the reaction against free trade. Britain, secure in its industrial equipment and world-wide mercantile marine, and Holland, with its command over important tropical products, could for some time afford to keep an open door and admit free access to their dependencies, but other powers, less fortunately situated, wanted colonies as close markets for their protected industries. This international rivalry for the possession of dependencies was in part responsible for the outbreak of war in 1914. Among the numerous reactions of the 'war to end war' was a new stimulus to the idea of international trusteeship in respect of 'backward peoples, not yet able to stand by themselves in the conditions of the modern world'. This found expression in the Mandates System, by which the colonies of the defeated powers were distributed among the victors to be administered in accordance with mandates from the League of Nations. The arrangements then sanctioned aggravated instead of allaying colonial rivalry. Germany wanted to regain its colonies; Italy was ambitious to extend its empire; Japan aspired to political and economic control over the Far East. Here again the depression of the thirties marks a turning-point. Colonial powers and their dependencies alike lost their accustomed markets, and tried to restore prosperity by quotas and other devices. This concentrated attention on the advantages of colonial rule, and exacerbated colonial rivalry, and, as the conflict of interest between the 'haves' and 'have-nots' grew more acute, the powers lined up into the groups which made war possible in 1939. Then the collapse of western rule in the Tropical Far East in 1942 emphasized another danger to security, the resentment of colonial relations among the inhabitants of tropical dependencies. Inevitably a colonial power is linked up with one section in the plural society of the tropics; it has especially close associations with the

European capitalist section, and naturally incurs the suspicion of governing the country in the interest of that section. Political and economic control rest in the same hands. Only by dissociating itself so far as possible from direct political control can the colonial power justify itself to non-European elements in a dependency as representing the general interest. By recognizing some form of international supervision over colonial relations, colonial powers can both mitigate the rivalry of other powers and allay the suspicions of their subjects, and by the same means they strengthen themselves to resist any challenge to their rule. International supervision reinforces their moral and material strength.

Thus the logic of economic circumstance confirms the logic of history. The old East India Companies served a useful purpose in their time, but times changed and they outlived their usefulness. From the wider standpoint of the nation they became an intolerable nuisance by engendering corruption in home politics; they furnished a justification for reform by going bankrupt; and they stimulated a moral impulse to reform by their oppression of their subjects. Similarly at the present time, the relations between colonial powers and their dependencies have created an intolerable nuisance from the wider standpoint of world welfare; they no longer provide adequately for economic progress, and they have failed to secure the standard of welfare among dependent peoples that the modern world requires. Many recent pronouncements show that we have once again reached a stage where idealism is justified by common sense, and visions of harmonious international co-operation in colonial affairs have come within the field of practical politics.

The public acceptance of the new policy may perhaps be dated from the Atlantic Charter of 1941, which affirmed the principle of international responsibility for the welfare of all nations, notably in points 5 and 6, laying down that the signatory powers

'desire to bring about the fullest collaboration between all nations in the economic field, with the object of securing for all improved labour standards, economic advancement and social security.

'After the final destruction of Nazi tyranny they hope to see established a peace which will afford to all nations the means of dwelling in safety within their own boundaries, and which will afford the assurance that all men in all the lands may live out their lives in freedom from war and want.'

'Backward areas', the Charter implies, 'are intolerable, and prejudice the good relations between nations. Not only do the demands of security compel us to assume responsibility for the less fortunate colonial territories, but for economic reasons as well they must be integrated as healthy partners into a world economic system.'[1] This view has met with at least partial acceptance by the British Government. In March 1943 the Colonial Secretary, while emphasizing his belief that the administration of the British colonies must continue to be the sole responsibility of Britain, regarded close international co-operation as essential. A few days later this interpretation was reaffirmed by the Prime Minister. The principle of international responsibility obtained further recognition at the United Nations Conference on Food and Agriculture held at Hot Springs in May–June 1943. This was recommended in Resolution xxiv:

1. That the governments and authorities here represented, by virtue of their determination to achieve freedom from want for all peoples in all lands, affirm the principle of mutual responsibility and coordinated action:

(a) To promote the full and most advantageous employment of their own and all other people, and a general advance in the standards of living, thereby providing for an increase in both production and purchasing power;

(b) To promote the uninterrupted development and most advantageous use of agricultural and other material resources for the establishment of an equitable balance between agriculture and industry in the interest of all;

(c) To secure for agriculture the stimulus of additional purchasing power through the sound development of industry;

(d) To assist in the achievement of these ends by all appropriate means, including the supply of capital, equipment and technical skill;

(e) To maintain an equilibrium in balances of payments, and to achieve the orderly management of currencies and exchange;

(f) To improve the methods and reduce the cost of distribution in international trade;

(g) As an integral part of this programme, to reduce barriers of every kind to international trade, and to eliminate all forms of discriminatory restrictions thereon, including inequitable policies in international transportation, as effectively and rapidly as possible.

2. That these governments and authorities take, individually and in concert, whether by conference or otherwise, all necessary measures, both domestic and international, to secure the application of this principle and the attainment of these objectives.

[1] *International Action and the Colonies* (1943), p. 17.

Official approval of the policy of common action was carried a stage further by Britain in a pronouncement of the Colonial Secretary in July 1943.

'Developments of modern transport and modern communications have brought together vast areas which before were widely separated. Many of their problems today are common problems and can only be solved in co-operation, for problems of security, of transport, of health, etc. transcend the boundaries of political units. H.M.G. would therefore welcome the establishment of machinery which would enable such problems to be discussed and to be solved by common efforts. What they have in mind is the possibility of establishing Commissions for certain regions. These Commissions would comprise not only the States with Colonial Territories in the region, but also other States which have in the region a major strategic or economic interest. While each State would remain responsible for the administration of its own territory, such a Commission would provide effective and permanent machinery for consultation and collaboration so that the States concerned might work together to promote the well being of the Colonial territories. An important consideration in designing the machinery of each Commission will be to give the people of the Colonial territories an opportunity to be associated with its work.'

Thus the principle of international collaboration has been accepted.

4. International Supervision and Autonomy

In the near future, then, we are likely to see experiments in international supervision over colonial relations. On certain matters there seems to be general agreement. It is commonly accepted that international collaboration must be organized regionally; that, for example, there should be a Regional Council for the Tropical Far East, comprising the lands from Formosa down to Netherlands India and from Burma to the Philippines. There seems also to be general agreement that any such Regional Council would, at least in the first instance, be merely a local agent charged with exercising on behalf of a World Council or other global organization some measure of supervision over the political Governments within that region, and with offering advice and assistance to those Governments if they should consult it.

At a first glance there would seem ground to welcome such an organization as tending to separate political from economic control. But there is reason to apprehend that it might enable economic forces to act more freely by liberating them from such restraint as still exists. The British tradition of respect for law, the Dutch tradition of care for native custom, are peculiarly national traditions; in all such matters an international organ would represent merely the highest common factor among the constituent members and fail to reach so high a standard as any single colonial power. A society of nations tends to resemble a plural society with only economic interests in common, and this tendency gains strength in proportion to its comprehensiveness. Although British, Dutch, French and Americans all have their own peculiar ethics, they also have in common those principles of Christianity from which the West has learned its way of life. But what have they in common with Moslems, Hindus and Buddhists, with Turks and Indians, Burmese, Chinese, Japanese? In the development of the tropics by western enterprise, casual labour suffers most because no single employer is responsible for protecting it (even in his own interest) from economic forces. Similarly, under an international body, colonial peoples may well be more exposed to economic forces than under the protection of a single power; at the same time they will be less able to offer resistance to the combined forces of the modern world than to a single Government, and will have no court of appeal in world opinion such as denounced the rule of Leopold in the Congo. It is the interest of colonial powers rather than of dependencies that has brought international collaboration within the range of practical politics; these powers will carry most weight in the deliberations of any international council, and it may well prove that with the growth of international collaboration, colonial policy will be dominated even more than in the past by purely economic material considerations. 'The main objective of Regional Councils', it has been said, 'should be to speed up material development.'[1] Dutch Liberals during the mid-nineteenth century drew glowing pictures of the future of Java when State enterprise should be replaced by private enterprise, but the result was merely to increase the number of shareholders in the exploitation of the colonial estate. Similarly a regional council may do no more than increase the number of shareholders in the vast enterprise of developing the tropics as a business concern.

International supervision will not in itself affect the working of economic laws. The economic process of the survival of the cheapest will still operate, perhaps even more effectively. Merchants dealing in native produce want to obtain it as cheaply as possible. Employers

[1] Lord Listowel, quoted *Colonial Review*, June 1944, p 166

want cheap labour. Western shareholders want dividends. If economic development arouses native disaffection, western interests lie in keeping the people weak by depriving them of arms and by fostering divisions in a plural society, in security rather than in peace. In the name of welfare employers approve reforms that will produce healthier, more intelligent, more efficient and more docile employees; such reforms appeal also to western labour as likely to diminish the threat of cheap oriental competition. Importers will support plans to increase the buying power of natives. All these factors will operate in the future as in the past, and will tend in some measure and among some classes to raise the standard of living, so far as economic efficiency requires. There may be some appearance or illusion of enhancement of individual material welfare, but this will remain an illusion unless there is an enhancement of social welfare, and, if international supervision is to promote social welfare, it must aim first at promoting colonial autonomy.

It is not improbable that in such a regional council there would be some opposition to measures purporting to endow dependencies with political autonomy. In the past such measures have often, if not usually, been resisted by the European section of the plural society, even although the political reforms have in fact strengthened its control over economic activities. This section would exercise great influence over the deliberations of the council, and would probably still oppose political reforms, until convinced that they were propitious, or at least innocuous, to its interests. But it is not sufficient that international supervision should be directed towards effecting reforms in political machinery, because this, whatever its design, works only in accordance with the will directing it, and, in the absence of a common social will, the machinery would still be directed by economic forces in the interest of economic progress. In order to bring these forces under control, international supervision must be directed towards making dependencies capable of autonomy, and this will necessitate restrictions on capitalist activities that will certainly encounter resistance. There is then a very real danger that the regional council may develop into an unholy alliance, enforcing more rigorously than at present the economic and political control of the West over the tropics.

In numerous suggestions for international collaboration in colonial affairs, this gloomy prospect is foreshadowed. They dwell on the value of such collaboration in promoting security, economic progress and welfare, the kind of welfare that is needed for economic efficiency. At the Colonial Conference in Canada, Lord Hailey, in advocating the constitution of a Pacific Council, touched on these points and further emphasized the need for charging it with 'the periodic review of the progress made in the promotion of self-governing institutions in the dependencies and in the improvement in their standard of living'. But all the evidence that we have studied goes to show that in the plural society of tropical dependencies, western self-governing institutions foster division and unrest, and hinder the attainment of self-government; and, further, that an improvement in the general standard of living can be attained only through self-government. That the regional council should be charged with the periodic review of the progress made towards self-government would certainly be useful, but it may well be doubted whether a council, representing in the main colonial powers, would seriously attempt to endow dependencies with the reality of independence, or to promote social welfare. If, as is only too possible, the regional council aims merely at constructing the machinery of western self-governing institutions in tropical society, instead of attempting to reintegrate and consolidate society so that it shall be capable of independence, and is content to mitigate the ill-effects of economic development on individuals instead of trying to promote general welfare by social education, it will do more harm than good.

Yet history allows of hope. We have seen that parliamentary institutions have favoured colonial welfare because they compel rival economic interests to appeal to national and moral considerations in order to attract support. The maxim of divide and rule works both ways. If it is easier to keep people in subjection by dividing them, it should be easier for subject peoples to gain their independence when there is division among their rulers. In a regional council there would be a wide diversity of interest. Some members might wish to remove all barriers to trade; others would object to flooding tropical markets with cheap imports to the prejudice of western manufactures. Some members would advocate welfare measures enabling western enterprise to pay low wages; others, more sensitive to competition from cheap labour, would favour high wages. There would be contrary views as to the importance of protecting tropical industries. Some members would wish to promote welfare by compulsion, but the colonial power immediately responsible for enforcing welfare measures, but responsible also for maintaining peace and quiet, would be more alive to the need for fostering social demand as a sounder, if a slower, way to welfare. In these and other such differences of opinion both parties would look for support to members with little economic interest in the point at issue, and the principle of national autonomy would emerge as a criterion transcending economic values that all would recognize as valid. There are then grounds for hoping that international supervision would promote colonial autonomy, and a council which adopted this as its basic principle and main objective could do more than any single colonial power towards this end.

5. REGIONAL COUNCILS

Functions. The mere institution of such a council would indeed go far towards removing one of the main obstacles to colonial autonomy. In the plural society of tropical dependencies the Government is to some extent, and looks even more largely, identified with the European section of the community. This naturally breeds suspicion among the native community, and hampers the Government even when aiming to promote native interests. The acceptance of international supervision would tend to separate economic and political control, and would be a gesture of goodwill. The European community might object to any effective international supervision as prejudicial to their economic interests but, if the goal of policy be the creation of a common social will, it is necessary to impose due limitations on economic activities and especially on those of foreign capital. Another objection sometimes put forward is that the acceptance of international supervision would be derogatory to national prestige. But colonial powers have always claimed to intend the welfare of their dependencies, and their critics have usually been sceptical about these claims. A system of international supervision would enable colonial powers to justify their claims by bringing their achievements to the notice of a public body, and this would enhance and not diminish their prestige.

It is probably by enabling colonial powers to demonstrate their achievements that a regional council could do most to promote the welfare of dependencies. Many or most colonial problems are common to colonial relations in general, and they have most in common within definite geographical areas such as the Tropical Far East, which are marked out by nature as appropriate units for a regional council. At present each colonial power tries to solve its problem separately for each dependency. Little or nothing is known of what is being attempted elsewhere for the promotion of literacy, the improvement of rural hygiene, the prevention of agricultural indebtedness, or any of the many other difficult problems arising out of the impact of the modern West on tropical society. Every Government could learn much from the achievements of the others, and no less perhaps from their mistakes. A regional council would gradually accumulate a fund of knowledge and experience from which all the countries of the region, whether colonial or semi-colonial, could benefit.

If the council were required as its primary objective to aim at making the dependencies capable of independence, it would review and report on the progress in respect of social, economic and political reintegration. It would examine the precautions against social disintegration, the methods of social education adopted to remedy the evils consequent on atomization, and the steps taken to bring under the control of social will the economic forces acting on tropical society from within. It would study also the progress towards economic reintegration. It would examine too the reports from western enterprises showing what they had done to substitute local for imported labour and to train natives of the country for technical posts and for the management and direction of their business; and reports from the Governments concerned, explaining what assistance they had rendered in this matter and what supervision they had exercised over the economic forces impinging on the country from outside through the activities of western enterprise. Again in respect of political reintegration it would examine what was being done to foster a common social will among all sections of the community and, on the programme suggested in the last chapter, the progress accomplished through dual government, semi-colonial government, and conditional independence to complete autonomy. Also it would examine the position with reference to representation of the various communities, and to the expression of the common social will in a 'responsible' legislature.

So long as any form of dual government might be needed the council could be especially helpful in resolving differences between the representative of the colonial power and the representative of the people. Such differences would inevitably be not infrequent in the future as they have been between governors and legislatures in the past. In the past such differences have, if necessary, been decided by the colonial power, but a regional council should be able to intervene with greater impartiality and with a more intimate and wider knowledge of the circumstances. Moreover, in the past, such differences have usually been evaded by abstaining from necessary but difficult and contentious legislation. With a regional council to enquire why necessary measures were neglected, it would be more difficult to adopt the easy course of leaving economic forces in control by doing nothing.

The most prolific source of difficulties in the administration of tropical dependencies is inherent in their character as plural societies. So long as minor communities exist which do not accept the common tie of nationality or are not regarded as full citizens, special arrangements are necessary to protect their interests without encouraging particularism. It is with reference to such questions that differences between the members of the dual Government are likely to be most frequent and acute. But it is also in such matters that a regional council, dealing with similar problems in a number of cognate plural societies, could give the greatest help. In general it may be claimed that the constitution of a regional council would provoke emulation for the enhancement of welfare throughout the region, and at the same time facilitate the imposition of sanctions on governments and peoples which failed to keep step with the general advance towards full membership in modern world society.

Constitution. In projects of a new world order one often finds elaborate provision for constitutional forms, with little reference to the functions that the machinery will discharge. But, as we have already insisted, the sound principle of social engineering is first to consider the functions and then to devise the simplest machinery that will perform them adequately. We have assumed that, in the first instance, a regional council will act as the agent of a world society to receive reports from the Governments within its region and to offer them assistance and advice. It would appear sufficient therefore to appoint a permanent representative of the world society as president and chief executive of the regional council and to hold annual or other periodical meetings of representatives of the governments concerned. Probably various private bodies would soon press for occasional or permanent representation, and the organization would grow more elaborate. Almost certainly the regional council would soon go further than the passive acceptance and consideration of reports, and would develop an inspecting staff. The various Governments also, as they came to value the advice and assistance of the council, would desire fuller and more permanent representation. But

it is much easier to devise machinery than to make it work satisfactorily, and the less elaborate the constitution of the council is to
start with; the more likely it is to develop on sound lines.

6. BURMA, NETHERLANDS INDIA AND TROPICAL ECONOMY

Our attempt to see the problems of Burma in due perspective against
a wider background has led us through a far-ranging enquiry into
various aspects of colonial administration. This voyage of exploration
through tropical jungles may well seem unduly venturesome. Pronouncements on colonial policy may be digested in the study, 'but
policy is a matter not only of purpose but of performance, and it
must be judged by its operation in practice'.[1] One fact impressed on
us, however, by our experience is that the material for framing a
judgment on colonial practice is both insufficient and inaccurate. The
statistical material which a detached observer requires for an objective judgment is defective, and too often misleading. Even in
official circles, owing to the general lack of continuity in tropical
administration, few can know what is happening within their charges
until some incident provokes an enquiry, which not infrequently is
mainly concerned to gloze the facts. Moreover in British (though not
in Dutch) colonial administration, the tradition of official reticence,
valuable in Europe but disastrous in the tropics, seals the lips of those
best acquainted with affairs, and precludes informed and constructive
discussion while leaving the administration a target for ignorant and
malicious criticism.

Nevertheless our enquiry does point to certain general conclusions
of considerable interest and importance. For various reasons conditions in Burma and Netherlands India are especially instructive.
Social studies differ from those of natural science by the greater
difficulty of isolating significant factors; it is impossible to control
experiments under the conditions of the laboratory. But here we
have experimental conditions to our hand. Burma is an extreme
example of development by native enterprise under direct rule, and
Netherlands India of development by western enterprise under indirect rule. In other respects they are typical of the tropics in general.
Both have come suddenly into contact with the modern world. When
Europeans first arrived in British India, they had little superiority in
their command over material resources, and in some respects India

[1] *Britain and Her Dependencies*, p. 5.

was in advance of Europe. Modern India grew up with modern Europe. But Burma and, in effect, Netherlands India came into contact with the West only after the Industrial Revolution had transformed the relations between East and West; and it was not until after the opening of the Suez Canal that their contact with the West became so intimate as to affect the general masses of the people in their daily life. Again, British India has been protected against the solvent influence of economic forces by the shield of caste; Burma and Netherlands India have lacked this safeguard against social disintegration. Similarly the peoples of Africa and of the tropics generally have been brought suddenly and recently into contact with the modern world, and their social order, lacking the cement of caste, is readily liable to erosion.

In Burma the native Government refused to enter the modern world. This was a defiance of world society which carried its own penalty, and British intervention may fairly be claimed as an act of social justice. In the event British rule has destroyed the Burmese social order; in opening up Burma to the world it has purged the abuses of Burmese rule, but has swept away good and bad together. Possibly nothing less catastrophic would have cleared the way for reconstruction. But the destruction of an ancient civilization, slowly built up through long ages by the good will of successive generations, is an offence against humanity. Needs be that offences come, but those who, even as the instrument of social justice, destroy a civilization, thereby assume responsibilities which they can discharge only by building a new and more highly organized civilization in its place and, if they fail in this, must pay their reckoning with Nemesis. Doubtless in Africa western rule brings greater benefits and does less harm, because native civilization was on a lower plane than in eastern lands. It has frequently been claimed that British colonial administration shows to best advantage in dealing with primitive and backward peoples, and that Englishmen have been uniquely successful in dealing with 'the unspoilt native'.[1] But it is in the later stages that colonial rule is tested; the tree is known by its fruit. The same factors are operative in Africa as in Asia. African dependencies are now in much the same stage as Burma when, superficially, all seemed to be going well—up to about 1880 in Lower Burma and 1910 in Upper Burma. Of the dependencies colonized by western capital during the nineteenth century, Burma and Netherlands India are among the

[1] *Colonial Review*, Dec. 1943, p. 103; 1946, Cmd. Col. 198, p. 26.

oldest, and would seem accordingly to point a line to future developments in African dependencies which are a generation, or even two generations, younger.

In framing a balance sheet of tropical administration we must certainly place economic development to the credit side of the account. It is well that tropical lands and peoples should furnish their full contribution to the welfare of the world. With good reason we believe in the economic development of dependencies. We believe in it not merely because we find it profitable, yet the fact that we profit by it calls for a careful scrutiny of the results, lest the dazzle of gold should blind our eyes. That the development of tropical dependencies is profitable to colonial powers is no ground for condemning it. One may claim rather that it is sound as an economic proposition just because it is right in principle. 'Philanthropy and 5 %' is no mere catchword, for philanthropy which does not pay at least 5 % (though not necessarily to the philanthropist) is probably muddle-headed sentiment. In any case western men of business will not be restrained from developing the resources of the tropics wherever the material reward seems likely to repay their labour. Not infrequently, though perhaps less frequently than a generation back, administrators, civil servants, assume credit for the benefits of western rule in the tropics while holding business men responsible for its evil consequences. But business men come to the tropics on business. It is their function to develop the material resources of the tropics, and they must needs do it on business lines or they will be put out of business. It is as idle to blame the man of business, western or oriental, for conducting his business in the manner which the environment demands, as it is to blame the moneylender for entangling cultivators in debt, or the Javanese for breeding too freely and for economic apathy, or the Burman for the growth of crime, corruption and clerical unrest. These things are naturally engendered by the environment.

In western homogeneous societies the business man accepts the social obligations of his environment; and social will, enforced and reinforced by law, compels any who would disregard them to restrict their activities within the limits of social welfare. In the plural society of the tropics, the business man must still keep on the safe side of the law, but the law has no sanction in a common social will and in great measure reflects and subserves business interests. If the activities of the business man result in the depopulation of wide areas, the deterioration of subsistence conditions owing to the migration of labour, the social evils due to the removal from their families of large numbers of adult males and the difficult situations created by the aggregation of industrial populations divorced from the traditional controls of social life; if they lead to debt, agrarian distress and crime, or to over-population and economic apathy; if they entail the narrowing of native life, the restriction of native economic activities, the decay of native religions and cultural values and the degeneration and dis-appearance of the arts and crafts in which these values found ex-pression—these things are not his business. His duty, not only to his shareholders but to society, is to run his business on the most efficient and most profitable lines that the environment allows. This, however anti-social its effect in a tropical environment, is his social function. He is merely performing his functions in an environment which favours instead of restraining acquisition, exploitation and other anti-social effects of economic forces. These evils are inherent in a dis-tinctive tropical economy where, in a plural society, the social order is transformed into 'a capitalist structure with the business concern as subject, far more typical of capitalism than one can imagine in the so-called capitalist countries which have grown slowly out of the past and are still bound to it by a hundred roots'.

In politics as in law, men must be held to intend the natural con-sequences of their actions. The early Liberals could not easily foresee the further consequences of their doctrine. Adam Smith taught the world that economic freedom was the key alike to progress and wel-fare. In the world of Adam Smith that was very largely true, since he could take for granted the stable foundations of society. But in the tropics the Liberals built their house on sand. It had no founda-tions and had to be buttressed from outside by the command and, if necessary, the exercise of military force, force so commanding that there was rarely need to exercise it. Experience has made us wiser than our fathers. We have learned that it is necessary, in our own interest, to impose restrictions on economic freedom. We claim also to be better than our fathers, with higher ideals in tropical administra-tion; and we impose restrictions in the name of a moral obligation to promote native welfare. Yet we very readily come 'down from the region of moral obligation to the more familiar ground in which the issues that are debated, the standards that are applied, are those of our own domestic political life'.[1] Whereas formerly in the nineteenth

[1] Lord Hailey, quoted *Colonial Review*, March 1942, p. 155.

century economic freedom was congenial to British interests, now what may be termed Fabianism is congenial to the interests of colonial powers in general. We are content to preach material comfort, where the Liberals promised freedom and Spain salvation.

Modern colonial policy promulgates welfare measures to counter-act the ill-effects of economic development, but looks to pay for these measures by injecting capital to expedite development. Such measures can be justified to common sense on the ground that they are profitable and to the humanitarian conscience as instruments of welfare. Common sense and common humanity require that tropical regions should be efficiently developed by mitigating the natural evil consequences of development. But experience has demonstrated that economic and social services, otherwise than in response to a native demand for welfare, function chiefly if not solely to make enterprise more efficient, and also more profitable, by re-lieving it of charges that, in default of subventions, it would have to bear in its own interest; and the efficiency of enterprise is questionable where it must be subsidized from the public treasury or from private charity instead of bearing its own charges. One repeatedly finds measures described as generous when they compel natives of the tropics to pay for education, or sanitation, or agricultural or veterinary precautions which, however desirable in the interest of commerce or of the colonial power or of world welfare, the people themselves do not appreciate, and which serve in fact merely or mainly to enhance the efficiency and profits of western enterprise. Colonial powers feel even more virtuous when they contribute to the cost of colonial development and welfare, incidentally subsidizing home capital and labour. In the name of welfare, for example, we vote subsidies to aviation that will expedite the process of colonial development. Socialists would go so far as to equip dependencies 'altruistically' at British expense with a complete outfit of railways, irrigation works, schools, hospitals and so on. A bridge over the Zambesi, com-ments Lord Wedgwood, means to them work for the unemployed on Tees side.[1] These things may be good business for the British taxpayer (so far as the money is not wasted), for we all have a finger in the colonial pie. But they are not altruistic. They serve merely to speed up the development of the colonial estate and en-hance its value as a business concern to the colonial power. Once again, as so often in past colonial history, we seem to hear little Jack

[1] Lord Wedgwood, *Testament to Democracy* (n.d. 1942), p. 148.

Horner exclaiming, 'What a good boy am I!' as he pulls out a few more plums.

It is inevitable and desirable that backward regions shall be developed. Welfare measures are needed to oil the wheels of economic progress and to mitigate the consequences. Yet welfare measures which lubricate the machinery of production but have no root among the people multiply the complexity of social life, adding more stories to the alien superstructure, and there is a danger that the lubricant may turn out to be nitro-glycerine. If, then, statesmen responsible for colonial affairs sincerely treat the welfare of subject peoples as of paramount importance, they will make it an object of colonial policy to moderate the pace of progress, so far as circumstances permit.

Formerly the rate of progress was retarded by the difficulty of getting anything done, and it has been claimed, not unjustly, that the most important function of officials in the tropics is to put a brake on progress. This view was tenable in the nineteenth century and the days of *laissez-faire*, when progress consisted in removing obstructions that official inertia helped to conserve. But the modern solidarity of interest in colonial development among all classes in a democratic colonial power, however philosophically it may accept restrictions imposed in the name of welfare on dependent peoples, is impatient of restrictions which it does not recognize as necessary to its own welfare. Progress is more purposeful; a merely negative policy of obstruction is no longer sufficient, and there is a growing urgency to reconcile progress and welfare. It is important then to recognize, as our enquiry shows, that progress is not a condition of welfare, but welfare a condition of progress; the problem is human, not mechanical, and compulsory progress bears fruit in disaffection and unrest. If we are to reconcile progress and welfare in the tropics we must organize a demand for welfare among the people.

Now, if tropical peoples are to be enabled to promote their own welfare, it is necessary to create an environment in which they enjoy the requisite status, a sufficient motive and adequate means to do so. The promotion of welfare is possible only in an autonomous society. Liberals obeyed a healthy instinct in placing autonomy in the forefront of their programme. But they thought that economic freedom would lead automatically to political advancement, and introduced the machinery of western political institutions, trusting that by some inherent magic form would take effect in function. Experience has demonstrated their mistake. We know by now that economic freedom may, and in the tropics ordinarily does result in economic bondage to the moneylender or employer, and that, in social as in civil engineering, form does not give birth to function. Western political institutions have proved disappointing in the tropics, and consequently we now impose conditions on political advancement, postponing autonomy until some remote future when by welfare measures the people shall have been endowed with the qualities requisite for working western institutions. But welfare is the product of autonomy, and not autonomy of welfare. We have seen that the failure of western institutions in the tropics must be ascribed chiefly to the environment, the plural society of tropical economy in which the political institutions of western homogeneous society are unworkable. In such an environment western political institutions aggravate the internal tension in a society divided against itself, and are inconsistent with self-government; like welfare measures, they are perverted into an instrument of economic progress. In its political as in its economic aspect, modern colonial policy is based on the same fallacy as the older Liberal policy; it aims at adapting tropical society to western principles instead of adapting western principles to the intricate confederation of native and alien elements constituting tropical society.

Here then in brief are certain principles of tropical economy suggested by our enquiry into colonial policy and practice. In the western world during the past three hundred years, economic forces have been increasingly liberated from the restraint of custom and transferred to the control of reason. In fact, custom still retains great force, but we are apt to underrate its power because it is native to us and unnoticeable, like the air we breathe. Moreover, the reason by which we exercise control over economic forces is not the natural reason impelling man to seek his individual advantage regardless of other considerations, but what may be termed the social reason, which accepts as valid the obligations and restrictions commonly acknowledged by the peoples of modern Christendom. It is only in international relations, and in these only within limits (though, it would seem, expanding limits) that the natural law prevails. Through its vastly greater power over the material world consequent on the freer play of economic forces, the West has come to exercise dominion over the tropics in economic and, over the greater part, political affairs. The first effect of this is to expose the fabric of tropical society to the solvent influence of forces acting on it both from outside and from within. Economic forces are liberated from the customary restraints which preserved the native society from dissolution, and in the new colonial society the various elements recognize no common principle of social obligation by which the newly liberated forces may be brought under control. Thus, by a process of natural evolution, there comes into existence a plural society dominated by economic forces, and functioning as a business concern for the profit of economic enterprise instead of as a political organ for the promotion of the common welfare. Colonial policy may aim at promoting material welfare or political emancipation, but in practice these aims are conditioned and frustrated by the economic environment. These, so far as our analysis of colonial relations is valid, would seem to be the fundamental principles of tropical economy.

If tropical economy in general has these common features, then it should be possible to arrive at general principles of colonial policy. A colonial estate enhances the prestige and adds to the wealth of the colonial power. If the estate is to be managed in the interest of the colonial power, colonial policy will be directed towards making the dependency incapable of independence, inducing the people to acquiesce in foreign rule, and gaining their co-operation in developing the estate as a business concern. It will overthrow or undermine the native political organization, encourage social disintegration, and foster communal rivalry on the principle of divide and rule; it will restrict the privilege of bearing arms to particular communities, numerical or racial minorities, favour with high pay and valued distinctions those who as officials or otherwise assist in the maintenance of foreign rule, and relieve the public in general of restrictions on their economic activities. So far as may be serviceable to economic progress it will aim at protecting the people against economic forces, and at promoting health and education. A sound colonial policy on this interpretation will aim at what a French writer has criticized as the aim of Dutch colonial policy—to get 'milk from contented cows'.[1] But, as we have seen, these are the results in practice of the most enlightened modern colonial policy. Such a policy will be adopted most whole-heartedly if the colonial power can persuade itself that it is treating native interests as paramount, and the policy will be successful in proportion as the subject people can be induced to regard it as beneficent. Instinctively and inevitably political control is used to further the interests of the colonial power, and the only

[1] Bousquet, p. 155.

safeguard against the misuse of political control is to divorce it so far as possible from economic control. That would seem to be the first principle of colonial policy if it is to be directed in the interest of subject peoples; and the expedient of international collaboration in colonial affairs should be capable of application to that end.

Naturally we like to believe that our rule over dependent peoples is beneficial. But goodwill is no substitute for knowledge, and it is easier to believe in the efficacy of good intentions if we are sheltered from the shock of facts. At present colonial powers, while stressing in official pronouncements the benevolent aspirations of their policy, seem almost deliberately averse from providing material for a just appreciation of their practice. The system of training candidates for the administrative service in British colonies, suitable enough for the system of *laissez-faire* from which it is a survival, is behind the times now that public administration is a skilled profession, and colonial administration a very specialized branch of that profession. Their training does not equip them to acquire a knowledge of the people or an understanding of tropical economy; and, even if it were better adapted to that end, it would be nullified by the conditions under which they work, with constant transfers from place to place and job to job. But the outside world is dependent for its knowledge of colonial affairs on the statistics and reports which they compile. Formerly a colonial government would conceal itself, like a cuttlefish, behind a flood of ink; now it has brought its tactics up to date and puts up a smoke screen in the local legislature, taking refuge behind a fog of words. Both expedients are useful to make darkness palpable, and if the object of colonial practice were to conceal the working of colonial policy, it would be hard to improve on them. But if the good intentions animating colonial policy are to take effect in practice, we want light to see the fruit. Here again international collaboration should help to facilitate a comparative and scientific study of colonial rule.

Goodwill can effect little without knowledge, but both together are of small avail without an understanding of the problems to be solved. The most conspicuous feature of tropical society and the natural consequence of colonial rule is atomization, social disintegration, which debars the people from procuring their own welfare while frustrating endeavours to help them. If colonial policy be directed towards promoting the welfare of tropical dependencies the basic problem is reintegration. Its primary object must be to frame together into one political society with a common social will the diverse and conflicting elements which, taken together, have their nearest analogy in a confederation, but differ from a confederation in combining instability of union with inability to stand alone. The problem of reintegration has no counterpart in normal homogeneous western states, and demands an appropriate technique outside the range of political science in the West. In the West the basic problem of applied political science is how best to ascertain and give effect to the common social will; in the tropics the basic problem is how best to organize a common social will. As with fundamental changes in physical science, it requires a revolution, a new system of ideas and new line of approach, and not merely reforms. Disintegration is the natural and inevitable effect of economic forces that are subject to no restraint but that of law, and reintegration must be based on some principle transcending the sphere of economics. The only principle that hitherto has enabled the colonies of western powers to assert and maintain their independence is Christianity, which has demonstrated its political value in South America and the Philippines.

One of the early Christian Fathers claimed that the Roman Empire was a providential dispensation for the spread of Christianity, and a similar justification is sometimes advanced for the modern expansion of Europe. At the time of the second Burmese war it was suggested that one result would be the conversion of the Burmese to Christianity,[1] but these hopes have been conspicuously disappointed. In this matter Burma and China present an instructive contrast. Both the two great leaders of modern China, Sun Yat Sen and Chiang Kai Shek, were Christians. In Burma the first Burmese Governor was brought up as a Christian and so also was Dr Ba Maw, the first Premier after the separation of Burma from India. But the former was regarded as an instrument of British rule, and the latter had to proclaim himself a Buddhist in order to gain popular support. A Burmese Christian is regarded with suspicion by his fellow-countrymen. Similarly in Java missionaries, though regarded by the Dutch as almost disloyal in their 'ethical tendencies', are looked on by the people as 'servants of the capitalist system'.[2] In Buddhist or Moslem lands the introduction of Christianity multiplies divisions in the plural society, weakening instead of strengthening the social fibre. Moreover, as an instrument of colonial policy the propagation of Christianity by the Government is too dangerous; and for reintegra-

[1] Durand, II, 185.   [2] *Netherlands India*, p. 381.

tion it is necessary to adopt some principle that Christians and those of other creeds alike accept as valid.

We have seen that the Dutch claim to have achieved remarkable progress towards reintegration during the past ten years, not by the apparently easier device of 'injections' of capital, but by taking advantage of the difficulties under which capitalist interests laboured during the recent depression. They contend that by converting capitalists into nationalists and nationalists into capitalists they have induced all the several elements of the plural society to recognize the ties of a common nationality. This is a bold claim. The community of sentiment between the Javanese and the Dyaks of Borneo or the Papuans of New Guinea must be tenuous, yet, at least as regards Java, it is not impossible that, given appropriate measures in post-war reconstruction, history may substantiate their claim. It is not impossible that, by similarly taking advantage of the difficulties under which capitalist interests now lie in Burma, we might achieve a similar result. In any case, if we are to find some principle that all may accept as of superior validity to economic interest there would seem to be no practical alternative to the principle of nationalism, which, as Sir Ernest Barker has argued,[1] is a principle that Christians must acknowledge as part of the Divine ordering of world economy.

Nationalism must indeed figure largely in any project of reintegration, for the object of reintegration is the framing of a national society capable of independence, so far as any minor (or even major) power is capable of independence in the modern world. But a people is fully secure of independence only when a Government, based on popular consent, accepts the obligations of national existence in the modern world. Under native rule the people accept the customary restraints on which the existence of native society depends. Foreign rule liberates them from the bonds of custom, but the acceptance of new obligations requires a process of social education that is possible only under their own leaders. There must be leaders who have graduated as citizens of the modern world, and these must be enabled and encouraged to exert their influence among their people. It is not sufficient that a few men and women shall be brought to finish their studies in England, France or Holland. These, in fact, are just the countries where least is to be learned. It was from the example of Japan and Siam that we took the idea of

[1] Sir Ernest Barker, *Christianity and Nationality* (Burge Memorial Lectures, 1927–33), p. 25.

bringing men to Europe,[1] but we have copied them on a comparatively small scale and have been concerned rather to strengthen the ties, political and economic, with the dependencies rather than to make the dependencies capable of independence. Not infrequently the result is disaffection rather than affection, and the advantage of the dependency will best be served by sending men, as has been the practice of Japan and Siam, to the country where they will learn most; ordinarily, so far as regards administration, they will learn most in countries engaged in the solution of problems similar to their own, rather than in England, France or Holland where such problems have already been solved in by-gone ages. Dependencies not only need such men as leaders; they need also appropriate machinery for social education, probably somewhat along the lines invented by the Dutch, so as to bring the people as a whole into vital contact with the modern world.

Finally, and not of least importance, is the principle of continuity. It is not unnatural that the importance of this principle should escape notice in lands where the tradition of party rivalry, as in England between Tory and Whig, Conservative and Liberal, Capitalist and Socialist, figures so prominently in history, and has proved so stimulating to political evolution. Yet it is the social unity of western lands which allows of party rivalry because all are agreed on fundamental issues. In the divided plural society of tropical dependencies one must needs foster the social unity that is the happy heritage of western peoples. Western political societies survive by their inherent vigour, but in the tropics social will must be conserved and strengthened by artificial respiration until the patient can safely be left alone. Continually economic forces are active everywhere and by all means to disintegrate the social fabric and consume social vitality, and constant vigilance and unremitting activity are needed to defeat them. Political machinery, uninformed by living social will, is unavailing, because it is always condemned to fight a rearguard action on a changing front against new circumstances, to which, being only machinery, it cannot adapt itself. Social, economic and political reintegration demand the embodiment of social will in continuity of person, which is just what the machinery of western political institutions was intended to prevent. These institutions were invented by and for western peoples whose social heritage provided adequately for continuity of social will apart from continuity in the person of the ruler; and the English, who

[1] Curzon, *RPI* (India), 1897-1902, p. 470.

may claim the original invention, have been careful to maintain an element of personal continuity in the Crown. Dependencies, on the other hand, are distinguished by their lack of social will and the need for fostering stability, while the characteristic defect of colonial administration, from top to bottom, has always been discontinuity. This is aggravated by the introduction of western political institutions. Colonial powers when introducing them may hold firmly the belief in their innate value, inherited from the Liberal tradition, but in effect they multiply vacillation of policy and discord among the people, to the profit of the colonial power and the further enfeeblement of the dependency. In a stable society western democratic institutions are a sign of strength; but, where they are not a sign of strength, they are a source of weakness. Nevertheless subject peoples who fail to understand that only a strong social constitution can withstand the rigours of party strife, are usually too ready to seek the means of liberation in institutions that will perpetuate subjection until there is no remedy but revolution.

If, then, we are to accept the welfare of dependent peoples as the main objective of colonial rule, the principles briefly summarized above would seem to derive from the essential character of colonial relations and to hold good for colonial policy in general, though doubtless in practice requiring diverse and even contrary methods of application according to local circumstances. Yet it may seem idle to discuss colonial relations in terms of general principles. So long as colonies are valued for considerations of power, prestige or profit, realists will be satisfied with 'the good old rule, the simple plan, that they should take who have the power, and they should keep who can'. Even those who are less realist in their outlook readily believe what it is, or seems, advantageous to believe. They believe in welfare measures that make the colonial estate more profitable, and that such measures will promote autonomy; and they believe in autonomy on condition that it is autonomy 'within the empire'. They may accordingly be reluctant to accept the principles emerging from this survey which run counter to these comfortable doctrines. Yet our survey shows also good reason to believe that it is well for tropical dependencies to remain within the empire, attached to England, France or Holland, as the case may be. When, however, we try to impose this as a condition of autonomy, instead of aiming to equip dependent peoples for autonomy and leaving them to seek admission to the larger political system as a privilege, there spreads throughout the tropics, naturally and inevitably, a growing human reaction against western rule, that must lead finally to a general revolt against western civilization. Already, instinctively, we are taking precautions against this in projects of international co-operation among western powers for safeguarding security. But if we value peace rather than security, we shall aim at making dependencies capable as soon as possible of independence, not on altruistic grounds or as a grudging concession to nationalist agitation, but on our own initiative and in our own interest as a condition of world welfare, and in order to preserve those established political connections between Europe and the tropics which have come into existence through the temporary incapacity of tropical rulers and peoples to accept the conditions of modern civilization. No one who has made a serious study of the problem is likely to underestimate its difficulties, but the chief obstacle is the reluctance, mistaken and largely subconscious, of colonial powers to seek an effective solution. Given the necessary creative impulse, goodwill can find a way and the difficulties will prove less formidable than many like to think. That we shall seek and find a solution depends on the evidence of things unseen.

APPENDIX I

Commodity	1868–9	1872–3	1903–4	1913–14	1926–7	1936–7
	Native Produce					
1. Rice Products						
Grain	20·55	29·40	144·74	258·21	381·71	209·17
Fodder	—	—	4·19	6·51	9·78	9·25
Total	*20·55*	*29·40*	*148·93*	*264·72*	*391·49*	*218·42*
2. Other Agricultural Products						
Other grain	—·	·23	2·65	5·03	8·17	13·09
Cotton: Raw	·73	2·88	3·23	8·98	12·77	12·70
Manufactures	·07	·02	·03	·06	1·07	·29
Seeds	—	·23	·06	4·17	·56	·31
Oil-cake	—	—	—	2·17	5·22	4·13
Oils (vegetable)	·01	·02	·01	·06	·04	·28
Fruit and vegetables	·03	·02	·04	·45	2·08	3·01
Spices	·03	·06	·34	·40	·48	1·33
Tobacco	·02	·04	·66	2·47	3·08	·72
Total	*·91*	*3·52*	*7·04*	*23·79*	*33·48*	*35·87*
3. Other Rural Products						
Coir and cordage	—	—	·01	·15	·33	·26
Dye-stuffs	1·77	2·28	2·46	1·48	2·16	1·21
Fisheries: Manure	—	—	·11	·36	·24	·07
Other products	—	—	·38	·32	·48	·18
Cattle: Hides and skins	·18	·80	2·73	8·57	4·01	2·11
Bone-meal	—	—	—	—	—	·10
Lac	·08	·29	1·51	·37	4·62	·69
Tea	·01	·17	·01	·01	(a)	(a)
Mineral oil	·13	·27	(a)	(a)	(a)	(a)
Ores and metals	—	·08	(a)	(a)	(a)	(a)
Precious stones, jade, etc.	·82	·63	(a)	(a)	(a)	(a)
Total	*3·00*	*4·52*	*7·21*	*11·27*	*11·85*	*4·63*
Total, Native Produce	**24·46**	**37·45**	**163·18**	**299·79**	**436·82**	**258·92**
	Capitalist Produce					
4. Forest Products						
Wood and timber	6·87	6·98	16·55	22·02	47·75	37·81
Railway plant, etc.	—	—	·21	·25	1·51	—
Matches	—	—	—	—	·60	1·92
Total	*6·87*	*6·98*	*16·76*	*22·27*	*49·87*	*39·73*
5. Plantation Products						
Rubber	—	—	·12	1·65	11·88	6·99
Tea	(b)	(b)	(b)	(b)	·16	·44
Total	—	—	*·12*	*1·65*	*12·04*	*7·43*
6. Oil-well Products						
Mineral oil	(b)	(b)	20·08	44·07	91·79	173·44
Candles	—	—	·89	3·64	2·07	1·28
Paraffin wax	—	—	·64	6·61	16·14	18·92
Total	—	—	*21·61*	*54·33*	*110·00*	*193·64*
7. Mineral Products						
Metals and ores	(b)	(b)	·33	5·26	41·39	51·29
Precious stones, jade, etc.	(b)	(b)	·83	·40	·47	·12
Total	—	—	*1·16*	*5·66*	*41·86*	*51·41*
Total, Capitalist Produce	**6·87**	**6·98**	**39·66**	**83·91**	**213·78**	**292·21**
8. Other produce (unclassed)	·94	·70	*1·84*	*2·52*	*4·13*	*4·14*
Total Exports	**32·28**	**45·13**	**204·69**	**386·23**	**654·74**	**555·27**

(a) Included under capitalist produce; (b) Under native produce.

SEABORNE TRADE OF BURMA, 1869–1937: IMPORTS (MERCHANDISE)
(MILLION RUPEES)

Commodity	1868–9	1872–3	1903–4	1913–14	1926–7	1936–7
	Consumption Goods					
1. (a) Food: Staples						
Grain, pulse, etc.	·07	·05	· 4·91	8·59	12·11	5·29
Oil	·28	·38	5·69	3·11	6·57	5·29
Oil-seeds	·02	·06	1·46	1·09	5·31	1·67
Fruit, vegetables	·56	·47	2·91	5·29	8·28	4·81
Fish	—	—	3·79	5·28	8·56	4·99
Salt	·48	·63	·87	1·44	2·34	1·56
Total	*1·41*	*1·59*	*19·65*	*24·80*	*43·18*	*23·62*
(b) Food: Luxuries						
Alcoholic liquors	1·28	1·22	3·90	5·15	6·10	2·62
Coffee and tea	·10	·14	·54	1·61	3·79	2·07
Provisions:						
Fruit (tinned)	—	—	—	—	·28	·18
Fish (tinned)	—	—	—	2·06	2·96	1·11
Others	·52	·66	7·74	15·43	19·10	12·12
Spices	1·61	1·39	5·89	7·46	12·75	4·72
Sugar	·33	·31	3·84	6·69	10·66	5·33
Tobacco	1·35	1·30	5·87	9·67	14·85	8·76
Total	*5·20*	*5·03*	*27·78*	*48·07*	*70·49*	*36·91*
Total food	*6·62*	*6·62*	*47·43*	*72·87*	*113·67*	*60·53*
2. (a) Clothing: Staples						
Cotton goods	9·85	10·18	30·77	62·19	84·18	45·47
(b) Clothing: Luxuries						
Silk goods	2·82	4·37	7·09	8·82	6·26	·49
Artificial silk	—	—	—	—	2·38	1·51
Woollen goods	1·26	1·13	3·40	5·93	8·50	2·43
Apparel, etc.*	·53	·71	3·31	4·71	5·31	4·48
Boots and shoes	·09	·11	1·15	2·07	2·49	1·37
Dyes	·03	·03	·13	·25	·56	·41
Total	*4·75*	*6·36*	*15·08*	*21·79*	*25·51*	*10·69*
Total clothing	*14·60*	*16·54*	*45·85*	*83·98*	*109·69*	*56·16*
3. Household goods:						
Earthenware	·25	·30	·85	1·97	2·27	·95
Glassware	·16	·16	·81	1·41	1·68	·84
Hardware, etc.	—	—	3·86	7·29	10·45	5·37
Soap	·05	·06	·48	1·65	3·51	·16
Lighting: Candles	·11	·23	·20	·16	·03	·01
Matches	·04	·11	1·20	1·58	1·66	·10
Kerosene	—	—	1·34	·57	·63	·76
Umbrellas	·10	·19	1·28	2·03	1·38	·50
Books	·03	·02	·20	·27	·61	·53
Total household goods	*·74*	*1·08*	*10·23*	*16·95*	*22·23*	*9·23*
TOTAL CONSUMPTION GOODS	**21·95**	**24·25**	**103·51**	**173·80**	**245·59**	**125·92**

* Includes Haberdashery.

SEABORNE TRADE OF BURMA, 1869–1937: IMPORTS (MERCHANDISE)
(MILLION RUPEES)

Commodity	1868–9	1872–3	1903–4	1913–14	1926–7	1936–7
			Production Goods			
4. Transport						
Cycles (pedal)	—	—	—	·33	·69	·58
Motor vehicles	—	—	—	1·30	5·79	2·25
Aircraft	—	—	—	—	—	·25
Carriages, etc.*	·02	·03	·69	·63	1·55	3·01
Rubber tyres	—	—	—	·06	1·71	1·25
Petrol	—	—	—	·24	2·94	5·65
Ships	—	·60	2·39	1·46	·12	·35
Railway plant	—	—	·14	2·24	3·03	·07
Coal	·41	·53	3·93	6·90	10·73	4·72
Total Transport	·44	1·16	7·15	13·16	26·58	18·13
5. Industry						
Building and Engineering	·02	·03	·48	1·94	3·90	2·36
Stone and marble	—	·03	·21	·21	·20	·04
Metals	1·50	1·51	11·81	16·90	25·04	13·99
Machinery, millwork	·36	·81	3·52	4·98	19·46	14·75
Belting	—	—	—	·63	1·18	·40
Packing	—	—	—	·10	·03	·03
Lubricants	—	—	·09	·27	1·23	·98
Paint	·09	·06	·60	1·07	1·74	1·32
Pitch, tar, etc.	·02	·02	·20	·19	·07	·05
Coir and cordage	·05	·07	1·16	1·97	2·83	1·25
Jute, gunnybags, etc.	1·27	2·58	6·85	17·42	27·63	13·36
Chemicals	—	—	·86	·94	1·79	2·22
Instruments	·03	·03	·68	1·79	5·39	4·11
Total Industry	3·35	5·15	26·48	48·42	90·50	54·87
TOTAL PRODUCTION GOODS	**3·78**	**6·31**	**33·63**	**61·59**	**117·08**	**73·01**
6. Other Imports (unclassed)	*1·85*	*1·69*	*8·22*	*18·66*	*23·83*	*18·88*
TOTAL IMPORTS	**27·59**	**32·25**	**145·36**	**254·06**	**386·50**	**217·81**

* 'Carriages' include unspecified vehicles. The decline under Shipping and Railway Plant is due partly to local construction, partly to redistribution of items over Metals and Machinery, and partly to the replacement of foreign imports by Indian imports, including undifferentiated items.

APPENDIX II

DISTRIBUTION OF SEABORNE TRADE OF BURMA, 1869–1937. EXPORTS OF
MERCHANDISE (MILLION RUPEES)

	1868–9	1872–3	1903–4	1913–14	1926–7	1936–7
Europe						
U.K.	21·4	29·6	25·4	36·3	55·5	61·0
Eire	—	—	—	—	—	·5
Austria-Hungary	—	—	9·0	20·9	2·2	—
Belgium	—	—	1·7	3·9	10·3	5·1
France	·4	—	1·0	4·3	·5	·5
Germany	·4	·2	17·5	34·8	52·3	11·3
Holland	—	—	8·5	29·9	15·0	9·0
Italy	—	—	·9	2·0	3·9	1·6
Elsewhere	·1	1·4	2·7	6·8	7·3	7·1
Total: Europe	*22·4*	*31·2*	*66·7*	*139·0*	*147·1*	*96·1*
Africa						
Egypt	—	—	2·9	5·3	9·1	·9
Elsewhere	—	—	3·4	6·3	16·2	11·3
Total: Africa	—	*·1*	*6·4*	*11·6*	*25·4*	*12·2*
America						
Canada	—	—	·3	1·4	·3	1·7
U.S.A.	—	—	·1	2·2	2·5	·7
Elsewhere	—	—	3·5	2·5	23·3	9·4
Total: America	*·1*	*·1*	*3·9*	*6·1*	*26·1*	*11·8*
TOTAL: WEST	**22·5**	**31·5**	**77·0**	**156·8**	**198·6**	**120·1**
Asia						
India	8·2	7·6	48·1	150·0	262·0	280·5
Aden	—	—	—	—	—	·6
Ceylon	·1	·2	2·8	7·1	49·9	27·6
Straits	1·7	5·3	34·4	34·1	45·9	24·7
F.M.S.	—	—	—	·6	6·4	5·6
Neth. India	—	·1	2·1	5·0	16·9	3·3
Siam	—	—	·1	·3	1·6	·1
French Indo-China	—	—	—	—	—	—
Philippines	—	—	4·1	·1	—	·7
China	—	·8	3·3	1·8	29·2	2·9
Hong-Kong	—	—	—	4·8	2·8	1·3
Japan	—	—	30·7	19·3	32·2	22·2
Japanese Empire	—	—	—	—	10·6	—
Elsewhere	—	·4	3·2	5·9	·5	1·9
Total: Asia	*10·1*	*14·4*	*128·7*	*229·0*	*458·1*	*371·4*
Australasia	—	—	*1·0*	*3·3*	*2·9*	*·9*
TOTAL: EAST	**10·1**	**14·4**	**129·7**	**232·4**	**461·0**	**372·3**
TOTAL EXPORTS	**32·6**	**45·9**	**206·7**	**389·1**	**659·5**	**492·5***

* Excludes duty on oil products, Rs. 65·7 mil.

DISTRIBUTION OF SEABORNE TRADE OF BURMA, 1869–1937. IMPORTS OF MERCHANDISE (MILLION RUPEES)

	1868–9	1872–3	1903–4	1913–14	1926–7	1936–7
Europe						
U.K.	10·2	13·5	48·5	89·1	104·6	41·3
Austria-Hungary	—	—	1·4	2·4	·3	·2
Belgium	—	—	3·1	8·6	7·6	3·8
France	—	—	1·8	1·6	3·0	·7
Germany	·1	·5	4·9	11·4	15·2	5·8
Holland	—	·2	2·7	6·3	10·0	2·7
Italy	—	—	·2	1·7	4·7	·5
Elsewhere	·1	—	—	2·3	6·2	3·6
Total: Europe	10·5	14·2	62·7	123·3	151·6	58·6
Africa						
Egypt	—	—	—	·2	·8	·2
Elsewhere	—	—	—	—	·1	·5
Total: Africa	—	—	—	·2	1·0	·7
America						
Canada	—	—	—	·1	2·7	·1
U.S.A.	—	—	2·5	5·8	18·3	7·1
Elsewhere	—	—	—	—	—	—
Total: America	·2	—	2·5	5·9	21·0	7·3
TOTAL: WEST	10·7	14·2	65·3	129·5	173·6	66·7
Asia						
India	14·1	15·3	62·7	94·0	153·3	109·3
Aden, etc.	—	—	—	—	—	·7
Iran	—	—	—	—	—	5·6
Ceylon	—	—	·1	·2	·3	·5
Straits	2·6	2·6	9·7	8·1	12·6	6·3
F.M.S.	—	—	—	—	—	—
Neth. India	—	—	·7	4·9	9·5	·7
Siam	—	—	—	·1	·1	—
French Indo-China	—	—	—	—	—	—
Philippines	—	—	—	—	—	—
China	—	—	1·7	1·9	3·7	·6
Hong-Kong	—	—	—	3·7	3·3	2·8
Japan	—	—	5·0	10·5	26·9	23·9
Elsewhere	—	—	—	·4	2·7	—
Total: Asia	16·9	18·0	79·9	124·0	212·5	150·5
Australasia	—	—	·1	·6	·8	·6
TOTAL: EAST	16·9	18·0	80·0	124·6	213·3	151·1
TOTAL IMPORTS	27·6	32·2	145·3	254·1	386·9	217·8

LIST OF REFERENCES

This list contains only those authorities which in the footnotes are given in an abbreviated form, omitting those for which full particulars are given.

Agriculture in Burma, Papers for the Royal Commission on Agriculture, 1926-8. (Rangoon, 1927.)
Astor, Lord (ed.). The Colonial Problem. (1937.)
Banerjee, A. C. Annexation of Burma. (Calcutta, 1944.)
—— The Eastern Frontier of British India. (Calcutta, 1946.)
BBG. British Burma Gazetteer. 2 vols. (Rangoon, 1879, 1880.)
Bell, K. N. and Morell, W. P. British Colonial Policy. (1928.)
Boeke, J. H. The Structure of Netherlands Indian Economy. (New York, 1942.)
Boulger, D. C. Lord William Bentinck. (1892.)
Bousquet, G. H. La Politique Musulmane et Coloniale des Pays-Bas. (Paris, 1938.)
Bradley, E. (ed.). The University outside Europe. (1939.)
Bright, John. Speeches. 2 vols. (1868.)
Burns, Sir A. C. M. History of Nigeria. (1942.)
Butler, Capt. J. Gazetteer of the Mergui District. (Rangoon, 1884.)
Callis, H. G. Foreign Trade in South-East Asia. (New York, 1941.)
CBC. Report of the Bribery and Corruption Enquiry Committee. (Rangoon, 1941.)
CBE. Report of the Burma Provincial Banking Enquiry Committee, 1924-30. (Rangoon, 1930.)
Chhibber, H. L. The Mineral Resources of Burma. (1934.)
CII. Report of the Imperial Idea Committee. (Rangoon, 1917.)
CISM. Report of the Committee of Enquiry into the Indigenous System of Medicine. (Rangoon, 1931.)
CLA. Report of the Land and Agriculture Committee. (Rangoon, 1938.)
Collis, M. Trials in Burma. (1938.)
Corr.T.D. Correspondence of the Commissioner, Tenasserim Division, 1825-6 to 1842-3. (Rangoon, 1915.)
Cotton, J. S. Mountstuart Elphinstone. (1892.)
Craddock, Sir Reginald. The Dilemma in India. (1929.)
Crosthwaite, Sir Charles. The Pacification of Burma. (1912.)
CRT. Report of the Committee of Enquiry into the Rice Trade. (Rangoon, 1934.)
CVS. Report of the Committee of Enquiry into the Village System. (Rangoon, 1941.)
CVV. Report of the Committee of Enquiry into Vernacular and Vocational Instruction. (Rangoon, 1936.)
Curtis, L. Dyarchy. (1920.)
Curzon, Lord. Resolution on Education, 1904. (Appendix to the Report on Public Instruction in India, 1897-1902.)
de la Court, J. F. H. A. Paedagogische richtlignen voor Indonesië. (Deventer, 1945.)
Desai, W. S. History of the British Residency in Burma, 1828-40. (Rangoon, 1939.)
Djajadiningrat, R. L. From Illiteracy to University. (New York, n.d. [1944].)
Durand, H. M. Life and Letters of Sir M. Durand. 2 vols. (1883.)
Fabian Colonial Bureau. International Action and the Colonies. (1943.)
Forbes, Capt. C. J. F. S. British Burma. (1878.)
Frankel, S. H. Capital Investment in Africa. (1938.)
Freytag, Dr W. The Spiritual Revolution in the East. (1940.)

Furnivall, J. S. Netherlands India. (1939.)
—— The Fashioning of Leviathan: Early British Rule in Burma. (Rangoon, 1939.)
—— Progress and Welfare in South-East Asia. (New York, 1941.)
—— Educational Progress in South-East Asia. (New York, 1943.)
Fytche, Sir A. Burma, Past and Present. 2 vols. (1878.)
Gleig, Rev. J. R. Life of Sir Thomas Munro. (1849.)
Gouger, H. A Personal Narrative of Two Years' Imprisonment in Burma. (1864.)
Hailey, Lord. African Survey. (1938.)
—— Britain and Her Dependencies. (1943.)
Hall, D. G. E. The Dalhousie-Phayre Correspondence, 1852–6. (1932.)
Hart, G. H. C. Towards Economic Democracy in the Netherlands Indies. (New York, 1942.)
Harvey, G. E. History of Burma. (1925.)
—— Burma, 1782–1852. (Cambridge History of India, v.)
—— Burma, 1852–1918. (Cambridge History of India, vi.)
—— British Rule in Burma, 1824–1942. (1946.)
Hinden, Dr R. Plan for Africa. (1941.)
HIOC. Hollandsch-Inlandsch Onderwijs-Commissie, Résumé, and Eindrapport. (Batavia, 1930–1.)
Huxley, J. On Living in a Revolution. (1944.)
Hydrick, J. L. Rural Hygiene in the Netherlands East Indies. (New York, 1942.)
IG. Imperial Gazetteer of India. (1907.)
ISC. Report and Proceedings of the Indian Statutory Commission, 1930.
Jardine, Sir John. Notes on Buddhist Law, i–viii. (Rangoon, 1882–3.)
JBRS. Journal of the Burma Research Society.
JRCAS. Journal of the Royal Central Asian Society.
Keesing, F. M. The South Seas in the Modern World. (n.d. [1941].)
Landon, K. P. Siam in Transition. (1939.)
Leach, J. B. The Future of Burma. (Rangoon, 1936.)
Macaulay, R. H. History of the Bombay-Burma Trading Corporation, 1864–1910. (n.d.)
McCully, B. T. English Education and the Origins of Indian Nationalism. (New York, 1940.)
Malcolm, G. A. The Commonwealth of the Philippines. (1936.)
Mass Education in African Society. (H.M.S.O. Colonial No. 186, 1944.)
Mayhew, A. M. Education in the Colonial Empire. (1938.)
—— The Education of India. (1926.)
Mills, L. A. British Rule in Eastern Asia. (1942.)
Mitchell, K. L. Industrialisation of the Western Pacific. (New York, 1942.)
MMR. Annual Report on the Material and Moral Progress of India.
O'Malley, L. S. S. The Indian Civil Service, 1600–1930. (1931.)
Post-War Training for the Colonial Service. (H.M.S.O. 1945.)
RAB. Annual Report on the Administration of Burma. (Rangoon.)
RCLI. Report and Proceedings of the Royal Commission on Labour in India. (1931.)
Read, M. Native Standards of Living and African Culture Change. (1938.)
Ross of Blandensburg, Major Sir J. F. G. The Marquess of Hastings. (1893.)
RPI. Annual (Quinquennial) Report on the Progress of Public Instruction (or Education).
RRA. Annual Report on the Revenue Administration of Burma.
RTC. Annual Report of Maritime Trade and Customs (or Navigation).
Ru.LB. Rulings of the Chief Court of Lower Burma. (Rangoon.)
Ru.PJ. Printed Judgments of the Judicial Commissioner of Lower Burma, 1892–9.
Ru.SJ. Selected Judgments of the Judicial Commissioner of British (or Lower) Burma, 1870–92.

Ru.UB. Rulings of the Judicial Commissioner of Upper Burma.

Schrieke, Dr B. (ed.). The Effect of Western Influence on Native Civilisations in the Malay Archipelago. (Batavia, 1929.)

Sidney, R. C. H. In British Malaya To-day. (1927.)

Sitsen, P. W. H. Industrial Development of the Netherlands Indies. (New York, n.d. [1944].)

SL. Selected Correspondence of the Commissioner of Tenasserim, 1825-6 to 1842-3.

Smeaton, D. M. The Loyal Karens of Burma. (1887.)

Social Policy in Dependent Territories. (I.L.O. Montreal, 1944.)

Teeling, L. W. B. Gods of To-morrow. (1936.)

Trant, T. A. Two Years in Ava. (1827.)

UBG. Upper Burma Gazetteer. 5 vols. (Rangoon, 1900.)

Vandenbosch, A. The Dutch East Indies. (1938.)

Visman, Verslag van de Commissie tot Bestudeering van Staatsrechtlijke Hervormingen. (The Visman Committee.) 2 vols. (Batavia, 1942.)

Vlekke, Dr B. H. M. Nusantara. (Harvard, 1943.)

Wickizer, V. D. and Bennett, M. K. The Rice Economy of Monsoon Asia. (Stanford Univ. 1941.)

Wilson, G. and N. The Analysis of Social Change. (1945.)

INDEX

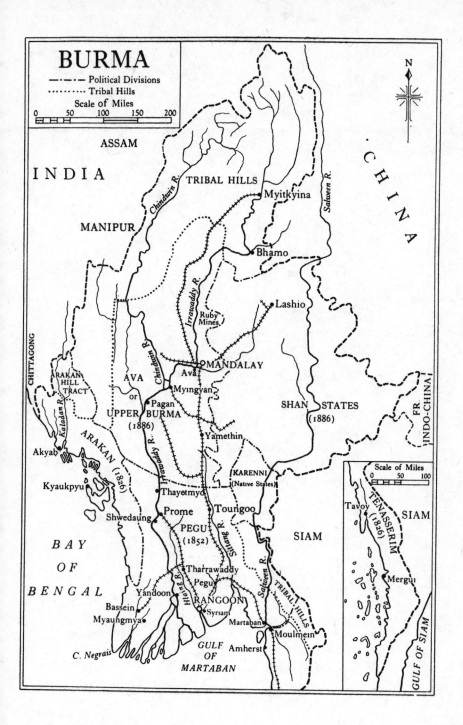

BURMA

- —·—· Political Divisions
- ········ Tribal Hills

Scale of Miles

0   50   100   150   200

N

ASSAM

I N D I A

TRIBAL HILLS

MANIPUR

Chindwin R.

Myitkyina

Salween R.

C H I N A

Bhamo

Lashio

Irrawaddy R.

Ruby Mines

CHITTAGONG

ARAKAN HILL TRACT

Kaladan R.

AVA

Chindwin R.

Ava

MANDALAY

Myingyan

or

Pagan

UPPER BURMA

(1886)

SHAN STATES

(1886)

FR. INDO-CHINA

Akyab

ARAKAN (1826)

Yamethin

Kyaukpyu

Irrawaddy R.

KARENNI

(Native States)

Scale of Miles

0   50   100

Thayetmyo

Prome

Toungoo

Shwedaung

PEGU

(1852)

Sittang R.

SIAM

Tavoy

TENASSERIM

(1826)

SIAM

B A Y

O F

B E N G A L

Tharrawaddy

Pegu

Salween R.

TRIBAL HILLS

Mergui

Hlaing R.

Yandoon

RANGOON

Bassein

Syriam

Myaungmya

Martaban

C. Negrais

GULF

OF

MARTABAN

Amherst

Moulmein

GULF OF SIAM